ALL GLORY TO ŚRĪ GURU AND GAURĀṄGA

ŚRĪMAD BHĀGAVATAM

of

KṚṢṆA-DVAIPĀYANA VYĀSA

ऋषभ उवाच
नायं देहो देहभाजां नृलोके
कष्टान् कामानर्हते विड्भुजां ये ।
तपो दिव्यं पुत्रका येन सत्त्वं
शुद्ध्येद्यस्माद् ब्रह्मसौख्यं त्वनन्तम् ॥ १ ॥

ṛṣabha uvāca
nāyaṁ deho deha-bhājāṁ nṛloke
kaṣṭān kāmān arhate viḍ-bhujāṁ ye
tapo divyaṁ putrakā yena sattvaṁ
śuddhyed yasmād brahma-saukhyaṁ tv anantam

(p.164)

BOOKS by
His Divine Grace A.C. Bhaktivedanta Swami Prabhupāda

Bhagavad-gītā As It Is
Śrīmad-Bhāgavatam, Cantos 1-5 (15 Vols.)
Śrī Caitanya-caritāmṛta (17 Vols.)
Teachings of Lord Caitanya
The Nectar of Devotion
Śrī Īśopaniṣad
Easy Journey to Other Planets
Kṛṣṇa Consciousness: The Topmost Yoga System
Kṛṣṇa, The Supreme Personality of Godhead (3 Vols.)
Transcendental Teachings of Prahlāda Mahārāja
Kṛṣṇa, the Reservoir of Pleasure
The Perfection of Yoga
Beyond Birth and Death
On the Way to Kṛṣṇa
Rāja-vidyā: The King of Knowledge
Elevation to Kṛṣṇa Consciousness
Kṛṣṇa Consciousness: The Matchless Gift
Back to Godhead Magazine (Founder)

A complete catalogue is available upon request.

The Bhaktivedanta Book Trust
3764 Watseka Avenue
Los Angeles, California 90034

ŚRĪMAD BHĀGAVATAM

Fifth Canto

"The Creative Impetus"

(Part One—Chapters 1-13)

With the Original Sanskrit Text, Its Roman Transliteration, Synonyms, Translation and Elaborate Purports by

His Divine Grace
A.C. Bhaktivedanta Swami Prabhupāda
Founder-*Ācārya* of the International Society for Krishna Consciousness

THE BHAKTIVEDANTA BOOK TRUST
New York · Los Angeles · London · Bombay

Readers interested in the subject matter of this book
are invited by the International Society for Krishna Consciousness
to correspond with its Secretary.

International Society for Krishna Consciousness
3764 Watseka Avenue
Los Angeles, California 90034

Library of Congress Catalogue Card Number: 73-169353
International Standard Book Number: 0-912776-78-1

First printing, 1975: 20,000 copies

Printed in the United States of America

Table of Contents

CHAPTER THREE
Ṛṣabhadeva's Appearance in the Womb of Merudevī, the Wife of King Nābhi

CHAPTER FOUR
The Characteristics of Ṛṣabhadeva, the Supreme Personality of Godhead

CHAPTER FIVE
Lord Ṛṣabhadeva's Teachings to His Sons

CHAPTER SIX
The Activities of Lord Ṛṣabhadeva

CHAPTER SEVEN
The Activities of King Bharata

CHAPTER EIGHT
A Description of the Character of Bharata Mahārāja

CHAPTER NINE
The Supreme Character of Jaḍa Bharata

CHAPTER TEN
The Discussion Between Jaḍa Bharata and Mahārāja Rahūgaṇa

CHAPTER ELEVEN
Jaḍa Bharata Instructs King Rahūgaṇa

CHAPTER TWELVE
Conversation Between Mahārāja Rahūgaṇa and Jaḍa Bharata

Table of Contents

CHAPTER THIRTEEN

Further Talks Between King Rahūgaṇa and Jaḍa Bharata

Appendixes

Preface

We must know the present need of human society. And what is that need? Human society is no longer bounded by geographical limits to particular countries or communities. Human society is broader than in the Middle Ages, and the world tendency is toward one state or one human society. The ideals of spiritual communism, according to *Śrīmad-Bhāgavatam*, are based more or less on the oneness of the entire human society, nay, on the entire energy of living beings. The need is felt by great thinkers to make this a successful ideology. *Śrīmad-Bhāgavatam* will fill this need in human society. It begins, therefore, with the aphorism of Vedānta philosophy (*janmādy asya yataḥ*) to establish the ideal of a common cause.

Human society, at the present moment, is not in the darkness of oblivion. It has made rapid progress in the field of material comforts, education and economic development throughout the entire world. But there is a pinprick somewhere in the social body at large, and therefore there are large-scale quarrels, even over less important issues. There is need of a clue as to how humanity can become one in peace, friendship and prosperity with a common cause. *Śrīmad-Bhāgavatam* will fill this need, for it is a cultural presentation for the re-spiritualization of the entire human society.

Śrīmad-Bhāgavatam should be introduced also in the schools and colleges, for it is recommended by the great student devotee Prahlāda Mahārāja in order to change the demonic face of society.

kaumāra ācaret prājño
dharmān bhāgavatān iha
durlabhaṁ mānuṣaṁ janma
tad apy adhruvam arthadam
(*Bhāg.* 7.6.1)

Disparity in human society is due to lack of principles in a godless civilization. There is God, or the Almighty One, from whom everything emanates, by whom everything is maintained and in whom everything is merged to rest. Material science has tried to find the ultimate source of creation very insufficiently, but it is a fact that there is one ultimate source of everything that be. This ultimate source is explained rationally and authoritatively in the beautiful *Bhāgavatam* or *Śrīmad-Bhāgavatam.*

Śrīmad-Bhāgavatam is the transcendental science not only for knowing the ultimate source of everything but also for knowing our relation with Him and our duty towards perfection of the human society on the basis of this perfect knowledge. It is powerful reading matter in the Sanskrit language, and it is now rendered into English elaborately so that simply by a careful reading one will know God perfectly well, so much so that the reader will be sufficiently educated to defend himself from the onslaught of atheists. Over and above this, the reader will be able to convert others to accept God as a concrete principle.

Śrīmad-Bhāgavatam begins with the definition of the ultimate source. It is a bona fide commentary on the *Vedānta-sūtra* by the same author, Śrīla Vyāsadeva, and gradually it develops into nine cantos up to the highest state of God realization. The only qualification one needs to study this great book of transcendental knowledge is to proceed step by step cautiously and not jump forward haphazardly as with an ordinary book. It should be gone through chapter by chapter, one after another. The reading matter is so arranged with its original Sanskrit text, its English transliteration, synonyms, translation and purports so that one is sure to become a God realized soul at the end of finishing the first nine cantos.

The Tenth Canto is distinct from the first nine cantos, because it deals directly with the transcendental activities of the Personality of Godhead Śrī Kṛṣṇa. One will be unable to capture the effects of the Tenth Canto without going through the first nine cantos. The book is complete in twelve cantos, each independent, but it is good for all to read them in small installments one after another.

I must admit my frailties in presenting *Śrīmad-Bhāgavatam,* but still I am hopeful of its good reception by the thinkers and leaders of society on the strength of the following statement of *Śrīmad-Bhāgavatam.*

tad vāg-visargo janatāgha-viplavo
yasmin pratiślokam abaddhavaty api

nāmāny anantasya yaśo 'nkitāni yac
chṛṇvanti gāyanti gṛṇanti sādhavaḥ
(*Bhāg.* 1.5.11)

"On the other hand, that literature which is full with descriptions of the transcendental glories of the name, fame, form and pastimes of the unlimited Supreme Lord is a transcendental creation meant to bring about a revolution in the impious life of a misdirected civilization. Such transcendental literatures, even though irregularly composed, are heard, sung and accepted by purified men who are thoroughly honest."

Oṁ tat sat

A. C. Bhaktivedanta Swami

Introduction

"This *Bhāgavata Purāṇa* is as brilliant as the sun, and it has arisen just after the departure of Lord Kṛṣṇa to His own abode, accompanied by religion, knowledge, etc. Persons who have lost their vision due to the dense darkness of ignorance in the age of Kali shall get light from this *Purāṇa.*" (*Śrīmad-Bhāgavatam* 1.3.43)

The timeless wisdom of India is expressed in the *Vedas,* ancient Sanskrit texts that touch upon all fields of human knowledge. Originally preserved through oral tradition, the *Vedas* were first put into writing five thousand years ago by Śrīla Vyāsadeva, the "literary incarnation of God." After compiling the *Vedas,* Vyāsadeva set forth their essence in the aphorisms known as *Vedānta-sūtras. Śrīmad-Bhāgavatam* is Vyāsadeva's commentary on his own *Vedānta-sūtras.* It was written in the maturity of his spiritual life under the direction of Nārada Muni, his spiritual master. Referred to as "the ripened fruit of the tree of Vedic literature," *Śrīmad-Bhāgavatam* is the most complete and authoritative exposition of Vedic knowledge.

After compiling the *Bhāgavatam,* Vyāsa impressed the synopsis of it upon his son, the sage Śukadeva Gosvāmī. Śukadeva Gosvāmī subsequently recited the entire *Bhāgavatam* to Mahārāja Parīkṣit in an assembly of learned saints on the bank of the Ganges at Hastināpura (now Delhi). Mahārāja Parīkṣit was the emperor of the world and was a great *rājarṣi* (saintly king). Having received a warning that he would die within a week, he renounced his entire kingdom and retired to the bank of the Ganges to fast until death and receive spiritual enlightenment. The *Bhāgavatam* begins with Emperor Parīkṣit's sober inquiry to Śukadeva Gosvāmī:

> "You are the spiritual master of great saints and devotees. I am therefore begging you to show the way of perfection for all persons, and especially for one who is about to die. Please let me know what a man should hear, chant, remember and worship, and also what he should not do. Please explain all this to me."

Śukadeva Gosvāmī's answer to this question, and numerous other questions posed by Mahārāja Parīkṣit, concerning everything from the nature of the self to the origin of the universe, held the assembled sages in rapt attention continuously for the seven days leading to the King's death. The sage Sūta Gosvāmī, who was present on the bank of the Ganges when Śukadeva Gosvāmī first recited *Śrīmad-Bhāgavatam*, later repeated the *Bhāgavatam* before a gathering of sages in the forest of Naimiṣāraṇya. Those sages, concerned about the spiritual welfare of the people in general, had gathered to perform a long, continuous chain of sacrifices to counteract the degrading influence of the incipient age of Kali. In response to the sages' request that he speak the essence of Vedic wisdom, Sūta Gosvāmī repeated from memory the entire eighteen thousand verses of *Śrīmad-Bhāgavatam*, as spoken by Śukadeva Gosvāmī to Mahārāja Parīkṣit.

The reader of *Śrīmad-Bhāgavatam* hears Sūta Gosvāmī relate the questions of Mahārāja Parīkṣit and the answers of Śukadeva Gosvāmī. Also, Sūta Gosvāmī sometimes responds directly to questions put by Śaunaka Ṛṣi, the spokesman for the sages gathered at Naimiṣāraṇya. One therefore simultaneously hears two dialogues: one between Mahārāja Parīkṣit and Śukadeva Gosvāmī on the bank of the Ganges, and another at Naimiṣāraṇya between Sūta Gosvāmī and the sages at Naimiṣāraṇya Forest, headed by Śaunaka Ṛṣi. Furthermore, while instructing King Parīkṣit, Śukadeva Gosvāmī often relates historical episodes and gives accounts of lengthy philosophical discussions between such great souls as the saint Maitreya and his disciple Vidura. With this understanding of the history of the *Bhāgavatam*, the reader will easily be able to follow its intermingling of dialogues and events from various sources. Since philosophical wisdom, not chronological order, is most important in the text, one need only be attentive to the subject matter of *Śrīmad-Bhāgavatam* to appreciate fully its profound message.

It should also be noted that the volumes of the *Bhāgavatam* need not be read consecutively, starting with the first and proceeding to the last. The translator of this edition compares the *Bhāgavatam* to sugar candy—wherever you taste it, you will find it equally sweet and relishable.

This edition of the *Bhāgavatam* is the first complete English translation of this important text with an elaborate commentary, and it is the first widely available to the English-speaking public. It is the product of the scholarly and devotional effort of His Divine Grace A. C. Bhaktivedanta Swami Prabhupāda, the world's most distinguished teacher of Indian religious and philosophical thought. His consummate Sanskrit scholarship and intimate familiarity with Vedic culture and thought as well as the modern way of life combine to reveal to the West a magnificent exposition of this important classic.

Readers will find this work of value for many reasons. For those interested in the classical roots of Indian civilization, it serves as a vast reservoir of detailed information on virtually every one of its aspects. For students of comparative philosophy and religion, the *Bhāgavatam* offers a penetrating view into the meaning of India's profound spiritual heritage. To sociologists and anthropologists, the *Bhāgavatam* reveals the practical workings of a peaceful and scientifically organized Vedic culture, whose institutions were integrated on the basis of a highly developed spiritual world view. Students of literature will discover the *Bhāgavatam* to be a masterpiece of majestic poetry. For students of psychology, the text provides important perspectives on the nature of consciousness, human behavior and the philosophical study of identity. Finally, to those seeking spiritual insight, the *Bhāgavatam* offers simple and practical guidance for attainment of the highest self-knowledge and realization of the Absolute Truth. The entire multivolume text, presented by the Bhaktivedanta Book Trust, promises to occupy a significant place in the intellectual, cultural and spiritual life of modern man for a long time to come.

—The Publishers

His Divine Grace
A. C. Bhaktivedanta Swami Prabhupāda
Founder-Ācārya of the International Society for Krishna Consciousness

PLATE ONE

"Prince Priyavrata was a great devotee because he sought the lotus feet of Nārada, his spiritual master, and thus achieved the highest perfection in transcendental knowledge. The Prince's father, Svāyambhuva Manu, asked him to take charge of ruling the world. He tried to convince Priyavrata that this was his duty as indicated in the revealed scriptures. Prince Priyavrata, however, was continuously practicing *bhakti-yoga* and therefore, although the order of his father could not be rejected, the Prince did not welcome it. Thus he very conscientiously raised the question of whether he might be diverted from devotional service by accepting the responsibility of ruling over the world. The first created being and most powerful demigod in this universe is Lord Brahmā, who is always responsible for developing universal affairs. This supremely powerful Lord Brahmā, accompanied by his associates and the personified *Vedas*, left his own abode in the highest planetary system and descended to the place of Prince Priyavrata's meditation to convince Priyavrata that it was necessary for him to follow the Vedic injunctions and accept the responsibility of ruling over the world. Lord Brahmā, the father of Nārada Muni, is the supreme person within this universe. As soon as Nārada saw the great swan, he could understand that Lord Brahmā had arrived. Therefore he immediately stood up, along with Svāyambhuva Manu and his son Priyavrata, whom Nārada was instructing. Then they folded their hands and began to worship Lord Brahmā with great respect." *(pp.11–17)*

PLATE TWO

"While so excellently ruling the universe, King Priyavrata once became dissatisfied with the circumambulation of the most powerful sun-god. In circling Sumeru Hill on his chariot, the sun-god illuminates all the surrounding planetary systems. However, when the sun is on the northern side of the hill, the south receives less light, and when the sun is in the south, the north receives less. King Priyavrata disliked this situation and therefore decided to make daylight in the part of the universe where there was night. He followed the orbit of the sun-god on a brilliant chariot and thus fulfilled his desire. He could perform such wonderful activities because of the power he had achieved by worshiping the Supreme Personality of Godhead." *(p.57)*

PLATE THREE

"Mahārāja Nābhi, the son of Agnīdhra, wished to have sons, and therefore he attentively began to offer prayers and worship the Supreme Personality of Godhead, Lord Viṣṇu, the master and enjoyer of all sacrifices. Mahārāja Nābhi's wife, Merudevī, who had not given birth to any children at that time, also worshiped Lord Viṣṇu along with her husband. When Mahārāja Nābhi worshiped and offered prayers to the Lord with great faith and devotion and with a pure uncontaminated mind, superficially performing some *yajña* in the line of Pravargya, the kind Supreme Personality of Godhead, due to His affection for His devotees, appeared before King Nābhi in His unconquerable and captivating form with four hands. In this way, to fulfill the desire of His devotee, the Supreme Personality of Godhead manifested Himself in His beautiful body before His devotee. Lord Viṣṇu was very bright, and He appeared to be the best of all personalities. Around the lower portion of His body, He wore a yellow silken garment. On His chest was the mark of Śrīvātsa, which always displays beauty. He carried a conchshell, lotus flower, disc and club, and He wore a garland of forest flowers and the Kaustubha gem. He was beautifully decorated with a helmet, earrings, bangles, belt, pearl necklace, armlets, ankle bells and other bodily ornaments bedecked with radiant jewels. Seeing the Lord present before them, King Nābhi and his priests and associates felt just like poor people who had suddenly attained great riches. They received the Lord and respectfully bent their heads and offered Him things in worship." *(pp.110–113)*

PLATE FOUR

"Once while touring the world, Lord Ṛṣabhadeva, the Supreme Lord, reached a place known as Brahmāvarta. There was a great conference of learned *brāhmaṇas* at that place, and all the King's sons attentively heard the instructions of the *brāhmaṇas* there. At that assembly, within the hearing of the citizens, Ṛṣabhadeva instructed His sons, although they were already well-behaved, devoted and qualified. He instructed them so that in the future they could rule the world very perfectly. The instructions of Lord Ṛṣabhadeva to His sons are very valuable if one wants to live peacefully within this world, which is full of miseries." *(pp.161–162)*

PLATE FIVE

"After accepting the feature of *avadhūta,* a great saintly person without material cares, Lord Ṛṣabhadeva passed through human society like a blind, deaf and dumb man, an idle stone, a ghost or a madman. Although people called Him such names, He remained silent and did not speak to anyone. Wherever He traveled, all bad elements surrounded Him, just as the flies surround the body of an elephant coming from a forest. He was always being threatened, beaten, urinated upon and spat upon. Sometimes people threw stones, stool and dust at Him, and sometimes people passed foul air before Him. Thus people called Him many bad names and gave Him a great deal of trouble, but He did not care about this, for He understood that the body is simply meant for such an end. He was situated on the spiritual platform, and, being in His spiritual glory, He did not care for all these material insults. In other words, He completely understood that matter and spirit are separate, and He had no bodily conception. Thus, without being angry at anyone, He walked through the whole world alone." *(pp.208–209)*

Pandu das

PLATE SIX

"The most exalted devotee, Mahārāja Bharata, was constantly engaged in the devotional service of the Lord. Naturally his love for Vāsudeva, Kṛṣṇa, increased more and more and melted his heart. Consequently he gradually lost all attachment for regulative duties. The hairs of his body stood on end, and all the ecstatic bodily symptoms were manifest. Once the great King Bharata, while sitting on the bank of the Gaṇḍakī River, saw a small deer, bereft of its mother, floating down the river. Seeing this, he felt great compassion. Like a sincere friend, he lifted the infant deer from the waves, and, knowing it to be motherless, brought it to his *āśrama*. Gradually Mahārāja Bharata became very affectionate toward the deer. He began to raise it and maintain it by giving it grass. He was always careful to protect it from the attacks of tigers and other animals. When it itched, he petted it, and in this way he always tried to keep it in a comfortable condition. He sometimes kissed it out of love. Being attached to raising the deer, Mahārāja Bharata forgot the rules and regulations for the advancement of spiritual life, and he gradually forgot to worship the Supreme Personality of Godhead. After a few days, he forgot everything about his spiritual advancement." *(pp.264–275)*

PLATE SEVEN

"The followers and servants of the dacoit chief bound Jaḍa Bhārata with ropes and brought him to the temple of the goddess Kālī. All the thieves, according to their imaginative ritual for killing animalistic men, bathed, dressed and decorated Jaḍa Bhārata with ornaments befitting an animal. Then they brought him before the goddess Kālī, and began worshiping the deity with various offerings before killing the man-animal. At this time, one of the thieves, acting as the chief priest, was ready to offer the blood of Jaḍa Bharata, whom they imagined to be an animal-man, to the goddess Kālī to drink as a liquor. He therefore took up a very fearsome sword, which was very sharp and, consecrating it by the *mantra* of Bhadra Kālī, raised it to kill Jaḍa Bharata. The goddess Kālī could immediately understand that these sinful dacoits were about to kill a great devotee of the Lord, and she could not bear this. Suddenly the deity's body burst asunder, and the goddess Kālī personally emerged from it in a body burning with an intense and intolerable effulgence. Intolerant of the offenses committed, the infuriated goddess Kālī flashed her eyes and displayed her fierce and curved teeth. Her reddish eyes glowed, and she displayed her fearsome features. She assumed a frightening body, as if she were prepared to destroy the entire creation. Leaping violently from the altar, she immediately decapitated all the rogues and thieves with the very sword with which they had intended to kill Jaḍa Bharata. She then began to drink the hot blood that flowed from the necks of the beheaded rogues and thieves as if this blood were liquor. Indeed, she drank this intoxicant with her associates who were witches and female demons. Becoming intoxicated with this blood, they all began to sing very loudly and dance as though prepared to annihilate the entire universe. At the same time, they began to play with the heads of the rogues and thieves, tossing them about as if they were balls." *(pp.322–329)*

CHAPTER ONE

The Activities of Mahārāja Priyavrata

This chapter describes how King Priyavrata enjoyed royal opulence and majesty and then returned to full knowledge. King Priyavrata was detached from worldly opulence, and then he became attached to his kingdom, but finally he again became detached from material enjoyment and thus achieved liberation. When King Parīkṣit heard about this, he was struck with wonder, but he was somewhat bewildered as to how a devotee with no attachment for material enjoyment could later become attached to it. Thus in astonishment he questioned Śukadeva Gosvāmī about this.

In response to the King's inquiries, Śukadeva Gosvāmī said that devotional service, being transcendental, cannot be deviated by any material influences. Priyavrata had received transcendental knowledge from the instructions of Nārada, and therefore he did not want to enter a materialistic life of enjoyment in a kingdom. He accepted the kingdom, however, at the request of such superior demigods as Lord Brahmā and Lord Indra, the King of heaven.

Everything is under the control of the Supreme Personality of Godhead, the supreme controller, and everyone must work accordingly. Just as a bull is controlled by a rope tied to its nose, so all conditioned souls are forced to work under the spells of the modes of nature. A civilized man, therefore, works according to the institution of *varṇa* and *āśrama.* Even in materialistic life, however, no one is free to act. Everyone is compelled to accept a certain type of body offered by the Supreme Lord and thus be allotted different grades of happiness and distress. Therefore even if one artificially leaves home and goes to the forest, he again becomes attached to materialistic life. Family life is compared to a fortress for practicing sense control. When the senses are controlled, one may live either at home or in the forest; there is no difference.

When Mahārāja Priyavrata, following the instruction of Lord Brahmā, accepted the royal throne, his father, Manu, left home for the forest.

Mahārāja Priyavrata then married Barhiṣmatī, the daughter of Viśvakarmā. In the womb of Barhiṣmatī he begot ten sons, named Āgnīdhra, Idhmajihva, Yajñabāhu, Mahāvīra, Hiraṇyaretā, Ghṛtapṛṣṭha, Savana, Medhātithi, Vītihotra and Kavi. He also begot one daughter, whose name was Ūrjasvatī. Mahārāja Priyavrata lived with his wife and family for many thousands of years. The impressions from the rims of Mahārāja Priyavrata's chariot wheels created seven oceans and seven islands. Of the ten sons of Priyavrata, three sons named Kavi, Mahāvīra and Savana accepted *sannyāsa,* the fourth order of life, and the remaining seven sons became the rulers of the seven islands. Mahārāja Priyavrata also had a second wife, in whom he begot three sons named Uttama, Raivata and Tāmasa. All of them were elevated to the post of Manu. Śukadeva Gosvāmī thus described how Mahārāja Priyavrata achieved liberation.

TEXT 1

राजोवाच
प्रियव्रतो भागवत आत्मारामः कथं मुने ।
गृहेऽरमत यन्मूलः कर्मबन्धः पराभवः ॥ १ ॥

rājovāca
priyavrato bhāgavata
ātmārāmaḥ kathaṁ mune
gṛhe 'ramata yan-mūlaḥ
karma-bandhaḥ parābhavaḥ

rājā uvāca—King Parīkṣit said; *priya-vrataḥ*—King Priyavrata; *bhāgavataḥ*—the great devotee; *ātma-ārāmaḥ*—who takes pleasure in self-realization; *katham*—why; *mune*—O great sage; *gṛhe*—at home; *aramata*—enjoyed; *yat-mūlaḥ*—having which as the root cause; *karma-bandhaḥ*—the bondage of fruitive activities; *parābhavaḥ*—the defeat of one's human mission.

TRANSLATION

King Parīkṣit inquired from Śukadeva Gosvāmī: O great sage, why did King Priyavrata, who was a great, self-realized devotee of

the Lord, remain in household life, which is the root cause of the bondage of karma [fruitive activities] and which defeats the mission of human life?

PURPORT

In the Fourth Canto, Śrīla Śukadeva Gosvāmī explains that Nārada Muni perfectly instructed King Priyavrata about the mission of human life. The mission of human life is to realize one's self and then gradually to go back home, back to Godhead. Since Nārada Muni instructed the King fully on this subject, why did he again enter household life, which is the main cause of material bondage? Mahārāja Parīkṣit was greatly astonished that King Priyavrata remained in household life, especially since he was not only a self-realized soul but also a first-class devotee of the Lord. A devotee actually has no attraction for household life, but surprisingly, King Priyavrata enjoyed household life very much. One may argue, "Why is it wrong to enjoy household life?" The reply is that in household life one becomes bound by the results of fruitive activities. The essence of household life is sense enjoyment, and as long as one engrosses his mind in working hard for sense enjoyment, one becomes bound by the reactions of fruitive activities. This ignorance of self-realization is the greatest defeat in human life. The human form of life is especially meant for getting out of the bondage of fruitive activities, but as long as one is forgetful of his life's mission and acts like an ordinary animal—eating, sleeping, mating and defending—he must continue his conditioned life of material existence. Such a life is called *svarūpa-vismṛti*, forgetfulness of one's real constitutional position. Therefore in Vedic civilization one is trained in the very beginning of life as a *brahmacārī*. A *brahmacārī* must execute austerities and refrain from sex indulgence. Therefore if one is completely trained in the principles of *brahmacarya*, he generally does not enter household life. He is then called a *naiṣṭhika-brahmacārī*, which indicates total celibacy. King Parīkṣit was thus astonished that the great King Priyavrata, although trained in the principles of *naiṣṭhika-brahmacarya*, entered household life.

The words *bhāgavata ātmārāmaḥ* are very significant in this verse. If one is self-satisfied as is the Supreme Personality of Godhead, he is called *bhāgavata ātmārāmaḥ*. There are different types of satisfaction. *Karmīs* are satisfied in their fruitive activities, *jñānīs* are satisfied to merge into the effulgence of Brahman, and devotees are satisfied to engage in the Lord's service. The Lord is self-satisfied because He is fully opulent, and one who is satisfied by serving Him is called *bhāgavata ātmārāmaḥ. Manuṣyāṇāṁ sahasreṣu:* out of many thousands of persons, one may endeavor for liberation, and of many thousands of persons attempting to become liberated, one may achieve liberation from the anxieties of material existence and become self-satisfied. Even that satisfaction, however, is not the ultimate satisfaction. The *jñānīs* and the *karmīs* have desires, as do the *yogīs*, but devotees have no desires. Satisfaction in the service of the Lord is called *akāma*, freedom from desire, and this is the ultimate satisfaction. Therefore Mahārāja Parīkṣit inquired, "How could one who was fully satisfied on the highest platform be satisfied with family life?"

The word *parābhavaḥ* in this verse is also significant. When one is satisfied in family life, he is doomed because he must already have forgotten his relationship with the Lord. Prahlāda Mahārāja describes how the activities of family life implicate one more and more. *Ātma-pātaṁ gṛham andha-kūpam:* household life is like a dark well. If one falls into this well, his spiritual death is assured. How Priyavrata Mahārāja remained a liberated *paramahaṁsa* even within family life is described in the next verse.

TEXT 2

न नूनं मुक्तसङ्गानां तादृशानां द्विजर्षभ ।
गृहेष्वभिनिवेशोऽयं पुंसां भवितुमर्हति ॥ २ ॥

na nūnaṁ mukta-saṅgānāṁ
tādṛśānāṁ dvijarṣabha
gṛheṣv abhiniveśo 'yaṁ
puṁsāṁ bhavitum arhati

na—not; *nūnam*—certainly; *mukta-saṅgānām*—who are free from attachment; *tādṛśānām*—such; *dvija-ṛṣabha*—O greatest of the *brāhmaṇas; gṛheṣu*—to family life; *abhiniveśaḥ*—excessive attachment; *ayam*—this; *puṁsām*—of persons; *bhavitum*—to be; *arhati*—is possible.

TRANSLATION

Devotees are certainly liberated persons. Therefore, O greatest of the brāhmaṇas, they cannot possibly be absorbed in family affairs.

PURPORT

In *Bhakti-rasāmṛta-sindhu* it is said that by executing devotional service to the Lord, one can understand the transcendental position of the living being and the Supreme Personality of Godhead. The Supreme Personality of Godhead cannot be understood by any means except *bhakti.* The Lord confirms this in *Śrīmad-Bhāgavatam* (11.14.21). *Bhaktyāham ekayā grāhyaḥ:* "Only by executing devotional service can one appreciate Me." Similarly, in *Bhagavad-gītā* (18.55) Lord Kṛṣṇa says, *bhaktyā mām abhijānāti:* "Simply by discharging devotional service, one can understand Me." Thus for a *bhakta* to become attached to family affairs is impossible, since a *bhakta* and his associates are liberated. Everyone is searching after *ānanda,* or bliss, but in the material world there can never be any bliss. It is only possible in devotional service. Attachment for family affairs and devotional service are incompatible. Therefore Mahārāja Parīkṣit was somewhat surprised to hear that Mahārāja Priyavrata was simultaneously attached to devotional service and to family life.

TEXT 3

महतां खलु विप्रर्षे उत्तमश्लोकपादयोः ।
छायानिर्वृतचित्तानां न कुटुम्बे स्पृहामतिः ॥ ३ ॥

mahatāṁ khalu viprarṣe
uttamaśloka-pādayoḥ
chāyā-nirvṛta-cittānāṁ
na kuṭumbe spṛhā-matiḥ

mahatām—of great devotees; *khalu*—certainly; *vipra-ṛṣe*—O great sage among the *brāhmaṇas; uttama-śloka-pādayoḥ*—of the lotus feet of the Supreme Personality of Godhead; *chāyā*—by the shade; *nirvṛta*—satiated; *cittānām*—whose consciousness; *na*—never; *kuṭumbe*—to family members; *spṛhā-matiḥ*—consciousness with attachment.

TRANSLATION

Elevated mahātmās who have taken shelter of the lotus feet of the Supreme Personality of Godhead are fully satiated by the shade of those lotus feet. Their consciousness cannot possibly become attached to family members.

PURPORT

Śrīla Narottama dāsa Ṭhākura has sung, *nitāi pada-kamala, koṭī-candra suśītala, ye chāyāya jagat juḍāya.* He describes the shade of the lotus feet of Lord Nityānanda as being so nice and cooling that all materialists, who are always in the blazing fire of material activities, may come under the shade of His lotus feet and be fully relieved and satiated. The distinction between family life and spiritual life can be experienced by any person who has undergone the tribulations of living with a family. One who comes under the shelter of the lotus feet of the Lord never becomes attracted by the activities of family life. As stated in *Bhagavad-gītā* (2.59), *paraṁ dṛṣṭvā nivartate:* one gives up lower engagements when he experiences a higher taste. Thus one becomes detached from family life as soon as he comes under the shelter of the lotus feet of the Lord.

TEXT 4

संशयोऽयं महान् ब्रह्मन्दारागारसुतादिषु ।
सक्तस्य यत्सिद्धिरभूत्कृष्णे च मतिरच्युता ॥ ४ ॥

saṁśayo 'yaṁ mahān brahman
dārāgāra-sutādiṣu
saktasya yat siddhir abhūt
kṛṣṇe ca matir acyutā

saṁśayaḥ—doubt; *ayam*—this; *mahān*—great; *brahman*—O *brāhmaṇa; dāra*—to the wife; *āgāra*—home; *suta*—children; *ādiṣu*—and so on; *saktasya*—of a person attached; *yat*—because; *siddhiḥ*—perfection; *abhūt*—became; *kṛṣṇe*—unto Kṛṣṇa; *ca*—also; *matiḥ*—attachment; *acyutā*—infallible.

TRANSLATION

The King continued: O great brāhmaṇa, this is my great doubt. How was it possible for a person like King Priyavrata, who was so attached to wife, children and home, to achieve the topmost infallible perfection in Kṛṣṇa consciousness?

PURPORT

King Parīkṣit wondered how a person so attached to wife, children and home could become so perfectly Kṛṣṇa conscious. Prahlāda Mahārāja has said:

matir na kṛṣṇe parataḥ svato vā
mitho 'bhipadyeta gṛhavratānām

A *gṛhavrata*, one who has taken a vow to execute family duties, has no chance to become Kṛṣṇa conscious. This is because most *gṛhavratas* are guided by sense gratification and therefore gradually glide down to the darkest regions of material existence (*adānta-gobhir viśatāṁ tamisram*). How can they possibly become perfect in Kṛṣṇa consciousness? Mahārāja Parīkṣit asked Śukadeva Gosvāmī to resolve this great doubt.

TEXT 5

श्रीशुक उवाच

बाढमुक्तं भगवत उत्तमश्लोकस्य श्रीमच्चरणारविन्दमकरन्दरस आवेशित-चेतसो भागवतपरमहंस दयितकथां किञ्चिदन्तरायविहतां स्वां शिवतमां पदवीं न प्रायेण हिन्वन्ति ॥ ५ ॥

śrī-śuka uvāca
bāḍham uktaṁ bhagavata uttamaślokasya śrīmac-caraṇāravinda-makaranda-rasa āveśita-cetaso bhāgavata-paramahaṁsa-dayita-kathāṁ kiñcid antarāya-vihatāṁ svāṁ śivatamāṁ padavīṁ na prāyeṇa hinvanti.

śrī-śukaḥ uvāca—Śrī Śukadeva Gosvāmī said; *bāḍham*—correct; *uktam*—what you have said; *bhagavataḥ*—of the Personality of Godhead;

uttama-ślokasya—who is praised with excellent verses; *śrīmat-caraṇa-aravinda*—of the feet, which are just like the most beautiful fragrant lotus flowers; *makaranda*—honey; *rase*—in the nectar; *āveśita*—absorbed; *cetasaḥ*—whose hearts; *bhāgavata*—to the devotees; *parama-haṁsa*—liberated persons; *dayita*—pleasing; *kathām*—glorification; *kiñcit*—sometimes; *antarāya*—by impediments; *vihatām*—checked; *svām*—own; *śiva-tamām*—most exalted; *padavīm*—position; *na*—do not; *prāyeṇa*—almost always; *hinvanti*—give up.

TRANSLATION

Śrī Śukadeva Gosvāmī said: What you have said is correct. The glories of the Supreme Personality of Godhead, who is praised in eloquent, transcendental verses by such exalted personalities as Brahmā, are very pleasing to great devotees and liberated persons. One who is attached to the nectarean honey of the Lord's lotus feet, and whose mind is always absorbed in His glories, may sometimes be checked by some impediment, but he still never gives up the exalted position he has acquired.

PURPORT

Śrī Śukadeva Gosvāmī accepted both of the King's propositions—that a person who is advanced in Kṛṣṇa consciousness cannot embrace materialistic life again and that one who has embraced materialistic life cannot take up Kṛṣṇa consciousness at any stage of his existence. Although accepting both these statements, Śukadeva Gosvāmī qualified them by saying that a person who has once absorbed his mind in the glories of the Supreme Personality of Godhead may sometimes be influenced by impediments, but he still does not give up his exalted devotional position.

According to Śrīla Viśvanātha Cakravartī Ṭhākura, there are two kinds of impediments to devotional service. The first is an offense at the lotus feet of a Vaiṣṇava. This is called *vaiṣṇava-aparādha*. Śrī Caitanya Mahāprabhu warned His devotees not to commit *vaiṣṇava-aparādha*, which He described as the mad elephant offense. When a mad elephant enters a beautiful garden, it destroys everything, leaving a barren field. Similarly, the power of *vaiṣṇava-aparādha* is so great that even an advanced devotee becomes almost devoid of his spiritual assets if he commits it. Since Kṛṣṇa consciousness is eternal, it cannot be destroyed altogether, but advancement may be checked for the time being. Thus *vaiṣṇava-aparādha* is one kind of impediment to devotional service. Sometimes, however, the Supreme Personality of Godhead or His devotee desires to impede one's devotional service. For example, Hiraṇyakaśipu and Hiraṇyākṣa were formerly Jaya and Vijaya, the gatekeepers in Vaikuṇṭha, but by the desire of the Lord, they became His enemies for three lives. Thus the desire of the Lord is another kind of impediment. But in both cases, the pure devotee, once advanced in Kṛṣṇa consciousness, cannot be lost. Following the orders of his superiors (Svāyambhuva and Lord Brahmā), Priyavrata accepted family life, but this did not mean he lost his position in devotional service. Kṛṣṇa consciousness is perfect and eternal, and therefore it cannot be lost under any circumstances. Because the material world is full of obstructions to advancement in Kṛṣṇa consciousness, there may appear to be many impediments, yet Kṛṣṇa, the Supreme Personality of Godhead, declares in *Bhagavad-gītā* (9.31), *kaunteya pratijānīhi na me bhaktaḥ praṇaśyati:* once one has taken shelter at the lotus feet of the Lord, he cannot be lost.

In this verse, the word *śivatamām* is very significant. *Śivatamām* means "the most auspicious." The devotional path is so auspicious that a devotee cannot be lost under any circumstances. This is described in the *Śrīmad Bhagavad-gītā* by the Lord Himself. *Pārtha naiveha nāmutra vināśas tasya vidyate:* "My dear Arjuna, for a devotee there is no question of being lost, either in this life or in the next." (Bg. 6.40) In *Bhagavad-gītā* (6.43) the Lord clearly explains how this is so.

tatra taṁ buddhi-saṁyogaṁ
labhate paurva-dehikam
yatate ca tato bhūyaḥ
saṁsiddhau kuru-nandana

By the order of the Lord, a perfect devotee sometimes comes to this material world like an ordinary human being. Because of his previous practice, such a perfect devotee naturally becomes attached to devotional service, apparently without cause. Despite all kinds of impediments due to surrounding circumstances, he automatically perseveres in devotional service and gradually advances until he once again becomes perfect. Bilvamaṅgala Ṭhākura had been an advanced devotee in his previous life, but in his next life he became greatly fallen and was attached to a prostitute. Suddenly, however, his entire behavior was changed by the words of the very prostitute who had so much attracted him, and he became a great devotee. In the lives of exalted devotees, there are many such instances, proving that once one has taken to the shelter of the lotus feet of the Lord, he cannot be lost (*kaunteya pratijānīhi na me bhaktaḥ praṇaśyati*).

The fact is, however, that one becomes a devotee when he is completely freed from all reactions to sinful life. As Kṛṣṇa states in *Bhagavad-gītā* (7.28):

yeṣām tv anta-gataṁ pāpaṁ
janānāṁ puṇya-karmaṇām
te dvanda-moha-nirmuktā
bhajante māṁ dṛḍha-vratāḥ

"Persons who have acted piously in previous lives and in this life, whose sinful actions are completely eradicated and who are freed from the duality of illusion, engage themselves in My service with determination." On the other hand, as Prahlāda Mahārāja said:

matir na kṛṣṇe parataḥ svato vā
mitho 'bhipadyeta gṛhavratānām

A person who is too attached to materialistic family life—home, family, wife, children and so on—cannot develop Kṛṣṇa consciousness.

These apparent contradictions are resolved in the life of a devotee by the grace of the Supreme Lord, and therefore a devotee is never bereft of his position on the path of liberation, which is described in this verse as *śivatamāṁ padavīm.*

TEXT 6

यर्हि वाव ह राजन् स राजपुत्रः प्रियव्रतः परमभागवतो
नारदस्य चरणोपसेवयाञ्जसावगतपरमार्थसतत्त्वो ब्रह्मसत्रेण दीक्षिष्यमाणो-
ऽवनितलपरिपालनायाम्नातप्रवरगुणगणैकान्तभाजनतया स्वपित्रोपामन्त्रितो
भगवति वासुदेव एवाव्यवधानसमाधियोगेन समावेशितसकलकारकक्रिया-

कलापो नैवाभ्यनन्दद्यद्यपि तदप्रत्याम्नातव्यं तदधिकरण आत्मनोऽन्यस्माद
सतोऽपि पराभवमन्वीक्षमाणः ॥ ६ ॥

yarhi vāva ha rājan sa rāja-putraḥ priyavrataḥ parama-bhāgavato nāradasya caraṇopasevayāñjasāvagata-paramārtha-satattvo brahma-satreṇa dīkṣiṣyamāṇo 'vani-tala-paripālanāyāmnāta-pravara-guṇa-gaṇaikānta-bhājanatayā sva-pitropāmantrito bhagavati vāsudeva evāvyavadhāna-samādhi-yogena samāveśita-sakala-kāraka-kriyā-kalāpo naivābhyanandad yadyapi tad apratyāmnātavyaṁ tad-adhikaraṇa ātmano 'nyasmād asato 'pi parābhavam anvīkṣamāṇaḥ.

yarhi—because; *vāva ha*—indeed; *rājan*—O King; *saḥ*—he; *rāja-putraḥ*—the Prince; *priyavrataḥ*—Priyavrata; *parama*—supreme; *bhāgavataḥ*—devotee; *nāradasya*—of Nārada; *caraṇa*—the lotus feet; *upasevayā*—by serving; *añjasā*—quickly; *avagata*—became aware of; *parama-artha*—transcendental subject matter; *sa-tattvaḥ*—with all knowable facts; *brahma-satreṇa*—by continuous discussion of the Supreme; *dīkṣiṣyamāṇaḥ*—desiring to fully dedicate himself; *avani-tala*—the surface of the globe; *paripālanāya*—to rule over; *āmnāta*—directed in the revealed scriptures; *pravara*—highest; *guṇa*—of qualities; *gaṇa*—the sum total; *ekānta*—without deviation; *bhājanatayā*—because of his possessing; *sva-pitrā*—by his father; *upāmantritaḥ*—being asked; *bhavagati*—in the Supreme Personality of Godhead; *vāsudeve*—the all-pervading Lord; *eva*—certainly; *avyavadhāna*—without cessation; *samādhi-yogena*—by practicing *yoga* in complete absorption; *samāveśita*—completely dedicated; *sakala*—all; *kāraka*—senses; *kriyā-kalāpaḥ*—whose total activities; *na*—not; *eva*—thus; *abhyanandat*—welcomed; *yadyapi*—although; *tat*—that; *apratyāmnātavyam*—not to be rejected for any reason; *tat-adhikaraṇe*—in occupying that post; *ātmanaḥ*—of himself; *anyasmāt*—by other engagements; *asataḥ*—material; *api*—certainly; *parābhavam*—deterioration; *anvīkṣamāṇaḥ*—foreseeing.

TRANSLATION

Śukadeva Gosvāmī continued: My dear King, Prince Priyavrata was a great devotee because he sought the lotus feet of Nārada, his spiritual master, and thus achieved the highest perfection in tran-

scendental knowledge. With advanced knowledge, he always engaged in discussing spiritual subjects and did not divert his attention to anything else. The Prince's father then asked him to take charge of ruling the world. He tried to convince Priyavrata that this was his duty as indicated in the revealed scriptures. Prince Priyavrata, however, was continuously practicing bhakti-yoga by constantly remembering the Supreme Personality of Godhead, thus engaging all his senses in the service of the Lord. Therefore, although the order of his father could not be rejected, the Prince did not welcome it. Thus he very conscientiously raised the question of whether he might be diverted from devotional service by accepting the responsibility of ruling over the world.

PURPORT

Śrīla Narottama dāsa Ṭhākura has sung, *chāḍiyā vaiṣṇava-sevā nistāra pāyeche kebā:* "Without serving the lotus feet of a pure Vaiṣṇava or spiritual master, no one has ever attained perfect liberation from material bondage." Prince Priyavrata regularly served the lotus feet of Nārada, and thus the Prince perfectly understood transcendental subjects in truth (*sa-tattvaḥ*). The word *sa-tattvaḥ* means that Priyavrata knew all the facts about the spirit soul, the Supreme Personality of Godhead, and the relationship between the spirit soul and the Supreme Personality of Godhead, and he also knew all about this material world and the relationship of the spirit soul and the Supreme Lord within the material world. Thus the Prince decided to engage himself only in rendering service to the Lord.

When Priyavrata's father, Svāyambhuva Manu, requested him to accept the responsibility of ruling over the world, he did not welcome the suggestion. This is the symptom of a great, liberated devotee. Even though engaged in worldly affairs, he does not take pleasure in them, but remains always absorbed in the Lord's service. While thus serving the Lord, he deals externally with worldly affairs without being affected. For example, although he has no attraction for his children, he cares for them and educates them to become devotees. Similarly, he speaks to his wife with affectionate words, but he is not attached to her. By rendering devotional service, a devotee acquires all the good qualities of the

Supreme Lord. Lord Kṛṣṇa had sixteen thousand wives, all of them very beautiful, and although He dealt with each of them as a beloved husband, He was not attracted or attached to any of them. In the same way, although a devotee may enter family life and act very affectionately toward his wife and children, he is never attached to these activities.

This verse states that by serving the lotus feet of his spiritual master, Prince Priyavrata very soon attained the perfectional stage of Kṛṣṇa consciousness. This is the only way to advance in spiritual life. As stated in the *Vedas:*

yasya deve parā bhaktir
yathā deve tathā gurau
tasyaite kathitā hy arthāḥ
prakāśante mahātmanaḥ

"If one has unflinching faith in the Supreme Lord and the spiritual master, the essence of all Vedic knowledge is revealed to him." (*Śvetāśvatara Upaniṣad* 6.23) A devotee always thinks of the Lord continuously. While chanting the Hare Kṛṣṇa *mantra*, the words Kṛṣṇa and Hare immediately remind him of all the Lord's activities. Since his entire life is engaged in the service of the Lord, a devotee cannot forget the Lord at any time. Just as an ordinary man always engages his mind in material activities, a devotee always engages his mind in spiritual activities. This is called *brahma-satra*, or meditating upon the Supreme Lord always. Prince Priyavrata was perfectly initiated into this practice by Śrī Nārada.

TEXT 7

अथ ह भगवानादिदेव एतस्य गुणविसर्गस्य परिबृंहणानुध्यानव्यवसित सकलजगदभिप्राय आत्मयोनिरखिलनिगमनिजगणपरिवेष्टितः स्वभवनादवततार॥७॥

atha ha bhagavān ādi-deva etasya guṇa-visargasya
paribṛṁhaṇānudhyāna-vyavasita-sakala-jagad-abhiprāya ātma-yonir
akhila-nigama-nija-gaṇa-pariveṣṭitaḥ sva-bhavanād avatatāra.

atha—thus; *ha*—indeed; *bhagavān*—the most powerful; *ādi-devaḥ*—the first demigod; *etasya*—of this universe; *guṇa-visargasya*—the creation of the three modes of material nature; *paribṛṁhaṇa*—the welfare; *anudhyāna*—always thinking of; *vyavasita*—known; *sakala*—whole; *jagat*—of the universe; *abhiprāyaḥ*—by whom the ultimate purpose; *ātma*—the Supreme Self; *yoniḥ*—whose source of birth; *akhila*—all; *nigama*—by the *Vedas; nija-gaṇa*—by personal associates; *pariveṣṭitaḥ*—being surrounded; *sva-bhavanāt*—from his own abode; *avatatāra*—descended.

TRANSLATION

Śrī Śukadeva Gosvāmī continued: The first created being and most powerful demigod in this universe is Lord Brahmā, who is always responsible for developing universal affairs. Born directly from the Supreme Personality of Godhead, he dedicates his activities to the welfare of the entire universe, for he knows the purpose of the universal creation. This supremely powerful Lord Brahmā, accompanied by his associates and the personified Vedas, left his own abode in the highest planetary system and descended to the place of Prince Priyavrata's meditation.

PURPORT

Lord Viṣṇu, the Supreme Self (*ātmā*), is the source of everything, as explained in the *Vedānta-sūtra: janmādy asya yataḥ.* Because Brahmā was born directly from Lord Viṣṇu, he is called *ātma-yoni.* He is also called *bhagavān,* although generally *bhagavān* refers to the Supreme Personality of Godhead (Viṣṇu or Lord Kṛṣṇa). Sometimes great personalities—such as demigods like Lord Brahmā, Nārada or Lord Śiva—are also addressed as *bhagavān* because they carry out the purpose of the Supreme Personality of Godhead. Lord Brahmā is called *bhagavān* because he is the secondary creator of this universe. He is always thinking of how to improve the situation of the conditioned souls who have come to the material world to enjoy material activities. For this reason, he disseminates the Vedic knowledge throughout the universe for everyone's guidance.

Vedic knowledge is divided into two parts: *pravṛtti-mārga* and *nivṛtti-mārga. Nivṛtti-mārga* is the path of negating sense enjoyment, and *pravṛtti-mārga* is the path by which the living entities are given a chance to enjoy and at the same time are directed in such a way that they can go back home, back to Godhead. Because ruling over this universe is a great responsibility, Brahmā must force many Manus in different ages to take charge of universal affairs. Under each Manu there are different kings who also execute the purpose of Lord Brahmā. It is understood from previous explanations that the father of Dhruva Mahārāja, King Uttānapāda, ruled over the universe because his elder brother, Priyavrata, practiced austerity from the very beginning of his life. Thus up to the point of the Pracetās, the kings of the universe were all descendants of Uttānapāda Mahārāja. Since there were no suitable kings after the Pracetās, Svāyambhuva Manu went to the Gandhamādana Hill to bring back his eldest son, Priyavrata, who was meditating there. Svāyambhuva Manu requested Priyavrata to rule over the universe. When he refused, Lord Brahmā descended from the supreme planetary system, known as Satyaloka, to request Priyavrata to accept the order. Lord Brahmā did not come alone. He came with other great sages like Marīci, Ātreya and Vasiṣṭha. To convince Priyavrata that it was necessary for him to follow the Vedic injunctions and accept the responsibility of ruling over the world, Lord Brahmā also brought with him the personified *Vedas*, his constant associates.

A significant word in this verse is *sva-bhavanāt*, indicating that Lord Brahmā descended from his own abode. Every demigod has his own abode. Indra, the King of the demigods, has his own abode, as do Candra, the lord of the moon planet, and Sūrya, the predominating deity of the sun planet. There are many millions of demigods, and the stars and planets are their respective homes. This is confirmed in *Bhagavad-gītā. Yānti deva-vratā devān:* "Those who worship the demigods go to their different planetary systems." Lord Brahmā's abode, the highest planetary system, is called Satyaloka or sometimes Brahmaloka. Brahmaloka usually refers to the spiritual world. The abode of Lord Brahmā is Satyaloka, but because Lord Brahmā resides there, it is also sometimes called Brahmaloka.

TEXT 8

स तत्र तत्र गगनतल उडुपतिरिव विमानावलिभिरनुपथममरपरिवृढैरभिपूज्यमानः
पथि पथि च वरूथशः सिद्धगन्धर्वसाध्यचारणमुनिगणैरुपगीयमानो गन्ध-
मादनद्रोणीमवभासयन्नुपससर्प ॥ ८ ॥

sa tatra tatra gagana-tala uḍu-patir iva vimānāvalibhir anupatham amara-parivṛḍhair abhipūjyamānaḥ pathi pathi ca varūthaśaḥ siddha-gandharva-sādhya-cāraṇa-muni-gaṇair upagīyamāno gandha-mādana-droṇīm avabhāsayann upasasarpa.

saḥ—he (Lord Brahmā); *tatra tatra*—here and there; *gagana-tale*—under the canopy of the sky; *uḍu-patiḥ*—the moon; *iva*—like; *vimāna-āvalibhiḥ*—in their different airplanes; *anupatham*—along the path; *amara*—of the demigods; *parivṛḍhaiḥ*—by the leaders; *abhipūjyamānaḥ*—being worshiped; *pathi pathi*—on the way, one after another; *ca*—also; *varūthaśaḥ*—in groups; *siddha*—by the residents of Siddhaloka; *gandharva*—by the residents of Gandharvaloka; *sādhya*—by the residents of Sādhyaloka; *cāraṇa*—by the residents of Cāraṇaloka; *muni-gaṇaiḥ*—and by great sages; *upagīyamānaḥ*—being worshiped; *gandha-mādana*—of the planet where the Gandhamādana Hill is found; *droṇīm*—the border; *avabhāsayan*—illuminating; *upasasarpa*—he approached.

TRANSLATION

As Lord Brahmā descended on his carrier, the great swan, all the residents of the planets named Siddhaloka, Gandharvaloka, Sādhyaloka and Cāraṇaloka, as well as great sages and demigods flying in their different airplanes, assembled within the canopy of the sky to receive Lord Brahmā and worship him. As he received respect and adoration from the residents of the various planets, Lord Brahmā appeared just like the full moon surrounded by illuminating stars. Lord Brahmā's great swan then arrived at the border of Gandhamādana Hill and approached Prince Priyavrata, who was sitting there.

PURPORT

It appears from this description that there is regular interplanetary travel between the planets of the demigods. Another significant point is that there is a planet covered mostly by great mountains, one of which is Gandhamādana Hill. Three great personalities—Priyavrata, Nārada and Svāyambhuva Manu—were sitting on this hill. According to *Brahma-*

saṁhitā, each universe is filled with different planetary systems, and every system has a unique opulence. For example, on Siddhaloka, all the residents are very advanced in the powers of mystic *yoga.* They can fly from one planet to another without airplanes or other flying machines. Similarly, the residents of Gandharvaloka are expert in musical science, and those on Sādhyaloka are all great saints. The interplanetary system undoubtedly exists, and residents of different planets may go from one to another. On this earth, however, we have not invented any machine that can go directly from one planet to another, although an unsuccessful attempt has been made to go directly to the moon.

TEXT 9

तत्र ह वा एनं देवर्षिर्हंसयानेन पितरं भगवन्तं हिरण्यगर्भमुपलभमानः
सहसैवोत्थायार्हणेन सह पितापुत्राभ्यामवहिताञ्जलिरुपतस्थे ॥ ९ ॥

tatra ha vā enaṁ devarṣir haṁsa-yānena pitaraṁ bhagavantaṁ
hiraṇya-garbham upalabhamānaḥ sahasaivotthāyārhaṇena saha pitā-
putrābhyām avahitāñjalir upatasthe.

tatra—there; *ha vā*—certainly; *enam*—him; *deva-ṛṣiḥ*—the great saint Nārada; *haṁsa-yānena*—by the swan carrier; *pitaram*—his father; *bhagavantam*—most powerful; *hiraṇya-garbham*—Lord Brahmā; *upalabhamānaḥ*—understanding; *sahasā eva*—immediately; *utthāya*—having stood up; *arhaṇena*—with paraphernalia for worship; *saha*—accompanied; *pitā-putrābhyām*—by Priyavrata and his father, Svāyambhuva Manu; *avahita-añjaliḥ*—with respect and folded hands; *upatasthe*—worshiped.

TRANSLATION

Lord Brahmā, the father of Nārada Muni, is the supreme person within this universe. As soon as Nārada saw the great swan, he could understand that Lord Brahmā had arrived. Therefore he immediately stood up, along with Svāyambhuva Manu and his son Priyavrata, whom Nārada was instructing. Then they folded their hands and began to worship Lord Brahmā with great respect.

PURPORT

As stated in the previous verse, Lord Brahmā was accompanied by other demigods, but his specific carrier was the great swan. Therefore as soon as Nārada Muni saw the swan, he could understand that his father, Lord Brahmā, who is also known as Hiraṇyagarbha, was arriving. Thus he immediately stood up with Svāyambhuva Manu and his son Priyavrata to receive Lord Brahmā and offer him respect.

TEXT 10

भगवानपि भारत तदुपनीतार्हणः सूक्तवाकेनातितरामुदितगुणगणावतार-सुजयः प्रियव्रतमादि पुरुषस्तं सदयहासावलोक इति होवाच ॥ १० ॥

bhagavān api bhārata tad-upanītārhaṇaḥ sūkta-vākenātitarām udita-guṇa-gaṇāvatāra-sujayaḥ priyavratam ādi-puruṣas taṁ sadaya-hāsāvaloka iti hovāca.

bhagavān—Lord Brahmā; *api*—moreover; *bhārata*—O King Parīkṣit; *tat*—by them; *upanīta*—brought forward; *arhaṇaḥ*—worshipable paraphernalia; *sūkta*—according to Vedic etiquette; *vākena*—by language; *atitarām*—highly; *udita*—praised; *guṇa-gaṇa*—qualities; *avatāra*—because of the descent; *su-jayaḥ*—whose glories; *priyavratam*—unto Priyavrata; *ādi-puruṣaḥ*—the original person; *tam*—unto him; *sa-daya*—with compassion; *hāsa*—smiling; *avalokaḥ*—whose looking; *iti*—thus; *ha*—certainly; *uvāca*—said.

TRANSLATION

My dear King Parīkṣit, because Lord Brahmā had finally descended from Satyaloka to Bhūloka, Nārada Muni, Prince Priyavrata and Svāyambhuva Manu came forward to offer him objects of worship and to praise him in highly qualified language, according to Vedic etiquette. At that time, Lord Brahmā, the original person of this universe, felt compassion for Priyavrata and, looking upon him with a smiling face, spoke to him as follows.

PURPORT

That Lord Brahmā descended from Satyaloka to see Priyavrata indicates that the matter was very serious. Nārada Muni had come to advise

Priyavrata about the value of spiritual life, knowledge, renunciation and *bhakti*, and Lord Brahmā knew that Nārada's instructions were very impressive. Therefore unless Lord Brahmā personally went to Gandhamādana Hill to request Priyavrata, Lord Brahmā knew that Prince Priyavrata would not accept his father's order. Brahmā's purpose was to break Priyavrata's determination. Therefore Brahmā first looked upon Priyavrata with compassion. His smile and compassionate features also indicated that although Brahmā would request Priyavrata to accept household life, Priyavrata would not be out of touch with devotional service. By the blessings of a Vaiṣṇava, everything is possible. This is described in *Bhakti-rasāmṛta-sindhu* as *kṛpā-siddhi*, or perfection attained simply by the blessings of a superior person. One usually becomes liberated and perfect by executing the regulative principles set down in the *śāstras*. Nonetheless, many persons have achieved perfection simply by the blessings of a spiritual master or superior.

Priyavrata was the grandson of Lord Brahmā, and as joking competition sometimes takes place between grandson and grandfather, in this case also Priyavrata was determined to remain in meditation, whereas Brahmā was determined that he rule the universe. Thus Lord Brahmā's affectionate smile and glance meant, "My dear Priyavrata, you have decided not to accept household life, but I have decided to convince you that you must accept it." Actually, Brahmā had come to praise Priyavrata for his high standard of renunciation, austerity, penance and devotion so that he would not be deviated from devotional service, even though he would accept household life.

In this verse, one important word is *sūkta-vākena* (by Vedic hymns). In the *Vedas*, there is the following prayer to Lord Brahmā: *hiraṇya-garbhaḥ samavartatāgre bhūtasya jātaḥ patir eka āsīt.* Brahmā was received with the appropriate Vedic hymns, and because he was welcomed according to the Vedic etiquette, he was very pleased.

TEXT 11

श्रीभगवानुवाच
निबोध तातेदमृतं ब्रवीमि
मासूयितुं देवमर्हस्यप्रमेयम् ।

वयं भवस्ते तत एष महर्षि-
वहाम सर्वे विवशा यस्य दिष्टम् ॥११॥

śrī-bhagavān uvāca
nibodha tatedam ṛtaṁ bravīmi
māsūyituṁ devam arhasy aprameyam
vayaṁ bhavas te tata eṣa maharṣir
vahāma sarve vivaśā yasya diṣṭam

śrī-bhagavān uvāca—the supreme person, Lord Brahmā, said; *nibodha*—kindly hear with attention; *tata*—my dear son; *idam*—this; *ṛtam*—true; *bravīmi*—I am speaking; *mā*—not; *asūyitum*—to be jealous of; *devam*—the Supreme Personality of Godhead; *arhasi*—you ought; *aprameyam*—who is beyond our experimental knowledge; *vayam*—we; *bhavaḥ*—Lord Śiva; *te*—your; *tataḥ*—father; *eṣaḥ*—this; *mahā-ṛṣiḥ*—Nārada; *vahāmaḥ*—carry out; *sarve*—all; *vivaśāḥ*—unable to deviate; *yasya*—of whom; *diṣṭam*—the order.

TRANSLATION

Lord Brahmā, the supreme person within this universe, said: My dear Priyavrata, kindly hear attentively what I shall say to you. Do not be jealous of the Supreme Lord, who is beyond our experimental measurements. All of us, including Lord Śiva, your father and the great sage Mahārṣi Nārada, must carry out the order of the Supreme. We cannot deviate from His order.

PURPORT

Of the twelve great authorities in devotional service, four—Lord Brahmā himself, his son Nārada, Svāyambhuva Manu and Lord Śiva—were present before Priyavrata. They were accompanied by many other authoritative sages. Brahmā first wanted to impress upon Priyavrata that although these great personalities are all authorities, they cannot possibly disobey the orders of the Supreme Personality of Godhead, who is described in this verse as *deva*, which means "always glorious." The power, glory and potencies of the Supreme Personality of Godhead can never be diminished. In the *Īśopaniṣad*, the Lord is described as *apāpa-*

viddha, which indicates that He is never affected by anything materially considered sinful. Similarly, *Śrīmad-Bhāgavatam* describes the Supreme Personality of Godhead as being so powerful that nothing we might consider abominable can affect Him. An example sometimes given to explain the position of the Supreme Lord is that of the sun, which evaporates urine from the earth but is never affected by contamination. The Supreme Lord can never be accused of doing anything wrong.

When Lord Brahmā went to induce Priyavrata to accept the responsibility for ruling the universe, he did not go whimsically; he was following the dictations of the Supreme Lord. Indeed, Brahmā and other genuine authorities never do anything without His permission. The Supreme Lord is situated in everyone's heart. In the beginning of *Śrīmad-Bhāgavatam* it is said, *tene brahma hṛdā ya ādi-kavaye:* the Lord dictated Vedic knowledge to Brahmā through his heart. The more a living entity is purified by devotional service, the more he comes in direct contact with the Supreme Personality of Godhead, as confirmed in *Śrīmad Bhagavad-gītā:*

teṣāṁ satata-yuktānāṁ
bhajatāṁ prīti-pūrvakam
dadāmi buddhi-yogaṁ taṁ
yena mām upayānti te

"To those who are constantly devoted and worship Me with love, I give the understanding by which they can come to Me." (Bg. 10.10) Lord Brahmā, therefore, had not come to Priyavrata by his own whims; rather, it is understood that he had been ordered to persuade Priyavrata by the Supreme Personality of Godhead, whose activities cannot be understood by material senses and who is therefore described herein as *aprameya*. Thus Lord Brahmā first advised Priyavrata to hear his words with attention and without envy.

Why one is induced to perform certain acts despite his desire to do something else is indicated herein. One cannot disobey the orders of the Supreme Lord, even if one is as powerful as Lord Śiva, Lord Brahmā, Manu or the great sage Nārada. All these authorities are certainly very powerful, but they do not have the power to disobey the orders of the

Supreme Personality of Godhead. Since Lord Brahmā had come to Priyavrata in accordance with the orders of the Supreme Lord, he first wanted to dispel any suspicions that he might be acting as Priyavrata's enemy. Lord Brahmā was following the orders of the Supreme Lord, and therefore it would be worthwhile for Priyavrata to accept Lord Brahmā's order, as the Lord desired.

TEXT 12

न तस्य कश्चित्तपसा विद्यया वा
न योगवीर्येण मनीषया वा ।
नैवार्थधर्मैः परतः स्वतो वा
कृतं विहन्तुं तनुभृद्विभूयात् ॥१२॥

na tasya kaścit tapasā vidyayā vā
na yoga-vīryeṇa manīṣayā vā
naivārtha-dharmaiḥ parataḥ svato vā
kṛtaṁ vihantuṁ tanu-bhṛd vibhūyāt

na—never; *tasya*—His; *kaścit*—anyone; *tapasā*—by austerity; *vidyayā*—by education; *vā*—or; *na*—never; *yoga*—by power of mystic *yoga; vīryeṇa*—by personal strength; *manīṣayā*—by intelligence; *vā*—or; *na*—never; *eva*—certainly; *artha*—by material opulence; *dharmaiḥ*—by the power of religion; *parataḥ*—by any external power; *svataḥ*—by personal endeavor; *vā*—or; *kṛtam*—the order; *vihantum*—to avoid; *tanu-bhṛt*—a living entity who has accepted a material body; *vibhūyāt*—is able.

TRANSLATION

One cannot avoid the order of the Supreme Personality of Godhead, not by the strength of severe austerities, an exalted Vedic education, or the power of mystic yoga, physical prowess or intellectual activities. Nor can one use his power of religion, his material opulence or any other means, either by himself or with the help of others, to defy the orders of the Supreme Lord. That is not possible for any living being, from Brahmā down to the ant.

PURPORT

In the *Garga Upaniṣad*, Gargamuni says to his wife, *etasya vā akṣarasya praśāsane gargi sūryā-candramasau vidhṛtau tiṣṭhataḥ:* "My dear Gargī, everything is under the control of the Supreme Personality of Godhead. Even the sun, the moon and other controllers and demigods like Lord Brahmā and King Indra are all under His control." An ordinary human being or animal who has accepted a material body cannot go beyond the jurisdiction of the Supreme Personality of Godhead's control. A material body includes senses. However, the sense activities of so-called scientists who try to be free from God's law or the laws of nature are useless. This is also confirmed in *Bhagavad-gītā* (7.14). *Mama māyā duratyayā:* it is impossible to surpass the control of material nature, for the Supreme Personality of Godhead is working behind it. Sometimes we are proud of our austerities, penances and mystic yogic powers, but it is clearly stated herein that one cannot surpass the laws and directions of the Supreme Personality of Godhead, either by dint of mystic power, a scientific education, or austerities and penances. It is impossible.

The word *manīṣayā* ("by intelligence") is of special significance. Priyavrata might argue that Lord Brahmā was requesting him to accept family life and the responsibility for ruling a kingdom, although Nārada Muni had advised him not to enter household life and be entangled in material affairs. Whom to accept would be a puzzle for Priyavrata because both Lord Brahmā and Nārada Muni are authorities. Under the circumstances, the use of the word *manīṣayā* is very appropriate, for it indicates that since both Nārada Muni and Lord Brahmā are authorized to give instruction, Priyavrata should neglect neither of them but should use his intelligence to follow the advice of both. To solve such dilemmas, Śrīla Rūpa Gosvāmī has given a very clear conception of intelligence. He says:

anāsaktasya viṣayān
yathārham upayuñjataḥ
nirbandhaḥ kṛṣṇa-sambandhe
yuktaṁ vairāgyam ucyate

Viṣayān, material affairs, should be accepted without attachment. and everything should be dovetailed with the service of the Lord. That is real intelligence (*manīṣā*). Becoming a family man or king in the material world is not harmful if one accepts everything for Kṛṣṇa's service. That necessitates clear intelligence. Māyāvādī philosophers say, *brahma satyaṁ jagan mithyā:* this material world is false, and only the Absolute Truth is real. However, an intelligent devotee in the line of Lord Brahmā and the great sage Nārada—or, in other words, in the Brahma-sampradāya—does not consider this world false. That which is created by the Supreme Personality of Godhead cannot be false, but using it for enjoyment is. Everything is meant to be enjoyed by the Supreme Personality of Godhead, as confirmed in *Bhagavad-gītā* (5.29). *Bhoktāraṁ yajña-tapasāṁ sarva-loka-maheśvaram:* the Supreme Personality of Godhead is the supreme proprietor and enjoyer, and therefore everything should be dovetailed for His enjoyment and service. Regardless of one's circumstances, favorable or unfavorable, one should use everything to serve the Supreme Lord. That is the perfect way to use one's intelligence.

TEXT 13

भवाय नाशाय च कर्म कर्तुं
शोकाय मोहाय सदा भयाय ।
सुखाय दुःखाय च देहयोग-
मव्यक्तदिष्टं जनताङ्ग धत्ते ॥१३॥

bhavāya nāśāya ca karma kartuṁ
śokāya mohāya sadā bhayāya
sukhāya duḥkhāya ca deha-yogam
avyakta-diṣṭaṁ janatāṅga dhatte

bhavāya—for birth; *nāśāya*—for death; *ca*—also; *karma*—activity; *kartum*—to do; *śokāya*—for bereavement; *mohāya*—for illuson; *sadā*—always; *bhayāya*—for fear; *sukhāya*—for happiness; *duḥkhāya*—for distress; *ca*—also; *deha-yogam*—connection with a material body; *avyakta*—by the Supreme Personality of Godhead; *diṣṭam*—directed; *janatā*—the living entities; *aṅga*—O Priyavrata; *dhatte*—accept.

TRANSLATION

My dear Priyavrata, by the order of the Supreme Personality of Godhead, all living entities accept different types of bodies for birth and death, activity, lamentation, illusion, fear of future dangers, and happiness and distress.

PURPORT

Every living entity who has come to this material world has come here for material enjoyment, but according to his own *karma*, activities, he must accept a certain type of body given to him by material nature under the order of the Supreme Personality of Godhead. As stated in *Bhagavad-gītā* (3.27), *prakṛteḥ kriyamāṇāni guṇaiḥ karmāṇi sarvaśaḥ:* everything is being done by *prakṛti*, material nature, under the direction of the Supreme Lord. Modern scientists do not know why there are varieties of bodies in 8,400,000 forms. The fact is that all these bodies are ordained for the living entities by the Supreme Personality of Godhead according to the living entities' desires. He gives the living entities freedom to act as they like, but on the other hand they must accept a body according to the reactions of their activities. Thus there are different types of bodies. Some living entities have short durations of life, whereas others live for fantastic durations. Every one of them, however, from Brahmā down to the ant, acts according to the direction of the Supreme Personality of Godhead, who is sitting in everyone's heart. As confirmed in *Bhagavad-gītā* (15.15):

sarvasya cāhaṁ hṛdi sanniviṣṭo
mattaḥ smṛtir jñānam apohanaṁ ca

"I am seated in everyone's heart, and from Me come remembrance, knowledge and forgetfulness." It is not a fact, however, that the Supreme Personality of Godhead gives direction to certain living entities in one way and other living entities in another way. The truth is that every living entity has a certain desire, and the Supreme Lord gives him a chance to fulfill it. The best course, therefore, is to surrender unto the Supreme Personality of Godhead and act according to His desire. One who does so is liberated.

TEXT 14

यद्वाचि तन्त्यां गुणकर्मदामभिः
सुदुस्तरैर्वत्स वयं सुयोजिताः ।
सर्वे वहामो बलिमीश्वराय
प्रोता नसीव द्विपदे चतुष्पदः ॥१४॥

yad-vāci tantyāṁ guṇa-karma-dāmabhiḥ
sudustarair vatsa vayaṁ suyojitāḥ
sarve vahāmo balim īśvarāya
protā nasīva dvi-pade catuṣ-padaḥ

yat—of whom; *vāci*—in the form of Vedic instruction; *tantyām*—to a long rope; *guṇa*—of quality; *karma*—and work; *dāmabhiḥ*—by the ropes; *su-dustaraiḥ*—very difficult to avoid; *vatsa*—my dear boy; *vayam*—we; *su-yojitāḥ*—are engaged; *sarve*—all; *vahāmaḥ*—carry out; *balim*—orders to please Him; *īśvarāya*—unto the Supreme Personality of Godhead; *protāḥ*—being bound; *nasi*—in the nose; *iva*—like; *dvi-pade*—to the two-legged (driver); *catuḥ-padaḥ*—the four-legged (bulls).

TRANSLATION

My dear boy, all of us are bound by the Vedic injunctions to the divisions of varṇāśrama according to our qualities and work. These divisions are difficult to avoid because they are scientifically arranged. We must therefore carry out our duties of varṇāśrama-dharma, like bulls obliged to move according to the direction of a driver pulling on ropes knotted to their noses.

PURPORT

In this verse, the words *tantyāṁ guṇa-karma-dāmabhiḥ* are very important. We each get a body according to our association with the *guṇas*, the qualities or modes of material nature, and we act accordingly. As stated in *Bhagavad-gītā*, the four orders of the social system—namely *brāhmaṇa, kṣatriya, vaiśya* and *śūdra*— are arranged according to *guṇa* and *karma*, their qualities and work. There is some controversy about this, however, because some say that since one receives a body according to the *guṇa* and *karma* of his past life, it is one's birth that determines his social status. Others say, however, that one's birth according to the *guṇa* and *karma* of his past life is not the essential consideration, since one can change his *guṇa* and *karma* even in this life. Thus they say that the four divisions of the social order—*brāhmaṇa, kṣatriya, vaiśya* and *śūdra*— should be arranged according to the *guṇa* and *karma* of this life. This version is confirmed in *Śrīmad-Bhāgavatam* by Nārada Muni. While instructing Mahārāja Yudhiṣṭhira about the symptoms of *guṇa* and *karma*, Nārada Muni said that these symptoms must govern the division of society. In other words, if a person born in the family of a *brāhmaṇa* has the symptoms of a *śūdra*, he should be designated as a *śūdra*. Similarly, if a *śūdra* has brahminical qualities, he should be designated a *brāhmaṇa*.

The *varṇāśrama* system is scientific. Therefore if we accept the divisions of *varṇa* and *āśrama* according to the Vedic instructions, our lives will be successful. Unless human society is thus divided and arranged, it cannot be perfect. As stated in the *Viṣṇu Purāṇa* (3.8.9):

varṇāśramācāravatā
puruṣeṇa paraḥ pumān
viṣṇur ārādhyate panthā
nānyat tat-toṣa-kāraṇam

"The Supreme Personality of Godhead, Lord Viṣṇu, is worshiped by the proper execution of prescribed duties in the system of *varṇa* and *āśrama*. There is no other way to satisfy the Supreme Personality of Godhead. One must be situated in the institution of the four *varṇas* and *āśramas*." All of human society is meant to worship Lord Viṣṇu. At the present moment, however, human society does not know that this is the ultimate goal or perfection of life. Therefore instead of worshiping Lord Viṣṇu, people have been educated to worship matter. According to the direction of modern society, men think they can advance in civilization by manipulating matter to build skyscrapers, big roads, automobiles and so on. Such a civilization must certainly be called materialistic because its people do not know the goal of life. The goal of life is to reach Viṣṇu, but instead of reaching Viṣṇu, people are bewildered by the external manifestation of the material energy. Therefore progress in material advancement is blind, and the leaders of such material advancement are also blind. They are leading their followers in the wrong way.

It is best, therefore, to accept the injunctions of the *Vedas*, which are mentioned in this verse as *yad-vāci*. In accordance with those injunctions, everyone should find out whether he is a *brāhmaṇa*, *kṣatriya*, *vaiśya* or *śūdra* and should thus be educated accordingly. Then his life will be successful. Otherwise, all of human society will be confused. If human society is divided scientifically according to *varṇa* and *āśrama*, and if the Vedic directions are followed, one's life, regardless of his position, will be successful. It is not that *brāhmaṇas* will be elevated to the transcendental platform but not the *śūdras*. If the Vedic injunctions are followed, all of them—*brāhmaṇas*, *kṣatriyas*, *vaiśyas* and *śūdras*—will be elevated to the transcendental platform, and their lives will be successful. The injunctions in the *Vedas* are explicit directions from the Supreme Personality of Godhead. The example cited in this verse is that bulls tied by ropes in their nostrils move according to the direction of the driver. Similarly, if we move according to the instructions of the *Vedas*, the perfect paths for our lives will be set. Otherwise, if we do not move in that way but act according to our whimsical ideas, our lives will be spoiled by confusion and will end in despair. Actually, because people at the present moment are not following the instructions of the *Vedas*, they are all confused. We must therefore accept this instruction by Lord Brahmā to Priyavrata as the factual scientific direction leading to the success of life. This is also confirmed in *Bhagavad-gītā* (16.23):

yaḥ śāstra-vidhim utsṛjya
vartate kāma-kārataḥ
na sa siddhim avāpnoti
na sukhaṁ na parāṁ gatim

If we do not live according to the injunctions of the *śāstras*, the *Vedas*, we shall never achieve success in life, to say nothing of happiness or elevation to higher statuses of living.

TEXT 15

ईशाभिसृष्टं ह्यवरुन्ध्महेऽङ्ग
दुःखं सुखं वा गुणकर्मसङ्गात् ।
आस्थाय तत्तद्यदयुङ्क्त नाथ-
श्चक्षुष्मतान्धा इव नीयमानाः ॥१५॥

īśābhisṛṣṭaṁ hy avarundhmahe 'ṅga
duḥkhaṁ sukhaṁ vā guṇa-karma-saṅgāt
āsthāya tat tad yad ayuṅkta nāthaś
cakṣuṣmatāndhā iva nīyamānāḥ

īśa-abhisṛṣṭam—created or given by the Lord; *hi*—certainly; *avarundhmahe*—we have to accept; *aṅga*—my dear Priyavrata; *duḥkham*—distress; *sukham*—happiness; *vā*—or; *guṇa-karma*—with quality and work; *saṅgāt*—by association; *āsthāya*—being situated in; *tat tat*—that condition; *yat*—which body; *ayuṅkta*—He gave; *nāthaḥ*—the Supreme Lord; *cakṣuṣmatā*—by a person having eyes; *andhāḥ*—blind men; *iva*—like; *nīyamānāḥ*—being conducted.

TRANSLATION

My dear Priyavrata, according to our association with different modes of material nature, the Supreme Personality of Godhead gives us our specific bodies and the happiness and distress we achieve. One must therefore remain situated as he is and be conducted by the Supreme Personality of Godhead, exactly as a blind man is led by a person who has eyes with which to see.

PURPORT

By material means, one cannot avoid the happiness and distress unique to his particular body. There are 8,400,000 bodily forms, each destined to enjoy and suffer a certain amount of happiness and distress. This we cannot change, for the happiness and distress are ordained by the Supreme Personality of Godhead, in accordance with whose decision we have received our bodies. Since we cannot avoid the plan of the Supreme Godhead, we must agree to be directed by Him, just as a blind man is led by a person who has eyes. Under any circumstances, if we remain in the condition allotted to us by the Supreme Lord and follow His instructions, we will become perfect. The main purpose of life is to follow the instructions of the Supreme Personality of Godhead. It is such instructions that constitute one's religion or occupational duty.

In *Bhagavad-gītā*, therefore, Lord Kṛṣṇa says, *sarva-dharmān parityajya mām ekaṁ śaraṇaṁ vraja:* "Give up all other engagements. Simply surrender unto Me and follow Me." (Bg. 18.66) This process of surrendering by following the instructions of the Supreme Personality of Godhead is not meant for any particular caste or creed. A *brāhmaṇa* can surrender, and so can a *kṣatriya, vaiśya* or *śūdra.* Everyone can adopt this process. As stated in this verse, *cakṣuṣmatāndhā iva nīyamānāḥ:* one should follow the Lord the way a blind man follows a person who has eyes. If we follow the Supreme Personality of Godhead by following the directions He gives in the *Vedas* and *Bhagavad-gītā,* our lives will be successful. The Lord therefore says:

man-manā bhava mad-bhakto
mad-yājī māṁ namaskuru
mām evaiṣyasi satyaṁ te
pratijāne priyo 'si me

"Always think of Me, become My devotee, and offer respect and obeisances unto Me. Then you will certainly come back home, back to Godhead. I promise you this because you are My very dear friend." (Bg. 18.65) This instruction is meant for everyone—*brāhmaṇa, kṣatriya, vaiśya* or *śūdra.* If anyone, from any division of life, surrenders to the Supreme Personality of Godhead and follows His instructions, his life will be successful.

The previous verse has given the analogy of bulls moving under the direction of the driver of a bullock cart. The bulls, being completely surrendered to the driver, remain wherever he wants to place them and eat whatever he wants them to eat. Similarly, being completely surrendered to the Supreme Personality of Godhead, we should not aspire for happiness, or regret distress; we must be satisfied with the position allotted to us by the Lord. We should follow the path of devotional service and not be dissatisfied with the happiness and distress He has given. People in the material modes of passion and ignorance generally cannot understand the plan of the Supreme Personality of Godhead with its 8,400,000 forms of life, but the human form affords one the special privilege to understand this plan, engage in devotional service and elevate oneself to the highest position of perfection by following the Lord's instructions. The entire world is working under the influence of the modes of material nature, especially ignorance and passion, but if people engage in hearing and chanting about the glories of the Supreme Lord, their lives can be successful, and they can be elevated to the highest perfection. In the *Bṛhan-nāradīya Purāṇa*, therefore, it is said:

harer nāma harer nāma
harer nāmaiva kevalam
kalau nāsty eva nāsty eva
nāsty eva gatir anyathā

"In this age of Kali, there is no other way, no other way, no other way for spiritual perfection than the holy name, the holy name, the holy name of the Lord." Everyone should be given the chance to hear the holy names of the Supreme Personality of Godhead, for thus one will gradually come to understand his real position in life and be elevated to the transcendental position above the mode of goodness. Thus all impediments to his progress will be cut to pieces. In conclusion, therefore, we must be satisfied in whatever position we have been put into by the Supreme Personality of Godhead, and we should try to engage ourselves in His devotional service. Then our lives will be successful.

TEXT 16

मुक्तोऽपि तावद्बिभृयात्स्वदेह-
मारब्धमश्नन्नभिमानशून्यः ।
यथानुभूतं प्रतियातनिद्रः
किं त्वन्यदेहाय गुणान्न वृङ्क्ते ॥१६॥

mukto 'pi tāvad bibhṛyāt sva-deham
ārabdham aśnann abhimāna-śūnyaḥ
yathānubhūtaṁ pratiyāta-nidraḥ
kiṁ tv anya-dehāya guṇān na vṛṅkte

muktaḥ—a liberated person; *api*—even; *tāvat*—so long; *bibhṛyāt*—must maintain; *sva-deham*—his own body; *ārabdham*—obtained as a result of past activity; *aśnan*—accepting; *abhimāna-śūnyaḥ*—without erroneous conceptions; *yathā*—as; *anubhūtam*—what was perceived; *pratiyāta-nidraḥ*—one who has awakened from sleep; *kim tu*—but; *anya-dehāya*—for another material body; *guṇān*—the material qualities; *na*—never; *vṛṅkte*—enjoys.

TRANSLATION

Even if one is liberated, he nevertheless accepts the body he has received according to his past karma. Without misconceptions, however, he regards his enjoyment and suffering due to that karma the way an awakened person regards a dream he had while sleeping. He thus remains steadfast and never works to achieve another material body under the influence of the three modes of material nature.

PURPORT

The difference between a liberated and conditioned soul is that the conditioned soul is under the concept of bodily life, whereas a liberated person knows that he is not the body but a spirit, different from the body. Priyavrata might have thought that although a conditioned soul is forced to act according to the laws of nature, why should he, who was far advanced in spiritual understanding, accept the same kind of bondage and impediments to spiritual advancement? To answer this doubt, Lord Brahmā informed him that even those who are liberated do not resent accepting, in the present body, the results of their past activities. While sleeping, one dreams many unreal things, but when he awakens he disregards them and makes progress in factual life. Similarly, a liberated person—one who has completely understood that he is not the body but a spirit soul—disregards past activities performed in ignorance and performs his present activities in such a way that they produce no reactions.

This is described in *Bhagavad-gītā* (3.9). *Yajñārthāt karmaṇo 'nyatra loko 'yaṁ karma-bandhanaḥ:* if one performs activities for the satisfaction of the Supreme Personality, the *yajña-puruṣa,* his work does not produce reactions, whereas *karmīs,* who act for themselves, are bound by the reactions of their work. A liberated person, therefore, does not think about whatever he has ignorantly done in the past; instead, he acts in such a way that he will not produce another body by fruitive activities. As clearly mentioned in *Bhagavad-gītā:*

mām ca yo 'vyabhicāreṇa
bhakti-yogena sevate
sa guṇān samatītyaitān
brahma-bhūyāya kalpate

"One who engages in full devotional service, who does not fall down in any circumstance, at once transcends the modes of material nature and thus comes to the level of Brahman." (Bg. 14.26) Regardless of what we have done in our past lives, if we engage ourselves in unalloyed devotional service to the Lord in this life, we will always be situated in the *brahma-bhūta* (liberated) state, free from reactions, and will not be obliged to accept another material body. *Tyaktvā dehaṁ punar janma naiti mām eti so 'rjuna* (Bg. 4.9). After giving up the body, one who has acted in that way does not accept another material body, but instead goes back home, back to Godhead.

TEXT 17

भयं प्रमत्तस्य वनेष्वपि स्याद्
यतः स आस्ते सहषटसपत्नः ।
जितेन्द्रियस्यात्मरतेर्बुधस्य
गृहाश्रमः किं नु करोत्यवद्यम् ॥१७॥

bhayaṁ pramattasya vaneṣv api syād
yataḥ sa āste saha-ṣaṭ-sapatnaḥ
jitendriyasyātma-rater budhasya
gṛhāśramaḥ kiṁ nu karoty avadyam

bhayam—fear; *pramattasya*—of one who is bewildered; *vaneṣu*—in forests; *api*—even; *syāt*—there must be; *yataḥ*—because; *saḥ*—he (one who is not self-controlled); *āste*—is existing; *saha*—with; *ṣaṭ-sapatnaḥ*—six co-wives; *jita-indriyasya*—for one who has already conquered the senses; *ātma-rateḥ*—self-satisfied; *budhasya*—for such a learned man; *gṛha-āśramaḥ*—household life; *kim*—what; *nu*—indeed; *karoti*—can do; *avadyam*—harm.

TRANSLATION

Even if he goes from forest to forest, one who is not self-controlled must always fear material bondage because he is living with six co-wives—the mind and knowledge-acquiring senses. Even householder life, however, cannot harm a self-satisfied, learned man who has conquered his senses.

PURPORT

Śrīla Narottama dāsa Ṭhākura has sung, *gṛhe vā vanete thāke, 'hā gaurāṅga' bale ḍāke:* whether one is situated in the forest or at home, if he is engaged in the devotional service of Lord Caitanya, he is a liberated person. Here this is also repeated. For one who has not controlled his senses, going to the forest to become a so-called *yogī* is meaningless. Because his uncontrolled mind and senses are going with him, he cannot achieve anything, even by giving up household life and staying in the forest. Formerly many mercantile men from the up-country of India used to go to Bengal, and thus there is a familiar saying, "If you go to Bengal, your fortune will go with you." Our first concern, therefore, should be to control the senses, and since the senses cannot be controlled unless engaged in the devotional service of the Lord, our most important duty is to engage the senses in devotional service. *Hṛṣīkeṇa hṛṣīkeśa-sevanaṁ bhaktir ucyate: bhakti* means engagement of the purified senses in the service of the Lord.

Herein Lord Brahmā indicates that instead of going to the forest with uncontrolled senses, it is better and more secure to engage the senses in the service of the Lord. Even household life can do no harm to a self-controlled person acting in this way; it cannot force him into material bondage. Śrīla Rūpa Gosvāmī has further enunciated this position:

īhā yasya harer dāsye
karmaṇā manasā girā
nikhilāsv apy avasthāsu
jīvan-muktaḥ sa ucyate

"Regardless of one's circumstances, if one fully engages his activities, mind and words in the devotional service of the Lord, he should be understood to be a liberated person." Śrīla Bhaktivinoda Ṭhākura was a responsible officer and a householder, yet his service to the cause of expanding the mission of Lord Caitanya Mahāprabhu is unique. Śrīla Prabodhānanda Sarasvatī Ṭhākura says, *durdāntendriya-kāla-sarpa-paṭalī protkhāta-daṁṣṭrāyate.* The sense organs are certainly our greatest enemies, and they are therefore compared to venomous serpents. However, if a venomous serpent is bereft of its poison fangs, it is no longer fearful. Similarly, if the senses are engaged in the service of the Lord, there is no need to fear their activities. The devotees in the Kṛṣṇa consciousness movement move within this material world, but because their senses are fully engaged in the service of the Lord, they are always aloof from the material world. They are always living in a transcendental position.

TEXT 18

यः षट् सपत्नान् विजिगीषमाणो
गृहेषु निर्विश्य यतेत पूर्वम् ।
अत्येति दुर्गाश्रित ऊर्जितारीन्
क्षीणेषु कामं विचरेद्विपश्चित् ॥१८॥

yaḥ ṣaṭ sapatnān vijigīṣamāṇo
gṛheṣu nirviśya yateta pūrvam
atyeti durgāśrita ūrjitārīn
kṣīṇeṣu kāmaṁ vicared vipaścit

yaḥ—anyone who; *ṣaṭ*—six; *sapatnān*—adversaries; *vijigīṣamāṇaḥ*—desiring to conquer; *gṛheṣu*—in household life; *nir-*

viśya—having entered; *yateta*—must try; *pūrvam*—first; *atyeti*—conquers; *durga-āśritaḥ*—being in a fortified place; *ūrjita-arīn*—very strong enemies; *kṣīṇeṣu*—decreased; *kāmam*—lusty desires; *vicaret*—can go; *vipaścit*—the most experienced, learned.

TRANSLATION

One who is situated in household life and who systematically conquers his mind and five sense organs is like a king in his fortress who conquers his powerful enemies. After one has been trained in household life and his lusty desires have decreased, he can move anywhere without danger.

PURPORT

The Vedic system of four *varṇas* and four *āśramas* is very scientific, and its entire purpose is to enable one to control the senses. Before entering household life (*gṛhastha-āśrama*), a student is fully trained to become *jitendriya*, a conqueror of the senses. Such a mature student is allowed to become a householder, and because he was first trained in conquering his senses, he retires from household life and becomes *vānaprastha* as soon as the strong waves of youthful life are past and he reaches the verge of old age at fifty years or slightly more. Then, after being further trained, he accepts *sannyāsa*. He is then a fully learned and renounced person who can move anywhere and everywhere without fear of being captivated by material desires. The senses are considered very powerful enemies. As a king in a strong fortress can conquer powerful enemies, so a householder in *gṛhastha-āśrama*, household life, can conquer the lusty desires of youth and be very secure when he takes *vānaprastha* and *sannyāsa*.

TEXT 19

त्वं त्वब्जनाभाङ्घ्रिसरोजकोश-
दुर्गाश्रितो निर्जितषट्सपत्नः ।
भुङ्क्ष्वेह भोगान् पुरुषातिदिष्टान्
विमुक्तसङ्गः प्रकृतिं भजस्व ॥१९॥

tvaṁ tv abja-nābhāṅghri-saroja-kośa-
durgāśrito nirjita-ṣaṭ-sapatnaḥ
bhuṅkṣveha bhogān puruṣātidiṣṭān
vimukta-saṅgaḥ prakṛtiṁ bhajasva

tvam—yourself; *tu*—then; *abja-nābha*—of the Supreme Personality of Godhead, whose navel is like a lotus flower; *aṅghri*—feet; *saroja*—lotus; *kośa*—hole; *durga*—the stronghold; *āśritaḥ*—taken shelter of; *nirjita*—conquered; *ṣaṭ-sapatnaḥ*—the six enemies (the mind and five senses); *bhuṅkṣva*—enjoy; *iha*—in this material world; *bhogān*—enjoyable things; *puruṣa*—by the Supreme Person; *atidiṣṭān*—extraordinarily ordered; *vimukta*—liberated; *saṅgaḥ*—from material association; *prakṛtim*—constitutional position; *bhajasva*—enjoy.

TRANSLATION

Lord Brahmā continued: My dear Priyavrata, seek shelter inside the opening in the lotus of the feet of the Lord, whose navel is also like a lotus. Thus conquer the six sense organs [the mind and knowledge-acquiring senses]. Accept material enjoyment because the Lord, extraordinarily, has ordered you to do this. You will thus always be liberated from material association and be able to carry out the Lord's orders in your constitutional position.

PURPORT

There are three kinds of men within this material world. Those who are trying to enjoy the senses to the utmost are called *karmīs,* above them are the *jñānīs,* who try to conquer the urges of the senses, and above them are the *yogīs,* who have already conquered the senses. None of them, however, are situated in a transcendental position. Only devotees, who belong to none of the above-mentioned groups, are transcendental. As explained in *Bhagavad-gītā* (14.26):

māṁ ca yo 'vyabhicāreṇa
bhakti-yogena sevate
sa guṇān samatītyaitān
brahma-bhūyāya kalpate

"One who engages in full devotional service, who does not fall down in any circumstance, at once transcends the modes of material nature and thus comes to the level of Brahman." Lord Brahmā herein advises Priyavrata to remain transcendental in the fortress not of family life but of the lotus feet of the Lord (*abja-nābhāṅghri-saroja*). When a bumblebee enters the opening of a lotus flower and drinks its honey, it is fully protected by the petals of the lotus. The bee is undisturbed by sunshine and other external influences. Similarly, one who always seeks shelter at the lotus feet of the Personality of Godhead is protected from all dangers. It is therefore said in *Śrīmad-Bhāgavatam* (10.14.58):

samāśritā ye pada-pallava-plavaṁ
mahat-padaṁ puṇya-yaśo murāreḥ
bhavāmbudhir vatsa-padaṁ paraṁ padaṁ
padaṁ padaṁ yad vipadāṁ na teṣām

For one who has taken shelter of the lotus feet of the Lord, everything becomes easier. Indeed, even crossing the great ocean of nescience (*bhavāmbudhi*) is exactly like crossing the hoofprint created by a calf (*vatsa-padam*). For such a devotee, there is no question of remaining in a place where every step is dangerous.

Our actual duty is to carry out the supreme order of the Personality of Godhead. If we are fixed in our determination to carry out the supreme order of the Lord, we are always secure, regardless of where we are situated, whether in hell or in heaven. Herein the words *prakṛtiṁ bhajasva* are very significant. *Prakṛtim* refers to one's constitutional position. Every living entity has the constitutional position of being an eternal servant of God. Therefore Lord Brahmā advised Priyavrata, "Be situated in your original position as an eternal servant of the Lord. If you carry out His orders, you will never fall, even in the midst of material enjoyment." Material enjoyment achieved by dint of one's fruitive activities differs from material enjoyment given by the Supreme Personality of Godhead. A devotee sometimes appears to be in a very opulent position, but he accepts that position to follow the orders of the Supreme Personality of Godhead. Therefore a devotee is never affected by material influences. The devotees in the Kṛṣṇa consciousness movement are preaching all over the world in accordance with the order of Śrī Caitanya Mahāprabhu.

They have to meet many *karmīs*, but by the mercy of Śrī Caitanya Mahāprabhu, they are unaffected by material influences. He has blessed them, as described in the *Caitanya-caritāmṛta* (*Madhya* 7.129):

kabhu nā bādhibe tomāra viṣaya-taraṅga
punarapi ei ṭhāñi pābe mora saṅge

A sincere devotee who engages in the service of Lord Śrī Caitanya Mahāprabhu by preaching His cult all over the world will never be affected by *viṣaya-taraṅga*, material influences. On the contrary, in due course of time he will return to the shelter of the lotus feet of Lord Śrī Caitanya Mahāprabhu and will thus have perpetual association with Him.

TEXT 20

श्रीशुक उवाच

इति समभिहितो महाभागवतो भगवतस्त्रिभुवनगुरोरनुशासनमात्मनो
लघुतयावनतशिरोधरो बाढमिति सबहुमानमुवाह ॥ २० ॥

śrī-śuka uvāca
iti samabhihito mahā-bhāgavato bhagavatas tri-bhuvana-guror anuśāsanam ātmano laghutayāvanata-śirodharo bāḍham iti sabahu-mānam uvāha.

śrī-śukaḥ uvāca—Śrī Śukadeva Gosvāmī said; *iti*—thus; *samabhihitaḥ*—completely instructed; *mahā-bhāgavataḥ*—the great devotee; *bhagavataḥ*—of the most powerful Lord Brahmā; *tri-bhuvana*—of the three worlds; *guroḥ*—the spiritual master; *anuśāsanam*—the order; *ātmanaḥ*—of himself; *laghutayā*—because of inferiority; *avanata*—bowed down; *śirodharaḥ*—his head; *bāḍham*—yes, sir; *iti*—thus; *sa-bahu-mānam*—with great respect; *uvāha*—carried out.

TRANSLATION

Śrī Śukadeva Gosvāmī continued: After thus being fully instructed by Lord Brahmā, who is the spiritual master of the three

worlds, Priyavrata, his own position being inferior, offered obeisances, accepted the order and carried it out with great respect.

PURPORT

Śrī Priyavrata was the grandson of Lord Brahmā. Therefore according to social etiquette, his position was inferior. It is the duty of the inferior to carry out the order of the superior with great respect. Priyavrata therefore immediately said, "Yes, sir. I shall carry out your order." Priyavrata is described as a *mahā-bhāgavata,* a great devotee. The duty of a great devotee is to carry out the order of the spiritual master, or the spiritual master of the spiritual master in the *paramparā* system. As described in *Bhagavad-gītā* (4.2), *evaṁ paramparā prāptam:* one has to receive the instructions of the Supreme Lord through the disciplic chain of spiritual masters. A devotee of the Lord always considers himself a servant of the servant of the servant of the Lord.

TEXT 21

भगवानपि मनुना यथावदुपकल्पितापचितिः प्रियव्रतनारदयोरविषमम-
भिसमीक्षमाणयोरात्मसमवस्थानमवाङ्मनसं क्षयमव्यवहृतं प्रवर्तयन्नगमत ॥२१॥

bhagavān api manunā yathāvad upakalpitāpacitiḥ priyavrata-
nāradayor aviṣamam abhisamīkṣamāṇayor ātmasam avasthānam avāṅ-
manasaṁ kṣayam avyavahṛtaṁ pravartayann agamat.

bhagavān—the most powerful Lord Brahmā; *api*—also; *manunā*—by Manu; *yathāvat*—as deserved; *upakalpita-apacitiḥ*—being worshiped; *priyavrata-nāradayoḥ*—in the presence of Priyavrata and Nārada; *aviṣamam*—without aversion; *abhisamīkṣamāṇayoḥ*—looking on; *ātmasam*—just suitable for his position; *avasthānam*—to his abode; *a-vāk-manasam*—beyond the description of mind and words; *kṣayam*—the planet; *avyavahṛtam*—extraordinarily situated; *pravartayan*—departing; *agamat*—returned.

TRANSLATION

Lord Brahmā was then worshiped by Manu, who respectfully satisfied him as well as he could. Priyavrata and Nārada also looked

upon Brahmā with no tinges of resentment. Having engaged Priyavrata in accepting his father's request, Lord Brahmā returned to his abode, Satyaloka, which is indescribable by the endeavor of mundane mind or words.

PURPORT

Manu was certainly very satisfied that Lord Brahmā had persuaded his son Priyavrata to take the responsibility for ruling the world. Priyavrata and Nārada were also very satisfied. Although Brahmā had forced Priyavrata to accept the management of worldly affairs, thus breaking his vow to remain *brahmacārī* and completely engage in devotional service, Nārada and Priyavrata did not look upon Brahmā with resentment. Nārada was not at all sorry that he had been frustrated in making Priyavrata a disciple. Both Priyavrata and Nārada were exalted personalities who knew how to respect Lord Brahmā. Therefore instead of looking upon Brahmā with resentment, they very feelingly offered him their respect. Lord Brahmā then returned to his celestial abode, known as Satyaloka, which is described here as being impeccable and being unapproachable by words.

It is stated in this verse that Lord Brahmā returned to his residence, which is as important as his own personality. Lord Brahmā is the creator of this universe and the most exalted personality within it. His lifetime is described in *Bhagavad-gītā* (8.17). *Sahasra-yuga-paryantam ahar yad brahmaṇo viduḥ.* The total duration of the four yugas is 4,300,000 years, and when that is multiplied a thousand times, it equals twelve hours in the life of Brahmā. Therefore we cannot factually comprehend even twelve hours of Brahmā's life, to say nothing of the one hundred years that constitute his entire lifetime. How, then, can we understand his abode? The Vedic literatures describe that in Satyaloka there is no birth, death, old age or disease. In other words, since Satyaloka is situated next to Brahmaloka, or the Brahman effulgence, it is almost as good as Vaikuṇṭhaloka. Lord Brahmā's abode is practically indescribable from our present status. Therefore it has been described as *avāṅ-manasa-gocara*, or beyond the description of our words and the imagination of our minds. The Vedic literatures thus describe the abode of Lord Brahmā: *yad vai parārdhyaṁ tad upārameṣṭhyaṁ na yatra śoko na jarā na mṛtyur nārtir na codvegaḥ.* "In Satyaloka, which is situated many millions and billions of years away, there is no lamentation, nor is there old age, death, anxiety or the influence of enemies."

TEXT 22

मनुरपि परेणैवं प्रतिसन्धितमनोरथः सुरर्षिवरानुमतेनात्मजमखिलधरामण्डल-
स्थितिगुप्तय आस्थाप्य स्वयमतिविषमविषयविषजलाशयाशाया उपरराम॥२२॥

manur api pareṇaivaṁ pratisandhita-manorathaḥ surarṣi-
varānumatenātmajam akhila-dharā-maṇḍala-sthiti-guptaya āsthāpya
svayam ati-viṣama-viṣaya-viṣa-jalāśayāśāyā upararāma.

manuḥ—Svāyambhuva Manu; *api*—also; *pareṇa*—by Lord Brahmā; *evam*—thus; *pratisandhita*—executed; *manaḥ-rathaḥ*—his mental aspiration; *sura-ṛṣi-vara*—of the great sage Nārada; *anumatena*—by the permission; *ātma-jam*—his son; *akhila*—of the entire universe; *dharā-maṇḍala*—of planets; *sthiti*—maintenance; *guptaye*—for the protection; *āsthāpya*—establishing; *svayam*—personally; *ati-viṣama*—very dangerous; *viṣaya*—material affairs; *viṣa*—of poison; *jala-āśaya*—ocean; *āśāyāḥ*—from desires; *upararāma*—got relief.

TRANSLATION

Svāyambhuva Manu, with the assistance of Lord Brahmā, thus fulfilled his desires. With the permission of the great sage Nārada, he delivered to his son the governmental responsibility for maintaining and protecting all the planets of the universe. He thus achieved relief from the most dangerous, poisonous ocean of material desires.

PURPORT

Svāyambhuva Manu was practically hopeless because such a great personality as Nārada was instructing his son Priyavrata not to accept household life. Now he was very pleased that Lord Brahmā had interfered by inducing his son to accept the responsibility for ruling the government of the universe. From *Bhagavad-gītā* we get information that Vaivasvata Manu was the son of the sun-god and that his son, Mahārāja Ikṣvāku, ruled this planet earth. Svāyambhuva Manu, however, appears to have been in charge of the entire universe, and he entrusted to his son, Mahārāja Priyavrata, the responsibility for maintaining and protecting all the planetary systems. *Dharā-maṇḍala* means "planet." This earth, for instance, is called *dharā-maṇḍala. Akhila,* however, means "all" or "universal." It is therefore difficult to understand where Mahārāja Priyavrata was situated, but from this literature his position certainly appears greater than that of Vaivasvata Manu, for he was entrusted with all the planetary systems of the entire universe.

Another significant statement is that Svāyambhuva Manu took great satisfaction from abnegating the responsibility for ruling all the planetary systems of the universe. At present, politicians are very eager to take charge of the government, and they engage their men in canvassing from door to door to get votes to win the post of president or a similar exalted office. On the contrary, however, herein we find that King Priyavrata had to be persuaded by Lord Brahmā to accept the post of emperor of the entire universe. Similarly, his father, Svāyambhuva Manu, felt relieved to entrust the universal government to Priyavrata. Thus it is evident that the kings and executive heads of government in the Vedic age never accepted their positions for sense enjoyment. Such exalted kings, who were known as *rājarṣis,* ruled only to maintain and protect the kingdom for the welfare of the citizens. The history of Priyavrata and Svāyambhuva Manu describes how exemplary, responsible monarchs performed the duties of government with disinterest, keeping themselves always aloof from the contamination of material attachment.

Material affairs have herein been compared to an ocean of poison. They have been described in a similar way by Śrīla Narottama dāsa Ṭhākura in one of his songs:

saṁsāra-viṣānale, divā-niśi hiyā jvale,
juḍāite nā kainu upāya

"My heart is always burning in the fire of material existence, and I have made no provisions for getting out of it."

golokera prema-dhana, hari-nāma-saṅkīrtana,
rati nā janmila kene tāya

"The only remedy is *hari-nāma-saṅkīrtana*, the chanting of the Hare Kṛṣṇa *mahā-mantra*, which is imported from the spiritual world, Goloka Vṛndāvana. How unfortunate I am that I have no attraction for this." Manu wanted to seek shelter at the lotus feet of the Lord, and therefore when his son Priyavrata took charge of his worldly affairs, Manu was very relieved. That is the system of Vedic civilization. At the end of life, one must free himself from worldly affairs and completely engage in the service of the Lord.

The word *surarṣi-vara-anumatena* is also significant. Manu entrusted the government to his son with the permission of the great saint Nārada. This is particularly mentioned because although Nārada wanted Priyavrata to become free from all material affairs, when Priyavrata took charge of the universe by the request of Lord Brahmā and Manu, Nārada was also very pleased.

TEXT 23

इति ह वाव स जगतीपतिरीश्वरेच्छयाधिनिवेशितकर्माधिकारोऽखिलजगद्बन्ध-
ध्वंसनपरानुभावस्य भगवत आदिपुरुषस्याङ्घ्रियुगलानवरतध्यानानुभावेन
परिरन्धितकषायाशयोऽवदातोऽपि मानवर्धनो महतां महीतलमनुशशास ॥ २३ ॥

iti ha vāva sa jagatī-patir īśvarecchayādhiniveśita-karmādhikāro
'khila-jagad-bandha-dhvaṁsana-parānubhāvasya bhagavata ādi-
puruṣasyāṅghri-yugalānavarata-dhyānānubhāvena parirandhita-
kaṣāyāśayo 'vadāto 'pi māna-vardhano mahatāṁ mahītalam anuśaśāsa.

iti—thus; *ha vāva*—indeed; *saḥ*—he; *jagatī-patiḥ*—the emperor of the whole universe; *īśvara-icchayā*—by the order of the Supreme Personality of Godhead; *adhiniveśita*—completely engaged; *karma-adhikāraḥ*—in material affairs; *akhila-jagat*—of the entire universe; *bandha*—bondage; *dhvaṁsana*—destroying; *para*—transcendental; *anubhāvasya*—whose influence; *bhagavataḥ*—of the Supreme Personality of Godhead; *ādi-puruṣasya*—the original person; *aṅghri*—on the lotus feet; *yugala*—two; *anavarata*—constant; *dhyāna-anubhāvena*—by meditation; *parirandhita*—destroyed; *kaṣāya*—all the dirty things; *āśayaḥ*—in his heart; *avadātaḥ*—completely pure; *api*—

although; *māna-vardhanaḥ*—just to give honor; *mahatām*—to superiors; *mahītalam*—the material world; *anuśaśāsa*—ruled.

TRANSLATION

Following the order of the Supreme Personality of Godhead, Mahārāja Priyavrata fully engaged in worldly affairs, yet he always thought of the lotus feet of the Lord, which are the cause of liberation from all material attachment. Although Priyavrata Mahārāja was completely freed from all material contamination, he ruled the material world just to honor the orders of his superiors.

PURPORT

The words *māna-vardhano mahatām* ("just to show honor to superiors") are very significant. Although Mahārāja Priyavrata was already a liberated person and had no attraction for material things, he engaged himself fully in governmental affairs just to show respect to Lord Brahmā. Arjuna had also acted in the same way. Arjuna had no desire to participate in political affairs or the fighting at Kurukṣetra, but when ordered to do so by the Supreme Lord, Kṛṣṇa, he executed those duties very nicely. One who always thinks of the lotus feet of the Lord is certainly above all the contamination of the material world. As stated in *Bhagavad-gītā:*

yoginām api sarveṣāṁ
mad-gatenāntarātmanā
śraddhāvān bhajate yo māṁ
sa me yuktatamo mataḥ

"Of all *yogīs*, he who always abides in Me with great faith, worshiping Me in transcendental loving service, is most intimately united with Me in *yoga* and is the highest of all." (Bg. 6.47) Mahārāja Priyavrata, therefore, was a liberated person and was among the highest of *yogīs*, yet superficially he became the emperor of the universe in accordance with the order of Lord Brahmā. Showing respect to his superior in this way was another of his extraordinary qualifications. As stated in *Śrīmad-Bhāgavatam* (6.17.28):

nārāyaṇa-parāḥ sarve
na kutaścana bibhyati
svargāpavarga-narkeṣv
api tulyārtha-darśinaḥ

A devotee who is actually advanced is not afraid of anything, provided he has the opportunity to execute the order of the Supreme Personality of Godhead. This is the proper explanation of why Priyavrata engaged in worldly affairs although he was a liberated person. Also, only because of this principle does a *mahā-bhāgavata,* who has nothing to do with the material world, come down to the second platform of devotional service to preach the glories of the Lord all over the world.

TEXT 24

अथ च दुहितरं प्रजापतेर्विश्वकर्मण उपयेमे बर्हिष्मतीं नाम तस्यामु ह वाव आत्मजानात्मसमानशीलगुणकर्मरूपवीर्योदारान्दश भावयाम्बभूव कन्यां च यवीयसीमूर्जस्वतीं नाम ॥ २४ ॥

atha ca duhitaraṁ prajāpater viśvakarmaṇa upayeme barhiṣmatīṁ nāma tasyām u ha vāva ātmajān ātma-samāna-śīla-guṇa-karma-rūpa-vīryodārān daśa bhāvayām babhūva kanyāṁ ca yavīyasīm ūrjasvatīṁ nāma.

atha—thereafter; *ca*—also; *duhitaram*—the daughter; *prajāpateḥ*—of one of the *prajāpatis* entrusted with increasing population; *viśvakarmaṇaḥ*—named Viśvakarmā; *upayeme*—married; *barhiṣmatīm*—Barhiṣmatī; *nāma*—named; *tasyām*—in her; *u ha*—as it is celebrated; *vāva*—wonderful; *ātma-jān*—sons; *ātma-samāna*—exactly equal to him; *śīla*—character; *guṇa*—quality; *karma*—activities; *rūpa*—beauty; *vīrya*—prowess; *udārān*—whose magnanimity; *daśa*—ten; *bhāvayām babhūva*—he begot; *kanyām*—daughter; *ca*—also; *yavīyasīm*—the youngest of all; *ūrjasvatīm*—Ūrjasvatī; *nāma*—named.

TRANSLATION

Thereafter, Mahārāja Priyavrata married Barhiṣmatī, the daughter of the prajāpati named Viśvakarmā. In her he begot ten

sons equal to him in beauty, character, magnanimity and other qualities. He also begot a daughter, the youngest of all, named Ūrjasvatī.

PURPORT

Mahārāja Priyavrata not only carried out the order of Lord Brahmā by accepting the duties of government, but also married Barhiṣmatī, the daughter of Viśvakarmā, one of the *prajāpatis.* Since Mahārāja Priyavrata was fully trained in transcendental knowledge, he could have returned home and conducted the business of government as a *brahmacārī.* Instead, however, when he returned to household life, he accepted a wife also. The principle is that when one becomes a *gṛhastha,* he must live perfectly in that order, which means he must live peacefully with a wife and children. When Caitanya Mahāprabhu's first wife died, His mother requested Him to marry for a second time. He was twenty years old and was going to take *sannyāsa* at the age of twenty-four, yet by the request of His mother, He married. "As long as I am in household life," He told His mother, "I must have a wife, for household life does not mean staying in a house. Real household life means living in a house with a wife."

Three words in this verse are very significant—*u ha vāva.* These words are used to express wonder. Priyavrata Mahārāja had taken a vow of renunciation, but accepting a wife and begetting children have nothing to do with the path of renunciation; these are activities on the path of enjoyment. It was a source of great wonder, therefore, that Priyavrata Mahārāja, who had followed the path of renunciation, had now accepted the path of enjoyment.

Sometimes we are criticized because although I am a *sannyāsī,* I have taken part in the marriage ceremonies of my disciples. It must be explained, however, that since we have started a Kṛṣṇa conscious society and since a human society must also have ideal marriages, to correctly establish an ideal society we must take part in marrying some of its members, although we have taken to the path of renunciation. This may be astonishing to persons who are not very interested in establishing *daiva-varṇāśrama,* the transcendental system of four social orders and four spiritual orders. Śrīla Bhaktisiddhānta Sarasvatī Ṭhākura, however, wanted to reestablish *daiva-varṇāśrama.* In *daiva-varṇāśrama* there cannot be acknowledgement of social status according to birthright because in *Bhagavad-gītā* it is said that the determining considerations are *guṇa* and *karma*, one's qualities and work. It is this *daiva-varṇāśrama* that should be established all over the world to continue a perfect society for Kṛṣṇa consciousness. This may be astonishing to foolish critics, but it is one of the functions of a Kṛṣṇa conscious society.

TEXT 25

आग्नीध्रेध्मजिह्वयज्ञबाहुमहावीरहिरण्यरेतोघृतपृष्ठसवनमेधातिथिवीतिहोत्रकवय इति सर्व एवाग्निनामानः ॥२५॥

āgnīdhredhmajihva-yajñabāhu-mahāvīra-hiraṇyareto-ghṛtapṛṣṭha-savana-medhātithi-vītihotra-kavaya iti sarva evāgni-nāmānaḥ.

āgnīdhra—Āgnīdhra; *idhma-jihva*—Idhmajihva; *yajña-bāhu*—Yajñabāhu; *mahā-vīra*—Mahāvīra; *hiraṇya-retaḥ*—Hiraṇyaretā; *ghṛta-pṛṣṭha*—Ghṛtapṛṣṭha; *savana*—Savana; *medhā-tithi*—Medhātithi; *vīti-hotra*—Vītihotra; *kavayaḥ*—and Kavi; *iti*—thus; *sarve*—all these; *eva*—certainly; *agni*—of the demigod controlling fire; *nāmānaḥ*—names.

TRANSLATION

The ten sons of Mahārāja Priyavrata were named Āgnīdhra, Idhmajihva, Yajñabāhu, Mahāvīra, Hiraṇyaretā, Ghṛtapṛṣṭha, Savana, Medhātithi, Vītihotra and Kavi. These are also names of Agni, the fire-god.

TEXT 26

एतेषां कविर्महावीरः सवन इति त्रय आसन्नूर्ध्वरेतसस्त आत्मविद्यायामर्भ-भावादारभ्य कृतपरिचयाः पारमहंस्यमेवाश्रममभजन् ॥ २६ ॥

eteṣāṁ kavir mahāvīraḥ savana iti traya āsann ūrdhva-retasas ta ātma-vidyāyām arbha-bhāvād ārabhya kṛta-paricayāḥ pāramahaṁsyam evāśramam abhajan.

eteṣām—of these; *kaviḥ*—Kavi; *mahāvīraḥ*—Mahāvīra; *savanaḥ*—Savana; *iti*—thus; *trayaḥ*—three; *āsan*—were; *ūrdhva-retasaḥ*—completely celibate; *te*—they; *ātma-vidyāyām*—in transcendental knowledge; *arbha-bhāvāt*—from childhood; *ārabhya*—beginning; *kṛta-paricayāḥ*—very well versed; *pāramahaṁsyam*—of the highest spiritual perfection of human life; *eva*—certainly; *āśramam*—the order; *abhajan*—executed.

TRANSLATION

Three among these ten—namely Kavi, Mahāvīra and Savana—lived in complete celibacy. Thus trained in brahmacārī life from the beginning of childhood, they were very conversant with the highest perfection, known as the paramahaṁsa-āśrama.

PURPORT

The word *ūrdhva-retasaḥ* in this verse is very significant. *Ūrdhva-retaḥ* refers to one who can control sex life and who instead of wasting semen by discharging it, can use this most important substance accumulated in the body to enrich the brain. One who can completely control sex life is able to work wonderfully with his brain, especially in remembering. Thus students who simply hear Vedic instructions once from their teacher could remember them verbatim without needing to read books, which therefore did not exist in former times.

Another significant word is *arbha-bhāvāt,* which means "from very childhood." Another meaning is "from being very affectionate to children." In other words, *paramahaṁsa* life is dedicated for the benefit of others. Just as a father sacrifices many things out of affection for his son, great saintly persons sacrifice all kinds of bodily comforts for the benefit of human society. In this connection there is a verse concerning the six Gosvāmīs:

tyaktvā tūrṇam aśeṣa-maṇḍala-pati-śreṇīṁ sadā tucchavat
bhūtvā dīna-gaṇeśakau karuṇayā kaupīna-kanthāśritau

Because of their compassion for the poor fallen souls, the six Gosvāmīs gave up their exalted positions as ministers and took vows as mendicants.

Thus minimizing their bodily wants as far as possible, they each accepted only a loincloth and a begging bowl. Thus they remained in Vṛndāvana to execute the orders of Śrī Caitanya Mahāprabhu by compiling and publishing various Vaiṣṇava literatures.

TEXT 27

तस्मिन्नु ह वा उपशमशीलाः परमर्षयः सकलजीवनिकायावासस्य भगवतो
वासुदेवस्य भीतानां शरणभूतस्य श्रीमच्चरणारविन्दाविरतस्मरणाविगलितपरम-
भक्तियोगानुभावेन परिभावितान्तर्हृदयाधिगते भगवति सर्वेषां भूतानामा-
त्मभूते प्रत्यगात्मन्येवात्मनस्तादात्म्यमविशेषेण समीयुः ॥ २७ ॥

tasminn u ha vā upaśama-śīlāḥ paramarṣayaḥ sakala-jīva-
nikāyāvāsasya bhagavato vāsudevasya bhītānāṁ śaraṇa-bhūtasya
śrīmac-caraṇāravindāvirata-smaraṇāvigalita-parama-bhakti-yogānu-
bhāvena paribhāvitāntar-hṛdayādhigate bhagavati sarveṣāṁ bhūtānām
ātma-bhūte pratyag-ātmany evātmanas tādātmyam aviśeṣeṇa samīyuḥ.

tasmin—in that *paramahaṁsa-āśrama; u*—certainly; *ha*—so celebrated; *vā*—indeed; *upaśama-śīlāḥ*—in the renounced order of life; *parama-ṛṣayaḥ*—the great sages; *sakala*—all; *jīva*—of living entities; *nikāya*—in total; *āvāsasya*—the residence; *bhagavataḥ*—of the Supreme Personality of Godhead; *vāsudevasya*—Lord Vāsudeva; *bhītānām*—of those afraid of material existence; *śaraṇa-bhūtasya*—the one who is the only shelter; *śrīmat*—of the Supreme Personality of Godhead; *caraṇa-aravinda*—the lotus feet; *avirata*—constantly; *smaraṇa*—remembering; *avigalita*—completely uncontaminated; *parama*—supreme; *bhakti-yoga*—of mystic devotional service; *anubhāvena*—by the prowess; *paribhāvita*—purified; *antaḥ*—within; *hṛdaya*—the heart; *adhigate*—perceived; *bhagavati*—the Supreme Personality of Godhead; *sarveṣām*—of all; *bhūtānām*—living entities; *ātma-bhūte*—situated within the body; *pratyak*—directly; *ātmani*—with the Supreme Supersoul; *eva*—certainly; *ātmanaḥ*—of the self; *tādātmyam*—qualitative equality; *aviśeṣeṇa*—without differences; *samīyuḥ*—realized.

TRANSLATION

Thus situated in the renounced order from the beginning of their lives, all three of them completely controlled the activities of their senses and thus became great saints. They concentrated their minds always upon the lotus feet of the Supreme Personality of Godhead, who is the resting place of the totality of living entities and who is therefore celebrated as Vāsudeva. Lord Vāsudeva is the only shelter of those who are actually afraid of material existence. By constantly thinking of His lotus feet, these three sons of Mahārāja Priyavrata became advanced in pure devotional service. By the prowess of their devotional service, they could directly perceive the Supreme Personality of Godhead, who is situated in everyone's heart as the Supersoul, and realize that there was qualitatively no difference between themselves and Him.

PURPORT

The *paramahaṁsa* stage is the topmost position in renounced life. In *sannyāsa*, the renounced order, there are four stages—*kuṭīcaka*, *bahūdaka*, *parivrājakācārya* and *paramahaṁsa*. According to the Vedic system, when one accepts the renounced order, he stays outside his village in a cottage, and his necessities, especially his food, are supplied from home. This is called the *kuṭīcaka* stage. When a *sannyāsī* advances further, he no longer accepts anything from home; instead, he collects his necessities, especially his food, from many places. This system is called *mādhukarī*, which literally means "the profession of the bumblebees." As bumblebees collect honey from many flowers, a little from each, so a *sannyāsī* should beg from door to door but not accept very much food from any particular house; he should collect a little bit from every house. This is called the *bahūdaka* stage. When a *sannyāsī* is still more experienced, he travels all over the world to preach the glories of Lord Vāsudeva. He is then known as *parivrājakācārya*. The *sannyāsī* reaches the *paramahaṁsa* stage when he finishes his preaching work and sits down in one place, strictly for the sake of advancing in spiritual life. An actual *paramahaṁsa* is one who completely controls his senses and engages in the unalloyed service of the Lord. Therefore all three of these sons of Priyavrata, namely Kavi, Mahāvīra and Savana, were situated in the *paramahaṁsa* stage from the very beginning. Their senses could not disturb them, for their senses were completely engaged in serving the Lord. Therefore the three brothers are described in this verse as *upaśama-śīlāḥ. Upaśama* means "completely subdued." Because they completely subdued their senses, they are understood to have been great sages and saints.

After subduing their senses, the three brothers concentrated their minds upon the lotus feet of Vāsudeva, Lord Kṛṣṇa. As stated in *Bhagavad-gītā* (7.19), *vāsudevaḥ sarvam iti.* The lotus feet of Vāsudeva are everything. Lord Vāsudeva is the reservoir of all living entities. When this cosmic manifestation is dissolved, all living entities enter the supreme body of the Lord, Garbhodakaśāyī Viṣṇu, who merges within the body of Mahā-Viṣṇu. Both of these *viṣṇu-tattvas* are *vāsudeva-tattvas,* and therefore the great sages Kavi, Mahāvīra and Savana concentrated always upon the lotus feet of Lord Vāsudeva, Kṛṣṇa. In this way they could understand that the Supersoul within the heart is the Supreme Personality of Godhead, and they could recognize their identity with Him. The complete description of this realization is that simply by discharging the unalloyed form of devotional service, one can realize his self completely. The *parama-bhakti-yoga* mentioned in this verse means that a living entity, by dint of unalloyed devotional service, has no other interest than the service of the Lord, as described in *Bhagavad-gītā* (*vāsudevaḥ sarvam iti*). By *parama-bhakti-yoga,* by elevating oneself to the highest platform of loving service, one can automatically be relieved from the bodily concept of life and see the Supreme Personality of Godhead face to face. As confirmed in *Brahma-saṁhitā:*

premāñjana-cchurita-bhakti-vilocanena
santaḥ sadaiva hṛdayeṣu vilokayanti
yaṁ śyāmasundaram acintya-guṇa-svarūpaṁ
govindam ādi-puruṣaṁ tam ahaṁ bhajāmi

An advanced devotee, who is known as a *sat,* or saint, can always see within his heart the Supreme Personality of Godhead, face to face. Kṛṣṇa, Śyāmasundara, expands Himself by His plenary portion, and thus a devotee can always see Him within his heart.

TEXT 28

अन्यस्यामपि जायायां त्रयः पुत्रा आसन्नुत्तमस्तामसो रैवत इति
मन्वन्तराधिपतयः ॥२८ ॥

anyasyām api jāyāyāṁ trayaḥ putrā āsann uttamas tāmaso raivata iti
manvantarādhipatayaḥ

anyasyām—other; *api*—also; *jāyāyām*—in the wife; *trayaḥ*—three; *putrāḥ*—sons; *āsan*—there were; *uttamaḥ tāmasaḥ raivataḥ*—Uttama, Tāmasa and Raivata; *iti*—thus; *manu-antara*—of the *manvantara* millennium; *adhipatayaḥ*—rulers.

TRANSLATION

In his other wife, Mahārāja Priyavrata begot three sons, named Uttama, Tāmasa and Raivata. All of them later took charge of manvantara millenniums.

PURPORT

In every day of Brahmā there are fourteen *manvantaras.* The duration of one *manvantara,* the lifespan of one Manu, is seventy-one *yugas,* and each *yuga* is 4,320,000 years. Almost all the Manus selected to rule the *manvantaras* came from the family of Mahārāja Priyavrata. Three of them are particularly mentioned herein, namely Uttama, Tāmasa and Raivata.

TEXT 29

एवमुपशमायनेषु स्वतनयेष्वथ जगतीपतिर्जगतीमर्बुदान्येकादश
परिवत्सराणामव्याहताखिलपुरुषकारसारसम्भृतदोर्दण्डयुगलापीडितमौर्वीगुण-
स्तनितविरमितधर्मप्रतिपक्षो बर्हिष्मत्याश्चानुदिनमेधमानप्रमोदप्रसरणयौषिण्य-
व्रीडाप्रमुषितहासावलोकरुचिरक्ष्वेल्यादिभिः पराभूयमानविवेक इवानव-
बुध्यमान इव महामना बुभुजे ॥ २९ ॥

evam upaśamāyaneṣu sva-tanayeṣv atha jagatī-patir jagatīm arbudāny ekādaśa parivatsarāṇām avyāhatākhila-puruṣa-kāra-sāra-sambhṛta-dor-daṇḍa-yugalāpīḍita-maurvī-guṇa-stanita-viramita-dharma-pratipakṣo barhiṣmatyāś cānudinam edhamāna-pramoda-prasaraṇa-yauṣiṇya-vrīḍā-pramuṣita-hāsāvaloka-rucira-kṣvely-ādibhiḥ parābhūyamāna-viveka ivānavabudhyamāna iva mahāmanā bubhuje.

evam—thus; *upaśama-ayaneṣu*—all well qualified; *sva-tanayeṣu*—his own sons; *atha*—thereafter; *jagatī-patiḥ*—the master of the universe; *jagatīm*—the universe; *arbudāni*—*arbudas* (one *arbuda* equals 100,000,000); *ekādaśa*—eleven; *parivatsarāṇām*—of years; *avyāhata*—without being interrupted; *akhila*—universal; *puruṣa-kāra*—prowess; *sāra*—strength; *sambhṛta*—endowed with; *doḥ-daṇḍaḥ*—of powerful arms; *yugala*—by the pair; *āpīḍita*—being drawn; *maurvī-guṇa*—of the bowstring; *stanita*—by the loud sound; *viramita*—defeated; *dharma*—religious principles; *pratipakṣaḥ*—those who are against; *barhiṣmatyāḥ*—of his wife Barhiṣmatī; *ca*—and; *anudinam*—daily; *edhamāna*—increasing; *pramoda*—pleasing intercourse; *prasaraṇa*—amiability; *yauṣiṇya*—feminine behavior; *vrīḍā*—by shyness; *pramuṣita*—held back; *hāsa*—laughing; *avaloka*—glancing; *rucira*—pleasing; *kṣveli-ādibhiḥ*—by exchanges of loving propensities; *parābhūyamāna*—being defeated; *vivekaḥ*—his true knowledge; *iva*—like; *anavabudhyamānaḥ*—a less intelligent person; *iva*—like; *mahā-manāḥ*—the great soul; *bubhuje*—ruled.

TRANSLATION

After Kavi, Mahāvīra and Savana were completely trained in the paramahaṁsa stage of life, Mahārāja Priyavrata ruled the universe for eleven arbudas of years. Whenever he was determined to fix his arrow upon his bowstring with his two powerful arms, all opponents of the regulative principles of religious life would flee from his presence in fear of the unparalleled prowess he displayed in ruling the universe. He greatly loved his wife Barhiṣmatī, and with the increase of days, their exchange of nuptial love also increased. By her feminine behavior as she dressed herself, walked, got up, smiled, laughed, and glanced about, Queen Barhiṣmatī in-

creased his energy. Thus although he was a great soul, he appeared lost in the feminine conduct of his wife. He behaved with her just like an ordinary man, but actually he was a great soul.

PURPORT

In this verse, the word *dharma-pratipakṣaḥ* ("opponents of religious principles") refers not to a particular faith, but to *varṇāśrama-dharma*, the division of society, socially and spiritually, into four *varṇas* (*brāhmaṇa, kṣatriya, vaiśya* and *śūdra*) and four *āśramas* (*brahmacarya, gṛhastha, vānaprastha* and *sannyāsa*). To maintain proper social order and help the citizens gradually progress toward the goal of life—namely spiritual understanding—the principles of *varṇāśrama-dharma* must be accepted. From this verse, Mahārāja Priyavrata appears to have been so strict in maintaining this institution of *varṇāśrama-dharma* that anyone neglecting it would immediately flee from his presence as soon as the King warned him by fighting or administering light punishment. Indeed, Mahārāja Priyavrata would not have to fight, for simply because of his strong determination, they dared not disobey the rules and regulations of *varṇāśrama-dharma.* It is said that unless human society is regulated by *varṇāśrama-dharma,* it is no better than a bestial society of cats and dogs. Mahārāja Priyavrata, therefore, strictly maintained *varṇāśrama-dharma* by his extraordinary, unparalleled prowess.

To maintain such a life of strict vigilance, one needs encouragement from his wife. In the *varṇāśrama-dharma* system, certain classes, such as the *brāhmaṇas* and *sannyāsīs,* do not need encouragement from the opposite sex. *Kṣatriyas* and *gṛhasthas,* however, actually need the encouragement of their wives in order to execute their duties. Indeed, a *gṛhastha* or *kṣatriya* cannot properly execute his responsibilities without the association of his wife. Śrī Caitanya Mahāprabhu personally admitted that a *gṛhastha* must live with a wife. *Kṣatriyas* were even allowed to have many wives to encourage them in discharging the duties of government. The association of a good wife is necessary in a life of *karma* and political affairs. To execute his duties properly, therefore, Mahārāja Priyavrata took advantage of his good wife Barhiṣmatī, who was always very expert in pleasing her great husband by properly dressing herself.

smiling, and exhibiting her feminine bodily features. Queen Barhiṣmatī always kept Mahārāja Priyavrata very encouraged, and thus he executed his governmental duty very properly. In this verse *iva* has twice been used to indicate that Mahārāja Priyavrata acted exactly like a henpecked husband and thereby seemed to have lost his sense of human responsibility. Actually, however, he was fully conscious of his position as a spirit soul, although he seemingly behaved like an acquiescent *karmī* husband. Mahārāja Priyavrata thus ruled the universe for eleven *arbudas* of years. One *arbuda* consists of 100,000,000 years, and Mahārāja Priyavrata ruled the universe for eleven such *arbudas*.

TEXT 30

**यावदवभासयति सुरगिरिमनुपरिक्रामन् भगवानादित्यो वसुधातलमर्धेनैव
प्रतपत्यर्धेनावच्छादयति तदा हि भगवदुपासनोपचितातिपुरुषप्रभावस्तदनभिनन्दन्
समजवेन रथेन ज्योतिर्मयेन रजनीमपि दिनं करिष्यामीति सप्तकृत्वस्तरणिम
नुपर्यक्रामद् द्वितीय इव पतङ्गः ॥ ३० ॥**

yāvad avabhāsayati sura-girim anuparikrāman bhagavān ādityo vasudhā-talam ardhenaiva pratapaty ardhenāvacchādayati tadā hi bhagavad-upāsanopacitāti-puruṣa-prabhāvas tad anabhinandan samajavena rathena jyotirmayena rajanīm api dinaṁ kariṣyāmīti sapta-kṛt vastaraṇim anuparyakrāmad dvitīya iva pataṅgaḥ.

yāvat—so long; *avabhāsayati*—illuminates; *sura-girim*—the Sumeru Hill; *anuparikrāman*—by circumambulating; *bhagavān*—the most powerful; *ādityaḥ*—sun-god; *vasudhā-talam*—the lower planetary system; *ardhena*—by half; *eva*—certainly; *pratapati*—makes dazzling; *ardhena*—by half; *avacchādayati*—covers with darkness; *tadā*—at that time; *hi*—certainly; *bhagavat-upāsanā*—by worshiping the Supreme Personality of Godhead; *upacita*—by satisfying Him perfectly; *ati-puruṣa*—superhuman; *prabhāvaḥ*—influence; *tat*—that; *anabhinandan*—without appreciating; *samajavena*—by equally powerful; *rathena*—on a chariot; *jyotiḥ-mayena*—dazzling; *rajanīm*—night; *api*—also; *dinam*—day; *kariṣyāmi*—I shall make it; *iti*—thus; *sapta-kṛt*—seven times; *vastaraṇim*—exactly following the orbit of the sun;

anuparyakrāmat—circumambulated; *dvitīyaḥ*—second; *iva*—like; *pataṅgaḥ*—sun.

TRANSLATION

While so excellently ruling the universe, King Priyavrata once became dissatisfied with the circumambulation of the most powerful sun-god. Encircling Sumeru Hill on his chariot, the sun-god illuminates all the surrounding planetary systems. However, when the sun is on the northern side of the hill, the south receives less light, and when the sun is in the south, the north receives less. King Priyavrata disliked this situation and therefore decided to make daylight in the part of the universe where there was night. He followed the orbit of the sun-god on a brilliant chariot and thus fulfilled his desire. He could perform such wonderful activities because of the power he had achieved by worshiping the Supreme Personality of Godhead.

PURPORT

There is a Bengali saying which describes that someone is so powerful that he can make the night day and the day night. That saying is current because of the prowess of Priyavrata. His activities demonstrate how powerful he became by worshiping the Supreme Personality of Godhead. Lord Kṛṣṇa is known as Yogeśvara, the master of all mystic powers. In *Bhagavad-gītā* (18.78) it is said wherever there is the master of all mystic powers (*yatra yogeśvaraḥ kṛṣṇaḥ*), victory, fortune and all other opulences are present. Devotional service is so powerful. When a devotee achieves what he wants to accomplish, it is not by his own mystic power but by the grace of the master of mystic power, Lord Kṛṣṇa; by His grace, a devotee can accomplish wonderful things unimaginable even to the most powerful scientist.

From the description in this verse, it appears that the sun moves. According to modern astronomers, the sun is fixed in one place, surrounded by the solar system, but here we find that the sun is not stationary: it is rotating in a prescribed orbit. This fact is corroborated by *Brahma-saṁhitā* (5.52). *Yasyājñayā bhramati saṁbhṛta-kāla-cakraḥ:* the sun is rotating in its fixed orbit in accordance with the order of the Supreme Personality of Godhead. According to *Jyotir Veda,* the science of astronomy in the Vedic literature, the sun moves for six months on the northern side of the Sumeru Hill and for six months on the southern side. We have practical experience on this planet that when there is summer in the north there is winter in the south and vice versa. Modern materialistic scientists sometimes present themselves as knowing all the ingredients of the sun, yet they are unable to offer a second sun like Mahārāja Priyavrata's.

Although Mahārāja Priyavrata devised a very powerful chariot as brilliant as the sun, he had no desire to compete with the sun-god, for a Vaiṣṇava never wants to supersede another Vaiṣṇava. His purpose was to give abundant benefits in material existence. Śrīla Viśvanātha Cakravartī Ṭhākura remarks that in the months of April and May the rays of Mahārāja Priyavrata's brilliant sun were as pleasing as the rays of the moon, and in October and November, both morning and evening, that sun provided more warmth than the sunshine. In short, Mahārāja Priyavrata was extremely powerful, and his actions extended his power in all directions.

TEXT 31

ये वा उ ह तद्रथचरणनेमिकृतपरिखातास्ते सप्त सिन्धव आसन् यत एव कृताः सप्त भुवो द्वीपाः ॥ ३१ ॥

ye vā u ha tad-ratha-caraṇa-nemi-kṛta-parikhātās te sapta sindhava āsan yata eva kṛtāḥ sapta bhuvo dvīpāḥ.

ye—that; *vā u ha*—certainly; *tat-ratha*—of his chariot; *caraṇa*—of the wheels; *nemi*—by the rims; *kṛta*—made; *parikhātāḥ*—trenches; *te*—those; *sapta*—seven; *sindhavaḥ*—oceans; *āsan*—became; *yataḥ*—because of which; *eva*—certainly; *kṛtāḥ*—were made; *sapta*—seven; *bhuvaḥ*—of the Bhū-maṇḍala; *dvīpāḥ*—islands.

TRANSLATION

When Priyavrata drove his chariot behind the sun, the rims of his chariot wheels created impressions that later became seven

oceans, dividing the planetary system known as Bhū-maṇḍala into seven islands.

PURPORT

Sometimes the planets in outer space are called islands. We have experience of various types of islands in the ocean, and similarly the various planets, divided into fourteen *lokas*, are islands in the ocean of space. As Priyavrata drove his chariot behind the sun, he created seven different types of oceans and planetary systems, which altogether are known as Bhū-maṇḍala, or Bhūloka. In the Gāyatrī *mantra*, we chant, *oṁ bhūr bhuvaḥ svaḥ tat savitur vareṇyam.* Above the Bhuloka planetary system is Bhuvarloka, and above that is Svargaloka, the heavenly planetary system. All these planetary systems are controlled by Savitā, the sun-god. By chanting the Gāyatrī *mantra* just after rising early in the morning, one worships the sun-god.

TEXT 32

जम्बूप्लक्षशाल्मलिकुशक्रौञ्चशाकपुष्करसंज्ञास्तेषां परिमाणं पूर्वस्मात्पूर्वस्मादुत्तर
उत्तरो यथासंख्यं द्विगुणमानेन बहिः समन्तत उपक्लृप्ताः ॥ ३२ ॥

jambū-plakṣa-śālmali-kuśa-krauñca-śāka-puṣkara-saṁjñās teṣāṁ parimāṇaṁ pūrvasmāt pūrvasmād uttara uttaro yathā-saṅkhyaṁ dvi-guṇa-mānena bahiḥ samantata upakḷptāḥ.

jambū—Jambū; *plakṣa*—Plakṣa; *śālmali*—Śālmali; *kuśa*—Kuśa; *krauñca*—Krauñca; *śāka*—Śāka; *puṣkara*—Puṣkara; *saṁjñāḥ*—known as; *teṣām*—of them; *parimāṇam*—measurement; *pūrvasmāt pūrvasmāt*—from the former; *uttaraḥ uttaraḥ*—the following; *yathā*—according to; *saṅkhyam*—number; *dvi-guṇa*—twice as much; *mānena*—with a measure; *bahiḥ*—outside; *samantataḥ*—all around; *upakḷptāḥ*—produced.

TRANSLATION

The names of the islands are Jambū, Plakṣa, Śālmali, Kuśa, Krauñca, Śāka and Puṣkara. Each island is twice as large as the one

preceding it, and each is surrounded by a liquid substance, beyond which is the next island.

PURPORT

The ocean in each planetary system has a different type of liquid. How they are situated is explained in the next verse.

TEXT 33

क्षारोदेक्षुरसोदसुरोदघृतोदक्षीरोददधिमण्डोदशुद्धोदाः सप्त जलधयः सप्त
द्वीपपरिखा इवाभ्यन्तरद्वीपसमाना एकैकश्येन यथानुपूर्वं सप्तस्वपि
बहिर्द्वीपेषु पृथक्परित उपकल्पितास्तेषु जम्ब्वादिषु बर्हिष्मतीपतिरनुव्रताना
त्मजानाग्नीध्रेध्मजिह्वयज्ञबाहुहिरण्यरेतोघृतपृष्ठमेधातिथिवीतिहोत्रसंज्ञान् यथा
संख्येनैकैकस्मिन्नेकमेवाधिपतिं विदधे ॥ ३३ ॥

kṣārodekṣu-rasoda-suroda-ghṛtoda-kṣīroda-dadhi-maṇḍoda-śuddhodāḥ sapta jaladhayaḥ sapta dvīpa-parikhā ivābhyantara-dvīpa-samānā ekaikaśyena yathānupūrvaṁ saptasv api bahir dvīpeṣu pṛthak parita upakalpitās teṣu jambv-ādiṣu barhiṣmatī-patir anuvratānātmajān āgnīdhredhmajihva-yajñabāhu-hiraṇyareto ghṛtapṛṣṭha-medhātithi-vītihotra-saṁjñān yathā-saṅkhyenaikaikasminn ekam evādhi-patiṁ vidadhe.

kṣāra—salt; *uda*—water; *ikṣu-rasa*—the liquid extract from sugarcane; *uda*—water; *surā*—liquor; *uda*—water; *ghṛta*—clarified butter; *uda*—water; *kṣīra*—milk; *uda*—water; *dadhi-maṇḍa*—emulsified yogurt; *uda*—water; *śuddha-udāḥ*—and drinking water; *sapta*—seven; *jala-dhayaḥ*—oceans; *sapta*—seven; *dvīpa*—islands; *parikhāḥ*—trenches; *iva*—like; *abhyantara*—internal; *dvīpa*—islands; *samānāḥ*—equal to; *eka-ekaśyena*—one after another; *yathā-anupūrvam*—in chronological order; *saptasu*—seven; *api*—although; *bahiḥ*—outside; *dvīpeṣu*—in islands; *pṛthak*—separate; *paritaḥ*—all around; *upakalpitāḥ*—situated; *teṣu*—within them; *jambū-ādiṣu*—beginning with Jambū; *barhiṣmatī*—of Barhiṣmatī; *patiḥ*—the husband; *anuvratān*—who were actually followers of the father's principles;

ātma-jān—sons; *āgnīdhra-idhmajihva-yajñabāhu-hiraṇyaretaḥ-ghṛtapṛṣṭha-medhātithi-vītihotra-saṁjñān*—named Āgnīdhra, Idhmajihva, Yajñabāhu, Hiraṇyaretā, Ghṛtapṛṣṭha, Medhātithi and Vītihotra; *yathā-saṅkhyena*—by the same number; *eka-ekasmin*—in each island; *ekam*—one; *eva*—certainly; *adhi-patim*—king; *vidadhe*—he made.

TRANSLATION

The seven oceans respectively contain salt water, sugarcane juice, liquor, clarified butter, milk, emulsified yogurt, and sweet drinking water. All the islands are completely surrounded by these oceans, and each ocean is equal in breadth to the island it surrounds. Mahārāja Priyavrata, the husband of Queen Barhiṣmatī, gave sovereignty over these islands to his respective sons, namely Āgnīdhra, Idhmajihva, Yajñabāhu, Hiraṇyaretā, Ghṛtapṛṣṭha, Medhātithi and Vītihotra. Thus they all became kings by the order of their father.

PURPORT

It is to be understood that all the *dvīpas*, or islands, are surrounded by different types of oceans, and it is said herein that the breadth of each ocean is the same as that of the island it surrounds. The length of the oceans, however, cannot equal the length of the islands. According to Vīrarāghava Ācārya, the breadth of the first island is 100,000 *yojanas*. One *yojana* equals eight miles, and therefore the breadth of the first island is calculated to be 800,000 miles. The water surrounding it must have the same breadth, but its length must be different.

TEXT 34

दुहितरं चोर्जस्वतीं नामोशनसे प्रायच्छद्यस्यामासीद् देवयानी नाम काव्यसुता ॥ ३४ ॥

duhitaraṁ corjasvatīṁ nāmośanase prāyacchad yasyām āsīd devayānī nāma kāvya-sutā.

duhitaram—the daughter; *ca*—also; *ūrjasvatīm*—Ūrjasvatī; *nāma*—named; *uśanase*—unto the great sage Uśanā (Śukrācārya); *prāyac-*

chat—he gave; *yasyām*—unto whom; *āsīt*—there was; *devayānī*—Devayānī; *nāma*—named; *kāvya-sutā*—the daughter of Śukrācārya.

TRANSLATION

King Priyavrata then gave his daughter, Ūrjasvatī, in marriage to Śukrācārya, who begot in her a daughter named Devayānī.

TEXT 35

नैवंविधः पुरुषकार उरुक्रमस्य
पुंसां तदङ्घ्रिरजसा जितषड्गुणानाम् ।
चित्रं विदूरविगतः सकृदाददीत
यन्नामधेयमधुना स जहाति बन्धम् ॥३५॥

naivaṁ-vidhaḥ puruṣa-kāra urukramasya
puṁsāṁ tad-aṅghri-rajasā jita-ṣaḍ-guṇānām
citraṁ vidūra-vigataḥ sakṛd ādadīta
yan-nāmadheyam adhunā sa jahāti bandham

na—not; *evam-vidhaḥ*—like that; *puruṣa-kāraḥ*—personal influence; *uru-kramasya*—of the Supreme Personality of Godhead; *puṁsām*—of the devotees; *tat-aṅghri*—of His lotus feet; *rajasā*—by the dust; *jita-ṣaṭ-guṇānām*—who have conquered the influence of the six kinds of material whips; *citram*—wonderful; *vidūra-vigataḥ*—the fifth-grade person, or the untouchable; *sakṛt*—only once; *ādadīta*—if he utters; *yat*—whose; *nāmadheyam*—holy name; *adhunā*—immediately; *saḥ*—he; *jahāti*—gives up; *bandham*—material bondage.

TRANSLATION

My dear King, a devotee who has taken shelter of the dust from the lotus feet of the Lord can transcend the influence of the six material whips—namely hunger, thirst, lamentation, illusion, old age and death—and he can conquer the mind and five senses. However, this is not very wonderful for a pure devotee of the Lord because even a person beyond the jurisdiction of the four castes—

in other words, an untouchable—is immediately relieved of bondage to material existence if he utters the holy name of the Lord even once.

PURPORT

Śukadeva Gosvāmī was speaking to Mahārāja Parīkṣit about the activities of King Priyavrata, and since the King might have had doubts about these wonderful, uncommon activities, Śukadeva Gosvāmī reassured him. "My dear King," he said, "don't be doubtful about the wonderful activities of Priyavrata. For a devotee of the Supreme Personality of Godhead, everything is possible because the Lord is also known as Urukrama." Urukrama is a name for Lord Vāmanadeva, who performed the wonderful act of occupying the three worlds with three footsteps. Lord Vāmanadeva requested three paces of land from Mahārāja Bali, and when Mahārāja Bali agreed to grant them, the Lord immediately covered the entire world with two footsteps, and for His third step He placed His foot upon Bali Mahārāja's head. Śrī Jayadeva Gosvāmī says:

chalayasi vikramaṇe balim adbhuta-vāmana
pada-nakha-nīra-janita-jana-pāvana
keśava dhṛta-vamāna-rūpa jaya jagadīśa hare

"All glories to Lord Keśava, who assumed the form of a dwarf. O Lord of the universe, who takes away everything inauspicious for the devotees! O wonderful Vāmanadeva! You tricked the great demon Bali Mahārāja by Your steps. The water that touched the nails of Your lotus feet when You pierced through the covering of the universe purifies all living entities in the form of the River Ganges."

Since the Supreme Lord is all-powerful, He can do things that seem wonderful for a common man. Similarly, a devotee who has taken shelter at the lotus feet of the Lord can also do wonderful things, unimaginable to a common man, by the grace of the dust of those lotus feet. Caitanya Mahāprabhu therefore teaches us to take shelter of the Lord's lotus feet:

ayi nanda-tanuja kiṅkaraṁ
patitaṁ māṁ viṣame bhavāṁbudhau

kṛpayā tava pāda-paṅkaja-
sthita-dhūlī-sadṛśaṁ vicintaya

"O son of Nanda Mahārāja, I am Your eternal servant, yet somehow or other I have fallen into the ocean of birth and death. Please pick me up from this ocean of death and place me as one of the atoms of Your lotus feet." Lord Caitanya teaches us to come in touch with the dust of the Lord's lotus feet, for then there will undoubtedly be all success.

Because of the material body, every living entity in material existence is always disturbed by *ṣaḍ-guṇa,* six whips—hunger, thirst, lamentation, illusion, invalidity and death. Furthermore, another *ṣaḍ-guṇa* are the mind and five sense organs. Not to speak of a sanctified devotee, even a *caṇḍāla,* an outcaste, who is untouchable, is immediately freed from material bondage if he utters the holy name of the Lord even once. Sometimes caste *brāhmaṇas* argue that unless one changes his body he cannot be accepted as a *brāhmaṇa,* for since the present body is obtained as a result of past actions, one who has in the past acted as a *brāhmaṇa* takes birth in a *brāhmaṇa* family. Therefore, they contend, without such a brahminical body, one cannot be accepted as a *brāhmaṇa.* Herein it is said, however, that even *vidūra-vigata,* a *caṇḍāla*—a fifth-class untouchable—is freed if he utters the holy name even once. Being freed means that he immediately changes his body. Sanātana Gosvāmī confirms this:

yathā kāñcanatāṁ yāti
kāṁsyaṁ rasa-vidhānataḥ
tathā dīkṣā-vidhānena
dvijatvaṁ jāyate nṛṇām

When a person, even though a *caṇḍāla,* is initiated by a pure devotee into chanting the holy name of the Lord, his body changes as he follows the instructions of the spiritual master. Although one cannot see how his body has changed, we must accept, on the grounds of the authoritative statements of the *śāstras,* that he changes his body. This is to be understood without arguments. This verse clearly says, *sa jahāti bandham:* "He gives up his material bondage." The body is a symbolic representation of material bondage according to one's *karma.* Although sometimes we cannot see the gross body changing, chanting the holy name of the Supreme Lord immediately changes the subtle body, and because the subtle body changes, the living entity is immediately freed from material bondage. After all, changes of the gross body are conducted by the subtle body. After the destruction of the gross body, the subtle body takes the living entity from his present gross body to another. In the subtle body, the mind is predominant, and therefore if one's mind is always absorbed in remembering the activities or the lotus feet of the Lord, he is to be understood to have already changed his present body and become purified. Therefore it is irrefutable that a *caṇḍāla*, or any fallen or lowborn person, can become a *brāhmaṇa* simply by the method of bona fide initiation.

TEXT 36

स एवमपरिमितबलपराक्रम एकदा तु देवर्षिचरणानुशयनानुपतितगुण-
विसर्गसंसर्गेणानिर्वृतमिवात्मानं मन्यमान आत्मनिर्वेद इदमाह ॥३६॥

sa evam aparimita-bala-parākrama ekadā tu devarṣi-
caraṇānuśayanānu-patita-guṇa-visarga-saṁsargeṇānirvṛtam
ivātmānaṁ manyamāna ātma-nirveda idam āha.

saḥ—he (Mahārāja Priyavrata); *evam*—thus; *aparimita*—unparalleled; *bala*—strength; *parākramaḥ*—whose influence; *ekadā*—once upon a time; *tu*—then; *deva-ṛṣi*—of the great saint Nārada; *caraṇa-anuśayana*—surrendering unto the lotus feet; *anu*—thereafter; *patita*—fallen down; *guṇa-visarga*—with material affairs (created by the three material modes of nature); *saṁsargeṇa*—by connection; *anirvṛtam*—not satisfied; *iva*—like; *ātmānam*—himself; *manyamānaḥ*—thinking like that; *ātma*—self; *nirvedaḥ*—possessing renunciation; *idam*—this; *āha*—said.

TRANSLATION

While enjoying his material opulences with full strength and influence, Mahārāja Priyavrata once began to consider that although he had fully surrendered to the great saint Nārada and was actually

on the path of Kṛṣṇa consciousness, he had somehow become again entangled in material activities. Thus his mind now became restless, and he began to speak in a spirit of renunciation.

PURPORT

In *Śrīmad-Bhāgavatam* (1.5.17) it is said:

tyaktvā sva-dharmaṁ caraṇāmbujaṁ harer
bhajann apakvo 'tha patet tato yadi
yatra kva vābhadram abhūd amuṣya kiṁ
ko vārtha āpto 'bhajatāṁ sva-dharmataḥ

"One who has forsaken his material occupations to engage in the devotional service of the Lord may sometimes fall down while in an immature stage, yet there is no danger of his being unsuccessful. On the other hand, a nondevotee, though fully engaged in occupational duties, does not gain anything." If one somehow or other comes to the shelter of a great Vaiṣṇava, takes to Kṛṣṇa consciousness because of sentiment or realization, but in course of time falls down because of immature understanding, he is not actually fallen, for his having engaged in Kṛṣṇa consciousness is a permanent asset. If one falls down, therefore, his progress might be checked for a certain time, but it will again become manifest at an opportune moment. Although Priyavrata Mahārāja was serving according to the instructions of Nārada Muni meant for going back home, back to Godhead, he returned to material affairs at the request of his father. In due course of time, however, his consciousness for serving Kṛṣṇa reawakened by the grace of his spiritual master, Nārada.

As stated in *Bhagavad-gītā* (6.41), *śucīnāṁ śrīmatāṁ gehe yoga-bhraṣṭo 'bhijāyate.* One who falls down from the process of *bhakti-yoga* is again offered the opulence of the demigods, and after enjoying such material opulence, he is given a chance to take birth in a noble family of a pure *brāhmaṇa,* or in a rich family, to be given the chance to revive his Kṛṣṇa consciousness. This actually happened in the life of Priyavrata; he is a most glorious example of this truth. In due course of time, he no longer wanted to enjoy his material opulences and his wife, kingdom and sons; instead, he wanted to renounce them all. Therefore, after having described the material opulences of Mahārāja Priyavrata, Śukadeva Gosvāmī, in this verse, describes his tendency for renunciation.

The words *devarṣi-caraṇānuśayana* indicate that Mahārāja Priyavrata, having fully surrendered to the great sage Devarṣi Nārada, was strictly following all the devotional processes and regulative principles under his direction. In regard to strictly following the regulative principles, Śrīla Viśvanātha Cakravartī Ṭhākura says; *daṇḍavat-praṇāmās tān anupatitaḥ.* By immediately offering obeisances (*daṇḍavat*) unto the spiritual master and by strictly following his directions, the student becomes advanced. Mahārāja Priyavrata was doing all these things regularly.

As long as one is in the material world, he has to be under the influence of the modes of material nature (*guṇa-visarga*). It is not that Mahārāja Priyavrata was freed from material influence because he possessed all material opulences. In this material world, both the very poor man and the very rich man are under material influences, for both wealth and poverty are creations of the modes of material nature. As stated in *Bhagavad-gītā* (3.27), *prakṛteḥ kriyamāṇāni guṇaiḥ karmāṇi sarvaśaḥ.* According to the modes of material nature we acquire, the material nature gives us facility for material enjoyment.

TEXT 37

**अहो असाध्वनुष्ठितं यदभिनिवेशितोऽहमिन्द्रियैरविद्यारचितविषमविषयान्ध-
कूपे तदलमलममुष्या वनिताया विनोदमृगं मां धिग्धिगिति गर्हयाञ्चकार
॥ ३७ ॥**

*aho asādhv anuṣṭhitaṁ yad abhiniveśito 'ham indriyair avidyā-racita-
viṣama-viṣayāndha-kūpe tad alam alam amuṣyā vanitāyā vinoda-
mṛgaṁ māṁ dhig dhig iti garhayāṁ cakāra.*

aho—alas; *asādhu*—not good; *anuṣṭhitam*—executed; *yat*—because; *abhiniveśitaḥ*—being completely absorbed; *aham*—I; *indriyaiḥ*—for sense gratification; *avidyā*—by nescience; *racita*—made; *viṣama*—causing distress; *viṣaya*—sense gratification; *andha-kūpe*—in the dark well; *tat*—that; *alam*—insignificant; *alam*—of no importance;

amuṣyāḥ—of that; *vanitāyāḥ*—wife; *vinoda-mṛgam*—just like a dancing monkey; *mām*—unto me; *dhik*—all condemnation; *dhik*—all condemnation; *iti*—thus; *garhayām*—criticism; *cakāra*—he did.

TRANSLATION

The King thus began criticizing himself: Alas, how condemned I have become because of my sense gratification! I have now fallen into material enjoyment, which is exactly like a covered well. I have had enough! I am not going to enjoy any more. Just see how I have become like a dancing monkey in the hands of my wife. Because of this, I am condemned.

PURPORT

How condemned is the advancement of material knowledge can be understood from the behavior of Mahārāja Priyavrata. He performed such wonderful acts as creating another sun, which shined during the night, and creating a chariot so great that its wheels formed vast oceans. These activities are so great that modern scientists cannot even imagine how such things can be done. Mahārāja Priyavrata acted very wonderfully in the material field of activities, but because he was dealing in sense gratification—ruling his kingdom and dancing to the indications of his beautiful wife—he personally condemned himself. When we think about this example of Mahārāja Priyavrata, we can just consider how degraded is the modern civilization of materialistic advancement. Modern so-called scientists and other materialists are very satisfied because they can construct great bridges, roads and machines, but such activities are nothing comparable to those of Mahārāja Priyavrata. If Mahārāja Priyavrata could condemn himself in spite of his wonderful activities, how condemned we are in our so-called advancement of material civilization. We can conclude that such advancement has nothing to do with the problems of the living entity entangled within this material world. Unfortunately, modern man does not understand his entanglement and how condemned he is, nor does he know what kind of body he is going to have in the next life. From a spiritual point of view, a great kingdom, beautiful wife and wonderful material activities are all impediments to spiritual advancement. Mahārāja Priyavrata had served the great sage Nārada sincerely.

Therefore even though he had accepted material opulences, he could not be deviated from his own task. He again became Kṛṣṇa conscious. As confirmed in *Bhagavad-gītā:*

nehābhikrama-nāśo 'sti
pratyavāyo na vidyate
svalpam apy asya dharmasya
trāyate mahato bhayāt

"In devotional service there is no loss or diminution, and even a small service rendered in devotional life is sufficient to save one from the greatest danger." (Bg. 2.40) Such renunciation as Mahārāja Priyavrata's is possible only by the grace of the Supreme Personality of Godhead. Generally when people are powerful or when they have a beautiful wife, a beautiful home and material popularity, they become more and more entangled. Priyavrata Mahārāja, however, having been completely trained by the great sage Nārada, revived his Kṛṣṇa consciousness in spite of all impediments.

TEXT 38

परदेवताप्रसादाधिगतात्मप्रत्यवमर्शेनानुप्रवृत्तेभ्यः पुत्रेभ्य इमां यथादायं विभज्य भुक्तभोगां च महिषीं मृतकमिव सहमहाविभूतिमपहाय स्वयं निहितनिर्वेदो हृदि गृहीतहरिविहारानुभावो भगवतो नारदस्य पदवीं पुनरेवानुससार ॥ ३८ ॥

para-devatā-prasādādhigatātma-pratyavamarśenānupravṛttebhyaḥ putrebhya imāṁ yathā-dāyaṁ vibhajya bhukta-bhogāṁ ca mahiṣīṁ mṛtakam iva saha mahā-vibhūtim apahāya svayaṁ nihita-nirvedo hṛdi gṛhīta-hari-vihārānubhāvo bhagavato nāradasya padavīṁ punar evānusasāra.

para-devatā—of the Supreme Personality of Godhead; *prasāda*—by the mercy; *adhigata*—obtained; *ātma-pratyavamarśena*—by self-realization; *anupravṛttebhyaḥ*—who exactly follow his path;

putrebhyaḥ—unto his sons; *imām*—this earth; *yathā-dāyam*—exactly according to the inheritance; *vibhajya*—dividing; *bhukta-bhogām*—whom he enjoyed in so many ways; *ca*—also; *mahiṣīm*—the Queen; *mṛtakam iva*—exactly like a dead body; *saha*—with; *mahā-vibhūtim*—great opulence; *apahāya*—giving up; *svayam*—himself; *nihita*—perfectly taken to; *nirvedaḥ*—renunciation; *hṛdi*—in the heart; *gṛhīta*—accepted; *hari*—of the Supreme Personality of Godhead; *vihāra*—pastimes; *anubhāvaḥ*—in such an attitude; *bhagavataḥ*—of the great saintly person; *nāradasya*—of Saint Nārada; *padavīm*—position; *punaḥ*—again; *eva*—certainly; *anusasāra*—began to follow.

TRANSLATION

By the grace of the Supreme Personality of Godhead, Mahārāja Priyavrata reawakened to his senses. He divided all his earthly possessions among his obedient sons. He gave up everything, including his wife, with whom he had enjoyed so much sense gratification, and his great and opulent kingdom, and he completely renounced all attachment. His heart, having been cleansed, became a place of pastimes for the Supreme Personality of Godhead. Thus he was able to return to the path of Kṛṣṇa consciousness, spiritual life, and resume the position he had attained by the grace of the great saint Nārada.

PURPORT

As enunciated by Śrī Caitanya Mahāprabhu in His *Śikṣāṣṭaka, ceto-darpaṇa-mārjanaṁ bhava-mahādāvāgni-nirvāpaṇam:* as soon as one's heart is cleansed, the blazing fire of material existence is immediately extinguished. Our hearts are meant for the pastimes of the Supreme Personality of Godhead. This means that one should be fully Kṛṣṇa conscious, thinking of Kṛṣṇa, as He Himself advises (*man-manā bhava mad-bhakto mad-yājī māṁ namaskuru*). This should be our only business. One whose heart is not clean cannot think of the transcendental pastimes of the Supreme Lord, but if one can once again place the Supreme Personality of Godhead in his heart, he very easily becomes qualified to renounce material attachment. Māyāvādī philosophers, *yogīs* and *jñānīs* try to give up this material world simply by saying, *brahma satyaṁ jagan mithyā:* "This world is false. There is no use of it. Let us take to Brahman." Such theoretical knowledge will not help us. If we believe that Brahman is the real truth, we have to place within our hearts the lotus feet of Śrī Kṛṣṇa, as Mahārāja Ambarīṣa did (*sa vai manaḥ kṛṣṇa-padāravindayoḥ*). One has to fix the lotus feet of the Lord within his heart. Then he gets the strength to be freed from material entanglement.

Mahārāja Priyavrata was able to give up his opulent kingdom, and he also gave up the association of his beautiful wife as if she were a dead body. However beautiful one's wife and however attractive her bodily features, one is no longer interested in her when her body is dead. We praise a beautiful woman for her body, but that same body, when bereft of a spirit soul, is no longer interesting to any lusty man. Mahārāja Priyavrata was so strong, by the grace of the Lord, that even though his beautiful wife was alive, he could give up her association exactly like one who is forced to give up the association of a dead wife. Śrī Caitanya Mahāprabhu said:

na dhanaṁ na janaṁ na sundarīṁ
kavitāṁ vā jagadīśa kāmaye
mama janmani janmanīśvare
bhavatād bhaktir ahaitukī tvayi

"O almighty Lord, I have no desire to accumulate wealth, nor do I desire beautiful women, nor do I want any number of followers. I only want Your causeless devotional service birth after birth." For one who desires to advance in spiritual life, attachment to material opulence and attachment to a beautiful wife are two great impediments. Such attachments are condemned even more than suicide. Therefore anyone desiring to cross beyond material nescience must, by the grace of Kṛṣṇa, be freed from attachment to women and money. When Mahārāja Priyavrata became completely free from these attachments, he could again peacefully follow the principles instructed by the great sage Nārada.

TEXT 39

तस्य ह वा एते श्लोकाः—
प्रियव्रतकृतं कर्म को नु कुर्याद्विनेश्वरम् ।
यो नेमिनिम्नैरकरोच्छायां घ्नन् सप्त वारिधीन् ॥३९॥

tasya ha vā ete ślokāḥ—
priyavrata-kṛtaṁ karma
ko nu kuryād vineśvaram
yo nemi-nimnair akaroc
chāyāṁ ghnan sapta vāridhīn

tasya—his; *ha vā*—certainly; *ete*—all these; *ślokāḥ*—verses; *priyavrata*—by King Priyavrata; *kṛtam*—done; *karma*—activities; *kaḥ*—who; *nu*—then; *kuryāt*—can execute; *vinā*—without; *īśvaram*—the Supreme Personality of Godhead; *yaḥ*—one who; *nemi*—of the rim of the wheels of his chariot; *nimnaiḥ*—by the depressions; *akarot*—made; *chāyām*—darkness; *ghnan*—dissipating; *sapta*—seven; *vāridhīn*—oceans.

TRANSLATION

There are many famous verses regarding Mahārāja Priyavrata's activities:

"No one but the Supreme Personality of Godhead could do what Mahārāja Priyavrata has done. Mahārāja Priyavrata dissipated the darkness of night, and with the rims of his great chariot, he excavated seven oceans."

PURPORT

There are many excellent verses, famous all over the world, concerning the activities of Mahārāja Priyavrata. He is so celebrated that his activities are compared to those of the Supreme Personality of Godhead. Sometimes a sincere servant and devotee of the Lord is also called *bhagavān.* Śrī Nārada is called *bhagavān,* and Lord Śiva and Vyāsadeva are also sometimes called *bhagavān.* This designation, *bhagavān,* is sometimes conferred upon a pure devotee by the grace of the Lord so that he will be very highly esteemed. Mahārāja Priyavrata was such a devotee.

TEXT 40

भूसंस्थानं कृतं येन सरिद्गिरिवनादिभिः ।
सीमा च भूतनिर्वृत्यै द्वीपे द्वीपे विभागशः ॥४०॥

bhū-saṁsthānaṁ kṛtaṁ yena
sarid-giri-vanādibhiḥ
sīmā ca bhūta-nirvṛtyai
dvīpe dvīpe vibhāgaśaḥ

bhū-saṁsthānam—the situation of the earth; *kṛtam*—done; *yena*—by whom; *sarit*—by rivers; *giri*—by hills and mountains; *vana-ādibhiḥ*—by forests and so on; *sīmā*—boundaries; *ca*—also; *bhūta*—of different nations; *nirvṛtyai*—to stop fighting; *dvīpe dvīpe*—on the various islands; *vibhāgaśaḥ*—separately.

TRANSLATION

"To stop the quarreling among different peoples, Mahārāja Priyavrata marked boundaries at rivers and at the edges of mountains and forests so that no one would trespass upon another's property."

PURPORT

The example set by Mahārāja Priyavrata in marking off different states is still followed. As indicated here, different classes of men are destined to live in different areas, and therefore the boundaries of various tracts of land, which are described here as islands, should be defined by different rivers, forests and hills. This is also mentioned in relation to Mahārāja Pṛthu, who was born from the dead body of his father by the manipulation of great sages. Mahārāja Pṛthu's father was very sinful, and therefore a black man called Niṣāda was first born from his dead body. The Naiṣāda race was given a place in the forest because by nature they are thieves and rogues. As animals are given places in various forests and hills, men who are like animals are also destined to live there. One cannot be promoted to civilized life unless one comes to Kṛṣṇa consciousness, for by nature one is destined to live in a particular situation according to one's *karma* and association with the modes of nature. If men want to live in harmony and peace, they must take to Kṛṣṇa consciousness, for they cannot achieve the highest standard while absorbed in the bodily concept of life. Mahārāja Priyavrata divided the surface of the globe into different islands so that each class of men would live peacefully and not clash with the others. The modern idea of nationhood has gradually developed from the divisions made by Mahārāja Priyavrata.

TEXT 41

भौमं दिव्यं मानुषं च महित्वं कर्मयोगजम् ।
यश्चक्रे निरयौपम्यं पुरुषानुजनप्रियः ॥४१॥

bhaumaṁ divyaṁ mānuṣaṁ ca
mahitvaṁ karma-yogajam
yaś cakre nirayaupamyaṁ
puruṣānujana-priyaḥ

bhaumam—of the lower planets; *divyam*—heavenly; *mānuṣam*—of human beings; *ca*—also; *mahitvam*—all opulences; *karma*—by fruitive activities; *yoga*—by mystic power; *jam*—born; *yaḥ*—one who; *cakre*—did; *niraya*—with hell; *aupamyam*—comparison or equality; *puruṣa*—of the Supreme Personality of Godhead; *anujana*—to the devotee; *priyaḥ*—most dear.

TRANSLATION

"As a great follower and devotee of the sage Nārada, Mahārāja Priyavrata considered hellish the opulences he had achieved by dint of fruitive activities and mystic power, whether in the lower or heavenly planetary systems or in human society."

PURPORT

Śrīla Rūpa Gosvāmī has said that the position of a devotee is so superexcellent that a devotee does not consider any material opulence worth having. There are different types of opulences on earth, in the heavenly planets and even in the lower planetary system, known as Pātāla. A devotee, however, knows that they are all material, and consequently he is not at all interested in them. As stated in *Bhagavad-gītā*, *paraṁ dṛṣṭvā nivartate*. Sometimes *yogīs* and *jñānīs* voluntarily give up all material opulences to practice their system of liberation and taste spiritual bliss. However, they frequently fall down because artificial renunciation of material opulences cannot endure. One must have a superior taste in spiritual life; then he can give up material opulence. Mahārāja Priyavrata had already tasted spiritual bliss, and therefore he had no interest in any of the material achievements available in the lower, higher or middle planetary systems.

Thus end the Bhaktivedanta purports to the Fifth Canto, First Chapter, of Śrīmad-Bhāgavatam, *entitled "The Activities of Mahārāja Priyavrata."*

CHAPTER TWO

The Activities of Mahārāja Āgnīdhra

In this chapter, the character of Mahārāja Āgnīdhra is described. When Mahārāja Priyavrata went off for spiritual realization, his son Āgnīdhra became the ruler of Jambūdvīpa, in accordance with Mahārāja Priyavrata's instructions, and maintained its residents with the same affection a father feels for his sons. Once Mahārāja Āgnīdhra desired to have a son, and therefore he entered a cave of Mandara Mountain to practice austerity. Understanding his desire, Lord Brahmā sent a celestial girl named Pūrvacitti to Āgnīdhra's hermitage. After dressing herself very attractively, she presented herself before him with various feminine movements, and Āgnīdhra was naturally attracted to her. The girl's actions, expressions, smile, sweet words and moving eyes were fascinating to him. Āgnīdhra was expert in flattery. Thus he attracted the celestial girl, who was pleased to accept him as her husband because of his mellifluous words. She enjoyed royal happiness with Āgnīdhra for many years before returning to her abode in the heavenly planets. In her womb Āgnīdhra begot nine sons—Nābhi, Kiṁpuruṣa, Harivarṣa, Ilāvṛta, Ramyaka, Hiraṇmaya, Kuru, Bhadrāśva and Ketumāla. He gave them nine islands with names corresponding to theirs. Āgnīdhra, however, his senses unsatisfied, was always thinking of his celestial wife, and therefore in his next life he was born in her celestial planet. After the death of Āgnīdhra, his nine sons married nine daughters of Meru named Merudevī, Pratirūpā, Ugradaṁṣṭrī, Latā, Ramyā, Śyāmā, Nārī, Bhadrā and Devavīti.

TEXT 1

श्रीशुक उवाच

एवं पितरि सम्प्रवृत्ते तदनुशासने वर्तमान आग्नीध्रो जम्बूद्वीपौकसः
प्रजा औरसवद्धर्मावेक्षमाणः पर्यगोपायत् ॥ १ ॥

śrī-śuka uvāca
evaṁ pitari sampravṛtte tad-anuśāsane vartamāna āgnīdhro
jambūdvīpaukasaḥ prajā aurasavad dharmāvekṣamāṇaḥ paryagopāyat.

śrī-śukaḥ—Śrī Śukadeva Gosvāmī; *uvāca*—said; *evam*—thus; *pitari*—when his father; *sampravṛtte*—took to the path of liberation; *tat-anuśāsane*—according to his order; *vartamānaḥ*—situated; *āgnīdhraḥ*—King Āgnīdhra; *jambū-dvīpa-okasaḥ*—the inhabitants of Jambūdvīpa; *prajāḥ*—citizens; *aurasa-vat*—as if they were his sons; *dharma*—religious principles; *avekṣamāṇaḥ*—strictly observing; *paryagopāyat*—completely protected.

TRANSLATION

Śrī Śukadeva Gosvāmī continued: After his father, Mahārāja Priyavrata, departed to follow the path of spiritual life by undergoing austerities, King Āgnīdhra completely obeyed his order. Strictly observing the principles of religion, he gave full protection to the inhabitants of Jambūdvīpa as if they were his own begotten sons.

PURPORT

Following the instruction of his father, Mahārāja Priyavrata, Mahārāja Āgnīdhra ruled the inhabitants of Jambūdvīpa according to religious principles. These principles are exactly contrary to the modern principles of faithlessness. As clearly stated here, the King protected the citizens the way a father protects his begotten children. How he ruled the citizens is also described here—*dharmāvekṣamāṇaḥ*, strictly according to religious principles. It is the duty of the executive head of a state to see that the citizens strictly follow religious principles. The Vedic religious principles begin with *varṇāśrama-dharma*, the duties of the four *varṇas* and four *āśramas*. *Dharma* refers to principles given by the Supreme Personality of Godhead. The first principle of *dharma*, or religion, is to observe the duties of the four orders as enjoined by the Supreme Personality of Godhead. According to people's qualities and activities, society should be divided into *brāhmaṇas*, *kṣatriyas*, *vaiśyas* and *śūdras* and then again into *brahmacārīs*, *gṛhasthas*, *vānaprasthas* and *sannyāsīs*. These are religious principles, and it is the duty of the head of state to see that his citizens strictly follow them. He should not merely act officially; he should be like a father who is always a well-wisher of his sons. Such a father strictly observes whether his sons are performing their duties, and sometimes he also punishes them.

Just contrary to the principles mentioned here, the presidents and chief executives in the age of Kali are simply tax collectors who do not care whether religious principles are observed. Indeed, the chief executives of the present day introduce all kinds of sinful activity, especially illicit sex, intoxication, animal killing and gambling. These sinful activities are now very prominently manifested in India. Although a hundred years ago these four principles of sinful life were strictly prohibited in the families of India, they have now been introduced into every Indian family; therefore they cannot follow religious principles. In contrast to the principles of the kings of old, the modern state is concerned only with propaganda for levying taxes and is no longer responsible for the spiritual welfare of the citizens. The state is now callous to religious principles. *Śrīmad-Bhāgavatam* predicts that in Kali-yuga the government will be entrusted with *dasyu-dharma*, which means the occupational duty of rogues and thieves. Modern heads of state are rogues and thieves who plunder the citizens instead of giving them protection. Rogues and thieves plunder without regard for law, but in this age of Kali, as stated in *Śrīmad-Bhāgavatam*, the lawmakers themselves plunder the citizens. The next prediction to be fulfilled, which is already coming to pass, is that because of the sinful activities of the citizens and the government, rain will become increasingly scarce. Gradually there will be complete drought and no production of food grains. People will be reduced to eating flesh and seeds, and many good, spiritually inclined people will have to forsake their homes because they will be too harassed by drought, taxation and famine. The Kṛṣṇa consciousness movement is the only hope to save the world from such devastation. It is the most scientific and authorized movement for the actual welfare of the whole human society.

TEXT 2

स च कदाचित्पितृलोककामः सुरवरवनिताक्रीडाचलद्रोण्यां भगवन्तं विश्व-
सृजां पतिमाभृतपरिचर्योपकरण आत्मैकाग्र्येण तपस्व्याराधयाम्बभूव ॥ २ ॥

sa ca kadācit pitṛloka-kāmaḥ sura-vara-vanitākrīḍācala-droṇyāṁ bhagavantaṁ viśva-sṛjāṁ patim ābhṛta-paricaryopakaraṇa ātmaikāgryeṇa tapasvy ārādhayām babhūva.

saḥ—he (King Āgnīdhra); *ca*—also; *kadācit*—once upon a time; *pitṛ-loka*—the Pitṛloka planet; *kāmaḥ*—desiring; *sura-vara*—of the great demigods; *vanitā*—the women; *ākrīḍā*—the place of pastimes; *acala-droṇyām*—in one valley of the Mandara Hill; *bhagavantam*—unto the most powerful (Lord Brahmā); *viśva-sṛjām*—of personalities who have created this universe; *patim*—the master; *ābhṛta*—having collected; *paricaryā-upakaraṇaḥ*—ingredients for worship; *ātma*—of the mind; *eka-agryeṇa*—with full attention; *tapasvī*—one who executes austerity; *ārādhayām babhūva*—became engaged in worshiping.

TRANSLATION

Desiring to get a perfect son and become an inhabitant of Pitṛloka, Mahārāja Āgnīdhra once worshiped Lord Brahmā, the master of those in charge of material creation. He went to a valley of Mandara Hill, where the damsels of the heavenly planets come down to stroll. There he collected garden flowers and other necessary paraphernalia and then engaged in severe austerities and worship.

PURPORT

The King became *pitṛloka-kāma,* or desirous of being transferred to the planet named Pitṛloka. Pitṛloka is mentioned in *Bhagavad-gītā (yānti deva-vratā devān pitṝn yānti pitṛ-vratāḥ).* To go to this planet, one needs very good sons who can make offerings to Lord Viṣṇu and then offer the remnants to their forefathers. The purpose of the *śrāddha* ceremony is to please the Supreme Personality of Godhead, Lord Viṣṇu, so that after pleasing Him one may offer *prasāda* to one's forefathers and in this way make them happy. The inhabitants of Pitṛloka are generally men of the *karma-kāṇḍīya,* or fruitive activities category, who have been transferred there because of their pious activities. They can stay there as long as their descendants offer them *viṣṇu-prasāda.* Everyone in heavenly planets such as Pitṛloka, however, must return to earth after exhausting the effects of his pious acts. As confirmed in *Bhagavad-gītā* (9.21), *kṣīṇe puṇye martya-lokaṁ viśanti:* persons who perform pious acts are transferred to higher planets, but when the effects of their pious acts are over, they are again transferred to earth.

Since Mahārāja Priyavrata was a great devotee, how could he have begotten a son who desired to be transferred to Pitṛloka? Lord Kṛṣṇa says, *pitṝn yānti pitṛ-vratāḥ:* persons who desire to go to Pitṛloka are transferred there. Similarly, *yānti mad-yājino 'pi mām:* persons who desire to be transferred to the spiritual planets, Vaikuṇṭhalokas, can also go there. Since Mahārāja Āgnīdhra was the son of a Vaiṣṇava, he should have desired to be transferred to the spiritual world, Vaikuṇṭhaloka. Why, then, did he desire to be transferred to Pitṛloka? In answer to this, Gosvāmī Giridhara, one of the *Bhāgavatam* commentators, remarks that Āgnīdhra was born when Mahārāja Priyavrata was infatuated by lusty desires. This may be accepted as a fact because sons are begotten with different mentalities according to the time of their conception. According to the Vedic system, therefore, before a child is conceived, the *garbhādhāna-saṁskāra* is performed. This ceremony molds the mentality of the father in such a way that when he plants his seed in the womb of his wife, he will beget a child whose mind will be completely saturated with a devotional attitude. At the present moment, however, there are no such *garbhādhāna-saṁskāras*, and therefore people generally have a lusty attitude when they beget children. Especially in this age of Kali, there are no *garbhādhāna* ceremonies; everyone enjoys sex with his wife like a cat or dog. Therefore according to śāstric injunctions, almost all the people of this age belong to the *śūdra* category. Of course, although Mahārāja Āgnīdhra had a desire to be transferred to Pitṛloka, this does not mean that his mentality was that of a *śūdra;* he was a *kṣatriya.*

Mahārāja Āgnīdhra desired to be transferred to Pitṛloka, and therefore he needed a wife because anyone desiring to be transferred to Pitṛloka must leave behind a good son to offer yearly *piṇḍa*, or *prasāda* from Lord Viṣṇu. To have a good son, Mahārāja Āgnīdhra wanted a wife from a family of demigods. Therefore he went to Mandara Hill, where the women of the demigods generally come, to worship Lord Brahmā. In *Bhagavad-gītā* (4.12) it is said, *kāṅkṣantaḥ karmaṇāṁ siddhiṁ yajanta iha devatāḥ:* materialists who want quick results in the material world worship demigods. This is also confirmed in *Śrīmad-Bhāgavatam. Śrī-aiśvarya-prajepsavaḥ:* those who desire beautiful wives, substantial wealth and many sons worship the demigods, but an intelligent devotee, instead of being entangled by the happiness of this material world in the form of a beautiful wife, material opulence and children, desires to be immediately transferred back home, back to Godhead. Thus he worships the Supreme Personality of Godhead, Viṣṇu.

TEXT 3

तदुपलभ्य भगवानादिपुरुषः सदसि गायन्तीं पूर्वचित्तिं नामाप्सरसमभियापयामास ॥३॥

tad upalabhya bhagavān ādi-puruṣaḥ sadasi gāyantīṁ pūrvacittiṁ nāmāpsarasam abhiyāpayām āsa.

tat—that; *upalabhya*—understanding; *bhagavān*—the most powerful; *ādi-puruṣaḥ*—the first created being within this universe; *sadasi*—in his assembly; *gāyantīm*—dancing girl; *pūrvacittim*—Pūrvacitti; *nāma*—named; *apsarasam*—the heavenly dancing girl; *abhiyāpayām āsa*—sent down.

TRANSLATION

Understanding King Āgnīdhra's desire, the first and most powerful created being of this universe, Lord Brahmā, selected the best of the dancing girls in his assembly, whose name was Pūrvacitti, and sent her to the King.

PURPORT

In this verse, the words *bhagavān ādi-puruṣaḥ* are significant. *Bhagavān ādi-puruṣaḥ* is Lord Kṛṣṇa. *Govindam ādi-puruṣaṁ tam ahaṁ bhajāmi.* Lord Kṛṣṇa is the original person. In *Bhagavad-gītā,* He is also addressed by Arjuna as *puruṣam ādyam,* the original person, and He is called Bhagavān. In this verse, however, we see that Lord Brahmā is described as *bhagavān ādi-puruṣaḥ.* The reason he is called *bhagavān* is that he fully represents the Supreme Personality of Godhead and is the first-born creature in this universe. Lord Brahmā could understand Mahārāja Āgnīdhra's desire because he is as powerful as Lord Viṣṇu. As Lord Viṣṇu, situated as Paramātmā, can understand the desire of the living entity, so Lord Brahmā can also understand the living entity's desire, for Viṣṇu, as a via medium, informs him. As stated in *Śrīmad-Bhāgavatam* (1.1.1), *tene brahma hṛdā ya ādi-kavaye:* Lord Viṣṇu informs Lord Brahmā of everything from within his heart. Because Mahārāja Āgnīdhra specifically worshiped Lord Brahmā, Lord Brahmā was pleased, and he sent Pūrvacitti, the Apsarā, to satisfy him.

TEXT 4

सा च तदाश्रमोपवनमतिरमणीयं विविधनिबिडविटपिविटपनिकरसंश्लिष्टपुरटल-
तारूढस्थलविहङ्गममिथुनैः प्रोच्यमानश्रुतिभिः प्रतिबोध्यमानसलिलकुक्कुटकार-
ण्डवकलहंसादिभिर्विचित्रमुपकूजितामलजलाशयकमलाकरमुपबभ्राम ॥४॥

sā ca tad-āśramopavanam ati-ramaṇīyaṁ vividha-nibiḍa-viṭapi-viṭapa-nikara-saṁśliṣṭa-puraṭa-latārūḍha-sthala-vihaṅgama-mithunaiḥ procyamāna-śrutibhiḥ pratibodhyamāna-salila-kukkuṭa-kāraṇḍava-kalahaṁsādibhir vicitram upakūjitāmala-jalāśaya-kamalākaram upababhrāma.

sā—she (Pūrvacitti); *ca*—also; *tat*—of Mahārāja Āgnīdhra; *āśrama*—of the place of meditation; *upavanam*—the park; *ati*—very; *ramaṇīyam*—beautiful; *vividha*—varieties of; *nibiḍa*—dense; *viṭapi*—trees; *viṭapa*—of branches and twigs; *nikara*—masses; *saṁśliṣṭa*—attached; *puraṭa*—golden; *latā*—with creepers; *ārūḍha*—going high; *sthala-vihaṅgama*—of land birds; *mithunaiḥ*—with pairs; *procyamāna*—vibrating; *śrutibhiḥ*—pleasing sounds; *pratibodhyamāna*—responding; *salila-kukkuṭa*—water fowl; *kāraṇḍava*—ducks; *kalahaṁsa*—with various kinds of swans; *ādibhiḥ*—and so on; *vicitram*—variegated; *upakūjita*—resounding with the vibration; *amala*—clear; *jala-āśaya*—in the lake; *kamala-ākaram*—the source of lotus flowers; *upababhrāma*—began to walk in.

TRANSLATION

The Apsarā sent by Lord Brahmā began strolling in a beautiful park near the place where the King was meditating and worshiping. The park was beautiful because of its dense green foliage and golden creepers. There were pairs of varied birds such as peacocks, and in a lake there were ducks and swans, all vibrating very sweet sounds. Thus the park was magnificently beautiful because of the foliage, the clear water, the lotus flowers and the sweet singing of various kinds of birds.

TEXT 5

तस्याः सुललितगमनपदविन्यासगतिविलासायाश्चानुपदं खणखणायमानरुचिर-
चरणाभरणस्वनमुपाकर्ण्य नरदेवकुमारः समाधियोगेनामीलितनयननलिन-
मुकुलयुगलमीषद्विकचय्य व्यचष्ट ॥५॥

tasyāḥ sulalita-gamana-pada-vinyāsa-gati-vilāsāyāś cānupadaṁ
khaṇa-khaṇāyamāna-rucira-caraṇābharaṇa-svanam upākarṇya
naradeva-kumāraḥ samādhi-yogenāmīlita-nayana-nalina-mukula-
yugalam īṣad vikacayya vyacaṣṭa.

tasyāḥ—of her (Pūrvacitti); *sulalita*—in a very beautiful; *gamana*—movements; *pada-vinyāsa*—with styles of walking; *gati*—in the progression; *vilāsāyāḥ*—whose pastime; *ca*—also; *anupadam*—with every step; *khaṇa-khaṇāyamāna*—making a tinkling sound; *rucira*—very pleasing; *caraṇa-ābharaṇa*—of the ornaments on the feet; *svanam*—the sound; *upākarṇya*—hearing; *naradeva-kumāraḥ*—the Prince; *samādhi*—in ecstasy; *yogena*—by controlling the senses; *āmīlita*—half-open; *nayana*—eyes; *nalina*—of lotus; *mukula*—buds; *yugalam*—like a pair; *īṣat*—slightly; *vikacayya*—opening; *vyacaṣta*—saw.

TRANSLATION

As Pūrvacitti passed by on the road in a very beautiful style and mood of her own, the pleasing ornaments on her ankles tinkled with her every step. Although Prince Āgnīdhra was controlling his

senses, practicing yoga with half-open eyes, he could see her with his lotuslike eyes, and when he heard the sweet tinkling of her bangles, he opened his eyes slightly more and could see that she was just nearby.

PURPORT

It is said that *yogīs* always think of the Supreme Personality of Godhead within their hearts. *Dhyānāvasthita-tad-gatena manasā paśyanti yaṁ yoginaḥ* (*Bhāg.* 12.13.1). The Supreme Personality of Godhead is always observed by *yogīs* who practice controlling the venomous senses. As recommended in *Bhagavad-gītā, yogīs* should practice *samprekṣya nāsikāgram,* keeping their eyes half-open. If the eyes are closed completely, there will be a tendency to sleep. So-called *yogīs* sometimes practice a fashionable form of *yoga* by closing their eyes and meditating, but we have actually seen such so-called *yogīs* sleeping and snoring while meditating. This is not the practice of *yoga.* To actually practice *yoga,* one should keep his eyes half-open and gaze at the tip of his nose.

Although Āgnīdhra, the son of Priyavrata, was practicing mystic *yoga* and trying to control his senses, the tinkling sound of Pūrvacitti's ankle bells disturbed his practice. *Yoga indriya-saṁyamaḥ:* actual *yoga* practice means controlling the senses. One must practice mystic *yoga,* to control the senses, but the sense control of a devotee who fully engages in the service of the Lord with his purified senses (*hṛṣīkeṇa hṛṣikeśa-sevanam*) can never be disturbed. Śrīla Prabodhānanda Sarasvatī therefore stated, *durdāntendriya-kāla-sarpa-paṭalī protkhāta-daṁṣṭrā-yate* (*Caitanya-candrāmṛta* 5). The practice of *yoga* is undoubtedly good because it controls the senses, which are like venomous serpents. When one engages in devotional service, however, completely employing all the activities of the senses in the service of the Lord, the venomous quality of the senses is completely nullified. It is explained that a serpent is to be feared because of its poison fangs, but if those fangs are broken, the serpent, although it seems fearsome, is not at all dangerous. Devotees, therefore, may see hundreds and thousands of beautiful women with fascinating bodily movements and gestures but not be allured, whereas such women would make ordinary *yogīs* fall. Even the advanced *yogī* Viśvāmitra broke his mystic practice to unite with Menakā and beget a child known as Śakuntalā. The practice of mystic *yoga*, therefore, is not sufficiently strong to control the senses. Another example is Prince Āgnīdhra, whose attention was drawn to the movements of Pūrvacitti, the Apsarā, simply because he heard the tinkling of her ankle bells. In the same way that Viśvāmitra Muni was attracted by the tinkling bangles of Menakā, Prince Āgnīdhra, upon hearing the tinkling bangles of Pūrvacitti, immediately opened his eyes to see her beautiful movements as she walked. The prince was also very handsome. As described herein, his eyes were just like the buds of lotus flowers. As he opened his lotuslike eyes, he could immediately see that the Apsarā was present by his side.

TEXT 6

तामेवाविदूरे मधुकरीमिव सुमनस उपजिघ्रन्तीं दिविजमनुजमनोनयनाह्लाद-
दुघैर्गतिविहारव्रीडाविनयावलोकसुस्वराक्षरावयवैर्मनसि नृणां कुसुमायुधस्य ।
विदधतीं विवरं निजमुखविगलितामृतासवसहासभाषणामोदमदान्धमधुकर-
निकरोपरोधेन द्रुतपदविन्यासेन वल्गुस्पन्दनस्तनकलशकबरभाररशनां देवीं
तदवलोकनेन विवृतावसरस्य भगवतो मकरध्वजस्य वशमुपनीतो ।
जडवदिति होवाच ॥ ६ ॥

tām evāvidūre madhukarīm iva sumanasa upajighrantīṁ divija-manuja-mano-nayanāhlāda-dughair gati-vihāra-vrīḍā-vinayāvaloka-susvarākṣarāvayavair manasi nṛṇāṁ kusumāyudhasya vidadhatīṁ vivaraṁ nija-mukha-vigalitāmṛtāsava-sahāsa-bhāṣaṇāmoda-madāndha-madhukara-nikaroparodhena druta-pada-vinyāsena valgu-spandana-stana-kalaśa-kabara-bhāra-raśanāṁ devīṁ tad-avalokanena vivṛtāvasarasya bhagavato makara-dhvajasya vaśam upanīto jaḍavad iti hovāca.

tām—to her; *eva*—indeed; *avidūre*—nearby; *madhukarīm iva*—like a honeybee; *sumanasaḥ*—beautiful flowers; *upajighrantīm*—smelling; *divi-ja*—of those born in the heavenly planets; *manu-ja*—of those born in human society; *manaḥ*—mind; *nayana*—for the eyes; *āhlāda*—

pleasure; *dughaiḥ*—producing; *gati*—by her movement; *vihāra*—by pastimes; *vrīḍā*—by shyness; *vinaya*—by humility; *avaloka*—by glancing; *su-svara-akṣara*—by her sweet voice; *avayavaiḥ*—and by the limbs of the body; *manasi*—in the mind; *nṛṇām*—of men; *kusuma-āyudhasya*—of Cupid, who has a flower arrow in his hand; *vidadhatīm*—making; *vivaram*—aural reception; *nija-mukha*—from her own mouth; *vigalita*—pouring out; *amṛta-āsava*—nectar like honey; *sa-hāsa*—in her smiling; *bhāṣaṇa*—and talking; *āmoda*—by the pleasure; *mada-andha*—blinded by intoxication; *madhukara*—of bees; *nikara*—by groups; *uparodhena*—because of being surrounded; *druta*—hasty; *pada*—of feet; *vinyāsena*—by stylish stepping; *valgu*—a little; *spandana*—moving; *stana*—breasts; *kalaśa*—like waterpots; *kabara*—of her braids of hair; *bhāra*—weight; *raśanām*—the belt upon the hips; *devīm*—the goddess; *tat-avalokanena*—simply by seeing her; *vivṛta-avasarasya*—taking the opportunity of; *bhagavataḥ*—of the greatly powerful; *makara-dhvajasya*—of Cupid; *vaśam*—under the control; *upanītaḥ*—being brought in; *jaḍa-vat*—as if stunned; *iti*—thus; *ha*—certainly; *uvāca*—he said.

TRANSLATION

Like a honeybee, the Apsarā smelled the beautiful and attractive flowers. She could attract the minds and vision of both humans and demigods by her playful movements, her shyness and humility, her glances, the very pleasing sounds that poured from her mouth as she spoke, and the motion of her limbs. By all these qualities, she opened for Cupid, who bears an arrow of flowers, a path of aural reception into the minds of men. When she spoke, nectar seemed to flow from her mouth. As she breathed, the bees, mad for the taste of her breath, tried to hover about her beautiful lotuslike eyes. Disturbed by the bees, she tried to move hastily, but as she raised her feet to walk quickly, her hair, the belt on her hips, and her breasts, which were like water jugs, also moved in a way that made her extremely beautiful and attractive. Indeed, she seemed to be making a path for the entrance of Cupid, who is most powerful. Therefore the prince, completely subdued by seeing her, spoke to her as follows.

PURPORT

How a beautiful woman's movements and gestures, her hair and the structure of her breasts, hips and other bodily features attract the minds not only of men but of demigods also is very finely described in this statement. The words *divija* and *manuja* specifically emphasize that the attraction of feminine gestures is powerful everywhere within this material world, both on this planet and in the higher planetary systems. It is said that the standard of living in the higher planetary systems is thousands and thousands of times higher than the standard of living on this planet. Therefore the beautiful bodily features of the women there are also thousands and thousands of times more attractive than the features of the women on earth. The creator has constructed women in such a way that their beautiful voices and movements and the beautiful features of their hips, their breasts, and the other parts of their bodies attract the members of the opposite sex, both on earth and on other planets, and awaken their lusty desires. When one is controlled by Cupid or the beauty of women, he becomes stunned like matter such as stone. Captivated by the material movements of women, he wants to remain in this material world. Thus one's promotion to the spiritual world is checked simply by seeing the beautiful bodily structure and movements of women. Śrī Caitanya Mahāprabhu has therefore warned all devotees to beware of the attraction of beautiful women and materialistic civilization. Śrī Caitanya Mahāprabhu even refused to see Pratāparudra Mahārāja because he was a very opulent person in the material world. Lord Caitanya said in this connection, *niṣkiñcanasya bhagavad-bhajanonmukhasya:* those who are engaged in the devotional service of the Lord because they are very serious about going back home, back to Godhead, should be very careful to avoid seeing the beautiful gestures of women and should also avoid seeing persons who are very rich.

niṣkiñcanasya bhagavad-bhajanonmukhasya
pāraṁ paraṁ jigamiṣor bhava-sāgarasya
sandarśanaṁ viṣayiṇām atha yoṣitāṁ ca
hā hanta hanta viṣa-bhakṣaṇato 'py asādhu

"Alas, for a person who is seriously desiring to cross the material ocean and engage in the transcendental loving service of the Lord without material motives, seeing a materialist engaged in sense gratification or seeing a woman who is similarly interested is more abominable than drinking poison willingly." (*Caitanya-caritāmṛta, Madhya* 11.8) One who is serious about going back home, back to Godhead, should not contemplate the attractive features of women and the opulence of rich men. Such contemplation will check one's advancement in spiritual life. Once a devotee is fixed in Kṛṣṇa consciousness, however, these attractions will not agitate his mind.

TEXT 7

का त्वं चिकीर्षसि च किं मुनिवर्य शैले
मायासि कापि भगवत्परदेवतायाः ।
विज्ये बिभर्षि धनुषी सुहृदात्मनोऽर्थे
किं वा मृगान्मृगयसे विपिने प्रमत्तान् ॥ ७ ॥

kā tvaṁ cikīrṣasi ca kiṁ muni-varya śaile
māyāsi kāpi bhagavat-para-devatāyāḥ
vijye bibharṣi dhanuṣī suhṛd-ātmano 'rthe
kiṁ vā mṛgān mṛgayase vipine pramattān

kā—who; *tvam*—are you; *cikīrṣasi*—are you trying to do; *ca*—also; *kim*—what; *muni-varya*—O best of *munis; śaile*—on this hill; *māyā*—illusory potency; *asi*—are you; *kāpi*—some; *bhagavat*—the Supreme Personality of Godhead; *para-devatāyāḥ*—of the transcendental Lord; *vijye*—without strings; *bibharṣi*—you are carrying; *dhanuṣī*—two bows; *suhṛt*—of a friend; *ātmanaḥ*—of yourself; *arthe*—for the sake; *kim vā*—or; *mṛgān*—forest animals; *mṛgayase*—are you trying to hunt; *vipine*—in this forest; *pramattān*—who are materially maddened.

TRANSLATION

The Prince mistakenly addressed the Apsarā: O best of saintly persons, who are you? Why are you on this hill, and what do you want to do? Are you one of the illusory potencies of the Supreme Personality of Godhead? You seem to be carrying two bows without strings. What is the reason you carry these bows? Is it for some

purpose of your own or for the sake of a friend? Perhaps you carry them to kill the mad animals in this forest.

PURPORT

While undergoing severe penances in the forest, Āgnīdhra was captivated by the movements of Pūrvacitti, the girl sent by Lord Brahmā. As stated in *Bhagavad-gītā, kāmais tais tair hṛta-jñānāḥ:* when one becomes lusty, he loses his intelligence. Therefore Āgnīdhra, having lost his intelligence, could not distinguish whether Pūrvacitti was male or female. He mistook her for a *muni-putra,* the son of a saintly person in the forest, and addressed her as *muni-varya.* Because of her personal beauty, however, he could not believe her to be a boy. He therefore began studying her features. First he saw her two eyebrows, which were so expressive that he wondered whether he or she might be the *māyā* of the Supreme Personality of Godhead. The words used in this connection are *bhagavat-para-devatāyāḥ. Devatāḥ,* the demigods, all belong to this material world, whereas Bhagavān, the Supreme Personality of Godhead, Kṛṣṇa, is always beyond this material world and is therefore known as *para-devatā.* The material world is certainly created by *māyā,* but it is created under the direction of *para-devatā,* the Supreme Personality of Godhead. As confirmed in *Bhagavad-gītā* (*mayādhyakṣeṇa prakṛtiḥ sūyate sa-carācaram*), *māyā* is not the ultimate authority for the creation of this material world. *Māyā* acts on behalf of Kṛṣṇa.

Pūrvacitti's eyebrows were so beautiful that Āgnīdhra compared them to bows without strings. He therefore asked her whether they were to be used for her own purposes or for the sake of someone else. Her eyebrows were like bows meant to kill animals in the forest. This material world is like a great forest, and its inhabitants are like forest animals such as deer and tigers meant to be killed. The killers are the eyebrows of beautiful women. Captivated by the beauty of the fair sex, all the men of the world are killed by bows without strings, but cannot see how they are killed by *māyā.* It is a fact, however, that they are being killed (*bhūtvā bhūtvā pralīyate*). By dint of his *tapasya,* Āgnīdhra could understand how *māyā* acts under the direction of the Supreme Personality of Godhead.

The word *pramattān* is also significant. *Pramatta* refers to one who cannot control his senses. The entire material world is being exploited by people who are *pramatta,* or *vimūḍha.* Prahlāda Mahārāja therefore said:

śoce tato vimukha-cetasa indriyārtha-
māyā-sukhāya bharam udvahato vimūḍhān

"They are rotting in material activities for transient material pleasure and spoiling their lives toiling all day and night simply for sense gratification, with no attachment for love of Godhead. I am simply lamenting for them and devising various plans to deliver them from the clutches of *māyā.*" (*Bhāg.* 7.9.43) *Karmīs* who act very seriously for sense gratification are always referred to in the *śāstras* by such terms as *pramatta, vimukha* and *vimūḍha.* They are killed by *māyā.* However, one who is *apramatta,* a sane, sober person, a *dhīra,* knows very well that a human being's primary duty is to render service to the Supreme Person. *Māyā* is always ready to kill those who are *pramatta* with her invisible bows and arrows. Āgnīdhra questioned Pūrvacitti about this.

TEXT 8

बाणाविमौ भगवतः शतपत्रपत्रौ
शान्तावपुङ्खरुचिरावतितिग्मदन्तौ ।
कस्मै युयुङ्क्षसि वने विचरन्न विद्मः
क्षेमाय नो जडधियां तव विक्रमोऽस्तु॥ ८ ॥

bāṇāv imau bhagavataḥ śata-patra-patrau
śāntāv apuṅkha-rucirāv ati-tigma-dantau
kasmai yuyuṅkṣasi vane vicaran na vidmaḥ
kṣemāya no jaḍa-dhiyāṁ tava vikramo 'stu

bāṇau—two arrows; *imau*—these; *bhagavataḥ*—of you, the most powerful; *śata-patra-patrau*—having feathers like the petals of a lotus flower; *śāntau*—peaceful; *apuṅkha*—without a shaft; *rucirau*—very beautiful; *ati-tigma-dantau*—having a very sharp point; *kasmai*—whom; *yuyuṅkṣasi*—you want to pierce; *vane*—in the forest; *vicaran*—loitering; *na vidmaḥ*—we cannot understand; *kṣemāya*—for welfare; *naḥ*—of us; *jaḍa-dhiyām*—who are dull-headed; *tava*—your; *vikramaḥ*—prowess; *astu*—may be.

TRANSLATION

Then Āgnīdhra observed the glancing eyes of Pūrvacitti and said: My dear friend, you have two very powerful arrows, namely your glancing eyes. Those arrows have feathers like the petals of a lotus flower. Although they have no shafts, they are very beautiful, and they have very sharp, piercing points. They appear very peaceful, and thus it seems that they will not be shot at anyone. You must be loitering in this forest to shoot those arrows at someone, but I cannot understand whom. My intelligence is dull, and I cannot combat you. Indeed, no one can equal you in prowess, and therefore I pray that your prowess will be for my good fortune.

PURPORT

Āgnīdhra thus began appreciating Pūrvacitti's powerful glance upon him. He compared her glancing eyes to very sharp arrows. Although her eyes were as beautiful as lotuses, they were simultaneously like shaftless arrows, and Āgnīdhra was therefore afraid of them. He hoped that her glances upon him would be favorable because he was already captivated, and the more captivated he became, the more impossible it would be for him to remain without her. Āgnīdhra therefore prayed to Pūrvacitti that her glances at him would be auspicious, not futile. In other words, he prayed that she would become his wife.

TEXT 9

शिष्या इमे भगवतः परितः पठन्ति
गायन्ति साम सरहस्यमजस्रमीशम् ।
युष्मच्छिखाविलुलिताः सुमनोऽभिवृष्टीः
सर्वे भजन्त्यृषिगणा इव वेदशाखाः ॥ ९ ॥

śiṣyā ime bhagavataḥ paritaḥ paṭhanti
gāyanti sāma sarahasyam ajasram īśam
yuṣmac-chikhā-vilulitāḥ sumano 'bhivṛṣṭīḥ
sarve bhajanty ṛṣi-gaṇā iva veda-śākhāḥ

śiṣyāḥ—disciples, followers; *ime*—these; *bhagavataḥ*—of your worshipable self; *paritaḥ*—surrounding; *paṭhanti*—are reciting; *gāyanti*—are singing; *sāma*—the *Sāma Veda; sa-rahasyam*—with the confidential portion; *ajasram*—incessantly; *īśam*—unto the Lord; *yuṣmat*—your; *śikhā*—from bunches of hair; *vilulitāḥ*—fallen; *sumanaḥ*—of flowers; *abhivṛṣṭīḥ*—showers; *sarve*—all; *bhajanti*—enjoy, resort to; *ṛṣi-gaṇāḥ*—sages; *iva*—like; *veda-śākhāḥ*—branches of Vedic literature.

TRANSLATION

Seeing the bumblebees following Pūrvacitti, Mahārāja Āgnīdhra said: My dear Lord, the bumblebees surrounding your body are like disciples surrounding your worshipable self. They are incessantly chanting the mantras of the Sāma Veda and the Upaniṣads, thus offering prayers to you. Just as great sages resort to the branches of Vedic literatures, the bumblebees are enjoying the showers of flowers falling from your hair.

TEXT 10

वाचं परं चरणपञ्जरतित्तिरीणां
ब्रह्मन्नरूपमुखरां शृणवाम तुभ्यम् ।
लब्धा कदम्बरुचिरङ्कविटङ्कबिम्बे
यस्यामलातपरिधिः क्व च वल्कलं ते॥१०॥

vācaṁ paraṁ caraṇa-pañjara-tittirīṇāṁ
brahmann arūpa-mukharāṁ śṛṇavāma tubhyam
labdhā kadamba-rucir aṅka-viṭaṅka-bimbe
yasyām alāta-paridhiḥ kva ca valkalaṁ te

vācam—the resounding vibration; *param*—only; *caraṇa-pañjara*—of the ankle bells; *tittirīṇām*—of the *tittiri* birds; *brahman*—O *brāhmaṇa; arūpa*—without form; *mukharām*—able to be very distinctly heard; *śṛṇavāma*—I hear; *tubhyam*—your; *labdhā*—gotten; *kadamba*—like the *kadamba* flower; *ruciḥ*—lovely color; *aṅka-viṭaṅka-*

bimbe—on the beautiful circular hips; *yasyām*—on which; *alāta-paridhiḥ*—encirclement of burning cinders; *kva*—where; *ca*—also; *valkalam*—covering cloth; *te*—your.

TRANSLATION

O brāhmaṇa, I can simply hear the tinkling of your ankle bells. Within those bells, tittiri birds seem to be chirping among themselves. Although I do not see their forms, I can hear how they are chirping. When I look at your beautiful circular hips, I see they are the lovely color of kadamba flowers, and your waist is encircled by a belt of burning cinders. Indeed, you seem to have forgotten to dress yourself.

PURPORT

With lusty desires to see Pūrvacitti, Āgnīdhra especially gazed upon the girl's attractive hips and waist. When a man looks upon a woman with such lusty desires, he is captivated by her face, her breasts and her waist, for a woman first attracts a man to fulfill his sexual desires by the beautiful features of her face, by the beautiful slope of her breasts and also by her waist. Pūrvacitta was dressed in fine yellow silk, and therefore her hips looked like *kadamba* flowers. Because of her belt, her waist seemed to be encircled by burning cinders. She was fully dressed, but Āgnīdhra had become so lusty that he asked, "Why have you come naked?"

TEXT 11

किं सम्भृतं रुचिरयोर्द्विज शृङ्गयोस्ते
मध्ये कृशो वहसि यत्र दृशिः श्रिता मे ।
पङ्कोऽरुणः सुरभिरात्मविषाण ईदृग्
येनाश्रमं सुभग मे सुरभीकरोषि ॥ ११ ॥

kiṁ sambhṛtaṁ rucirayor dvija śṛṅgayos te
madhye kṛśo vahasi yatra dṛśiḥ śritā me
paṅko 'ruṇaḥ surabhir ātma-viṣāṇa īdṛg
yenāśramaṁ subhaga me surabhī-karoṣi

kim—what; *sambhṛtam*—filled; *rucirayoḥ*—very beautiful; *dvija*—O *brāhmaṇa; śṛṅgayoḥ*—within two horns; *te*—your; *madhye*—in the middle; *kṛśaḥ*—thin; *vahasi*—you are carrying; *yatra*—wherein; *dṛśiḥ*—eyes; *śritā*—attached; *me*—my; *paṅkaḥ*—powder; *aruṇaḥ*—red; *surabhiḥ*—fragrant; *ātma-viṣāṇe*—on the two horns; *īdṛk*—such; *yena*—by which; *āśramam*—place of residence; *su-bhaga*—O most fortunate one; *me*—my; *surabhī-karoṣi*—you are perfuming.

TRANSLATION

Āgnīdhra then praised Pūrvacitti's raised breasts. He said: My dear brāhmaṇa your waist is very thin, yet with great difficulty you are carefully carrying two horns, to which my eyes have become attracted. What is filling those two beautiful horns? You seem to have spread fragrant red powder upon them, powder that is like the rising morning sun. O most fortunate one, I beg to inquire where you have gotten this fragrant powder that is perfuming my āśrama, my place of residence.

PURPORT

Āgnīdhra appreciated Pūrvacitti's raised breasts. After seeing the girl's breasts, he became almost mad. Nevertheless, he could not recognize whether Pūrvacitti was a boy or a girl, for as a result of his austerity, he saw no distinction between the two. He therefore addressed her with the word *dvija,* "O *brāhmaṇa.*" Yet why should a *dvija,* a *brāhmaṇa* boy, have horns on his chest? Because the boy's waist was thin, Āgnīdhra thought, he was carrying the horns with great difficulty, and therefore they must be filled with something very valuable. Otherwise why would he carry them? When a woman's waist is thin and her breasts are full, she looks very attractive. Āgnīdhra, his eyes attracted, contemplated the heavy breasts on the girl's thin body and imagined how her back must sustain them. Āgnīdhra imagined that her raised breasts were two horns she had covered with cloth so that others would not see the valuables within them. Āgnīdhra, however, was very anxious to see them. Therefore he requested, "Please uncover them so that I can see what you are carrying. Rest assured that I shall not take it away. If you feel an inconvenience in removing the covering, I can help you; I myself can uncover them to see what valuable things those raised horns contain." He was also surprised to see the red dust of perfumed *kuṅkuma* spread over her breasts. Nevertheless, still considering Pūrvacitti a boy, Āgnīdhra addressed her as *subhaga*, most fortunate *muni*. The boy must have been fortunate; otherwise how simply by standing there could he perfume Āgnīdhra's entire *āśrama?*

TEXT 12

लोकं प्रदर्शय सुहृत्तम तावकं मे
यत्रत्य इत्थमुरसावयवावपूर्वौ ।
अस्मद्विधस्य मनउन्नयनौ बिभर्ति
बह्वद्भुतं सरसराससुधादि वक्त्रे ॥१२॥

lokaṁ pradarśaya suhṛttama tāvakaṁ me
yatratya ittham urasāvayavāv apūrvau
asmad-vidhasya mana-unnayanau bibharti
bahv adbhutaṁ sarasa-rāsa-sudhādi vaktre

lokam—residential place; *pradarśaya*—please show; *suhṛt-tama*—O best of friends; *tāvakam*—your; *me*—unto me; *yatratyaḥ*—a person born wherein; *ittham*—like this; *urasā*—by the chest; *avayavau*—two limbs (breasts); *apūrvau*—wonderful; *asmat-vidhasya*—of a person like me; *manaḥ-unnayanau*—very agitating to the mind; *bibharti*—sustains; *bahu*—many; *adbhutam*—wonderful; *sarasa*—sweet words; *rāsa*—amorous gestures like smiling; *sudhā-ādi*—such as nectar; *vaktre*—in the mouth.

TRANSLATION

O best friend, will you kindly show me the place where you reside? I cannot imagine how the residents of that place have gotten such wonderful bodily features as your raised breasts, which agitate the mind and eyes of a person like me who sees them. Judging by the sweet speech and kind smiles of those residents, I think that their mouths must contain nectar.

PURPORT

Still bewildered, Āgnīdhra wanted to see the place from which the *brāhmaṇa* boy had come, where the men had such raised breasts. Such attractive features, he thought, must be due to the severe austerities performed there. Āgnīdhra addressed the girl as *suhṛttama*, the best friend, so that she would not refuse to take him there. Not only was Āgnīdhra captivated by the girl's raised breasts; he was also attracted by her sweet speech. Nectar seemed to emanate from her mouth, and therefore he was increasingly surprised.

TEXT 13

का वाऽऽत्मवृत्तिरदनाद्धविरङ्ग वाति
विष्णोः कलास्यनिमिषोन्मकरौ च कर्णौ ।
उद्विग्नमीनयुगलं द्विजपङ्क्तिशोचि-
रासन्नभृङ्गनिकरं सर इन्मुखं ते ॥१३॥

kā vātma-vṛttir adanād dhavir aṅga vāti
viṣṇoḥ kalāsy animiṣonmakarau ca karṇau
udvigna-mīna-yugalaṁ dvija-paṅkti-śocir
āsanna-bhṛṅga-nikaraṁ sara in mukhaṁ te

kā—what; *vā*—and; *ātma-vṛttiḥ*—food for maintenance of the body; *adanāt*—by the chewing (of betel); *haviḥ*—pure sacrificial ingredients; *aṅga*—my dear friend; *vāti*—emanate; *viṣṇoḥ*—of Lord Viṣṇu; *kalā*—expansion of the body; *asi*—you are; *animiṣa*—without blinking; *unmakarau*—two brilliant sharks; *ca*—also; *karṇau*—two ears; *udvigna*—restless; *mīna-yugalam*—possessing two fish; *dvija-paṅkti*—of lines of teeth; *śociḥ*—beauty; *āsanna*—nearby; *bhṛṅga-nikaram*—possessing swarms of bumblebees; *saraḥ it*—like a lake; *mukham*—face; *te*—your.

TRANSLATION

My dear friend, what do you eat to maintain your body? Because you are chewing betel, a pleasing scent is emanating from your mouth. This proves that you always eat the remnants of food offered to Viṣṇu. Indeed, you must also be an expansion of Lord

Viṣṇu's body. Your face is as beautiful as a pleasing lake. Your jeweled earrings resemble two brilliant sharks with unblinking eyes like those of Viṣṇu, and your own eyes resemble two restless fish. Simultaneously, therefore, two sharks and two restless fish are swimming in the lake of your face. Besides them, the white rows of your teeth seem like rows of very beautiful swans in the water, and your scattered hair resembles swarms of bumblebees following the beauty of your face.

PURPORT

The devotees of Lord Viṣṇu are also His expansions. They are called *vibhinnāṁśa.* Lord Viṣṇu is offered all kinds of sacrificial ingredients, and because devotees always eat *prasāda,* the remnants of His food, the scent of sacrificial ingredients emanates not only from Viṣṇu but also from the devotees who eat the remnants of His food or the food of His devotees. Āgnīdhra considered Pūrvacitti an expansion of Lord Viṣṇu because of the pleasing scent of her body. Aside from that, because of her jeweled earrings, shaped like sharks, because of her scattered hair, resembling bumblebees mad after the scent of her body, and because of the white rows of her teeth, which resembled swans, Āgnīdhra compared Pūrvacitti's face to a beautiful lake decorated with lotus flowers, fish, swans and bumblebees.

TEXT 14

योऽसौ त्वया करसरोजहतः पतङ्गो
दिक्षु भ्रमन् भ्रमत एजयतेऽक्षिणी मे ।
मुक्तं न ते स्मरसि वक्रजटावरूथं
कष्टोऽनिलो हरति लम्पट एष नीवीम्॥१४॥

yo 'sau tvayā kara-saroja-hataḥ pataṅgo
dikṣu bhraman bhramata ejayate 'kṣiṇī me
muktaṁ na te smarasi vakra-jaṭā-varūthaṁ
kaṣṭo 'nilo harati lampaṭa eṣa nīvīm

yaḥ—which; *asau*—that; *tvayā*—by you; *kara-saroja*—with the lotus palm; *hataḥ*—struck; *pataṅgaḥ*—the ball; *dikṣu*—in all directions; *bhraman*—moving; *bhramataḥ*—restless; *ejayate*—disturbs; *akṣiṇī*—eyes; *me*—of me; *muktam*—scattered; *na*—not; *te*—your; *smarasi*—are you mindful of; *vakra*—curling; *jaṭā*—of hair; *varūtham*—bunches; *kaṣṭaḥ*—giving trouble; *anilaḥ*—wind; *harati*—takes away; *lampaṭaḥ*—like a man attached to women; *eṣaḥ*—this; *nīvīm*—lower garment.

TRANSLATION

My mind is already restless, and by playing with a ball, moving it all about with your lotuslike palm, you are also agitating my eyes. Your curling black hair is now scattered, but you are not attentive to arranging it. Are you not going to arrange it? Like a man attached to women, the most cunning wind is trying to take off your lower garment. Are you not mindful of it?

PURPORT

The girl Pūrvacitti was playing with a ball in her hand, and the ball seemed like nothing but another lotus flower captured by her lotuslike palm. Because of her movements, her hair was loose, and the belt holding her cloth was giving way, as if the cunning wind were trying to make her naked. Yet she paid no attention to arranging her hair or fixing her dress. As Āgnīdhra tried to see the girl's naked beauty, his eyes were very agitated by her movements.

TEXT 15

रूपं तपोधन तपश्चरतां तपोघ्नं
ह्येतत्तु केन तपसा भवतोपलब्धम् ।
चर्तुं तपोऽर्हसि मया सह मित्र मह्यं
किं वा प्रसीदति स वै भवभावनो मे ॥१५॥

rūpaṁ tapodhana tapaś caratāṁ tapoghnaṁ
hy etat tu kena tapasā bhavatopalabdham

cartuṁ tapo 'rhasi mayā saha mitra mahyaṁ
kiṁ vā prasīdati sa vai bhava-bhāvano me

rūpam—beauty; *tapaḥ-dhana*—O best of the sages performing austerity; *tapaḥ caratām*—of persons engaged in executing austerities and penances; *tapaḥ-ghnam*—which dismantles the austerities; *hi*—certainly; *etat*—this; *tu*—indeed; *kena*—by what; *tapasā*—austerity; *bhavatā*—by you; *upalabdham*—achieved; *cartum*—to execute; *tapaḥ*—austerity; *arhasi*—you ought; *mayā saha*—with me; *mitra*—my dear friend; *mahyam*—unto me; *kim vā*—or maybe; *prasīdati*—is pleased; *saḥ*—he; *vai*—certainly; *bhava-bhāvanaḥ*—the creator of this universe; *me*—with me.

TRANSLATION

O best among those performing austerities, where did you get this wonderful beauty that dismantles the austerities performed by others? Where have you learned this art? What austerity have you undergone to achieve this beauty, my dear friend? I desire that you join me to perform austerity and penance, for it may be that the creator of the universe, Lord Brahmā, being pleased with me, has sent you to become my wife.

PURPORT

Āgnīdhra appreciated the wonderful beauty of Pūrvacitti. Indeed, he was surprised to see such exceptional beauty, which must have been the result of past austerities and penances. He therefore asked the girl whether she had achieved such beauty just to break the penances and austerities of others. He thought that Lord Brahmā, the creator of the universe, might have been pleased with him and might therefore have sent her to become his wife. He requested Pūrvacitti to become his wife so that together they could perform austerities and penances in family life. In other words, a suitable wife helps her husband perform penances and austerities in household life if both of them are on the same elevated platform of spiritual understanding. Without spiritual understanding, husband and wife cannot be equally situated. Lord Brahmā, the creator of the universe, is interested in good progeny. Therefore unless he is pleased, one cannot get a suitable wife. In fact, Lord Brahmā is worshiped in marriage ceremonies. In India even today, wedding invitations are still issued with a picture of Lord Brahmā on the face of the card.

TEXT 16

न त्वां त्यजामि दयितं द्विजदेवदत्तं
यस्मिन्मनो दृगपि नो न वियाति लग्नम् ।
मां चारुशृङ्गयर्हसि नेतुमनुव्रतं ते
चित्तं यतः प्रतिसरन्तु शिवाः सचिव्यः ॥ १६ ॥

na tvāṁ tyajāmi dayitaṁ dvija-deva-dattaṁ
yasmin mano dṛg api no na viyāti lagnam
māṁ cāru-śṛṅgy arhasi netum anuvrataṁ te
cittaṁ yataḥ pratisarantu śivāḥ sacivyaḥ

na—not; *tvām*—you; *tyajāmi*—I shall give up; *dayitam*—very dear; *dvija-deva*—by Lord Brahmā, the demigod worshiped by the *brāhmaṇas; dattam*—given; *yasmin*—unto whom; *manaḥ*—mind; *dṛk*—eyes; *api*—also; *naḥ*—my; *na viyāti*—do not go away; *lagnam*—tightly attached; *mām*—me; *cāru-śṛṅgi*—O woman with beautiful raised breasts; *arhasi*—you ought; *netum*—to lead; *anuvratam*—follower; *te*—your; *cittam*—desire; *yataḥ*—wherever; *pratisarantu*—may follow; *śivāḥ*—favorable; *sacivyaḥ*—friends.

TRANSLATION

Lord Brahmā, who is worshiped by the brāhmaṇas, has very mercifully given you to me, and that is why I have met you. I do not want to give up your company, for my mind and eyes are fixed upon you and cannot be drawn away. O woman with beautiful raised breasts, I am your follower. You may take me wherever you like, and your friends may also follow me.

PURPORT

Now Āgnīdhra frankly admits his weakness. He was attracted to Pūrvacitti, and therefore before she could say, "But I have no business with you," he expressed his desire to be united with her. He was so attracted that he was ready to go anywhere, hell or heaven, in her company. When one is absorbed in lust and the influence of sex, one surrenders to the feet of a woman without reservations. Śrīla Madhvācārya remarks in this connection that when one engages in joking and talking like a crazy person, one may say anything and everything, but his words will be meaningless.

TEXT 17

श्रीशुक उवाच

इति ललनानुनयातिविशारदो ग्राम्यवैदग्ध्यया परिभाषया तां विबुधवधूं विबुधमतिरधिसभाजयामास ॥१७॥

śrī-śuka uvāca
iti lalanānunayāti-viśārado grāmya-vaidagdhyayā paribhāṣayā tāṁ vibudha-vadhūṁ vibudha-matir adhisabhājayām āsa.

śrī-śukaḥ uvāca—Śukadeva Gosvāmī said; *iti*—thus; *lalanā*—women; *anunaya*—in winning over; *ati-viśāradaḥ*—very expert; *grāmya-vaidagdhyayā*—expert in fulfilling one's material desires; *paribhāṣayā*—by selected words; *tām*—her; *vibudha-vadhūm*—the celestial girl; *vibudha-matiḥ*—Āgnīdhra, who possessed intelligence like that of the demigods; *adhisabhājayām āsa*—gained the favor of.

TRANSLATION

Śukadeva Gosvāmī continued: Mahārāja Āgnīdhra, whose intelligence was like that of a demigod, knew the art of flattering women to win them to his side. He therefore pleased that celestial girl with his lusty words and gained her favor.

PURPORT

Since King Āgnīdhra was a devotee, he actually had no attraction for material enjoyment, but because he wanted a wife for progeny and Lord Brahmā had sent Pūrvacitti for this purpose, he expertly pleased her with flattering words. Women are attracted by a man's flattering words. One who is expert in this art of flattery is called *vidagdha.*

TEXT 18

सा च ततस्तस्य वीरयूथपतेर्बुद्धिशीलरूपवयःश्रियौदार्येण पराक्षिप्तमनास्तेन
सहायुतायुतपरिवत्सरोपलक्षणं कालं जम्बूद्वीपपतिना भौमस्वर्गभोगान् बुभुजे
॥१८॥

sā ca tatas tasya vīra-yūtha-pater buddhi-śīla-rūpa-vayaḥ-
śriyaudāryeṇa parākṣipta-manās tena sahāyutāyuta-
parivatsaropalakṣaṇaṁ kālaṁ jambūdvīpa-patinā bhauma-svarga-
bhogān bubhuje.

sā—she; *ca*—also; *tataḥ*—thereafter; *tasya*—of him; *vīra-yūtha-pateḥ*—the master of heroes; *buddhi*—by the intelligence; *śīla*—behavior; *rūpa*—beauty; *vayaḥ*—youth; *śriyā*—opulence; *audāryeṇa*—and by the magnanimity; *parākṣipta*—attracted; *manāḥ*—her mind; *tena saha*—with him; *ayuta*—ten thousand; *ayuta*—ten thousand; *parivatsara*—years; *upalakṣaṇam*—extending; *kālam*—time; *jambūdvīpa-patinā*—with the King of Jambūdvīpa; *bhauma*—earthly; *svarga*—heavenly; *bhogān*—pleasures; *bubhuje*—enjoyed.

TRANSLATION

Attracted by the intelligence, learning, youth, beauty, behavior, opulence and magnanimity of Āgnīdhra, the King of Jambūdvīpa and master of all heroes, Pūrvacitti lived with him for many thousands of years and luxuriously enjoyed both worldly and heavenly happiness.

PURPORT

By the grace of Lord Brahmā, King Āgnīdhra and the heavenly girl. Pūrvacitti, found their union quite suitable. Thus they enjoyed worldly and heavenly happiness for many thousands of years.

TEXT 19

तस्यामु ह वा आत्मजान् स राजवर आग्नीध्रो नाभिकिम्पुरुषहरिवर्षेलावृतरम्यक-
हिरण्मयकुरुभद्राश्वकेतुमालसंज्ञान्नव पुत्रानजनयत् ॥१९॥

tasyām u ha vā ātmajān sa rāja-vara āgnīdhro nābhi-kiṁpuruṣa-harivarṣelāvṛta-ramyaka-hiraṇmaya-kuru-bhadrāśva-ketumāla-saṁjñān nava putrān ajanayat.

tasyām—in her; *u ha vā*—certainly; *ātma-jān*—sons; *saḥ*—he; *rāja-varaḥ*—the best of kings; *āgnīdhraḥ*—Āgnīdhra; *nābhi*—Nābhi; *kiṁ-puruṣa*—Kiṁpuruṣa; *hari-varṣa*—Harivarṣa; *ilāvṛta*—Ilāvṛta; *ramyaka*—Ramyaka; *hiraṇmaya*—Hiraṇmaya; *kuru*—Kuru; *bhadrāśva*—Bhadrāśva; *ketu-māla*—Ketumāla; *saṁjñān*—named; *nava*—nine; *putrān*—sons; *ajanayat*—begot.

TRANSLATION

In the womb of Pūrvacitti, Mahārāja Āgnīdhra, the best of kings, begot nine sons, named Nābhi, Kiṁpuruṣa, Harivarṣa, Ilāvṛta, Ramyaka, Hiraṇmaya, Kuru, Bhadrāśva and Ketumāla.

TEXT 20

सा सूत्वाथ सुतान्नवानुवत्सरं गृह एवापहाय पूर्वचित्तिर्भूय एवाजं
देवमुपतस्थे ॥२०॥

sā sūtvātha sutān navānuvatsaraṁ gṛha evāpahāya pūrvacittir bhūya evājaṁ devam upatasthe.

sā—she; *sūtvā*—after giving birth to; *atha*—thereafter; *sutān*—sons; *nava*—nine; *anuvatsaram*—year after year; *gṛhe*—at home; *eva*—certainly; *apahāya*—leaving; *pūrvacittiḥ*—Pūrvacitti; *bhūyaḥ*—again; *eva*—certainly; *ajam*—Lord Brahmā; *devam*—the demigod; *upatasthe*—approached.

TRANSLATION

Pūrvacitti gave birth to these nine sons, one each year, but after they grew up, she left them at home and again approached Lord Brahmā to worship him.

PURPORT

There are many instances in which Apsarās, heavenly angels, have descended to this earth by the order of a superior demigod like Lord Brahmā or Lord Indra, have followed the demigod's order by marrying someone and giving birth to children, and have then returned to their celestial homes. For example, after Menakā, the celestial woman who had come to delude Viśvāmitra Muni, gave birth to the child Śakuntalā, she left both the child and her husband and returned to the heavenly planets. Pūrvacitti did not remain permanently with Mahārāja Āgnīdhra. After cooperating in his household affairs, she left Mahārāja Āgnīdhra and all nine sons and returned to Brahmā to worship him.

TEXT 21

आग्नीध्रसुतास्ते मातुरनुग्रहादौत्पत्तिकेनैव संहननबलोपेताः पित्रा विभक्ता आत्मतुल्यनामानि यथाभागं जम्बूद्वीपवर्षाणि बुभुजुः ॥ २१ ॥

āgnīdhra-sutās te mātur anugrahād autpattikenaiva saṁhanana-balopetāḥ pitrā vibhaktā ātma-tulya-nāmāni yathā-bhāgaṁ jambūdvīpa-varṣāṇi bubhujuḥ.

āgnīdhra-sutāḥ—the sons of Mahārāja Āgnīdhra; *te*—they; *mātuḥ*—of the mother; *anugrahāt*—by the mercy or by drinking the breast milk; *autpattikena*—naturally; *eva*—certainly; *saṁhanana*—well-built body; *bala*—strength; *upetāḥ*—obtained; *pitrā*—by the father; *vibhaktāḥ*—divided; *ātma-tulya*—following their own; *nāmāni*—possessing names; *yathā-bhāgam*—divided properly; *jambūdvīpa-varṣāṇi*—different parts of Jambūdvīpa (probably Asia and Europe combined together); *bubhujuḥ*—ruled.

TRANSLATION

Because of drinking the breast milk of their mother, the nine sons of Āgnīdhra naturally had strong, well-built bodies. Their father gave them each a kingdom in a different part of Jambūdvīpa. The kingdoms were named according to the names of the sons. Thus the sons of Āgnīdhra ruled the kingdoms they received from their father.

PURPORT

The *ācāryas* specifically mention that in this verse the words *mātuḥ anugrahāt* ("by the mercy of their mother") refer to the breast milk of their mother. In India it is a common belief that if a baby is fed his mother's milk for at least six months, his body will be very strong. Besides that, it is mentioned herein that all the sons of Āgnīdhra were endowed with the nature of their mother. *Bhagavad-gītā* (1.40) also declares, *strīṣu duṣṭāsu vārṣṇeya jāyate varṇa-saṅkaraḥ:* when women are polluted, *varṇa-saṅkara,* unqualified children, are generated, and when the *varṇa-saṅkara* population increases, the entire world becomes hellish. Therefore, according to *Manu-saṁhitā,* a woman needs a great deal of protection in order to remain pure and chaste so that her children can be fully engaged for the benefit of human society.

TEXT 22

आग्नीध्रो राजातृप्तः कामानामप्सरसमेवानुदिनमधिमन्यमानस्तस्याः
सलोकतां श्रुतिभिरवारुन्ध यत्र पितरो मादयन्ते ॥ २२ ॥

āgnīdhro rājātṛptaḥ kāmānām apsarasam evānudinam adhi-
manyamānas tasyāḥ salokatāṁ śrutibhir avārundha yatra pitaro
mādayante.

āgnīdhraḥ—Āgnīdhra; *rājā*—the King; *atṛptaḥ*—not satisfied; *kāmānām*—with sense gratification; *apsarasam*—the celestial woman (Pūrvacitti); *eva*—certainly; *anudinam*—day after day; *adhi*—exceedingly; *manyamānaḥ*—thinking of; *tasyāḥ*—of her; *sa-lokatām*—promotion to the same planet; *śrutibhiḥ*—by the *Vedas; avārundha*—

got; *yatra*—where; *pitaraḥ*—the forefathers; *mādayante*—take pleasure.

TRANSLATION

After Pūrvacitti's departure, King Āgnīdhra, his lusty desires not at all satisfied, always thought of her. Therefore, in accordance with the Vedic injunctions, the King, after his death, was promoted to the same planet as his celestial wife. That planet, which is called Pitṛloka, is where the pitās, the forefathers, live in great delight.

PURPORT

If one always thinks of something, he certainly gets a related body after death. Mahārāja Āgnīdhra was always thinking of Pitṛloka, the place where his wife had returned. Therefore after his death he achieved that same planet, probably to live with her again. *Bhagavad-gītā* also says:

yaṁ yaṁ vāpi smaran bhāvaṁ
tyajaty ante kalevaram
taṁ tam evaiti kaunteya
sadā tad-bhāva-bhāvitaḥ

"Whatever state of being one remembers when he quits his body, that state he will attain without fail." (Bg. 8.6) We can naturally conclude that if we always think of Kṛṣṇa or become fully Kṛṣṇa conscious, we can be promoted to the planet of Goloka Vṛndāvana, where Kṛṣṇa eternally lives.

TEXT 23

सम्परेते पितरि नव भ्रातरो मेरुदुहितॄर्मेरुदेवीं प्रतिरूपामुग्रदंष्ट्रीं लतां रम्यां
श्यामां नारीं भद्रां देववीतिमितिसंज्ञा नवोदवहन् ॥२३॥

samparete pitari nava bhrātaro meru-duhitṝr merudevīṁ pratirūpām ugradaṁṣṭrīṁ latāṁ ramyāṁ śyāmāṁ nārīṁ bhadrāṁ devavītim iti saṁjñā navodavahan.

samparete pitari—after the departure of their father; *nava*—nine; *bhrātaraḥ*—brothers; *meru-duhitṝḥ*—the daughters of Meru; *meru-devīm*—Merudevī; *prati-rūpām*—Pratirūpā; *ugra-daṁṣṭrīm*—Ugradaṁṣṭrī; *latām*—Latā; *ramyām*—Ramyā; *śyāmām*—Śyāmā; *nārīm*—Nārī; *bhadrām*—Bhadrā; *deva-vītim*—Devavīti; *iti*—thus; *saṁjñāḥ*—the names; *nava*—nine; *udavahan*—married.

TRANSLATION

After the departure of their father, the nine brothers married the nine daughters of Meru named Merudevī, Pratirūpā, Ugradaṁṣṭrī, Latā, Ramyā, Śyāmā, Nārī, Bhadrā and Devavīti.

Thus end the Bhaktivedanta purports of the Fifth Canto, Second Chapter, of the Śrīmad-Bhāgavatam, *entitled "The Activities of Mahārāja Āgnīdhra."*

CHAPTER THREE

Ṛṣabhadeva's Appearance in the Womb of Merudevī, the Wife of King Nābhi

In this chapter the spotless character of King Nābhi, the oldest son of Āgnīdhra, is described. Wanting to have sons, Mahārāja Nābhi underwent severe austerities and penances. He performed many sacrifices along with his wife and worshiped Lord Viṣṇu, master of all sacrifices. Being very kind to His devotees, the Supreme Personality of Godhead was very pleased with the austerities of Mahārāja Nābhi. He personally appeared before the King in His four-handed feature, and the priests, who were performing the sacrifices, began to offer their prayers unto Him. They prayed for a son like the Lord, and Lord Viṣṇu agreed to take birth in the womb of Merudevī, the wife of King Nābhi, and incarnate as King Ṛṣabhadeva.

TEXT 1

श्रीशुक उवाच

नाभिरपत्यकामोऽप्रजया मेरुदेव्या भगवन्तं यज्ञपुरुषमवहितात्मायजत ॥ १ ॥

śrī-śuka uvāca
nābhir apatya-kāmo 'prajayā merudevyā bhagavantaṁ
yajña-puruṣam avahitātmāyajata.

śrī-śukaḥ uvāca—Śukadeva Gosvāmī said; *nābhiḥ*—the son of Mahārāja Āgnīdhra; *apatya-kāmaḥ*—desiring to have sons; *aprajayā*—who had not given birth to any children; *merudevyā*—with Merudevī; *bhagavantam*—the Supreme Personality of Godhead; *yajña-puruṣam*—Lord Viṣṇu, the master and enjoyer of all performances of sacrifice;

avahita-ātmā—with great attention; *ayajata*—offered prayers and worshiped.

TRANSLATION

Śukadeva Gosvāmī continued to speak: Mahārāja Nābhi, the son of Āgnīdhra, wished to have sons, and therefore he attentively began to offer prayers and worship the Supreme Personality of Godhead, Lord Viṣṇu, the master and enjoyer of all sacrifices. Mahārāja Nābhi's wife, Merudevī, who had not given birth to any children at that time, also worshiped Lord Viṣṇu along with her husband.

TEXT 2

तस्य ह वाव श्रद्धया विशुद्धभावेन यजतः प्रवर्ग्येषु प्रचरत्सु द्रव्यदेशकाल-
मन्त्रर्त्विग्दक्षिणाविधानयोगोपपत्त्या दुरधिगमो ऽपि भगवान् भागवतवात्सल्यतया
सुप्रतीक आत्मानमपराजितं निजजनाभिप्रेतार्थविधित्सया गृहीतहृदयो हृदयङ्गमं
मनोनयनानन्दनावयवाभिराममाविश्चकार ॥ २ ॥

tasya ha vāva śraddhayā viśuddha-bhāvena yajataḥ pravargyeṣu
pracaratsu dravya-deśa-kāla-mantrartvig-dakṣiṇā-vidhāna-
yogopapattyā duradhigamo 'pi bhagavān bhāgavata-vātsalyatayā
supratīka ātmānam aparājitaṁ nija-janābhipretārtha-vidhitsayā gṛhīta-
hṛdayo hṛdayaṅgamaṁ mano-nayanānandanāvayavābhirāmam
āviścakāra.

tasya—when he (Nābhi); *ha vāva*—certainly; *śraddhayā*—with great faith and devotion; *viśuddha-bhāvena*—with a pure, uncontaminated mind; *yajataḥ*—was worshiping; *pravargyeṣu*—while the fruitive activities called *pravargya; pracaratsu*—were being performed; *dravya*—the ingredients; *deśa*—place; *kāla*—time; *mantra*—hymns; *ṛtvik*—priests conducting the ceremony; *dakṣiṇā*—gifts to the priests; *vidhāna*—regulative principles; *yoga*—and of the means; *upapattyā*—by the performance; *duradhigamaḥ*—not obtainable; *api*—although; *bhagavān*—the Supreme Personality of Godhead; *bhāgavata-vātsalyatayā*—because of His being very affectionate to His devotee; *su-*

pratīkaḥ—possessing a very beautiful form; *ātmānam*—Himself; *aparājitam*—not to be conquered by anyone; *nija-jana*—of His devotee; *abhipreta-artha*—the desire; *vidhitsayā*—to fulfill; *gṛhīta-hṛdayaḥ*—His heart being attracted; *hṛdayaṅgamam*—captivating; *manaḥ-nayana-ānandana*—pleasing to the mind and eyes; *avayava*—by the limbs; *abhirāmam*—beautiful; *āviścakāra*—manifested.

TRANSLATION

In the performance of a sacrifice, there are seven transcendental means to obtain the mercy of the Supreme Personality of Godhead: (1) by sacrificing valuable things or eatables, (2) by acting in terms of place, (3) by acting in terms of time, (4) by offering hymns, (5) by going through the the priest, (6) by offering gifts to the priests and (7) by observing the regulative principles. However, one cannot always obtain the Supreme Lord through this paraphernalia. Nonetheless, the Lord is affectionate to His devotee; therefore when Mahārāja Nābhi, who was a devotee, worshiped and offered prayers to the Lord with great faith and devotion and with a pure uncontaminated mind, superficially performing some yajña in the line of pravargya, the kind Supreme Personality of Godhead, due to His affection for His devotees, appeared before King Nābhi in His unconquerable and captivating form with four hands. In this way, to fulfill the desire of His devotee, the Supreme Personality of Godhead manifested Himself in His beautiful body before His devotee. This body pleases the mind and eyes of the devotees.

PURPORT

In *Bhagavad-gītā* it is clearly said:

bhaktyā mām abhijānāti
yāvān yaś cāsmi tattvataḥ
tato māṁ tattvato jñātvā
viśate tad-anantaram

"One can understand the Supreme Personality as He is only by devotional service. And when one is in full consciousness of the Supreme

Lord by such devotion, he can enter into the kingdom of God." (Bg. 18.55)

One can understand and see the Supreme Personality of Godhead through the process of devotional service, and not in any other way. Although Mahārāja Nābhi performed prescribed duties and sacrifices, it should still be considered that the Lord appeared before him not due to his sacrifices but because of his devotional service. It was for this reason that the Lord agreed to appear before him in His beautiful bodily features. As stated in *Brahma-saṁhitā* (5.30), the Supreme Lord in His original nature is very beautiful. *Veṇuṁ kvaṇantam aravinda-dalāyatākṣaṁ barhāvataṁsam asitāmbuda-sundarāṅgam:* the Supreme Personality of Godhead, although blackish, is very, very beautiful.

TEXT 3

अथ ह तमाविष्कृतभुजयुगलद्वयं हिरण्मयं पुरुषविशेषं कपिशकौशेयाम्बरधरमुरसि
विलसच्छ्रीवत्सललामं दरवरवनरुहवनमालाच्छूर्यमृतमणिगदादिभिरुपलक्षितं
स्फुटकिरणप्रवरमुकुटकुण्डलकटककटिसूत्रहारकेयूरनूपुराद्यङ्गभूषणविभूषितमृ -
त्विक्सदस्यगृहपतयोऽधना इवोत्तमधनमुपलभ्य सबहुमानमर्हणेनावनतशीर्षाण
उपतस्थुः ॥ ३ ॥

atha ha tam āviṣkṛta-bhuja-yugala-dvayaṁ hiraṇmayaṁ puruṣa-viśesaṁ kapiśa-kauśeyāmbara-dharam urasi vilasac-chrīvatsa-lalāmaṁ daravara-vanaruha-vana-mālācchūry-amṛta-maṇi-gadādibhir upalakṣitaṁ sphuṭa-kiraṇa-pravara-mukuṭa-kuṇḍala-kaṭaka-kaṭi-sūtra-hāra-keyūra-nūpurādy-aṅga-bhūṣana-vibhūṣitam ṛtvik-sadasya-gṛha-patayo 'dhanā ivottama-dhanam upalabhya sabahu-mānam arhaṇenāvanata-śīrṣāṇa upatasthuḥ.

atha—thereafter; *ha*—certainly; *tam*—Him; *āviṣkṛta-bhuja-yugala-dvayam*—who manifested Himself with four arms; *hiraṇmayam*—very bright; *puruṣa-viśeṣam*—the topmost of all living beings, Puruṣottama; *kapiśa-kauśeya-ambara-dharam*—wearing a yellow silk garment; *urasi*—on the chest; *vilasat*—beautiful; *śrīvatsa*—called Śrīvatsa; *lalāmam*—possessing the mark; *dara-vara*—by a conchshell; *vana-ruha*—lotus flower; *vana-mālā*—garland of forest flowers; *acchūri*—

disc; *amṛta-maṇi*—the Kaustubha gem; *gadā-ādibhiḥ*—and by a club and other symbols; *upalakṣitam*—symptomized; *sphuṭa-kiraṇa*—radiant; *pravara*—excellent; *mukuṭa*—helmet; *kuṇḍala*—earrings; *kaṭaka*—bracelets; *kaṭi-sūtra*—girdle; *hāra*—necklace; *keyūra*—armlets; *nūpura*—ankle bells; *ādi*—and so on; *aṅga*—of the body; *bhūṣaṇa*—with ornaments; *vibhūṣitam*—decorated; *ṛtvik*—the priests; *sadasya*—associates; *gṛha-patayaḥ*—and King Nābhi; *adhanāḥ*—poor persons; *iva*—like; *uttama-dhanam*—a great treasure; *upalabhya*—having achieved; *sa-bahu-mānam*—with great regard; *arhaṇena*—with ingredients for worship; *avanata*—bent; *śīrṣāṇaḥ*—their heads; *upatasthuḥ*—worshiped.

TRANSLATION

Lord Viṣṇu appeared before King Nābhi with four arms. He was very bright, and He appeared to be the best of all personalities. Around the lower portion of His body, He wore a yellow silken garment. On His chest was the mark of Śrīvatsa, which always displays beauty. He carried a conchshell, lotus flower, disc and club, and He wore a garland of forest flowers and the Kaustubha gem. He was beautifully decorated with a helmet, earrings, bangles, belt, pearl necklace, armlets, ankle bells and other bodily ornaments bedecked with radiant jewels. Seeing the Lord present before them, King Nābhi and his priests and associates felt just like poor people who have suddenly attained great riches. They received the Lord and respectfully bent their heads and offered Him things in worship.

PURPORT

It is distinctly mentioned here that the Supreme Personality of Godhead did not appear as an ordinary human being. He appeared before King Nābhi and his associates as the best of all personalities (Puruṣottama). As stated in the *Vedas: Nityo nityānāṁ cetanaś cetanānām.* The Supreme Personality of Godhead is also a living being, but He is the supreme living being. In *Bhagavad-gītā* (7.7), Lord Kṛṣṇa Himself says, *mattaḥ parataraṁ nānyat kiñcid asti dhanañjaya:* "O conquerer of wealth [Arjuna], there is no truth superior to Me." No one is more attractive or more authoritative than Lord Kṛṣṇa. That is one of the differences between God and an ordinary living being. According to this description of the transcendental body of Lord Viṣṇu, the Lord can easily be distinguished from all other living beings. Consequently Mahārāja Nābhi and his priests and associates all offered the Lord obeisances and began to worship Him with various things. As stated in *Bhagavad-gītā* (6.22), *yaṁ labdhvā cāparaṁ lābhaṁ manyate nādhikaṁ tataḥ.* That is, "Upon gaining this, one thinks that there is no greater gain." When one realizes God and sees the Lord face to face, one certainly thinks that he has gained the best of all things. *Raso 'py asya paraṁ dṛṣṭvā nivartate:* when one experiences a higher taste, his consciousness is fixed. After seeing the Supreme Personality of Godhead, one ceases to be attracted by anything material. One then remains steady in his worship of the Supreme Personality of Godhead.

TEXTS 4-5

ऋत्विज ऊचुः

अर्हसि मुहुरर्हत्तमार्हणमस्माकमनुपथानां नमो नम इत्येतावत्सदुपशिक्षितं
को ऽर्हति पुमान् प्रकृतिगुणव्यतिकरमतिरनीश ईश्वरस्य परस्य प्रकृतिपुरुषयो
रर्वाक्तनाभिर्नामरूपाकृतिभी रूपनिरूपणम् ॥ ४ ॥ सकलजननिकायवृजिन-
निरसनशिवतमप्रवरगुणगणैकदेशकथनादृते ॥ ५ ॥

ṛtvija ūcuḥ

arhasi muhur arhattamārhaṇam asmākam anupathānāṁ namo nama ity etāvat sad-upaśikṣitaṁ ko 'rhati pumān prakṛti-guṇa-vyatikara-matir anīśa īśvarasya parasya prakṛti-puruṣayor arvāktanābhir nāma-rūpākṛtibhī rūpa-nirūpaṇam. sakala-jana-nikāya-vṛjina-nirasana-śivatama-pravara-guṇa-gaṇaika-deśa-kathanād ṛte.

ṛtvijaḥ ūcuḥ—the priests said; *arhasi*—please (accept); *muhuḥ*—again and again; *arhat-tama*—O most exalted, worshipable person; *arhaṇam*—offering of worship; *asmākam*—of us; *anupathānām*—who are Your servants; *namaḥ*—respectful obeisances; *namaḥ*—respectful obeisances; *iti*—thus; *etāvat*—so far; *sat*—by exalted personalities; *upaśikṣitam*—instructed; *kaḥ*—what; *arhati*—is able (to make);

pumān—man; *prakṛti*—of material nature; *guṇa*—of the modes; *vyatikara*—in the transformations; *matiḥ*—whose mind (is absorbed); *anīśaḥ*—who is most incapable; *īśvarasya*—of the Supreme Personality of Godhead; *parasya*—beyond; *prakṛti-puruṣayoḥ*—the jurisdiction of the three modes of material nature; *arvāktanābhiḥ*—which do not reach up to, or which are of this material world; *nāma-rūpa-ākṛtibhiḥ*—by names, forms and qualities; *rūpa*—of Your nature or position; *nirūpaṇam*—ascertainment, perception; *sakala*—all; *jana-nikāya*—of mankind; *vṛjina*—sinful actions; *nirasana*—which wipe out; *śiva-tama*—most auspicious; *pravara*—excellent; *guṇa-gaṇa*—of the transcendental qualities; *eka-deśa*—one part; *kathanāt*—by speaking; *ṛte*—except.

TRANSLATION

The priests began to offer prayers to the Lord, saying: O most worshipable one, we are simply Your servants. Although You are full in Yourself, please, out of Your causeless mercy, accept a little service from us, Your eternal servants. We are not actually aware of Your transcendental form, but we can simply offer our respectful obeisances again and again, as instructed by the Vedic literatures and authorized ācāryas. Materialistic living entities are very much attracted to the modes of material nature, and therefore they are never perfect, but You are above the jurisdiction of all material conceptions. Your name, form and qualities are all transcendental and beyond the conception of experimental knowledge. Indeed, who can conceive of You? In the material world we can perceive only material names and qualities. We have no other power than to offer our respectful obeisances and prayers unto You, the transcendental person. The chanting of Your auspicious transcendental qualities will wipe out the sins of all mankind. That is the most auspicious activity for us, and we can thus partially understand Your supernatural position.

PURPORT

The Supreme Personality of Godhead has nothing to do with material perception. Even the impersonalist Śaṅkarācārya says, *nārāyaṇaḥ paro 'vyaktāt:* "Nārāyaṇa, the Supreme Personality of Godhead, is beyond the material conception." We cannot concoct the form and attributes of the Supreme Personality of Godhead. We must simply accept the description given in Vedic literatures about the Lord's form and activities. As stated in *Brahma-saṁhitā* (5.29):

cintāmaṇi-prakara-sadmasu kalpa-vṛkṣa-
lakṣāvṛteṣu surabhīr abhipālayantam
lakṣmī-sahasra-śata-sambhrama-sevyamānaṁ
govindam ādi-puruṣaṁ tam ahaṁ bhajāmi

"I worship Govinda, the primeval Lord, the first progenitor, who is tending the cows, yielding all desires, in abodes built with spiritual gems and surrounded by millions of purpose trees. He is always served with great reverence and affection by hundreds and thousands of goddesses of fortune." We can have some conception of the Absolute Truth, His form and His attributes simply by reading the descriptions given in Vedic literatures and authoritative statements given by exalted personalities like Brahmā, Nārada, Śukadeva Gosvāmī and others. Śrīla Rūpa Gosvāmī says, *ataḥ śrī-kṛṣṇa-nāmādi na bhaved grāhyam indriyaiḥ:* "We cannot conceive the name, form and qualities of Śrī Kṛṣṇa through our material senses." Because of this, other names for the Lord are *adhokṣaja* and *aprākṛta,* which indicate that He is beyond any material senses. Out of His causeless mercy upon His devotees, the Lord appeared before Mahārāja Nābhi. Similarly, when we are engaged in the Lord's devotional service, the Lord reveals Himself to us. *Sevonmukhe hi jihvādau svayam eva sphuraty adaḥ.* This is the only way to understand the Supreme Personality of Godhead. As confirmed in *Bhagavad-gītā, bhaktyā mām abhijānāti yāvān yaś cāsmi tattvataḥ:* one can understand the Supreme Personality of Godhead through devotional service. There is no other way. We have to hear from the authorities and from the *śāstras* and consider the Supreme Lord in terms of their statements. We cannot imagine or concoct forms and attributes of the Lord.

TEXT 6

परिजनानुरागविरचितशबलसंशब्दसलिलसितकिसलयतुलसिकादूर्वाङ्कुरैरपि
सम्भृतया सपर्यया किल परम परितुष्यसि ।६।

parijanānurāga-viracita-śabala-saṁśabda-salila-sita-kisalaya-tulasikā-dūrvāṅkurair api sambhṛtayā saparyayā kila parama paritusyasi.

parijana—by Your servants; *anurāga*—in great ecstasy; *viracita*—executed; *śabala*—with a faltering voice; *saṁśabda*—with prayers; *salila*—water; *sita-kisalaya*—twigs bearing new leaves; *tulasikā*—*tulasī* leaves; *dūrvā-aṅkuraiḥ*—and with newly grown grass; *api*—also; *sambhṛtayā*—performed; *saparyayā*—by worship; *kila*—indeed; *parama*—O Supreme Lord; *parituṣyasi*—You become satisfied.

TRANSLATION

O Supreme Lord, You are full in every respect. You are certainly very satisfied when Your devotees offer You prayers with faltering voices and in ecstasy bring You tulasī leaves, water, twigs bearing new leaves, and newly grown grass. This surely makes You satisfied.

PURPORT

One does not need great wealth, education or opulence to satisfy the Supreme Personality of Godhead. If one is fully absorbed in love and ecstasy, he need offer only a flower and a little water. As stated in *Bhagavad-gītā, patraṁ puṣpaṁ phalaṁ toyaṁ yo me bhaktyā prayacchati:* "If one offers Me with love and devotion a leaf, a flower, fruit or water, I will accept it." (Bg. 9.26)

The Supreme Lord can be pleased only by devotional service; therefore it is said here that the Lord is surely satisfied by devotion and nothing else. Quoting from the *Gautamīya-tantra*, the *Hari-bhakti-vilāsa* states:

tulasī-dala-mātreṇa
jalasya culukena vā
vikrīṇīte svam ātmānaṁ
bhaktebhyo bhakta-vatsalaḥ

"Śrī Kṛṣṇa, who is very affectionate toward His devotees, sells Himself to a devotee who offers merely a *tulasī* leaf and a palmful of water." The Supreme Lord is causelessly merciful upon His devotee, so much so that even the poorest of men can offer Him a little water and a flower in devotion and thus please Him. This is due to His affectionate dealings with His devotees.

TEXT 7

अथानयापि न भवत इज्ययोरुभारभरया समुचितमर्थमिहोपलभामहे ॥७॥

athānayāpi na bhavata ijyayoru-bhāra-bharayā samucitam artham ihopalabhāmahe.

atha—otherwise; *anayā*—this; *api*—even; *na*—not; *bhavataḥ*—of Your exalted personality; *ijyayā*—by performance of sacrifice; *uru-bhāra-bharayā*—encumbered by much paraphernalia; *samucitam*—required; *artham*—use; *iha*—here; *upalabhāmahe*—we can see.

TRANSLATION

We have engaged in Your worship with many things and have offered sacrifices unto You, but we think that there is no need for so many arrangements to please Your Lordship.

PURPORT

Śrīla Rūpa Gosvāmī says that if one is offered varied foods but has no appetite, the offering has no value. In a big sacrificial ceremony there may be many things accumulated to satisfy the Supreme Personality of Godhead, but if there is no devotion, attachment or love for the Lord, the arrangement is useless. The Lord is complete in Himself, and He does not need anything from us. However, if we offer Him a little water, a flower and a *tulasī* leaf, He will accept them. *Bhakti*, devotional service, is the main way to satisfy the Supreme Personality of Godhead. It is not a question of arranging huge sacrifices. The priests were regretful, thinking that they were not on the path of devotional service and that their sacrifice was not pleasing to the Lord.

TEXT 8

आत्मन एवानुसवनमञ्जसाव्यतिरेकेण बोभूयमानाशेषपुरुषार्थस्वरूपस्य किन्तु नाथाशिष आशासानानामेतदभिसंराधनमात्रं भवितुमर्हति ॥ ८ ॥

ātmana evānusavanam añjasāvyatirekeṇa bobhūyamānāśeṣa-puruṣārtha-svarūpasya kintu nāthāśiṣa āśāsānānām etad abhisaṁrādhana-mātraṁ bhavitum arhati.

ātmanaḥ—self-sufficiently; *eva*—certainly; *anusavanam*—at every moment; *añjasā*—directly; *avyatirekeṇa*—without stopping; *bobhūyamāna*—increasing; *aśeṣa*—unlimitedly; *puruṣa-artha*—the goals of life; *sva-rūpasya*—Your actual identity; *kintu*—but; *nātha*—O Lord; *āśiṣaḥ*—benedictions for material enjoyment; *āśāsānānām*—of us, who are always desiring; *etat*—this; *abhisaṁrādhana*—for getting Your mercy; *mātram*—only; *bhavitum arhati*—can be.

TRANSLATION

All of life's goals and opulences are directly, self-sufficiently, unceasingly and unlimitedly increasing in You at every moment. Indeed, You are unlimited enjoyment and blissful existence itself. As far as we are concerned, O Lord, we are always after material enjoyment. You do not need all these sacrificial arrangements, but they are meant for us so that we may be benedicted by Your Lordship. All these sacrifices are performed for our fruitive results, and they are not actually needed by You.

PURPORT

Being self-sufficient, the Supreme Lord does not need huge sacrifices. Fruitive activity for a more opulent life is for those who desire such material opulence for their interest. *Yajñārthāt karmaṇo 'nyatra loko 'yaṁ karma-bandhanaḥ:* if we do not act to satisfy the Supreme Lord, we engage in *māyā's* activities. We may construct a gorgeous temple and spend thousands of dollars, but such a temple is not required by the Lord. The Lord has many millions of temples for His residence, and He does not need our attempt. He does not require opulent activity at all.

Such engagement is meant for our benefit. If we engage our money in constructing a gorgeous temple, we are freed from the reactions of our endeavors. This is for our benefit. In addition, if we attempt to do something nice for the Supreme Lord, He is pleased with us and gives us His benediction. In conclusion, the gorgeous arrangements are not for the Lord's sake but for our own. If we somehow or other receive blessings and benedictions from the Lord, our consciousness can be purified and we can become eligible to return home, back to Godhead.

TEXT 9

तद्यथा बालिशानां स्वयमात्मनः श्रेयः परमविदुषां परमपरमपुरुष प्रकर्ष-करुणया स्वमहिमानं चापवर्गाख्यमुपकल्पयिष्यन् स्वयं नापचित एवेतरवदिहोपलक्षितः ॥ ९ ॥

tad yathā bāliśānāṁ svayam ātmanaḥ śreyaḥ param aviduṣāṁ parama-parama-puruṣa prakarṣa-karuṇayā sva-mahimānaṁ cāpavargākhyam upakalpayiṣyan svayaṁ nāpacita evetaravad ihopalakṣitaḥ.

tat—that; *yathā*—as; *bāliśānām*—of the fools; *svayam*—by Yourself; *ātmanaḥ*—own; *śreyaḥ*—welfare; *param*—ultimate; *aviduṣām*—of persons who do not know; *parama-parama-puruṣa*—O Lord of lords; *prakarṣa-karuṇayā*—by abundant causeless mercy; *sva-mahimānam*—Your personal glory; *ca*—and; *apavarga-ākhyam*—called *apavarga* (liberation); *upakalpayiṣyan*—desiring to give; *svayam*—personally; *na apacitaḥ*—not properly worshiped; *eva*—although; *itara-vat*—like an ordinary person; *iha*—here; *upalakṣitaḥ*—(You are) present and seen (by us).

TRANSLATION

O Lord of lords, we are completely ignorant of the execution of dharma, artha, kāma and mokṣa, the process of liberation, because we do not actually know the goal of life. You have appeared personally before us like a person soliciting worship, but actually You are present here just so we can see You. You have come out of Your abundant and causeless mercy in order to serve our purpose, our

interest, and give us the benefit of Your personal glory called apavarga, liberation. You have come, although You are not properly worshiped by us due to our ignorance.

PURPORT

Lord Viṣṇu was personally present at the sacrificial arena, but this does not mean that He had any interest in His own personal benefit. Similarly, the *arcā-vigraha,* the Deity in the temple, is present for the same purpose. Out of His causeless mercy, the Supreme Personality of Godhead presents Himself before us so that we can see Him. Since we have no transcendental vision, we cannot see the spiritual *sac-cid-ānanda-vigraha* of the Lord; therefore, out of His causeless mercy He comes in a form we can see. We can only see material things like stone and wood, and therefore He accepts a form of stone and wood and thus accepts our service in the temple. This is an exhibition of the Lord's causeless mercy. Although He has no interest in such things, in order to receive our loving service, He agrees to act as He does. We cannot actually offer suitable paraphernalia for the Lord's worship because we are completely ignorant. It was out of His causeless mercy that the Lord appeared in the sacrificial arena of Mahārāja Nābhi.

TEXT 10

अथायमेव वरो ह्यर्हत्तम यर्हि बर्हिषि राजर्षेर्वरदर्षभो भवान्निजपुरुषेक्षणविषय आसीत् ॥ १० ॥

athāyam eva varo hy arhattama yarhi barhiṣi rājarṣer varadarṣabho
bhavān nija-puruṣekṣaṇa-viṣaya āsīt.

atha—then; *ayam*—this; *eva*—certainly; *varaḥ*—benediction; *hi*—indeed; *arhat-tama*—O most worshipable of the worshipable; *yarhi*—because; *barhiṣi*—in the sacrifice; *rāja-ṛṣeḥ*—of King Nābhi; *varada-ṛṣabhaḥ*—the best of the benefactors; *bhavān*—Your Lordship; *nija-puruṣa*—of Your devotees; *īkṣaṇa-viṣayaḥ*—the object of the sight; *āsīt*—has become.

TRANSLATION

O most worshipable of all, You are the best of all benefactors, and Your appearance at saintly King Nābhi's sacrificial arena is meant for our benediction. Because You have been seen by us, You have bestowed upon us the most valuable benediction.

PURPORT

Nija-puruṣa-īkṣaṇa-viṣaya. In *Bhagavad-gītā* (9.29) Kṛṣṇa says, *samo 'haṁ sarva-bhūteṣu:* "I envy no one, nor am I partial to anyone. I am equal to all. But whoever renders service unto Me in devotion is a friend, is in Me, and I am also a friend to him."

The Supreme Personality of Godhead is equal to everyone. In that sense, He has no enemies and no friends. Everyone is enjoying the fruitive reactions of his own work, and the Lord, within everyone's heart, is observing and giving everyone the desired result. However, just as the devotees are always anxious to see the Supreme Lord satisfied in every way, similarly the Supreme Lord is very anxious to present Himself before His devotees. Śrī Kṛṣṇa says in *Bhagavad-gītā* (4.8):

paritrāṇāya sādhūnāṁ
vināśāya ca duṣkṛtām
dharma-saṁsthāpanārthāya
sambhavāmi yuge yuge

"To deliver the pious and to annihilate the miscreants, as well as to reestablish the principles of religion, I advent Myself millennium after millennium."

Thus Kṛṣṇa's appearance is for the deliverance and satisfaction of His devotees. Actually He does not advent Himself simply to kill the demons, for that can be done by His agents. Lord Viṣṇu's appearance at the sacrificial arena of Mahārāja Nābhi was just to please the King and his assistants. Otherwise there was no reason for His being present there.

TEXT 11

असङ्गनिशितज्ञानानलविधूताशेषमलानां भवत्स्वभावानामात्मारामाणां
मुनीनामनवरतपरिगुणितगुणगण परममङ्गलायनगुणगणकथनो ऽसि ॥ ११ ॥

asaṅga-niśita-jñānānala-vidhūtāśeṣa-malānāṁ bhavat-svabhāvānām ātmārāmāṇāṁ munīnām anavarata-pariguṇita-guṇa-gaṇa parama-maṅgalāyana-guṇa-gaṇa-kathano 'si.

asaṅga—by detachment; *niśita*—strengthened; *jñāna*—of knowledge; *anala*—by the fire; *vidhūta*—removed; *aśeṣa*—unlimited; *malānām*—whose dirty things; *bhavat-svabhāvānām*—who have attained Your qualities; *ātma-ārāmāṇām*—who are self-satisfied; *munīnām*—of great sages; *anavarata*—incessantly; *pariguṇita*—recounted; *guṇa-gaṇa*—O Lord, whose spiritual qualities; *parama-maṅgala*—supreme bliss; *āyana*—produces; *guṇa-gaṇa-kathanaḥ*—He, the chanting of whose attributes; *asi*—You are.

TRANSLATION

Dear Lord, all the great sages who are thoughtful and saintly persons incessantly recount Your spiritual qualities. These sages have already burned up all the unlimited dirty things and, by the fire of knowledge, strengthened their detachment from the material world. Thus they have attained Your qualities and are self-satisfied. Yet even for those who feel spiritual bliss in chanting Your attributes, Your personal presence is very rare.

PURPORT

The priests in Mahārāja Nābhi's sacrificial arena appreciated the personal presence of the Supreme Lord Viṣṇu, and they considered themselves very much obliged. The Lord's appearance is rare even for great saintly persons who have become completely detached from this material world and whose hearts are clean due to constantly chanting the glories of the Lord. Such people are satisfied by chanting the transcendental qualities of the Lord. The Lord's personal presence is not actually required. The priests are pointing out that the Lord's personal presence is very rare even for such elevated sages but that He was so kind to them that now He was personally present. Therefore the priests were very much obliged.

TEXT 12

अथ कथञ्चित्स्खलनक्षुत्पतनजृम्भणदुरवस्थानादिषु विवशानां नः स्मरणाय ज्वरमरणदशायामपि सकलकश्मलनिरसनानि तव गुणकृतनामधेयानि वचन-गोचराणि भवन्तु ॥ १२ ॥

atha kathañcit skhalana-kṣut-patana-jṛmbhaṇa-duravasthānādiṣu vivaśānāṁ naḥ smaraṇāya jvara-maraṇa-daśāyām api sakala-kaśmala-nirasanāni tava guṇa-kṛta-nāmadheyāni vacana-gocarāṇi bhavantu.

atha—still; *kathañcit*—somehow or other; *skhalana*—stumbling; *kṣut*—hunger; *patana*—falling down; *jṛmbhaṇa*—yawning; *duravasthāna*—because of being placed in an undesirable position; *ādiṣu*—and so on; *vivaśānām*—unable; *naḥ*—of ourselves; *smaraṇāya*—to remember; *jvara-maraṇa-daśāyām*—in the case of having a high fever at the time of death; *api*—also; *sakala*—all; *kaśmala*—sins; *nirasanāni*—which can dispel; *tava*—Your; *guṇa*—attributes; *kṛta*—activities; *nāmadheyāni*—names; *vacana-gocarāṇi*—possible to be uttered; *bhavantu*—let them become.

TRANSLATION

Dear Lord, we may not be able to remember Your name, form and qualities due to stumbling, hunger, falling down, yawning or being in a miserable diseased condition at the time of death when there is a high fever. We therefore pray unto You, O Lord, for You are very affectionate to Your devotees. Please help us remember You and utter Your holy names, attributes and activities, which can dispel all the reactions of our sinful lives.

PURPORT

The real success in life is *ante nārāyaṇa-smṛti*—remembering the holy name, attributes, activities and form of the Lord at the time of death. Although we may be engaged in the Lord's devotional service in the temple, material conditions are so tough and inevitable that we may forget the Lord at the time of death due to a diseased condition or mental derangement. Therefore we should pray to the Lord to be able to remember His lotus feet without fail at the time of death, when we are in such a precarious condition. In this regard, one may also see *Śrīmad-Bhāgavatam* (6.2.9-10 and 14-15).

TEXT 13

किञ्चायं राजर्षिरपत्यकामः प्रजां भवादृशीमाशासान ईश्वरमाशिषां स्वर्गापवर्गयोरपि भवन्तमुपधावति प्रजायामर्थप्रत्ययो धनदमिवाधनः फलीकरणम् ॥१३॥

kiñcāyaṁ rājarṣir apatya-kāmaḥ prajāṁ bhavādṛśīm āśāsāna
īśvaram āśiṣāṁ svargāpavargayor api bhavantam upadhāvati prajāyām
artha-pratyayo dhanadam ivādhanaḥ phalīkaraṇam.

kiñca—moreover; *ayam*—this; *rāja-ṛṣiḥ*—pious King (Nābhi); *apatya-kāmaḥ*—desiring offspring; *prajām*—a son; *bhavādṛśīm*—exactly like You; *āśāsānaḥ*—hoping for; *īśvaram*—the supreme controller; *āśiṣām*—of benedictions; *svarga-apavargayoḥ*—of the heavenly planets and liberation; *api*—although; *bhavantam*—You; *upadhāvati*—worships; *prajāyām*—children; *artha-pratyayaḥ*—regarding as the ultimate goal of life; *dhana-dam*—unto a person who can give immense wealth as charity; *iva*—like; *adhanaḥ*—a poor man; *phalīkaraṇam*—a little husk.

TRANSLATION

Dear Lord, here is the great King Nābhi, whose ultimate goal in life is to have a son like You. Your Lordship, his position is like that of a person approaching a very rich man and begging for a little grain. Mahārāja Nābhi is so desirous of having a son that he is worshiping You for a son, although You can offer him any exalted position, including elevation to the heavenly planets or liberation back to Godhead.

PURPORT

The priests were a little ashamed that King Nābhi was performing a great sacrifice just to ask the Lord's benediction for a son. The Lord could offer him promotion to the heavenly planets or the Vaikuṇṭha planets. Śrī Caitanya Mahāprabhu has taught us how to approach the Supreme Lord and ask Him for the ultimate benediction. He said: *na dhanaṁ na janaṁ na sundarīṁ kavitāṁ vā jagad-īśa kāmaye.* He did not want to ask the Supreme Lord for anything material. Material opulence means riches, a nice family, a good wife and many followers, but an intelligent devotee doesn't ask the Supreme Lord for anything material. His only prayer is: *mama janmani janmanīśvare bhavatād bhaktir ahaitukī tvayi.* He wants to be engaged perpetually in the loving service of the Lord. He does not want promotion to the heavenly planets or *mukti,* liberation from material bondage. If this were the case, Śrī Caitanya Mahāprabhu would not have said, *mama janmani janmani.* It doesn't matter to a devotee whether or not he takes birth life after life, as long as he remains a devotee. Actually eternal liberty means returning home, back to Godhead. A devotee is never concerned about anything material. Although Nābhi Mahārāja wanted a son like Viṣṇu, wanting a son like God is also a form of sense gratification. A pure devotee wants only to engage in the Lord's loving service.

TEXT 14

**को वा इह तेऽपराजितोऽपराजितया माययानवसितपदव्यानावृतमतिर्विषय-
विषरयानावृतप्रकृतिरनुपासितमहच्चरणः ॥ १४ ॥**

ko vā iha te 'parājito 'parājitayā māyayānavasita-padavyānāvṛta-matir
viṣaya-viṣa-rayānāvṛta-prakṛtir anupāsita-mahac-caraṇaḥ.

kaḥ vā—who is that person; *iha*—within this material world; *te*—of Your Lordship; *aparājitaḥ*—not conquered; *aparājitayā*—by the unconquerable; *māyayā*—illusory energy; *anavasita-padavya*—whose path cannot be ascertained; *anāvṛta-matiḥ*—whose intelligence is not bewildered; *viṣaya-viṣa*—of material enjoyment, which is like poison; *raya*—by the course; *anāvṛta*—not covered; *prakṛtiḥ*—whose nature; *anupāsita*—without worshiping; *mahat-caraṇaḥ*—the lotus feet of great devotees.

TRANSLATION

Dear Lord, unless one worships the lotus feet of great devotees, one will be conquered by the illusory energy, and his intelligence will be bewildered. Indeed, who has not been carried away by the waves of material enjoyment, which are like poison? Your illusory energy is unconquerable. No one can see the path of this material energy or tell how it is working.

PURPORT

Mahārāja Nābhi was inclined to performing great sacrifices for begetting a son. The son might be as good as the Supreme Personality of Godhead, but such a material desire—be it great or insignificant—is brought about by the influence of *māyā.* A devotee does not at all desire anything for sense gratification. Devotion is therefore explained as devoid of material desires (*anyābhilāṣitā-śūnya*). Everyone is subjected to the influence of *māyā* and entangled in all kinds of material desire, and Mahārāja Nābhi was no exception. Freedom from *māyā's* influence is possible when one engages in the service of the great devotees (*mahac-caraṇa-sevā*). Without worshiping the lotus feet of a great devotee, one cannot be freed from *māyā's* influence. Śrīla Narottama dāsa Ṭhākura therefore says, *chāḍiyā vaiṣṇava-sevā nistāra pāyeche kebā:* "Who has been freed from *māyā's* clutches without serving the lotus feet of a Vaiṣṇava?" *Māyā* is *aparājita*, and her influence is also *aparājita.* As confirmed in *Bhagavad-gītā* (7.14):

daivī hy eṣā guṇamayī
mama māyā duratyayā

"This divine energy of Mine, consisting of the three modes of material nature, is difficult to overcome."

Only a devotee can surpass *māyā's* great influence. It was no fault on Mahārāja Nābhi's part that he wanted a son. He wanted a son like the Supreme Personality of Godhead, who is the best of all sons. By the association of the Lord's devotee, one no longer desires material opulence. This is confirmed in *Caitanya-caritāmṛta* (*Madhya* 22.54):

"sādhu-saṅga", "sādhu-saṅga" sarva-śāstre kaya
lava-mātra sādhu-saṅge sarva-siddhi haya

and *Madhya* 22.51:

mahat-kṛpā vinā kona karme 'bhakti' naya
kṛṣṇa-bhakti dūre rahu, saṁsāra nahe kṣaya

If one is serious about escaping *māyā's* influence and returning home, back to Godhead, one must associate with a *sādhu* (devotee). That is the verdict of all scriptures. By the slight association of a devotee, one can be freed from the clutches of *māyā.* Without the mercy of the pure devotee, one cannot get freedom by any means. Certainly a pure devotee's association is necessary in order to obtain the loving service of the Lord. One cannot be freed from *māyā's* clutches without *sādhu-saṅga,* the benediction of a great devotee. In *Śrīmad-Bhāgavatam* (7.5.32) Prahlāda Mahārāja says:

naiṣāṁ matis tāvad urukramāṅghriṁ
spṛśaty anarthāpagamo yad arthaḥ
mahīyasāṁ pāda-rajo-'bhiṣekaṁ
niṣkiñcanānāṁ na vṛṇīta yāvat

One cannot become the Lord's pure devotee without taking the dust of a great devotee on his head (*pāda-rajo-'bhiṣekam*). A pure devotee is *niṣkiñcana;* he has no material desire to enjoy the material world. One has to take shelter of such a pure devotee in order to attain his qualities. The pure devotee is always free from the clutches of *māyā* and her influence.

TEXT 15

यदु ह वाव तव पुनरदभ्रकर्तरिह समाहूतस्तत्रार्थधियां मन्दानां नस्तद्यद्देवहेलनं देव-
देवार्हसि साम्येन सर्वान् प्रतिवोढुमविदुषाम् ॥१५॥

yad u ha vāva tava punar adabhra-kartar iha samāhūtas tatrārtha-dhiyāṁ mandānāṁ nas tad yad deva-helanaṁ deva-devārhasi sāmyena sarvān prativoḍhum aviduṣām.

yat—because; *u ha vāva*—indeed; *tava*—Your; *punaḥ*—again; *adabhra-kartaḥ*—O Lord, who performs many activities; *iha*—here, in this arena of sacrifice; *samāhūtaḥ*—invited; *tatra*—therefore; *artha-dhiyām*—who aspire to fulfill material desires; *mandānām*—not very intelligent; *naḥ*—of us; *tat*—that; *yat*—which; *deva-helanam*—disrespect of the Supreme Personality of Godhead; *deva-deva*—Lord of lords; *arhasi*—please; *sāmyena*—because of Your equipoised position; *sarvān*—everything; *prativoḍhum*—tolerate; *aviduṣām*—of us, who are all ignorant.

TRANSLATION

O Lord, You perform many wonderful activities. Our only aim was to acquire a son by performing this great sacrifice; therefore our intelligence is not very sharp. We are not experienced in ascertaining life's goal. By inviting You to this negligible sacrifice for some material motive, we have certainly committed a great offense at Your lotus feet. Therefore, O Lord of lords, please excuse our offense because of Your causeless mercy and equal mind.

PURPORT

The priests were certainly unhappy to have called the Supreme Lord from Vaikuṇṭha for such an insignificant reason. A pure devotee never wants to see the Lord unnecessarily. The Lord is engaged in various activities, and the pure devotee does not want to see Him whimsically, for his own sense gratification. The pure devotee simply depends on the Lord's mercy, and when the Lord is pleased, he can see Him face to face. The Lord is unseen even by demigods like Lord Brahmā and Lord Śiva. By calling on the Supreme Lord, the priests of Nābhi Mahārāja proved themselves unintelligent; nonetheless, the Lord came out of His causeless mercy. All of them therefore wanted to be excused by the Lord.

Worship of the Supreme Lord for material gain is not approved by authorities. As stated in *Bhagavad-gītā* (7.16):

catur-vidhā bhajante māṁ
janāḥ sukṛtino 'rjuna
ārto jijñāsur arthārthī
jñānī ca bharatarṣabha

"O best among the Bharatas [Arjuna], four kinds of pious men render devotional service unto Me—the distressed, the desirer of wealth, the inquisitive, and he who is searching for knowledge of the Absolute."

Initiation into *bhakti* begins when one is in a distressed condition or in want of money, or when one is inquisitive to understand the Absolute Truth. Nonetheless, people who approach the Supreme Lord in this way are not actually devotees. They are accepted as pious (*sukṛtinaḥ*) due to their inquiring about the Absolute Truth, the Supreme Personality of Godhead. Not knowing the various activities and engagements of the Lord, such people unnecessarily disturb the Lord for material gain. However, the Lord is so kind that even though disturbed, He fulfills the desires of such beggars. The pure devotee is *anyābhilāṣitā-śūnya;* he has no motive behind his worship. He is not conducted by the influence of *māyā* in the form of *karma* or *jñāna.* The pure devotee is always prepared to execute the order of the Lord without personal consideration. The *ṛtvijaḥ,* the priests at the sacrifice, knew very well the distinction between *karma* and *bhakti,* and because they considered themselves under the influence of *karma,* fruitive activity, they begged the Lord's pardon. They knew that the Lord had been invited to come for some paltry reason.

TEXT 16

श्रीशुक उवाच

इति निगदेनाभिष्टूयमानो भगवाननिमिषर्षभो वर्षधराभिवादिताभिवन्दित-
चरणः सदयमिदमाह ।१६।

śrī-śuka uvāca
iti nigadenābhiṣṭūyamāno bhagavān animiṣarṣabho varṣa-
dharābhivāditābhivandita-caraṇaḥ sadayam idam āha.

śrī-śukaḥ uvāca—Śrī Śukadeva Gosvāmī said; *iti*—thus; *nigadena*—by prayers in prose; *abhiṣṭūyamānaḥ*—being worshiped; *bhagavān*—the Supreme Personality of Godhead; *animiṣa-ṛṣabhaḥ*—the chief of all the demigods; *varṣa-dhara*—by King Nābhi, the Emperor of Bhārata-varṣa; *abhivādita*—worshiped; *abhivandita*—were bowed down to; *caraṇaḥ*—whose feet; *sadayam*—kindly; *idam*—this; *āha*—said.

TRANSLATION

Śrī Śukadeva Gosvāmī said: The priests, who were even worshiped by King Nābhi, the Emperor of Bhārata-varṣa, offered prayers in prose [generally they were in poetry] and bowed down at the Lord's lotus feet. The Lord of lords, the ruler of the demigods, was very pleased with them, and He began to speak as follows.

TEXT 17

श्रीभगवानुवाच

अहो बताहमृषयो भवद्भिरवितथगीर्भिर्वरमसुलभमभियाचितो यद्-
मुष्यात्मजो मया सदृशो भूयादिति ममाहमेवाभिरूपः कैवल्यादथापि ब्रह्मवादो
न मृषा भवितुमर्हति ममैव हि मुखं यद् द्विजदेवकुलम् ॥१७॥

śrī-bhagavān uvāca
aho batāham ṛṣayo bhavadbhir avitatha-gīrbhir varam asulabham
abhiyācito yad amuṣyātmajo mayā sadṛśo bhūyād iti mamāham
evābhirūpaḥ kaivalyād athāpi brahma-vādo na mṛṣā bhavitum arhati
mamaiva hi mukhaṁ yad dvija-deva-kulam.

śrī-bhagavān uvāca—the Supreme Personality of Godhead said; *aho*—alas; *bata*—certainly I am pleased; *aham*—I; *ṛṣayaḥ*—O great sages; *bhavadbhiḥ*—by you; *avitatha-gīrbhiḥ*—whose words are all true; *varam*—for a benediction; *asulabham*—very difficult to achieve; *abhiyācitaḥ*—have been requested; *yat*—that; *amuṣya*—of King Nābhi; *ātma-jaḥ*—a son; *mayā sadṛśaḥ*—like Me; *bhūyāt*—there may be; *iti*—thus; *mama*—My; *aham*—I; *eva*—only; *abhirūpaḥ*—equal; *kaivalyāt*—because of being without a second; *athāpi*—nevertheless; *brahma-vādaḥ*—the words spoken by exalted *brāhmaṇas; na*—not; *mṛṣā*—false; *bhavitum*—to become; *arhati*—ought; *mama*—My; *eva*—certainly; *hi*—because; *mukham*—mouth; *yat*—that; *dvija-deva-kulam*—the class of pure *brāhmaṇas.*

TRANSLATION

The Supreme Personality of Godhead replied: O great sages, I am certainly very pleased with your prayers. You are all truthful.

You have prayed for the benediction of a son like Me for King Nābhi, but this is very difficult to obtain. Since I am the Supreme Person without a second and since no one is equal to Me, another personality like Me is not possible to find. In any case, because you are all qualified brāhmaṇas, your vibrations should not prove untrue. I consider the brāhmaṇas who are well qualified with brahminical qualities to be as good as My own mouth.

PURPORT

The word *avitatha-gīrbhiḥ* means "they whose spoken vibrations cannot be nullified." The *brāhmaṇas* (*dvija*, the twiceborn), are given a chance by the śāstric regulations to become almost as powerful as the Supreme Lord. Whatever a *brāhmaṇa* speaks cannot be nullified or changed in any circumstance. According to the Vedic injunctions, a *brāhmaṇa* is the mouth of the Supreme Personality of Godhead; therefore in all rituals a *brāhmaṇa* is offered food (*brāhmaṇa-bhojana*) because when a *brāhmaṇa* eats, it is considered that the Supreme Lord Himself eats. Similarly, whatever a *brāhmaṇa* speaks cannot be changed. It must act. The learned sages who were priests at Mahārāja Nābhi's sacrifice were not only *brāhmaṇas* but were so qualified that they were like *devas*, demigods, or God Himself. If this were not the case, how could they invite Lord Viṣṇu to come to the sacrificial arena? God is one, and God does not belong to this or that religion. In Kali-yuga, different religious sects consider their God to be different from the God of others, but that is not possible. God is one, and He is appreciated according to different angles of vision. In this verse the word *kaivalyāt* means that God has no competitor. There is only one God. In the *Śvetāśvatara Upaniṣad* (6.8) it is said, *na tat-samaś cābhyadhikaś ca dṛśyate:* "No one is found to be equal to Him or greater than Him." That is the definition of God.

TEXT 18

तत आग्नीध्रीयेंऽशकलयावतरिष्याम्यात्मतुल्यमनुपलभमानः ॥१८॥

tata āgnīdhrīye 'ṁśa-kalayāvatariṣyāmy ātma-tulyam anupalabhamānaḥ.

tataḥ—therefore; *āgnīdhrīye*—in the wife of Nābhi, the son of Āgnīdhra; *aṁśa-kalayā*—by an expansion of My personal form; *avatariṣyāmi*—I shall advent Myself; *ātma-tulyam*—My equal; *anupalabhamānaḥ*—not finding.

TRANSLATION

Since I cannot find anyone equal to Me, I shall personally expand Myself into a plenary portion and thus advent Myself in the womb of Merudevī, the wife of Mahārāja Nābhi, the son of Āgnīdhra.

PURPORT

This is an example of the omnipotence of the Supreme Personality of Godhead. Although He is one without a second, He expands Himself by *svāṁśa*, His personal expansion, and sometimes by *vibhinnāṁśa*, or His separated expansion. Lord Viṣṇu herein agrees to send His personal expansion as the son of Merudevī, the wife of Mahārāja Nābhi, who is the son of Āgnīdhra. The *ṛtvijaḥ*, the priests, knew that God is one, yet they prayed for the Supreme Lord to become the son of Mahārāja Nābhi to let the world know that the Absolute Truth, the Supreme Personality of Godhead, is one without a second. When He incarnates, He expands Himself in different potencies.

TEXT 19

श्रीशुक उवाच

इति निशामयन्त्या मेरुदेव्याः पतिमभिधायान्तर्दधे भगवान् ॥१९॥

śrī-śuka uvāca
iti niśāmayantyā merudevyāḥ patim abhidhāyāntardadhe bhagavān.

śrī-śukaḥ uvāca—Śrī Śukadeva Gosvāmī said; *iti*—thus; *niśāmayantyāḥ*—who was listening; *merudevyāḥ*—in the presence of Merudevī; *patim*—unto her husband; *abhidhāya*—having spoken; *antardadhe*—disappeared; *bhagavān*—the Supreme Personality of Godhead.

TRANSLATION

Śukadeva Gosvāmī continued: After saying this, the Lord disappeared. The wife of King Nābhi, Queen Merudevī, was sitting by the side of her husband, and consequently she could hear everything the Supreme Lord had spoken.

PURPORT

According to the Vedic injunctions, one should perform sacrifices in the company of one's own wife. *Sapatnīko dharmam ācaret:* religious rituals should be performed with one's wife; therefore Mahārāja Nābhi conducted his great sacrifice with his wife by his side.

TEXT 20

बर्हिषि तस्मिन्नेव विष्णुदत्त भगवान् परमर्षिभिः प्रसादितो नाभेः प्रियचिकीर्षया
तदवरोधायने मेरुदेव्यां धर्मान्दर्शयितुकामो वातरशनानां श्रमणानामृषीणामू-
र्ध्वमन्थिनां शुक्लया तनुवावततार ॥२०॥

barhiṣi tasminn eva viṣṇudatta bhagavān paramarṣibhiḥ prasādito
nābheḥ priya-cikīrṣayā tad-avarodhāyane merudevyāṁ dharmān
darśayitu-kāmo vāta-raśanānāṁ śramaṇānām ṛṣīṇām ūrdhva-
manthināṁ śuklayā tanuvāvatatāra.

barhiṣi—in the arena of sacrifice; *tasmin*—that; *eva*—in this way; *viṣṇu-datta*—O Mahārāja Parīkṣit; *bhagavān*—the Supreme Personality of Godhead; *parama-ṛṣibhiḥ*—by the great *ṛṣis; prasāditaḥ*—being pleased; *nābheḥ priya-cikīrṣayā*—to please King Nābhi; *tat-avarodhāyane*—in his wife; *merudevyām*—Merudevī; *dharmān*—the principles of religion; *darśayitu-kāmaḥ*—desiring to exhibit how to perform; *vāta-raśanānām*—of the *sannyāsīs* (who have almost no cloth); *śramaṇānām*—of the *vānaprasthas; ṛṣīṇām*—of the great sages; *ūrdhva-manthinām*—of the *brahmacārīs; śuklayā tanuvā*—in His original spiritual form, which is above the modes of material nature; *avatatāra*—appeared as an incarnation.

TRANSLATION

O Viṣṇudatta, Parīkṣit Mahārāja, the Supreme Personality of Godhead was pleased by the great sages at that sacrifice. Consequently the Lord decided to personally exhibit the method of executing religious principles [as observed by brahmacārīs, sannyāsīs, vānaprasthas and gṛhasthas engaged in rituals] and also satisfy Mahārāja Nābhi's desire. Consequently He appeared as the son of Merudevī in His original spiritual form, which is above the modes of material nature.

PURPORT

When the Supreme Lord appears or descends as an incarnation within this material world, He does not accept a body made of the three modes of material nature (*sattva-guṇa, rajo-guṇa* and *tamo-guṇa*). Māyāvādī philosophers say that the impersonal God appears in this material world by accepting a body in the *sattva-guṇa*. Śrīla Viśvanātha Cakravartī states that the word *śukla* means "consisting of *śuddha-sattva.*" Lord Viṣṇu descends in His *śuddha-sattva* form. *Śuddha-sattva* refers to the *sattva-guṇa* which is never contaminated. In this material world, even the mode of goodness (*sattva-guṇa*) is contaminated by tinges of *rajo-guṇa* and *tamo-guṇa*. When *sattva-guṇa* is never contaminated by *rajo-guṇa* and *tamo-guṇa*, it is called *śuddha-sattva. Sattvaṁ viśuddhaṁ vasudeva-śabditam* (*Bhāg.* 4.3.23). That is the platform of *vasudeva*, whereby the Supreme Personality of Godhead, Vāsudeva, can be experienced. In *Bhagavad-gītā* (4.7) Śrī Kṛṣṇa Himself says:

yadā yadā hi dharmasya
glānir bhavati bhārata
abhyutthānam adharmasya
tadātmānaṁ sṛjāmy aham

"Whenever and wherever there is a decline in religious practice, O descendant of Bharata, and a predominant rise of irreligion—at that time I descend Myself."

Unlike ordinary living entities, the Supreme Lord is not forced by the modes of material nature to appear. He appears *dharmān darśayitu-*

kāma—to show how to execute the functions of a human being. The word *dharma* is meant for human beings and is never used in connection with beings inferior to human beings, such as animals. Unfortunately, without being guided by the Supreme Lord, human beings sometimes manufacture a process of *dharma* by concoction. Actually *dharma* cannot be made by man. *Dharmaṁ tu sākṣād bhagavat-praṇītam.* (*Bhāg.* 6.3.19) *Dharma* is given by the Supreme Personality of Godhead, just as the law is given by the state government. Man-made *dharma* has no meaning. *Śrīmad-Bhāgavatam* refers to man-made *dharma* as *kaitava-dharma,* cheating religion. The Supreme Lord sends an *avatāra* (incarnation) to teach human society the proper way to execute religious principles. Such religious principles are *bhakti-mārga.* As the Supreme Lord Himself says in *Bhagavad-gītā: sarva-dharmān parityajya mām ekaṁ śaraṇaṁ vraja.* The son of Mahārāja Nābhi, Ṛṣabhadeva, appeared on this earth to preach the principles of religion. That will be explained in the Fifth Chapter of this Fifth Canto.

Thus end the Bhaktivedanta purports of the Fifth Canto, Third Chapter, of the Śrīmad-Bhāgavatam, *entitled "Ṛṣabhadeva's Appearance in the Womb of Merudevī, the wife of King Nābhi."*

CHAPTER FOUR

The Characteristics of Ṛṣabhadeva, the Supreme Personality of Godhead

In this chapter, Ṛṣabhadeva, the son of Mahārāja Nābhi, begot a hundred sons, and during the reign of those sons the world was very happy in all respects. When Ṛṣabhadeva appeared as the son of Mahārāja Nābhi, He was appreciated by the people as the most exalted and beautiful personality of that age. His poise, influence, strength, enthusiasm, bodily luster and other transcendental qualities were beyond compare. The word *ṛṣabha* refers to the best, or the supreme. Due to the superexcellent attributes of the son of Mahārāja Nābhi, the King named his son Ṛṣabha, or "the best." His influence was incomparable. Although there was a scarcity of rain, Ṛṣabhadeva did not care for Indra, the King of heaven, who is in charge of supplying rain. Through His own potency, Ṛṣabhadeva sumptuously covered Ajanābha with ample rain. Upon receiving Ṛṣabhadeva, who is the Supreme Personality of Godhead, as his son, King Nābhi began to raise Him very carefully. After that, he entrusted the ruling power to Him and, retiring from family life, lived at Badarikāśrama completely engaged in the worship of Vāsudeva, the Supreme Lord. To follow social customs, Lord Ṛṣabhadeva for a while became a student in the *gurukula*, and after returning, He followed the orders of His *guru* and accepted a wife named Jayantī, who had been given to Him by the King of heaven, Indra. He begot a hundred sons in the womb of Jayantī. Of these hundred sons, the eldest was known as Bharata. Since the reign of Mahārāja Bharata, this planet has been called Bhārata-varṣa. Ṛṣabhadeva's other sons were headed by Kuśāvarta, Ilāvarta, Brahmāvarta, Malaya, Ketu, Bhadrasena, Indraspṛk, Vidarbha and Kīkaṭa. There were also other sons named Kavi, Havi, Antarikṣa, Prabuddha, Pippalāyana, Āvirhotra, Drumila, Camasa and Karabhājana. Instead of ruling the kingdom, these nine became mendicant preachers of Kṛṣṇa consciousness, following the religious precepts of the *Bhāgavatam.* Their characteristics and activities are described in the

Eleventh Canto of *Śrīmad-Bhāgavatam* during the talks between Vasudeva and Nārada at Kurukṣetra. To teach the general populace, King Ṛṣabhadeva performed many sacrifices and taught His sons how to rule the citizens.

TEXT 1

श्रीशुक उवाच

अथ ह तमुत्पत्त्यैवाभिव्यज्यमानभगवल्लक्षणं साम्योपशमवैराग्यैश्वर्यमहा-
विभूतिभिरनुदिनमेध मानानुभावं प्रकृतयः प्रजा ब्राह्मणा देवताश्चावनितल-
समवनायातितरां जगृधुः ॥ १ ॥

śrī-śuka uvāca
atha ha tam utpattyaivābhivyajyamāna-bhagaval-lakṣaṇaṁ
sāmyopaśama-vairāgyaiśvarya-mahā-vibhūtibhir anudinam
edhamānānubhāvaṁ prakṛtayaḥ prajā brāhmaṇā devatāś cāvani-tala-
samavanāyātitarāṁ jagṛdhuḥ.

śrī-śukaḥ uvāca—Śrī Śukadeva Gosvāmī said; *atha ha*—thus (after the Supreme Personality of Godhead appeared); *tam*—Him; *utpattyā*—from the beginning of His appearance; *eva*—even; *abhivyajyamāna*—distinctly manifested; *bhagavat-lakṣaṇam*—possessing the symptoms of the Supreme Personality of Godhead; *sāmya*—equal to everyone; *upaśama*—completely peaceful, in control of the senses and mind; *vairāgya*—renunciation; *aiśvarya*—opulences; *mahā-vibhūtibhiḥ*—with great attributes; *anudinam*—day after day; *edhamāna*—increasing; *anubhāvam*—His power; *prakṛtayaḥ*—the ministers; *prajāḥ*—the citizens; *brāhmaṇāḥ*—the learned scholars in full knowledge of Brahman; *devatāḥ*—the demigods; *ca*—and; *avani-tala*—the surface of the globe; *samavanāya*—to rule; *atitarām*—greatly; *jagṛdhuḥ*—desired.

TRANSLATION

Śrī Śukadeva Gosvāmī said: As soon as the Lord was born as the son of Mahārāja Nābhi, He manifested symptoms of the Supreme Lord, such as marks on the bottoms of His feet [the flag,

thunderbolt, etc.]. This son was equal to everyone and very peaceful. He could control His senses and His mind, and, possessing all opulence, He did not hanker for material enjoyment. Endowed with all these attributes, the son of Mahārāja Nābhi became more powerful day after day. Due to this, the citizens, learned brāhmaṇas, demigods and ministers wanted Ṛṣabhadeva to be appointed ruler of the earth.

PURPORT

In these days of cheap incarnations, it is very interesting to note the bodily symptoms found in an incarnation. From the very beginning of His birth, it was observed that Ṛṣabhadeva's feet were marked with the transcendental signs (a flag, thunderbolt, lotus flower, etc.). In addition to this, as the Lord began to grow, He became very prominent. He was equal to everyone. He did not favor one person and neglect another. An incarnation of God must have the six opulences—wealth, strength, knowledge, beauty, fame and renunciation. It is said that although Ṛṣabhadeva was endowed with all opulences, He was not at all attached to material enjoyment. He was self-controlled and therefore liked by everyone. Due to His superexcellent qualities, everyone wanted Him to rule the earth. An incarnation of God has to be accepted by experienced people and by the symptoms described in the *śāstras.* An incarnation is not accepted simply by the adulation of foolish people.

TEXT 2

तस्य ह वा इत्थं वर्ष्मणा वरीयसा बृहच्छ्लोकेन चौजसा बलेन श्रिया यशसा वीर्य-शौर्याभ्यां च पिता ऋषभ इतीदं नाम चकार ॥ २ ॥

tasya ha vā itthaṁ varṣmaṇā varīyasā bṛhac-chlokena caujasā balena
śriyā yaśasā vīrya-śauryābhyāṁ ca pitā ṛṣabha itīdaṁ nāma cakāra.

tasya—of Him; *ha vā*—certainly; *ittham*—thus; *varṣmaṇā*—by the bodily features; *varīyasā*—most exalted; *bṛhat-ślokena*—decorated with all the high qualities described by poets; *ca*—also; *ojasā*—by prowess; *balena*—by strength; *śriyā*—by beauty; *yaśasā*—by fame; *vīrya-śauryābhyām*—by influence and heroism; *ca*—and; *pitā*—the father

(Mahārāja Nābhi); *ṛṣabhaḥ*—the best; *iti*—thus; *idam*—this; *nāma*—name; *cakāra*—gave.

TRANSLATION

When the son of Mahārāja Nābhi became visible, He evinced all good qualities described by the great poets—namely, a well-built body with all the symptoms of the Godhead, prowess, strength, beauty, name, fame, influence and enthusiasm. When the father, Mahārāja Nābhi, saw all these qualities, he thought his son to be the best of human beings or the supreme being. Therefore he gave Him the name Ṛṣabha.

PURPORT

To accept someone as God or an incarnation of God, one must observe the symptoms of God in his body. All the symptoms were found in the body of Mahārāja Nābhi's extraordinarily powerful son. His body was well structured, and He displayed all the transcendental qualities. He showed great influence, and He could control His mind and senses. Consequently He was named Ṛṣabha, which indicates that He was the supreme living being.

TEXT 3

यस्य हीन्द्रः स्पर्धमानो भगवान् वर्षे न ववर्ष तदवधार्य भगवानृ
षभदेवो योगेश्वरः प्रहस्यात्मयोगमायया स्ववर्षमजनाभं नामाभ्यवर्षत्॥ ३ ॥

yasya hīndraḥ spardhamāno bhagavān varṣe na vavarṣa tad
avadhārya bhagavān ṛṣabhadevo yogeśvaraḥ prahasyātma-
yogamāyayā sva-varṣam ajanābhaṁ nāmābhyavarṣat.

yasya—of whom; *hi*—indeed; *indraḥ*—King Indra of heaven; *spardhamānaḥ*—being envious; *bhagavān*—very opulent; *varṣe*—on Bhārata-varṣa; *na vavarṣa*—did not pour water; *tat*—that; *avadhārya*—knowing; *bhagavān*—the Supreme Personality of Godhead; *ṛṣabha-devaḥ*—Ṛṣabhadeva; *yoga-īśvaraḥ*—the master of all mystic power; *prahasya*—smiling; *ātma-yoga-māyayā*—by His own spiritual potency; *sva-varṣam*—on His place; *ajanābham*—Ajanābha; *nāma*—named; *abhyavarṣat*—He poured water.

TRANSLATION

Indra, the King of heaven, who is very materially opulent, became envious of King Ṛṣabhadeva. Consequently he stopped pouring water on the planet known as Bhārata-varṣa. At that time the Supreme Lord, Ṛṣabhadeva, the master of all mystic power, understood King Indra's purpose and smiled a little. Then, by His own prowess, through yogamāyā [His internal potency], He profusely poured water upon His own place, which was known as Ajanābha.

PURPORT

We find the word *bhagavān* used twice in this verse. Both King Indra and Ṛṣabhadeva, the incarnation of the Supreme Lord, are described as *bhagavān.* Sometimes Nārada and Lord Brahmā are also addressed as *bhagavān.* The word *bhagavān* means that one is a very opulent and powerful person like Lord Brahmā, Lord Śiva, Nārada or Indra. They are all addressed as *bhagavān* due to their extraordinary opulence. King Ṛṣabhadeva is an incarnation of the Supreme Lord, and therefore He was the original Bhagavān. Consequently He is described herein as *yogeśvara,* which indicates that He has the most powerful spiritual potency. He is not dependent on King Indra for water. He can supply water Himself, and He did so in this case. In *Bhagavad-gītā,* it is stated: *yajñād bhavati parjanyaḥ.* Due to the performance of *yajña,* clouds of water are manifest in the sky. Clouds and rainfall are under the management of Indra, the heavenly King, but when Indra is neglectful, the Supreme Lord Himself, who is also known as *yajña* or *yajña-pati,* takes the task upon Himself. Consequently there was sufficient rainfall in the place named Ajanābha. When *yajña-pati* wants to, He can do anything without the help of any subordinate. Therefore the Supreme Lord is known as almighty. In the present age of Kali there will eventually be a great scarcity of water (*anāvṛṣṭi*), for the general populace, due to ignorance and the scarcity of yajñic ingredients, will neglect to perform *yajñas. Śrīmad-Bhāgavatam* therefore advises: *yajñaiḥ saṅkīrtana-prāyaiḥ yajanti hi sumedhasaḥ.* After all, *yajña* is meant to satisfy the Supreme Personality of Godhead. In this age of Kali, there is great scarcity and ignorance; nonetheless, everyone can perform *saṅkīrtana-yajña.* Every family in every society can conduct *saṅkīrtana-yajña* at least every evening. In this way there will be no disturbance or scarcity of rain. It is essential for the people in this age to perform the *saṅkīrtana-yajña* in order to be materially happy and to advance spiritually.

TEXT 4

नाभिस्तु यथाभिलषितं सुप्रजस्त्वमवरुध्यातिप्रमोदभरविह्वलो गद्गदाक्षरया
गिरा स्वैरं गृहीत नरलोकसधर्मं भगवन्तं पुराणपुरुषं मायाविलसितमतिर्वत्स
तातेति सानुरागमुपलालयन् परां निर्वृतिमुपगतः ॥ ४ ॥

nābhis tu yathābhilaṣitaṁ suprajastvam avarudhyāti-pramoda-bhara-
vihvalo gadgadākṣarayā girā svairaṁ gṛhīta-naraloka-sadharmaṁ
bhagavantaṁ purāṇa-puruṣaṁ māyā-vilasita-matir vatsa tāteti
sānurāgam upalālayan parāṁ nirvṛtim upagataḥ.

nābhiḥ—King Nābhi; *tu*—certainly; *yathā-abhilaṣitam*—according to his desire; *su-prajastvam*—the most beautiful son; *avarudhya*—getting; *ati-pramoda*—of great jubilation; *bhara*—by an excess; *vihvalaḥ*—being overwhelmed; *gadgada-akṣarayā*—faltering in ecstasy; *girā*—with a voice; *svairam*—by His independent will; *gṛhīta*—accepted; *nara-loka-sadharmam*—acting as if a human being; *bhagavantam*—the Supreme Personality of Godhead; *purāṇa-puruṣam*—the oldest among living beings; *māyā*—by *yogamāyā; vilasita*—bewildered; *matiḥ*—his mentality; *vatsa*—my dear son; *tāta*—my darling; *iti*—thus; *sa-anurāgam*—with great affection; *upalālayan*—raising; *parām*—transcendental; *nirvṛtim*—bliss; *upagataḥ*—achieved.

TRANSLATION

Due to getting a perfect son according to his desire, King Nābhi was always overwhelmed with transcendental bliss and was very affectionate to his son. It was with ecstasy and a faltering voice that he addressed Him, "My dear son, my darling." This mentality was brought about by yogamāyā, whereby he accepted the Supreme Lord, the supreme father, as his own son. Out of His supreme good will, the Lord became his son and dealt with everyone as if He were an ordinary human being. Thus King Nābhi began to raise

his transcendental son with great affection, and he was overwhelmed with transcendental bliss, joy and devotion.

PURPORT

The word *māyā* is used in the sense of illusion. Considering the Supreme Personality of Godhead to be his own son, Mahārāja Nābhi was certainly in illusion, but this was transcendental illusion. This illusion is required; otherwise how can one accept the supreme father as his own son? The Supreme Lord appears as the son of one of His devotees, just as Lord Kṛṣṇa appeared as the son of Yaśodā and Nanda Mahārāja. These devotees could never think of their son as the Supreme Personality of Godhead, for such appreciation would hamper their relationship of paternal love.

TEXT 5

**विदितानुरागमापौरप्रकृति जनपदो राजा नाभिरात्मजं समयसेतु-
रक्षायामभिषिच्य ब्राह्मणेषूपनिधाय सह मेरुदेव्या विशालायां प्रसन्न-
निपुणेन तपसा समाधियोगेन नरनारायणाख्यं भगवन्तं वासुदेवमुपासीनः
कालेन तन्महिमानमवाप ॥ ५ ॥**

viditānurāgam āpaura-prakṛti jana-pado rājā nābhir ātmajaṁ samaya-setu-rakṣāyām abhiṣicya brāhmaṇeṣūpanidhāya saha merudevyā viśālāyāṁ prasanna-nipuṇena tapasā samādhi-yogena nara-nārāyaṇākhyaṁ bhagavantaṁ vāsudevam upāsīnaḥ kālena tan-mahimānam avāpa.

vidita—known very well; *anurāgam*—popularity; *āpaura-prakṛti*—among all the citizens and government officers; *jana-padaḥ*—desiring to serve the people in general; *rājā*—the King; *nābhiḥ*—Nābhi; *ātmajam*—his son; *samaya-setu-rakṣāyām*—to protect the people strictly according to the Vedic principles of religious life; *abhiṣicya*—enthroning; *brāhmaṇeṣu*—to the learned *brāhmaṇas;* *upanidhāya*—entrusting; *saha*—with; *merudevyā*—his wife, Merudevī; *viśālāyām*—in Badarikāśrama; *prasanna-nipuṇena*—performed with great satisfaction and expertise; *tapasā*—by austerities and penances; *samādhi-yogena*—by full *samādhi; nara-nārāyaṇa-ākhyam*—named Nara-Nārāyaṇa; *bhagavantam*—the Supreme Personality of Godhead; *vāsudevam*—Kṛṣṇa; *upāsīnaḥ*—worshiping; *kālena*—in due course of time; *tat-mahimānam*—His glorious abode, the spiritual world, Vaikuṇṭha; *avāpa*—achieved.

TRANSLATION

King Nābhi understood that his son, Ṛṣabhadeva, was very popular among the citizens and among government officers and ministers. Understanding the popularity of his son, Mahārāja Nābhi enthroned Him as the emperor of the world to give protection to the general populace in terms of the Vedic religious system. To do this, he entrusted Him into the hands of learned brāhmaṇas, who would guide Him in administrating the government. Then Mahārāja Nābhi and his wife, Merudevī, went to Badarikāśrama in the Himalaya Mountains, where the King engaged Himself very expertly in austerities and penances with great jubilation. In full samādhi he worshiped the Supreme Personality of Godhead, Nara-Nārāyaṇa, who is Kṛṣṇa in His plenary expansion. By doing so, in course of time Mahārāja Nābhi was elevated to the spiritual world known as Vaikuṇṭha.

PURPORT

When Mahārāja Nābhi saw that his son Ṛṣabhadeva was popular with the general populace and the governmental servants, he chose to install Him on the imperial throne. In addition, he wanted to entrust his son into the hands of the learned *brāhmaṇas.* This means that a monarch was supposed to govern strictly according to Vedic principles under the guidance of learned *brāhmaṇas,* who could advise Him according to the standard Vedic scriptures like *Manu-smṛti* and similar *śāstras.* It is the duty of the king to rule the citizens according to Vedic principles. According to Vedic principles, society is divided into four categories—*brāhmaṇa, kṣatriya, vaiśya* and *śūdra. Cātur-varṇyaṁ .nayā sṛṣṭaṁ guṇa-karma-vibhāgaśaḥ.* After dividing society in this way, it is the king's duty to see that everyone executes Vedic principles according to his caste. A *brāhmaṇa* must perform the duty of a *brāhmaṇa* without cheating the public. It is not that one attains the name of a *brāhmaṇa* without the qualifications. It is the king's duty to see that everyone engages in his occupational duty according to Vedic principles. In addition, retirement at the end of life is compulsory. Mahārāja Nābhi, although still a king, retired from family life and went with his wife to a place called Badarikāśrama in the Himalayas, where the Deity Nara-Nārāyaṇa is worshiped. The words *prasanna-nipuṇena tapasā* indicate that the King accepted all kinds of austerity very expertly and jubilantly. He did not at all mind leaving his comfortable life at home, although he was the emperor. Despite undergoing severe austerities and penances, he felt very pleased at Badarikāśrama, and he did everything there expertly. In this way, being fully absorbed in Kṛṣṇa consciousness (*samādhi-yoga*), always thinking of Kṛṣṇa, Vāsudeva, Mahārāja Nābhi attained success at the end of his life and was promoted to the spiritual world, Vaikuṇṭhaloka.

This is the way of Vedic life. One must stop the process of repeated birth and death and return home, back to Godhead. The words *tan-mahimānam avāpa* are significant in this regard. Śrīla Śrīdhara Svāmī says that *mahimā* means liberation in this life. We should act in such a way in this life that after giving up this body, we will become liberated from the bondage of repeated birth and death. This is called *jīvan-mukti.* Śrīla Vīrarāghava Ācārya states that in the *Chāndogya Upaniṣad* there are eight symptoms of a *jīvan-mukta,* a person who is already liberated even when living in this body. The first symptom of one so liberated is that he is freed from all sinful activity (*apahata-pāpa*). As long as one is under the clutches of *māyā* in the material energy, one has to engage in sinful activity. *Bhagavad-gītā* describes such people as *duṣkṛtinaḥ,* which indicates that they are always engaged in sinful activity. One who is liberated in this life does not commit any sinful activities. Sinful activity involves illicit sex, meat-eating, intoxication and gambling. Another symptom of a liberated person is *vijara,* which indicates that he is not subjected to the miseries of old age. Another symptom is *vimṛtyu.* A liberated person prepares himself in such a way that he does not take on any more material bodies, which are destined to die. In other words, he does not fall down again to repeat birth and death. Another symptom is *viśoka,* which indicates that he is callous to material distress and happiness. Another is *vijighatsa,* which indicates that he no longer desires material enjoyment. Another symptom is *apipātā,* which means that he has no desire other than to engage in the devotional service of Kṛṣṇa, his dearmost pursuable Lord. A further symptom is *satya-kāma,* which indicates that all his desires are directed to the Supreme Truth, Kṛṣṇa. He does not want anything else. He is *satya-saṅkalpa.* Whatever he desires is fulfilled by the grace of Kṛṣṇa. First of all, he does not desire anything for his material benefit, and secondly if he desires anything at all, he simply desires to serve the Supreme Lord. That desire is fulfilled by the Lord's grace. That is called *satya-saṅkalpa.* Śrīla Viśvanātha Cakravartī points out that the word *mahimā* means returning to the spiritual world, back home, back to Vaikuṇṭha. Śrī Śukadeva says that the word *mahimā* means that the devotee attains the qualities of the Supreme Personality of Godhead. This is called *sadharma,* or "the same quality." Just as Kṛṣṇa is never born and never dies, His devotees who return to Godhead never die and never take birth within the material world.

TEXT 6

यस्य ह पाण्डवेय श्लोकावुदाहरन्ति—
को नु तत्कर्म राजर्षेर्नाभेरन्वाचरेत्पुमान् ।
अपत्यतामगाद्यस्य हरिः शुद्धेन कर्मणा ॥ ६ ॥

yasya ha pāṇḍaveya ślokāv udāharanti—
ko nu tat karma rājarṣer
nābher anv ācaret pumān
apatyatām agād yasya
hariḥ śuddhena karmaṇā

yasya—of whom; *ha*—indeed; *pāṇḍaveya*—O Mahārāja Parīkṣit; *ślokau*—two verses; *udāharanti*—recite; *kaḥ*—who; *nu*—then; *tat*—that; *karma*—work; *rāja-ṛṣeḥ*—of the pious King; *nābheḥ*—Nābhi; *anu*—following; *ācaret*—could execute; *pumān*—a man; *apatyatām*—sonhood; *agāt*—accepted; *yasya*—whose; *hariḥ*—the Supreme Personality of Godhead; *śuddhena*—pure, executed in devotional service; *karmaṇā*—by activities.

TRANSLATION

O Mahārāja Parīkṣit, to glorify Mahārāja Nābhi, the old sages composed two verses. One of them is this: "Who can attain the perfection of Mahārāja Nābhi? Who can attain his activities? Because of his devotional service, the Supreme Personality of Godhead agreed to become his son."

PURPORT

The words *śuddhena karmaṇā* are significant in this verse. If work is not carried out in devotional service, it is contaminated by the modes of material nature. That is explained in *Bhagavad-gītā: yajñārthāt karmaṇo 'nyatra loko 'yaṁ karma-bandhanaḥ.* Activities performed only for the satisfaction of the Supreme Lord are pure and are not contaminated by the modes of material nature. All other activities are contaminated by the modes of ignorance and passion, as well as goodness. All material activities meant for satisfying the senses are contaminated, and Mahārāja Nābhi did not perform anything contaminated. He simply executed his transcendental activities even when performing *yajña.* Consequently he obtained the Supreme Lord as his son.

TEXT 7

ब्रह्मण्योऽन्यः कुतो नाभेर्विप्रा मङ्गलपूजिताः ।
यस्य बर्हिषि यज्ञेशं दर्शयामासुरोजसा ॥ ७ ॥

brahmaṇyo 'nyaḥ kuto nābher
viprā maṅgala-pūjitāḥ
yasya barhiṣi yajñeśaṁ
darśayām āsur ojasā

brahmaṇyaḥ—a devotee of the *brāhmaṇas; anyaḥ*—any other: *kutaḥ*—where is; *nābheḥ*—besides Mahārāja Nābhi; *viprāḥ*—the *brāhmaṇas; maṅgala-pūjitāḥ*—well worshiped and satisfied: *yasya*—of whom; *barhiṣi*—in the sacrificial arena; *yajña-īśam*—the Supreme Personality of Godhead, the enjoyer of all sacrificial ceremonies: *darśayām āsuḥ*—showed; *ojasā*—by their brahminical prowess.

TRANSLATION

[The second prayer is this.] "Who is a better worshiper of brāhmaṇas than Mahārāja Nābhi? Because he worshiped the qualified brāhmaṇas to their full satisfaction, the brāhmaṇas, by their brahminical prowess, showed Mahārāja Nābhi the Supreme Personality of Godhead, Nārāyaṇa, in person."

PURPORT

The *brāhmaṇas* engaged as priests in the sacrificial ceremony were not ordinary *brāhmaṇas.* They were so powerful that they could bring forth the Supreme Personality of Godhead by their prayers. Thus Mahārāja Nābhi was able to see the Lord face to face. Unless one is a Vaiṣṇava, he cannot call forth the Supreme Personality of Godhead. The Lord does not accept an invitation unless one is a Vaiṣṇava. Therefore it is said in *Padma Purāṇa:*

ṣaṭ-karma-nipuṇo vipro
mantra-tantra-viśāradaḥ
avaiṣṇavo gurur na syād
vaiṣṇavaḥ śva-paco guruḥ

"A scholarly *brāhmaṇa* expert in all subjects of Vedic knowledge is unfit to become a spiritual master without being a Vaiṣṇava, but a person born in a family of a lower caste can become a spiritual master if he is a Vaiṣṇava." These *brāhmaṇas* were certainly very expert in chanting the Vedic *mantras.* They were competent in the performance of the Vedic rituals, and over and above this they were Vaiṣṇavas. Therefore by their spiritual powers they could call on the Supreme Personality of Godhead and enable their disciple, Mahārāja Nābhi, to see the Lord face to face. Śrīla Viśvanātha Cakravartī Ṭhākura comments that the word *ojasā* means "by dint of devotional service."

TEXT 8

अथ ह भगवानृषभदेवः स्ववर्षं कर्मक्षेत्रमनुमन्यमानः प्रदर्शितगुरुकुल-
वासो लब्धवरैर्गुरुभिरनुज्ञातो गृहमेधिनां धर्माननुशिक्षमाणो जयन्त्यामिन्द्र-

दत्तायामुभयलक्षणं कर्म समाम्नायाम्नातमभियुञ्जन्नात्मजानामात्मसमानानां शतं जनयामास ॥ ८ ॥

atha ha bhagavān ṛṣabhadevaḥ sva-varṣaṁ karma-kṣetram anumanyamānaḥ pradarśita-gurukula-vāso labdha-varair gurubhir anujñāto gṛhamedhināṁ dharmān anuśikṣamāṇo jayantyām indra-dattāyām ubhaya-lakṣaṇaṁ karma samāmnāyāmnātam abhiyuñjann ātmajānām ātma-samānānāṁ śataṁ janayām āsa.

atha—thereupon (after the departure of his father); *ha*—indeed; *bhagavān*—the Supreme Personality of Godhead; *ṛṣabha-devaḥ*—Ṛṣabhadeva; *sva*—His own; *varṣam*—kingdom; *karma-kṣetram*—the field of activities; *anumanyamānaḥ*—accepting as; *pradarśita*—shown as an example; *guru-kula-vāsaḥ*—lived at the *gurukula; labdha*—having achieved; *varaiḥ*—gifts; *gurubhiḥ*—by the spiritual masters; *anujñātaḥ*—being ordered; *gṛha-medhinām*—of the householders; *dharmān*—duties; *anuśikṣamāṇaḥ*—teaching by example; *jayantyām*—in His wife, Jayantī; *indra-dattāyām*—offered by Lord Indra; *ubhaya-lakṣaṇam*—of both types; *karma*—activities; *samāmnāyāmnātam*—mentioned in the scriptures; *abhiyuñjan*—performing; *ātmajānām*—sons; *ātma-samānānām*—exactly like Himself; *śatam*—one hundred; *janayām āsa*—begot.

TRANSLATION

After Nābhi Mahārāja departed for Badarikāśrama, the Supreme Lord, Ṛṣabhadeva, understood that His kingdom was His field of activities. He therefore showed Himself as an example and taught the duties of a householder by first accepting brahmacarya under the direction of spiritual masters. He also went to live at the spiritual masters' place, gurukula. After His education was finished, He gave gifts (guru-dakṣiṇā) to His spiritual masters and then accepted the life of a householder. He took a wife named Jayantī and begot one hundred sons who were as powerful and qualified as He Himself. His wife Jayantī had been offered to Him by Indra, the King of heaven. Ṛṣabhadeva and Jayantī performed

householder life in an examplary way, carrying out ritualistic activities ordained by the śruti and smṛti śāstra.

PURPORT

Being an incarnation of the Supreme Personality of Godhead, Ṛṣabhadeva had nothing to do with material affairs. As stated in *Bhagavad-gītā, paritrāṇāya sādhūnāṁ vināśāya ca duṣkṛtām:* the purpose of an incarnation is to liberate His devotees and to stop the demoniac activities of nondevotees. These are the two functions of the Supreme Lord when He incarnates. Śrī Caitanya Mahāprabhu has said that in order to preach, one must live a practical life and show people how to do things. *Āpani ācari' bhakti śikhāimu sabāre.* One cannot teach others unless he behaves the same way himself. Ṛṣabhadeva was an ideal king, and He took His education in the *gurukula,* although He was already educated because the Supreme Lord is omniscient. Although Ṛṣabhadeva had nothing to learn from *gurukula,* He went there just to teach the people in general how to take an education from the right source, from Vedic teachers. He then entered householder life and lived according to the principles of Vedic knowledge—*śruti* and *smṛti.* In his *Bhakti-rasāmṛta-sindhu* (1.2.10) Śrīla Rūpa Gosvāmī, quoting the *Skanda Purāṇa,* states:

śruti-smṛti-purāṇādi-
pañcarātra-vidhiṁ vinā
aikāntikī harer bhaktir
utpātāyaiva kalpate

Human society must follow the instructions received from *śruti* and *smṛti,* Vedic literature. Practically applied in life this is worship of the Supreme Personality of Godhead according to the *pāñcarātrika-vidhi.* Every human being must advance his spiritual life and at the end return home, back to Godhead. Mahārāja Ṛṣabhadeva strictly followed all these principles. He remained an ideal *gṛhastha* and taught His sons how to become perfect in spiritual life. These are some examples of how He ruled the earth and completed His mission as an incarnation.

TEXT 9

येषां खलु महायोगी भरतो ज्येष्ठः श्रेष्ठगुण आसीद्येनेदं वर्षं भारतमिति व्यपदिशन्ति ॥ ९ ॥

yeṣāṁ khalu mahā-yogī bharato jyeṣṭhaḥ śreṣṭha-guṇa āsīd yenedaṁ varṣaṁ bhāratam iti vyapadiśanti.

yeṣām—of whom; *khalu*—indeed; *mahā-yogī*—a very highly exalted devotee of the Lord; *bharataḥ*—Bharata; *jyeṣṭhaḥ*—the eldest; *śreṣṭha-guṇaḥ*—qualified with the best attributes; *āsīt*—was; *yena*—by whom; *idam*—this; *varṣam*—planet; *bhāratam*—Bhārata; *iti*—thus; *vyapadiśanti*—people call.

TRANSLATION

Of Ṛṣabhadeva's one hundred sons, the eldest, named Bharata, was a great, exalted devotee qualified with the best attributes. In his honor, this planet has become known as Bhārata-varṣa.

PURPORT

This planet known as Bhārata-varṣa is also called *puṇya-bhūmi*, the pious land. At the present moment Bhārata-bhūmi, or Bhārata-varṣa, is a small piece of land extending from the Himalaya Mountains to Cape Comorin. Sometimes this peninsula is called *puṇya-bhūmi*. Śrī Caitanya Mahāprabhu has given special importance to the people of this land.

bhārata-bhūmite haila manuṣya-janma yāra
janma sārthaka kari' kara para-upakāra

"One who has taken his birth as a human being in the land of India (Bhārata-varṣa) should make his life successful and work for the benefit of all other people." (Cc. *Ādi* 9.41) The inhabitants of this piece of land are very fortunate. They can purify their existence by accepting this Kṛṣṇa consciousness movement and go outside Bhārata-bhūmi (India) and preach this cult to benefit the whole world.

TEXT 10

तमनु कुशावर्त इलावर्तो ब्रह्मावर्तो मलयः केतुर्भद्रसेन इन्द्रस्पृग्विदर्भः कीकट इति नव नवति प्रधानाः ॥ १० ॥

tam anu kuśāvarta ilāvarto brahmāvarto malayaḥ ketur bhadrasena indrasprg vidarbhaḥ kīkaṭa iti nava navati pradhānāḥ.

tam—him; *anu*—following; *kuśāvarta*—Kuśāvarta; *ilāvartaḥ*—Ilāvarta; *brahmāvartaḥ*—Brahmāvarta; *malayaḥ*—Malaya; *ketuḥ*—Ketu; *bhadra-senaḥ*—Bhadrasena; *indra-spṛk*—Indraspṛk; *vidarbhaḥ*—Vidarbha; *kīkaṭaḥ*—Kīkaṭa; *iti*—thus; *nava*—nine; *navati*—ninety; *pradhānāḥ*—older than.

TRANSLATION

Following Bharata, there were ninety-nine other sons. Among these were nine elderly sons, named Kuśāvarta, Ilāvarta, Brahmāvarta, Malaya, Ketu, Bhadrasena, Indraspṛk, Vidarbha and Kīkaṭa.

TEXTS 11-12

कविर्हविरन्तरिक्षः प्रबुद्धः पिप्पलायनः ।
आविर्होत्रोऽथ द्रुमिलश्चमसः करभाजनः ॥११॥

इति भागवतधर्मदर्शना नव महाभागवतास्तेषां सुचरितं भगवन्महिमोपबृंहितं वसुदेवनारदसंवादमुपशमायनमुपरिष्टाद्वर्णयिष्यामः ॥ १२ ॥

kavir havir antarikṣaḥ
prabuddhaḥ pippalāyanaḥ
āvirhotro 'tha drumilaś
camasaḥ karabhājanaḥ

iti bhāgavata-dharma-darśanā nava mahā-bhāgavatās teṣāṁ sucaritaṁ bhagavan-mahimopabṛṁhitaṁ vasudeva-nārada-saṁvādam upaśamāyanam upariṣṭād varṇayiṣyāmaḥ.

kaviḥ—Kavi; *haviḥ*—Havi; *antarikṣaḥ*—Antarikṣa; *prabuddhaḥ*—Prabuddha; *pippalāyanaḥ*—Pippalāyana; *āvirhotraḥ*—Āvirhotra; *atha*—also; *drumilaḥ*—Drumila; *camasaḥ*—Camasa; *karabhājanaḥ*—Karabhājana; *iti*—thus; *bhāgavata-dharma-darśanāḥ*—authorized preachers of *Śrīmad-Bhāgavatam; nava*—nine; *mahā-bhāgavatāḥ*—highly advanced devotees; *teṣām*—of them; *sucaritam*—good characteristics; *bhagavat-mahimā-upabṛṁhitam*—accompanied by the glories of the Supreme Lord; *vasudeva-nārada-saṁvādam*—within the conversation between Vasudeva and Nārada; *upaśamāyanam*—which gives full satisfaction to the mind; *upariṣṭāt*—hereafter (in the Eleventh Canto); *varṇayiṣyāmaḥ*—I shall vividly explain.

TRANSLATION

In addition to these sons were Kavi, Havi, Antarikṣa, Prabuddha, Pippalāyana, Āvirhotra, Drumila, Camasa and Karabhājana. These were all very exalted, advanced devotees and authorized preachers of Śrīmad-Bhāgavatam. These devotees were glorified due to their strong devotion to Vāsudeva, the Supreme Personality of Godhead. Therefore they were very exalted. To satisfy the mind perfectly, I [Śukadeva Gosvāmī] shall hereafter describe the characteristics of these nine devotees when I discuss the conversation between Nārada and Vasudeva.

TEXT 13

यवीयांस एकाशीतिर्जायन्तेयाः पितुरादेशकरा महाशालीना महाश्रोत्रिया यज्ञशीलाः कर्मविशुद्धा ब्राह्मणा बभूवुः ॥ १३ ॥

yavīyāṁsa ekāśītir jāyanteyāḥ pitur ādeśakarā mahā-śālīnā mahā-śrotriyā yajña-śīlāḥ karma-viśuddhā brāhmaṇā babhūvuḥ.

yavīyāṁsaḥ—younger; *ekāśītiḥ*—numbering eighty-one; *jāyanteyāḥ*—the sons of Jayantī, the wife of Ṛṣabhadeva; *pituḥ*—of their father; *ādeśakarāḥ*—following the order; *mahā-śālīnāḥ*—well behaved, well cultured; *mahā-śrotriyāḥ*—extremely learned in Vedic knowledge; *yajña-śīlāḥ*—expert in performing ritualistic ceremonies; *karma-viśud-*

dhāḥ—very pure in their activities; *brāhmaṇāḥ*—qualified *brāhmaṇas; babhūvuḥ*—became.

TRANSLATION

In addition to these nineteen sons mentioned above, there were eighty-one younger ones, all born of Ṛṣabhadeva and Jayantī. According to the order of their father, they became well cultured, well behaved, very pure in their activities and expert in Vedic knowledge and the performance of Vedic rituals. Thus they all became perfectly qualified brāhmaṇas.

PURPORT

From this verse we have good information of how the castes are qualified according to quality and work. Ṛṣabhadeva, a king, was certainly a *kṣatriya.* He had a hundred sons, and out of these, ten were engaged as *kṣatriyas* and ruled the planet. Nine sons became good preachers of *Śrīmad-Bhāgavatam* (*mahā-bhāgavatas*), and this indicates that they were above the position of *brāhmaṇas.* The other eighty-one sons became highly qualified *brāhmaṇas.* These are some practical examples of how one can become fit for a certain type of activity by qualification, not by birth. All the sons of Mahārāja Ṛṣabhadeva were *kṣatriyas* by birth, but by quality some of them became *kṣatriyas*, and some became *brāhmaṇas.* Nine became preachers of *Śrīmad-Bhāgavatam* (*bhāgavata-dharma-darśanāḥ*), which means that they were above the categories of *kṣatriya* and *brāhmaṇa.*

TEXT 14

भगवानृषभसंज्ञ आत्मतन्त्रः स्वयं नित्यनिवृत्तानर्थपरम्परः
केवलानन्दानुभव ईश्वर एव विपरीतवत्कर्माण्यारभमाणः कालेनानुगतं
धर्ममाचरणेनोपशिक्षयन्नतद्विदां सम उपशान्तो मैत्रः कारुणिको धर्मार्थ-
यशःप्रजानन्दामृतावरोधेन गृहेषु लोकं नियमयत् ॥ १४ ॥

bhagavān ṛṣabha-saṁjña ātma-tantraḥ svayaṁ nitya-nivṛttānartha-paramparaḥ kevalānandānubhava īśvara eva viparītavat karmāṇy ārabhamāṇaḥ kālenānugataṁ dharmam ācaraṇenopaśikṣayann atad-vidāṁ sama upaśānto maitraḥ kāruṇiko dharmārtha-yaśaḥ-prajānan-dāmṛtāvarodhena gṛheṣu lokaṁ niyamayat.

bhagavān—the Supreme Personality of Godhead; *ṛṣabha*—Ṛṣabha; *saṁjñaḥ*—named; *ātma-tantraḥ*—fully independent; *svayam*—personally; *nitya*—eternally; *nivṛtta*—free from; *anartha*—of things not wanted (birth, old age, disease and death); *paramparaḥ*—the continual succession, one after another; *kevala*—only; *ānanda-anubhavaḥ*—full of transcendental bliss; *īśvaraḥ*—the Supreme Lord, the controller; *eva*—indeed; *viparīta-vat*—just like the opposite; *karmāṇi*—material activities; *ārabhamāṇaḥ*—performing; *kālena*—in course of time; *anugatam*—neglected; *dharmam*—the *varṇāśrama-dharma; ācaraṇena*—by executing; *upaśikṣayan*—teaching; *a-tat-vidām*—persons who are in ignorance; *samaḥ*—equipoised; *upaśāntaḥ*—undisturbed by the material senses; *maitraḥ*—very friendly to everyone; *kāruṇikaḥ*—very merciful to all; *dharma*—religious principles; *artha*—economic development; *yaśaḥ*—reputation; *prajā*—sons and daughters; *ānanda*—material pleasure; *amṛta*—eternal life; *avarodhena*—for achieving; *gṛheṣu*—in household life; *lokam*—the people in general; *niyamayat*—He regulated.

TRANSLATION

Being an incarnation of the Supreme Personality of Godhead, Lord Ṛṣabhadeva was fully independent because His form was spiritual, eternal and full of transcendental bliss. He eternally had nothing to do with the four principles of material misery [birth, death, old age and disease]. Nor was He materially attached. He was always equipoised, and He saw everyone on the same level. He was unhappy to see others unhappy, and He was the well-wisher of all living entities. Although He was a perfect personality, the Supreme Lord and controller of all, He nonetheless acted as if He were an ordinary conditioned soul. Therefore He strictly followed the principles of varṇāśrama-dharma and acted accordingly. In due course of time, the principles of varṇāśrama-dharma had become neglected; therefore through His personal characteristics and behavior, He taught the ignorant public how to perform duties

within the varṇāśrama-dharma. In this way He regulated the general populace in householder life, enabling them to develop religion and economic well-being and to attain reputations, sons and daughters, material pleasure and finally eternal life. By His instructions, He showed how people could remain householders and at the same time become perfect by following the principles of varṇāśrama-dharma.

PURPORT

The *varṇāśrama-dharma* is meant for imperfect, conditioned souls. It trains them to become spiritually advanced in order to return home, back to Godhead. A civilization that does not know the highest aim of life is no better than an animal society. As stated in *Śrīmad-Bhāgavatam: na te viduḥ svārtha-gatiṁ hi viṣṇum.* A human society is meant for elevation to spiritual knowledge so that all of the people can be freed from the clutches of birth, death, old age and disease. The *varṇāśrama-dharma* enables human society to become perfectly fit for getting out of the clutches of *māyā*, and by following the regulative principles of *varṇāśrama-dharma*, one can become successful. In this regard, see *Bhagavad-gītā* (3.21-24).

TEXT 15

यद्यच्छीर्षण्याचरितं तत्तदनुवर्तते लोकः॥ १५॥

yad yac chīrṣaṇyācaritaṁ tat tad anuvartate lokaḥ.

yat yat—whatever; *śīrṣaṇya*—by the leading personalities; *ācaritam*—performed; *tat tat*—that; *anuvartate*—follow; *lokaḥ*—the people in general.

TRANSLATION

Whatever action is performed by a great man, common men follow.

PURPORT

A similar verse is also found in *Bhagavad-gītā* (3.21). It is essential for human society to have a section of men perfectly trained as qualified *brāhmaṇas* according to the instructions of Vedic knowledge. Those below the brahminical qualification—administrators, merchants and workers—should take instructions from those ideal people who are considered to be intellectuals. In this way, everyone can be elevated to the highest transcendental position and be freed from material attachment. The material world is described by Lord Kṛṣṇa Himself as *duḥkhālayam aśāśvatam*, a temporary place of misery. No one can stay here, even if he makes a compromise with misery. One has to give up this body and accept another, which may not even be a human body. As soon as one gets a material body, he becomes *deha-bhṛt*, or *dehī*. In other words, he is subjected to all the material conditions. The leaders of society must be so ideal that by following them one can be relieved from the clutches of material existence.

TEXT 16

यद्यपि स्वविदितं सकलधर्मं ब्राह्मं गुह्यं ब्राह्मणैर्दर्शितमार्गेण सामादिभिरुपायै-र्जनतामनुशशास ॥१६॥

yadyapi sva-viditaṁ sakala-dharmaṁ brāhmaṁ guhyaṁ brāhmaṇair darśita-mārgeṇa sāmādibhir upāyair janatām anuśaśāsa.

yadyapi—although; *sva-viditam*—known by Him; *sakala-dharmam*—which includes all different types of occupational duties; *brāhmam*—Vedic instruction; *guhyam*—very confidential; *brāhmaṇaiḥ*—by the *brāhmaṇas; darśita-mārgeṇa*—by the path showed; *sāma-ādibhiḥ*—*sāma, dama, titikṣā* (controlling the mind, controlling the senses, practicing tolerance) and so on; *upāyaiḥ*—by the means; *janatām*—the people in general; *anuśaśāsa*—he ruled over.

TRANSLATION

Although Lord Ṛṣabhadeva knew everything about confidential Vedic knowledge, which includes information about all types of occupational duties, He still maintained Himself as a kṣatriya and followed the instructions of the brāhmaṇas as they related to mind control, sense control, tolerance and so forth. Thus He ruled the people according to the system of varṇāśrama-dharma, which

enjoins that the brāhmaṇas instruct the kṣatriyas and the kṣatriyas administer to the state through the vaiśyas and śūdras.

PURPORT

Although Ṛṣabhadeva knew all the Vedic instructions perfectly well, He nonetheless followed the instructions of the *brāhmaṇas* in order to perfectly maintain the social order. The *brāhmaṇas* would give advice according to the *śāstras*, and all the other castes would follow. The word *brahma* means "perfect knowledge of all activities," and this knowledge is very confidentially described in the Vedic literatures. Men trained perfectly as *brāhmaṇas* should know all Vedic literature, and the benefit derived from this literature should be distributed to the general populace. The general populace should follow the perfect *brāhmaṇa.* In this way, one can learn how to control the mind and senses and thus gradually advance to spiritual perfection.

TEXT 17

द्रव्यदेशकालवयःश्रद्धर्त्विग्विविधोद्देशोपचितैः सर्वैरपि क्रतुभिर्यथोपदेशं
शतकृत्व इयाज ॥ १७ ॥

dravya-deśa-kāla-vayaḥ-śraddhartvig-vividhoddeśopacitaiḥ sarvair api kratubhir yathopadeśaṁ śata-kṛtva iyāja.

dravya—the ingredients for performing *yajña; deśa*—the particular place, a holy place or a temple; *kāla*—the suitable time, such as springtime; *vayaḥ*—the age, especially youth; *śraddhā*—faith in goodness, not in passion and ignorance; *ṛtvik*—the priests; *vividha-uddeśa*—worshiping different demigods for different purposes; *upacitaiḥ*—enriched by; *sarvaiḥ*—all kinds of; *api*—certainly; *kratubhiḥ*—by sacrificial ceremonies; *yathā-upadeśam*—according to the instruction; *śata-kṛtvaḥ*—one hundred times; *iyāja*—He worshiped.

TRANSLATION

Lord Ṛṣabhadeva performed all kinds of sacrifices one hundred times according to the instructions of the Vedic literatures. Thus He satisfied Lord Viṣṇu in every respect. All the rituals were

enriched by first-class ingredients. They were executed in holy places according to the proper time by priests who were all young and faithful. In this way Lord Viṣṇu was worshiped, and the prasāda was offered to all the demigods. Thus the functions and festivals were all successful.

PURPORT

It is said, *kaumāra ācaret prājño dharmān bhāgavatān iha* (*Bhāg.* 7.6.1). A ritual should be performed by young men, even boys, at a tender age in order for the ritual to be performed successfully. From childhood, people should be trained in Vedic culture, especially in devotional service. In this way, one can perfect one's life. A Vaiṣṇava does not disrespect the demigods, but on the other hand he is not so foolish that he accepts each and every demigod as the Supreme Lord. The Supreme Lord is master of all demigods; therefore the demigods are His servants. The Vaiṣṇava accepts them as servants of the Supreme Lord, and he worships them directly. In the *Brahma-saṁhitā,* the important demigods—Lord Śiva, Lord Brahmā and even the incarnations and expansions of Lord Kṛṣṇa like Mahā-Viṣṇu, Garbhodakaśāyī Viṣṇu and all the other *viṣṇu-tattvas,* as well as the *śakti-tattvas* like Durgādevī—are all worshiped by the process of worshiping Govinda with the words *govindam ādi-puruṣaṁ tam ahaṁ bhajāmi.* A Vaiṣṇava worships the demigods in relation to Govinda, not independently. Vaiṣṇavas are not so foolish that they consider the demigods independent of the Supreme Personality of Godhead. This is confirmed in *Caitanya-caritāmṛta. Ekale īśvara kṛṣṇa, āra saba bhṛtya:* the supreme master is Kṛṣṇa, and all others are His servants.

TEXT 18

भगवतर्षभेण परिरक्ष्यमाण एतस्मिन् वर्षे न कश्चन पुरुषो वाञ्छत्य-
विद्यमानमिवात्मनोऽन्यस्मात्कथञ्चन किमपि कर्हिचिदवेक्षते भर्तर्यनुसवनं
विजृम्भितस्नेहातिशयमन्तरेण ॥ १८ ॥

bhagavatarṣabheṇa parirakṣyamāṇa etasmin varṣe na kaścana puruṣo
vāñchaty avidyamānam ivātmano 'nyasmāt kathañcana kimapi
karhicid avekṣate bhartary anusavanaṁ vijṛmbhita-snehātiśayam antareṇa.

bhagavatā—by the Supreme Personality of Godhead; *ṛṣabheṇa*—King Ṛṣabha; *parirakṣyamāṇe*—being protected; *etasmin*—on this; *varṣe*—planet; *na*—not; *kaścana*—anyone; *puruṣaḥ*—even a common man; *vāñchati*—desires; *avidyamānam*—not existing in reality; *iva*—as if; *ātmanaḥ*—for himself; *anyasmāt*—from anyone else; *kathañcana*—by any means; *kimapi*—anything; *karhicit*—at any time; *avekṣate*—does care to see; *bhartari*—toward the master; *anusavanam*—always; *vijṛmbhita*—expanding; *sneha-atiśayam*—very great affection; *antareṇa*—within one's self.

TRANSLATION

No one likes to possess anything that is like a will-o'-the-wisp or a flower in the sky, for everyone knows very well that such things do not exist. When Lord Ṛṣabhadeva ruled this planet of Bhārata-varṣa, even common men did not want to ask for anything, at any time or by any means. No one ever asks for a will-o'-the-wisp. In other words, everyone was completely satisfied, and therefore there was no chance of anyone's asking for anything. The people were absorbed in great affection for the King. Since this affection was always expanding, they were not inclined to ask for anything.

PURPORT

In Bengal the word *ghoḍā-ḍimba* is used, which means "the egg of a horse." Since a horse never lays an egg, the word *ghoḍā-ḍimba* actually has no meaning. In Sanskrit there is a word *kha-puṣpa*, which means "the flower in the sky." No flower grows in the sky; therefore no one is interested in asking for *kha-puṣpa* or *ghoḍā-ḍimba*. During the reign of Mahārāja Ṛṣabhadeva, people were so well equipped that they did not want to ask for anything. They were immensely supplied with all necessities for life due to King Ṛṣabhadeva's good government. Consequently everyone felt full satisfaction and did not want anything. This is the perfection of government. If the citizens are unhappy due to bad government, the heads of government are condemned. During these democratic days, monarchy is disliked by the people, but here is an example of how an emperor of the whole world kept all the citizens fully satisfied by supplying the necessities of life and following the Vedic principles. Thus everyone was happy during the reign of Mahārāja Ṛṣabhadeva, the Supreme Personality of Godhead.

TEXT 19

स कदाचिदटमानो भगवानृषभो ब्रह्मावर्तगतो ब्रह्मर्षिप्रवरसभायां प्रजानां
निशामयन्तीनामात्मजानवहितात्मनः प्रश्रयप्रणयभरसुयन्त्रितानप्युपशिक्ष-
यन्निति होवाच ।१९।

sa kadācid aṭamāno bhagavān ṛṣabho brahmāvarta-gato brahmarṣi-
pravara-sabhāyāṁ prajānāṁ niśāmayantīnām ātmajān avahitātmanaḥ
praśraya-praṇaya-bhara-suyantritān apy upaśikṣayann iti hovāca.

saḥ—He; *kadācit*—once; *aṭamānaḥ*—while on tour; *bhagavān*—the Supreme Personality of Godhead; *ṛṣabhaḥ*—Lord Ṛṣabha; *brahmāvarta-gataḥ*—when He reached the place known as Brahmāvarta (identified by some as Burma and by others as a place near Kanpura, Uttar Pradesh); *brahma-ṛṣi-pravara-sabhāyām*—in a meeting of first-class *brāhmaṇas; prajānām*—while the citizens; *niśāmayantīnām*—were hearing; *ātmajān*—His sons; *avahita-ātmanaḥ*—attentive; *praśraya*—of good behavior; *praṇaya*—of devotion; *bhara*—by an abundance; *su-yantritān*—well controlled; *api*—although; *upaśikṣayan*—teaching; *iti*—thus; *ha*—certainly; *uvāca*—said.

TRANSLATION

Once while touring the world, Lord Ṛṣabhadeva, the Supreme Lord, reached a place known as Brahmāvarta. There was a great conference of learned brāhmaṇas at that place, and all the King's sons attentively heard the instructions of the brāhmaṇas there. At that assembly, within the hearing of the citizens, Ṛṣabhadeva instructed His sons, although they were already very well behaved, devoted and qualified. He instructed them so that in the future they could rule the world very perfectly. Thus he spoke as follows.

PURPORT

The instructions of Lord Ṛṣabhadeva to His sons are very valuable if one wants to live peacefully within this world, which is full of miseries. In the next chapter, Lord Ṛṣabhadeva gives His sons these valuable instructions.

Thus end the Bhaktivedanta purports of the Fifth Canto, Fourth Chapter, of the Śrīmad-Bhāgavatam, *entitled "The Characteristics of Ṛṣabhadeva, the Supreme Personality of Godhead."*

CHAPTER FIVE

Lord Ṛṣabhadeva's Teachings to His Sons

In this chapter there is a description of *bhāgavata-dharma*, religious principles in devotional service that transcend religious principles for liberation and the mitigation of material misery. It is stated in this chapter that a human being should not work hard like dogs and hogs for sense gratification. The human life is especially meant for the revival of our relationship with the Supreme Lord, and to this end all kinds of austerities and penances should be accepted. By austere activities, one's heart can be cleansed of material contamination, and as a result one can be situated on the spiritual platform. To attain this perfection, one has to take shelter of a devotee and serve him. Then the door of liberation will be open. Those who are materially attached to women and sense gratification gradually become entangled in material consciousness and suffer the miseries of birth, old age, disease and death. Those who are engaged in the general welfare of all and who are not attached to children and family are called *mahātmās*. Those who are engaged in sense gratification, who act piously or impiously, cannot understand the purpose of the soul. Therefore they should approach a highly elevated devotee and accept him as a spiritual master. By his association, one will be able to understand the purpose of life. Under the instructions of such a spiritual master, one can attain devotional service to the Lord, detachment from material things, and tolerance of material misery and distress. One can then see all living entities equally, and one becomes very eager to know about transcendental subject matters. Endeavoring persistently for the satisfaction of Kṛṣṇa, one becomes detached from wife, children and home. He is not interested in wasting time. In this way one becomes self-realized. A person advanced in spiritual knowledge does not engage anyone in material activity. And one who cannot deliver another person by instructing him in devotional service should not become a spiritual master, father, mother, demigod or husband. Instructing His one hundred sons, Lord Ṛṣabhadeva advised them to accept their eldest brother, Bharata, as their guide and lord, and thereby serve him. Of all living entities, the *brāhmaṇas* are the best, and above the *brāhmaṇas* the Vaiṣṇavas are situated in an even better position. Serving a Vaiṣṇava means serving the Supreme Personality of Godhead. Thus Śukadeva Gosvāmī describes the characteristics of Bharata Mahārāja and the sacrificial performance executed by Lord Ṛṣabhadeva for the instruction of the general populace.

TEXT 1

ऋषभ उवाच
नायं देहो देहभाजां नृलोके
कष्टान् कामानर्हते विड्भुजां ये ।
तपो दिव्यं पुत्रका येन सत्त्वं
शुद्ध्येद्यस्माद् ब्रह्मसौख्यं त्वनन्तम् ॥ १ ॥

ṛṣabha uvāca
nāyaṁ deho deha-bhājāṁ nṛloke
kaṣṭān kāmān arhate viḍ-bhujāṁ ye
tapo divyaṁ putrakā yena sattvaṁ
śuddhyed yasmād brahma-saukhyaṁ tv anantam

ṛṣabhaḥ uvāca—Lord Ṛṣabhadeva said; *na*—not; *ayam*—this; *dehaḥ*—body; *deha-bhājām*—of all living entities who have accepted material bodies; *nṛ-loke*—in this world; *kaṣṭān*—troublesome; *kāmān*—sense gratification; *arhate*—deserves; *viṭ-bhujām*—of stool-eaters; *ye*—which; *tapaḥ*—austerities and penances; *divyam*—divine; *putrakāḥ*—My dear sons; *yena*—by which; *sattvam*—the heart; *śuddhyet*—becomes purified; *yasmāt*—from which; *brahma-saukhyam*—spiritual happiness; *tu*—certainly; *anantam*—unending.

TRANSLATION

Lord Ṛṣabhadeva told His sons: My dear boys, of all the living entities who have accepted material bodies in this world, one who has been awarded this human form should not work hard day and

night simply for sense gratification, which is available even for dogs and hogs that eat stool. One should engage in penance and austerity to attain the divine position of devotional service. By such activity, one's heart is purified, and when one attains this position, he attains eternal, blissful life, which is transcendental to material happiness and which continues forever.

PURPORT

In this verse Lord Ṛṣabhadeva tells His sons about the importance of human life. The word *deha-bhāk* refers to anyone who accepts a material body, but the living entity who is awarded the human form must act differently from animals. Animals like dogs and hogs enjoy sense gratification by eating stool. After undergoing severe hardships all day, human beings are trying to enjoy themselves at night by eating, drinking, having sex and sleeping. At the same time, they have to properly defend themselves. However, this is not human civilization. Human life means voluntarily practicing suffering for the advancement of spiritual life. There is, of course, suffering in the lives of animals and plants, which are suffering due to their past misdeeds. However, human beings should voluntarily accept suffering in the form of austerities and penances in order to attain the divine life. After attaining the divine life, one can enjoy happiness eternally. After all, every living entity is trying to enjoy happiness, but as long as one is encaged in the material body, he has to suffer different kinds of misery. A higher sense is present in the human form. We should act according to superior advice in order to attain eternal happiness and go back to Godhead.

It is significant in this verse that the government and the natural guardian, the father, should educate subordinates and raise them to Kṛṣṇa consciousness. Devoid of Kṛṣṇa consciousness, every living being suffers in this cycle of birth and death perpetually. To relieve them from this bondage and enable them to become blissful and happy, *bhakti-yoga* should be taught. A foolish civilization neglects to teach people how to rise to the platform of *bhakti-yoga.* Without Kṛṣṇa consciousness, a person is no better than a hog or dog. The instructions of Ṛṣabhadeva are very essential at the present moment. People are being educated and trained to work very hard for sense gratification, and there is no sublime aim in life. A man travels to earn his livelihood, leaving home early in the morning, catching a local train and being packed in a compartment. He has to stand for an hour or two in order to reach his place of business. Then again he takes a bus to get to the office. At the office he works hard from nine to five; then he takes two or three hours to return home. After eating, he has sex and goes to sleep. For all this hardship, his only happiness is a little sex. *Yan maithunādi-gṛhamedhi-sukhaṁ hi tuccham.* Ṛṣabhadeva clearly states that human life is not meant for this kind of existence, which is enjoyed even by dogs and hogs. Indeed, dogs and hogs do not have to work so hard for sex. A human being should try to live in a different way and should not try to imitate dogs and hogs. The alternative is mentioned. Human life is meant for *tapasya,* austerity and penance. By *tapasya,* one can get out of the material clutches. When one is situated in Kṛṣṇa consciousness, devotional service, his happiness is guaranteed eternally. By taking to *bhakti-yoga,* devotional service, one's existence is purified. The living entity is seeking happiness life after life, but he can make a solution to all his problems simply by practicing *bhakti-yoga.* Then he immediately becomes eligible to return home, back to Godhead. As confirmed in *Bhagavad-gītā* (4.9):

janma karma ca me divyam
evaṁ yo vetti tattvataḥ
tyaktvā dehaṁ punar janma
naiti mām eti so 'rjuna

"One who knows the transcendental nature of My appearance and activities does not, upon leaving the body, take his birth again in this material world, but attains My eternal abode, O Arjuna."

TEXT 2

महत्सेवां द्वारमाहुर्विमुक्ते-
स्तमोद्वारं योषितां सङ्गिसङ्गम् ।
महान्तस्ते समचित्ताः प्रशान्ता
विमन्यवः सुहृदः साधवो ये ॥ २ ॥

mahat-sevāṁ dvāram āhur vimuktes
tamo-dvāraṁ yoṣitāṁ saṅgi-saṅgam

mahāntas te sama-cittāḥ praśāntā
vimanyavaḥ suhṛdaḥ sādhavo ye

mahat-sevām—service to the spiritually advanced persons called *mahātmās; dvāram*—the way; *āhuḥ*—they say; *vimukteḥ*—of liberation; *tamaḥ-dvāram*—the way to the dungeon of a dark, hellish condition of life; *yoṣitām*—of women; *saṅgi*—of associates; *saṅgam*—association; *mahāntaḥ*—highly advanced in spiritual understanding; *te*—they; *sama-cittāḥ*—persons who see everyone in a spiritual identity; *praśāntāḥ*—very peaceful, situated in Brahman or Bhagavān; *vimanyavaḥ*—without anger (one must distribute Kṛṣṇa consciousness to persons who are hostile without becoming angry at them); *suhṛdaḥ*—well-wishers of everyone; *sādhavaḥ*—qualified devotees, without abominable behavior; *ye*—they who.

TRANSLATION

One can attain the path of liberation from material bondage only by rendering service to highly advanced spiritual personalities. These personalities are impersonalists and devotees. Whether one wants to merge into the Lord's existence or wants to associate with the Personality of Godhead, one should render service to the mahātmās. For those who are not interested in such activities, who associate with people fond of women and sex, the path to hell is wide open. The mahātmās are equipoised. They do not see any difference between one living entity and another. They are very peaceful and are fully engaged in devotional service. They are devoid of anger, and they work for the benefit of everyone. They do not behave in any abominable way. Such people are known as mahātmās.

PURPORT

The human body is like a junction. One may either take the path of liberation or the path leading to a hellish condition. How one can take these paths is described herein. On the path of liberation, one associates with *mahātmās,* and on the path of bondage one associates with those attached to sense gratification and women. There are two types of *mahātmās*—the impersonalist and the devotee. Although their ultimate goal is different, the process of emancipation is almost the same. Both want eternal happiness. One seeks happiness in impersonal Brahman, and the other seeks happiness in the association of the Supreme Personality of Godhead. As described in the first verse: *brahma-saukhyam.* Brahman means spiritual or eternal; both the impersonalist and the devotee seek eternal blissful life. In any case, it is advised that one become perfect. In the words of *Caitanya-caritāmṛta* (*Madhya* 22.87):

asat-saṅga-tyāga,——ei vaiṣṇava-ācāra
'strī-saṅgī'——eka asādhu, 'kṛṣṇābhakta' āra

To remain unattached to the modes of material nature, one should avoid associating with those who are *asat,* materialistic. There are two kinds of materialists. One is attached to women and sense gratification, and the other is simply a nondevotee. On the positive side is association with *mahātmās,* and on the negative side is the avoidance of nondevotees and women-hunters.

TEXT 3

ये वा मयीशे कृतसौहृदार्था
जनेषु देहम्भरवार्तिकेषु ।
गृहेषु जायात्मजरातिमत्सु
न प्रीतियुक्ता यावदर्थाश्च लोके ॥ ३ ॥

ye vā mayīśe kṛta-sauhṛdārthā
janeṣu dehambhara-vārtikeṣu
gṛheṣu jāyātmaja-rātimatsu
na prīti-yuktā yāvad-arthāś ca loke

ye—those who; *vā*—or; *mayi*—unto Me; *īśe*—the Supreme Personality of Godhead; *kṛta-sauhṛda-arthāḥ*—very eager to develop love (in a relationship of *dāsya, sakhya, vātsalya* or *mādhurya*); *janeṣu*—to people; *dehambhara-vārtikeṣu*—who are interested only in maintaining the body, not in spiritual salvation; *gṛheṣu*—to the home; *jāyā*—wife; *ātma-ja*—children; *rāti*—wealth or friends; *matsu*—consisting of; *na*—

not; *prīti-yuktāḥ*—very attached; *yāvat-arthāḥ*—who live by collecting only as much as required; *ca*—and; *loke*—in the material world.

TRANSLATION

Those who are interested in reviving Kṛṣṇa consciousness and increasing their love of Godhead do not like to do anything that is not related to Kṛṣṇa. They are not interested in mingling with people who are busy maintaining their bodies, eating, sleeping, mating and defending. They are not attached to their homes, although they may be householders. Nor are they attached to wives, children, friends or wealth. At the same time, they are not indifferent to the execution of their duties. Such people are interested in collecting only enough money to keep the body and soul together.

PURPORT

Whether he is an impersonalist or a devotee, one who is actually interested in advancing spiritually should not mingle with those who are simply interested in maintaining the body by means of the so-called advancement of civilization. Those who are interested in spiritual life should not be attached to homely comforts in the company of wife, children, friends and so forth. Even if one is a *gṛhastha* and has to earn his livelihood, he should be satisfied by collecting only enough money to maintain body and soul together. One should not have more than that nor less than that. As indicated herein, a householder should endeavor to earn money for the execution of *bhakti-yoga—śravaṇaṁ kīrtanaṁ viṣṇoḥ smaraṇaṁ pāda-sevanam/ arcanaṁ vandanaṁ dāsyaṁ sakhyam ātma-nivedanam.* A householder should lead such a life that he gets full opportunity to hear and chant. He should worship the Deity at home, observe festivals, invite friends in and give them *prasāda.* A householder should earn money for this purpose, not for sense gratification.

TEXT 4

नूनं प्रमत्तः कुरुते विकर्म
यदिन्द्रियप्रीतय आपृणोति ।

न साधु मन्ये यत आत्मनोऽय-
मसन्नपि क्लेशद आस देहः ॥ ४ ॥

nūnaṁ pramattaḥ kurute vikarma
yad indriya-prītaya āpṛṇoti
na sādhu manye yata ātmano 'yam
asann api kleśada āsa dehaḥ

nūnam—indeed; *pramattaḥ*—mad; *kurute*—performs; *vikarma*—sinful activities forbidden in the scriptures; *yat*—when; *indriya-prītaye*—for sense gratification; *āpṛṇoti*—engages; *na*—not; *sādhu*—befitting; *manye*—I think; *yataḥ*—by which; *ātmanaḥ*—of the soul; *ayam*—this; *asan*—being temporary; *api*—although; *kleśa-daḥ*—giving misery; *āsa*—became possible; *dehaḥ*—the body.

TRANSLATION

When a person considers sense gratification the aim of life, he certainly becomes mad after materialistic living and engages in all kinds of sinful activity. He does not know that due to his past misdeeds he has already received a body which, although temporary, is the cause of his misery. Actually the living entity should not have taken on a material body, but he has been awarded the material body for sense gratification. Therefore I think it not befitting an intelligent man to involve himself again in the activities of sense gratification by which he perpetually gets material bodies one after another.

PURPORT

Begging, borrowing and stealing to live for sense gratification is condemned in this verse because such consciousness leads one to a dark, hellish condition. The four sinful activities are illicit sex, meat-eating, intoxication and gambling. These are the means by which one gets another material body that is full of miseries. In the *Vedas* it is said: *asaṅgo hy ayaṁ puruṣaḥ.* The living entity is not really connected with this material world, but due to his tendency to enjoy the material senses, he is put into the material condition. One should perfect his life by associating with devotees. He should not become further implicated in the material body.

TEXT 5

पराभवस्तावदबोधजातो
यावन्न जिज्ञासत आत्मतत्त्वम् ।
यावत्क्रियास्तावदिदं मनो वै
कर्मात्मकं येन शरीरबन्धः ॥ ५ ॥

parābhavas tāvad abodha-jāto
yāvan na jijñāsata ātma-tattvam
yāvat kriyās tāvad idaṁ mano vai
karmātmakaṁ yena śarīra-bandhaḥ

parābhavaḥ—defeat, misery; *tāvat*—so long; *abodha-jātaḥ*—produced from ignorance; *yāvat*—as long as; *na*—not; *jijñāsate*—inquires about; *ātma-tattvam*—the truth of the self; *yāvat*—as long as; *kriyāḥ*—fruitive activities; *tāvat*—so long; *idam*—this; *manaḥ*—mind; *vai*—indeed; *karma-ātmakam*—absorbed in material activities; *yena*—by which; *śarīra-bandhaḥ*—bondage in this material body.

TRANSLATION

As long as one does not inquire about the spiritual values of life, one is defeated and subjected to miseries arising from ignorance. Be it sinful or pious, karma has its resultant actions. If a person is engaged in any kind of karma, his mind is called karmātmaka, colored with fruitive activity. As long as the mind is impure, consciousness is unclear, and as long as one is absorbed in fruitive activity, he has to accept a material body.

PURPORT

Generally people think that one should act very piously in order to be relieved from misery, but this is not a fact. Even though one engages in pious activity and speculation, he is nonetheless defeated. His only aim should be emancipation from the clutches of *māyā* and all material activities. Speculative knowledge and pious activity do not solve the problems of material life. One should be inquisitive to understand his spiritual position. As stated in *Bhagavad-gītā* (4.37):

yathaidhāṁsi samiddho 'gnir
bhasmasāt kurute 'rjuna
jñānāgniḥ sarva-karmāṇi
bhasmasāt kurute tathā

"As a blazing fire turns firewood to ashes, O Arjuna, so does the fire of knowledge burn to ashes all reactions to material activities."

Unless one understands the self and its activities, one has to be considered in material bondage. In *Śrīmad-Bhāgavatam* (10.2.32) it is also said: *ye 'nye 'ravindākṣa vimukta-māninas tvayy asta-bhāvād aviśud-dha-buddhayaḥ.* A person who doesn't have knowledge of devotional service may think himself liberated, but actually he is not. *Āruhya kṛc-chreṇa paraṁ padaṁ tataḥ patanty adho 'nādṛta-yuṣmad-aṅghrayaḥ:* such people may approach the impersonal Brahman effulgence, but they fall down again into material enjoyment because they have no knowledge of devotional service. As long as one is interested in *karma* and *jñāna,* he continues enduring the miseries of material life—birth, old age, disease and death. *Karmīs* certainly take on one body after another. As far as *jñānīs* are concerned, unless they are promoted to the topmost understanding, they must return to the material world. As explained in *Bhagavad-gītā* (7.19): *bahūnāṁ janmanāṁ ante jñānavān māṁ pra-padyate.* The point is to know Kṛṣṇa, Vāsudeva, as everything and surrender unto Him. *Karmīs* do not know this, but a devotee who is one hundred percent engaged in the devotional service of the Lord knows fully what is *karma* and *jñāna;* therefore a pure devotee is no longer interested in *karma* or *jñāna. Anyābhilāṣitā-śūnyaṁ jñāna-karmādy-anāvṛtam.* The real *bhakta* is untouched by any tinge of *karma* and *jñāna.* His only purpose in life is to serve the Lord.

TEXT 6

एवं मनः कर्मवशं प्रयुङ्क्ते
अविद्ययाऽऽत्मन्युपधीयमाने

प्रीतिर्न यावन्मयि वासुदेवे
न मुच्यते देहयोगेन तावत् ॥ ६ ॥

evaṁ manaḥ karma-vaśaṁ prayuṅkte
avidyayātmany upadhīyamāne
prītir na yāvan mayi vāsudeve
na mucyate deha-yogena tāvat

evam—thus; *manaḥ*—the mind; *karma-vaśam*—subjugated by fruitive activities; *prayuṅkte*—acts; *avidyayā*—by ignorance; *ātmani*—when the living entity; *upadhīyamāne*—is covered; *prītiḥ*—love; *na*—not; *yāvat*—as long as; *mayi*—unto Me; *vāsudeve*—Vāsudeva, Kṛṣṇa; *na*—not; *mucyate*—is delivered; *deha-yogena*—from contact with the material body; *tāvat*—so long.

TRANSLATION

When the living entity is covered by the mode of ignorance, he does not understand the individual living being and the supreme living being, and his mind is subjugated to fruitive activity. Therefore, until one has love for Lord Vāsudeva, who is none other than Myself, he is certainly not delivered from having to accept a material body again and again.

PURPORT

When the mind is polluted by fruitive activity, the living entity wants to be elevated from one material position to another. Generally everyone is involved in working hard day and night to improve his economic condition. Even when one understands the Vedic rituals, he becomes interested in promotion to heavenly planets, not knowing that one's real interest lies in returning home, back to Godhead. By acting on the platform of fruitive activity, one wanders throughout the universe in different species and forms. Unless he comes in contact with a devotee of the Lord, a *guru*, he does not become attached to the service of Lord Vāsudeva. Knowledge of Vāsudeva requires many births to understand. As confirmed in *Bhagavad-gītā* (7.19): *vāsudevaḥ sarvam iti sa mahātmā sudurlabhaḥ.* After struggling for existence for many births, one may take shelter at the lotus feet of Vāsudeva, Kṛṣṇa. When this happens, one actually becomes wise and surrenders unto Him. That is the only way to stop the repetition of birth and death. This is confirmed in *Caitanya-caritāmṛta* (*Madhya* 19.151) in the instructions given by Śrī Caitanya Mahāprabhu to Śrīla Rūpa Gosvāmī at Daśāśvamedha-ghāṭa.

brahmāṇḍa bhramite kona bhāgyavān jīva
guru-kṛṣṇa-prasāde pāya bhakti-latā-bīja

The living entity wanders throughout different planets in different forms and bodies, but if by chance he comes in contact with a bona fide spiritual master, by the grace of the spiritual master he receives Lord Kṛṣṇa's shelter, and his devotional life begins.

TEXT 7

यदा न पश्यत्ययथा गुणेहां
स्वार्थे प्रमत्तः सहसा विपश्चित् ।
गतस्मृतिर्विन्दति तत्र तापा-
नासाद्य मैथुन्यमगारमज्ञः ॥ ७ ॥

yadā na paśyaty ayathā guṇehāṁ
svārthe pramattaḥ sahasā vipaścit
gata-smṛtir vindati tatra tāpān
āsādya maithunyam agāram ajñaḥ

yadā—when; *na*—not; *paśyati*—sees; *ayathā*—unnecessary; *guṇa-īhām*—endeavor to satisfy the senses; *sva-arthe*—in self-interest; *pramattaḥ*—mad; *sahasā*—very soon; *vipaścit*—even one advanced in knowledge; *gata-smṛtiḥ*—being forgetful; *vindati*—gets; *tatra*—there; *tāpān*—material miseries; *āsādya*—getting; *maithunyam*—based on sexual intercourse; *agāram*—a home; *ajñaḥ*—being foolish.

TRANSLATION

Even though one may be very learned and wise, he is mad if he does not understand that the endeavor for sense gratification is a

useless waste of time. Being forgetful of his own interest, he tries to be happy in the material world, centering his interests around his home, which is based on sexual intercourse and which brings him all kinds of material miseries. In this way one is no better than a foolish animal.

PURPORT

In the lowest stage of devotional life, one is not an unalloyed devotee. *Anyābhilāṣitā-śūnyaṁ jñāna-karmādy-anāvṛtam:* to be an unalloyed devotee, one must be freed from all material desires and untouched by fruitive activity and speculative knowledge. On the lower platform, one may sometimes be interested in philosophical speculation with a tinge of devotion. However, at that stage one is still interested in sense gratification and is contaminated by the modes of material nature. The influence of *māyā* is so strong that even a person advanced in knowledge actually forgets that he is Kṛṣṇa's eternal servant. Therefore he remains satisfied in his householder life, which is centered around sexual intercourse. Conceding to a life of sex, he agrees to suffer all kinds of material miseries. Due to ignorance, one is thus bound by the chain of material laws.

TEXT 8

पुंसः स्त्रिया मिथुनीभावमेतं
तयोर्मिथो हृदयग्रन्थिमाहुः ।
अतो गृहक्षेत्रसुताप्तवित्तै-
र्जनस्य मोहोऽयमहं ममेति ॥ ८ ॥

puṁsaḥ striyā mithunī-bhāvam etaṁ
tayor mitho hṛdaya-granthim āhuḥ
ato gṛha-kṣetra-sutāpta-vittair
janasya moho 'yam ahaṁ mameti

puṁsaḥ—of a male; *striyāḥ*—of a female; *mithunī-bhāvam*—attraction for sexual life; *etam*—this; *tayoḥ*—of both of them; *mithaḥ*—between one another; *hṛdaya-granthim*—the knot of the hearts; *āhuḥ*—they call; *ataḥ*—thereafter; *gṛha*—by home; *kṣetra*—field; *suta*—

children; *āpta*—relatives; *vittaiḥ*—and by wealth; *janasya*—of the living being; *mohaḥ*—illusion; *ayam*—this; *aham*—I; *mama*—mine; *iti*—thus.

TRANSLATION

The attraction between male and female is the basic principle of material existence. On the basis of this misconception, which ties together the hearts of the male and female, one becomes attracted to his body, home, property, children, relatives and wealth. In this way one increases life's illusions and thinks in terms of "I and mine."

PURPORT

Sex serves as the natural attraction between man and woman, and when they are married, their relationship becomes more involved. Due to the entangling relationship between man and woman, there is a sense of illusion whereby one thinks, "This man is my husband," or "This woman is my wife." This is called *hṛdaya-granthi,* "the hard knot in the heart." This knot is very difficult to undo, even though a man and woman separate either for the principles of *varṇāśrama* or simply to get a divorce. In any case, the man always thinks of the woman, and the woman always thinks of the man. Thus a person becomes materially attached to family, property and children, although all of these are temporary. The possessor unfortunately identifies with his property and wealth. Sometimes, even after renunciation, one becomes attached to a temple or to the few things that constitute the property of a *sannyāsī,* but such attachment is not as strong as family attachment. The attachment to the family is the strongest illusion. In the *Satya-saṁhitā,* it is stated:

brahmādyā yājñavalkādyā
mucyante strī-sahāyinaḥ
bodhyante kecanaiteṣāṁ
viśeṣam ca vido viduḥ

Sometimes it is found among exalted personalities like Lord Brahmā that the wife and children are not a cause of bondage. On the contrary, the wife actually helps further spiritual life and liberation. Nonetheless, most people are bound by the knots of the marital relationship, and consequently they forget their relationship with Kṛṣṇa.

TEXT 9

यदा मनोहृदयग्रन्थिरस्य
कर्मानुबद्धो दृढ आश्लथेत ।
तदा जनः सम्परिवर्ततेऽस्माद्
मुक्तः परं यात्यतिहाय हेतुम् ॥ ९ ॥

yadā mano-hṛdaya-granthir asya
karmānubaddho dṛḍha āślatheta
tadā janaḥ samparivartate 'smād
muktaḥ paraṁ yāty atihāya hetum

yadā—when; *manaḥ*—the mind; *hṛdaya-granthiḥ*—the knot in the heart; *asya*—of this person; *karma-anubaddhaḥ*—bound by the results of his past deeds; *dṛḍhaḥ*—very strong; *āślatheta*—becomes slackened: *tadā*—at that time; *janaḥ*—the conditioned soul; *samparivartate*—turns away; *asmāt*—from this attachment for sex life; *muktaḥ*—liberated: *param*—to the transcendental world; *yāti*—goes; *atihāya*—giving up: *hetum*—the original cause.

TRANSLATION

When the strong knot in the heart of a person implicated in material life due to the results of past action is slackened, one turns away from his attachment to home, wife and children. In this way, one gives up the basic principle of illusion [I and mine] and becomes liberated. Thus one goes to the transcendental world.

PURPORT

When, by associating with *sādhus* and engaging in devotional service. one is gradually freed from the material conception due to knowledge. practice and detachment, the knot of attachment in the heart is slackened. Thus one can get freed from conditional life and become eligible to return home, back to Godhead.

TEXTS 10-13

हंसे गुरौ मयि भक्त्यानुवृत्या
वितृष्णया द्वन्द्वतितिक्षया च ।
सर्वत्र जन्तोर्व्यसनावगत्या
जिज्ञासया तपसेहानिवृत्त्या ॥१०॥
मत्कर्मभिर्मत्कथया च नित्यं
मद्देवसङ्गाद् गुणकीर्तनान्मे ।
निर्वैरसाम्योपशमेन पुत्रा
जिहासया देहगेहात्मबुद्धेः ॥११॥
अध्यात्मयोगेन विविक्तसेवया
प्राणेन्द्रियात्माभिजयेन सध्र्यक् ।
सच्छ्रद्धया ब्रह्मचर्येण शश्वद्
असम्प्रमादेन यमेन वाचाम् ॥१२॥
सर्वत्र मद्भावविचक्षणेन
ज्ञानेन विज्ञानविराजितेन ।
योगेन धृत्युद्यमसत्त्वयुक्तो
लिङ्गं व्यपोहेत्कुशलोऽहमाख्यम् ॥१३॥

haṁse gurau mayi bhaktyānuvṛtyā
vitṛṣṇayā dvandva-titikṣayā ca
sarvatra jantor vyasanāvagatyā
jijñāsayā tapasehā-nivṛttyā

mat-karmabhir mat-kathayā ca nityaṁ
mad-deva-saṅgād guṇa-kīrtanān me
nirvaira-sāmyopaśamena putrā
jihāsayā deha-gehātma-buddheḥ

adhyātma-yogena vivikta-sevayā
prāṇendriyātmābhijayena sadhryak
sac-chraddhayā brahmacaryeṇa śaśvad
asampramādena yamena vācām

sarvatra mad-bhāva-vicakṣaṇena
jñānena vijñāna-virājitena
yogena dhṛty-udyama-sattva-yukto
liṅgaṁ vyapohet kuśalo 'ham-ākhyam

haṁse—who is a *paramahaṁsa,* or the most exalted, spiritually advanced person; *gurau*—to the spiritual master; *mayi*—unto Me, the Supreme Personality of Godhead; *bhaktyā*—by devotional service; *anuvṛtyā*—by following; *vitṛṣṇayā*—by detachment from sense gratification; *dvandva*—of the dualities of the material world; *titikṣayā*—by tolerance; *ca*—also; *sarvatra*—everywhere; *jantoḥ*—of the living entity; *vyasana*—the miserable condition of life; *avagatyā*—by realizing; *jijñāsayā*—by inquiring about the truth; *tapasā*—by practicing austerities and penances; *īhā-nivṛttyā*—by giving up the endeavor for sense enjoyment; *mat-karmabhiḥ*—by working for Me; *mat-kathayā*—by hearing topics about Me; *ca*—also; *nityam*—always; *mat-deva-saṅgāt*—by association with My devotees; *guṇa-kīrtanāt me*—by chanting and glorifying My transcendental qualities; *nirvaira*—being without enmity; *sāmya*—seeing everyone equally by spiritual understanding; *upaśamena*—by subduing anger, lamentation and so on; *putrāḥ*—O sons; *jihāsayā*—by desiring to give up; *deha*—with the body; *geha*—with the home; *ātma-buddheḥ*—identification of the self; *adhyātma-yogena*—by study of the revealed scriptures; *vivikta-sevayā*—by living in a solitary place; *prāṇa*—the life air; *indriya*—the senses; *ātma*—the mind; *abhijayena*—by controlling; *sadhryak*—completely; *sat-śraddhayā*—by developing faith in the scriptures; *brahmacaryeṇa*—by observing celibacy; *śaśvat*—always; *asampramādena*—by not being bewildered; *yamena*—by restraint; *vācām*—of words; *sarvatra*—everywhere; *mat-bhāva*—thinking of Me; *vicakṣaṇena*—by observing; *jñānena*—by development of knowledge; *vijñāna*—by practical application of knowledge; *virājitena*—illumined;

yogena—by practice of *bhakti-yoga; dhṛti*—patience; *udyama*—enthusiasm; *sattva*—discretion; *yuktaḥ*—endowed with; *liṅgam*—the cause of material bondage; *vyapohet*—one can give up; *kuśalaḥ*—in full auspiciousness; *aham-ākhyam*—false ego, false identification with the material world.

TRANSLATION

O My sons, you should accept a highly elevated paramahaṁsa, a spiritually advanced spiritual master. In this way, you should place your faith and love in Me, the Supreme Personality of Godhead. You should detest sense gratification and tolerate the duality of pleasure and pain, which are like the seasonal changes of summer and winter. Try to realize the miserable condition of living entities, who are miserable even in the higher planetary systems. Philosophically inquire about the truth. Then undergo all kinds of austerities and penances for the sake of devotional service. Give up the endeavor for sense enjoyment and engage in the service of the Lord. Listen to discussions about the Supreme Personality of Godhead, and always associate with devotees. Chant about and glorify the Supreme Lord, and look upon everyone equally on the spiritual platform. Give up enmity and subdue anger and lamentation. Abandon identifying the self with the body and the home, and practice reading the revealed scriptures. Live in a secluded place and practice the process by which you can completely control your life air, mind and senses. Have full faith in the revealed scriptures, the Vedic literatures, and always observe celibacy. Perform your prescribed duties and avoid unnecessary talks. Always thinking of the Supreme Personality of Godhead, acquire knowledge from the right source. Thus practicing bhakti-yoga, you will patiently and enthusiastically be elevated in knowledge and will be able to give up the false ego.

PURPORT

In these four verses, Ṛṣabhadeva tells His sons how they can be freed from the false identification arising from false ego and material conditional life. One gradually becomes liberated by practicing as mentioned above. All these prescribed methods enable one to give up the material body (*liṅgaṁ vyapohet*) and be situated in his original spiritual body. First of all one has to accept a bona fide spiritual master. This is advocated by Śrīla Rūpa Gosvāmī in his *Bhakti-rasāmṛta-sindhu: śrī-guru-pādāśrayaḥ.* To be freed from the entanglement of the material world, one has to approach a spiritual master. *Tad-vijñānārthaṁ sa gurum evābhigacchet.* By questioning the spiritual master and by serving him, one can advance in spiritual life. When one engages in devotional service, naturally the attraction for personal comfort—for eating, sleeping and dressing—is reduced. By associating with the devotee, a spiritual standard is maintained. The word *mad-deva-saṅgāt* is very important. There are many so-called religions devoted to the worship of various demigods, but here good association means association with one who simply accepts Kṛṣṇa as his worshipable Deity.

Another important item is *dvandva-titikṣā.* As long as one is situated in the material world, there must be pleasure and pain arising from the material body. As Kṛṣṇa advises in *Bhagavad-gītā, tāṁs titikṣasva bhārata.* One has to learn how to tolerate the temporary pains and pleasures of this material world. One must also be detached from his family and practice celibacy. Sex with one's wife according to the scriptural injunctions is also accepted as *brahmacarya* (celibacy), but illicit sex is opposed to religious principles, and it hampers advancement in spiritual consciousness. Another important word is *vijñāna-virājita.* Everything should be done very scientifically and consciously. One should be a realized soul. In this way, one can give up the entanglement of material bondage.

As Śrī Madhvācārya points out, the sum and substance of these four *ślokas* is that one should refrain from acting out of a desire for sense gratification and should instead always engage in the Lord's loving service. In other words, *bhakti-yoga* is the acknowledged path of liberation. Śrīla Madhvācārya quotes from the *Adhyātma:*

ātmano 'vihitaṁ karma
varjayitvānya-karmaṇaḥ
kāmasya ca parityāgo
nirīhety āhur uttamāḥ

One should perform activities only for the benefit of the soul; any other activity should be given up. When a person is situated in this way, he is said to be desireless. Actually a living entity cannot be totally desireless, but when he desires the benefit of the soul and nothing else, he is said to be desireless.

Spiritual knowledge is *jñāna-vijñāna-samanvitam.* When one is fully equipped with *jñāna* and *vijñāna,* he is perfect. *Jñāna* means that one understands the Supreme Personality of Godhead, Viṣṇu, to be the Supreme Being. *Vijñāna* refers to the activities that liberate one from the ignorance of material existence. As stated in *Śrīmad-Bhāgavatam* (2.9.31): *jñānaṁ parama-guhyaṁ me yad vijñāna-samanvitam.* Knowledge of the Supreme Lord is very confidential, and the supreme knowledge by which one understands Him furthers the liberation of all living entities. This knowledge is *vijñāna.* As confirmed in *Bhagavad-gītā* (4.9):

janma karma ca me divyam
evaṁ yo vetti tattvataḥ
tyaktvā dehaṁ punar janma
naiti mām eti so 'rjuna

"One who knows the transcendental nature of My appearance and activities does not, upon leaving the body, take his birth again in this material world, but attains My eternal abode, O Arjuna."

TEXT 14

कर्माशयं हृदयग्रन्थिबन्ध-
मविद्ययाऽऽसादितमप्रमत्तः ।
अनेन योगेन यथोपदेशं
सम्यग्व्यपोह्योपरमेत योगात् ॥१४॥

karmāśayaṁ hṛdaya-granthi-bandham
avidyayāsāditam apramattaḥ
anena yogena yathopadeśaṁ
samyag vyapohyoparameta yogāt

karma-āśayam—the desire for fruitive activities; *hṛdaya-granthi*—the knot in the heart; *bandham*—bondage; *avidyayā*—because of ignorance; *āsāditam*—brought about; *apramattaḥ*—not being covered by ignorance or illusion, very careful; *anena*—by this; *yogena*—practice of *yoga; yathā-upadeśam*—as advised; *samyak*—completely; *vyapohya*—becoming free from; *uparameta*—one should desist; *yogāt*—from the practice of *yoga*, the means of liberation.

TRANSLATION

As I have advised you, My dear sons, you should act accordingly. Be very careful. By these means you will be freed from the ignorance of the desire for fruitive activity, and the knot of bondage in the heart will be completely severed. For further advancement, you should also give up the means. That is, you should not become attached to the process of liberation itself.

PURPORT

The process of liberation is *brahma-jijñāsā*, the search for the Absolute Truth. Generally *brahma-jijñāsā* is called *neti neti*, the process by which one analyzes existence to search out the Absolute Truth. This method continues as long as one is not situated in his spiritual life. Spiritual life is *brahma-bhūta*, the self-realized state. In the words of *Bhagavad-gītā* (18.54):

brahma-bhūtaḥ prasannātmā
na śocati na kāṅkṣati
samaḥ sarveṣu bhūteṣu
mad-bhaktiṁ labhate parām

"One who is thus transcendentally situated at once realizes the Supreme Brahman and becomes fully joyful. He never laments nor desires to have anything; he is equally disposed to every living entity. In that state, he attains pure devotional service unto Me."

The idea is to enter into the *parā bhakti*, the transcendental devotional service of the Supreme Lord. To attain this, one must analyze one's existence, but when one is actually engaged in devotional service, he should not bother seeking out knowledge. By simply engaging in devotional service undeviatingly, one will always remain in the liberated condition.

māṁ ca yo 'vyabhicāreṇa
bhakti-yogena sevate
sa guṇān samatītyaitān
brahma-bhūyāya kalpate
(Bg. 14.26)

The unflinching execution of devotional service is in itself *brahma-bhūta.* Another important feature in this connection is *anena yogena yathopadeśam.* The instructions received from the spiritual master must be followed immediately. One should not deviate from or surpass the instructions of the spiritual master. One should not be simply intent on consulting books but should simultaneously execute the spiritual master's order (*yathopadeśam*). Mystic power should be achieved to enable one to give up the material conception, but when one actually engages in devotional service, one does not need to practice the mystic *yoga* system. The point is that one can give up the practice of *yoga,* but devotional service cannot be given up. As stated in *Śrīmad-Bhāgavatam* (1.7.10):

ātmārāmāś ca munayo
nirgranthā apy urukrame
kurvanty ahaitukīṁ bhaktim
ittham-bhūta-guṇo hariḥ

Even those who are liberated (*ātmārāma*) must always engage in devotional service. One may give up the practice of *yoga* when one is self-realized, but at no stage can one give up devotional service. All other activities for self-realization, including *yoga* and philosophical speculation, may be given up, but devotional service must be retained at all times.

TEXT 15

पुत्रांश्च शिष्यांश्च नृपो गुरुर्वा
मल्लोककामो मदनुग्रहार्थः ।

इत्थं विमन्युरनुशिष्यादतज्ज्ञान्
न योजयेत्कर्मसु कर्ममूढान् ।
कं योजयन्मनुजोऽर्थं लभेत
निपातयन्नष्टदृशं हि गर्ते ॥१५॥

putrāṁś ca śiṣyāṁś ca nṛpo gurur vā
mal-loka-kāmo mad-anugrahārthaḥ
itthaṁ vimanyur anuśiṣyād ataj-jñān
na yojayet karmasu karma-mūḍhān
kaṁ yojayan manujo 'rthaṁ labheta
nipātayan naṣṭa-dṛśaṁ hi garte

putrān—the sons; *ca*—and; *śiṣyān*—the disciples; *ca*—and; *nṛpaḥ*—the king; *guruḥ*—the spiritual master; *vā*—or; *mat-loka-kāmaḥ*—desiring to go to My abode; *mat-anugraha-arthaḥ*—thinking that to achieve My mercy is the aim of life; *ittham*—in this manner; *vimanyuḥ*—free from anger; *anuśiṣyāt*—should instruct; *a-tat-jñān*—bereft of spiritual knowledge; *na*—not; *yojayet*—should engage; *karmasu*—in fruitive activities; *karma-mūḍhān*—simply engaged in pious or impious activities; *kam*—what; *yojayan*—engaging; *manu-jaḥ*—a man; *artham*—benefit; *labheta*—can achieve; *nipātayan*—causing to fall; *naṣṭa-dṛśam*—one who is already bereft of his transcendental sight; *hi*—indeed; *garte*—in the hole.

TRANSLATION

If one is serious about going back home, back to Godhead, he must consider the mercy of the Supreme Personality of Godhead the summum bonum and chief aim of life. If he is a father instructing his sons, a spiritual master instructing his disciples, or a king instructing his citizens, he must instruct them as I have advised. Without being angry, he should continue giving instructions, even if his disciple, son or citizen is sometimes unable to follow his order. Ignorant people who engage in pious and impious activities should be engaged in devotional service by all means. They should always avoid fruitive activity. If one puts into

the bondage of karmic activity his disciple, son or citizen who is bereft of transcendental vision, how will one profit? It is like leading a blind man to a dark well and causing him to fall in.

PURPORT

It is stated in *Bhagavad-gītā* (3.26):

na buddhi-bhedaṁ janayed
ajñānāṁ karma-saṅginām
joṣayet sarva-karmāṇi
vidvān yuktaḥ samācaran

"Let not the wise disrupt the minds of the ignorant who are attached to fruitive action. They should be encouraged not to refrain from work, but to work in the spirit of devotion."

TEXT 16

लोकः स्वयं श्रेयसि नष्टदृष्टि-
र्योऽर्थान् समीहेत निकामकामः ।
अन्योन्यवैरः सुखलेशहेतो-
रनन्तदुःखं च न वेद मूढः ॥१६॥

lokaḥ svayaṁ śreyasi naṣṭa-dṛṣṭir
yo 'rthān samīheta nikāma-kāmaḥ
anyonya-vairaḥ sukha-leśa-hetor
ananta-duḥkhaṁ ca na veda mūḍhaḥ

lokaḥ—people; *svayam*—personally; *śreyasi*—of the path of auspiciousness; *naṣṭa-dṛṣṭiḥ*—who have lost sight; *yaḥ*—who; *arthān*—things meant for sense gratification; *samīheta*—desire; *nikāma-kāmaḥ*—having too many lusty desires for sense enjoyment; *anyonya-vairaḥ*—being envious of one another; *sukha-leśa-hetoḥ*—simply for temporary material happiness; *ananta-duḥkham*—unlimited sufferings; *ca*—also; *na*—do not; *veda*—know; *mūḍhaḥ*—foolish.

TRANSLATION

Due to ignorance, the materialistic person does not know anything about his real self-interest, the auspicious path in life. He is simply bound to material enjoyment by lusty desires, and all his plans are made for this purpose. For temporary sense gratification, such a person creates a society of envy, and due to this mentality, he plunges into the ocean of suffering. Such a foolish person does not even know about this.

PURPORT

The word *naṣṭa-dṛṣṭiḥ,* meaning "one who has no eyes to see the future," is very significant in this verse. Life goes on from one body to another, and the activities performed in this life are enjoyed or suffered in the next life, if not later in this life. One who is unintelligent, who has no eyes to see the future, simply creates enmity and fights with others for sense gratification. As a result, one suffers in the next life, but due to being like a blind man, he continues to act in such a way that he suffers unlimitedly. Such a person is a *mūḍha,* one who simply wastes his time and does not understand the Lord's devotional service. As stated in *Bhagavad-gītā* (7.25):

nāhaṁ prakāśaḥ sarvasya
yogamāyā-samāvṛtaḥ
mūḍho 'yaṁ nābhijānāti
loko mām ajam avyayam

"I am never manifest to the foolish and unintelligent. For them I am covered by My eternal creative potency [*yogamāyā*]; and so the deluded world knows Me not, who am unborn and infallible."

In the *Kaṭha Upaniṣad* it is also said: *avidyāyām antare vartamānāḥ svayaṁ dhīrāḥ paṇḍitaṁ manyamānāḥ.* Although ignorant, people still go to other blind men for leadership. As a result, both are subjected to miserable conditions. The blind lead the blind into the ditch.

TEXT 17

कस्तं स्वयं तदभिज्ञो विपश्चिद्
अविद्यायामन्तरे वर्तमानम् ।

दृष्ट्वा पुनस्तं सघृणः कुबुद्धिं
प्रयोजयेदुत्पथगं यथान्धम् ॥१७॥

kas taṁ svayaṁ tad-abhijño vipaścid
avidyāyām antare vartamānam
dṛṣṭvā punas taṁ saghṛṇaḥ kubuddhiṁ
prayojayed utpathagaṁ yathāndham

kaḥ—who is that person; *tam*—him; *svayam*—personally; *tat-abhijñaḥ*—knowing spiritual knowledge; *vipaścit*—a learned scholar; *avidyāyām antare*—in ignorance; *vartamānam*—existing; *dṛṣṭvā*—seeing; *punaḥ*—again; *tam*—him; *sa-ghṛṇaḥ*—very merciful; *ku-buddhim*—who is addicted to the path of *saṁsāra; prayojayet*—would engage; *utpatha-gam*—who is proceeding on the wrong path; *yathā*—like; *andham*—a blind man.

TRANSLATION

If someone is ignorant and addicted to the path of saṁsāra, how can one who is actually learned, merciful and advanced in spiritual knowledge engage him in fruitive activity and thus further entangle him in material existence? If a blind man is walking down the wrong path, how can a gentleman allow him to continue on his way to danger? How can he approve this method? No wise or kind man can allow this.

TEXT 18

गुरुर्न स स्यात्स्वजनो न स स्यात्
पिता न स स्याज्जननी न सा स्यात् ।
दैवं न तत्स्यान्न पतिश्च स स्या-
न्न मोचयेद्यः समुपेतमृत्युम् ॥१८॥

gurur na sa syāt sva-jano na sa syāt
pitā na sa syāj jananī na sā syāt
daivaṁ na tat syān na patiś ca sa syān
na mocayed yaḥ samupeta-mṛtyum

guruḥ—a spiritual master; *na*—not; *saḥ*—he; *syāt*—should become; *sva-janaḥ*—a relative; *na*—not; *saḥ*—such a person; *syāt*—should become; *pitā*—a father; *na*—not; *saḥ*—he; *syāt*—should become; *jananī*—a mother; *na*—not; *sā*—she; *syāt*—should become; *daivam*—the worshipable deity; *na*—not; *tat*—that; *syāt*—should become; *na*—not; *patiḥ*—a husband; *ca*—also; *saḥ*—he; *syāt*—should become; *na*—not; *mocayet*—can deliver; *yaḥ*—who; *samupeta-mṛtyum*—one who is on the path of repeated birth and death.

TRANSLATION

"One who cannot deliver his dependents from the path of repeated birth and death should never become a spiritual master, a father, a husband, a mother or a worshipable demigod.

PURPORT

There are many spiritual masters, but Ṛṣabhadeva advises that one should not become a spiritual master if he is unable to save his disciple from the path of birth and death. Unless one is a pure devotee of Kṛṣṇa, he cannot save himself from the path of repeated birth and death. *Tyaktvā dehaṁ punar janma naiti mām eti so 'rjuna.* One can stop birth and death only by returning home, back to Godhead. However, who can go back to Godhead unless he understands the Supreme Lord in truth? *Janma karma ca me divyam evaṁ yo vetti tattvataḥ.*

We have many instances in history illustrating Ṛṣabhadeva's instructions. Śukrācārya was rejected by Bali Mahārāja due to his inability to save Bali Mahārāja from the path of repeated birth and death. Śukrācārya was not a pure devotee, he was more or less inclined to fruitive activity, and he objected when Bali Mahārāja promised to give everything to Lord Viṣṇu. Actually one is supposed to give everything to the Lord because everything belongs to the Lord. Consequently, the Supreme Lord advises in *Bhagavad-gītā* (9.27):

yat karoṣi yad aśnāsi
yaj juhoṣi dadāsi yat
yat tapasyasi kaunteya
tat kuruṣva mad-arpaṇam

"O son of Kuntī, all that you do, all that you eat, all that you offer and give away, as well as all austerities that you may perform, should be done as an offering unto Me." This is *bhakti.* Unless one is devoted, he cannot give everything to the Supreme Lord. Unless one can do so, he cannot become a spiritual master, husband, father or mother. Similarly, the wives of the *brāhmaṇas* who were performing sacrifices gave up their relatives just to satisfy Kṛṣṇa. This is an example of a wife rejecting a husband who cannot deliver her from the impending dangers of birth and death. Similarly, Prahlāda Mahārāja rejected his father, and Bharata Mahārāja rejected his mother (*jananī na sā syāt*). The word *daivam* indicates a demigod or one who accepts worship from a dependent. Ordinarily, the spiritual master, husband, father, mother or superior relative accepts worship from an inferior relative, but here Ṛṣabhadeva forbids this. First the father, spiritual master or husband must be able to release the dependent from repeated birth and death. If he cannot do this, he plunges himself into the ocean of reproachment for his unlawful activities. Everyone should be very responsible and take charge of his dependents just as a spiritual master takes charge of his disciple or a father takes charge of his son. All these responsibilities cannot be discharged honestly unless one can save the dependent from repeated birth and death.

TEXT 19

इदं शरीरं मम दुर्विभाव्यं
सत्त्वं हि मे हृदयं यत्र धर्मः ।
पृष्ठे कृतो मे यदधर्म आराद्
अतो हि मामृषभं प्राहुरार्याः ॥१९॥

idaṁ śarīraṁ mama durvibhāvyaṁ
sattvaṁ hi me hṛdayaṁ yatra dharmaḥ
pṛṣṭhe kṛto me yad adharma ārād
ato hi māṁ ṛṣabhaṁ prāhur āryāḥ

idam—this; *śarīram*—transcendental body, *sac-cid-ānanda-vigraha; mama*—My; *durvibhāvyam*—inconceivable; *sattvam*—with no tinge of the material modes of nature; *hi*—indeed; *me*—My; *hṛdayam*—heart; *yatra*—wherein; *dharmaḥ*—the real platform of religion, *bhakti-yoga;* *pṛṣṭhe*—on the back; *kṛtaḥ*—made; *me*—by Me; *yat*—because; *adharmaḥ*—irreligion; *ārāt*—far away; *ataḥ*—therefore; *hi*—indeed; *mām*—Me; *ṛṣabham*—the best of the living beings; *prāhuḥ*—call; *āryāḥ*—those who are advanced in spiritual life, or the respectable superiors.

TRANSLATION

My transcendental body [sac-cid-ānanda-vigraha] looks exactly like a human form, but it is not a material human body. It is inconceivable. I am not forced by nature to accept a particular type of body; I take on a body by My own sweet will. My heart is also spiritual, and I always think of the welfare of My devotees. Therefore within My heart can be found the process of devotional service, which is meant for the devotees. Far from My heart have I abandoned irreligion [adharma] and nondevotional activities. They do not appeal to Me. Due to all these transcendental qualities, people generally pray to Me as Ṛṣabhadeva, the Supreme Personality of Godhead, the best of all living entities.

PURPORT

In this verse the words *idaṁ śarīraṁ mama durvibhāvyam* are very significant. Generally we experience two energies—material energy and spiritual energy. We have some experience of the material energy (earth, water, air, fire, ether, mind, intelligence and ego) because in the material world everyone's body is composed of these elements. Within the material body is the spirit soul, but we cannot see it with the material eyes. When we see a body full of spiritual energy, it is very difficult for us to understand how the spiritual energy can have a body. It is said that Lord Ṛṣabhadeva's body is completely spiritual; therefore for a materialistic person, it is very difficult to understand. For a materialistic person, the completely spiritual body is inconceivable. We have to accept the version of the *Vedas* when our experimental perception cannot understand a subject. As stated in *Brahma-saṁhitā: īśvaraḥ paramaḥ kṛṣṇaḥ sac-cid-ānanda-vigrahaḥ.* The Supreme Lord has a body with form, but that body is not composed of material elements. It is made of spiritual bliss, eternity and living force. By the inconceivable energy of the Supreme Personality of Godhead, the Lord can appear before us in His original spiritual body, but because we have no experience of the spiritual body, we are sometimes bewildered and see the form of the Lord as material. The Māyāvādī philosophers are completely unable to conceive of a spiritual body. They say that the spirit is always impersonal, and whenever they see something personal, they take it for granted that it is material. In *Bhagavad-gītā* (9.11) it is said:

avajānanti māṁ mūḍhā
mānuṣīṁ tanum āśritam
paraṁ bhāvam ajānanto
mama bhūta-maheśvaram

"Fools deride Me when I descend in the human form. They do not know My transcendental nature and My supreme dominion over all that be."

Unintelligent people think that the Supreme Lord accepts a body composed of the material energy. We can easily understand the material body, but we cannot understand the spiritual body. Therefore Ṛṣabhadeva says: *idaṁ śarīraṁ mama durvibhāvyam.* In the spiritual world, everyone has a spiritual body. There is no conception of material existence there. In the spiritual world there is only service and the receiving of service. There is only *sevya, sevā,* and *sevaka*—the person served, the process of service and the servant. These three items are completely spiritual, and therefore the spiritual world is called absolute. There is no tinge of material contamination there. Being completely transcendental to the material conception, Lord Ṛṣabhadeva states that His heart is composed of *dharma. Dharma* is explained in *Bhagavad-gītā* (18.66): *sarva-dharmān parityajya mām ekaṁ śaraṇaṁ vraja.* In the spiritual world, every living entity is surrendered to the Supreme Lord and is completely on the spiritual platform. Although there are servitors, the served and service, all are spiritual and variegated. At the present moment, due to our material conception, everything is *durvibhāvya,* inconceivable. Being the Supreme, the Lord is called Ṛṣabha, the best. In terms of the Vedic language, *nityo nityānām.* We are also spiritual, but we are subordinate. Kṛṣṇa, the Supreme Lord, is the foremost living entity. The word *ṛṣabha* means "the chief," or "the supreme," and indicates the Supreme Being, or God Himself.

TEXT 20

तस्माद्भवन्तो हृदयेन जाताः
सर्वे महीयांसममुं सनाभम् ।
अक्लिष्टबुद्ध्या भरतं भजध्वं
शुश्रूषणं तद्भरणं प्रजानाम् ॥२०॥

tasmād bhavanto hṛdayena jātāḥ
sarve mahīyāṁsam amuṁ sanābham
akliṣṭa-buddhyā bharataṁ bhajadhvaṁ
śuśrūṣaṇaṁ tad bharaṇaṁ prajānām

tasmāt—therefore (because I am the Supreme); *bhavantaḥ*—you; *hṛdayena*—from My heart; *jātāḥ*—born; *sarve*—all; *mahīyāṁsam*—the best; *amum*—that; *sa-nābham*—brother; *akliṣṭa-buddhyā*—with your intelligence, without material contamination; *bharatam*—Bharata; *bhajadhvam*—just try to serve; *śuśrūṣaṇam*—service; *tat*—that; *bharaṇam prajānām*—ruling over the citizens.

TRANSLATION

My dear boys, you are all born of My heart, which is the seat of all spiritual qualities. Therefore you should not be like materialistic and envious men. You should accept your eldest brother, Bharata, who is exalted in devotional service. If you engage yourselves in Bharata's service, your service to him will include My service, and you will rule the citizens automatically.

PURPORT

In this verse the word *hṛdaya* indicates the heart, which is also called *uraḥ*, the chest. The heart is situated within the chest, and although instrumentally the son is born with the aid of the genitals, he is actually born from within the heart. According to the heart's situation, the semen takes the form of a body. Therefore according to the Vedic system, when one begets a child his heart should be purified through the ritualistic ceremony known as *garbhādhāna*. Ṛṣabhadeva's heart was always uncontaminated and spiritual. Consequently all the sons born from the heart of Ṛṣabhadeva were spiritually inclined. Nonetheless, Ṛṣabhadeva suggested that His eldest son was superior, and He advised the others to serve him. All the brothers of Bharata Mahārāja were advised by Ṛṣabhadeva to adhere to Bharata's service. The question may be asked why one should be attached to family members, for in the beginning it was advised that one should not be attached to home and family. However, it is also advised, *mahīyasām pāda-rajo-'bhiṣeka*—one has to serve the *mahīyān*, one who is very spiritually advanced. *Mahat-sevāṁ dvāram āhur vimukteḥ:* by serving the *mahat*, the exalted devotee, one's path for liberation is open. The family of Ṛṣabhadeva should not be compared to an ordinary materialistic family. Bharata Mahārāja, Ṛṣabhadeva's eldest son, was specifically very exalted. For this reason the other sons were advised to serve him for his pleasure. That was to be their duty.

The Supreme Lord was advising Bharata Mahārāja to be the chief ruler of the planet. This is the real plan of the Supreme Lord. In the Battle of Kurukṣetra, we find that Lord Kṛṣṇa wanted Mahārāja Yudhiṣṭhira to be the supreme emperor of this planet. He never wanted Duryodhana to take the post. As stated in the previous verse, Lord Ṛṣabhadeva's heart is *hṛdayaṁ yatra dharmaḥ*. The characteristic *dharma* is also explained in *Bhagavad-gītā:* surrender unto the Supreme Personality of Godhead. To protect *dharma* (*paritrāṇāya sādhūnām*), the Lord always wants the ruler of the earth to be a devotee. Then everything goes on nicely for the benefit of everyone. As soon as a demon rules the earth, everything becomes chaotic. At the present moment, the world is inclined toward the democratic process, but the people in general are all contaminated by the modes of passion and ignorance. Consequently they cannot select the right person to head the government. The president is selected by the votes of ignorant *śūdras;* therefore another *śūdra* is elected, and immediately the entire government becomes polluted. If people strictly followed the principles of *Bhagavad-gītā*, they would elect a person who is the Lord's devotee. Then automatically there would be good government. Ṛṣabhadeva therefore recommended Bharata Mahārāja as the emperor of this planet. Serving a devotee means serving the Supreme Lord, for a devotee always represents the Lord. When a devotee is in charge, the government is always congenial and beneficial for everyone.

TEXTS 21-22

भूतेषु वीरुद्भ्य उदुत्तमा ये
सरीसृपास्तेषु सबोधनिष्ठाः ।
ततो मनुष्याः प्रमथास्ततोऽपि
गन्धर्वसिद्धा विबुधानुगा ये ॥२१॥
देवासुरेभ्यो मघवत्प्रधाना
दक्षादयो ब्रह्मसुतास्तु तेषाम् ।
भवः परः सोऽथ विरिञ्चवीर्यः
स मत्परोऽहं द्विजदेवदेवः ॥२२॥

bhūteṣu vīrudbhya uduttamā ye
sarīsṛpās teṣu sabodha-niṣṭhāḥ
tato manuṣyāḥ pramathās tato 'pi
gandharva-siddhā vibudhānugā ye

devāsurebhyo maghavat-pradhānā
dakṣādayo brahma-sutās tu teṣām
bhavaḥ paraḥ so 'tha viriñca-vīryaḥ
sa mat-paro 'haṁ dvija-deva-devaḥ

bhūteṣu—among things generated (with and without symptoms of life); *vīrudbhyaḥ*—than the plants; *uduttamāḥ*—far superior; *ye*—those who; *sarīsṛpāḥ*—moving entities like worms and snakes; *teṣu*—of them; *sa-bodha-niṣṭhāḥ*—those who have developed intelligence; *tataḥ*—than them; *manuṣyāḥ*—the human beings; *pramathāḥ*—the ghostly spirits; *tataḥ api*—better than them; *gandharva*—the inhabitants of Gandharvaloka (appointed singers in the planets of the demigods); *siddhāḥ*—the inhabitants of Siddhaloka, who have all mystic powers; *vibudha-anugāḥ*—the Kinnaras; *ye*—those who; *deva*—the demigods; *asurebhyaḥ*—than the *asuras; maghavat-pradhānāḥ*—headed by Indra; *dakṣa-ādayaḥ*—beginning with Dakṣa; *brahma-sutāḥ*—the direct sons of Brahmā; *tu*—then; *teṣām*—of them; *bhavaḥ*—Lord Śiva; *paraḥ*—the best; *saḥ*—he (Lord Śiva); *atha*—moreover; *viriñca-vīryaḥ*—producing from Lord Brahmā; *saḥ*—he (Brahmā); *mat-paraḥ*—My devotee; *aham*—I; *dvija-deva-devaḥ*—a worshiper of the *brāhmaṇas*, or the Lord of the *brāhmaṇas*.

TRANSLATION

Of the two energies manifest [spirit and dull matter], beings possessing living force [vegetables, grass, trees and plants] are superior to dull matter [stone, earth, etc.]. Superior to nonmoving plants and vegetables are worms and snakes, which can move. Superior to worms and snakes are animals that have developed intelligence. Superior to animals are human beings, and superior to human beings are ghosts because they have no material bodies. Superior to ghosts are the Gandharvas, and superior to them are the Siddhas. Superior to the Siddhas are the Kinnaras, and superior to them are the asuras. Superior to the asuras are the demigods, and of the demigods, Indra, the King of heaven, is supreme. Superior to Indra are the direct sons of Lord Brahmā, sons like King Dakṣa, and supreme among Brahmā's sons is Lord Śiva. Since Lord Śiva is the son of Lord Brahmā, Brahmā is considered superior, but Brahmā is also subordinate to Me, the Supreme Personality of Godhead. Because I am inclined to the brāhmaṇas, the brāhmaṇas are best of all.

PURPORT

In this verse the *brāhmaṇas* are given a position superior to that of the Supreme Lord. The idea is that the government should be conducted under the guidance of the *brāhmaṇas.* Although Ṛṣabhadeva recommended His eldest son, Bharata, as emperor of the earth, he still had to follow the instructions of the *brāhmaṇas* in order to govern the world perfectly. The Lord is worshiped as *brahmaṇya-deva.* The Lord is very fond of devotees, or *brāhmaṇas.* This does not refer to so-called caste *brāhmaṇas*, but to qualified *brāhmaṇas.* A *brāhmaṇa* should be qualified with the eight qualities mentioned in text 24, such as *śama, dama, satya* and *titikṣā.* The *brāhmaṇas* should always be worshiped, and under their guidance the ruler should discharge his duty and rule the citizens. Unfortunately, in this age of Kali, the executive is not selected by very intelligent people, nor is he guided by qualified *brāhmaṇas.* Consequently, chaos results. The mass of people should be educated in Kṛṣṇa consciousness so that according to the democratic process they can select a first-class devotee like Bharata Mahārāja to head the government. If the head of the state is headed by qualified *brāhmaṇas,* everything is completely perfect.

In this verse, the evolutionary process is indirectly mentioned. The modern theory that life evolves from matter is to some extent supported in this verse because it is stated, *bhūteṣu vīrudbhyaḥ.* That is, the living entities evolve from vegetables, grass, plants and trees, which are superior to dull matter. In other words, matter also has the potency to manifest living entities in the form of vegetables. In this sense, life comes out of matter, but matter also comes out of life. As Kṛṣṇa says in *Bhagavad-gītā* (10.8), *ahaṁ sarvasya prabhavo mattaḥ sarvaṁ pravartate:* "I am the source of all spiritual and material worlds. Everything emanates from Me."

There are two energies—material and spiritual—and both originally come from Kṛṣṇa. Kṛṣṇa is the supreme living being. Although it may be said that in the material world a living force is generated from matter, it must be admitted that originally matter is generated from the supreme living being. *Nityo nityānāṁ cetanaś cetanānām.* The conclusion is that everything, both material and spiritual, is generated from the Supreme Being. From the evolutionary point of view, perfection is reached when the living entity attains the platform of a *brāhmaṇa.* A *brāhmaṇa* is a worshiper of the Supreme Brahman, and the Supreme Brahman worships the *brāhmaṇa.* In other words, the devotee is subordinate to the Supreme Lord, and the Lord is inclined to see to the satisfaction of His devotee. A *brāhmaṇa* is called *dvija-deva,* and the Lord is called *dvija-deva-deva.* He is the Lord of *brāhmaṇas.*

The evolutionary process is also explained in *Caitanya-caritāmṛta* (*Madhya,* Chapter Nineteen), wherein it is said that there are two types of living entities—moving and nonmoving. Among moving entities, there are birds, beasts, aquatics, human beings and so on. Of these, the human beings are supposed to be the best, but they are few. Of these small numbers of human beings, there are many low-class human beings like *mlecchas*, Pulindas, *bauddhas* and *śabaras*. The human being elevated enough to accept the Vedic principles is superior. Among those who accept the Vedic principles generally known as *varṇāśrama* (presently known as the Hindu system), few actually follow these principles. Of those who actually follow the Vedic principles, most perform fruitive activity or pious activity for elevation to a high position. *Manuṣyāṇāṁ sahasreṣu kaścid yatati siddhaye:* out of many attached to fruitive activity, one may be a *jñānī*—that is, one philosophically inclined and superior to the *karmīs*. *Yatatām api siddhānāṁ kaścin māṁ vetti tattvataḥ:* out of many *jñānīs*, one may be liberated from material bondage, and out of many millions of liberated *jñānīs*, one may become a devotee of Kṛṣṇa.

TEXT 23

न ब्राह्मणैस्तुलये भूतमन्यत्
पश्यामि विप्राः किमतः परं तु ।
यस्मिन्नृभिः प्रहुतं श्रद्धयाह-
मश्नामि कामं न तथाग्निहोत्रे ॥२३॥

na brāhmaṇais tulaye bhūtam anyat
paśyāmi viprāḥ kim ataḥ paraṁ tu
yasmin nṛbhiḥ prahutaṁ śraddhayāham
aśnāmi kāmaṁ na tathāgni-hotre

na—not; *brāhmaṇaiḥ*—with the *brāhmaṇas; tulaye*—I count as equal; *bhūtam*—entity; *anyat*—other; *paśyāmi*—I can see; *viprāḥ*—O assembled *brāhmaṇas; kim*—anything; *ataḥ*—to the *brāhmaṇas; param*—superior; *tu*—certainly; *yasmin*—through whom; *nṛbhiḥ*—by people; *prahutam*—food offered after ritualistic ceremonies are properly performed; *śraddhayā*—with faith and love; *aham*—I; *aśnāmi*—eat; *kāmam*—with full satisfaction; *na*—not; *tathā*—in that way; *agni-hotre*—in the fire sacrifice.

TRANSLATION

O respectful brāhmaṇas, as far as I am concerned, no one is equal or superior to the brāhmaṇas in this world. I do not find anyone comparable to them. When people know My motive after performing rituals according to the Vedic principles, they offer food to Me with faith and love through the mouth of a brāhmaṇa. When food is thus offered unto Me, I eat it with full satisfaction. Indeed, I derive more pleasure from food offered in that way than from the food offered in the sacrificial fire.

PURPORT

According to the Vedic system, after the sacrificial ceremony the *brāhmaṇas* are invited to eat the remnants of the offered food. When the *brāhmaṇas* eat the food, it is to be considered directly eaten by the Supreme Lord. Thus no one can be compared to qualified *brāhmaṇas.* The perfection of evolution is to be situated on the brahminical platform. Any civilization not based on brahminical culture or guided by *brāhmaṇas* is certainly a condemned civilization. Presently human civilization is based on sense gratification, and consequently more and more people are becoming addicted to different types of things. No one respects brahminical culture. Demoniac civilization is attached to *ugra-karma,* horrible activities, and big industries are created to satisfy unfathomable lusty desires. Consequently the people are greatly harassed by governmental taxation. The people are irreligious and do not perform the sacrifices recommended in *Bhagavad-gītā. Yajñād bhavati parjanyaḥ:* by the performance of sacrifice, clouds form and rain falls. Due to sufficient rainfall, there is sufficient production of food. Guided by the *brāhmaṇas,* society should follow the principles of *Bhagavad-gītā.* Then people will become very happy. *Annād bhavanti bhūtāni:* when animals and man are sufficiently fed with grains, they become stronger, their hearts become tranquil and their brains peaceful. They can then advance in spiritual life, life's ultimate destination.

TEXT 24

धृता तनूरुशती मे पुराणी
येनेह सत्त्वं परमं पवित्रम् ।

शमो दमः सत्यमनुग्रहश्च
तपस्तितिक्षानुभवश्च यत्र ॥२४॥

dhṛtā tanūr uśatī me purāṇī
yeneha sattvaṁ paramaṁ pavitram
śamo damaḥ satyam anugrahaś ca
tapas titikṣānubhavaś ca yatra

dhṛtā—maintained by transcendental education; *tanūḥ*—body; *uśatī*—free from material contamination; *me*—My; *purāṇī*—eternal; *yena*—by whom; *iha*—in this material world; *sattvam*—the mode of goodness; *paramam*—supreme; *pavitram*—purified; *śamaḥ*—control of the mind; *damaḥ*—control of the senses; *satyam*—truthfulness; *anugrahaḥ*—mercy; *ca*—and; *tapaḥ*—austerity; *titikṣā*—tolerance; *anubhavaḥ*—realization of God and the living entity; *ca*—and; *yatra*—wherein.

TRANSLATION

The Vedas are My eternal transcendental sound incarnation. Therefore the Vedas are śabda-brahma. In this world, the brāhmaṇas thoroughly study all the Vedas, and because they assimilate the Vedic conclusions, they are also to be considered the Vedas personified. The brāhmaṇas are situated in the supreme transcendental mode of nature—sattva-guṇa. Because of this, they are fixed in mind control [śama], sense control [dama], and truthfulness [satya]. They describe the Vedas in their original sense, and out of mercy [anugraha] they preach the purpose of the Vedas to all conditioned souls. They practice penance [tapasya] and tolerance [titikṣā], and they realize the position of the living entity and the Supreme Lord [anubhava]. These are the eight qualifications of the brāhmaṇas. Therefore among all living entities, no one is superior to the brāhmaṇas.

PURPORT

This is a true description of a *brāhmaṇa.* A *brāhmaṇa* is one who has assimilated the Vedic conclusions by practicing mind and sense control.

He speaks the true version of all the *Vedas*. As confirmed in the *Bhagavad-gītā* (15.15): *vedaiś ca sarvair aham eva vedyaḥ*. By studying all the *Vedas*, one should come to understand the transcendental position of Lord Śrī Kṛṣṇa. One who actually assimilated the essence of the *Vedas* can preach the truth. He is compassionate to conditioned souls who are suffering the threefold miseries of this conditional world due to their not being Kṛṣṇa conscious. A *brāhmaṇa* should take pity on the people and preach Kṛṣṇa consciousness in order to elevate them. Śrī Kṛṣṇa Himself, the Supreme Personality of Godhead, personally descends into this universe from the spiritual kingdom to teach conditioned souls about the values of spiritual life. He tries to induce them to surrender unto Him. Similarly, the *brāhmaṇas* do the same thing. After assimilating the Vedic instructions, they assist the Supreme Lord in His endeavor to deliver conditioned souls. The *brāhmaṇas* are very dear to the Supreme Lord due to their high *sattva-guṇa* qualities, and they also engage in welfare activities for all conditioned souls in the material world.

TEXT 25

मत्तोऽप्यनन्तात्परतः परस्मात्
स्वर्गापवर्गाधिपतेर्न किञ्चित् ।
येषां किमु स्यादितरेण तेषा-
मकिञ्चनानां मयि भक्तिभाजाम् ॥२५॥

matto 'py anantāt parataḥ parasmāt
svargāpavargādhipater na kiñcit
yeṣāṁ kim u syād itareṇa teṣām
akiñcanānāṁ mayi bhakti-bhājām

mattaḥ—from Me; *api*—even; *anantāt*—unlimited in strength and opulence; *parataḥ parasmāt*—higher than the highest; *svarga-apavarga-adhipateḥ*—able to bestow happiness obtainable by living in the heavenly kingdom, by liberation, or by enjoyment of material comfort and then liberation; *na*—not; *kiñcit*—anything; *yeṣām*—of whom; *kim*—what need; *u*—oh; *syāt*—can there be; *itareṇa*—with any other;

teṣām—of them; *akiñcanānām*—without needs or without possessions; *mayi*—unto Me; *bhakti-bhājām*—executing devotional service.

TRANSLATION

I am fully opulent, almighty and superior to Lord Brahmā and Indra, the King of the heavenly planets. I am also the bestower of all happiness obtained in the heavenly kingdom and by liberation. Nonetheless, the brāhmaṇas do not seek material comforts from Me. They are very pure and do not want to possess anything. They simply engage in My devotional service. What is the need of their asking for material benefits from anyone else?

PURPORT

The perfect brahminical qualification is stated herein: *akiñcanānāṁ mayi bhakti-bhājām.* The *brāhmaṇas* are always engaged in the devotional service of the Lord; consequently they have no material wants, nor do they possess material things. In *Caitanya-caritāmṛta* (*Madhya* 11.8), Caitanya Mahāprabhu explains the position of pure Vaiṣṇavas who are anxious to return home, back to Godhead. *Niṣkiñcanasya bhagavad-bhajanonmukhasya.* Those who actually want to return back to Godhead are *niṣkiñcana*—that is, they have no desire for material comfort. Śrī Caitanya Mahāprabhu advises, *sandarśanaṁ viṣayiṇām atha yoṣitāṁ ca hā hanta hanta viṣa-bhakṣaṇato 'py asādhu:* material opulence and sense gratification through the association of women are more dangerous than poison. *Brāhmaṇas* who are pure Vaiṣṇavas always engage in the Lord's service and are devoid of any desire for material gain. The *brāhmaṇas* do not worship demigods like Lord Brahmā, Indra or Lord Śiva for any material comfort. They do not even ask the Supreme Lord for material profit; therefore it is concluded that the *brāhmaṇas* are the supreme living entities of this world. Śrī Kapiladeva also confirms this in *Śrīmad-Bhāgavatam* (3.29.33):

tasmān mayy arpitāśeṣa-
kriyārthātmā nirantaraḥ
mayy arpitātmanaḥ puṁso
mayi sannyasta-karmaṇaḥ

na paśyāmi paraṁ bhūtam
akartuḥ sama-darśanāt

The *brāhmaṇas* are always dedicated to the Lord's service with their bodies, words and mind. There is no better person than a *brāhmaṇa* who thus engages himself and dedicates himself to the Supreme Lord.

TEXT 26

सर्वाणि मद्धिष्ण्यतया भवद्भि-
श्चराणि भूतानि सुता ध्रुवाणि ।
सम्भावितव्यानि पदे पदे वो
विविक्तदृग्भिस्तदु हार्हणं मे ॥२६॥

sarvāṇi mad-dhiṣṇyatayā bhavadbhiś
carāṇi bhūtāni sutā dhruvāṇi
sambhāvitavyāni pade pade vo
vivikta-dṛgbhis tad u hārhaṇaṁ me

sarvāṇi—all; *mat-dhiṣṇyatayā*—because of being My sitting place; *bhavadbhiḥ*—by you; *carāṇi*—that move; *bhūtāni*—living entities; *sutāḥ*—My dear sons; *dhruvāṇi*—that do not move; *sambhāvitavyāni*—to be respected; *pade pade*—at every moment; *vaḥ*—by you; *vivikta-dṛgbhiḥ*—possessing clear vision and understanding (that the Supreme Personality of Godhead in His Paramātmā feature is situated everywhere); *tat u*—that indirectly; *ha*—certainly; *arhaṇam*—offering respect; *me*—unto Me.

TRANSLATION

My dear sons, you should not envy any living entity—be he moving or nonmoving. Knowing that I am situated in them, you should offer respect to all of them at every moment. In this way, you offer respect to Me.

PURPORT

In this verse the word *vivikta-dṛgbhiḥ*, meaning without envy, is used. All living entities are the abode of the Supreme Personality of Godhead in His Paramātmā feature. As confirmed in *Brahma-saṁhitā: aṇḍāntara-sthaṁ paramāṇu-cayāntara-stham.* The Lord is situated in this universe as Garbhodakaśāyī Viṣṇu and Kṣīrodakaśāyī Viṣṇu. He is also situated within every atom. According to the Vedic statement: *īśāvāsyam idaṁ sarvam.* The Supreme Lord is situated everywhere, and wherever He is situated is His temple. We even offer respects to a temple from a distant place, and all living entities should similarly be offered respect. This is different from the theory of pantheism, which holds that everything is God. Everything has a relationship with God because God is situated everywhere. We should not make any particular distinction between the poor and the rich like the foolish worshipers of *daridra-nārāyaṇa.* Nārāyaṇa is present in the rich as well as the poor. One should not simply think Nārāyaṇa is situated among the poor. He is everywhere. An advanced devotee will offer respects to everyone—even to cats and dogs.

vidyā-vinaya-sampanne
brāhmaṇe gavi hastini
śuni caiva śva-pāke ca
paṇḍitāḥ sama-darśinaḥ

"The humble sage, by virtue of true knowledge, sees with equal vision a learned and gentle *brāhmaṇa*, a cow, an elephant, a dog and a dog-eater [outcaste]." (Bg. 5.18) This *sama-darśinaḥ*, equal vision, should not be mistaken to mean that the individual is the same as the Supreme Lord. They are always distinct. Every individual person is different from the Supreme Lord. It is a mistake to equate the individual living entity with the Supreme Lord on the plea of *vivikta-dṛk, sama-dṛk.* The Lord is always in an exalted position, even though He agrees to live everywhere. Śrīla Madhvācārya, quoting *Padma Purāṇa*, states: *vivikta-dṛṣṭi-jīvānāṁ dhiṣṇyatayā parameśvarasya bheda-dṛṣṭiḥ.* "One who has clear vision and who is devoid of envy can see that the Supreme Lord is separate from all living entities, although He is situated in every living entity." Madhvācārya further quotes from *Padma Purāṇa:*

upapādayet parātmānaṁ
jīvebhyo yaḥ pade pade
bhedenaiva na caitasmāt
priyo viṣṇos tu kaścana

"One who sees the living entity and the Supreme Lord as always distinct is very dear to the Lord." *Padma Purāṇa* also states, *yo hareś caiva jīvānāṁ bheda-vaktā hareḥ priyaḥ:* "One who preaches that the living entities are separate from the Supreme Lord is very dear to Lord Viṣṇu."

TEXT 27

मनोवचोदृक्करणेहितस्य
साक्षात्कृतं मे परिबर्हणं हि ।
विना पुमान् येन महाविमोहात्
कृतान्तपाशान्न विमोक्तुमीशेत् ॥२७॥

mano-vaco-dṛk-karaṇehitasya
sākṣāt-kṛtaṁ me paribarhaṇaṁ hi
vinā pumān yena mahā-vimohāt
kṛtānta-pāśān na vimoktum īśet

manaḥ—mind; *vacaḥ*—words; *dṛk*—sight; *karaṇa*—of the senses; *īhitasya*—of all activities (for maintenance of body, society, friendship and so on); *sākṣāt-kṛtam*—directly offered; *me*—of Me; *paribarhaṇam*—worship; *hi*—because; *vinā*—without; *pumān*—any person; *yena*—which; *mahā-vimohāt*—from the great illusion; *kṛtānta-pāśāt*—exactly like the stringent rope of Yamarāja; *na*—not; *vimoktum*—to become free; *īśet*—becomes able.

TRANSLATION

The true activity of the sense organs—mind, sight, words and all the knowledge-gathering and working senses—is to engage fully in My service. Unless his senses are thus engaged, a living entity cannot think of getting out of the great entanglement of material existence, which is exactly like Yamarāja's stringent rope.

PURPORT

As stated in the *Nārada-pañcarātra:*

sarvopādhi-vinirmuktaṁ
tat-paratvena nirmalam

hṛṣīkeṇa hṛṣīkeśa-
sevanaṁ bhaktir ucyate

This is the conclusion of *bhakti.* All the time, Lord Ṛṣabhadeva has been stressing devotional service, and now He is concluding by saying that all the senses should be engaged in the Lord's service. There are five senses by which we gather knowledge and five senses with which we work. These ten senses and the mind should be fully engaged in the Lord's service. Without engaging them in this way, one cannot get out of the clutches of *māyā.*

TEXT 28

श्रीशुक उवाच

एवमनुशास्यात्मजान् स्वयमनुशिष्टानपि लोकानुशासनार्थं महानुभावः
परमसुहृद्भगवानृषभापदेश उपशमशीलानामुपरतकर्मणां महामुनीनां भक्तिज्ञान-
वैराग्यलक्षणं पारमहंस्यधर्ममुपशिक्षमाणः स्वतनयशतज्येष्ठं परमभागवतं
भगवज्जनपरायणं भरतं धरणिपालनायाभिषिच्य स्वयं भवन एवोर्वरित-
शरीरमात्रपरिग्रह उन्मत्त इव गगनपरिधानः प्रकीर्णकेश आत्मन्या-
रोपिताहवनीयो ब्रह्मावर्तात्प्रवव्राज॥२८॥

śrī-śuka uvāca
evam anuśāsyātmajān svayam anuśiṣṭān api lokānuśāsanārthaṁ mahānubhāvaḥ parama-suhṛd bhagavān ṛṣabhāpadeśa upaśama-śīlānām uparata-karmaṇāṁ mahā-munīnāṁ bhakti-jñāna-vairāgya-lakṣaṇaṁ pāramahaṁsya-dharmam upaśikṣamāṇaḥ sva-tanaya-śata-jyeṣṭhaṁ parama-bhāgavataṁ bhagavaj-jana-parāyaṇaṁ bharataṁ dharaṇi-pālanāyābhiṣicya svayaṁ bhavana evorvarita-śarīra-mātra-parigraha unmatta iva gagana-paridhānaḥ prakīrṇa-keśa ātmany āropitāhavanīyo brahmāvartāt pravavrāja.

śrī-śukaḥ uvāca—Śrī Śukadeva Gosvāmī said; *evam*—in this way; *anuśāsya*—after instructing; *ātma-jān*—His sons; *svayam*—personally; *anuśiṣṭān*—highly educated in culture; *api*—although; *loka-anuśāsana-artham*—just to instruct the people; *mahā-anubhāvaḥ*—the great personality; *parama-suhṛt*—everyone's sublime well-wisher; *bhagavān*—the Supreme Personality of Godhead; *ṛṣabha-apadeśaḥ*—who is celebrated and known as Ṛṣabhadeva; *upaśama-śīlānām*—of persons who have no desire for material enjoyment; *uparata-karmaṇām*—who are no longer interested in fruitive activities; *mahā-munīnām*—who are *sannyāsīs; bhakti*—devotional service; *jñāna*—perfect knowledge; *vairāgya*—detachment; *lakṣaṇam*—characterized by; *pāramahaṁsya*—of the best of human beings; *dharmam*—the duties; *upaśikṣamāṇaḥ*—instructing; *sva-tanaya*—of His sons; *śata*—hundred; *jyeṣṭham*—the eldest; *parama-bhāgavatam*—a topmost devotee of the Lord; *bhagavat-jana-parāyaṇam*—a follower of the devotees of the Lord, *brāhmaṇas* and Vaiṣṇavas; *bharatam*—Bharata Mahārāja; *dharaṇi-pālanāya*—with a view to ruling the world; *abhiṣicya*—placing on the throne; *svayam*—personally; *bhavane*—at home; *eva*—although; *urvarita*—remaining; *śarīra-mātra*—the body only; *parigrahaḥ*—accepting; *unmattaḥ*—a madman; *iva*—exactly like; *gagana-paridhānaḥ*—taking the sky as His dress; *prakīrṇa-keśaḥ*—having scattered hair; *ātmani*—in Himself; *āropita*—keeping; *āhavanīyaḥ*—the Vedic fire; *brahmāvartāt*—from the place known as Brahmāvarta; *pravavrāja*—began to travel all over the world.

TRANSLATION

Śukadeva Gosvāmī said: Thus the great well-wisher of everyone, the Supreme Lord Ṛṣabhadeva, instructed His own sons. Although they were perfectly educated and cultured, He instructed them just to set an example of how a father should instruct his sons before retiring from family life. Sannyāsīs, who are no longer bound by fruitive activity and who have taken to devotional service after all their material desires have been vanquished, also learn by these instructions. Lord Ṛṣabhadeva instructed His one hundred sons, of whom the eldest, Bharata, was a very advanced devotee and a follower of Vaiṣṇavas. In order to rule the whole world, the Lord enthroned His eldest son on the royal seat. Thereafter, although still at home, Lord Ṛṣabhadeva lived like a madman, naked and with disheveled hair. Then the Lord took the sacrificial fire within Himself, and He left Brahmāvarta to tour the whole world.

PURPORT

Actually the instructions given to Lord Ṛṣabhadeva's sons were not exactly meant for His sons because they were already educated and highly advanced in knowledge. Rather, these instructions were meant for *sannyāsīs* who intend to become advanced devotees. *Sannyāsīs* must abide by Lord Ṛṣabhadeva's instructions while on the path of devotional service. Lord Ṛṣabhadeva retired from family life and lived like a naked madman even while still with His family.

TEXT 29

जडान्धमूकबधिरपिशाचोन्मादकवदवधूतवेषोऽभिभाष्यमाणोऽपि जनानां गृहीतमौनव्रतस्तूष्णीं बभूव ॥२९॥

jaḍāndha-mūka-badhira-piśāconmādakavad-avadhūta-veṣo
'bhibhāṣyamāṇo 'pi janānāṁ gṛhīta-mauna-vratas tūṣṇīṁ babhūva.

jaḍa—idle; *andha*—blind; *mūka*—dumb; *badhira*—deaf; *piśāca*—ghost; *unmādaka*—a madman; *vat*—like; *avadhūta-veṣaḥ*—appearing like an *avadhūta* (having no concern with the material world); *abhibhāṣyamāṇaḥ*—being thus addressed (as deaf, dumb and blind); *api*—although; *janānām*—by the people; *gṛhīta*—took; *mauna*—of silence; *vrataḥ*—the vow; *tūṣṇīm babhūva*—He remained silent.

TRANSLATION

After accepting the feature of avadhūta, a great saintly person without material cares, Lord Ṛṣabhadeva passed through human society like a blind, deaf and dumb man, an idle stone, a ghost or a madman. Although people called Him such names, He remained silent and did not speak to anyone.

PURPORT

The word *avadhūta* refers to one who does not care for social conventions, particularly the *varṇāśrama-dharma*. However, such a person may be situated fully within himself and be satisfied with the Supreme Personality of Godhead, on whom he meditates. In other words, one who has surpassed the rules and regulations of *varṇāśrama-dharma* is called *avadhūta*. Such a person has already surpassed the clutches of *māyā*, and he lives completely separate and independent.

TEXT 30

तत्र तत्र पुरग्रामाकरखेटवाटखर्वटशिबिरव्रजघोषसार्थगिरिवनाश्रमादिष्वनुपथ
मवनिचरापसदैः परिभूयमानो मक्षिकाभिरिव वनगजस्तर्जनताडनावमेहन-
ष्ठीवनग्रावशकृद्रजःप्रक्षेपपूतिवातदुरुक्तैस्तदविगणयन्नेवासत्संस्थान एतस्मिन्
देहोपलक्षणे सदपदेश उभयानुभवस्वरूपेण स्वमहिमावस्थानेनासमारोपिताहं-
ममाभिमानत्वादविखण्डितमनाः पृथिवीमेकचरः परिबभ्राम ॥३०॥

tatra tatra pura-grāmākara-kheṭa-vāṭa-kharvaṭa-śibira-vraja-ghoṣa-sārtha-giri-vanāśramādiṣv anupatham avanicarāpasadaiḥ paribhūyamāno makṣikābhir iva vana-gajas tarjana-tāḍanāvamehana-ṣṭhīvana-grāva-śakṛd-rajaḥ-prakṣepa-pūti-vāta-duruktais tad aviganayann evāsat-saṁsthāna etasmin dehopalakṣaṇe sad-apadeśa ubhayānubhava-svarūpeṇa sva-mahimāvasthānenāsamāropitāhaṁ-mamābhimānatvād avikhaṇḍita-manāḥ pṛthivīm eka-caraḥ paribabhrāma.

tatra tatra—here and there; *pura*—cities; *grāma*—villages; *ākara*—mines; *kheṭa*—agricultural places; *vāṭa*—gardens; *kharvaṭa*—villages in valleys; *śibira*—military encampments; *vraja*—cow pens; *ghoṣa*—residential places of cowherd men; *sārtha*—resting places for pilgrims; *giri*—hills; *vana*—forests; *āśrama*—in the residential places of hermits; *ādiṣu*—and so on; *anupatham*—as He passed through; *avanicara-apasadaiḥ*—by undesirable elements, wicked persons; *pari-bhūyamānaḥ*—being surrounded; *makṣikābhiḥ*—by flies; *iva*—like; *vana-gajaḥ*—an elephant coming from the forest; *tarjana*—by threats; *tāḍana*—beating; *avamehana*—passing urine on the body; *ṣṭhīvana*—spitting on the body; *grāva-śakṛt*—stones and stool; *rajaḥ*—dust; *prak-ṣepa*—throwing; *pūti-vāta*—passing air over the body; *duruktaiḥ*—and by bad words; *tat*—that; *avigaṇayan*—without caring about; *eva*—thus; *asat-saṁsthāne*—habitat not fit for a gentleman; *etasmin*—in this; *deha-upalakṣaṇe*—in the shape of the material body; *sat-apadeśe*—

called real; *ubhaya-anubhava-svarūpeṇa*—by understanding the proper situation of the body and the soul; *sva-mahima*—in His personal glory; *avasthānena*—by being situated; *asamāropita-aham-mama-abhimānatvāt*—from not accepting the misconception of "I and mine"; *avikhaṇḍita-manāḥ*—undisturbed in mind; *pṛthivīm*—all over the world; *eka-caraḥ*—alone; *paribabhrāma*—He wandered.

TRANSLATION

Ṛṣabhadeva began to tour through cities, villages, mines, countrysides, valleys, gardens, military camps, cow pens, the homes of cowherd men, transient hotels, hills, forests and hermitages. Wherever He traveled, all bad elements surrounded Him, just as flies surround the body of an elephant coming from a forest. He was always being threatened, beaten, urinated upon and spat upon. Sometimes people threw stones, stool and dust at Him, and sometimes people passed foul air before Him. Thus people called Him many bad names and gave Him a great deal of trouble, but He did not care about this, for He understood that the body is simply meant for such an end. He was situated on the spiritual platform, and, being in His spiritual glory, He did not care for all these material insults. In other words, He completely understood that matter and spirit are separate, and He had no bodily conception. Thus, without being angry at anyone, He walked through the whole world alone.

PURPORT

Narottama dāsa Ṭhākura says: *deha-smṛti nāhi yāra, saṁsāra bandhana kāhāṅ tāra.* When a person fully realizes that the material body and world are temporary, he is not concerned with pain and pleasures of the body. As Śrī Kṛṣṇa advises in *Bhagavad-gītā* (2.14):

mātrā-sparśās tu kaunteya
śītoṣṇa-sukha-duḥkha-dāḥ
āgamāpāyino 'nityās
tāṁs titikṣasva bhārata

"O son of Kuntī, the nonpermanent appearance of happiness and distress, and their disappearance in due course, are like the appearance and disappearance of winter and summer seasons. They arise from sense perception, O scion of Bharata, and one must learn to tolerate them without being disturbed."

As far as Ṛṣabhadeva is concerned, it has already been explained: *idaṁ śarīraṁ mama durvibhāvyam.* He did not at all possess a material body; and therefore He was tolerant of all the trouble offered to Him by the bad elements in society. Consequently He could tolerate people's throwing stool and dust upon Him and beating Him. His body was transcendental and consequently did not at all suffer pain. He was always situated in His spiritual bliss. As stated in *Bhagavad-gītā* (18.61):

īśvaraḥ sarva-bhūtānāṁ
hṛd-deśe 'rjuna tiṣṭhati
bhrāmayan sarva-bhūtāni
yantrārūḍhāni māyayā

"The Supreme Lord is situated in everyone's heart, O Arjuna, and is directing the wanderings of all living entities, who are seated as on a machine, made of the material energy."

Since the Lord is situated in everyone's heart, He is in the heart of hogs and dogs also. If hogs and dogs in their material bodies live in filthy places, one should not think that the Supreme Personality of Godhead in His Paramātmā feature also lives in a filthy place. Although Lord Ṛṣabhadeva was maltreated by the bad elements of the world, He was not at all affected. Therefore it is stated here, *sva-mahima-avasthānena:* "He was situated in His own glory." He was never saddened due to being insulted in the many ways described above.

TEXT 31

अतिसुकुमारकरचरणोरःस्थलविपुलबाह्वंसगलवदनाद्यवयवविन्यासः प्रकृति-
सुन्दरस्वभावहाससुमुखो नवनलिनदलायमानशिशिरतारारुणायतनयन-
रुचिरः सदृशसुभगकपोलकर्णकण्ठनासो विगूढस्मितवदनमहोत्सवेन

पुरवनितानां मनसि कुसुमशरासनमुपदधानः परागवलम्बमानकुटिलजटिलकपिशकेशभूरिभारोऽवधूतमलिननिजशरीरेण ग्रहगृहीत इवादृश्यत ॥ ३१ ॥

ati-sukumāra-kara-caraṇoraḥ-sthala-vipula-bāhv-aṁsa-gala-vadanādy-avayava-vinyāsaḥ prakṛti-sundara-svabhāva-hāsa-sumukho nava-nalina-dalāyamāna-śiśira-tārāruṇāyata-nayana-ruciraḥ sadṛśa-subhaga-kapola-karṇa-kaṇṭha-nāso vigūḍha-smita-vadana-mahotsavena pura-vanitānāṁ manasi kusuma-śarāsanam upadadhānaḥ parāg-avalambamāna-kuṭila-jaṭila-kapiśa-keśa-bhūri-bhāro 'vadhūta-malina-nija-śarīreṇa graha-gṛhīta ivādṛśyata.

ati-su-kumāra—very delicate; *kara*—hands; *caraṇa*—feet; *uraḥ-sthala*—chest; *vipula*—long; *bāhu*—arms; *aṁsa*—shoulders; *gala*—neck; *vadana*—face; *ādi*—and so on; *avayava*—limbs; *vinyāsaḥ*—properly situated; *prakṛti*—by nature; *sundara*—lovely; *sva-bhāva*—natural; *hāsa*—with smiling; *su-mukhaḥ*—His beautiful mouth; *nava-nalina-dalāyamāna*—appearing like the petals of a new lotus flower; *śiśira*—taking away all miseries; *tāra*—the irises; *aruṇa*—reddish; *āyata*—spread wide; *nayana*—with eyes; *ruciraḥ*—lovely; *sadṛśa*—such; *subhaga*—beauty; *kapola*—forehead; *karṇa*—ears; *kaṇṭha*—neck; *nāsaḥ*—His nose; *vigūḍha-smita*—by deep smiling; *vadana*—by His face; *mahā-utsavena*—appearing like a festival; *pura-vanitānām*—of women within household life; *manasi*—in the heart; *kusuma-śarāsanam*—Cupid; *upadadhānaḥ*—awakening; *parāk*—all around; *avalambamāna*—spread; *kuṭila*—curly; *jaṭila*—matted; *kapiśa*—brown; *keśa*—of hair; *bhūri-bhāraḥ*—possessing a great abundance; *avadhūta*—neglected; *malina*—dirty; *nija-śarīreṇa*—by His body; *graha-gṛhītaḥ*—haunted by a ghost; *iva*—as if; *adṛśyata*—He appeared.

TRANSLATION

Lord Ṛṣabhadeva's hands, feet and chest were very long. His shoulders, face and limbs were all very delicate and symmetrically proportioned. His mouth was beautifully decorated with His natural smile, and He appeared all the more lovely with His reddish eyes spread wide like the petals of a newly grown lotus flower covered with dew in the early morning. The irises of His eyes were

so pleasing that they removed all the troubles of everyone who saw Him. His forehead, ears, neck, nose and all His other features were very beautiful. His gentle smile always made His face beautiful, so much so that He even attracted the hearts of married women. It was as though they had been pierced by arrows of Cupid. About His head was an abundance of curly, matted brown hair. His hair was disheveled because His body was dirty and not taken care of. He appeared as if He were haunted by a ghost.

PURPORT

Although Lord Ṛṣabhadeva's body was very much neglected, His transcendental features were so attractive that even married women were attracted to Him. His beauty and dirtiness combined to make His beautiful body appear as though it were haunted by a ghost.

TEXT 32

यर्हि वाव स भगवान् लोकमिमं योगस्याद्धा प्रतीपमिवाचक्षाण-स्तत्प्रतिक्रियाकर्म बीभत्सितमिति व्रतमाजगरमास्थितः शयान एवाश्नाति पिबति खादत्यवमेहति हदति स्म चेष्टमान उच्चरित आदिग्धोद्देशः ॥ ३२

yarhi vāva sa bhagavān lokam imaṁ yogasyāddhā pratīpam ivācakṣāṇas tat-pratikriyā-karma bībhatsitam iti vratam ājagaram āsthitaḥ śayāna evāśnāti pibati khādaty avamehati hadati sma ceṣṭamāna uccarita ādigdhoddeśaḥ.

yarhi vāva—when; *saḥ*—He; *bhagavān*—the Personality of Godhead; *lokam*—the people in general; *imam*—this; *yogasya*—to the performance of *yoga; addhā*—directly; *pratīpam*—antagonistic; *iva*—like; *ācakṣāṇaḥ*—observed; *tat*—of that; *pratikriyā*—for counteraction; *karma*—activity; *bībhatsitam*—abominable; *iti*—thus; *vratam*—the behavior; *ājagaram*—of a python (to stay in one place); *āsthitaḥ*—accepting; *śayānaḥ*—lying down; *eva*—indeed; *aśnāti*—eats; *pibati*—drinks; *khādati*—chews; *avamehati*—passes urine; *hadati*—passes stool; *sma*—thus; *ceṣṭamānaḥ*—rolling; *uccarite*—in the stool and urine; *ādigdha-uddeśaḥ*—His body thus smeared.

TRANSLATION

When Lord Ṛṣabhadeva saw that the general populace was very antagonistic to His execution of mystic yoga, He accepted the behavior of a python in order to counteract their opposition. Thus He stayed in one place and lay down. While lying down, He ate and drank, and He passed stool and urine and rolled in it. Indeed, He smeared His whole body with His own stool and urine so that opposing elements might not come and disturb Him.

PURPORT

According to one's destiny, one enjoys allotted happiness and distress, even though one keeps himself in one place. This is the injunction of the *śāstras.* When one is spiritually situated, he may stay in one place, and all his necessities will be supplied by the arrangement of the supreme controller. Unless one is a preacher, there is no need to travel all over the world. A person can stay in one place and execute devotional service suitably according to time and circumstance. When Ṛṣabhadeva saw that He was simply being disturbed by traveling throughout the world, He decided to lie down in one place like a python. Thus He ate, drank, and He passed stool and urine and smeared His body with them so that people would not disturb Him.

TEXT 33

तस्य ह यः पुरीषसुरभिसौगन्ध्यवायुस्तं देशं दशयोजनं समन्तात् सुरभिं चकार ॥ ३३ ॥

tasya ha yaḥ purīṣa-surabhi-saugandhya-vāyus taṁ deśaṁ daśa-yojanaṁ samantāt surabhiṁ cakāra.

tasya—His; *ha*—indeed; *yaḥ*—which; *purīṣa*—of the stool; *surabhi*—by the aroma; *saugandhya*—possessing a good fragrance; *vāyuḥ*—the air; *tam*—that; *deśam*—country; *daśa*—up to ten; *yojanam*—*yojanas* (one *yojana* equals eight miles); *samantāt*—all around; *surabhim*—aromatic; *cakāra*—made.

TRANSLATION

Because Lord Ṛṣabhadeva remained in that condition, the public did not disturb Him, but no bad aroma emanated from His stool and urine. Quite the contrary, His stool and urine were so aromatic that they filled eighty miles of the countryside with a pleasant fragrance.

PURPORT

From this we can certainly assume that Lord Ṛṣabhadeva was transcendentally blissful. His stool and urine were so completely different from material stool and urine that they were aromatic. Even in the material world, cow dung is accepted as purified and antiseptic. A person can keep stacks of cow dung in one place, and it will not create a bad odor to disturb anyone. We can take it for granted that in the spiritual world, stool and urine are also pleasantly scented. Indeed, the entire atmosphere became very pleasant due to Lord Ṛṣabhadeva's stool and urine.

TEXT 34

एवं गोमृगकाकचर्यया व्रजंस्तिष्ठन्नासीनः शयानः काकमृगगोचरितः
पिबति खादत्यवमेहति स्म ॥३४॥

evaṁ go-mṛga-kāka-caryayā vrajaṁs tiṣṭhann āsīnaḥ śayānaḥ kāka-mṛga-go-caritaḥ pibati khādaty avamehati sma.

evam—thus; *go*—of cows; *mṛga*—deer; *kāka*—crows; *caryayā*—by the activities; *vrajan*—moving; *tiṣṭhan*—standing; *āsīnaḥ*—sitting; *śayānaḥ*—lying down; *kāka-mṛga-go-caritaḥ*—behaving exactly like the crows, deer and cows; *pibati*—drinks; *khādati*—eats; *avamehati*—passes urine; *sma*—He did so.

TRANSLATION

In this way Lord Ṛṣabhadeva followed the behavior of cows, deer and crows. Sometimes He moved or walked, and sometimes He sat down in one place. Sometimes He lay down, behaving

exactly like cows, deer and crows. In that way, He ate, drank, passed stool and urine and cheated the people in this way.

PURPORT

Being the Supreme Personality of Godhead, Lord Ṛṣabhadeva possessed a transcendental, spiritual body. Since the general public could not appreciate His behavior and mystic *yoga* practice, they began to disturb Him. To cheat them, He behaved like crows, cows and deer.

TEXT 35

इति नानायोगचर्याचरणो भगवान् कैवल्यपतिरृषभोऽविरतपरममहानन्दानुभव
आत्मनि सर्वेषां भूतानामात्मभूते भगवति वासुदेव आत्मनोऽव्यवधानानन्त-
रोदरभावेन सिद्धसमस्तार्थपरिपूर्णो योगैश्वर्याणि वैहायसमनोजवान्तर्धानपरकाय-
प्रवेशदूरग्रहणादीनि यदृच्छयोपगतानि नाञ्जसा नृप हृदयेनाभ्यनन्दत् ॥३५॥

iti nānā-yoga-caryācaraṇo bhagavān kaivalya-patir ṛṣabho 'virata-parama-mahānandānubhava ātmani sarveṣāṁ bhūtānām ātma-bhūte bhagavati vāsudeva ātmano 'vyavadhānānanta-rodara-bhāvena siddha-samastārtha-paripūrṇo yogaiśvaryāṇi vaihāyasa-mano-javāntardhāna-parakāya-praveśa-dūra-grahaṇādīni yadṛcchayopagatāni nāñjasā nṛpa hṛdayenābhyanandat.

iti—thus; *nānā*—various; *yoga*—of mystic *yoga; caryā*—performances; *ācaraṇaḥ*—practicing; *bhagavān*—the Supreme Personality of Godhead; *kaivalya-patiḥ*—the master of *kaivalya,* oneness, or the giver of *sāyujya-mukti; ṛṣabhaḥ*—Lord Ṛṣabha; *avirata*—incessantly; *parama*—supreme; *mahā*—great; *ānanda-anubhavaḥ*—feeling transcendental bliss; *ātmani*—in the Supreme Soul; *sarveṣām*—of all; *bhūtānām*—living entities; *ātma-bhūte*—situated in the heart; *bhagavati*—unto the Supreme Personality of Godhead; *vāsudeve*—Kṛṣṇa, the son of Vasudeva; *ātmanaḥ*—of Himself; *avyavadhāna*—by the non-difference of constitution; *ananta*—unlimited; *rodara*—like crying, laughing and shivering; *bhāvena*—by the symptoms of love; *siddha*—completely perfect; *samasta*—all; *artha*—with desirable opulences; *paripūrṇaḥ*—full; *yoga-aiśvaryāṇi*—the mystic powers; *vaihāyasa*—

flying in the sky; *manaḥ-java*—traveling at the speed of mind; *antardhāna*—the ability to disappear; *parakāya-praveśa*—the ability to enter another's body; *dūra-grahaṇa*—the ability to perceive things far, far away; *ādīni*—and others; *yadṛcchayā*—without difficulty, automatically; *upagatāni*—achieved; *na*—not; *añjasā*—directly; *nṛpa*—O King Parīkṣit; *hṛdayena*—within the heart; *abhyanandat*—accepted.

TRANSLATION

O King Parīkṣit, just to show all the yogīs the mystic process, Lord Ṛṣabhadeva, the partial expansion of Lord Kṛṣṇa, performed wonderful activities. Actually He was the master of liberation and was fully absorbed in transcendental bliss, which increased a thousandfold. Lord Kṛṣṇa, Vāsudeva, the son of Vasudeva, is the original source of Lord Ṛṣabhadeva. There is no difference in Their constitution, and consequently Lord Ṛṣabhadeva awakened the loving symptoms of crying, laughing and shivering. He was always absorbed in transcendental love. Due to this, all mystic powers automatically approached Him, such as the ability to travel in outer space at the speed of mind, to appear and disappear, to enter the bodies of others, and to see things far, far away. Although He could do all this, He did not exercise these powers.

PURPORT

In the *Caitanya-caritāmṛta* (*Madhya* 19.149) it is said:

kṛṣṇa-bhakta——niṣkāma, ataeva 'śānta'
bhukti-mukti-siddhi-kāmī——sakali 'aśānta'

The word *śānta* means completely peaceful. Unless all one's desires are fulfilled, one cannot be peaceful. Everyone is trying to fulfill his aspirations and desires, be they material or spiritual. Those in the material world are *aśānta* (without peace) because they have so many desires to fulfill. The pure devotee, however, is without desire. *Anyābhilāṣitā-śūnya:* a pure devotee is completely free from all kinds of material desire. *Karmīs*, on the other hand, are simply full of desires because they try to enjoy sense gratification. They are not peaceful in this life, nor the next, during the past, present or future. Similarly, *jñānīs* are always aspiring after liberation and trying to become one with the Supreme. *Yogīs* are aspiring after many *siddhis* (powers)—*aṇimā, laghimā, prāpti,* etc. However, a devotee is not at all interested in these things because he is fully dependent on the mercy of Kṛṣṇa. Kṛṣṇa is *yogeśvara,* the possessor of all mystic powers (*siddhis*), and He is *ātmārāma,* fully self-satisfied. The *yoga-siddhis* are described in this verse. One can fly in outer space without the aid of a machine, and he can travel at the speed of mind. This means that as soon as a *yogī* desires to go somewhere within this universe or even beyond this universe, he can do so immediately. One cannot estimate the speed of mind, for within a second the mind can go many millions of miles. Sometimes *yogīs* enter into the bodies of other people and act as they desire when their bodies are not working properly. When the body becomes old, a perfect *yogī* can find a young, able body. Giving up his old body, the *yogī* can enter into the young body and act as he pleases. Being a plenary expansion of Lord Vāsudeva, Lord Ṛṣabhadeva possessed all these mystic *yoga* powers, but He was satisfied with His devotional love of Kṛṣṇa, which was evinced by the ecstatic symptoms, such as crying, laughing and shivering.

Thus end the Bhaktivedanta purports of the Fifth Canto, Fifth Chapter of the Śrīmad-Bhāgavatam *entitled "Lord Ṛṣabhadeva's Teachings to His Sons."*

CHAPTER SIX

The Activities of Lord Ṛṣabhadeva

This chapter tells how Lord Ṛṣabhadeva left His body. He was not attached to His body even when it was being burned up in a forest fire. When the seed of fruitive activity is burned by the fire of knowledge, the spiritual properties and mystic powers are automatically manifest, yet *bhakti-yoga* is not affected by these mystic powers. An ordinary *yogī* is captivated by mystic powers and his progress checked; therefore a perfect *yogī* does not welcome them. Because the mind is restless and undependable, it must remain always under control. Even the mind of the advanced *yogī* Saubhari created such a disturbance that he lost his yogic mystic powers. Due to a restless mind, even a very advanced *yogī* can fall down. The mind is so restless that it induces even a perfect *yogī* to be controlled by the senses. Therefore Lord Ṛṣabhadeva, for the instruction of all *yogīs*, showed the process of quitting the body. While traveling in South India, through the provinces of Karṇāṭa, Koṅka, Veṅka and Kuṭaka, Lord Ṛṣabhadeva arrived in the neighborhood of Kuṭakācala. Suddenly there was a forest fire that burned the forest and Lord Ṛṣabhadeva's body to ashes. The pastimes of Lord Ṛṣabhadeva as a liberated soul were known by the King of Koṅka, Veṅka and Kuṭaka. This King's name was Arhat. He later became captivated by the illusory energy, and in this condition he set forth the basic principles of Jainism. Lord Ṛṣabhadeva set forth the principles of religion that can free one from material bondage, and He put an end to all kinds of atheistic activities. On this earth, the place known as Bhārata-varṣa was a very pious land because the Supreme Lord appeared there when He wanted to incarnate.

Lord Ṛṣabhadeva neglected all the mystic powers for which the so-called *yogīs* hanker. Because of the beauty of devotional service, devotees are not at all interested in so-called mystic power. The master of all yogic power, Lord Kṛṣṇa, can exhibit all powers on behalf of His devotee. Devotional service is more valuable than yogic mystic powers. Devotees who are sometimes misled aspire for liberation and mystic powers. The

Supreme Lord gives these devotees whatever they desire, but they cannot attain the most important function of devotional service. Devotional service to the Lord is guaranteed for those who do not desire liberation and mystic power.

TEXT 1

राजोवाच

न नूनं भगव आत्मारामाणां योगसमीरितज्ञानावभर्जितकर्मबीजानामैश्वर्याणि पुनः क्लेशदानि भवितुमर्हन्ति यदृच्छयोपगतानि ॥ १ ॥

rājovāca

na nūnaṁ bhagava ātmārāmāṇāṁ yoga-samīrita-jñānāvabharjita-karma-bījānām aiśvaryāṇi punaḥ kleśadāni bhavitum arhanti yadṛc-chayopagatāni.

rājā uvāca—King Parīkṣit inquired; *na*—not; *nūnam*—indeed; *bhagavaḥ*—O most powerful Śukadeva Gosvāmī; *ātmārāmāṇām*—of pure devotees simply engaged in devotional service; *yoga-samīrita*—achieved by practice of *yoga; jñāna*—by knowledge; *avabharjita*—burned; *karma-bījānām*—of those whose seeds of fruitive activities; *aiśvaryāṇi*—the mystic powers; *punaḥ*—again; *kleśadāni*—sources of distress; *bhavitum*—to become; *arhanti*—are able; *yadṛcchayā*—automatically; *upagatāni*—achieved.

TRANSLATION

King Parīkṣit asked Śukadeva Gosvāmī: My dear Lord, for those who are completely pure in heart, knowledge is attained by the practice of bhakti-yoga, and attachment for fruitive activity is completely burned to ashes. For such people, the powers of mystic yoga automatically arise. They do not cause distress. Why, then, did Ṛṣabhadeva neglect them?

PURPORT

A pure devotee is constantly engaged in the service of the Supreme Personality of Godhead. Whatever is necessary for the discharge of devotional service is automatically attained, though it may appear to be the result of mystic *yoga* power. Sometimes a *yogī* displays a little yogic power by manufacturing gold. A little quantity of gold captivates foolish people, and thus the *yogī* gets many followers, who are willing to accept such a tiny person as the Supreme Personality of Godhead. Such a *yogī* may also advertise himself as Bhagavān. However, a devotee does not have to exhibit such magical wonders. Without practicing the mystic yogic process, he achieves even greater opulence all over the world. Under the circumstances, Lord Ṛṣabhadeva refused to manifest mystic yogic perfections, and Mahārāja Parīkṣit asked why He did not accept them, since, for a devotee, they are not at all disturbing. A devotee is never distressed or satisfied by material opulence. His concern is how to please the Supreme Personality of Godhead. If, by the grace of the Supreme Lord, a devotee achieves extraordinary opulence, he utilizes the opportunity for the Lord's service. He is not disturbed by the opulence.

TEXT 2

ऋषिरुवाच

सत्यमुक्तं किन्त्विह वा एके न मनसोऽद्धा विश्रम्भमनवस्थानस्य शठकिरात इव सङ्गच्छन्ते ॥ २ ॥

ṛṣir uvāca
satyam uktaṁ kintv iha vā eke na manaso 'ddhā viśrambham anavasthānasya śaṭha-kirāta iva saṅgacchante.

ṛṣiḥ uvāca—Śukadeva Gosvāmī said; *satyam*—the correct thing; *uktam*—have said; *kintu*—but; *iha*—in this material world; *vā*—either; *eke*—some; *na*—not; *manasaḥ*—of the mind; *addhā*—directly; *viśrambham*—faithful; *anavasthānasya*—being unsteady; *śaṭha*—very cunning; *kirātaḥ*—a hunter; *iva*—like; *saṅgacchante*—become.

TRANSLATION

Śrīla Śukadeva Gosvāmī replied: My dear King, you have spoken correctly. However, after capturing animals, a cunning hunter does not put faith in them, for they might run away. Similarly,

those who are advanced in spiritual life do not put faith in the mind. Indeed, they always remain vigilant and watch the mind's action.

PURPORT

In *Bhagavad-gītā* (18.5) Lord Kṛṣṇa says:

yajña-dāna-tapaḥ-karma
na tyājyaṁ kāryam eva tat
yajño dānaṁ tapaś caiva
pāvanāni manīṣiṇām

"Acts of sacrifice, charity and penance are not to be given up but should be performed. Indeed, sacrifice, charity and penance purify even the great souls."

Even one who has renounced the world and has taken *sannyāsa* should not renounce chanting the Hare Kṛṣṇa *mahā-mantra.* Renunciation does not mean that one has to renounce *saṅkīrtana-yajña.* Similarly, one should not renounce charity or *tapasya.* The *yoga* system for control of the mind and senses must be strictly followed. Lord Ṛṣabhadeva showed how severe types of *tapasya* could be performed, and He set an example for all others.

TEXT 3

तथा चोक्तम्—
न कुर्यात्कर्हिचित्सख्यं मनसि ह्यनवस्थिते ।
यद्विश्रम्भाच्चिराच्चीर्णं चस्कन्द तप ऐश्वरम् ॥ ३ ॥

tathā coktam—
na kuryāt karhicit sakhyaṁ
manasi hy anavasthite
yad-viśrambhāc cirāc cīrṇaṁ
caskanda tapa aiśvaram

tathā—so; *ca*—and; *uktam*—it is said; *na*—never; *kuryāt*—should do; *karhicit*—at any time or with anyone; *sakhyam*—friendship;

manasi—in the mind; *hi*—certainly; *anavasthite*—which is very restless; *yat*—in which; *viśrambhāt*—from placing too much faith; *cirāt*—for a long time; *cīrṇam*—practiced; *caskanda*—became disturbed; *tapaḥ*—the austerity; *aiśvaram*—of great personalities like Lord Śiva and the great sage Saubhari.

TRANSLATION

All the learned scholars have given their opinion. The mind is by nature very restless, and one should not make friends with it. If we place full confidence in the mind, it may cheat us at any moment. Even Lord Śiva became agitated upon seeing the Mohinī form of Lord Kṛṣṇa, and Saubhari Muni also fell down from the mature stage of yogic perfection.

PURPORT

The first business of one trying to advance in spiritual life is to control the mind and senses. As Śrī Kṛṣṇa says in *Bhagavad-gītā* (15.7):

mamaivāṁśo jīva-loke
jīva-bhūtaḥ sanātanaḥ
manaḥ ṣaṣṭhānīndriyāṇi
prakṛti-sthāni karṣati

Although the living entities are part and parcel of the Supreme Lord and are therefore in a transcendental position, they are still suffering in this material world and struggling for existence due to the mind and the senses. To get out of this false struggle for existence and become happy in the material world, one has to control the mind and senses and be detached from material conditions. One should never neglect austerities and penances; one should always perform them. Lord Ṛṣabhadeva personally showed us how to do this. In the *Śrīmad-Bhāgavatam* (9.19.17) it is specifically stated:

mātrā svasrā duhitrā vā
nāviviktāsano bhavet
balavān indriya-grāmo
vidvāṁsam api karṣati

A *gṛhastha, vānaprastha, sannyāsī* and *brahmacārī* should be very careful when associating with women. One is forbidden to sit down in a solitary place even with one's mother, sister or daughter. In our Kṛṣṇa consciousness movement it has been very difficult to disassociate ourselves from women in our society, especially in Western countries. We are therefore sometimes criticized, but nonetheless we are trying to give everyone a chance to chant the Hare Kṛṣṇa *mahā-mantra* and thus advance spiritually. If we stick to the principle of chanting the Hare Kṛṣṇa *mahā-mantra* offenselessly, then, by the grace of Śrīla Haridāsa Ṭhākura, we may be saved from the allurement of women. However, if we are not very strict in chanting the Hare Kṛṣṇa *mahā-mantra,* we may at any time fall victim to women.

TEXT 4

नित्यं ददाति कामस्यच्छिद्रं तमनु येऽरयः ।
योगिनः कृतमैत्रस्य पत्युर्जायेव पुंश्चली ॥ ४ ॥

nityaṁ dadāti kāmasya
cchidraṁ tam anu ye 'rayaḥ
yoginaḥ kṛta-maitrasya
patyur jāyeva puṁścalī

nityam—always; *dadāti*—gives; *kāmasya*—of lust; *chidram*—facility; *tam*—that (lust); *anu*—following; *ye*—those; *arayaḥ*—enemies; *yoginaḥ*—of the *yogīs* or persons trying to advance in spiritual life; *kṛta-maitrasya*—having put faith in the mind; *patyuḥ*—of the husband; *jāyā iva*—like the wife; *puṁścalī*—who is unchaste or easily carried away by other men.

TRANSLATION

An unchaste woman is very easily carried away by paramours, and it sometimes happens that her husband is violently killed by her paramours. If the yogī gives his mind a chance and does not restrain it, his mind will give facility to enemies like lust, anger and greed, and they will doubtlessly kill the yogī.

PURPORT

In this verse the word *puṁścalī* refers to a woman who is easily carried away by men. Such a woman is never to be trusted. Unfortunately, in the present age, women are never controlled. According to the directions of the *śāstras*, women are never to be given freedom. When a child, a woman must be strictly controlled by her father. When she is young, she must be strictly controlled by her husband, and when she is old, she must be controlled by her elderly sons. If she is given independence and allowed to mingle unrestrictedly with men, she will be spoiled. A spoiled woman, being manipulated by paramours, might even kill her husband. This example is given here because a *yogī* desiring to get free from material conditions must always keep his mind under control. Śrīla Bhaktisiddhānta Sarasvatī Ṭhākura used to say that in the morning our first business should be to beat the mind with shoes a hundred times, and, before going to bed, to beat the mind a hundred times with a broomstick. In this way one's mind can be kept under control. An uncontrolled mind and an unchaste wife are the same. An unchaste wife can kill her husband at any time, and an uncontrolled mind, followed by lust, anger, greed, madness, envy and illusion, can certainly kill the *yogī*. When the *yogī* is controlled by the mind, he falls down into the material condition. One should be very careful of the mind, just as a husband should be careful of an unchaste wife.

TEXT 5

कामो मन्युर्मदो लोभः शोकमोहभयादयः ।
कर्मबन्धश्च यन्मूलः स्वीकुर्यात्को नु तद् बुधः ॥ ५ ॥

kāmo manyur mado lobhaḥ
śoka-moha-bhayādayaḥ
karma-bandhaś ca yan-mūlaḥ
svīkuryāt ko nu tad budhaḥ

kāmaḥ—lust; *manyuḥ*—anger; *madaḥ*—pride; *lobhaḥ*—greed; *śoka*—lamentation; *moha*—illusion; *bhaya*—fear; *ādayaḥ*—all these together; *karma-bandhaḥ*—bondage to fruitive activities; *ca*—and; *yat-*

mūlaḥ—the origin of which; *svīkuryāt*—would accept; *kaḥ*—who; *nu*—indeed; *tat*—that mind; *budhaḥ*—if one is learned.

TRANSLATION

The mind is the root cause of lust, anger, pride, greed, lamentation, illusion and fear. Combined, these constitute bondage to fruitive activity. What learned man would put faith in the mind?

PURPORT

The mind is the original cause of material bondage. It is followed by many enemies, such as anger, pride, greed, lamentation, illusion and fear. The best way to control the mind is to engage it always in Kṛṣṇa consciousness (*sa vai manaḥ kṛṣṇa-padāravindayoḥ*). Since the followers of the mind bring about material bondage, we should be very careful not to trust the mind.

TEXT 6

अथैवमखिललोकपालललामोऽपि विलक्षणैर्जडवदवधूतवेषभाषाचरितैर-
विलक्षितभगवत्प्रभावो योगिनां साम्परायविधिमनुशिक्षयन् स्वकलेवरं
जिहासुरात्मन्यात्मानमसंव्यवहितमनर्थान्तरभावेनान्वीक्षमाण
उपरतानुवृत्तिरुपरराम ॥६॥

athaivam akhila-loka-pāla-lalāmo 'pi vilakṣaṇair jaḍavad avadhūta-
veṣa-bhāṣā-caritair avilakṣita-bhagavat-prabhāvo yogināṁ sāmparāya-
vidhim anuśikṣayan sva-kalevaraṁ jihāsur ātmany ātmānam
asaṁvyavahitam anarthāntara-bhāvenānvīkṣamāṇa uparatānuvṛttir
upararāma.

atha—thereafter; *evam*—in this way; *akhila-loka-pāla-lalāmaḥ*—the head of all kings and monarchs of the universe; *api*—although; *vilakṣaṇaiḥ*—various; *jaḍa-vat*—as if stupid; *avadhūta-veṣa-bhāṣā-caritaiḥ*—by the dress, language and characteristics of an *avadhūta;* *avilakṣita-bhagavat-prabhāvaḥ*—hiding the opulence of the Supreme Personality of Godhead (keeping Himself like an ordinary human being); *yoginām*—of the *yogīs; sāmparāya-vidhim*—the method of giving up this material body; *anuśikṣayan*—teaching; *sva-kalevaram*—His own personal body, which is not at all material; *jihāsuḥ*—desiring to give up like an ordinary human being; *ātmani*—unto Vāsudeva, the original person; *ātmānam*—Himself, Lord Ṛṣabhadeva, being an *āveśa-avatāra* of Lord Viṣṇu; *asaṁvyavahitam*—without intervention by the illusory energy; *anartha-antara-bhāvena*—Himself in the status of Viṣṇu; *anvīkṣamāṇaḥ*—always seeing; *uparata-anuvṛttiḥ*—who was acting as if giving up His material body; *upararāma*—ceased His pastimes as the King of this planet.

TRANSLATION

Lord Ṛṣabhadeva was the head of all kings and emperors within this universe, but assuming the dress and language of an avadhūta, He acted as if dull and materially bound. Consequently no one could observe His divine opulence. He adopted this behavior just to teach yogīs how to give up the body. Nonetheless, He maintained His original position as a plenary expansion of Lord Vāsudeva, Kṛṣṇa. Remaining always in that state, He gave up His pastimes as Lord Ṛṣabhadeva within the material world. If, following in the footsteps of Lord Ṛṣabhadeva, one can give up his subtle body, there is no chance that one will accept a material body again.

PURPORT

As Lord Kṛṣṇa says in *Bhagavad-gītā* (4.9):

janma karma ca me divyam
evaṁ yo vetti tattvataḥ
tyaktvā dehaṁ punar janma
naiti mām eti so 'rjuna

"One who knows the transcendental nature of My appearance and activities does not, upon leaving the body, take his birth again in this material world, but attains My eternal abode, O Arjuna."

This is possible simply by keeping oneself an eternal servant of the Supreme Lord. One must understand his constitutional position and the constitutional position of the Supreme Lord as well. Both have the same spiritual identity. Maintaining oneself as a servant of the Supreme Lord, one should avoid rebirth in this material world. If one keeps himself spiritually fit and thinks of himself as an eternal servant of the Supreme Lord, he will be successful at the time he has to give up the material body.

TEXT 7

तस्य ह वा एवं मुक्तलिङ्गस्य भगवत ऋषभस्य योगमायावासनया देह
इमां जगतीमभिमानाभासेन संक्रममाणः कोङ्कवेङ्ककुटकान्दक्षिणकर्णाटका
न्देशान् यदृच्छयोपगतः कुटकाचलोपवन आस्यकृताश्मकवल उन्माद इव
मुक्तमूर्धजोऽसंवीत एव विचचार ॥ ७ ॥

tasya ha vā evaṁ mukta-liṅgasya bhagavata ṛṣabhasya yogamāyā-
vāsanayā deha imāṁ jagatīm abhimānābhāsena saṅkramamāṇaḥ
koṅka-veṅka-kuṭakān dakṣiṇa-karṇāṭakān deśān yadṛcchayopagataḥ
kuṭakācalopavana āsya kṛtāśma-kavala unmāda iva mukta-mūrdhajo
'saṁvīta eva vicacāra.

tasya—of Him (Lord Ṛṣabhadeva); *ha vā*—as it were; *evam*—thus; *mukta-liṅgasya*—who had no identification with the gross and subtle body; *bhagavataḥ*—of the Supreme Personality of Godhead; *ṛṣabhasya*—of Lord Ṛṣabhadeva; *yoga-māyā-vāsanayā*—by the accomplishment of *yogamāyā* for the purpose of the Lord's pastimes; *dehaḥ*—body; *imām*—this; *jagatīm*—earth; *abhimāna-ābhāsena*—with the apparent conception of having a body of material elements; *saṅkramamāṇaḥ*—traveling; *koṅka-veṅka-kuṭakān*—Koṅka, Veṅka and Kuṭaka; *dakṣiṇa*—in South India; *karṇāṭakān*—in the province of Karṇāṭa *deśān*—all the countries; *yadṛcchayā*—of His own accord; *upagataḥ*—reached; *kuṭakācala-upavane*—a forest near Kuṭakācala; *āsya*—within the mouth; *kṛta-aśma-kavalaḥ*—having put a mouthful of stone; *unmādaḥ iva*—just like a madman; *mukta-mūrdhajaḥ*—having scattered hair; *asaṁvītaḥ*—naked; *eva*—just; *vicacāra*—traveled.

TRANSLATION

Actually Lord Ṛṣabhadeva had no material body, but due to yogamāyā, He considered His body material, and therefore,

because He played like an ordinary human being, He gave up the mentality of identifying with it. Following this principle, He began to wander all over the world. While traveling, He came to the province of Karṇāṭa in South India and passed through Koṅka, Veṅka and Kuṭaka. He had no plan to travel this way, but He arrived near Kuṭakācala and entered a forest there. He placed stones within His mouth and began to wander through the forest, naked and with His hair disheveled like a madman.

TEXT 8

अथ समीरवेगविधूतवेणुविकर्षणजातोग्रदावानलस्तद्वनमालेलिहानः सह तेन ददाह ॥८॥

atha samīra-vega-vidhūta-veṇu-vikarṣaṇa-jātogra-dāvānalas tad vanam ālelihānaḥ saha tena dadāha.

atha—thereafter; *samīra-vega*—by the force of the wind; *vidhūta*—tossed about; *veṇu*—of bamboos; *vikarṣaṇa*—by the rubbing; *jāta*—produced; *ugra*—fierce; *dāva-analaḥ*—a forest fire; *tat*—that; *vanam*—forest near Kuṭakācala; *ālelihānaḥ*—devouring all around; *saha*—with; *tena*—that body; *dadāha*—burned to ashes.

TRANSLATION

While He was wandering about, a wild forest fire began. This fire was caused by the friction of bamboos, which were being blown by the wind. In that fire, the entire forest near Kuṭakācala and the body of Lord Ṛṣabhadeva were burnt to ashes.

PURPORT

Such a forest fire can burn the external bodies of animals, but Lord Ṛṣabhadeva was not burned, although He apparently seemed so. Lord Ṛṣabhadeva is the Supersoul of all living entities within the forest, and His soul is never burned by fire. As stated in *Bhagavad-gītā, adāhyo 'yam*—the soul is never burned by fire. Due to Lord Ṛṣabhadeva's presence, all the animals in the forest were also liberated from material encagement.

TEXT 9

यस्य किलानुचरितमुपाकर्ण्य कोङ्कवेङ्ककुटकानां राजार्हन्नामोपशिक्ष्य कलावधर्म उत्कृष्यमाणे भवितव्येन विमोहितः स्वधर्मपथमकुतोभयमपहाय कुपथपाखण्डमसमञ्जसं निजमनीषया मन्दः सम्प्रवर्तयिष्यते ॥ ९ ॥

yasya kilānucaritam upākarṇya koṅka-veṅka-kuṭakānāṁ rājārhan-
nāmopaśikṣya kalāv adharma utkṛṣyamāṇe bhavitavyena vimohitaḥ
sva-dharma-patham akuto-bhayam apahāya kupatha-pākhaṇḍam
asamañjasaṁ nija-manīṣayā mandaḥ sampravartayiṣyate.

yasya—of whom (Lord Ṛṣabhadeva); *kila anucaritam*—pastimes as a *paramahaṁsa*, above all regulative *varṇāśrama* principles; *upākarṇya*—hearing; *koṅka-veṅka-kuṭakānām*—of Koṅka, Veṅka and Kuṭaka; *rājā*—the King; *arhat-nāma*—whose name was Arhat (now known as the Jain); *upaśikṣya*—imitating the activities of Lord Ṛṣabhadeva in His *paramahaṁsa* feature; *kalau*—in this age of Kali; *adharme utkṛṣyamāṇe*—because of increasing irreligious life; *bhavitavyena*—by that which was about to happen; *vimohitaḥ*—bewildered; *sva-dharma-patham*—the path of religion; *akutaḥ-bhayam*—which is free from all kinds of fearful danger; *apahāya*—giving up (such practices as cleanliness, truthfulness, control of the senses and mind, simplicity, the principles of religion, and practical application of knowledge); *ku-patha-pākhaṇḍam*—the wrong path of atheism; *asamañjasam*—improper or against the Vedic literature; *nija-manīṣayā*—by his own fertile brain; *mandaḥ*—most foolish; *sampravartayiṣyate*—will introduce.

TRANSLATION

Śukadeva Gosvāmī continued speaking to Mahārāja Parīkṣit: My dear King, the King of Koṅka, Veṅka and Kuṭaka whose name was Arhat, heard of the activities of Ṛṣabhadeva and, imitating Ṛṣabhadeva's principles, introduced a new system of religion. Taking advantage of Kali-yuga, the age of sinful activity, King Arhat, being bewildered, gave up the Vedic principles, which are free from risk, and concocted a new system of religion opposed to

the Vedas. That was the beginning of the Jain dharma. Many other so-called religions followed this atheistic system.

PURPORT

When Lord Śrī Kṛṣṇa was present on this planet, a person named Pauṇḍraka imitated the four-handed Nārāyaṇa and declared himself the Supreme Personality of Godhead. He desired to compete with Kṛṣṇa. Similarly, during the time of Lord Ṛṣabhadeva, the King of Koṅka and Veṅka acted like a *paramahaṁsa* and imitated Lord Ṛṣabhadeva. He introduced a system of religion and took advantage of the fallen condition of the people in this age of Kali. It is said in Vedic literatures that people in this age will be more inclined to accept anyone as the Supreme Lord and accept any religious system opposed to Vedic principles. The people in this age are described as *mandāḥ sumanda-matayaḥ.* Generally they have no spiritual culture, and therefore they are very fallen. Due to this, they will accept any religious system. Due to their misfortune, they forget the Vedic principles. Following non-Vedic principles in this age, they think themselves the Supreme Lord and thus spread the cult of atheism all over the world.

TEXT 10

येन ह वाव कलौ मनुजापसदा देवमायामोहिताः स्वविधिनियोगशौच-
चारित्रविहीना देवहेलनान्यपव्रतानि निजनिजेच्छया गृह्णाना
अस्नानानाचमनाशौचकेशोल्लुञ्चनादीनि कलिनाधर्मबहुलेनोपहतधियो
ब्रह्मब्राह्मणयज्ञपुरुषलोकविदूषकाः प्रायेण भविष्यन्ति ॥ १० ॥

yena ha vāva kalau manujāpasadā deva-māyā-mohitāḥ sva-vidhi-
niyoga-śauca-cāritra-vihīnā deva-helanāny apavratāni nija-nijecchayā
gṛhṇānā asnānānācamanāśauca-keśolluñcanādīni kalinādharma-
bahulenopahata-dhiyo brahma-brāhmaṇa-yajña-puruṣa-loka-
vidūṣakāḥ prāyeṇa bhaviṣyanti.

yena—by which pseudo religious system; *ha vāva*—certainly; *kalau*—in this age of Kali; *manuja-apasadāḥ*—the most condemned men; *deva-māyā-mohitāḥ*—bewildered by the external energy, or illusory energy, of the Supreme Personality of Godhead; *sva-vidhi-niyoga-śauca-cāritra-vihīnāḥ*—without character, cleanliness, and the rules and regulations given according to one's own duty in life; *deva-helanāni*—negligent of the Supreme Personality of Godhead; *apavratāni*—impious vows; *nija-nija-icchayā*—by their own desires; *gṛhṇānāḥ*—accepting; *asnāna-anācamana-aśauca-keśa-ulluñcana-ādīni*—concocted religious principles such as no bathing, no washing of the mouth, being unclean and plucking out the hair; *kalinā*—by the age of Kali; *adharma-bahulena*—with an abundance of irreligion; *upahata-dhiyaḥ*—whose pure consciousness is destroyed; *brahma-brāhmaṇa-yajña-puruṣa-loka-vidūṣakāḥ*—blasphemous toward the *Vedas*, the strict *brāhmaṇas*, ritualistic ceremonies such as sacrifice, and toward the Supreme Personality of Godhead and the devotees; *prāyeṇa*—almost entirely; *bhaviṣyanti*—will become.

TRANSLATION

People who are lowest among men and bewildered by the illusory energy of the Supreme Lord will give up the original varṇāśrama-dharma and its rules and regulations. They will abandon bathing three times daily and worshiping the Lord. Abandoning cleanliness and neglecting the Supreme Lord, they will accept nonsensical principles. Not regularly bathing or washing their mouths regularly, they will always remain unclean, and they will pluck out their hair. Following a concocted religion, they will flourish. During this age of Kali, people are more inclined to irreligious systems. Consequently these people will naturally deride Vedic authority, the followers of Vedic authority, the brāhmaṇas, the Supreme Personality of Godhead and the devotees.

PURPORT

Presently the hippies in the Western countries fit this description. They are irresponsible and unregulated. They do not bathe, and they deride standard Vedic knowledge. They concoct new life-styles and religions. There are many hippie groups at the present moment, but they all originated from King Arhat, who imitated the activities of Lord Ṛṣabhadeva, who was situated on the *paramahaṁsa* stage. King Arhat did not care for the fact that although Lord Ṛṣabhadeva acted like a madman, His stool and urine were nonetheless aromatic, so much so that they nicely scented the countryside for miles around. The followers of King Arhat went under the name Jains, and they were later followed by many others, particularly by the hippies, who are more or less offshoots of Māyāvāda philosophy because they think themselves the Supreme Personality of Godhead. Such people do not respect the real followers of Vedic principles, the ideal *brāhmaṇas*. Nor do they have respect for the Supreme Personality of Godhead, the Supreme Brahman. Due to the influence of this age of Kali, they are apt to concoct false religious systems.

TEXT 11

ते च ह्यर्वाक्तनया निजलोकयात्रयान्धपरम्परयाऽऽश्वस्तास्तमस्यन्धे स्वयमेव प्रपतिष्यन्ति ॥ ११ ॥

te ca hy arvāktanayā nija-loka-yātrayāndha-paramparayāśvastās
tamasy andhe svayam eva prapatiṣyanti.

te—those people not following the Vedic principles; *ca*—and; *hi*—certainly; *arvāktanayā*—deviating from the eternal principles of Vedic religion; *nija-loka-yātrayā*—by a practice arrived at by their own mental concoction; *andha-paramparayā*—by a disciplic succession of blind, ignorant people; *āśvastāḥ*—being encouraged; *tamasi*—into the darkness of ignorance; *andhe*—blindness; *svayam eva*—themselves; *prapatiṣyanti*—will fall down.

TRANSLATION

Low-class people, due to their gross ignorance, introduce a system of religion that deviates from the Vedic principles. Following their own mental concoctions, they automatically fall down into the darkest regions of existence.

PURPORT

In this connection, one may see *Bhagavad-gītā*, Chapter Sixteen, where there is a description of the downfall of the *asuras* (16.16 and 16.23).

TEXT 12

अयमवतारो रजसोपप्लुतकैवल्योपशिक्षणार्थः ॥ १२ ॥

ayam avatāro rajasopapluta-kaivalyopaśikṣaṇārthaḥ.

ayam avatāraḥ—this incarnation (Lord Ṛṣabhadeva); *rajasā*—by the mode of passion; *upapluta*—overwhelmed; *kaivalya-upaśikṣaṇa-arthaḥ*—to teach people the path of liberation.

TRANSLATION

In this age of Kali, people are overwhelmed by the modes of passion and ignorance. Lord Ṛṣabhadeva incarnated Himself to deliver them from the clutches of māyā.

PURPORT

The symptoms of Kali-yuga are predicted in the Twelfth Canto, Third Chapter, of *Śrīmad-Bhāgavatam. Lāvaṇyaṁ keśa-dhāraṇam.* It is predicted how fallen souls will behave. They will keep their hair long and consider themselves very beautiful, or they will pluck out their hair as the Jains do. They will keep themselves unclean and will not wash their mouths. Jains refer to Lord Ṛṣabhadeva as their original preceptor. If such people are serious followers of Ṛṣabhadeva, they must also take His instructions. In the Fifth Chapter of this canto, Ṛṣabhadeva gave His one hundred sons instructions whereby they could become free from the clutches of *māyā.* If one actually follows Ṛṣabhadeva, he will certainly be delivered from the clutches of *māyā* and return home, back to Godhead. If one strictly follows the instructions of Ṛṣabhadeva given in the Fifth Chapter, he will certainly be liberated. Lord Ṛṣabhadeva incarnated specifically to deliver these fallen souls.

TEXT 13

तस्यानुगुणान् श्लोकान् गायन्ति—

अहो भुवः सप्तसमुद्रवत्या

द्वीपेषु वर्षेष्वधिपुण्यमेतत् ।

गायन्ति यत्रत्यजना मुरारेः
कर्माणि भद्राण्यवतारवन्ति ॥१३॥

tasyānuguṇān ślokān gāyanti—
aho bhuvaḥ sapta-samudravatyā
dvīpeṣu varṣeṣv adhipuṇyam etat
gāyanti yatratya-janā murāreḥ
karmāṇi bhadrāṇy avatāravanti

tasya—of Him (Lord Ṛṣabhadeva); *anuguṇān*—conforming to the instructions for liberation; *ślokān*—verses; *gāyanti*—chant; *aho*—oh; *bhuvaḥ*—of this earthly planet; *sapta-samudra-vatyāḥ*—possessing seven seas; *dvīpeṣu*—among the islands; *varṣeṣu*—among the lands; *adhipuṇyam*—more pious than any other island; *etat*—this (Bhārata-varṣa); *gāyanti*—sing about; *yatratya-janāḥ*—the people of this tract of land; *murāreḥ*—of Murāri, the Supreme Personality of Godhead; *karmāṇi*—the activities; *bhadrāṇi*—all-auspicious; *avatāravanti*—in many incarnations such as Lord Ṛṣabhadeva.

TRANSLATION

Learned scholars chant about the transcendental qualities of Lord Ṛṣabhadeva in this way: "Oh, this earthly planet contains seven seas and many islands and lands, of which Bhārata-varṣa is considered the most pious. People of Bhārata-varṣa are accustomed to glorifying the activities of the Supreme Personality of Godhead in His incarnations as Lord Ṛṣabhadeva and others. All these activities are very auspicious for the welfare of humanity.

PURPORT

Śrī Caitanya Mahāprabhu said:

bhārata-bhūmite haila manuṣya-janma yāra
janma sārthaka kari' kara para-upakāra

As stated in this verse, Bhārata-varṣa is a most pious land. The followers of Vedic literature understand the Supreme Personality of Godhead in

His different incarnations, and they are privileged to glorify the Lord by following the directions of Vedic literature. After realizing the glories of human life, such people should take up the mission to spread the importance of human life throughout the whole world. This is the mission of Śrī Caitanya Mahāprabhu. The word *adhipuṇyam* indicates that there are certainly many other pious men throughout the world, but the people of Bhārata-varṣa are even more pious. Therefore they are fit to spread Kṛṣṇa Consciousness throughout the world for the benefit of all human society. Śrīla Madhvācārya also recognizes the land of Bhārata-varṣa: *viśeṣād bhārate puṇyam.* Throughout the world, there is no question of *bhagavad-bhakti* or devotional service, but the people of Bhārata-varṣa can easily understand the devotional service of the Lord. Thus every inhabitant of Bhārata-varṣa can perfect his life by discharging *bhagavad-bhakti* and then preaching this cult throughout the world for the benefit of everyone.

TEXT 14

अहो नु वंशो यशसावदातः
प्रैयव्रतो यत्र पुमान् पुराणः ।
कृतावतारः पुरुषः स आद्य-
श्चचार धर्मं यदकर्महेतुम् ॥१४॥

aho nu vaṁśo yaśasāvadātaḥ
praiyavrato yatra pumān purāṇaḥ
kṛtāvatāraḥ puruṣaḥ sa ādyaś
cacāra dharmaṁ yad akarma-hetum

aho—oh; *nu*—indeed; *vaṁśaḥ*—the dynasty; *yaśasā*—with widespread fame; *avadātaḥ*—fully pure; *praiyavrataḥ*—related to King Priyavrata; *yatra*—wherein; *pumān*—the Supreme Person; *purāṇaḥ*—the original; *kṛta-avatāraḥ*—descended as an incarnation; *puruṣaḥ*—the Supreme Personality of Godhead; *saḥ*—He; *ādyaḥ*—the original person; *cacāra*—executed; *dharmam*—religious principles; *yat*—from which; *akarma-hetum*—the cause of the end of fruitive activities.

TRANSLATION

"Oh, what shall I say of the dynasty of Priyavrata, which is pure and very much celebrated. In that dynasty, the Supreme Person, the original Personality of Godhead, descended as an incarnation and executed religious principles that could free one from the results of fruitive activity.

PURPORT

There are many dynasties in human society wherein the Supreme Lord descends as an incarnation. Lord Kṛṣṇa appeared in the Yadu dynasty, and Lord Rāmacandra appeared in the Ikṣvāku, or Raghu, dynasty. Similarly, Lord Ṛṣabhadeva appeared in the dynasty of King Priyavrata. All these dynasties are very famous, and of them the dynasty of Priyavrata is most famous.

TEXT 15

को न्वस्य काष्ठामपरोऽनुगच्छे-
न्मनोरथेनाप्यभवस्य योगी ।
यो योगमायाः स्पृहयत्युदस्ता
ह्यसत्तया येन कृतप्रयत्नाः ॥१५॥

ko nv asya kāṣṭhām aparo 'nugacchen
mano-rathenāpy abhavasya yogī
yo yoga-māyāḥ spṛhayaty udastā
hy asattayā yena kṛta-prayatnāḥ

kaḥ—who; *nu*—indeed; *asya*—of Lord Ṛṣabhadeva; *kāṣṭhām*—the example; *aparaḥ*—else; *anugacchet*—can follow; *manaḥ-rathena*—by the mind; *api*—even; *abhavasya*—of the unborn; *yogī*—the mystic; *yaḥ*—who; *yoga-māyāḥ*—the mystic perfections of *yoga; spṛhayati*—desires; *udastāḥ*—rejected by Ṛṣabhadeva; *hi*—certainly; *asattayā*—by the quality of being insubstantial; *yena*—by whom, Ṛṣabhadeva; *kṛta-prayatnāḥ*—although eager to serve.

TRANSLATION

"Who is that mystic yogī who can follow the examples of Lord Ṛṣabhadeva even with his mind? Lord Ṛṣabhadeva rejected all kinds of yogic perfection, which other yogīs hanker to attain. Who is that yogī who can compare to Lord Ṛṣabhadeva?"

PURPORT

Generally *yogīs* desire the yogic perfections of *aṇimā, laghimā, mahimā, prākāmya, prāpti, īśitva, vaśitva* and *kāmāvasāyitā.* Lord Ṛṣabhadeva, however, never aspired for all these material things. Such *siddhis* (perfections) are presented by the illusory energy of the Lord. The real purpose of the *yoga* system is to achieve the favor and shelter of the lotus feet of the Supreme Personality of Godhead, but this purpose is covered by the illusory energy of *yogamāyā.* So-called *yogīs* are therefore allured by the superficial material perfections of *aṇimā, laghimā, prāpti* and so forth. Consequently ordinary *yogīs* cannot compare to Lord Ṛṣabhadeva, the Supreme Personality of Godhead.

TEXT 16

इति ह स्म सकलवेदलोकदेवब्राह्मणगवां परमगुरोर्भगवत ऋषभाख्यस्य विशुद्धाचरितमीरितं पुंसां समस्तदुश्चरिताभिहरणं परममहा-मङ्गलायनमिदमनुश्रद्धयोपचितयानुशृणोत्याश्रावयति वावहितो भगवति तस्मिन् वासुदेव एकान्ततो भक्तिरनयोरपि समनुवर्तते ॥ १६ ॥

iti ha sma sakala-veda-loka-deva-brāhmaṇa-gavāṁ parama-guror bhagavata ṛṣabhākhyasya viśuddhācaritam īritaṁ puṁsāṁ samasta-duścaritābhiharaṇaṁ parama-mahā-maṅgalāyanam idam anuśraddhayopacitayānuśṛṇoty āśrāvayati vāvahito bhagavati tasmin vāsudeva ekāntato bhaktir anayor api samanuvartate.

iti—thus; *ha sma*—indeed; *sakala*—all; *veda*—of knowledge; *loka*—of people in general; *deva*—of the demigods; *brāhmaṇa*—of the *brāhmaṇas; gavām*—of the cows; *parama*—the supreme; *guroḥ*—master; *bhagavataḥ*—of the Supreme Personality of Godhead; *ṛṣabha-*

ākhyasya—whose name was Lord Ṛṣabhadeva; *viśuddha*—pure; *ācaritam*—activities; *īritam*—now explained; *puṁsām*—of every living entity; *samasta*—all; *duścarita*—sinful activities; *abhiharaṇam*—destroying; *parama*—foremost; *mahā*—great; *maṅgala*—of auspiciousness; *ayanam*—the shelter; *idam*—this; *anuśraddhayā*—with faith; *upacitayā*—increasing; *anuśṛṇoti*—hears from the authority; *āśrāvayati*—speaks to others; *vā*—or; *avahitaḥ*—being attentive; *bhagavati*—the Supreme Personality of Godhead; *tasmin*—unto Him; *vāsudeve*—to Lord Vāsudeva, Lord Kṛṣṇa; *eka-antataḥ*—unflinching; *bhaktiḥ*—devotion; *anayoḥ*—of both groups, the listeners and the speakers; *api*—certainly; *samanuvartate*—factually begins.

TRANSLATION

Śukadeva Gosvāmī continued: Lord Ṛṣabhadeva is the master of all Vedic knowledge, human beings, demigods, cows and brāhmaṇas. I have already explained His pure, transcendental activities, which will vanquish the sinful activities of all living entities. This narration of Lord Ṛṣabhadeva's pastimes is the reservoir of all auspicious things. Whoever attentively hears or speaks of them, following in the footsteps of the ācāryas, will certainly attain unalloyed devotional service at the lotus feet of Lord Vāsudeva, the Supreme Personality of Godhead.

PURPORT

The teachings of Lord Ṛṣabhadeva are for the people of all *yugas*—Satya-yuga, Tretā-yuga, Dvāpara-yuga and especially Kali-yuga. These instructions are so powerful that even in this age of Kali, one can attain perfection simply by explaining the instructions, following in the footsteps of the *ācāryas* or listening to the instructions with great attention. If one does so, one can attain the platform of pure devotional service to Lord Vāsudeva. The pastimes of the Supreme Personality of Godhead and His devotees are recorded in *Śrīmad-Bhāgavatam* so that those who recite these pastimes and listen to them will become purified. *Nityaṁ bhāgavata-sevayā.* As a matter of principle, devotees should read, speak and hear *Śrīmad-Bhāgavatam* persistently, twenty-four hours daily if possible. That is the recommendation of Śrī Caitanya Mahāprabhu.

Kīrtanīyaḥ sadā hariḥ. One should either chant the Hare Kṛṣṇa *mahā-mantra* or read *Śrīmad-Bhāgavatam* and thereby try to understand the characteristics and instructions of the Supreme Lord, who appeared as Lord Ṛṣabhadeva, Lord Kapila and Lord Kṛṣṇa. In this way one can become fully aware of the transcendental nature of the Supreme Personality of Godhead. As stated in *Bhagavad-gītā,* one who knows the transcendental nature of the Lord's birth and activities attains liberation from material bondage and returns to Godhead.

TEXT 17

यस्यामेव कवय आत्मानमविरतं विविधवृजिनसंसारपरितापोपतप्यमानमनुसवनं स्नापयन्तस्तयैव परया निर्वृत्या ह्यपवर्गमात्यन्तिकं परमपुरुषार्थमपि स्वयमासादितं नो एवाद्रियन्ते भगवदीयत्वेनैव परिसमाप्तसर्वार्थाः ॥ १७ ॥

yasyām eva kavaya ātmānam aviratam vividha-vṛjina-saṁsāra-paritāpopatapyamānam anusavanaṁ snāpayantas tayaiva parayā nirvṛtyā hy apavargam ātyantikaṁ parama-puruṣārtham api svayam āsāditaṁ no evādriyante bhagavadīyatvenaiva parisamāpta-sarvārthāḥ.

yasyām eva—in which (Kṛṣṇa consciousness or the nectar of devotional service); *kavayaḥ*—the advancement of learned scholars or philosophers in spiritual life; *ātmānam*—the self; *aviratam*—constantly; *vividha*—various; *vṛjina*—full of sins; *saṁsāra*—in material existence; *paritāpa*—from miserable conditions; *upatapyamānam*—suffering; *anusavanam*—without stopping; *snāpayantaḥ*—bathing; *tayā*—by that; *eva*—certainly; *parayā*—great; *nirvṛtyā*—with happiness; *hi*—certainly; *apavargam*—liberation; *ātyantikam*—uninterrupted; *parama-puruṣa-artham*—the best of all human achievements; *api*—although; *svayam*—itself; *āsāditam*—obtained; *no*—not; *eva*—certainly; *ādriyante*—endeavor to achieve; *bhagavadīyatvena eva*—because of a relationship with the Supreme Personality of Godhead; *parisamāpta-sarva-arthāḥ*—those who have ended all kinds of material desires.

TRANSLATION

Devotees always bathe themselves in devotional service in order to be relieved from the various tribulations of material existence. By doing this, the devotees enjoy supreme bliss, and liberation personified comes to serve them. Nonetheless, they do not accept that service, even if it is offered by the Supreme Personality of Godhead Himself. For the devotees, liberation [mukti] is very unimportant because, having attained the Lord's transcendental loving service, they have attained everything desirable and have transcended all material desires.

PURPORT

Devotional service unto the Lord is the highest attainment for anyone desiring liberation from the tribulations of material existence. As stated in *Bhagavad-gītā* (6.22), *yaṁ labdhvā cāparaṁ lābhaṁ manyate nādhikaṁ tataḥ:* "Gaining this, one thinks there is no greater gain." When one attains the service of the Lord, which is non-different from the Lord, one does not desire anything material. *Mukti* means relief from material existence. Bilvamaṅgala Ṭhākura says: *muktiḥ mukulitāñjaliḥ sevate 'smān.* For a devotee, *mukti* is not a very great achievement. *Mukti* means being situated in one's constitutional position. The constitutional position of every living being is that of the Lord's servant; therefore when a living entity is engaged in the Lord's loving service, he has already attained *mukti.* Consequently a devotee does not aspire for *mukti,* even if it is offered by the Supreme Lord Himself.

TEXT 18

राजन् पतिर्गुरुरलं भवतां यदूनां
दैवं प्रियः कुलपतिः क्व च किङ्करो वः ।
अस्त्वेवमङ्ग भगवान् भजतां मुकुन्दो
मुक्तिं ददाति कर्हिचित्स्म न भक्तियोगम् ॥ १८ ॥

rājan patir gurur alaṁ bhavatāṁ yadūnāṁ
daivaṁ priyaḥ kula-patiḥ kva ca kiṅkaro vaḥ

astv evam aṅga bhagavān bhajatāṁ mukundo
muktiṁ dadāti karhicit sma na bhakti-yogam

rājan—O my dear King; *patiḥ*—maintainer; *guruḥ*—spiritual master; *alam*—certainly; *bhavatām*—of you; *yadūnām*—the Yadu dynasty; *daivam*—the worshipable Deity; *priyaḥ*—very dear friend; *kula-patiḥ*—the master of the dynasty; *kva ca*—sometimes even; *kiṅkaraḥ*—servant; *vaḥ*—of you (the Pāṇḍavas); *astu*—to be sure; *evam*—thus; *aṅga*—O King; *bhagavān*—the Supreme Personality of Godhead; *bhajatām*—of those devotees engaged in service; *mukundaḥ*—the Lord, the Supreme Personality of Godhead; *muktim*—liberation; *dadāti*—delivers; *karhicit*—at any time; *sma*—indeed; *na*—not; *bhakti-yogam*—loving devotional service.

TRANSLATION

Śukadeva Gosvāmī continued: My dear King, the Supreme Person, Mukunda, is actually the maintainer of all the members of the Pāṇḍava and Yadu dynasties. He is your spiritual master, worshipable Deity, friend, and the director of your activities. To say nothing of this, He sometimes serves your family as a messenger or servant. This means He worked just as ordinary servants do. Those engaged in getting the Lord's favor attain liberation from the Lord very easily, but He does not very easily give the opportunity to render direct service unto Him.

PURPORT

While instructing Mahārāja Parīkṣit, Śukadeva Gosvāmī thought it wise to encourage the King because the King might be thinking of the glorious position of various royal dynasties. Especially glorious is the dynasty of Priyavrata, in which the Supreme Lord Ṛṣabhadeva incarnated. Similarly, the family of Uttānapāda Mahārāja, the father of Mahārāja Dhruva, is also glorious due to King Pṛthu's taking birth in it. The dynasty of Mahārāja Raghu is glorified because Lord Rāmacandra appeared in that family. As far as the Yadu and Kuru dynasties are concerned, they existed simultaneously, but of the two, the Yadu dynasty was more glorious due to the appearance of Lord Kṛṣṇa. Mahārāja

Parīkṣit might have been thinking that the Kuru dynasty was not as fortunate as the others because the Supreme Lord did not appear in that family, neither as Kṛṣṇa, Lord Rāmacandra, Lord Ṛṣabhadeva or Mahārāja Pṛthu. Therefore Parīkṣit Mahārāja was encouraged by Śukadeva Gosvāmī in this particular verse.

The Kuru dynasty may be considered more glorious due to the presence of devotees like the five Pāṇḍavas, who rendered unalloyed devotional service. Although Lord Kṛṣṇa did not appear in the Kuru dynasty, He was so obligated to the Pāṇḍavas' devotional service that He acted as a maintainer of the family and spiritual master of the Pāṇḍavas. Although He took birth in the Yadu dynasty, Lord Kṛṣṇa was more affectionate to the Pāṇḍavas. By His actions, Lord Kṛṣṇa proved that He was more inclined to the Kuru dynasty than the Yadu dynasty. Indeed, Lord Kṛṣṇa, indebted to the Pāṇḍavas' devotional service, sometimes acted as their messenger, and He guided them through many dangerous situations. Therefore Mahārāja Parīkṣit should not have been saddened because Lord Kṛṣṇa did not appear in his family. The Supreme Personality of Godhead is always inclined toward His pure devotees, and by His action it is clear that liberation is not very important for the devotees. Lord Kṛṣṇa easily gives one liberation, but He does not so easily give one the facility to become a devotee. *Muktiṁ dadāti karhicit sma na bhakti-yogam.* Directly or indirectly, it is proved that *bhakti-yoga* is the basis for the supreme relationship with the Supreme Lord. It is far superior to liberation. For a pure devotee of the Lord, *mukti* is automatically attained.

TEXT 19

नित्यानुभूतनिजलाभनिवृत्ततृष्णः
श्रेयस्यतद्रचनया चिरसुप्तबुद्धेः ।
लोकस्य यः करुणयाभयमात्मलोक-
माख्यान्नमो भगवते ऋषभाय तस्मै ॥१९॥

nityānubhūta-nija-lābha-nivṛtta-tṛṣṇaḥ
śreyasy atad-racanayā cira-supta-buddheḥ
lokasya yaḥ karuṇayābhayam ātma-lokam
ākhyān namo bhagavate ṛṣabhāya tasmai

nitya-anubhūta—due to being always conscious of His real identity; *nija-lābha-nivṛtta-tṛṣṇaḥ*—who was complete in Himself and had no other desire to fulfill; *śreyasi*—in life's genuine welfare; *a-tat-racanayā*—by expanding activities in the material field, mistaking the body for the self; *cira*—for a long time; *supta*—sleeping; *buddheḥ*—whose intelligence; *lokasya*—of men; *yaḥ*—who (Lord Ṛṣabhadeva); *karuṇayā*—by His causeless mercy; *abhayam*—fearlessness; *ātma-lokam*—the real identity of the self; *ākhyāt*—instructed; *namaḥ*—respectful obeisances; *bhagavate*—unto the Supreme Personality of Godhead; *ṛṣabhāya*—unto Lord Ṛṣabhadeva; *tasmai*—unto Him.

TRANSLATION

The Supreme Personality of Godhead, Lord Ṛṣabhadeva, was fully aware of His true identity; therefore He was self-sufficient, and He did not desire external gratification. There was no need for Him to aspire for success, since He was complete in Himself. Those who unnecessarily engage in bodily conceptions and create an atmosphere of materialism are always ignorant of their real self-interest. Out of His causeless mercy, Lord Ṛṣabhadeva taught the self's real identity and the goal of life. We therefore offer our respectful obeisances unto the Lord, who appeared as Lord Ṛṣabhadeva.

PURPORT

This is the summary of this chapter, in which the activities of Lord Ṛṣabhadeva are described. Being the Supreme Personality of Godhead Himself, Lord Ṛṣabhadeva is complete in Himself. We living entities, as parts and parcels of the Supreme Lord, should follow the instructions of Lord Ṛṣabhadeva and become self-sufficient. We should not create unnecessary demands due to the bodily conception. When one is self-realized, he is sufficiently satisfied due to being situated in his original spiritual position. As confirmed in *Bhagavad-gītā* (18.54): *Brahma-bhūtaḥ prasannātmā na śocati na kāṅkṣati.* This is the goal of all living entities. Even though one may be situated within this material world, he can become fully satisfied and devoid of hankering and lamentation simply by following the instructions of the Lord as set forth in

Bhagavad-gītā or *Śrīmad-Bhāgavatam.* Satisfaction through self-realization is called *svarūpānanda.* The conditioned soul, eternally sleeping in darkness, does not understand his self-interest. He simply tries to become happy by making material adjustments, but this is impossible. It is therefore said in *Śrīmad-Bhāgavatam, na te viduḥ svārtha-gatiṁ hi viṣṇum:* due to gross ignorance, the conditioned soul does not know that his real self-interest is to take shelter at the lotus feet of Lord Viṣṇu. To try to become happy by adjusting the material atmosphere is a useless endeavor. Indeed, it is impossible. By His personal behavior and instructions, Lord Ṛṣabhadeva enlightened the conditioned soul and showed him how to become self-sufficient in his spiritual identity.

Thus end the Bhaktivedanta purports of the Fifth Canto, Sixth Chapter, of the Śrīmad-Bhāgavatam, *entitled "The Activities of Lord Ṛṣabhadeva."*

CHAPTER SEVEN

The Activities of King Bharata

In this chapter, the activities of King Bharata Mahārāja, the emperor of the whole world, are described. Bharata Mahārāja performed various ritualistic ceremonies (Vedic *yajñas*) and satisfied the Supreme Lord by his different modes of worship. In due course of time, he left home and resided in Hardwar and passed his days in devotional activities. Being ordered by his father, Lord Ṛṣabhadeva, Bharata Mahārāja married Pañcajanī, the daughter of Viśvarūpa. After this, he ruled the whole world peacefully. Formerly this planet was known as Ajanābha, and after the reign of Bharata Mahārāja it became known as Bhārata-varṣa. Bharata Mahārāja begot five sons in the womb of Pañcajanī, and he named the sons Sumati, Rāṣṭrabhṛta, Sudarśana, Āvaraṇa and Dhūmraketu. Bharata Mahārāja was very rigid in executing religious principles and following in the footsteps of his father. He therefore ruled the citizens very successfully. Because he performed various *yajñas* to satisfy the Supreme Lord, he was personally very satisfied. Being of undisturbed mind, he increased his devotional activities unto Lord Vāsudeva. Bharata Mahārāja was competent in understanding the principles of saintly persons like Nārada, and he followed in the footsteps of the sages. He also kept Lord Vāsudeva constantly within his heart. After finishing his kingly duties, he divided his kingdom among his five sons. He then left home and went to the place of Pulaha known as Pulahāśrama. There he ate forest vegetables and fruits, and worshiped Lord Vāsudeva with everything available. Thus he increased his devotion toward Vāsudeva, and he automatically began to realize further his transcendental, blissful life. Due to his highly advanced spiritual position, there were sometimes visible in his body the *aṣṭa-sāttvika* transformations, such as ecstatic crying and bodily trembling, which are symptoms of love of Godhead. It is understood that Mahārāja Bharata worshiped the Supreme Lord with the *mantras* mentioned in the *Ṛg Veda*, generally known as Gāyatrī *mantra*, which aim at the Supreme Nārāyaṇa situated within the sun.

TEXT 1

श्रीशुक उवाच

भरतस्तु महाभागवतो यदा भगवतावनितलपरिपालनाय सञ्चिन्तित-स्तदनुशासनपरः पञ्चजनीं विश्वरूपदुहितरमुपयेमे ॥ १ ॥

śrī-śuka uvāca
bharatas tu mahā-bhāgavato yadā bhagavatāvani-tala-paripālanāya sañcintitas tad-anuśāsana-paraḥ pañcajanīṁ viśvarūpa-duhitaram upayeme.

śrī-śukaḥ uvāca—Śukadeva Gosvāmī said; *bharataḥ*—Mahārāja Bharata; *tu*—but; *mahā-bhāgavataḥ*—a *mahā-bhāgavata*, most exalted devotee of the Lord; *yadā*—when; *bhagavatā*—by the order of his father, Lord Ṛṣabhadeva; *avani-tala*—the surface of the globe; *paripālanāya*—for ruling over; *sañcintitaḥ*—made up his mind; *tat-anuśāsana-paraḥ*—engaged in governing the globe; *pañcajanīm*—Pañcajanī; *viśvarūpa-duhitaram*—the daughter of Viśvarūpa; *upayeme*—married.

TRANSLATION

Śukadeva Gosvāmī continued speaking to Mahārāja Parīkṣit: My dear King, Bharata Mahārāja was a topmost devotee. Following the orders of his father, who had already decided to install him on the throne, he began to rule the earth accordingly. When Bharata Mahārāja ruled the entire globe, he followed the orders of his father and married Pañcajanī, the daughter of Viśvarūpa.

TEXT 2

तस्यामु ह वा आत्मजान् कार्त्स्न्येनानुरूपानात्मनः पञ्च जनयामास भूतादिरिव भूतसूक्ष्माणि सुमतिं राष्ट्रभृतं सुदर्शनमावरणं धूम्रकेतुमिति ॥ २ ॥

tasyām u ha vā ātmajān kārtsnyenānurūpān ātmanaḥ pañca janayām āsa bhūtādir iva bhūta-sūkṣmāṇi. sumatiṁ rāṣṭrabhṛtaṁ sudarśanam āvaraṇaṁ dhūmraketum iti.

tasyām—in her womb; *u ha vā*—indeed; *ātma-jān*—sons; *kārtsnyena*—entirely; *anurūpān*—exactly like; *ātmanaḥ*—himself; *pañca*—five; *janayām āsa*—begot; *bhūta-ādiḥ iva*—like the false ego; *bhūta-sūkṣmāṇi*—the five subtle objects of sense perception; *su-matim*—Sumatim; *rāṣṭra-bhṛtam*—Rāṣṭrabhṛta; *su-darśanam*—Sudarśana; *āvaraṇam*—Āvaraṇa; *dhūmra-ketum*—Dhūmraketu; *iti*—thus.

TRANSLATION

Just as the false ego creates the subtle sense objects, Mahārāja Bharata created five sons in the womb of Pañcajanī, his wife. These sons were named Sumati, Rāṣṭrabhṛta, Sudarśana, Āvaraṇa and Dhūmraketu.

TEXT 3

अजनाभं नामैतद्वर्षं भारतमिति यत आरभ्य व्यपदिशन्ति ॥ ३ ॥

ajanābhaṁ nāmaitad varṣaṁ bhāratam iti yata ārabhya vyapadiśanti.

ajanābham—Ajanābha; *nāma*—by the name; *etat*—this; *varṣam*—island; *bhāratam*—Bhārata; *iti*—thus; *yataḥ*—from whom; *ārabhya*—beginning; *vyapadiśanti*—they celebrate.

TRANSLATION

Formerly this planet was known as Ajanābha-varṣa, but since Mahārāja Bharata's reign, it has become known as Bhārata-varṣa.

PURPORT

This planet was formerly known as Ajanābha because of the reign of King Nābhi. After Bharata Mahārāja ruled the planet, it became celebrated as Bhārata-varṣa.

TEXT 4

स बहुविन्महीपतिः पितृपितामहवदुरुवत्सलतया स्वे स्वे कर्मणि वर्तमानाः प्रजाः स्वधर्ममनुवर्तमानः पर्यपालयत् ॥ ४ ॥

sa bahuvin mahī-patiḥ pitṛ-pitāmahavad uru-vatsalatayā sve sve karmaṇi vartamānāḥ prajāḥ sva-dharmam anuvartamānaḥ paryapālayat.

saḥ—that King (Mahārāja Bharata); *bahu-vit*—being very advanced in knowledge; *mahī-patiḥ*—the ruler of the earth; *pitṛ*—father; *pitā-maha*—grandfather; *vat*—exactly like; *uru-vatsalatayā*—with the quality of being very affectionate to the citizens; *sve sve*—in their own respective; *karmaṇi*—duties; *vartamānāḥ*—remaining; *prajāḥ*—the citizens; *sva-dharmam anuvartamānaḥ*—being perfectly situated in his own occupational duty; *paryapālayat*—ruled.

TRANSLATION

Mahārāja Bharata was a very learned and experienced king on this earth. He perfectly ruled the citizens, being himself engaged in his own respective duties. Mahārāja Bharata was as affectionate to the citizens as his father and grandfather had been. Keeping them engaged in their occupational duties, he ruled the earth.

PURPORT

It is most important that the chief executive rule the citizens by keeping them fully engaged in their respective occupational duties. Some of the citizens were *brāhmaṇas*, some were *kṣatriyas*, and some were *vaiśyas* and *śūdras*. It is the duty of the government to see that the citizens act according to these material divisions for their spiritual advancement. No one should remain unemployed or unoccupied in any way. One must work as a *brāhmaṇa, kṣatriya, vaiśya* or *śūdra* on the material path, and on the spiritual path, everyone should act as a *brahmacārī, gṛhastha, vānaprastha* or *sannyāsī*. Although formerly the government was a monarchy, all the kings were very affectionate toward the citizens, and they strictly kept them engaged in their respective duties. Therefore society was very smoothly conducted.

TEXT 5

ईजे च भगवन्तं यज्ञक्रतुरूपं क्रतुभिरुच्चावचैः श्रद्धयाऽऽहृताग्निहोत्रदर्श-
पूर्णमासचातुर्मास्यपशुसोमानां प्रकृतिविकृतिभिरनुसवनं चातुर्होत्रविधिना ॥५॥

ῑje ca bhagavantaṁ yajña-kratu-rūpaṁ kratubhir uccāvacaiḥ śraddhayāhṛtāgnihotra-darśa-pūrṇamāsa-cāturmāsya-paśu-somānāṁ prakṛti-vikṛtibhir anusavanaṁ cāturhotra-vidhinā.

ῑje—worshiped; *ca*—also; *bhagavantam*—the Supreme Personality of Godhead; *yajña-kratu-rūpam*—having the form of sacrifices without animals and sacrifices with animals; *kratubhiḥ*—by such sacrifices; *uccāvacaiḥ*—very great and very small; *śraddhayā*—with faith; *āhṛta*—being performed; *agni-hotra*—of the *agnihotra-yajña; darśa*—of the *darśa-yajña; pūrṇamāsa*—of the *pūrṇamāsa-yajña; cāturmāsya*—of the *cāturmāsya-yajña; paśu-somānām*—of the *yajña* with animals and the *yajña* with *soma-rasa; prakṛti*—by full performances; *vikṛtibhiḥ*—and by partial performances; *anusavanam*—almost always; *cātuḥ-hotra-vidhinā*—by the regulative principles of sacrifice directed by four kinds of priests.

TRANSLATION

With great faith King Bharata performed various kinds of sacrifice. He performed the sacrifices known as agni-hotra, darśa, pūrṇamāsa, cāturmāsya, paśu-yajña [wherein a horse is sacrificed] and soma-yajña [wherein a kind of beverage is offered]. Sometimes these sacrifices were performed completely and sometimes partially. In any case, in all the sacrifices the regulations of cāturhotra were strictly followed. In this way Bharata Mahārāja worshiped the Supreme Personality of Godhead.

PURPORT

Animals like hogs and cows were offered in sacrifice to test the proper execution of the sacrifice. Otherwise, there was no purpose in killing the animal. Actually the animal was offered in the sacrificial fire to get a rejuvenated life. Generally an old animal was sacrificed in the fire, and it would come out again in a youthful body. Some of the rituals, however, did not require animal sacrifice. In the present age, animal sacrifices are forbidden. As stated by Śrī Caitanya Mahāprabhu:

aśvamedhaṁ gavālambhaṁ
sannyāsaṁ pala-paitṛkam

devareṇa sutotpattiṁ
kalau pañca vivarjayet

"In this age of Kali, five acts are forbidden: the offering of a horse in sacrifice, the offering of a cow in sacrifice, the acceptance of the order of *sannyāsa,* the offering of oblations of flesh to the forefathers, and a man's begetting children in his brother's wife." (Cc. *Ādi* 17.164) Such sacrifices are impossible in this age due to the scarcity of expert ***brāhmaṇas*** or *ṛtvijaḥ* who are able to take the responsibility. In the absence of these, the *saṅkīrtana-yajña* is recommended. *Yajñaiḥ saṅkīrtana-prāyair yajanti hi sumedhasaḥ* (*Bhāg.* 11.5.32). After all, sacrifices are executed to please the Supreme Personality of Godhead. *Yajñārtha-karma:* such activities should be carried out for the Supreme Lord's pleasure. In this age of Kali, the Supreme Lord in His incarnation of Śrī Caitanya Mahāprabhu should be worshiped with His associates by performance of *saṅkīrtana-yajña,* the congregational chanting of the Hare Kṛṣṇa *mantra.* This process is accepted by intelligent men. *Yajñaiḥ saṅkīrtana-prāyair yajanti hi sumedhasaḥ.* The word *sumedhasaḥ* refers to intelligent men who possess very good brain substance.

TEXT 6

सम्प्रचरत्सु नानायागेषु विरचिताङ्गक्रियेष्वपूर्वं यत्तत्क्रियाफलं धर्माख्यं
परे ब्रह्मणि यज्ञपुरुषे सर्वदेवतालिङ्गानां मन्त्राणामर्थनियामकतया
साक्षात्कर्तरि परदेवतायां भगवति वासुदेव एव भावयमान आत्मनैपुण्य-
मृदितकषायो हविःष्वध्वर्युभिर्गृह्यमाणेषु स यजमानो यज्ञभाजो
देवांस्तान् पुरुषावयवेष्वभ्यध्यायत् ॥ ६ ॥

sampracaratsu nānā-yāgeṣu viracitāṅga-kriyeṣv apūrvaṁ yat tat kriyā-phalaṁ dharmākhyaṁ pare brahmaṇi yajña-puruṣe sarva-devatā-liṅgānāṁ mantrāṇām artha-niyāma-katayā sākṣāt-kartari para-devatāyāṁ bhagavati vāsudeva eva bhāvayamāna ātma-naipuṇya-mṛdita-kaṣāyo haviḥṣv adhvaryubhir gṛhyamāṇeṣu sa yajamāno yajña-bhājo devāṁs tān puruṣāvayaveṣv abhyadhyāyat.

sampracaratsu—when beginning to perform; *nānā-yāgeṣu*—various kinds of sacrifice; *viracita-aṅga-kriyeṣu*—in which the supplementary rites were performed; *apūrvam*—remote; *yat*—whatever; *tat*—that; *kriyā-phalam*—the result of such sacrifice; *dharma-ākhyam*—by the name of religion; *pare*—unto the transcendence; *brahmaṇi*—the Supreme Lord; *yajña-puruṣe*—the enjoyer of all sacrifices; *sarva-devatā-liṅgānām*—which manifest all the demigods; *mantrāṇām*—of the Vedic hymns; *artha-niyāma-katayā*—due to being the controller of the objects; *sākṣāt-kartari*—directly the performer; *para-devatāyām*—the origin of all demigods; *bhagavati*—the Supreme Personality of Godhead; *vāsudeve*—unto Kṛṣṇa; *eva*—certainly; *bhāvayamānaḥ*—always thinking; *ātma-naipuṇya-mṛdita-kaṣāyaḥ*—freed from all lust and anger by his expertise in such thinking; *haviḥṣu*—the ingredients to be offered in the sacrifice; *adhvaryubhiḥ*—when the priests expert in the sacrifices mentioned in the *Atharva Veda; gṛhyamāṇeṣu*—taking; *saḥ*—Mahārāja Bharata; *yajamānaḥ*—the sacrificer; *yajña-bhājaḥ*—the recipients of the results of sacrifice; *devān*—all the demigods; *tān*—them; *puruṣa-avayaveṣu*—as different parts and limbs of the body of the Supreme Personality of Godhead, Govinda; *abhyadhyāyat*—he thought.

TRANSLATION

After performing the preliminaries of various sacrifices, Mahārāja Bharata offered the results in the name of religion to the Supreme Personality of Godhead, Vāsudeva. In other words, he performed all the yajñas for the satisfaction of Lord Vāsudeva, Kṛṣṇa. Mahārāja Bharata thought that since the demigods were different parts of Vāsudeva's body, He controls those who are explained in the Vedic mantras. By thinking in this way, Mahārāja Bharata was freed from all material contamination, such as attachment, lust and greed. When the priests were about to offer the sacrificial ingredients into the fire, Mahārāja Bharata expertly understood how the offering made to different demigods was simply an offering to the different limbs of the Lord. For instance, Indra is the arm of the Supreme Personality of Godhead, and Sūrya [the sun] is His eye. Thus Mahārāja Bharata considered that the

oblations offered to different demigods were actually offered unto the different limbs of Lord Vāsudeva.

PURPORT

The Supreme Personality of Godhead says that as long as one does not develop the pure devotional service of *śravaṇaṁ kīrtanam,* hearing and chanting, one must carry out his prescribed duties. Since Bharata Mahārāja was a great devotee, one may ask why he performed so many sacrifices that are actually meant for *karmīs.* The fact is that he was simply following the orders of Vāsudeva. As Kṛṣṇa says in *Bhagavad-gītā, sarva dharmān parityajya mām ekaṁ śaraṇaṁ vraja:* "Abandon all varieties of religion and just surrender unto Me." (Bg. 18.66) Whatever we do, we should constantly remember Vāsudeva. People are generally addicted to offering obeisances to various demigods, but Bharata Mahārāja simply wanted to please Lord Vāsudeva. As stated in *Bhagavad-gītā: bhoktāraṁ yajña-tapasāṁ sarva-loka-maheśvaram* (Bg. 5.29). A *yajña* may be carried out to satisfy a particular demigod, but when the *yajña* is offered to the *yajña-puruṣa,* Nārāyaṇa, the demigods are satisfied. The purpose of performing different *yajñas* is to satisfy the Supreme Lord. One may perform them in the name of different demigods or directly. If we directly offer oblations to the Supreme Personality of Godhead, the demigods are automatically satisfied. If we water the root of a tree, the branches, twigs, fruits and flowers are automatically satisfied. When one offers sacrifices to different demigods, one should remember that the demigods are simply parts of the body of the Supreme. If we worship the hand of a person, we intend to satisfy the person himself. If we massage a person's legs, we do not really serve the legs but the person who possesses the legs. All the demigods are different parts of the Lord, and if we offer service to them, we actually serve the Lord Himself. Demigod worship is mentioned in *Brahma-saṁhitā,* but actually the *ślokas* advocate worship of the Supreme Personality of Godhead, Govinda. For instance, worship of the goddess Durgā is mentioned this way in *Brahma-saṁhitā* (5.44):

sṛṣṭi-sthiti-pralaya-sādhana-śaktir ekā
chāyeva yasya bhuvanāni vibharti durgā

icchānurūpam api yasya ca ceṣṭate sā
govindam ādi-puruṣaṁ tam ahaṁ bhajāmi

Following the orders of Śrī Kṛṣṇa, the goddess Durgā creates, maintains and annihilates. Śrī Kṛṣṇa also confirms this statement in *Bhagavad-gītā. Mayādhyakṣeṇa prakṛtiḥ sūyate sa-carācaram:* "This material nature is working under My direction, O son of Kuntī, and it is producing all moving and unmoving beings." (Bg. 9.10)

We should worship the demigods in that spirit. Because the goddess Durgā satisfies Kṛṣṇa, we should therefore offer respects to goddess Durgā. Because Lord Śiva is nothing but Kṛṣṇa's functional body, we should therefore offer respects to Lord Śiva. Similarly, we should offer respects to Brahmā, Agni and Sūrya. There are many offerings to different demigods, and one should always remember that these offerings are usually meant to satisfy the Supreme Personality of Godhead. Bharata Mahārāja did not aspire to receive some benediction from demigods. His aim was to please the Supreme Lord. In the *Mahābhārata,* among the thousand names of Viṣṇu, it is said *yajña-bhug yajña-kṛd yajñaḥ.* The enjoyer of *yajña,* the performer of *yajña* and *yajña* itself are the Supreme Lord. The Supreme Lord is the performer of everything, but out of ignorance the living entity thinks that he is the actor. As long as we think we are the actors, we bring about *karma-bandha* (bondage to activity). If we act for *yajña,* for Kṛṣṇa, there is no *karma-bandha. Yajñārthāt karmaṇo 'nyatra loko 'yaṁ karma-bandhanaḥ:* "Work done as a sacrifice for Viṣṇu has to be performed. otherwise work binds one to this material world." (Bg. 3.9)

Following the instructions of Bharata Mahārāja, we should act not for our personal satisfaction but for the satisfaction of the Supreme Personality of Godhead. In *Bhagavad-gītā* (17.28) it is also stated:

aśraddhayā hutaṁ dattaṁ
tapas taptaṁ kṛtam ca yat
asad ity ucyate pārtha
na ca tat pretya no iha

Sacrifices, austerities and charities performed without faith in the Supreme Personality of Godhead are nonpermanent. Regardless of whatever rituals are performed, they are called *asat,* nonpermanent. They are therefore usless both in this life and the next.

Kings like Mahārāja Ambarīṣa and many other *rājarṣis* who were pure devotees of the Lord simply passed their time in the service of the Supreme Lord. When a pure devotee executes some service through the agency of another person, he should not be criticized, for his activities are meant for the satisfaction of the Supreme Lord. A devotee may have a priest perform some *karma-kāṇḍa,* and the priest may not be a pure Vaiṣṇava, but because the devotee wants to please the Supreme Lord, he should not be criticized. The word *apūrva* is very significant. The resultant actions of *karma* are called *apūrva.* When we act piously or impiously, immediate results do not ensue. We therefore wait for the results, which are called *apūrva.* The results are manifest in the future. Even the *smārtas* accept this *apūrva.* Pure devotees simply act for the pleasure of the Supreme Personality of Godhead; therefore the results of their activities are spiritual, or permanent. They are not like those of the *karmīs,* which are nonpermanent. This is confirmed in *Bhagavad-gītā* (4.23):

gata-saṅgasya muktasya
jñānāvasthita-cetasaḥ
yajñāyācarataḥ karma
samagraṁ pravilīyate

"The work of a man who is unattached to the modes of material nature and who is fully situated in transcendental knowledge merges entirely into transcendence."

A devotee is always free from material contamination. He is fully situated in knowledge, and therefore his sacrifices are intended for the satisfaction of the Supreme Personality of Godhead.

TEXT 7

एवं कर्मविशुद्धया विशुद्धसत्त्वस्यान्तर्हृदयाकाशशरीरे ब्रह्मणि भगवति वासुदेवे
महापुरुषरूपोपलक्षणे श्रीवत्सकौस्तुभवनमालारिदरगदादिभिरुपलक्षिते

निजपुरुषहृल्लिखितेनात्मनि पुरुषरूपेण विरोचमान उच्चैस्तरां भक्तिरनुदिनमेधमानरयाजायत ॥ ७ ॥

evaṁ karma-viśuddhyā viśuddha-sattvasyāntar-hṛdayākāśa-śarīre brahmaṇi bhagavati vāsudeve mahā-puruṣa-rūpopalakṣaṇe śrīvatsa-kaustubha-vana-mālāri-dara-gadādibhir upalakṣite nija-puruṣa-hṛl-likhitenātmani puruṣa-rūpeṇa virocamāna uccaistarāṁ bhaktir anudinam edhamāna-rayājāyata.

evam—thus; *karma-viśuddhyā*—by offering everything for the service of the Supreme Personality of Godhead and not desiring any results of his pious activities; *viśuddha-sattvasya*—of Bharata Mahārāja, whose existence was completely purified; *antaḥ-hṛdaya-ākāśa-śarīre*—the Supersoul within the heart, as meditated on by *yogīs; brahmaṇi*—into impersonal Brahman, which is worshiped by impersonalist *jñānīs; bhagavati*—unto the Supreme Personality of Godhead; *vāsudeve*—the son of Vasudeva, Lord Kṛṣṇa; *mahā-puruṣa*—of the Supreme Person; *rūpa*—of the form; *upalakṣaṇe*—having the symptoms; *śrīvatsa*—the mark on the chest of the Lord; *kaustubha*—the Kaustubha gem used by the Lord; *vana-mālā*—flower garland; *ari-dara*—by the disc and conchshell; *gadā-ādibhiḥ*—by the club and other symbols; *upalakṣite*—being recognized; *nija-puruṣa-hṛt-likhitena*—which is situated in the heart of His own devotee like an engraved picture; *ātmani*—in his own mind; *puruṣa-rūpeṇa*—by His personal form; *virocamāne*—shining; *uccaistarām*—on a very high level; *bhaktiḥ*—devotional service; *anudinam*—day after day; *edhamāna*—increasing; *rayā*—possessing force; *ajāyata*—appeared.

TRANSLATION

In this way, being purified by ritualistic sacrifices, the heart of Mahārāja Bharata was completely uncontaminated. His devotional service unto Vāsudeva, Lord Kṛṣṇa, increased day after day. Lord Kṛṣṇa, the son of Vasudeva, is the original Personality of Godhead manifest as the Supersoul [Paramātmā] as well as the impersonal Brahman. Yogīs meditate upon the localized Paramātmā situated in

the heart, jñānīs worship the impersonal Brahman as the Supreme Absolute Truth, and devotees worship Vāsudeva, the Supreme Personality of Godhead, whose transcendental body is described in the śāstras. His body is decorated with the Śrīvatsa, the Kaustubha jewel and a flower garland, and His hands hold a conchshell, disc, club and lotus flower. Devotees like Nārada always think of Him within their hearts.

PURPORT

Lord Vāsudeva, or Śrī Kṛṣṇa, the son of Vasudeva, is the Supreme Personality of Godhead. He is manifest within the hearts of *yogīs* in His Paramātmā feature, and He is worshiped as impersonal Brahman by *jñānīs.* The Paramātmā feature is described in the *śāstras* as having four hands, holding disc, conchshell, lotus flower and club. As confirmed in the *Śrīmad-Bhāgavatam* (2.2.8):

kecit sva-dehāntar-hṛdayāvakāśe
prādeśa-mātraṁ puruṣaṁ vasantam
catur-bhujaṁ kañja-rathāṅga-śaṅkha-
gadā-dharaṁ dhāraṇayā smaranti

Paramātmā is situated in the hearts of all living beings. He has four hands, which hold four symbolic weapons. All devotees who think of the Paramātmā within the heart worship the Supreme Personality of Godhead as the temple Deity. They also understand the impersonal features of the Lord and His bodily rays, the Brahman effulgence.

TEXT 8

एवं वर्षायुतसहस्रपर्यन्तावसितकर्मनिर्वाणावसरोऽधिभुज्यमानं स्वतनयेभ्यो रिक्थं पितृपैतामहं यथादायं विभज्य स्वयं सकलसम्पन्निकेतात्स्वनिकेतात् पुलहाश्रमं प्रवव्राज ॥ ८ ॥

evaṁ varṣāyuta-sahasra-paryantāvasita-karma-nirvāṇāvasaro 'dhibhujyamānaṁ sva-tanayebhyo rikthaṁ pitṛ-paitāmahaṁ yathā-dāyaṁ vibhajya svayaṁ sakala-sampan-niketāt sva-niketāt pulahāśramaṁ pravavrāja.

evam—thus being always engaged; *varṣa-ayuta-sahasra*—one thousand times ten thousand years; *paryanta*—until then; *avasita-karma-nirvāṇa-avasaraḥ*—Mahārāja Bharata who ascertained the moment of the end of his royal opulence; *adhibhujyamānam*—being enjoyed in this way for that duration; *sva-tanayebhyaḥ*—unto his own sons; *riktham*—the wealth; *pitṛ-paitāmaham*—which he received from his father and forefathers; *yathā-dāyam*—according to the *dāya-bhāk* laws of Manu; *vibhajya*—dividing; *svayam*—personally; *sakala-sampat*—of all kinds of opulence; *niketāt*—the abode; *sva-niketāt*—from his paternal home; *pulaha-āśramam pravavrāja*—he went to the *āśrama* of Pulaha in Hardwar (where the *śālagrāma-śilās* are obtainable).

TRANSLATION

Destiny fixed the time for Mahārāja Bharata's enjoyment of material opulence at one thousand times ten thousand years. When that period was finished, he retired from family life and divided the wealth he had received from his forefathers among his sons. He left his paternal home, the reservoir of all opulence, and started for Pulahāśrama, which is situated in Hardwar. The śālagrāma-śilās are obtainable there.

PURPORT

According to the law of *dāya-bhāk*, when one inherits an estate, he must hand it over to the next generation. Bharata Mahārāja did this properly. First he enjoyed his paternal property for one thousand times ten thousand years. At the time of his retirement, he divided this property among his sons and left for Pulaha-āśrama.

TEXT 9

यत्र ह वाव भगवान् हरिरद्यापि तत्रत्यानां निजजनानां वात्सल्येन संनिधाप्यत इच्छारूपेण ॥ ९ ॥

yatra ha vāva bhagavān harir adyāpi tatratyānāṁ nija-janānāṁ
vātsalyena sannidhāpyata icchā-rūpeṇa.

yatra—where; *ha vāva*—certainly; *bhagavān*—the Supreme Personality of Godhead; *hariḥ*—the Lord; *adya-api*—even today; *tatra-*

tyānām—residing in that place; *nija-janānām*—for His own devotees; *vātsalyena*—by His transcendental affection; *sannidhāpyate*—becomes visible; *icchā-rūpeṇa*—according to the desire of the devotee.

TRANSLATION

At Pulaha-āśrama, the Supreme Personality of Godhead, Hari, out of His transcendental affection for His devotee, becomes visible to His devotee, satisfying His devotee's desires.

PURPORT

The Lord always exists in different transcendental forms. As stated in *Brahma-saṁhitā* (5.39):

rāmādi-mūrtiṣu kalā-niyamena tiṣṭhan
nānāvatāram akarod bhuvaneṣu kintu
kṛṣṇaḥ svayaṁ samabhavat paramaḥ pumān yo
govindam ādi-puruṣaṁ tam ahaṁ bhajāmi

The Lord is situated as Himself, Lord Kṛṣṇa, the Supreme Personality of Godhead, and He is accompanied by His expansions like Lord Rāma, Baladeva, Saṅkarṣaṇa, Nārāyaṇa, Mahā-Viṣṇu and so forth. The devotees worship all these forms according to their liking, and the Lord, out of His affection, presents Himself as *arcā-vigraha.* He sometimes presents Himself personally before the devotee out of reciprocation or affection. A devotee is always fully surrendered to the loving service of the Lord, and the Lord is visible to the devotee according to the devotee's desires. He may be present in the form of Lord Rāma, Lord Kṛṣṇa, Lord Nṛsiṁhadeva and so on. Such is the exchange of love between the Lord and His devotees.

TEXT 10

यत्राश्रमपदान्युभयतोनाभिभिर्दृषच्चक्रैश्चक्रनदी नाम सरित्प्रवरा सर्वतः पवित्री-करोति ॥ १० ॥

yatrāśrama-padāny ubhayato nābhibhir dṛṣac-cakraiś cakra-nadī nāma sarit-pravarā sarvataḥ pavitrī-karoti.

yatra—where; *āśrama-padāni*—all hermitages; *ubhayataḥ*—both on top and below; *nābhibhiḥ*—like the symbolic mark of a navel; *dṛṣat*—visible; *cakraiḥ*—with the circles; *cakra-nadī*—the Cakra-nadī River (generally known as the Gaṇḍakī); *nāma*—of the name; *sarit-pravarā*—the most important river of all; *sarvataḥ*—everywhere; *pavitrī-karoti*—sanctifies.

TRANSLATION

In Pulaha-āśrama is the Gaṇḍakī River, which is the best of all rivers. The śālagrāma-śilā, the marble pebbles, purify all those places. On each and every marble pebble, up and down, circles like navels are visible.

PURPORT

Śālagrāma-śilā refers to pebbles that appear like stones with circles marked up and down. These are available in the river known as Gaṇḍakī-nadī. Wherever the waters of this river flow, the place becomes immediately sanctified.

TEXT 11

**तस्मिन् वाव किल स एकलः पुलहाश्रमोपवने विविधकुसुम-
किसलयतुलसिकाम्बुभिः कन्दमूलफलोपहारैश्च समीहमानो भगवत
आराधनं विविक्त उपरतविषयाभिलाष उपभृतोपशमः परां निर्वृतिमवाप ॥ ११ ॥**

*tasmin vāva kila sa ekalaḥ pulahāśramopavane vividha-kusuma-
kisalaya-tulasikāmbubhiḥ kanda-mūla-phalopahāraiś ca samīhamāno
bhagavata ārādhanaṁ vivikta uparata-viṣayābhilāṣa upabhṛtopaśamaḥ
parāṁ nirvṛtim avāpa.*

tasmin—in that *āśrama; vāva kila*—indeed; *saḥ*—Bharata Mahārāja; *ekalaḥ*—alone, only; *pulaha-āśrama-upavane*—in the gardens situated in Pulaha-āśrama; *vividha-kusuma-kisalaya-tulasikā-ambubhiḥ*—with varieties of flowers, twigs and *tulasī* leaves, as well as with water; *kanda-mūla-phala-upahāraiḥ*—by offerings of roots, bulbs and fruits; *ca*—and; *samīhamānaḥ*—performing; *bhagavataḥ*—of the Supreme

Personality of Godhead; *ārādhanam*—worshiping; *viviktaḥ*—purified; *uparata*—being freed from; *viṣaya-abhilāṣaḥ*—desire for material sense enjoyment; *upabhṛta*—increased; *upaśamaḥ*—tranquility; *parām*—transcendental; *nirvṛtim*—satisfaction; *avāpa*—he obtained.

TRANSLATION

In the gardens of Pulaha-āśrama, Mahārāja Bharata lived alone and collected a variety of flowers, twigs and tulasī leaves. He also collected the water of the Gaṇḍakī River, as well as various roots, fruits and bulbs. With these he offered food to the Supreme Personality of Godhead, Vāsudeva, and, worshiping Him, he remained satisfied. In this way his heart was completely uncontaminated, and he did not have the least desire for material enjoyment. All material desires vanished. In this steady position, he felt full satisfaction and was situated in devotional service.

PURPORT

Everyone is searching after peace of mind. This is obtainable only when one is completely freed from the desire for material sense gratification and is engaged in the devotional service of the Lord. As stated in *Bhagavad-gītā: patraṁ puṣpaṁ phalaṁ toyaṁ yo me bhaktyā prayacchati* (9.26). Worship of the Lord is not at all expensive. One can offer the Lord a leaf, a flower, a little fruit and some water. The Supreme Lord accepts these offerings when they are offered with love and devotion. In this way, one can become freed from material desires. As long as one maintains material desires, he cannot be happy. As soon as one engages in the devotional service of the Lord, his mind is purified of all material desires. Then one becomes fully satisfied.

sa vai puṁsāṁ paro dharmo
yato bhaktir adhokṣaje
ahaituky apratihatā
yayātmā suprasīdati

vāsudeve bhagavati
bhakti-yogaḥ prayojitaḥ

janayaty āśu vairāgyaṁ
jñānaṁ ca yad ahaitukam

"The supreme occupation [*dharma*] for all humanity is that by which men can attain to loving devotional service unto the transcendent Lord. Such devotional service must be unmotivated and uninterrupted in order to completely satisfy the self. By rendering devotional service unto the Personality of Godhead, Śrī Kṛṣṇa, one immediately acquires causeless knowledge and detachment from the world." (*Bhāg.* 1.2.6-7)

These are the instructions given in *Śrīmad-Bhāgavatam*, the supreme Vedic literature. One may not be able to go to Pulaha-āśrama, but wherever one is one can happily render devotional service to the Lord by adopting the processes mentioned above.

TEXT 12

तयेत्थमविरतपुरुषपरिचर्यया भगवति प्रवर्धमानानुरागभरद्रुतहृदयशैथिल्यः प्रहर्षवेगेनात्मन्युद्भिद्यमानरोमपुलककुलक औत्कण्ठ्यप्रवृत्तप्रणयबाष्पनिरुद्धावलोकनयन एवं निजरमणारुणचरणारविन्दानुध्यानपरिचितभक्तियोगेन परिप्लुतपरमाह्लादगम्भीरहृदयह्रदावगाढधिषणस्तामपि क्रियमाणां भगवत्सपर्यां न सस्मार॥१२॥

tayettham avirata-puruṣa-paricaryayā bhagavati pravardhamānā-
nurāga-bhara-druta-hṛdaya-śaithilyaḥ praharṣa-vegenātmany
udbhidyamāna-roma-pulaka-kulaka autkaṇṭhya-pravṛtta-praṇaya-
bāṣpa-niruddhāvaloka-nayana evaṁ nija-ramaṇāruṇa-
caraṇāravindānudhyāna-paricita-bhakti-yogena paripluta-
paramāhlāda-gambhīra-hṛdaya-hradāvagāḍha-dhiṣaṇas tām api
kriyamāṇāṁ bhagavat-saparyāṁ na sasmāra.

tayā—by that; *ittham*—in this manner; *avirata*—constant; *puruṣa*—of the Supreme Lord; *paricaryayā*—by service; *bhagavati*—unto the Supreme Personality of Godhead; *pravardhamāna*—constantly increasing; *anurāga*—of attachment; *bhara*—by the load; *druta*—melted; *hṛdaya*—heart; *śaithilyaḥ*—laxity; *praharṣa-vegena*—by the force of transcendental ecstasy; *ātmani*—in his body; *udbhidyamāna-roma-pulaka-kulakaḥ*—standing of the hair on end; *autkaṇṭhya*—because of intense longing; *pravṛtta*—produced; *praṇaya-bāṣpa-niruddha-avaloka-nayanaḥ*—awakening of tears of love in the eyes, obstructing the vision; *evam*—thus; *nija-ramaṇa-aruṇa-caraṇa-aravinda*—on the Lord's reddish lotus feet; *anudhyāna*—by meditating; *paricita*—increased; *bhakti-yogena*—by dint of devotional service; *paripluta*—spreading everywhere; *parama*—highest; *āhlāda*—of spiritual bliss; *gambhīra*—very deep; *hṛdaya-hrada*—in the heart, which is compared to a lake; *avagāḍha*—immersed; *dhiṣaṇaḥ*—whose intelligence; *tām*—that; *api*—although; *kriyamāṇām*—executing; *bhagavat*—of the Supreme Personality of Godhead; *saparyām*—the worship; *na*—not; *sasmāra*—remembered.

TRANSLATION

That most exalted devotee, Mahārāja Bharata, in this way engaged constantly in the devotional service of the Lord. Naturally his love for Vāsudeva, Kṛṣṇa, increased more and more and melted his heart. Consequently he gradually lost all attachment for regulative duties. The hairs of his body stood on end, and all the ecstatic bodily symptoms were manifest. Tears flowed from his eyes, so much so that he could not see anything. Thus he constantly meditated on the reddish lotus feet of the Lord. At that time, his heart, which was like a lake, was filled with the water of ecstatic love. When his mind was immersed in that lake, he even forgot the regulative service to the Lord.

PURPORT

When one is actually advanced in ecstatic love for Kṛṣṇa, eight transcendental, blissful symptoms are manifest in the body. Those are the symptoms of perfection arising from loving service to the Supreme Personality of Godhead. Since Mahārāja Bharata was constantly engaged in devotional service, all the symptoms of ecstatic love were manifest in his body.

TEXT 13

इत्थं धृतभगवद्व्रत ऐणेयाजिनवाससानुसवनाभिषेकार्द्रकपिशकुटिलजटाकलापेन च विरोचमानः सूर्यर्चा भगवन्तं हिरण्मयं पुरुषमुज्जिहाने सूर्यमण्डले-ऽभ्युपतिष्ठन्नेतदु होवाच—॥१३॥

itthaṁ dhṛta-bhagavad-vrata aiṇeyājina-vāsasānusavanābhiṣekārdra-kapiśa-kuṭila-jaṭā-kalāpena ca virocamānaḥ sūryarcā bhagavantaṁ hiraṇmayaṁ puruṣam ujjihāne sūrya-maṇḍale 'bhyupatiṣṭhann etad u hovāca.

ittham—in this way; *dhṛta-bhagavat-vrataḥ*—having accepted the vow to serve the Supreme Personality of Godhead; *aiṇeya-ajina-vāsasa*—with a dress of a deerskin; *anusavana*—three times in a day; *abhiṣeka*—by a bath; *ardra*—wet; *kapiśa*—tawny; *kuṭila-jaṭā*—of curling and matted hair; *kalāpena*—by masses; *ca*—and; *virocamānaḥ*—being very beautifully decorated; *sūryarcā*—by the Vedic hymns worshiping the expansion of Nārāyaṇa within the sun; *bhagavantam*—unto the Supreme Personality of Godhead; *hiraṇmayam*—the Lord, whose bodily hue is just like gold; *puruṣam*—the Supreme Personality of Godhead; *ujjihāne*—when rising; *sūrya-maṇḍale*—the sun globe; *abhyupatiṣṭhan*—worshiping; *etat*—this; *u ha*—certainly; *uvāca*—he recited.

TRANSLATION

Mahārāja Bharata appeared very beautiful. He had a wealth of curly hair on his head, which was wet from bathing three times daily. He dressed in a deerskin. He worshiped Lord Nārāyaṇa, whose body was composed of golden effulgence and who resided within the sun. Mahārāja Bharata worshiped Lord Nārāyaṇa by chanting the hymns given in the Ṛg Veda, and he recited the following verse as the sun rose.

PURPORT

The predominating Deity within the sun is Hiraṇmaya, Lord Nārāyaṇa. He is worshiped by the Gāyatrī *mantra: oṁ bhūr bhuvaḥ svaḥ tat savitur vareṇyaṁ bhargo devasya dhīmahi.* He is also worshiped by other hymns mentioned in the *Ṛg Veda,* for instance: *dhyeyaḥ sadā savitṛ-maṇḍala-madhya-vartī.* Within the sun, Lord Nārāyaṇa is situated, and He has a golden hue.

TEXT 14

परोरजः सवितुर्जातवेदो
देवस्य भर्गो मनसेदं जजान ।
सुरेतसादः पुनराविश्य चष्टे
हंसं गृध्राणं नृषद्रिङ्गिरामिमः ॥१४॥

paro-rajaḥ savitur jāta-vedo
devasya bhargo manasedaṁ jajāna
suretasādaḥ punar āviśya caṣṭe
haṁsaṁ gṛdhrāṇaṁ nṛṣad-riṅgirām imaḥ

paraḥ-rajaḥ—beyond the mode of passion (situated in the pure mode of goodness); *savituḥ*—of the one who illuminates the whole universe; *jāta-vedaḥ*—from which all the devotee's desires are fulfilled; *devasya*—of the Lord; *bhargaḥ*—the self-effulgence; *manasā*—simply by contemplating; *idam*—this universe; *jajāna*—created; *su-retasā*—by spiritual potency; *adaḥ*—this created world; *punaḥ*—again; *āviśya*—entering; *caṣṭe*—sees or maintains; *haṁsam*—the living entity; *gṛdhrāṇam*—desiring for material enjoyment; *nṛṣat*—to the intelligence; *riṅgirām*—to one who gives motion; *imaḥ*—let me offer my obeisances.

TRANSLATION

"The Supreme Personality of Godhead is situated in pure goodness. He illuminates the entire universe and bestows all benedictions upon His devotees. The Lord has created this universe from His own spiritual potency. According to His desire, the Lord entered this universe as the Supersoul, and by virtue of His different potencies, He is maintaining all living entities desiring material

enjoyment. Let me offer my respectful obeisances unto the Lord, who is the giver of intelligence."

PURPORT

The predominating Deity of the sun is another expansion of Nārāyaṇa, who is illuminating the entire universe. The Lord enters the hearts of all living entities as the Supersoul, and He gives them intelligence and fulfills their material desires. This is also confirmed in *Bhagavad-gītā. Sarvasya cāhaṁ hṛdi sanniviṣṭaḥ.* "I am sitting in everyone's heart." (Bg. 15.15)

As the Supersoul, the Lord enters the hearts of all living entities. As stated in *Brahma-saṁhitā* (5.35), *aṇḍāntara-stha-paramāṇu-cayāntara-stham:* "He enters the universe and the atom as well." In the *Ṛg Veda,* the predominating Deity of the sun is worshiped by this mantra: *dhyeyaḥ sadā savitṛ-maṇḍala-madhya-vartī nārāyaṇaḥ sarasijāsana-sanniviṣṭaḥ.* Nārāyaṇa sits on His lotus flower within the sun. By reciting this *mantra,* every living entity should take shelter of Nārāyaṇa just as the sun rises. According to modern scientists, the material world rests on the sun's effulgence. Due to the sunshine, all planets are rotating and vegetables are growing. We also have information that the moonshine helps vegetables and herbs grow. Actually Nārāyaṇa within the sun is maintaining the entire universe; therefore Nārāyaṇa should be worshiped by the Gāyatrī *mantra* or the *Ṛg mantra.*

Thus end the Bhaktivedanta purports of the Fifth Canto, Seventh Chapter, of the Śrīmad-Bhāgavatam, *entitled "The activities of King Bharata."*

CHAPTER EIGHT

A Description of the Character of Bharata Mahārāja

Although Bharata Mahārāja was very elevated, he fell down due to his attachment to a young deer. One day after Bharata Mahārāja had taken his bath as usual in the River Gaṇḍakī and was chanting his *mantra*, he saw a pregnant deer come to the river to drink water. Suddenly there could be heard the thundering roar of a lion, and the deer was so frightened that it immediately gave birth to its calf. It then crossed the river, but died immediately thereafter. Mahārāja Bharata took compassion upon the motherless calf, rescued it from the water, took it to his *āśrama* and cared for it affectionately. He gradually became attached to this young deer and always thought of it affectionately. As it grew up, it became Mahārāja Bharata's constant companion, and he always took care of it. Gradually he became so absorbed in thinking of this deer that his mind became agitated. As he became more attached to the deer, his devotional service slackened. Although he was able to give up his opulent kingdom, he became attached to the deer. Thus he fell down from his mystic *yoga* practice. Once when the deer was absent, Mahārāja Bharata was so disturbed that he began to search for it. While searching and lamenting the deer's absence, Mahārāja Bharata fell down and died. Because his mind was fully absorbed thinking of the deer, he naturally took his next birth from the womb of a deer. However, because he was considerably advanced spiritually, he did not forget his past activities, even though he was in the body of a deer. He could understand how he had fallen down from his exalted position, and remembering this, he left his mother deer and again went to Pulaha-āśrama. He finally ended his fruitive activities in the form of a deer, and when he died he was released from the deer's body.

TEXT 1

श्रीशुक उवाच
एकदा तु महानद्यां कृताभिषेकनैयमिकावश्यको ब्रह्माक्षरमभिगृणानो मुहूर्तत्रयमुदकान्त उपविवेश ॥ १ ॥

śrī-śuka uvāca
ekadā tu mahā-nadyāṁ kṛtābhiṣeka-naiyamikāvaśyako
brahmākṣaram abhigṛṇāno muhūrta-trayam udakānta upaviveśa.

śrī-śukaḥ uvāca—Śrī Śukadeva Gosvāmī said; *ekadā*—once upon a time; *tu*—but; *mahā-nadyām*—in the great river known as Gaṇḍakī; *kṛta-abhiṣeka-naiyamika-avaśyakaḥ*—having taken a bath after finishing the daily external duties such as passing stool and urine and brushing the teeth; *brahma-akṣaram*—the *praṇava-mantra* (*oṁ*); *abhigṛṇānaḥ*—chanting; *muhūrta-trayam*—for three minutes; *udaka-ante*—on the bank of the river; *upaviveśa*—he sat down.

TRANSLATION

Śrī Śukadeva Gosvāmī continued: My dear King, one day, after finishing his morning duties—evacuating, urinating and bathing—Mahārāja Bharata sat down on the bank of the River Gaṇḍakī for a few minutes and began chanting his mantra, beginning with oṁkāra.

TEXT 2

तत्र तदा राजन् हरिणी पिपासया जलाशयाभ्याशमेकैवोपजगाम ॥२॥

tatra tadā rājan hariṇī pipāsayā jalāśayābhyāśam ekaivopajagāma.

tatra—on the bank of the river; *tadā*—at the time; *rājan*—O King; *hariṇī*—a doe; *pipāsayā*—because of thirst; *jalāśaya-abhyāśam*—near the river; *eka*—one; *eva*—certainly; *upajagāma*—arrived.

TRANSLATION

O King, while Bharata Mahārāja was sitting on the bank of that river, a doe, being very thirsty, came there to drink.

TEXT 3

तया पेपीयमान उदके तावदेवाविदूरेण नदतो मृगपतेरुन्नादो लोकभयङ्कर उदपतत् ॥ ३ ॥

tayā pepīyamāna udake tāvad evāvidūreṇa nadato mṛga-pater unnādo loka-bhayaṅkara udapatat.

tayā—by the doe; *pepīyamāne*—being drunk with great satisfaction: *udake*—the water; *tāvat eva*—exactly at that time; *avidūreṇa*—very near; *nadataḥ*—roaring; *mṛga-pateḥ*—of one lion; *unnādaḥ*—the tumultuous sound; *loka-bhayam-kara*—very fearful to all living entities; *udapatat*—arose.

TRANSLATION

While the doe was drinking with great satisfaction, a lion, which was very close, roared very loudly. This was frightful to every living entity, and it was heard by the doe.

TEXT 4

तमुपश्रुत्य सा मृगवधूः प्रकृति विक्लवा चकितनिरीक्षणा सुतरामपिहरिभयाभिनिवेशव्यग्रहृदया पारिप्लवदृष्टिरगततृषा भयात् सहसैवोच्चक्राम ॥ ४ ॥

tam upaśrutya sā mṛga-vadhūḥ prakṛti-viklavā cakita-nirīkṣaṇā sutarām api hari-bhayābhiniveśa-vyagra-hṛdayā pāriplava-dṛṣṭir agata-tṛṣā bhayāt sahasaivoccakrāma.

tam upaśrutya—hearing that tumultuous sound: *sā*—that: *mṛga-vadhūḥ*—wife of a deer: *prakṛti-viklavā*—by nature always afraid of being killed by others: *cakita-nirīkṣaṇā*—having wandering eyes: *sutarām api*—almost immediately: *hari*—of the lion: *bhaya*—of fear: *abhiniveśa*—by the entrance: *vyagra-hṛdayā*—whose mind was agitated: *pāriplava-dṛṣṭiḥ*—whose eyes were moving to and fro: *agata-tṛṣā*—without fully satisfying the thirst: *bhayāt*—out of fear: *sahasā*—suddenly: *eva*—certainly: *uccakrāma*—crossed the river.

TRANSLATION

By nature the doe was always afraid of being killed by others, and it was always looking about suspiciously. When it heard the lion's tumultuous roar, it became very agitated. Looking here and there with disturbed eyes, the doe, although it had not fully satisfied itself by drinking water, suddenly leaped across the river.

TEXT 5

तस्या उत्पतन्त्या अन्तर्वत्न्या उरुभयावगलितो योनिनिर्गतो गर्भः स्रोतसि निपपात ॥ ५ ॥

tasyā utpatantyā antarvatnyā uru-bhayāvagalito yoni-nirgato garbhaḥ srotasi nipapāta.

tasyāḥ—of it; *utpatantyāḥ*—forcefully jumping up; *antarvatnyāḥ*—having a full womb; *uru-bhaya*—due to great fear; *avagalitaḥ*—having slipped out; *yoni-nirgataḥ*—coming out of the womb; *garbhaḥ*—the offspring; *srotasi*—in the flowing water; *nipapāta*—fell down.

TRANSLATION

The doe was pregnant, and when it jumped out of fear, the baby deer fell from its womb into the flowing waters of the river.

PURPORT

There is every chance of a woman's having a miscarriage if she experiences some ecstatic emotion or is frightened. Pregnant women should therefore be spared all these external influences.

TEXT 6

तत्प्रसवोत्सर्पणभयखेदातुरा स्वगणेन वियुज्यमाना कस्याञ्चिद्दर्यां कृष्णसारसती निपपाताथ च ममार ॥ ६ ॥

tat-prasavotsarpaṇa-bhaya-khedāturā sva-gaṇena viyujyamānā kasyāñcid daryāṁ kṛṣṇa-sārasatī nipapātātha ca mamāra.

tat-prasava—from untimely discharge of that (baby deer); *utsarpaṇa*—from jumping across the river; *bhaya*—and from fear; *kheda*—by exhaustion; *āturā*—afflicted; *sva-gaṇena*—from the flock of deer; *viyujyamānā*—being separated; *kasyāñcit*—in some; *daryām*—cave of a mountain; *kṛṣṇa-sārasatī*—the black doe; *nipapāta*—fell down; *atha*—therefore; *ca*—and; *mamāra*—died.

TRANSLATION

Being separated from its flock and distressed by its miscarriage, the black doe, having crossed the river, was very much distressed. Indeed, it fell down in a cave and died immediately.

TEXT 7

तं त्वेणकुणकं कृपणं स्रोतसानूह्यमानमभिवीक्ष्यापविद्धं बन्धुरिवानुकम्पया राजर्षिर्भरत आदाय मृतमातरमित्याश्रमपदमनयत् ॥ ७ ॥

taṁ tv eṇa-kuṇakaṁ kṛpaṇaṁ srotasānūhyamānam
abhivīkṣyāpaviddhaṁ bandhur ivānukampayā rājarṣir bharata ādāya
mṛta-mātaram ity āśrama-padam anayat.

tam—that; *tu*—but; *eṇa-kuṇakam*—the deer calf; *kṛpaṇam*—helpless; *srotasā*—by the waves; *anūhyamānam*—floating; *abhivīkṣya*—seeing; *apaviddham*—removed from its own kind; *bandhuḥ iva*—just like a friend; *anukampayā*—with compassion; *rāja-ṛṣiḥ bharataḥ*—the great, saintly King Bharata; *ādāya*—taking; *mṛta-mātaram*—who lost its mother; *iti*—thus thinking; *āśrama-padam*—to the *āśrama; anayat*—brought.

TRANSLATION

The great King Bharata, while sitting on the bank of the river, saw the small deer, bereft of its mother, floating down the river. Seeing this, he felt great compassion. Like a sincere friend, he lifted the infant deer from the waves, and, knowing it to be motherless, brought it to his āśrama.

PURPORT

The laws of nature work in subtle ways unknown to us. Mahārāja Bharata was a great king very advanced in devotional service. He had almost reached the point of loving service to the Supreme Lord, but even from that platform he could fall down onto the material platform. In *Bhagavad-gītā* we are therefore warned:

yaṁ hi na vyathayanty ete
puruṣaṁ puruṣarṣabha
sama-duḥkha-sukhaṁ dhīraṁ
so 'mṛtatvāya kalpate

"O best among men [Arjuna], the person who is not disturbed by happiness and distress and is steady in both is certainly eligible for liberation." (Bg. 2.15)

Spiritual salvation and liberation from material bondage must be worked out with great caution, otherwise a little discrepancy will cause one to fall down again into material existence. By studying the activities of Mahārāja Bharata, we can learn the art of becoming completely freed from all material attachment. As it will be revealed in later verses, Bharata Mahārāja had to accept the body of a deer due to being overly compassionate for this infant deer. We should be compassionate by raising one from the material platform to the spiritual platform; otherwise at any moment our spiritual advancement may be spoiled, and we may fall down onto the material platform. Mahārāja Bharata's compassion for the deer was the beginning of his falldown into the material world.

TEXT 8

तस्य ह वा एणकुणक उच्चैरेतस्मिन् कृतनिजाभिमानस्याहरहस्तत्पोषणपालन-
लालनप्रीणनानुध्यानेनात्मनियमाः सहयमाः पुरुषपरिचर्यादय एकैकशः
कतिपयेनाहर्गणेन वियुज्यमानाः किल सर्व एवोदवसन् ॥ ८ ॥

tasya ha vā eṇa-kuṇaka uccair etasmin kṛta-nijābhimānasyāhar-ahas tat-poṣaṇa-pālana-lālana-prīṇanānudhyānenātma-niyamāḥ saha-

yamāḥ puruṣa-paricaryādaya ekaikaśaḥ katipayenāhar-gaṇena viyujyamānāḥ kila sarva evodavasan.

tasya—of that King; *ha vā*—indeed; *eṇa-kuṇake*—in the deer calf; *uccaiḥ*—greatly; *etasmin*—in this; *kṛta-nija-abhimānasya*—who accepted the calf as his own son; *ahaḥ-ahaḥ*—every day; *tat-poṣaṇa*—maintaining that calf; *pālana*—protecting from dangers; *lālana*—raising it or showing love to it by kissing and so on; *prīṇana*—petting it in love; *anudhyānena*—by such attachment; *ātma-niyamāḥ*—his personal activities for taking care of his body; *saha-yamāḥ*—with his spiritual duties, such as nonviolence, tolerance and simplicity; *puruṣa-paricaryā-ādayaḥ*—worshiping the Supreme Personality of Godhead and performing other duties; *eka-ekaśaḥ*—every day; *katipayena*—with only a few; *ahaḥ-gaṇena*—days of time; *viyujyamānāḥ*—being given up; *kila*—indeed; *sarve*—all; *eva*—certainly; *udavasan*—became destroyed.

TRANSLATION

Gradually Mahārāja Bharata became very affectionate toward the deer. He began to raise it and maintain it by giving it grass. He was always careful to protect it from the attacks of tigers and other animals. When it itched, he petted it, and in this way he always tried to keep it in a comfortable condition. He sometimes kissed it out of love. Being attached to raising the deer, Mahārāja Bharata forgot the rules and regulations for the advancement of spiritual life, and he gradually forgot to worship the Supreme Personality of Godhead. After a few days, he forgot everything about his spiritual advancement.

PURPORT

From this we can understand how we have to be very cautious in executing our spiritual duties by observing the rules and regulations and regularly chanting the Hare Kṛṣṇa *mahā-mantra.* If we neglect doing this, we will eventually fall down. We must rise early in the morning, bathe, attend *maṅgala-ārati,* worship the Deities, chant the Hare Kṛṣṇa *mantra,* study the Vedic literatures and follow all the rules prescribed by the *ācāryas* and the spiritual master. If we deviate from this process, we may fall down, even though we may be very highly advanced. As stated in *Bhagavad-gītā* (18.5):

yajña-dāna-tapaḥ-karma
na tyājyaṁ kāryam eva tat
yajño dānaṁ tapaś caiva
pāvanāni manīṣiṇām

"Acts of sacrifice, charity and penance are not to be given up but should be performed. Indeed, sacrifice, charity and penance purify even the great soul." Even if one is in the renounced order, he should never give up the regulative principles. He should worship the Deity and give his time and life to the service of Kṛṣṇa. He should also continue following the rules and regulations of austerity and penance. These things cannot be given up. One should not think oneself very advanced simply because one has accepted the *sannyāsa* order. The activities of Bharata Mahārāja should be carefully studied for one's spiritual advancement.

TEXT 9

अहो बतायं हरिणकुणकः कृपण ईश्वररथचरणपरिभ्रमणरयेण स्वगणसुहृद्-
बन्धुभ्यः परिवर्जितः शरणं च मोपसादितो मामेव मातापितरौ भ्रातृज्ञातीन्
यौथिकांश्चैवोपेयाय नान्यं कञ्चन वेद मय्यतिविस्रब्धश्चात एव मया मत्परायणस्य
पोषणपालनप्रीणनलालनमनसूयुनानुष्ठेयं शरण्योपेक्षादोषविदुषा ॥ ९ ॥

aho batāyaṁ hariṇa-kuṇakaḥ kṛpaṇa īśvara-ratha-caraṇa-
paribhramaṇa-rayeṇa sva-gaṇa-suhṛd-bandhubhyaḥ parivarjitaḥ
śaraṇaṁ ca mopasādito mām eva mātā-pitarau bhrātṛ-jñātīn
yauthikāṁś caivopeyāya nānyaṁ kañcana veda mayy ati-visrabdhaś
cāta eva mayā mat-parāyaṇasya poṣaṇa-pālana-prīṇana-lālanam
anasūyunānuṣṭheyaṁ śaraṇyopekṣā-doṣa-viduṣā.

aho bata—alas; *ayam*—this; *hariṇa-kuṇakaḥ*—the deer calf; *kṛpaṇaḥ*—helpless; *īśvara-ratha-caraṇa-paribhramaṇa-rayeṇa*—by the force of the rotation of the time agent of the Supreme Personality of

Godhead, which is compared to the wheel of His chariot; *sva-gaṇa*—own kinsmen; *suhṛt*—and friends; *bandhubhyaḥ*—relatives; *parivarjitaḥ*—deprived of; *śaraṇam*—as shelter; *ca*—and; *mā*—me; *upasāditaḥ*—having obtained; *mām*—me; *eva*—alone; *mātā-pitarau*—father and mother; *bhrātṛ-jñātīn*—brothers and kinsmen; *yauthikān*—belonging to the herd; *ca*—also; *eva*—certainly; *upeyāya*—having gotten; *na*—not; *anyam*—anyone else; *kañcana*—some person; *veda*—it knows; *mayi*—in me; *ati*—very great; *visrabdhaḥ*—having faith; *ca*—and; *ataḥ eva*—therefore; *mayā*—by me; *mat-parāyaṇasya*—of one who is so dependent upon me; *poṣaṇa-pālana-prīṇana-lālanam*—raising, maintaining, petting and protecting; *anasūyunā*—who am without any grudge; *anuṣṭheyam*—to be executed; *śaraṇya*—the one who has taken shelter; *upekṣā*—of neglecting; *doṣa-viduṣā*—who knows the fault.

TRANSLATION

The great King Mahārāja Bharata began to think: Alas, this helpless young deer, by the force of time, an agent of the Supreme Personality of Godhead, has now lost its relatives and friends and has taken shelter of me. It does not know anyone but me, as I have become its father, mother, brother and relatives. This deer is thinking in this way, and it has full faith in me. It does not know anyone but me; therefore I should not be envious and think that for the deer my own welfare will be destroyed. I should certainly raise, protect, gratify and fondle it. When it has taken shelter with me, how can I neglect it? Even though the deer is disturbing my spiritual life, I realize that a helpless person who has taken shelter cannot be neglected. That would be a great fault.

PURPORT

When a person is advanced in spiritual consciousness or Kṛṣṇa consciousness, he naturally becomes very sympathetic toward all living entities suffering in the material world. Naturally such an advanced person thinks of the suffering of the people in general. However, if one does not know of the material sufferings of fallen souls and becomes sympathetic because of bodily comforts, as in the case of Bharata Mahārāja, such sympathy or compassion is the cause of one's downfall. If one is actually sympathetic to fallen, suffering humanity, he should try to elevate people from material consciousness to spiritual consciousness. As far as the deer was concerned, Bharata Mahārāja became very sympathetic, but he forgot that it was impossible for him to elevate a deer to spiritual consciousness, because, after all, a deer is but an animal. It was very dangerous for Bharata Mahārāja to sacrifice all his regulative principles simply to take care of an animal. The principles enunciated in *Bhagavad-gītā* should be followed. *Yaṁ hi na vyathayanty ete puruṣaṁ puruṣarṣabha.* As far as the material body is concerned, we cannot do anything for anyone. However, by the grace of Kṛṣṇa, we may raise a person to spiritual consciousness if we ourselves follow the rules and regulations. If we give up our own spiritual activities and simply become concerned with the bodily comforts of others, we will fall into a dangerous position.

TEXT 10

नूनं ह्यार्याः साधव उपशमशीलाः कृपणसुहृद एवंविधार्थे स्वार्थानपि गुरुतरानुपेक्षन्ते ॥ १० ॥

nūnaṁ hy āryāḥ sādhava upaśama-śīlāḥ kṛpaṇa-suhṛda evaṁ-
vidhārthe svārthān api gurutarān upekṣante.

nūnam—indeed; *hi*—certainly; *āryāḥ*—those who are advanced in civilization; *sādhavaḥ*—saintly persons; *upaśama-śīlāḥ*—even though completely in the renounced order of life; *kṛpaṇa-suhṛdaḥ*—the friends of the helpless; *evaṁ-vidha-arthe*—to execute such principles; *sva-arthān api*—even their own personal interests; *guru-tarān*—very important; *upekṣante*—neglect.

TRANSLATION

Even though one is in the renounced order, one who is advanced certainly feels compassion for suffering living entities. One should certainly neglect his own personal interests, although they may be very important, to protect one who has surrendered.

PURPORT

Māyā is very strong. In the name of philanthropy, altruism and communism, people are feeling compassion for suffering humanity throughout the world. Philanthropists and altruists do not realize that it is impossible to improve people's material conditions. Material conditions are already established by the superior administration according to one's *karma.* They cannot be changed. The only benefit we can render to suffering beings is to try to raise them to spiritual consciousness. Material comforts cannot be increased or decreased. It is therefore said in *Śrīmad-Bhāgavatam* (1.5.18), *tal labhyate duḥkhavad anyataḥ sukham:* "As far as material happiness is concerned, that comes without effort, just as tribulations come without effort." Material happiness and pain can be attained without endeavor. One should not bother for material activities. If one is at all sympathetic or able to do good to others, he should endeavor to raise people to Kṛṣṇa consciousness. In this way everyone advances spiritually by the grace of the Lord. For our instruction, Bharata Mahārāja acted in such a way. We should be very careful not to be misled by so-called welfare activities conducted in bodily terms. One should not give up his interest in attaining the favor of Lord Viṣṇu at any cost. Generally people do not know this, or they forget it. Consequently they sacrifice their original interest, the attainment of Viṣṇu's favor, and engage in philanthropic activities for bodily comfort.

TEXT 11

इति कृतानुषङ्ग आसनशयनाटनस्नानाशनादिषु सह मृगजहुना
स्नेहानुबद्धहृदय आसीत् ॥ ११ ॥

iti kṛtānuṣaṅga āsana-śayanāṭana-snānāśanādiṣu saha mṛga-jahunā snehānubaddha-hṛdaya āsīt.

iti—thus; *kṛta-anuṣaṅgaḥ*—having developed attachment; *āsana*—sitting; *śayana*—lying down; *aṭana*—walking; *snāna*—bathing; *āśana-ādiṣu*—while eating and so on; *saha mṛga-jahunā*—with the deer calf; *sneha-anubaddha*—captivated by affection; *hṛdayaḥ*—his heart; *āsīt*—became.

TRANSLATION

Due to attachment for the deer, Mahārāja Bharata lay down with it, walked about with it, bathed with it and even ate with it. Thus his heart became bound to the deer in affection.

TEXT 12

कुशकुसुमसमित्पलाशफलमूलोदकान्याहरिष्यमाणो वृकसालावृकादिभ्यो भयमाशंसमानो यदा सह हरिणकुणकेन वनं समाविशति ॥ १२ ॥

kuśa-kusuma-samit-palāśa-phala-mūlodakāny āhariṣyamāṇo vṛkasālā-vṛkādibhyo bhayam āśaṁsamāno yadā saha hariṇa-kuṇakena vanaṁ samāviśati.

kuśa—a kind of grass required for ritualistic ceremonies; *kusuma*—flowers; *samit*—firewood; *palāśa*—leaves; *phala-mūla*—fruits and roots; *udakāni*—and water; *āhariṣyamāṇaḥ*—desiring to collect; *vṛkasālā-vṛka*—from wolves and dogs; *ādibhyaḥ*—and other animals, such as tigers; *bhayam*—fear; *āśaṁsamānaḥ*—doubting; *yadā*—when; *saha*—with; *hariṇa-kuṇakena*—the deer calf; *vanam*—the forest; *samāviśati*—enters.

TRANSLATION

When Mahārāja Bharata wanted to enter the forest to collect kuśa grass, flowers, wood, leaves, fruits, roots and water, he would fear that dogs, jackals, tigers and other ferocious animals might kill the deer. He would therefore always take the deer with him when entering the forest.

PURPORT

How Mahārāja Bharata increased his affection for the deer is described herein. Even such an exalted personality as Bharata Mahārāja, who had attained loving affection for the Supreme Personality of Godhead, fell down from his position due to his affection for some animal. Consequently, as will be seen, he had to accept the body of a deer in his next life. Since this was the case with Bharata Mahārāja, what can we say of those who are not advanced in spiritual life but who become attached to cats and dogs? Due to their affection for their cats and dogs, they have to take the same bodily forms in the next life unless they clearly increase their affection and love for the Supreme Personality of Godhead. Unless we increase our faith in the Supreme Lord, we shall be attracted to many other things. That is the cause of our material bondage.

TEXT 13

पथिषु च मुग्धभावेन तत्र तत्र विषक्तमतिप्रणयभरहृदयः कार्पण्या-
त्स्कन्धेनोद्वहति एवमुत्सङ्ग उरसि चाधायोपलालयन्मुदं परमामवाप॥१३॥

pathiṣu ca mugdha-bhāvena tatra tatra viṣakta-mati-praṇaya-bhara-hṛdayaḥ kārpaṇyāt skandhenodvahati evam utsaṅga urasi cādhāyopalālayan mudaṁ paramām avāpa.

pathiṣu—on the forest paths; *ca*—also; *mugdha-bhāvena*—by the childish behavior of the deer; *tatra tatra*—here and there; *viṣakta-mati*—whose mind was too much attracted; *praṇaya*—with love; *bhara*—loaded; *hṛdayaḥ*—whose heart; *kārpaṇyāt*—because of affection and love; *skandhena*—by the shoulder; *udvahati*—carries; *evam*—in this way; *utsaṅge*—sometimes on the lap; *urasi*—on the chest while sleeping; *ca*—also; *ādhāya*—keeping; *upalālayan*—fondling; *mudam*—pleasure; *paramām*—very great; *avāpa*—he felt.

TRANSLATION

When entering the forest, the animal would appear very attractive to Mahārāja Bharata due to its childish behavior. Mahārāja Bharata would even take the deer on his shoulders and carry it due to affection. His heart was so filled with great love for the deer that he would sometimes keep it on his lap or, when sleeping, on his chest. In this way he felt great pleasure in fondling the animal.

PURPORT

Mahārāja Bharata left his home, wife, children, kingdom and everything else to advance his spiritual life in the forest, but again he fell victim to material affection due to his attachment to an insignificant pet deer. What, then, was the use of his renouncing his family? One who is serious in advancing his spiritual life should be very cautious not to become attached to anything but Kṛṣṇa. Sometimes, in order to preach, we have to accept many material activities, but we should remember that everything is for Kṛṣṇa. If we remember this, there is no chance of our being victimized by material activities.

TEXT 14

क्रियायां निर्वर्त्यमानायामन्तरालेऽप्युत्थायोत्थाय यदैनमभिचक्षीत तर्हि वाव स वर्षपतिः प्रकृतिस्थेन मनसा तस्मा आशिष आशास्ते स्वस्ति स्ताद्वत्स ते सर्वत इति ॥ १४ ॥

kriyāyāṁ nirvartyamānāyām antarāle 'py utthāyotthāya yadainam abhicakṣīta tarhi vāva sa varṣa-patiḥ prakṛti-sthena manasā tasmā āśiṣa āśāste svasti stād vatsa te sarvata iti.

kriyāyām—the activities of worshiping the Lord or performing ritualistic ceremonies; *nirvartyamānāyām*—even without finishing; *antarāle*—at intervals in the middle; *api*—although; *utthāya utthāya*—repeatedly getting up; *yadā*—when; *enam*—the deer calf; *abhicakṣīta*—would see; *tarhi vāva*—at that time; *saḥ*—he; *varṣa-patiḥ*—Mahārāja Bharata; *prakṛti-sthena*—happy; *manasā*—within his mind; *tasmai*—unto it; *āśiṣaḥ āśāste*—bestows benedictions; *svasti*—all auspiciousness; *stāt*—let there be; *vatsa*—O my dear calf; *te*—unto you; *sarvataḥ*—in all respects; *iti*—thus.

TRANSLATION

When Mahārāja Bharata was actually worshiping the Lord or was engaged in some ritualistic ceremony, although his activities were unfinished, he would still, at intervals, get up and see where the deer was. In this way he would look for it, and when he could see that the deer was comfortably situated, his mind and heart would be very satisfied, and he would bestow his blessings upon the deer, saying, "My dear calf, may you be happy in all respects."

PURPORT

Because his attraction for the deer was so intense, Bharata Mahārāja could not concentrate upon worshiping the Lord or performing his ritualistic ceremonies. Even though he was engaged in worshiping the Deity, his mind was restless due to his inordinate affection. While trying to meditate, he would simply think of the deer, wondering where it had gone. In other words, if one's mind is distracted from worship, a mere show of worship will not be of any benefit. The fact that Bharata Mahārāja had to get up at intervals to look for the deer was simply a sign that he had fallen down from the spiritual platform.

TEXT 15

अन्यदा भृशमुद्विग्नमना नष्टद्रविण इव कृपणः सकरुणमतितर्षेण हरिणकुणक विरहविह्वलहृदयसन्तापस्तमेवानुशोचन् किल कश्मलं महदभिरम्भित इति होवाच ॥ १५॥

anyadā bhṛśam udvigna-manā naṣṭa-draviṇa iva kṛpaṇaḥ sakaruṇam ati-tarṣeṇa hariṇa-kuṇaka-viraha-vihvala-hṛdaya-santāpas tam evānuśocan kila kaśmalaṁ mahad abhirambhita iti hovāca.

anyadā—sometimes (not seeing the calf); *bhṛśam*—very much; *udvigna-manāḥ*—his mind full of anxiety; *naṣṭa-draviṇaḥ*—who has lost his riches; *iva*—like; *kṛpaṇaḥ*—a miserly man; *sa-karuṇam*—piteously; *ati-tarṣeṇa*—with great anxiety; *hariṇa-kuṇaka*—from the calf of the deer; *viraha*—by separation; *vihvala*—agitated; *hṛdaya*—in mind or heart; *santāpaḥ*—whose affliction; *tam*—that calf; *eva*—only; *anuśocan*—continuously thinking of; *kila*—certainly; *kaśmalam*—illusion; *mahat*—very great; *abhirambhitaḥ*—obtained; *iti*—thus; *ha*—certainly; *uvāca*—said.

TRANSLATION

If Bharata Mahārāja sometimes could not see the deer, his mind would be very agitated. He would become like a miser, who, having obtained some riches, had lost them and had then become very unhappy. When the deer was gone, he would be filled with anxiety and would lament due to separation. Thus he would become illusioned and speak as follows.

PURPORT

If a poor man loses some money or gold, he at once becomes very agitated. Similarly, the mind of Mahārāja Bharata would become agitated when he did not see the deer. This is an example of how our attachment can be transferred. If our attachment is transferred to the Lord's service, we progress. Śrīla Rūpa Gosvāmī prayed to the Lord that he would be as naturally attracted to the Lord's service as young men and young women are naturally attracted to each other. Śrī Caitanya Mahāprabhu exhibited such attachment to the Lord when He jumped into the ocean or cried at night in separation. However, if our attachment is diverted to material things instead of to the Lord, we will fall down from the spiritual platform.

TEXT 16

अपि बत स वै कृपण एणबालको मृतहरिणीसुतोऽहो ममानार्यस्य शठकिरातमतेर-कृतसुकृतस्य कृतविस्रम्भ आत्मप्रत्ययेन तदविगणयन् सुजन इवागमिष्यति ॥१६॥

api bata sa vai kṛpaṇa eṇa-bālako mṛta-hariṇī-suto 'ho mamānāryasya
śaṭha-kirāta-mater akṛta-sukṛtasya kṛta-visrambha ātma-pratyayena
tad avigaṇayan sujana ivāgamiṣyati.

api—indeed; *bata*—alas; *saḥ*—that calf; *vai*—certainly; *kṛpaṇaḥ*—aggrieved; *eṇa-bālakaḥ*—the deer child; *mṛta-hariṇī-sutaḥ*—the calf of the dead doe; *aho*—oh; *mama*—of me; *anāryasya*—the most ill-behaved; *śaṭha*—of a cheater; *kirāta*—or of an uncivilized aborigine; *mateḥ*—whose mind is that; *akṛta-sukṛtasya*—who has no pious activities; *kṛta-visrambhaḥ*—putting all faith; *ātma-pratyayena*—by assuming me to be like himself; *tat avigaṇayan*—without thinking of all these things; *su-janaḥ iva*—like a perfect gentle person; *agamiṣyati*—will he again return.

TRANSLATION

Bharata Mahārāja would think: Alas, the deer is now helpless. I am now very unfortunate, and my mind is like a cunning hunter, for it is always filled with cheating propensities and cruelty. The deer has put its faith in me, just as a good man who has a natural interest in good behavior forgets the misbehavior of a cunning friend and puts his faith in him. Although I have proved faithless, will this deer return and place its faith in me?

PURPORT

Bharata Mahārāja was very noble and exalted, and therefore when the deer was absent from him he thought himself unworthy to give it protection. Due to his attachment for the animal, he thought that the animal was as noble and exalted as he himself was. According to the logic of *ātmavan manyate jagat*, everyone thinks of others according to his own position. Therefore Mahārāja Bharata felt that the deer had left him due to his negligence and that due to the animal's noble heart, it would again return.

TEXT 17

अपि क्षेमेणास्मिन्नाश्रमोपवने शष्पाणि चरन्तं देवगुप्तं द्रक्ष्यामि ॥१७॥

api kṣemeṇāsminn āśramopavane śaṣpāṇi carantaṁ deva-guptaṁ drakṣyāmi.

api—it may be; *kṣemeṇa*—with fearlessness because of the absence of tigers and other animals; *asmin*—in this; *āśrama-upavane*—garden of the hermitage; *śaṣpāṇi carantam*—walking and eating the soft grasses; *deva-guptam*—being protected by the demigods; *drakṣyāmi*—shall I see.

TRANSLATION

Alas, is it possible that I shall again see this animal protected by the Lord and fearless of tigers and other animals? Shall I again see him wandering in the garden eating soft grass?

PURPORT

Mahārāja Bharata thought that the animal was disappointed in his protection and had left him for the protection of a demigod. Regardless, he ardently desired to see the animal again within his *āśrama* eating the soft grass and not fearing tigers and other animals. Mahārāja Bharata could think only of the deer and how the animal could be protected from all kinds of inauspicious things. From the materialistic point of view, such kind thoughts may be very laudable, but from the spiritual point of view the King was actually falling from his exalted spiritual position and unnecessarily becoming attached to an animal. Thus degrading himself, he would have to accept an animal body.

TEXT 18

अपि च न वृकः सालावृकोऽन्यतमो वा नैकचर एकचरो वा भक्षयति ॥१८॥

api ca na vṛkaḥ sālā-vṛko 'nyatamo vā naika-cara eka-caro vā bhakṣayati.

api ca—or; *na*—not; *vṛkaḥ*—a wolf; *sālā-vṛkaḥ*—a dog; *anyatamaḥ*—any one of many; *vā*—or; *na-eka-caraḥ*—the hogs that flock together; *eka-caraḥ*—the tiger that wanders alone; *vā*—or; *bhakṣayati*—is eating (the poor creature).

TRANSLATION

I do not know, but the deer might have been eaten by a wolf or a dog or by the boars that flock together or the tiger who travels alone.

PURPORT

Tigers never wander in the forest in flocks. Each tiger wanders alone, but forest boars keep together. Similarly, hogs, wolves and dogs also do the same. Thus Mahārāja Bharata thought that the deer had been killed by some of the many ferocious animals within the forest.

TEXT 19

निम्लोचति ह भगवान् सकलजगत्क्षेमोदयस्त्रय्यात्माद्यापि मम न मृगवधून्यास आगच्छति ॥१९॥

nimlocati ha bhagavān sakala-jagat-kṣemodayas trayy-ātmādyāpi mama na mṛga-vadhū-nyāsa āgacchati.

nimlocati—sets; *ha*—alas; *bhagavān*—the Supreme Personality of Godhead, represented as the sun; *sakala-jagat*—of all the universe; *kṣema-udayaḥ*—who increases the auspiciousness; *trayī-ātmā*—who consists of the three *Vedas; adya api*—until now; *mama*—my; *na*—not; *mṛga-vadhū-nyāsaḥ*—this baby deer entrusted to me by its mother; *āgacchati*—has come back.

TRANSLATION

Alas, when the sun rises, all auspicious things begin. Unfortunately, they have not begun for me. The sun-god is the Vedas personified, but I am bereft of all Vedic principles. That sun-god is now setting, yet the poor animal who trusted in me since its mother died has not returned.

PURPORT

In the *Brahma-saṁhitā* (5.52), the sun is described as the eye of the Supreme Personality of Godhead.

yac-cakṣur eṣa savitā sakala-grahāṇāṁ
rājā samasta-sura-mūrtir aśeṣa-tejāḥ
yasyājñayā bhramati saṁbhṛta-kāla-cakro
govindam ādi-puruṣaṁ tam ahaṁ bhajāmi

As the sun arises, one should chant the Vedic *mantra* beginning with the Gāyatrī. The sun is the symbolic representation of the eyes of the Supreme Lord. Mahārāja Bharata lamented that although the sun was going to set, due to the poor animal's absence, he could not find anything auspicious. Bharata Mahārāja considered himself most unfortunate, for due to the animal's absence, there was nothing auspicious for him in the presence of the sun.

TEXT 20

अपिस्विदकृतसुकृतमागत्य मां सुखयिष्यति हरिणराजकुमारो
विविधरुचिरदर्शनीयनिजमृगदारकविनोदैरसन्तोषं स्वानामपनुदन्॥२०॥

api svid akṛta-sukṛtam āgatya māṁ sukhayiṣyati hariṇa-rāja-kumāro vividha-rucira-darśanīya-nija-mṛga-dāraka-vinodair asantoṣaṁ svānām apanudan.

api svit—whether it will; *akṛta-sukṛtam*—who has never executed any pious activities; *āgatya*—coming back; *mām*—to me; *sukhayiṣyati*—give pleasure; *hariṇa-rāja-kumāraḥ*—the deer, who was just like a prince because of my taking care of it exactly like a son; *vividha*—various; *rucira*—very pleasing; *darśanīya*—to be seen; *nija*—own; *mṛga-dāraka*—befitting the calf of the deer; *vinodaiḥ*—by pleasing activities; *asantoṣam*—the unhappiness; *svānām*—of his own kind; *apanudan*—driving away.

TRANSLATION

That deer is exactly like a prince. When will it return? When will it again display its personal activities, which are so pleasing? When will it again pacify a wounded heart like mine? I certainly must have no pious assets, otherwise the deer would have returned by now.

PURPORT

Out of strong affection, the King accepted the small deer as if it were a prince. This is called *moha.* Due to his anxiety over the deer's absence, the King addressed the animal as though it were his son. Out of affection, anyone can be addressed as anything.

TEXT 21

क्ष्वेलिकायां मां मृषासमाधिनाऽऽमीलितदृशं प्रेमसंरम्भेण चकितचकित आगत्य पृषदपरुषविषाणाग्रेण लुठति ॥ २१ ॥

kṣvelikāyāṁ māṁ mṛṣā-samādhināmīlita-dṛśaṁ prema-saṁrambheṇa cakita-cakita āgatya pṛṣad-aparuṣa-viṣāṇāgreṇa luṭhati.

kṣvelikāyām—while playing; *mām*—unto me; *mṛṣā*—feigning; *samādhinā*—by a meditational trance; *āmīlita-dṛśam*—with closed eyes;

prema-saṁrambheṇa—because of anger due to love; *cakita-cakitaḥ*—with fear; *āgatya*—coming; *pṛṣat*—like drops of water; *aparuṣa*—very soft; *viṣāṇa*—of the horns; *agreṇa*—by the point; *luṭhati*—touches my body.

TRANSLATION

Alas, the small deer, while playing with me and seeing me feigning meditation with closed eyes, would circumambulate me due to anger arising from love, and it would fearfully touch me with the points of its soft horns, which felt like drops of water.

PURPORT

Now King Bharata considers his meditation false. While engaged in meditation, he was actually thinking of his deer, and he would feel great pleasure when the animal pricked him with the points of its horns. Feigning meditation, the King would actually think of the animal, and this was but a sign of his downfall.

TEXT 22

आसादितहविषि बर्हिषि दूषिते मयोपालब्धो भीतभीतः सपद्युपरतरास ऋषिकुमारवदवहितकरणकलाप आस्ते ॥ २२ ॥

āsādita-haviṣi barhiṣi dūṣite mayopālabdho bhīta-bhītaḥ sapady
uparata-rāsa ṛṣi-kumāravad avahita-karaṇa-kalāpa āste.

āsādita—placed; *haviṣi*—all the ingredients to be offered in the sacrifice; *barhiṣi*—on the *kuśa* grass; *dūṣite*—when polluted; *mayā upalabdhaḥ*—being scolded by me; *bhīta-bhītaḥ*—in great fear; *sapadi*—immediately; *uparata-rāsaḥ*—stopped its playing; *ṛṣi-kumāra-vat*—exactly like the son or disciple of a saintly person; *avahita*—completely restrained; *karaṇa-kalāpaḥ*—all the senses; *āste*—sits.

TRANSLATION

When I placed all the sacrificial ingredients on the kuśa grass, the deer, when playing, would touch the grass with its teeth and

thus pollute it. When I chastised the deer by pushing it away, it would immediately become fearful and sit down motionless, exactly like the son of a saintly person. Thus it would stop its play.

PURPORT

Bharata Mahārāja was constantly thinking of the activities of the deer, forgetting that such meditation and diversion of attention was killing his progress in spiritual achievement.

TEXT 23

किं वा अरे आचरितं तपस्तपस्विन्यानया यदियमवनिः सविनयकृष्णसारतनयतनुतरसुभगशिवतमाखरखुरपदपङ्क्तिभिर्द्रविण विधुरातुरस्य कृपणस्य मम द्रविणपदवीं सूचयन्त्यात्मानं च सर्वतः कृतकौतुकं द्विजानां स्वर्गापवर्गकामानां देवयजनं करोति॥२३॥

kiṁ vā are ācaritaṁ tapas tapasvinyānayā yad iyam avaniḥ
savinaya-kṛṣṇa-sāra-tanaya-tanutara-subhaga-śivatamākhara-khura-
pada-paṅktibhir draviṇa-vidhurāturasya kṛpaṇasya mama draviṇa-
padavīṁ sūcayanty ātmānaṁ ca sarvataḥ kṛta-kautukaṁ dvijānāṁ
svargāpavarga-kāmānāṁ deva-yajanaṁ karoti.

kim vā—what; *are*—oh; *ācaritam*—practiced; *tapaḥ*—penance; *tapasvinyā*—by the most fortunate; *anayā*—this planet earth; *yat*—since; *iyam*—this; *avaniḥ*—earth; *sa-vinaya*—very mild and well-behaved; *kṛṣṇa-sāra-taṇaya*—of the calf of the black deer; *tanutara*—small; *subhaga*—beautiful; *śiva-tama*—most auspicious; *akhara*—soft; *khura*—of the hooves; *pada-paṅktibhiḥ*—by the series of the marks; *draviṇa-vidhura-āturasya*—who is very aggrieved because of loss of wealth; *kṛpaṇasya*—a most unhappy creature; *mama*—for me; *draviṇa-padavīm*—the way to achieve that wealth; *sūcayanti*—indicating; *ātmānam*—her own personal body; *ca*—and; *sarvataḥ*—on all sides; *kṛta-kautukam*—ornamented; *dvijānām*—of the *brāhmaṇas; svarga-apavarga-kāmānām*—who are desirous of achieving heavenly planets or liberation; *deva-yajanam*—a place of sacrifice to the demigods; *karoti*—it makes.

TRANSLATION

After speaking like a madman in this way, Mahārāja Bharata got up and went outside. Seeing the footprints of the deer on the ground, he praised the footprints out of love, saying: O unfortunate Bharata, your austerities and penances are very insignificant compared to the penance and austerity undergone by this earth planet. Due to the earth's severe penances, the footprints of this deer, which are small, beautiful, most auspicious and soft, are imprinted on the surface of this fortunate planet. This series of footprints show a person like me, who am bereaved due to loss of the deer, how the animal has passed through the forest and how I can regain my lost wealth. By these footprints, this land has become a proper place for brāhmaṇas who desire heavenly planets or liberation to execute sacrifices to the demigods.

PURPORT

It is said that when a person becomes overly involved in loving affairs, he forgets himself as well as others, and he forgets how to act and how to speak. It is said that once when a man's son was blind since birth, the father, out of staunch affection for the child, named him Padmalocana, or "lotus-eyed." This is the situation arising from blind love. Bharata Mahārāja gradually fell into this condition due to his material love for the deer. It is said in the *smṛti-śāstra:*

yasmin deśe mṛgaḥ kṛṣṇas
tasmin dharmānn ivodhata

"That tract of land wherein the footprints of a black deer can be seen is to be understood as a suitable place to execute religious rituals."

TEXT 24

अपिस्विदसौ भगवानुडुपतिरेनं मृगपतिभयान्मृतमातरं मृगबालकं
स्वाश्रमपरिभ्रष्टमनुकम्पया कृपणजनवत्सलः परिपाति ॥२४॥

api svid asau bhagavān uḍu-patir enaṁ mṛga-pati-bhayān mṛta-mātaraṁ mṛga-bālakaṁ svāśrama-paribhraṣṭam anukampayā kṛpaṇa-jana-vatsalaḥ paripāti.

api svit—can it be; *asau*—that; *bhagavān*—most powerful; *uḍu-patiḥ*—the moon; *enam*—this; *mṛga-pati-bhayāt*—because of fear of the lion; *mṛta-mātaram*—who lost its mother; *mṛga-bālakam*—the son of a deer; *sva-āśrama-paribhraṣṭam*—who strayed from its *āśrama; anukampayā*—out of compassion; *kṛpaṇa-jana-vatsalaḥ*—(the moon) who is very kind to the unhappy men; *paripāti*—now is protecting it.

TRANSLATION

Mahārāja Bharata continued to speak like a madman. Seeing above his head the dark marks on the rising moon, which resembled a deer, he said: Can it be that the moon, who is so kind to an unhappy man, might also be kind upon my deer, knowing that it has strayed from home and has become motherless? This moon has given the deer shelter near itself just to protect it from the fearful attacks of a lion.

TEXT 25

किं वाऽऽत्मजविश्लेषज्वरदवदहनशिखाभिरुपतप्यमानहृदयस्थलनलिनीकं मामुपसृतमृगीतनयं शिशिरशान्तानुरागगुणितनिजवदनसलिलामृतमयगभस्तिभिः स्वधयतीति च ॥२५॥

kim vātmaja-viśleṣa-jvara-dava-dahana-śikhābhir upatapyamāna-hṛdaya-sthala-nalinīkaṁ mām upasṛta-mṛgī-tanayaṁ śiśira-śāntānurāga-guṇita-nija-vadana-salilāmṛtamaya-gabhastibhiḥ svadhayatīti ca.

kim vā—or it may be; *ātma-ja*—from the son; *viśleṣa*—because of separation; *jvara*—the heat; *dava-dahana*—of the forest fire; *śikhābhiḥ*—by the flames; *upatapyamāna*—being burned; *hṛdaya*—the heart; *sthala-nalinīkam*—compared to a red lotus flower; *mām*—unto me; *upasṛta-mṛgī-tanayam*—to whom the son of the deer was so submissive; *śiśira-śānta*—which is so peaceful and cool; *anurāga*—out of love; *guṇita*—flowing; *nija-vadana-salila*—the water from its mouth; *amṛta-maya*—as good as nectar; *gabhastibhiḥ*—by the rays of the moon; *svadhayati*—is giving me pleasure; *iti*—thus; *ca*—and.

TRANSLATION

After perceiving the moonshine, Mahārāja Bharata continued speaking like a crazy person. He said: The deer's son was so submissive and dear to me that due to its separation I am feeling separation from my own son. Due to the burning fever of this separation, I am suffering as if enflamed by a forest fire. My heart, which is like the lily of the land, is now burning. Seeing me so distressed, the moon is certainly splashing its shining nectar upon me just as a friend throws water on another friend who has a high fever. In this way, the moon is bringing me happiness.

PURPORT

According to Ayur-vedic treatment, it is said that if one has a high fever, someone should splash him with water after gargling this water. In this way the fever subsides. Although Bharata Mahārāja was very aggrieved due to the separation of his so-called son, the deer, he thought that the moon was splashing gargled water on him from its mouth and that this water would subdue his high fever, which was raging due to separation from the deer.

TEXT 26

एवमघटमानमनोरथाकुलहृदयो मृगदारकाभासेन स्वारब्धकर्मणा
योगारम्भणतो विभ्रंशितः स योगतापसो भगवदाराधनलक्षणाच्च
कथमितरथा जात्यन्तर एणकुणक आसङ्गः साक्षान्निःश्रेयसप्रतिपक्षतया
प्राक्परित्यक्तदुस्त्यजहृदयाभिजातस्य तस्यैवमन्तरायविहत योगारम्भणस्य
राजर्षेर्भरतस्य तावन्मृगार्भकपोषणपालनप्रीणनलालनानुषङ्गेणाविगणयत
आत्मानमहिरिवाखुबिलं दुरतिक्रमः कालः करालरभस आपद्यत ॥२६॥

evam aghaṭamāna-manorathākula-hṛdayo mṛga-dārakābhāsena svārabdha-karmaṇā yogārambhaṇato vibhraṁśitaḥ sa yoga-tāpaso bhagavad-ārādhana-lakṣaṇāc ca katham itarathā jāty-antara eṇa-kuṇaka āsaṅgaḥ sākṣān niḥśreyasa-pratipakṣatayā prāk-parityakta-dustyaja-hṛdayābhijātasya tasyaivam antarāya-vihata-yogārambhaṇasya rājarṣer bharatasya tāvan mṛgārbhaka-poṣaṇa-pālana-prīṇana-lālanānuṣaṅgeṇāvigaṇayata ātmānam ahir ivākhu-bilaṁ duratikramaḥ kālaḥ karāla-rabhasa āpadyata.

evam—in that way; *aghaṭamāna*—impossible to be achieved; *manaḥ-ratha*—by desires, which are like mental chariots; *ākula*—aggrieved; *hṛdayaḥ*—whose heart; *mṛga-dāraka-ābhāsena*—resembling the son of a deer; *sva-ārabdha-karmaṇā*—by the bad results of his unseen fruitive actions; *yoga-ārambhaṇataḥ*—from the activities of *yoga* performances; *vibhraṁśitaḥ*—fallen down; *saḥ*—he (Mahārāja Bharata); *yoga-tāpasaḥ*—executing the activities of mystic *yoga* and austerities; *bhagavat-ārādhana-lakṣaṇāt*—from the activities of devotional service rendered to the Supreme Personality of Godhead; *ca*—and; *katham*—how; *itarathā*—else; *jāti-antare*—belonging to a different species of life; *eṇa-kuṇake*—to the body of a deer calf; *āsaṅgaḥ*—so much affectionate attachment; *sākṣāt*—directly; *niḥśreyasa*—to achieve the ultimate goal of life; *pratipakṣatayā*—with the quality of being an obstacle; *prāk*—who previously; *parityakta*—given up; *dustyaja*—although very difficult to give up; *hṛdaya-abhi-jātasya*—his sons, born of his own heart; *tasya*—of him; *evam*—thus; *antarāya*—by that obstacle; *vihata*—obstructed; *yoga-ārambhaṇasya*—whose path of executing the mystic *yoga* practices; *rāja-ṛṣeḥ*—of the great saintly King; *bharatasya*—of Mahārāja Bharata; *tāvat*—in that way; *mṛga-arbhaka*—the son of a deer; *poṣaṇa*—in maintaining; *pālana*—in protecting; *prīṇana*—in making happy; *lālana*—in fondling; *anuṣaṅgeṇa*—by constant absorption; *avigaṇayataḥ*—neglecting; *ātmānam*—his own soul; *ahiḥ iva*—like a serpent; *ākhu-bilam*—the hole of a mouse; *duratikramaḥ*—unsurpassable; *kālaḥ*—ultimate death; *karāla*—terrible; *rabhasaḥ*—having speed; *āpadyata*—arrived.

TRANSLATION

Śukadeva Gosvāmī continued: My dear King, in this way Bharata Mahārāja was overwhelmed by an uncontrollable desire which was

manifest in the form of the deer. Due to the fruitive results of his past deeds, he fell down from mystic yoga, austerity and worship of the Supreme Personality of Godhead. If it were not due to his past fruitive activity, how could he have been attracted to the deer after giving up the association of his own son and family, considering them stumbling blocks on the path of spiritual life? How could he show such uncontrollable affection for a deer? This was definitely due to his past karma. The King was so engrossed in petting and maintaining the deer that he fell down from his spiritual activities. In due course of time, insurmountable death, which is compared to a venomous snake that enters the hole created by a mouse, situated itself before him.

PURPORT

As will be seen in later verses, Bharata Mahārāja, at the time of death, would be forced to accept the body of a deer due to his attraction for the deer. In this regard, a question may be raised. How can a devotee be affected by his past misconduct and vicious activities? In *Brahma-saṁhitā* (5.54) it is said, *karmāṇi nirdahati kintu ca bhakti-bhājām:* "For those engaged in devotional service, *bhakti-bhajana*, the results of past deeds are indemnified." According to this, Bharata Mahārāja could not be punished for his past misdeeds. The conclusion must be that Mahārāja Bharata purposefully became over-addicted to the deer and neglected his spiritual advancement. To immediately rectify his mistake, for a short time he was awarded the body of a deer. This was just to increase his desire for mature devotional service. Although Bharata Mahārāja was awarded the body of an animal, he did not forget what had previously happened due to his purposeful mistake. He was very anxious to get out of his deer body, and this indicates that his affection for devotional service was intensified, so much so that he was quickly to attain perfection in a *brāhmaṇa* body in the next life. It is with this conviction that we declare in our *Back to Godhead* magazine that devotees like the *gosvāmīs* living in Vṛndāvana who purposely commit some sinful activity are born in the bodies of dogs, monkeys and tortoises in that holy land. Thus they take on these lower life forms for a short while, and after they give up those animal bodies, they are again promoted to the spiritual world. Such punishment is only for a short period, and it is not due to past *karma.* It may appear to be due to past *karma,* but it is offered to rectify the devotee and bring him to pure devotional service.

TEXT 27

तदानीमपि पार्श्ववर्तिनमात्मजमिवानुशोचन्तमभिवीक्षमाणो मृगएवाभिनिवेशित-
मना विसृज्य लोकमिमं सह मृगेण कलेवरं मृतमनु न मृतजन्मानुस्मृति-
रितरवन्मृगशरीरमवाप ॥२७॥

tadānīm api pārśva-vartinam ātmajam ivānuśocantam abhivīkṣamāṇo mṛga evābhiniveśita-manā visṛjya lokam imaṁ saha mṛgeṇa kalevaraṁ mṛtam anu na mṛta-janmānusmṛtir itaravan mṛga-śarīram avāpa.

tadānīm—at that time; *api*—indeed; *pārśva-vartinam*—by the side of his deathbed; *ātma-jam*—his own son; *iva*—like; *anuśocantam*—lamenting; *abhivīkṣamāṇaḥ*—seeing; *mṛge*—in the deer; *eva*—certainly; *abhiniveśita-manāḥ*—his mind was absorbed; *visṛjya*—giving up; *lokam*—world; *imam*—this; *saha*—with; *mṛgeṇa*—the deer; *kalevaram*—his body; *mṛtam*—died; *anu*—thereafter; *na*—not; *mṛta*—destroyed; *janma-anusmṛtiḥ*—remembrance of the incident before his death; *itara-vat*—like others; *mṛga-śarīram*—the body of a deer; *avāpa*—got.

TRANSLATION

At the time of death, the King saw that the deer was sitting by his side, exactly like his own son, and was lamenting his death. Actually the mind of the King was absorbed in the body of the deer, and consequently—like those bereft of Kṛṣṇa consciousness—he left the world, the deer, and his material body and acquired the body of a deer. However, there was one advantage. Although he lost his human body and received the body of a deer, he did not forget the incidents of his past life.

PURPORT

There was a difference between Bharata Mahārāja's acquiring a deer body and others' acquiring different bodies according to their mental condition at the time of death. After death, others forget everything that has happened in their past lives, but Bharata Mahārāja did not forget. According to *Bhagavad-gītā:*

yaṁ yaṁ vāpi smaran bhāvaṁ
tyajaty ante kalevaram
taṁ tam evaiti kaunteya
sadā tad-bhāva-bhāvitaḥ

"Whatever state of being one remembers when he quits his body, that state he will attain without fail." (Bg. 8.6)

After quitting his body, a person gets another body according to his mental condition at the time of death. At death, a person always thinks of that subject matter in which he has been engrossed during his life. According to this law, because Bharata Mahārāja was always thinking of the deer and forgetting his worship of the Supreme Lord, he acquired the body of a deer. However, due to his having been elevated to the topmost platform of devotional service, he did not forget the incidents of his past life. This special benediction saved him from further deterioration. Due to his past activities in devotional service, he became determined to finish his devotional service even in the body of a deer. It is therefore said in this verse, *mṛtam,* although he had died, *anu,* afterwards, *na mṛta-janmānusmṛtir itaravat,* he did not forget the incidents of his past life as others forget them. As stated in *Brahma-saṁhitā: karmāṇi nirdahati kintu ca bhakti-bhājām* (Bs. 5.54). It is proved herein that due to the grace of the Supreme Lord, a devotee is never vanquished. Due to his willful neglect of devotional service, a devotee may be punished for a short time, but he again revives his devotional service and returns home. back to Godhead.

TEXT 28

तत्रापि ह वा आत्मनो मृगत्वकारणं भगवदाराधनसमीहानुभावेनानुस्मृत्य भृशमनुतप्यमान आह ॥२८॥

tatrāpi ha vā ātmano mṛgatva-kāraṇaṁ bhagavad-ārādhana-samīhānubhāvenānusmṛtya bhṛśam anutapyamāna āha.

tatra api—in that birth; *ha vā*—indeed; *ātmanaḥ*—of himself; *mṛgatva-kāraṇam*—the cause of accepting the body of a deer; *bhagavat-ārādhana-samīhā*—of past activities in devotional service; *anubhāvena*—by consequence; *anusmṛtya*—remembering; *bhṛśam*—always; *anutapyamānaḥ*—repenting; *āha*—said.

TRANSLATION

Although in the body of a deer, Bharata Mahārāja, due to his rigid devotional service in his past life, could understand the cause of his birth in that body. Considering his past and present life, he constantly repented his activities, speaking in the following way.

PURPORT

This is a special concession for a devotee. Even if he attains a body that is nonhuman, by the grace of the Supreme Personality of Godhead he advances further in devotional service, whether by remembering his past life or by natural causes. It is not easy for a common man to remember the activities of his past life, but Bharata Mahārāja could remember his past activities due to his great sacrifices and engagement in devotional service.

TEXT 29

अहो कष्टं भ्रष्टोऽहमात्मवतामनुपथाद्यद्विमुक्तसमस्तसङ्गस्य विविक्तपुण्यारण्य-शरणस्यात्मवत आत्मनि सर्वेषामात्मनां भगवति वासुदेवे तदनुश्रवणमनन-सङ्कीर्तनाराधनानुस्मरणाभियोगेनाशून्यसकलयामेन कालेन समावेशितं समाहितं कार्त्स्न्येन मनस्तत्तु पुनर्ममाबुधस्यारान्मृगसुतमनु परिसुस्राव ॥२९॥

aho kaṣṭaṁ bhraṣṭo 'ham ātmavatām anupathād yad-vimukta-samasta-
saṅgasya vivikta-puṇyāraṇya-śaraṇasyātmavata ātmani sarveṣām
ātmanāṁ bhagavati vāsudeve tad-anuśravaṇa-manana-
saṅkīrtanārādhanānusmaraṇābhiyogenāśūnya-sakala-yāmena kālena
samāveśitaṁ samāhitaṁ kārtsnyena manas tat tu punar
mamābudhasyārān mṛga-sutam anu parisusrāva.

aho kaṣṭam—alas, what a miserable condition of life; *bhraṣṭaḥ*—fallen; *aham*—I (am); *ātma-vatām*—of great devotees who have achieved perfection; *anupathāt*—from the way of life; *yat*—from which; *vimukta-samasta-saṅgasya*—although having given up the association of my real sons and home; *vivikta*—solitary; *puṇya-araṇya*—of a sacred forest; *śaraṇasya*—who had taken shelter; *ātma-vataḥ*—of one who had become perfectly situated on the transcendental platform; *ātmani*—in the Supersoul; *sarveṣām*—of all; *ātmanām*—living entities; *bhagavati*—unto the Supreme Personality of Godhead; *vāsudeve*—Lord Vāsudeva; *tat*—of Him; *anuśravaṇa*—constantly hearing; *manana*—thinking; *saṅkīrtana*—chanting; *ārādhana*—worshiping; *anusmaraṇa*—constantly remembering; *abhiyogena*—by absorption in; *aśūnya*—filled; *sakala-yāmena*—in which all the hours; *kālena*—by time; *samāveśitam*—fully established; *samāhitam*—fixed; *kārtsnyena*—totally; *manaḥ*—the mind in such a situation; *tat*—that mind; *tu*—but; *punaḥ*—again; *mama*—of me; *abudhasya*—a great fool; *ārāt*—from a great distance; *mṛga-sutam*—the son of a deer; *anu*—being affected by; *parisusrāva*—fell down.

TRANSLATION

In the body of a deer, Bharata Mahārāja began to lament: What misfortune! I have fallen from the path of the self-realized. I gave up my real sons, wife and home to advance in spiritual life, and I took shelter in a solitary holy place in the forest. I became self-controlled and self-realized, and I engaged constantly in devotional service, hearing, thinking, chanting, worshiping and remembering the Supreme Personality of Godhead, Vāsudeva. I was successful in my attempt, so much so that my mind was always absorbed in devotional service. However, due to my personal foolishness, my mind again became attached—this time to a deer. Now I have obtained the body of a deer and have fallen far from my devotional practices.

PURPORT

Due to his stringent execution of devotional service, Mahārāja Bharata could remember the activities of his past life and how he was raised to the spiritual platform. Due to his foolishness, he became attached to an insignificant deer and thus fell down and had to accept the body of a deer. This is significant for every devotee. If we misuse our position and think that we are fully engaged in devotional service and can do whatever we like, we have to suffer like Bharata Mahārāja and be condemned to accept the type of body that impairs our devotional service. Only the human form is able to execute devotional service, but if we voluntarily give this up for sense gratification, we certainly have to be punished. This punishment is not exactly like that endured by an ordinary materialistic person. By the grace of the Supreme Lord, a devotee is punished in such a way that his eagerness to attain the lotus feet of Lord Vāsudeva is increased. By his intense desire, he returns home in the next lifetime. Devotional service is very completely described here: *tad-anuśravaṇa-manana-saṅkīrtanārādhanānusmaraṇābhiyogena.* The constant hearing and chanting of the glories of the Lord is recommended in *Bhagavad-gītā: satataṁ kīrtayanto māṁ yatantaś ca dṛḍha-vratāḥ.* Those who have taken to Kṛṣṇa consciousness should be very careful that not a single moment is wasted and that not a single moment is spent without chanting and remembering the Supreme Personality of Godhead and His activities. By His own actions and by the actions of His devotees, Kṛṣṇa teaches us how to become cautious in devotional service. Through the medium of Bharata Mahārāja, Kṛṣṇa teaches us that we must be careful in the discharge of devotional service. If we want to keep our minds completely fixed without deviation, we must engage them in devotional service full time. As far as the members of the International Society for Krishna Consciousness are concerned, they have sacrificed everything to push on this Kṛṣṇa consciousness movement. Yet they must take a lesson from the life of Bharata Mahārāja to be very cautious and to see that not a single moment is wasted in frivolous talk, sleep or voracious eating. Eating is not prohibited, but if we eat voraciously we shall certainly sleep more than required. Sense gratification ensues, and we may be degraded to a lower life form. In that way our spiritual progress may be checked at least for the time being. The best course is to take the advice of Śrīla Rūpa Gosvāmī: *avyartha-kālatvam.* We should see that every moment of our lives is utilized for the rendering of devotional service and nothing else. This is the secure position for one wanting to return home, back to Godhead.

TEXT 30

इत्येवं निगूढनिर्वेदो विसृज्य मृगीं मातरं पुनर्भगवत्-
क्षेत्रमुपशमशीलमुनिगणदयितं शालग्रामं पुलस्त्यपुलहाश्रमं कालञ्जरात्प्रत्या-
जगाम ॥३०॥

ity evaṁ nigūḍha-nirvedo visṛjya mṛgīṁ mātaraṁ punar bhagavat-kṣetram upaśama-śīla-muni-gaṇa-dayitaṁ śālagrāmaṁ pulastya-pulahāśramaṁ kālañjarāt pratyājagāma.

iti—thus; *evam*—in this way; *nigūḍha*—hidden; *nirvedaḥ*—completely unattached to material activities; *visṛjya*—giving up; *mṛgīm*—the deer; *mātaram*—its mother; *punaḥ*—again; *bhagavat-kṣetram*—the place where the Supreme Lord is worshiped; *upaśama-śīla*—completely detached from all material attachments; *muni-gaṇa-dayitam*—which is dear to the great saintly residents; *śālagrāmam*—the village known as Śālagrāma; *pulastya-pulaha-āśramam*—to the *āśrama* conducted by such great sages as Pulastya and Pulaha; *kālañjarāt*—from the Kālañjara Mountain, where he had taken his birth in the womb of a deer; *pratyā-jagāma*—he came back.

TRANSLATION

Although Bharata Mahārāja received the body of a deer, by constant repentance he became completely detached from all material things. He did not disclose these things to anyone, but he left his mother deer in a place known as Kālañjara Mountain, where he was born. He again went to the forest of Śālagrāma and to the āśrama of Pulastya and Pulaha.

PURPORT

It is significant that Mahārāja Bharata, by the grace of Vāsudeva, remembered his past life. He did not waste a moment; he returned to Pulaha-āśrama to the village known as Śālagrāma. Association is very meaningful; therefore ISKCON tries to perfect one who enters the society. The members of this society should always remember that the society is not like a free hotel. All the members should be very careful to execute their spiritual duties so that whoever comes will automatically become a devotee and will be able to return back to Godhead in this very life. Although Bharata Mahārāja acquired the body of a deer, he again left his hearth and home, in this case the Mountain Kālañjara. No one should be captivated by his birthplace and family; one should take shelter of the association of devotees and cultivate Kṛṣṇa consciousness.

TEXT 31

तस्मिन्नपि कालं प्रतीक्षमाणः सङ्गाच्च भृशमुद्विग्न आत्मसहचरः शुष्कपर्ण-
तृणवीरुधा वर्तमानो मृगत्वनिमित्तावसानमेव गणयन्मृगशरीरं
तीर्थोदकक्लिन्नमुत्ससर्ज ॥ ३१ ॥

tasminn api kālaṁ pratīkṣamāṇaḥ saṅgāc ca bhṛśam udvigna ātma-sahacaraḥ śuṣka-parṇa-tṛṇa-vīrudhā vartamāno mṛgatva-nimittāvasānam eva gaṇayan mṛga-śarīraṁ tīrthodaka-klinnam ut-sasarja.

tasmin api—in that *āśrama* (Pulaha-āśrama); *kālam*—the end of the duration of life in the deer body; *pratīkṣamāṇaḥ*—always waiting for; *saṅgāt*—from association; *ca*—and; *bhṛśam*—constantly; *udvignaḥ*—full of anxiety; *ātma-sahacaraḥ*—having the Supersoul as the only constant companion (no one should think of being alone); *śuṣka-parṇa-tṛṇa-vīrudhā*—by eating only the dry leaves and herbs; *vartamānaḥ*—existing; *mṛgatva-nimitta*—of the cause of a deer's body; *avasānam*—the end; *eva*—only; *gaṇayan*—considering; *mṛga-śarīram*—the body of a deer; *tīrtha-udaka-klinnam*—bathing in the water of that holy place; *utsasarja*—gave up.

TRANSLATION

Remaining in that āśrama, the great King Bharata Mahārāja was now very careful not to fall victim to bad association. Without disclosing his past to anyone, he remained in that āśrama and ate dry leaves only. He was not exactly alone, for he had the association of the Supersoul. In this way he waited for death in the body of a deer. Bathing in that holy place, he finally gave up that body.

PURPORT

Holy places like Vṛndāvana, Hardwar, Prayāga and Jagannātha Purī are especially meant for the execution of devotional service. Vṛndāvana specifically is the most exalted and preferred holy place for Vaiṣṇava devotees of Lord Kṛṣṇa who are aspiring to return back to Godhead, the Vaikuṇṭha planets. There are many devotees in Vṛndāvana who regularly bathe in the Yamunā, and this cleanses all the contamination of the material world. By constantly chanting and hearing the holy names and pastimes of the Supreme Lord, one certainly becomes purified and becomes a fit candidate for liberation. However, if one purposefully falls victim to sense gratification, he has to be punished, at least for one lifetime, like Bharata Mahārāja.

Thus end the Bhaktivedanta purports of the Fifth Canto, Eighth Chapter, of the Śrīmad-Bhāgavatam, *entitled "A Description of the Character of Bharata Mahārāja."*

CHAPTER NINE

The Supreme Character of Jaḍa Bharata

In this chapter Bharata Mahārāja's attainment of the body of a *brāhmaṇa* is described. In this body he remained like one dull, deaf and dumb, so much so that when he was brought before the goddess Kālī to be killed as a sacrifice, he never protested but remained silent. After having given up the body of a deer, he took birth in the womb of the youngest wife of a *brāhmaṇa*. In this life he could also remember the activities of his past life, and in order to avoid the influence of society, he remained like a deaf and dumb person. He was very careful not to fall down again. He did not mix with anyone who was not a devotee. This process should be adopted by every devotee. As advised by Śrī Caitanya Mahāprabhu: *asat-saṅga-tyāga,——ei vaiṣṇava-ācāra.* One should strictly avoid the company of nondevotees, even though they may be family members. When Bharata Mahārāja was in the body of a *brāhmaṇa*, the people in the neighborhood thought of him as a crazy, dull fellow, but within he was always chanting and remembering Vāsudeva, the Supreme Personality of Godhead. Although his father wanted to give him an education and purify him as a *brāhmaṇa* by offering him the sacred thread, he remained in such a way that his father and mother could understand that he was crazy and not interested in the reformatory method. Nonetheless, he remained fully Kṛṣṇa conscious, even without undergoing such official ceremonies. Due to his silence, some people who were no better than animals began to tease him in many ways, but he tolerated this. After the death of his father and mother, his stepmother and stepbrothers began to treat him very poorly. They would give him the most condemned food, but still he did not mind; he remained completely absorbed in Kṛṣṇa consciousness. He was ordered by his stepbrothers and mother to guard a paddy field one night, and at that time the leader of a dacoit party took him away and tried to kill him by offering him as a sacrifice before Bhadra Kālī. When the dacoits brought Bharata Mahārāja before the goddess Kālī and raised a chopper to kill him, the goddess Kālī became immediately alarmed due to the mistreatment of a devotee. She came out of the deity and, taking the chopper in her own hands, killed all the dacoits there. Thus a pure devotee of the Supreme Personality of Godhead can remain silent despite the mistreatment of nondevotees. Rogues and dacoits who misbehave toward a devotee are punished at last by the arrangement of the Supreme Personality of Godhead.

TEXTS 1-2

श्रीशुक उवाच

अथ कस्यचिद् द्विजवरस्याङ्गिरःप्रवरस्य शमदमतपःस्वाध्यायाध्ययनत्याग-
सन्तोषतितिक्षाप्रश्रयविद्यानसूयात्मज्ञानानन्दयुक्तस्यात्मसदृशश्रुतशीलाचाररूपौ-
दार्यगुणा नव सोदर्या अङ्गजा बभूवुर्मिथुनं च यवीयस्यां भार्यायाम्
॥ १ ॥ यस्तु तत्र पुमांस्तं परमभागवतं राजर्षिप्रवरं भरतमुत्सृष्टमृग-
शरीरं चरमशरीरेण विप्रत्वं गतमाहुः ॥ २ ॥

śrī-śuka uvāca
atha kasyacid dvija-varasyāṅgiraḥ-pravarasya śama-dama-tapaḥ-svādhyāyādhyayana-tyāga-santoṣa-titikṣā-praśraya-vidyānasūyātma-jñānānanda-yuktasyātma-sadṛśa-śruta-śīlācāra-rūpaudārya-guṇā nava sodaryā aṅgajā babhūvur mithunaṁ ca yavīyasyāṁ bhāryāyām. yas tu tatra pumāṁs taṁ parama-bhāgavataṁ rājarṣi-pravaraṁ bharatam utsṛṣṭa-mṛga-śarīraṁ carama-śarīreṇa vipratvaṁ gatam āhuḥ.

śrī-śukaḥ uvāca—Śukadeva Gosvāmī continued to speak; *atha*—thereafter; *kasyacit*—of some; *dvija-varasya—brāhmaṇa; aṅgiraḥ-pravarasya*—who came in the dynasty of the great saint Aṅgirā; *śama*—control of the mind; *dama*—control of the senses; *tapaḥ*—practice of austerities and penances; *svādhyāya*—recitation of the Vedic literatures; *adhyayana*—studying; *tyāga*—renunciation; *santoṣa*—satisfaction; *titikṣā*—tolerance; *praśraya*—very gentle; *vidyā*—knowledge; *anasūya*—without envy; *ātma-jñāna-ānanda*—satisfied in self-realization; *yuktasya*—who was qualified with; *ātma-sadṛśa*—and exactly like himself; *śruta*—in education; *śīla*—in character; *ācāra*—in behavior; *rūpa*—in beauty; *audārya*—in magnanimity; *guṇāḥ*—

possessing all these qualities; *nava sa-udaryāḥ*—nine brothers born of the same womb; *aṅga-jāḥ*—sons; *babhūvuḥ*—were born; *mithunam*—a twin brother and sister; *ca*—and; *yavīyasyām*—in the youngest; *bhāryāyām*—wife; *yaḥ*—who; *tu*—but; *tatra*—there; *pumān*—the male child; *tam*—him; *parama-bhāgavatam*—the most exalted devotee; *rāja-ṛṣi*—of saintly kings; *pravaram*—most honored; *bharatam*—Bharata Mahārāja; *utsṛṣṭa*—having given up; *mṛga-śarīram*—the body of a deer; *carama-śarīreṇa*—with the last body; *vipratvam*—being a *brāhmaṇa; gatam*—obtained; *āhuḥ*—they said.

TRANSLATION

Śrīla Śukadeva Gosvāmī continued: My dear King, after giving up the body of a deer, Bharata Mahārāja took birth in a very pure brāhmaṇa family. There was a brāhmaṇa who belonged to the dynasty of Aṅgirā. He was fully qualified with brahminical qualifications. He could control his mind and senses, and he had studied the Vedic literatures and other subsidiary literatures. He was expert in giving charity, and he was always satisfied, tolerant, very gentle, learned and nonenvious. He was self-realized and engaged in the devotional service of the Lord. He remained always in a trance. He had nine equally qualified sons by his first wife, and by his second wife he begot twins—a brother and a sister, of which the male child was said to be the topmost devotee and foremost of saintly kings—Bharata Mahārāja. This, then, is the story of the birth he took after giving up the body of a deer.

PURPORT

Bharata Mahārāja was a great devotee, but he did not attain success in one life. In *Bhagavad-gītā* it is said that a devotee who does not fulfill his devotional duties in one life is given the chance to be born in a fully qualified *brāhmaṇa* family or a rich *kṣatriya* or *vaiśya* family. *Śucīnāṁ śrīmatāṁ gehe* (Bg. 6.41). Bharata Mahārāja was the firstborn son of Mahārāja Ṛṣabha in a rich *kṣatriya* family, but due to his willful negligence of his spiritual duties and his excessive attachment to an insignificant deer, he was obliged to take birth as the son of a deer. However, due to his strong position as a devotee, he was gifted with the remembrance of his past life. Being repentant, he remained in a solitary forest and always thought of Kṛṣṇa. Then he was given the chance to take birth in a very good *brāhmaṇa* family.

TEXT 3

**तत्रापि स्वजनसङ्गाच्च भृशमुद्विजमानो भगवतः कर्मबन्धविध्वंसनश्रवणस्मरण-
गुणविवरणचरणारविन्दयुगलं मनसा विदधदात्मनः प्रतिघातमाशङ्कमानो
भगवदनुग्रहेणानुस्मृतस्वपूर्वजन्मावलिरात्मानमुन्मत्तजडान्धबधिरस्वरूपेण दर्शया-
मास लोकस्य ॥ ३ ॥**

tatrāpi svajana-saṅgāc ca bhṛśam udvijamāno bhagavataḥ karma-bandha-vidhvaṁsana-śravaṇa-smaraṇa-guṇa-vivaraṇa-caraṇāravinda-yugalaṁ manasā vidadhad ātmanaḥ pratighātam āśaṅkamāno bhagavad-anugraheṇānusmṛta-sva-pūrva-janmāvalir ātmānam unmatta-jaḍāndha-badhira-svarūpeṇa darśayām āsa lokasya.

tatra api—in that *brāhmaṇa* birth also; *sva-jana-saṅgāt*—from association with relatives and friends; *ca*—and; *bhṛśam*—greatly; *udvijamānaḥ*—being always afraid that he would fall down again; *bhagavataḥ*—of the Supreme Personality of Godhead; *karma-bandha*—the bondage of the reactions of fruitive activities; *vidhvaṁsana*—which vanquishes; *śravaṇa*—hearing; *smaraṇa*—remembering; *guṇa-vivaraṇa*—hearing descriptions of the qualities of the Lord; *caraṇa-aravinda*—lotus feet; *yugalam*—the two; *manasā*—with the mind; *vidadhat*—always thinking of; *ātmanaḥ*—of his soul; *pratighātam*—obstruction on the path of devotional service; *āśaṅkamānaḥ*—always fearing; *bhagavat-anugraheṇa*—by the special mercy of the Supreme Personality of Godhead; *anusmṛta*—remembered; *sva-pūrva*—his own previous; *janma-āvaliḥ*—string of births; *ātmānam*—himself; *unmatta*—mad; *jaḍa*—dull; *andha*—blind; *badhira*—and deaf; *sva-rūpeṇa*—with these features; *darśayām āsa*—he exhibited; *lokasya*—to people in general.

TRANSLATION

Due to his being especially gifted with the Lord's mercy, Bharata Mahārāja could remember the incidents of his past life. Although he received the body of a brāhmaṇa, he was still very much afraid

of his relatives and friends who were not devotees. He was always very cautious of such association because he feared that he would again fall down. Consequently he manifested himself before the public eye as a madman—dull, blind and deaf—so that others would not try to talk to him. In this way he saved himself from bad association. Within he was always thinking of the lotus feet of the Lord and chanting the Lord's glories, which save one from the bondage of fruitive action. In this way he saved himself from the onslaught of nondevotee associates.

PURPORT

Every living entity is bound by different activities due to association with the modes of nature. As stated in *Bhagavad-gītā, kāraṇaṁ guṇa-saṅgo 'sya sad-asad-yoni-janmasu:* "This is due to his association with that material nature. Thus he meets with good and evil among various species." (Bg. 13.22)

We get different types of bodies among 8,400,000 species according to our *karma. Karmaṇā daiva-netreṇa:* we work under the influence of material nature contaminated by the three modes, and thus we get a certain type of body according to superior order. This is called *karma-bandha.* To get out of this *karma-bandha,* one must engage himself in devotional service. Then one will not be affected by the modes of material nature.

māṁ ca yo 'vyabhicāreṇa
bhakti-yogena sevate
sa guṇān samatītyaitān
brahma-bhūyāya kalpate

"One who engages in full devotional service, who does not fall down in any circumstance, at once transcends the modes of material nature and thus comes to the level of Brahman." (Bg. 14.26) To remain immune from the material qualities, one must engage himself in devotional service—*śravaṇaṁ kīrtanaṁ viṣṇoḥ.* That is the perfection of life. When Mahārāja Bharata took birth as a *brāhmaṇa,* he was not very interested in the duties of a *brāhmaṇa,* but within he remained a pure Vaiṣṇava, always thinking of the lotus feet of the Lord. As advised in *Bhagavad-gītā:*

man-manā bhava mad-bhakto mad-yājī māṁ namaskuru. This is the only process by which one can be saved from the danger of repeated birth and death.

TEXT 4

तस्यापि ह वा आत्मजस्य विप्रः पुत्रस्नेहानुबद्धमना आसमावर्तनात्संस्कारान् यथोपदेशं विदधान उपनीतस्य च पुनः शौचाचमनादीन् कर्मनियमाननभिप्रेतानपि समशिक्षयदनुशिष्टेन हि भाव्यं पितुः पुत्रेणेति ॥ ४ ॥

tasyāpi ha vā ātmajasya vipraḥ putra-snehānubaddha-manā
āsamāvartanāt saṁskārān yathopadeśaṁ vidadhāna upanītasya ca
punaḥ śaucācamanādīn karma-niyamān anabhipretān api
samaśikṣayad anuśiṣṭena hi bhāvyaṁ pituḥ putreṇeti.

tasya—of him; *api ha vā*—certainly; *ātma-jasya*—of his son; *vipraḥ*—the *brāhmaṇa* father of Jaḍa Bharata (mad, crazy Bharata); *putra-sneha-anubaddha-manāḥ*—who was obliged by affection for his son; *ā-sama-āvartanāt*—until the end of the *brahmacarya-āśrama; saṁskārān*—the purificatory processes; *yathā-upadeśam*—as prescribed in the *śāstras; vidadhānaḥ*—performing; *upanītasya*—of one who has a sacred thread; *ca*—also; *punaḥ*—again; *śauca-ācamana-ādīn*—practice of cleanliness, washing of the mouth, legs and hands, etc.; *karma-niyamān*—the regulative principles of fruitive activities; *anabhipretān api*—although not wanted by Jaḍa Bharata; *samaśikṣayat*—taught; *anuśiṣṭena*—taught to follow the regulative principles; *hi*—indeed; *bhāvyam*—should be; *pituḥ*—from the father; *putreṇa*—the son; *iti*—thus.

TRANSLATION

The brāhmaṇa father's mind was always filled with affection for his son, Jaḍa Bharata [Bharata Mahārāja]. Therefore he was always attached to Jaḍa Bharata. Because Jaḍa Bharata was unfit to enter the gṛhastha-āśrama, he simply executed the purificatory process up to the end of the brahmacarya-āśrama. Although Jaḍa Bharata was unwilling to accept his father's instructions, the brāhmaṇa nonetheless instructed him in how to keep clean and how to wash, thinking that the son should be taught by the father.

PURPORT

Jaḍa Bharata was Bharata Mahārāja in the body of a *brāhmaṇa*, and he outwardly conducted himself as if he were dull, deaf, dumb and blind. Actually he was quite alert within. He knew perfectly well of the results of fruitive activity and the results of devotional service. In the body of a *brāhmaṇa*, Mahārāja Bharata was completely absorbed in devotional service within; therefore it was not at all necessary for him to execute the regulative principles of fruitive activity. As confirmed in *Śrīmad-Bhāgavatam: svanuṣṭhitasya dharmasya saṁsiddhir hari-toṣaṇam* (*Bhāg.* 1.2.13). One has to satisfy Hari, the Supreme Personality of Godhead. That is the perfection of the regulative principles of fruitive activity. Besides that, it is stated in *Śrīmad-Bhāgavatam:*

dharmaḥ svanuṣṭhitaḥ puṁsāṁ
viṣvaksena-kathāsu yaḥ
notpādayed yadi ratiṁ
śrama eva hi kevalam

"Duties [*dharma*] executed by men, regardless of occupation, are only so much useless labor if they do not provoke attraction for the message of the Supreme Lord." (*Bhāg.* 1.2.8) These *karma-kāṇḍa* activities are required as long as one has not developed Kṛṣṇa consciousness. If one is developed in Kṛṣṇa consciousness, there is no need to execute the prior regulative principles of *karma-kāṇḍa*. Śrīla Mādhavendra Purī said, "O regulative principles of *karma-kāṇḍa*, please excuse me. I cannot follow all these regulative principles, for I am fully engaged in devotional service." He expressed the desire to sit somehwere beneath a tree and continue chanting the Hare Kṛṣṇa *mahā-mantra*. Consequently he did not execute all the regulative principles. Similarly, Haridāsa Ṭhākura was born in a Mohammedan family. From the very beginning of his life he was never trained in the *karma-kāṇḍa* system, but because he was always chanting the holy name of the Lord, Śrī Caitanya Mahāprabhu accepted him as *nāmācārya*, the authority in chanting the holy name. As Jaḍa Bharata, Bharata Mahārāja was always engaged in devotional service within his mind. Since he had executed the regulative principles continuously for three lives, he was not interested in continuing to execute them, although his *brāhmaṇa* father wanted him to do so.

TEXT 5

स चापि तदु ह पितृसंनिधावेवासध्रीचीनमिव स्म करोति छन्दांस्यध्यापयिष्यन् सह व्याहृतिभिः सप्रणवशिरस्त्रिपदीं सावित्रीं ग्रैष्मवासन्तिकान्मासानधीयानमप्यसमवेतरूपं ग्राहयामास ॥ ५ ॥

sa cāpi tad u ha pitṛ-sannidhāv evāsadhrīcīnam iva sma karoti chandāṁsy adhyāpayiṣyan saha vyāhṛtibhiḥ sapraṇava-śiras tripadīṁ sāvitrīṁ graiṣma-vāsantikān māsān adhīyānam apy asamaveta-rūpaṁ grāhayām āsa.

saḥ—he (Jaḍa Bharata); *ca*—also; *api*—indeed; *tat u ha*—that which was instructed by his father; *pitṛ-sannidhau*—in the presence of his father; *eva*—even; *asadhrīcīnam iva*—not correct, as if he could not understand anything; *sma karoti*—used to perform; *chandāṁsi adhyāpayiṣyan*—desiring to teach him Vedic *mantras* during the months beginning with Śrāvaṇa or during the period of Cāturmāsya; *saha*—along with; *vyāhṛtibhiḥ*—the utterance of the names of the heavenly planets (*bhūḥ, bhuvaḥ, svaḥ*); *sa-praṇava-śiraḥ*—headed by *oṁkāra; tri-padīm*—three-footed; *sāvitrīm*—the Gāyatrī *mantra; graiṣma-vāsantikān*—for four months, beginning with Caitra, on the fifteenth of May; *māsān*—the months; *adhīyānam api*—although fully studying; *asamaveta-rūpam*—in an incomplete form; *grāhayām āsa*—he made him learn.

TRANSLATION

Jaḍa Bharata behaved before his father like a fool, despite his father's adequately instructing him in Vedic knowledge. He behaved in that way so that his father would know that he was unfit for instruction and would abandon the attempt to instruct him further. He would behave in a completely opposite way. Although instructed to wash his hands after evacuating, he would wash them before. Nonetheless, his father wanted to give him Vedic instruc-

tions during the spring and summer. He tried to teach him the Gāyatrī mantra along with oṁkāra and vyāhṛti, but after four months, his father still was not successful in instructing him.

TEXT 6

एवं स्वतनुज आत्मन्यनुरागावेशितचित्तः शौचाध्ययनव्रतनियम-
गुर्वनलशुश्रूषणाद्यौपकुर्वाणककर्माण्यनभियुक्तान्यपि समनुशिष्टेन
भाव्यमित्यसदाग्रहः पुत्रमनुशास्य स्वयं तावद् अनधिगतमनोरथः
कालेनाप्रमत्तेन स्वयं गृह एव प्रमत्त उपसंहृतः ॥ ६ ॥

evaṁ sva-tanuja ātmany anurāgāveśita-cittaḥ śaucādhyayana-vrata-niyama-gurv-anala-śuśrūṣaṇādy-aupakurvāṇaka-karmāṇy anabhiyuktāny api samanuśiṣṭena bhāvyam ity asad-āgrahaḥ putram anuśāsya svayaṁ tāvad anadhigata-manorathaḥ kālenāpramattena svayaṁ gṛha eva pramatta upasaṁhṛtaḥ.

evam—thus; *sva*—own; *tanu-je*—in his son, Jaḍa Bharata; *ātmani*—whom he considered to be himself; *anurāga-āveśita-cittaḥ*—the *brāhmaṇa* who was absorbed in love for his son; *śauca*—cleanliness; *adhyayana*—study of Vedic literature; *vrata*—accepting all the vows; *niyama*—regulative principles; *guru*—of the spiritual master; *anala*—of the fire; *śuśrūṣaṇa-ādi*—the service, etc.; *aupakurvāṇaka*—of the *brahmacarya-āśrama; karmāṇi*—all the activities; *anabhiyuktāni api*—although not liked by his son; *samanuśiṣṭena*—fully instructed; *bhāvyam*—should be; *iti*—thus; *asat-āgrahaḥ*—having unsuitable obstinacy; *putram*—his son; *anuśāsya*—instructing; *svayam*—himself; *tāvat*—in that way; *anadhigata-manorathaḥ*—not having fulfilled his desires; *kālena*—by the influence of time; *apramattena*—which is not forgetful; *svayam*—he himself; *gṛhe*—to his home; *eva*—certainly; *pramattaḥ*—being madly attached; *upasaṁhṛtaḥ*—died.

TRANSLATION

The brāhmaṇa father of Jaḍa Bharata considered his son his heart and soul, and therefore he was very much attached to him.

He thought it wise to educate his son properly, and being absorbed in this unsuccessful endeavor, he tried to teach his son the rules and regulations of brahmacarya—including the execution of the Vedic vows, cleanliness, study of the Vedas, the regulative methods, service to the spiritual master and the method of offering a fire sacrifice. He tried his best to teach his son in this way, but all his endeavors failed. In his heart he hoped that his son would be a learned scholar, but all his attempts were unsuccessful. Like everyone, this brāhmaṇa was attached to his home, and he had forgotten that someday he would die. Death, however, was not forgetful. At the proper time, death appeared and took him away.

PURPORT

Those too attached to family life, who forget that death comes in the future to take them away, become attached and unable to finish their duty as human beings. The duty of human life is to solve all the problems of life, but instead people remain attached to family affairs and duties. Although they forget death, death will not forget them. Suddenly they will be kicked off the platform of a peaceful family life. One may forget that he has to die, but death never forgets. Death comes always at the right time. The *brāhmaṇa* father of Jaḍa Bharata wanted to teach his son the process of *brahmacarya*, but he was unsuccessful due to his son's unwillingness to undergo the process of Vedic advancement. Jaḍa Bharata was simply concerned with returning home, back to Godhead, by executing devotional service through *śravaṇaṁ kīrtanaṁ viṣṇoḥ*. He did not care for the Vedic instructions of his father. When one is fully interested in the service of the Lord, he does not need to follow all the regulative principles enunciated in the *Vedas*. Of course, for an ordinary man, the Vedic principles are imperative. No one can avoid them. But when one has attained the perfection of devotional service, it is not very important to follow the Vedic principles. Lord Kṛṣṇa advised Arjuna to ascend to the platform of *nistraiguṇya*, the transcendental position above the Vedic principles.

traiguṇya-viṣayā vedā
nistraiguṇyo bhavārjuna
nirdvandvo nitya-sattva-stho
niryoga-kṣema ātmavān

"The *Vedas* mainly deal with the subject of the three modes of material nature. Rise above these modes, O Arjuna. Be transcendental to all of them. Be free from all dualities and from all anxieties for gain and safety, and be established in the Self." (Bg. 2.45)

TEXT 7

**अथ यवीयसी द्विजसती स्वगर्भजातं मिथुनं सपत्न्या उपन्यस्य स्वय-
मनुसंस्थया पतिलोकमगात् ॥ ७ ॥**

*atha yavīyasī dvija-satī sva-garbha-jātaṁ mithunaṁ sapatnyā
upanyasya svayam anusaṁsthayā patilokam agāt.*

atha—thereafter; *yavīyasī*—the youngest; *dvija-satī*—wife of the *brāhmaṇa; sva-garbha-jātam*—born of her womb; *mithunam*—the twins; *sapatnyai*—unto the co-wife; *upanyasya*—entrusting; *svayam*—personally; *anusaṁsthayā*—by following her husband; *pati-lokam*—the planet named Patiloka; *agāt*—went to.

TRANSLATION

Thereafter, the brāhmaṇa's younger wife, after entrusting her twin children—the boy and girl—to the elder wife, departed for Patiloka, voluntarily dying with her husband.

TEXT 8

**पितर्युपरते भ्रातर एनमतत्प्रभावविदस्त्रय्यां विद्यायामेव पर्यवसितमतयो
न परविद्यायां जडमतिरिति भ्रातुरनुशासननिर्बन्धान्न्यवृत्सन्त ॥ ८ ॥**

*pitary uparate bhrātara enam atat-prabhāva-vidas trayyāṁ
vidyāyām eva paryavasita-matayo na para-vidyāyāṁ jaḍa-matir iti
bhrātur anuśāsana-nirbandhān nyavṛtsanta.*

pitari uparate—after the death of the father; *bhrātaraḥ*—the stepbrothers; *enam*—unto this Bharata (Jaḍa Bharata); *a-tat-prabhāva-vidaḥ*—without understanding his exalted position; *trayyām*—of the three *Vedas; vidyāyām*—in the matter of material ritualistic knowledge;

eva—indeed; *paryavasita*—settled; *matayaḥ*—whose minds; *na*—not; *para-vidyāyām*—in the transcendental knowledge of spiritual life (devotional service); *jaḍa-matiḥ*—most dull intelligence; *iti*—thus; *bhrātuḥ*—their brother (Jaḍa Bharata); *anuśāsana-nirbandhāt*—from the endeavor to teach; *nyavṛtsanta*—stopped.

TRANSLATION

After the father died, the nine stepbrothers of Jaḍa Bharata, who considered Jaḍa Bharata dull and brainless, abandoned the father's attempt to give Jaḍa Bharata a complete education. The stepbrothers of Jaḍa Bharata were learned in the three Vedas—the Ṛg Veda, Sāma Veda and Yajur Veda—which very much encourage fruitive activity. The nine brothers were not at all spiritually enlightened in devotional service to the Lord. Consequently they could not understand the highly exalted position of Jaḍa Bharata.

TEXTS 9-10

स च प्राकृतैर्द्विपदपशुभिरुन्मत्तजडबधिरमूकेत्यभिभाष्यमाणो यदा तदनुरूपाणि प्रभाषते कर्माणि च कार्यमाणः परेच्छया करोति विष्टितो वेतनतो वा याच्ञया यदृच्छया वोपसादितमल्पं बहु मृष्टं कदन्नं वाभ्यवहरति परं नेन्द्रियप्रीतिनिमित्तम् । नित्यनिवृत्तनिमित्तस्वसिद्धविशुद्धानुभवानन्दस्वात्म-लाभाधिगमः सुखदुःखयोर्द्वन्द्वनिमित्तयोरसम्भावितदेहाभिमानः ॥ ९ ॥
शीतोष्णवातवर्षेषु वृष इवानावृताङ्गः पीनः संहननाङ्गः स्थण्डिलसंवेशनानुन्मर्दनामज्जनरजसा महामणिरिवानभिव्यक्तब्रह्मवर्चसः कुपटावृतकटिरुपवीतेनोरुमषिणा द्विजातिरिति ब्रह्मबन्धुरिति संज्ञयातज्ज्ञजनावमतो विचचार ॥ १० ॥

sa ca prākṛtair dvipada-paśubhir unmatta-jaḍa-badhira-mūkety
abhibhāṣyamāṇo yadā tad-anurūpāṇi prabhāṣate karmāṇi ca
kāryamāṇaḥ parecchayā karoti viṣṭito vetanato vā yācñayā yadṛcchayā
vopasāditam alpaṁ bahu mṛṣṭaṁ kadannaṁ vābhyavaharati paraṁ
nendriya-prīti-nimittam. nitya-nivṛtta-nimitta-sva-siddha-

viśuddhānubhavānanda-svātma-lābhādhigamaḥ sukha-duḥkhayor dvanda-nimittayor asambhāvita-dehābhimānaḥ. śītoṣṇa-vāta-varṣeṣu vṛṣa ivānāvṛtāṅgaḥ pīnaḥ saṁhananāṅgaḥ sthaṇḍila-saṁveśanānunmardanāmajjana-rajasā mahāmaṇir ivānabhivyakta-brahma-varcasaḥ kupaṭāvṛta-kaṭir upavītenoru-maṣiṇā dvijātir iti brahma-bandhur iti saṁjñayātaj-jñajanāvamato vicacāra.

saḥ ca—he also; *prākṛtaiḥ*—by common persons who have no access to spiritual knowledge; *dvi-pada-paśubhiḥ*—who are nothing but animals with two legs; *unmatta*—mad; *jaḍa*—dull; *badhira*—deaf; *mūka*—dumb; *iti*—thus; *abhibhāṣyamāṇaḥ*—being addressed; *yadā*—when; *tat-anurūpāṇi*—words suitable to reply to theirs; *prabhāṣate*—he used to speak; *karmāṇi*—activities; *ca*—also; *kāryamāṇaḥ*—being caused to execute; *para-icchayā*—by the order of others; *karoti*—he used to act; *viṣṭitaḥ*—by force; *vetanataḥ*—or by some wages; *vā*—either; *yācñayā*—by begging; *yadṛcchayā*—by its own accord; *vā*—or; *upasāditam*—gotten; *alpam*—a very small quantity; *bahu*—a large quantity; *mṛṣṭam*—very palatable; *kat-annam*—stale, tasteless foods; *vā*—or; *abhyavaharati*—he used to eat; *param*—only; *na*—not; *indriya-prīti-nimittam*—for the satisfaction of the senses; *nitya*—eternally; *nivṛtta*—stopped; *nimitta*—fruitive activity; *sva-siddha*—by self-accomplished; *viśuddha*—transcendental; *anubhava-ānanda*—blissful perception; *sva-ātma-lābha-adhigamaḥ*—who has achieved knowledge of the self; *sukha-duḥkhayoḥ*—in happiness and distress; *dvandva-nimittayoḥ*—in the causes of duality; *asambhāvita-deha-abhimānaḥ*—not identified with the body; *śīta*—in the winter; *uṣṇa*—in the summer; *vāta*—in the wind; *varṣeṣu*—in the rainfall; *vṛṣaḥ*—a bull; *iva*—like; *anāvṛta-aṅgaḥ*—uncovered body; *pīnaḥ*—very strong; *saṁhanana-aṅgaḥ*—whose limbs were firm; *sthaṇḍila-saṁveśana*—from lying down on the ground; *anunmardana*—without any massage; *amajjana*—without bathing; *rajasā*—by dirt; *mahā-maṇiḥ*—highly valuable gem; *iva*—like; *anabhivyakta*—unmanifested; *brahma-varcasaḥ*—spiritual splendor; *ku-paṭa-āvṛta*—covered by a dirty cloth; *kaṭiḥ*—whose loins; *upavītena*—with a sacred thread; *uru-maṣiṇā*—which was highly blackish due to dirt; *dvi-jātiḥ*—born in a *brāhmaṇa* family; *iti*—thus (saying out of contempt); *brahma-bandhuḥ*—a friend of a *brāhmaṇa; iti*—thus; *saṁjñayā*—by such names; *a-tat-jña-jana*—by persons not knowing his real position; *avamataḥ*—being disrespected; *vicacāra*—he wandered.

TRANSLATION

Degraded men are actually no better than animals. The only difference is that animals have four legs and such men have only two. These two-legged, animalistic men used to call Jaḍa Bharata mad, dull, deaf and dumb. They mistreated him, and Jaḍa Bharata behaved for them like a madman who was deaf, blind or dull. He did not protest or try to convince them that he was not so. If others wanted him to do something, he acted according to their desires. Whatever food he could acquire by begging or by wages, and whatever came of its own accord—be it a small quantity, palatable, stale or tasteless—he would accept and eat. He never ate anything for sense gratification because he was already liberated from the bodily conception, which induces one to accept palatable or unpalatable food. He was full in the transcendental consciousness of devotional service, and therefore he was unaffected by the dualities arising from the bodily conception. Actually his body was as strong as a bull's, and his limbs were very muscular. He didn't care for winter or summer, wind or rain, and he never covered his body at any time. He lay on the ground, and never smeared oil on his body or took a bath. Because his body was dirty, his spiritual effulgence and knowledge were covered, just as the splendor of a valuable gem is covered by dirt. He only wore a dirty loincloth and his sacred thread, which was blackish. Understanding that he was born in a brāhmaṇa family, people would call him a brahma-bandhu and other names. Being thus insulted and neglected by materialistic people, he wandered here and there.

PURPORT

Śrīla Narottama dāsa Ṭhākura has sung: *deha-smṛti nāhi yāra, saṁsāra-bandhana kāhāṅ tāra.* One who has no desire to maintain the body or who is not anxious to keep the body in order and who is satisfied in any condition must be either mad or liberated. Actually Bharata Mahārāja in his birth as Jaḍa Bharata was completely liberated from material dualities. He was a *paramahaṁsa* and therefore did not care for bodily comfort.

TEXT 11

यदा तु परत आहारं कर्मवेतनत ईहमानः स्वभ्रातृभिरपि केदारकर्मणि निरूपितस्तदपि करोति किन्तु न समं विषमं न्यूनमधिकमिति वेद कणपिण्याकफलीकरणकुल्माषस्थालीपुरीषादीन्यप्यमृतवदभ्यवहरति ॥ ११ ॥

yadā tu parata āhāraṁ karma-vetanata īhamānaḥ sva-bhrātṛbhir api kedāra-karmaṇi nirūpitas tad api karoti kintu na samaṁ viṣamaṁ nyūnam adhikam iti veda kaṇa-piṇyāka-phalī-karaṇa-kulmāṣa-sthālīpurīṣādīny apy amṛtavad abhyavaharati.

yadā—when; *tu*—but; *parataḥ*—from others; *āhāram*—food; *karma-vetanataḥ*—in exchange for wages from working; *īhamānaḥ*—looking for; *sva-bhrātṛbhiḥ api*—even by his own stepbrothers; *kedāra-karmaṇi*—in working in the field and adjusting the agricultural work; *nirūpitaḥ*—engaged; *tat api*—at that time also; *karoti*—he used to do; *kintu*—but; *na*—not; *samam*—level; *viṣamam*—uneven; *nyūnam*—deficient; *adhikam*—more raised; *iti*—thus; *veda*—he knew; *kaṇa*—broken rice; *piṇyāka*—oil cakes; *phalī-karaṇa*—the chaff of rice; *kulmāṣa*—worm-eaten grains; *sthālī-purīṣa-ādīni*—burned rice stuck to the pot and so on; *api*—even; *amṛta-vat*—like nectar; *abhyavaharati*—used to eat.

TRANSLATION

Jaḍa Bharata used to work only for food. His stepbrothers took advantage of this and engaged him in agricultural field work in exchange for some food, but actually he did not know how to work very well in the field. He did not know where to spread dirt or where to make the ground level or uneven. His brothers used to give him broken rice, oil cakes, the chaff of rice, worm-eaten grains and burned grains that had stuck to the pot, but he gladly accepted all this as if it were nectar. He did not hold any grudges and ate all this very gladly.

PURPORT

The platform of *paramahaṁsa* is described in *Bhagavad-gītā* (2.15): *sama-duḥkha-sukhaṁ dhīraṁ so 'mṛtatvāya kalpate.* When one is callous to all duality, the happiness and distress of this material world, one is fit for *amṛtatva*, eternal life. Bharata Mahārāja was determined to finish his business in this material world, and he did not at all care for the world of duality. He was complete in Kṛṣṇa consciousness and was oblivious to good and evil, happiness and distress. As stated in *Caitanya-caritāmṛta* (*Antya* 4.176):

'dvaite' bhadrābhadra-jñāna, saba-'manodharma'
'ei bhāla, ei manda',——saba 'bhrama'

"In the material world, conceptions of good and bad are all mental speculations. Therefore, saying, 'This is good and this is bad,' is all a mistake." One has to understand that in the material world of duality, to think that this is good or that this is bad is simply a mental concoction. However, one should not imitate this consciousness; one should actually be situated on the spiritual platform of neutrality.

TEXT 12

अथ कदाचित्कश्चिद् वृषलपतिर्भद्रकाल्यै पुरुषपशुमालभतापत्यकामः ॥१२॥

atha kadācit kaścid vṛṣala-patir bhadra-kālyai puruṣa-paśum ālabhatāpatya-kāmaḥ.

atha—thereafter; *kadācit*—at some time; *kaścit*—some; *vṛṣala-patiḥ*—the leader of *śūdras* engaged in plundering the property of others; *bhadra-kālyai*—unto the goddess known as Bhadra Kālī; *puruṣa-paśum*—an animal in the shape of a man; *ālabhata*—started to sacrifice; *apatya-kāmaḥ*—desiring a son.

TRANSLATION

At this time, being desirous of obtaining a son, a leader of dacoits who came from a śūdra family wanted to worship the goddess Bhadra Kālī by offering her in sacrifice a dull man, who is considered no better than an animal.

PURPORT

Low-class men such as *śūdras* worship demigods like goddess Kālī, or Bhadra Kālī, for the fulfillment of material desires. To this end, they sometimes kill a human being before the deity. They generally choose a person who is not very intelligent—in other words, an animal in the shape of a man.

TEXT 13

तस्य ह दैवमुक्तस्य पशोः पदवीं तदनुचराः परिधावन्तो निशि निशीथसमये
तमसाऽऽवृतायामनधिगतपशव आकस्मिकेन विधिना केदारान् वीरासनेन
मृगवराहादिभ्यः संरक्षमाणमङ्गिरःप्रवर सुतमपश्यन्॥ १३॥

tasya ha daiva-muktasya paśoḥ padavīṁ tad-anucarāḥ paridhāvanto
niśi niśītha-samaye tamasāvṛtāyām anadhigata-paśava ākasmikena
vidhinā kedārān vīrāsanena mṛga-varāhādibhyaḥ saṁrakṣamāṇam
aṅgiraḥ-pravara-sutam apaśyan.

tasya—of the leader of the dacoits; *ha*—certainly; *daiva-muktasya*—by chance having escaped; *paśoḥ*—of the human animal; *padavīm*—the path; *tat-anucarāḥ*—his followers or assistants; *paridhāvantaḥ*—searching here and there to find; *niśi*—at night; *niśītha-samaye*—at midnight; *tamasā āvṛtāyām*—being covered by darkness; *anadhigata-paśavaḥ*—not catching the man-animal; *ākasmikena vidhinā*—by the unexpected law of providence; *kedārān*—the fields; *vīra-āsanena*—by a seat on a raised place; *mṛga-varāha-ādibhyaḥ*—from the deer, wild pigs and so on; *saṁrakṣamāṇam*—protecting; *aṅgiraḥ-pravara-sutam*—the son of the *brāhmaṇa* descending from the Āṅgirā family; *apaśyan*—they found.

TRANSLATION

The leader of the dacoits captured a man-animal for sacrifice, but he escaped, and the leader ordered his followers to find him. They ran in different directions but could not find him. Wandering here and there in the middle of the night, covered by dense darkness, they came to a paddy field where they saw the exalted

son of the Āṅgirā family [Jaḍa Bharata], who was sitting in an elevated place guarding the field against the attacks of deer and wild pigs.

TEXT 14

अथ त एनमनवद्यलक्षणमवमृश्य भर्तृकर्मनिष्पत्तिं मन्यमाना बद्ध्वा रशनया चण्डिकागृहमुपनिन्युर्मुदा विकसितवदनाः ॥ १४ ॥

atha ta enam anavadya-lakṣaṇam avamṛśya bhartṛ-karma-niṣpattiṁ manyamānā baddhvā rasanayā caṇḍikā-gṛham upaninyur mudā vikasita-vadanāḥ.

atha—thereafter; *te*—they (the servants of the leader of the dacoits); *enam*—this (Jaḍa Bharata); *anavadya-lakṣaṇam*—as bearing the characteristics of a dull animal because of a fat body like a bull's and because of being deaf and dumb; *avamṛśya*—recognizing; *bhartṛ-karma-niṣpattim*—the accomplishment of their master's work; *manyamānāḥ*—understanding; *baddhvā*—binding tightly; *rasanayā*—with ropes; *caṇḍikā-gṛham*—to the temple of goddess Kālī; *upaninyuḥ*—brought; *mudā*—with great happiness; *vikasita-vadanāḥ*—with bright faces.

TRANSLATION

The followers and servants of the dacoit chief considered Jaḍa Bharata to possess qualities quite suitable for a man-animal, and they decided that he was a perfect choice for sacrifice. Their faces bright with happiness, they bound him with ropes and brought him to the temple of the goddess Kālī.

PURPORT

In some parts of India, animalistic men are still sacrificed before the goddess Kālī. However, such a sacrifice is only performed by *śūdras* and dacoits. Their business is to plunder the wealthy, and to become successful they offer an animalistic man before the goddess Kālī. It should be noted that they never sacrifice an intelligent man before the goddess.

In the body of a *brāhmaṇa*, Bharata Mahārāja appeared deaf and dumb, yet he was the most intelligent man in the world. Nonetheless, being completely surrendered unto the Supreme Personality of Godhead, he remained in that condition and did not protest being brought before the deity for slaughter. As we have learned from the previous verses, he was very strong and could have very easily avoided being bound with ropes, but he did not do anything. He simply depended on the Supreme Personality of Godhead for his protection. Śrīla Bhaktivinoda Ṭhākura describes surrender unto the Supreme Lord in this way:

mārabi rākhabi——yo icchā tohārā
nitya-dāsa-prati tuyā adhikārā

"My Lord, I am now surrendered unto You. I am Your eternal servant, and if You like You can kill me, or, if You like, You can protect me. In any case, I am fully surrendered unto You."

TEXT 15

अथ पणयस्तं स्वविधिनाभिषिच्याहतेन वाससाऽऽच्छाद्य
भूषणालेपस्रक्तिलकादिभिरुपस्कृतं भुक्तवन्तं धूपदीपमाल्यलाजकिसलया-
ङ्कुरफलोपहारोपेतया वैशससंस्थया महता गीतस्तुतिमृदङ्गपणवघोषेण च
पुरुषपशुं भद्रकाल्याः पुरत उपवेशयामासुः ॥ १५ ॥

atha paṇayas taṁ sva-vidhinābhiṣicyāhatena vāsasācchādya bhūṣaṇālepa-srak-tilakādibhir upaskṛtaṁ bhuktavantaṁ dhūpa-dīpa-mālya-lāja-kisalayāṅkura-phalopahāropetayā vaiśasa-saṁsthayā mahatā gīta-stuti-mṛdaṅga-paṇava-ghoṣeṇa ca puruṣa-paśuṁ bhadra-kālyāḥ purata upaveśayām āsuḥ.

atha—thereafter; *paṇayaḥ*—all the followers of the dacoit; *tam*—him (Jaḍa Bharata); *sva-vidhinā*—according to their own ritualistic principles; *abhiṣicya*—bathing; *ahatena*—with new; *vāsasā*—garments; *ācchādya*—covering; *bhūṣaṇa*—ornaments; *ālepa*—smearing the body with sandalwood pulp; *srak*—a flower garland; *tilaka-ādibhiḥ*—with markings on the body and so on; *upaskṛtam*—completely decorated; *bhuktavantam*—having eaten; *dhūpa*—with incense; *dīpa*—lamps; *mālya*—garlands; *lāja*—parched grain; *kisalaya-aṅkura*—twigs and sprouts; *phala*—fruits; *upahāra*—other paraphernalia; *upetayā*—fully equipped; *vaiśasa-saṁsthayā*—with complete arrangements for sacrifice; *mahatā*—great; *gīta-stuti*—of songs and prayers; *mṛdaṅga*—of the drums; *paṇava*—of the bugles; *ghoṣeṇa*—by vibration; *ca*—also; *puruṣa-paśum*—the man-animal; *bhadra-kālyāḥ*—of the goddess Kālī; *purataḥ*—just in front; *upaveśayām āsuḥ*—made him sit down.

TRANSLATION

After this, all the thieves, according to their imaginative ritual for killing animalistic men, bathed Jaḍa Bharata, dressed him in new clothes, decorated him with ornaments befitting an animal, smeared his body with scented oils and decorated him with tilaka, sandalwood pulp and garlands. They fed him sumptuously and then brought him before the goddess Kālī, offering her incense, lamps, garlands, parched grain, newly grown twigs, sprouts, fruits and flowers. In this way they worshiped the deity before killing the man-animal, and they vibrated songs and prayers and played drums and bugles. Jaḍa Bharata was then made to sit down before the deity.

PURPORT

In this verse the word *sva-vidhinā* (according to their own ritualistic principles) is very significant. According to the Vedic *śāstras*, everything must be done according to regulative principles, but here it is stated that the thieves and rogues devised their own process for killing an animalistic man. The tamasic *śāstras* give instructions for the sacrifice of an animal like a goat or buffalo before the goddess Kālī, but there is no mention of killing a man, however dull he may be. This process was manufactured by the dacoits themselves; therefore the word *sva-vidhinā* is used. Even at this time there are many sacrifices being conducted without reference to the Vedic scriptures. For instance, in Calcutta recently a slaughterhouse was being advertised as a temple of the goddess Kālī. Meat-eaters foolishly purchase meat from such shops, thinking it different from ordinary meat and taking it to be the *prasāda* of goddess

Kālī. The sacrifice of a goat or a similar animal before the goddess Kālī is mentioned in *śāstras* just to keep people from eating slaughterhouse meat and becoming responsible for the killing of animals. The conditioned soul has a natural tendency toward sex and meat-eating; consequently the *śāstras* grant them some concessions. Actually the *śāstras* aim at putting an end to these abominable activities, but they impart some regulative principles so that gradually meat-eaters and sex hunters will be rectified.

TEXT 16

अथ वृषलराजपणिः पुरुषपशोरसृगासवेन देवीं भद्रकालीं यक्ष्यमाण-
स्तदभिमन्त्रितमसिमतिकरालनिशितमुपाददे॥१६॥

atha vṛṣala-rāja-paṇiḥ puruṣa-paśor asṛg-āsavena devīṁ bhadra-kālīṁ
yakṣyamāṇas tad-abhimantritam asim ati-karāla-niśitam upādade.

atha—thereafter; *vṛṣala-rāja-paṇiḥ*—the so-called priest of the leader of the dacoits (one of the thieves); *puruṣa-paśoḥ*—of the animalistic man for being sacrificed (Bharata Mahārāja); *asṛk-āsavena*—with the liquor of blood; *devīm*—to the deity; *bhadra-kālīm*—the goddess Kālī; *yakṣyamāṇaḥ*—desiring to offer; *tat-abhimantritam*—consecrated by the *mantra* of Bhadra Kālī; *asim*—the sword; *ati-karāla*—very fearful; *niśitam*—finely sharpened; *upādade*—he took up.

TRANSLATION

At this time, one of the thieves, acting as the chief priest, was ready to offer the blood of Jaḍa Bharata, whom they imagined to be an animal-man, to the goddess Kālī to drink as a liquor. He therefore took up a very fearsome sword, which was very sharp and, consecrating it by the mantra of Bhadra Kālī, raised it to kill Jaḍa Bharata.

TEXT 17

इति तेषां वृषलानां रजस्तमःप्रकृतीनां धनमदरजउत्सिक्तमनसां भगवत्कलावीर-
कुलं कदर्थीकृत्योत्पथेन स्वैरं विहरतां हिंसाविहाराणां कर्मातिदारुणं यद्ब्रह्म-

भूतस्य साक्षाद्ब्रह्मर्षिसुतस्य निर्वैरस्य सर्वभूतसुहृदः सूनायामप्यननुमतमालम्भनं तदुपलभ्य ब्रह्मतेजसातिदुर्विषहेण दन्दह्यमानेन वपुषा सहसोच्चचाट सैव देवी भद्रकाली ॥ १७ ॥

iti teṣāṁ vṛṣalānāṁ rajas-tamaḥ-prakṛtīnāṁ dhana-mada-raja-utsikta-manasāṁ bhagavat-kalā-vīra-kulaṁ kadarthī-kṛtyotpathena svairaṁ viharatāṁ hiṁsā-vihārāṇāṁ karmāti-dāruṇaṁ yad brahma-bhūtasya sākṣād brahmarṣi-sutasya nirvairasya sarva-bhūta-suhṛdaḥ sūnāyām apy ananumatam ālambhanaṁ tad upalabhya brahma-tejasāti-durviṣaheṇa dandahyamānena vapuṣā sahasoccacāṭa saiva devī bhadra-kālī.

iti—thus; *teṣām*—of them; *vṛṣalānām*—the *śūdras,* by whom all religious principles are destroyed; *rajaḥ*—in passion; *tamaḥ*—in ignorance; *prakṛtīnām*—having natures; *dhana-mada*—in the form of infatuation by material wealth; *rajaḥ*—by passion; *utsikta*—puffed up; *manasām*—whose minds; *bhagavat-kalā*—an expansion of the plenary expansion of the Supreme Personality of Godhead; *vīra-kulam*—the group of elevated personalities (the *brāhmaṇas*); *kat-arthī-kṛtya*—disrespecting; *utpathena*—by a wrong path; *svairam*—independently; *viharatām*—who are proceeding; *hiṁsā-vihārāṇām*—whose business is to commit violence against others; *karma*—the activity; *ati-dāruṇam*—very fearful; *yat*—that which; *brahma-bhūtasya*—of a self-realized person born in a *brāhmaṇa* family; *sākṣāt*—directly; *brahma-ṛṣi-sutasya*—of the son born of a *brāhmaṇa* exalted in spiritual consciousness; *nirvairasya*—who had no enemies; *sarva-bhūta-suhṛdaḥ*—a well-wisher to all others; *sūnāyām*—at the last moment; *api*—even though; *ananumatam*—not being sanctioned by law; *ālambhanam*—against the desire of the Lord; *tat*—that; *upalabhya*—perceiving; *brahma-tejasā*—with the effulgence of spiritual bliss; *ati-durviṣaheṇa*—being too bright and unbearable; *dandahyamānena*—burning; *vapuṣā*—with a physical body; *sahasā*—suddenly; *uccacāṭa*—fractured (the deity); *sā*—she; *eva*—indeed; *devī*—the goddess; *bhadra-kālī*—Bhadra Kālī.

TRANSLATION

All the rogues and thieves who had made arrangements for the worship of goddess Kālī were low minded and bound to the modes

of passion and ignorance. They were overpowered by the desire to become very rich; therefore they had the audacity to disobey the injunctions of the Vedas, so much so that they were prepared to kill Jaḍa Bharata, a self-realized soul born in a brāhmaṇa family. Due to their envy, these dacoits brought him before the goddess Kālī for sacrifice. Such people are always addicted to envious activities, and therefore they dared to try to kill Jaḍa Bharata. Jaḍa Bharata was the best friend of all living entities. He was no one's enemy, and he was always absorbed in meditation on the Supreme Personality of Godhead. He was born of a good brāhmaṇa father, and killing him was forbidden, even though he might have been an enemy or aggressive person. In any case, there was no reason to kill Jaḍa Bharata, and the goddess Kālī could not bear this. She could immediately understand that these sinful dacoits were about to kill a great devotee of the Lord. Suddenly the deity's body burst asunder, and the goddess Kālī personally emerged from it in a body burning with an intense and intolerable effulgence.

PURPORT

According to the Vedic injunctions, only an aggressor can be killed. If a person comes with an intent to kill, one can immediately take action and kill in self-defense. It is also stated that one can be killed if he comes to set fire to the home or to pollute or kidnap one's wife. Lord Rāmacandra killed the entire family of Rāvaṇa because Rāvaṇa kidnapped His wife, Sītādevī. However, killing is not sanctioned in the *śāstras* for other purposes. The killing of animals in sacrifice to the demigods, who are expansions of the Supreme Personality of Godhead, is sanctioned for those who eat meat. This is a kind of restriction for meat-eating. In other words, the slaughter of animals is also restricted by certain rules and regulations in the *Vedas.* Considering these points, there was no reason to kill Jaḍa Bharata, who was born in a respectable, highly exalted *brāhmaṇa* family. He was a God-realized soul and a well-wisher to all living entities. The *Vedas* did not at all sanction the killing of Jaḍa Bharata by rogues and thieves. Consequently the goddess Bhadra Kālī emerged from the deity to give protection to the Lord's devotee. Śrīla Viśvanātha Cakravartī Ṭhākura explains that due to the Brahman effulgence of such a devotee as Jaḍa Bharata, the deity was fractured.

Only thieves and rogues in the modes of passion and ignorance and maddened by material opulence offer a man in sacrifice before the goddess Kālī. This is not sanctioned by the Vedic instructions. Presently there are many hundreds and thousands of slaughterhouses throughout the world that are maintained by a puffed-up population mad for material opulence. Such activities are never supported by the *Bhāgavata* school.

TEXT 18

**भृशममर्षरोषावेशरभसविलसितभ्रुकुटिविटपकुटिलदंष्ट्रारुणेक्षणाटोपातिभयानक-
वदना हन्तुकामेवेदं महाट्टहासमतिसंरम्भेण विमुञ्चन्ती तत
उत्पत्य पापीयसां दुष्टानां तेनैवासिना विवृक्णशीर्ष्णां गलात्स्रवन्तमसृगासव-
मत्युष्णं सह गणेन निपीयातिपानमदविह्वलोच्चैस्तरां स्वपार्षदैः सह जगौ ननर्त च
विजहार च शिरःकन्दुकलीलया ॥ १८ ॥**

*bhṛśam amarṣa-roṣāveśa-rabhasa-vilasita-bhru-kuṭi-viṭapa-kuṭila-
daṁṣṭrāruṇekṣaṇāṭopāti-bhayānaka-vadanā hantu-kāmevedaṁ
mahāṭṭa-hāsam ati-saṁrambheṇa vimuñcantī tata utpatya pāpīyasāṁ
duṣṭānāṁ tenaivāsinā vivṛkṇa-śīrṣṇāṁ galāt sravantam asṛg-āsavam
atyuṣṇaṁ saha gaṇena nipīyāti-pāna-mada-vihvaloccaistarāṁ sva-
pārṣadaiḥ saha jagau nanarta ca vijahāra ca śiraḥ-kanduka-līlayā.*

bhṛśam—very highly; *amarṣa*—in intolerance of the offenses; *roṣa*—in anger; *āveśa*—of her absorption; *rabhasa-vilasita*—expanded by the force; *bhru-kuṭi*—of her eyebrows; *viṭapa*—the branches; *kuṭila*—curved; *daṁṣṭra*—teeth; *aruṇa-īkṣaṇa*—of reddish eyes; *āṭopa*—by the agitation; *ati*—very much; *bhayānaka*—fearful; *vadanā*—having a face; *hantu-kāmā*—desirous to destroy; *iva*—as if; *idam*—this universe; *mahā-aṭṭa-hāsam*—a greatly fearful laugh; *ati*—great; *saṁrambheṇa*—because of anger; *vimuñcantī*—releasing; *tataḥ*—from that altar; *utpatya*—coming forth; *pāpīyasām*—of all the sinful; *duṣṭānām*—great offenders; *tena eva asinā*—by that same chopper; *vivṛkṇa*—separated; *śīrṣṇām*—whose heads; *galāt*—from the neck; *sravantam*—oozing out; *asṛk-āsavam*—the blood, compared to an intoxicating beverage; *ati-uṣṇam*—very hot; *saha*—with; *gaṇena*—her associates; *nipīya*—drinking; *ati-pāna*—from drinking so much; *mada*—by intoxication; *vihvalā*—overwhelmed; *uccaiḥ-tarām*—very loudly; *sva-pārṣadaiḥ*—her own associates; *saha*—with; *jagau*—sang; *nanarta*—danced; *ca*—also; *vijahāra*—played; *ca*—also; *śiraḥ-kanduka*—using the heads as balls; *līlayā*—by sports.

TRANSLATION

Intolerant of the offenses committed, the infuriated goddess Kālī flashed her eyes and displayed her fierce, curved teeth. Her reddish eyes glowed, and she displayed her fearsome features. She assumed a frightening body, as if she were prepared to destroy the entire creation. Leaping violently from the altar, she immediately decapitated all the rogues and thieves with the very sword with which they had intended to kill Jaḍa Bharata. She then began to drink the hot blood that flowed from the necks of the beheaded rogues and thieves, as if this blood were liquor. Indeed, she drank this intoxicant with her associates, who were witches and female demons. Becoming intoxicated with this blood, they all began to sing very loudly and dance as though prepared to annihilate the entire universe. At the same time, they began to play with the heads of the rogues and thieves, tossing them about as if they were balls.

PURPORT

It is evident from this verse that the devotees of goddess Kālī are not at all favored by her. It is goddess Kālī's work to kill and punish the demons. Goddess Kālī (Durgā) engages in decapitating many demons, dacoits and other unwanted elements in society. Neglecting Kṛṣṇa consciousness, foolish people try to satisfy the goddess by offering her many abominable things, but ultimately when there is a little discrepancy in this worship, the goddess punishes the worshiper by taking his life. Demoniac people worship goddess Kālī to obtain some material benefit, but they are not excused of the sins performed in the name of worship. To sacrifice a man or animal before the deity is specifically forbidden.

TEXT 19

एवमेव खलु महदभिचारातिक्रमः कार्त्स्न्येनात्मने फलति ॥ १९ ॥

evam eva khalu mahad-abhicārāti-kramaḥ kārtsnyenātmane phalati.

evam eva—in this way; *khalu*—indeed; *mahat*—to great personalities; *abhicāra*—in the form of envy; *ati-kramaḥ*—the limit of offense; *kārtsnyena*—always; *ātmane*—unto oneself; *phalati*—gives the result.

TRANSLATION

When an envious person commits an offense before a great personality, he is always punished in the way mentioned above.

TEXT 20

न वा एतद्विष्णुदत्त महदद्भुतं यदसम्भ्रमः स्वशिरश्छेदन आपतितेऽपि विमुक्तदेहाद्यात्मभावसुदृढहृदयग्रन्थीनां सर्वसत्त्वसुहृदात्मनां निर्वैराणां साक्षाद्भगवतानिमिषारिवरायुधेनाप्रमत्तेन तैस्तैर्भावैः परिरक्ष्यमाणानां तत्पादमूलमकुतश्चिद्भयमुपसृतानां भागवतपरमहंसानाम् ॥ २० ॥

na vā etad viṣṇudatta mahad-adbhutaṁ yad asambhramaḥ sva-śiraś-chedana āpatite 'pi vimukta-dehādy-ātma-bhāva-sudṛḍha-hṛdaya-granthīnāṁ sarva-sattva-suhṛd-ātmanāṁ nirvairāṇāṁ sākṣād bhagavatānimiṣāri-varāyudhenāpramattena tais tair bhāvaiḥ parirakṣyamāṇānāṁ tat-pāda-mūlam akutaścid-bhayam upasṛtānāṁ bhāgavata-paramahaṁsānām.

na—not; *vā*—or; *etat*—this; *viṣṇu-datta*—O Mahārāja Parīkṣit, who was protected by Lord Viṣṇu; *mahat*—a great; *adbhutam*—wonder; *yat*—which; *asambhramaḥ*—lack of perplexity; *sva-śiraḥ-chedane*—when the chopping off of the head; *āpatite*—was about to happen; *api*—even though; *vimukta*—completely liberated from; *deha-ādi-ātma-bhāva*—the false bodily concept of life; *su-dṛḍha*—very strong and tight; *hṛdaya-granthīnām*—of those whose knots within the heart; *sarva-sattva-suhṛt-ātmanām*—of persons who in their hearts always wish well to all living entities; *nirvairāṇām*—who do not find anyone as their enemy; *sākṣāt*—directly; *bhagavatā*—by the Supreme Personality of Godhead; *animiṣa*—invincible time; *ari-vara*—and the best of weapons, the Sudarśana *cakra; āyudhena*—by Him who possesses the weapons; *apramattena*—not agitated at any time; *taiḥ taiḥ*—by those respective; *bhāvaiḥ*—moods of the Supreme Personality of Godhead; *parirakṣyamāṇānām*—of persons who are protected; *tat-pāda-mūlam*—at the lotus feet of the Supreme Personality of Godhead; *akutaścit*—from nowhere; *bhayam*—fear; *upasṛtānām*—of those who have taken complete shelter; *bhāgavata*—of devotees of the Lord; *parama-haṁsānām*—of the most liberated persons.

TRANSLATION

Śukadeva Gosvāmī then said to Mahārāja Parīkṣit: O Viṣṇudatta, those who already know that the soul is separate from the body, who are liberated from the invincible knot in the heart, who are always engaged in welfare activities for all living entities and who never contemplate harming anyone are always protected by the Supreme Personality of Godhead, who carries His disc [the Sudarśana cakra] and acts as supreme time to kill the demons and protect His devotees. The devotees always take shelter at the lotus feet of the Lord. Therefore at all times, even if threatened by decapitation, they remain unagitated. For them, this is not at all wonderful.

PURPORT

These are some of the great qualities of a pure devotee of the Supreme Personality of Godhead. First, a devotee is firmly convinced of his spiritual identity. He never identifies with the body; he is firmly convinced that the spirit soul is different from the body. Consequently he fears nothing. Even though his life may be threatened, he is not at all afraid. He does not even treat an enemy like an enemy. Such are the qualifications of devotees. Devotees are always fully dependent on the Supreme Personality of Godhead, and the Lord is always eager to give them all protection in all circumstances.

Thus end the Bhaktivedanta purports of the Fifth Canto, Ninth Chapter, of the Śrīmad-Bhāgavatam, *entitled "The Supreme Character of Jaḍa Bharata."*

CHAPTER TEN

The Discussion Between Jaḍa Bharata and Mahārāja Rahūgaṇa

In this chapter Bharata Mahārāja, now Jaḍa Bharata, was successfully accepted by King Rahūgaṇa, ruler of the states known as Sindhu and Sauvīra. The King forced Jaḍa Bharata to carry his palanquin and chastised him because he did not carry it properly. A carrier of King Rahūgaṇa's palanquin was needed, and to fulfill this need the chief carriers found Jaḍa Bharata as the most likely person to do the work. He was therefore forced to carry the palanquin. Jaḍa Bharata, however, did not protest this proud order, but humbly accepted the job and carried the palanquin. While carrying it, however, he was very careful to see that he did not step on an ant, and whenever he saw one, he would stop until the ant had passed. Because of this, he could not keep pace with the other carriers. The King within the palanquin became very disturbed and chastised Jaḍa Bharata with filthy language, but Jaḍa Bharata, being completely freed from the bodily conception, did not protest; he proceeded carrying the palanquin. When he continued as before, the King threatened him with punishment, and being threatened by the King, Jaḍa Bharata began to talk. He protested against the filthy language used by the King when the King chastised him, and the King, hearing the instructions of Jaḍa Bharata, was awakened to his real knowledge. When he came to his consciousness, he understood that he had offended a great, learned and saintly person. At that time he very humbly and respectfully prayed to Jaḍa Bharata. He now wanted to understand the deep meaning of the philosophical words used by Jaḍa Bharata, and with great sincerity, he begged his pardon. He admitted that if one offends the lotus feet of a pure devotee, he is certainly punished by the trident of Lord Śiva.

TEXT 1

श्रीशुक उवाच

अथ सिन्धुसौवीरपते रहूगणस्य व्रजत इक्षुमत्यास्तटे तत्कुलपतिना शिबिकावाहपुरुषान्वेषणसमये दैवेनोपसादितः स द्विजवर उपलब्ध एष पीवा युवा संहननाङ्गो गोखरवद्धुरं वोढुमलमिति पूर्वविष्टिगृहीतैः सह गृहीतः प्रसभमतदर्ह उवाह शिबिकां स महानुभावः ॥ १ ॥

śrī-śuka uvāca
atha sindhu-sauvīra-pate rahūgaṇasya vrajata ikṣumatyās taṭe tat-kula-patinā śibikā-vāha-puruṣānveṣaṇa-samaye daivenopasāditaḥ sa dvija-vara upalabdha eṣa pīvā yuvā saṁhananāṅgo go-kharavad dhuraṁ voḍhum alam iti pūrva-viṣṭi-gṛhītaiḥ saha gṛhītaḥ prasabham atad-arha uvāha śibikāṁ sa mahānubhāvaḥ.

śrī-śukaḥ uvāca—Śukadeva Gosvāmī continued to speak: *atha*—thus; *sindhu-sauvīra-pateḥ*—of the ruler of the states known as Sindhu and Sauvīra; *rahū-gaṇasya*—the King known as Rahūgaṇa; *vrajataḥ*—while going (to the *āśrama* of Kapila); *ikṣu-matyāḥ taṭe*—on the bank of the river known as Ikṣumatī; *tat-kula-patinā*—by the leader of the palanquin carriers; *śibikā-vāha*—to become a carrier of the palanquin; *puruṣa-anveṣaṇa-samaye*—at the time of searching for a man; *daivena*—by chance; *upasāditaḥ*—led near; *saḥ*—that; *dvija-varaḥ*—Jaḍa Bharata, the son of a *brāhmaṇa; upalabdhaḥ*—obtained; *eṣaḥ*—this man; *pīvā*—very strong and stout; *yuvā*—young; *saṁhanana-aṅgaḥ*—having very firm limbs; *go-khara-vat*—like a cow or an ass; *dhuram*—a load; *voḍhum*—to carry; *alam*—able; *iti*—thus thinking; *pūrva-viṣṭi-gṛhītaiḥ*—others who were formerly forced to do the task; *saha*—with; *gṛhītaḥ*—being taken; *prasabham*—by force; *a-tat-arhaḥ*—although not fit for carrying the palanquin; *uvāha*—carried; *śibikām*—the palanquin; *saḥ*—he; *mahā-anubhāvaḥ*—a great soul.

TRANSLATION

Śukadeva Gosvāmī continued: My dear King, after this, King Rahūgaṇa, ruler of the states known as Sindhu and Sauvīra, was

going to Kapilāśrama. When the King's chief palanquin carriers reached the banks of the River Ikṣumatī, they needed another carrier. Therefore they began searching for someone, and by chance they came upon Jaḍa Bharata. They considered the fact that Jaḍa Bharata was very young and strong and had firm limbs. Like cows and asses, he was quite fit to carry loads. Thinking in this way, although the great soul Jaḍa Bharata was unfit for such work, they nonetheless unhesitatingly forced him to carry the palanquin.

TEXT 2

यदा हि द्विजवरस्येषुमात्रावलोकानुगतेर्न समाहिता पुरुषगतिस्तदा विषमगतां स्वशिबिकां रहूगण उपधार्य पुरुषानधिवहत आह हे वोढारः साध्वतिक्रमत किमिति विषममुह्यते यानमिति ॥ २ ॥

yadā hi dvija-varasyeṣu-mātrāvalokānugater na samāhitā puruṣa-gatis tadā viṣama-gatāṁ sva-śibikāṁ rahūgaṇa upadhārya puruṣān adhivahata āha he voḍhāraḥ sādhv atikramata kim iti viṣamam uhyate yānam iti.

yadā—when; *hi*—certainly; *dvija-varasya*—of Jaḍa Bharata; *iṣu-mātra*—the measurement of an arrow (three feet) ahead; *avaloka-anugateḥ*—from moving only after glancing; *na samāhitā*—not united; *puruṣa-gatiḥ*—the movement of the carriers; *tadā*—at that time; *viṣama-gatām*—becoming uneven; *sva-śibikām*—his own palanquin; *rahūgaṇaḥ*—King Rahūgaṇa; *upadhārya*—understanding; *puruṣān*—unto the men; *adhivahataḥ*—who were carrying the palanquin; *āha*—said; *he*—oh; *voḍhāraḥ*—carriers of the palanquin; *sādhu atikramata*—please walk evenly so that there will not be bouncing; *kim iti*—for what reason; *viṣamam*—uneven; *uhyate*—is being carried; *yānam*—the palanquin; *iti*—thus.

TRANSLATION

The palanquin, however, was very erratically carried by Jaḍa Bharata due to his sense of nonviolence. As he stepped forward, he checked before him every three feet to see whether he was about

to step on ants. Consequently he could not keep pace with the other carriers. Due to this, the palanquin was shaking, and King Rahūgaṇa immediately asked the carriers, "Why are you carrying this palanquin unevenly? Better carry it properly."

PURPORT

Although Jaḍa Bharata was forced to carry the palanquin, he did not give up his sympathetic feelings toward the poor ants passing on the road. A devotee of the Lord does not forget his devotional service and other favorable activities, even when he is in a most distressful condition. Jaḍa Bharata was a qualified *brāhmaṇa*, highly elevated in spiritual knowledge, yet he was forced to carry the palanquin. He did not mind this, but while walking on the road, he could not forget his duty to avoid killing even an ant. A Vaiṣṇava is never envious or unnecessarily violent. There were many ants on the path, but Jaḍa Bharata took care by looking ahead three feet. When the ants were no longer in his way, he would place his foot on the ground. A Vaiṣṇava is always very kind at heart to all living entities. In His *sāṅkhya-yoga*, Lord Kapiladeva explains: *suhṛdaḥ sarva-dehinām*. Living entities assume different bodily forms. Those who are not Vaiṣṇavas consider only human society worthy of their sympathy, but Kṛṣṇa claims to be the supreme father of all life forms. Consequently the Vaiṣṇava takes care not to annihilate untimely or unnecessarily any life form. All living entities have to fulfill a certain duration for being encaged in a particular type of material body. They have to finish the duration allotted a particular body before being promoted or evolved to another body. Killing an animal or any other living being simply places an impediment in the way of his completing his term of imprisonment in a certain body. One should therefore not kill bodies for one's sense gratification, for this will implicate one in sinful activity.

TEXT 3

अथ त ईश्वरवचः सोपालम्भमुपाकर्ण्योपायतुरीयाच्छङ्कितमनसस्तं विज्ञापयांबभूवुः ॥ ३ ॥

atha ta īśvara-vacaḥ sopālambham upākarṇyopāya-turīyāc chaṅkita-manasas taṁ vijñāpayāṁ babhūvuḥ.

atha—thus; *te*—they (the carriers of the palanquin); *īśvara-vacaḥ*—the words of the master, King Rahūgaṇa; *sa-upālambham*—with reproach; *upākarṇya*—hearing; *upāya*—the means; *turīyāt*—from the fourth one; *śaṅkita-manasaḥ*—whose minds were afraid; *tam*—him (the King); *vijñāpayām babhūvuḥ*—informed.

TRANSLATION

When the palanquin carriers heard the threatening words of Mahārāja Rahūgaṇa, they became very afraid of his punishment and began to speak to him as follows.

PURPORT

According to political science, a king sometimes tries to pacify his subordinates, sometimes chastises them, sometimes derides them and sometimes rewards them. In this way the king rules his subordinates. The bearers of the palanquin could understand that the King was angry and that he would chastise them.

TEXT 4

न वयं नरदेव प्रमत्ता भवन्नियमानुपथाः साध्वेव वहामः । अयमधुनैव नियुक्तोऽपि न द्रुतं व्रजति नानेन सह वोढुमु ह वयं पारयाम इति ॥ ४ ॥

na vayaṁ nara-deva pramattā bhavan-niyamānupathāḥ sādhv eva
vahāmaḥ. ayam adhunaiva niyukto 'pi na drutaṁ vrajati nānena saha
voḍhum u ha vayaṁ pārayāma iti.

na—not; *vayam*—we; *nara-deva*—O lord among human beings (the king is supposed to be the representative of *deva*, the Supreme Personality of Godhead); *pramattāḥ*—neglectful in our duties; *bhavat-niyama-anupathāḥ*—who are always obedient to your order; *sādhu*—properly; *eva*—certainly; *vahāmaḥ*—we are carrying; *ayam*—this man; *adhunā*—just recently; *eva*—indeed; *niyuktaḥ*—being engaged to work with us; *api*—although; *na*—not; *drutam*—very quickly; *vrajati*—works; *na*—not; *anena*—him; *saha*—with; *voḍhum*—to carry; *u ha*—oh; *vayam*—we; *pārayāmaḥ*—are able; *iti*—thus.

TRANSLATION

O lord, please note that we are not at all negligent in discharging our duties. We have been faithfully carrying this palanquin according to your desire, but this man who has been recently engaged to work with us cannot walk very swiftly. Therefore we are not able to carry the palanquin with him.

PURPORT

The other palanquin carriers were *śūdras*, whereas Jaḍa Bharata was not only a high-caste *brāhmaṇa* but also a great devotee. *Śūdras* do not sympathize with other living beings, but a Vaiṣṇava cannot act like a *śūdra*. Whenever a *śūdra* and a *brāhmaṇa* Vaiṣṇava are combined, there will certainly be imbalance in the execution of duties. The *śūdras* were walking with the palanquin without at all caring for the ants on the ground, but Jaḍa Bharata could not act like a *śūdra*, and therefore difficulty arose.

TEXT 5

सांसर्गिको दोष एव नूनमेकस्यापि सर्वेषां सांसर्गिकाणां
भवितुमर्हतीति निश्चित्य निशम्य कृपणवचो राजा रहूगण उपासित-
वृद्धोऽपि निसर्गेण बलात्कृत ईषदुत्थितमन्युरविस्पष्टब्रह्मतेजसं
जातवेदसमिव रजसाऽऽवृतमतिराह ॥ ५ ॥

sāṁsargiko doṣa eva nūnam ekasyāpi sarveṣāṁ sāṁsargikāṇāṁ
bhavitum arhatīti niścitya niśamya kṛpaṇa-vaco rājā rahūgaṇa upāsita-
vṛddho 'pi nisargeṇa balāt kṛta īṣad-utthita-manyur avispaṣṭa-brahma-
tejasaṁ jāta-vedasam iva rajasāvṛta-matir āha.

sāṁsargikaḥ—resulting from intimate association; *doṣaḥ*—a fault; *eva*—indeed; *nūnam*—certainly; *ekasya*—of one; *api*—although; *sarveṣām*—of all other; *sāṁsargikāṇām*—persons associated with him; *bhavitum*—to become; *arhati*—is able; *iti*—thus; *niścitya*—ascertaining; *niśamya*—by hearing; *kṛpaṇa-vacaḥ*—the words of the poor servants, who were very afraid of being punished; *rājā*—the King;

rahūgaṇaḥ—Rahūgaṇa; *upāsita-vṛddhaḥ*—having served and heard from many elderly sages; *api*—in spite of; *nisargeṇa*—by his personal nature, which was that of a *kṣatriya; balāt*—by force; *kṛtaḥ*—done; *īṣat*—slightly; *utthita*—awakened; *manyuḥ*—whose anger; *avispaṣṭa*—not being distinctly visible; *brahma-tejasam*—his (Jaḍa Bharata's) spiritual effulgence; *jāta-vedasam*—a fire covered by ashes in Vedic ritualistic ceremonies; *iva*—like; *rajasā āvṛta*—covered by the mode of passion; *matiḥ*—whose mind; *āha*—said.

TRANSLATION

King Rahūgaṇa could understand the speeches given by the carriers, who were afraid of being punished. He could also understand that simply due to the fault of one person, the palanquin was not being carried properly. Knowing this perfectly well and hearing their appeal, he became a little angry, although he was very advanced in political science and was very experienced. His anger arose due to his inborn nature as a king. Actually King Rahūgaṇa's mind was covered by the mode of passion, and he therefore spoke as follows to Jaḍa Bharata, whose Brahman effulgence was not clearly visible, being covered like a fire covered by ashes.

PURPORT

The distinction between *rajo-guṇa* and *sattva-guṇa* is explained in this verse. Although the King was very upright and advanced in political science and governmental management, he was nonetheless in the mode of passion, and therefore, due to a slight agitation, he became angry. Jaḍa Bharata, despite all kinds of injustice endured because of his deaf and dumb display, remained silent by the strength of his spiritual advancement. Nonetheless his *brahma-tejaḥ*, his Brahman effulgence, was indistinctly visible in his person.

TEXT 6

अहो कष्टं भ्रातर्व्यक्तमुरु परिश्रान्तो दीर्घमध्वानमेक एव ऊहिवान् सुचिरं
नातिपीवा न संहननाङ्गो जरसा चोपद्रुतो भवान् सखे नो एवापर एते

सङ्घट्टिन इति बहु विप्रलब्धोऽप्यविद्यया रचितद्रव्यगुणकर्माशयस्वचरमकलेवरे ऽवस्तुनि संस्थानविशेषेऽहं ममेत्यनध्यारोपितमिथ्याप्रत्ययो ब्रह्मभूतस्तूष्णीं शिबिकां पूर्ववदुवाह ॥ ६ ॥

aho kaṣṭaṁ bhrātar vyaktam uru-pariśrānto dīrgham adhvānam eka eva ūhivān suciraṁ nāti-pīvā na saṁhananāṅgo jarasā copadruto bhavān sakhe no evāpara ete saṅghaṭṭina iti bahu-vipralabdho 'py avidyayā racita-dravya-guṇa-karmāśaya-sva-carama-kalevare 'vastuni saṁsthāna-viśeṣe 'haṁ mamety anadhyāropita-mithyā-pratyayo brahma-bhūtas tūṣṇīṁ śibikāṁ pūrvavad uvāha.

aho—alas; *kaṣṭam*—how troublesome it is; *bhrātaḥ*—my dear brother; *vyaktam*—clearly; *uru*—very much; *pariśrāntaḥ*—fatigued; *dīrgham*—a long; *adhvānam*—path; *ekaḥ*—alone; *eva*—certainly; *ūhivān*—you have carried; *su-ciram*—for a long time; *na*—not; *ati-pīvā*—very strong and stout; *na*—nor; *saṁhanana-aṅgaḥ*—having a firm, tolerant body; *jarasā*—by old age; *ca*—also; *upadrutaḥ*—disturbed; *bhavān*—yourself; *sakhe*—my friend; *no eva*—not certainly; *apare*—the other; *ete*—all these; *saṅghaṭṭinaḥ*—co-workers; *iti*—thus; *bahu*—very much; *vipralabdhaḥ*—sarcastically criticized; *api*—although; *avidyayā*—by nescience; *racita*—manufactured; *dravya-guṇa-karma-āśaya*—in a combination of material elements, material qualities, and the results of past activities and desires; *sva-carama-kalevare*—in the body, which is moved by the subtle elements (mind, intelligence and ego); *avastuni*—in such physical things; *saṁsthāna-viśeṣe*—having a particular disposition; *aham mama*—I and mine; *iti*—in this way; *anadhyāropita*—not interposed; *mithyā*—false; *pratyayaḥ*—belief; *brahma-bhūtaḥ*—who was self-realized, standing on the Brahman platform; *tūṣṇīm*—being silent; *śibikām*—the palanquin; *pūrva-vat*—as before; *uvāha*—carried.

TRANSLATION

King Rahūgaṇa told Jaḍa Bharata: How troublesome this is, my dear brother. You certainly appear very fatigued because you have

carried this palanquin alone without assistance for a long time and for a long distance. Besides that, due to your old age you have become greatly troubled. My dear friend, I see that you are not very firm, nor very strong and stout. Aren't your fellow carriers cooperating with you?

In this way the King criticized Jaḍa Bharata with sarcastic words, yet despite being criticized in this way, Jaḍa Bharata had no bodily conception of the situation. He knew that he was not the body, for he had attained his spiritual identity. He was neither fat, lean nor thin, nor had he anything to do with a lump of matter, a combination of the five gross and three subtle elements. He had nothing to do with the material body and its two hands and legs. In other words, he had completely realized his spiritual identity [ahaṁ brahmāsmi]. He was therefore unaffected by this sarcastic criticism from the King. Without saying anything, he continued carrying the palanquin as before.

PURPORT

Jaḍa Bharata was completely liberated. He did not even care when the dacoits attempted to kill his body; he knew that he certainly was not the body. Even if the body were killed, he would not have cared, for he was thoroughly convinced of the proposition found in *Bhagavad-gītā* (2.20): *na hanyate hanyamāne śarīre.* He knew that he could not be killed even if his body were killed. Although he did not protest, the Supreme Personality of Godhead in His agent could not tolerate the injustice of the dacoits; therefore he was saved by the mercy of Kṛṣṇa, and the dacoits were killed. In this case, while carrying the palanquin, he also knew that he was not the body. This body was very strong and stout, in sound condition and quite competent to carry the palanquin. Due to his being freed from the bodily conception, the sarcastic words of the King did not at all affect him. The body is created according to one's *karma,* and material nature supplies the ingredients for the development of a certain type of body. The soul the body covers is different from the bodily construction; therefore anything favorable or mischievous done to the body does not affect the spirit soul. The Vedic injunction is *asaṅgo hy ayaṁ puruṣaḥ:* the spirit soul is always unaffected by material arrangements.

TEXT 7

अथ पुनः स्वशिबिकायां विषमगतायां प्रकुपित उवाच रहूगणः किमिदमरे त्वं जीवन्मृतो मां कदर्थीकृत्य भर्तृशासनमतिचरसि प्रमत्तस्य च ते करोमि चिकित्सां दण्डपाणिरिव जनताया यथा प्रकृतिं स्वां भजिष्यस इति ॥ ७ ॥

atha punaḥ sva-śibikāyāṁ viṣama-gatāyāṁ prakupita uvāca rahūgaṇaḥ kim idam are tvaṁ jīvan-mṛto māṁ kadarthī-kṛtya bhartṛ-śāsanam aticarasi pramattasya ca te karomi cikitsāṁ daṇḍa-pāṇir iva janatāyā yathā prakṛtiṁ svāṁ bhajiṣyasa iti.

atha—thereafter; *punaḥ*—again; *sva-śibikāyām*—in his own palanquin; *viṣama-gatāyām*—being unevenly carried because of Jaḍa Bharata's not walking properly; *prakupitaḥ*—becoming very angry; *uvāca*—said; *rahūgaṇaḥ*—King Rahūgaṇa; *kim idam*—what is this nonsense; *are*—O fool; *tvam*—you; *jīvat*—living; *mṛtaḥ*—dead; *mām*—me; *kat-arthī-kṛtya*—neglecting; *bhartṛ-śāsanam*—chastisement by the master; *aticarasi*—you are overstepping; *pramattasya*—who are almost crazy; *ca*—also; *te*—your; *karomi*—I shall do; *cikitsām*—proper treatment; *daṇḍa-pāṇiḥ iva*—like Yamarāja; *janatāyāḥ*—of the people in general; *yathā*—so that; *prakṛtim*—natural position; *svām*—your own; *bhajiṣyase*—you will take to; *iti*—thus.

TRANSLATION

Thereafter, when the King saw that his palanquin was still being shaken by the carriers, he became very angry and said: You rascal, what are you doing? Are you dead despite the life within your body? Do you not know that I am your master? You are disregarding me and are not carrying out my order. For this disobedience I shall now punish you just as Yamarāja, the superintendent of death, punishes sinful people. I shall give you proper treatment so that you will come to your senses and do the correct thing.

TEXT 8

एवं बह्वबद्धमपि भाषमाणं नरदेवाभिमानं रजसा तमसानुविद्धेन मदेन तिरस्कृताशेषभगवत्प्रियनिकेतं पण्डितमानिनं स भगवान् ब्राह्मणो ब्रह्मभूतः सर्वभूतसुहृदात्मा योगेश्वरचर्यायां नातिव्युत्पन्नमतिं स्मयमान इव विगतस्मय इदमाह ॥ ८ ॥

evaṁ bahv abaddham api bhāṣamāṇaṁ nara-devābhimānaṁ rajasā tamasānuviddhena madena tiraskṛtāśeṣa-bhagavat-priya-niketaṁ paṇḍita-māninaṁ sa bhagavān brāhmaṇo brahma-bhūta-sarva-bhūta-suhṛd-ātmā yogeśvara-caryāyāṁ nāti-vyutpanna-matiṁ smayamāna iva vigata-smaya idam āha.

evam—in this way; *bahu*—much; *abaddham*—nonsensical; *api*—although; *bhāṣamāṇam*—talking; *nara-deva-abhimānam*—King Rahūgaṇa, who thought himself the ruler; *rajasā*—by the material mode of passion; *tamasā*—as well as by the mode of ignorance; *anuviddhena*—being increased; *madena*—by madness; *tiraskṛta*—who rebuked; *aśeṣa*—innumerable; *bhagavat-priya-niketam*—devotees of the Lord; *paṇḍita-māninam*—considering himself a very learned scholar; *saḥ*—that; *bhagavān*—spiritually most powerful (Jaḍa Bharata); *brāhmaṇaḥ*—a fully qualified *brāhmaṇa; brahma-bhūta*—fully self-realized; *sarva-bhūta-suhṛt-ātmā*—who was thus the friend of all living entities; *yoga-īśvara*—of the most advanced mystic *yogīs; caryāyām*—in the behavior; *na ati-vyutpanna-matim*—unto King Rahūgaṇa, who was not actually experienced; *smayamānaḥ*—slightly smiling; *iva*—like; *vigata-smayaḥ*—who was relieved from all material pride; *idam*—this; *āha*—spoke.

TRANSLATION

Thinking himself a king, King Rahūgaṇa was in the bodily conception and was influenced by material nature's modes of passion and ignorance. Due to madness, he chastised Jaḍa Bharata with uncalled-for and contradictory words. Jaḍa Bharata was a topmost

devotee and the dear abode of the Supreme Personality of Godhead. Although considering himself very learned, the King did not know about the position of an advanced devotee situated in devotional service, nor did he know his characteristics. Jaḍa Bharata was the residence of the Supreme Personality of Godhead; he always carried the form of the Lord within his heart. He was the dear friend of all living beings, and he did not entertain any bodily conception. He therefore smiled and spoke the following words.

PURPORT

The distinction between a person in the bodily conception and a person beyond the bodily conception is presented in this verse. In the bodily conception, King Rahūgaṇa considered himself a king and chastised Jaḍa Bharata in so many unwanted ways. Being self-realized, Jaḍa Bharata, who was fully situated on the transcendental platform, did not at all become angry; instead, he smiled and began to deliver his teachings to King Rahūgaṇa. A highly advanced Vaiṣṇava devotee is a friend to all living entities, and consequently he is a friend to his enemies also. In fact, he does not consider anyone to be his enemy. *Suhṛdaḥ sarva-dehinām.* Sometimes a Vaiṣṇava becomes superficially angry at a non-devotee, but this is good for the nondevotee. We have several examples of this in Vedic literature. Once Nārada became angry with the two sons of Kuvera, Nalakuvera and Maṇigrīva, and he chastised them by turning them into trees. The result was that later they were liberated by Lord Śrī Kṛṣṇa. The devotee is situated on the absolute platform, and when he is angry or pleased, there is no difference, for in either case he bestows his benediction.

TEXT 9

ब्राह्मण उवाच

त्वयोदितं व्यक्तमविप्रलब्धं
भर्तुः स मे स्याद्यदि वीर भारः ।
गन्तुर्यदि स्यादधिगम्यमध्वा
पीवेति राशौ न विदां प्रवादः ॥ ९ ॥

brāhmaṇa uvāca
tvayoditaṁ vyaktam avipralabdhaṁ
bhartuḥ sa me syād yadi vīra bhāraḥ
gantur yadi syād adhigamyam adhvā
pīveti rāśau na vidāṁ pravādaḥ

brāhmaṇaḥ uvāca—the learned *brāhmaṇa* (Jaḍa Bharata) spoke; *tvayā*—by you; *uditam*—explained; *vyaktam*—very clearly; *avipralabdham*—without contradictions; *bhartuḥ*—of the bearer, the body; *saḥ*—that; *me*—mine; *syāt*—it would have been; *yadi*—if; *vīra*—O great hero (Mahārāja Rahūgaṇa); *bhāraḥ*—a load; *gantuḥ*—of the mover, also the body; *yadi*—if; *syāt*—it had been; *adhigamyam*—the object to be obtained; *adhvā*—the path; *pīvā*—very stout and strong; *iti*—thus; *rāśau*—in the body; *na*—not; *vidām*—of the self-realized persons; *pravādaḥ*—subject matter for discussion.

TRANSLATION

The great brāhmaṇa Jaḍa Bharata said: My dear King and hero, whatever you have spoken sarcastically is certainly true. Actually these are not simply words of chastisement, for the body is the carrier. The load carried by the body does not belong to me, for I am the spirit soul. There is no contradiction in your statements because I am different from the body. I am not the carrier of the palanquin; the body is the carrier. Certainly, as you have hinted, I have not labored carrying the palanquin, for I am detached from the body. You have said that I am not stout and strong, and these words are befitting a person who does not know the distinction between the body and the soul. The body may be fat or thin, but no learned man would say such things of the spirit soul. As far as the spirit soul is concerned, I am neither fat nor skinny; therefore you are correct when you say that I am not very stout. Also, if the object of this journey and the path leading there were mine, there would be many troubles for me, but because they relate not to me but to my body, there is no trouble at all.

PURPORT

In *Bhagavad-gītā* it is stated that one who is advanced in spiritual knowledge is not disturbed by the pains and pleasures of the material body. The material body is completely separate from the spirit soul, and the pains and pleasures of the body are superfluous. The practice of austerity and penance is meant for understanding the distinction between the body and the soul and how the soul can be unaffected by the pleasures and pains of the body. Jaḍa Bharata was actually situated on the platform of self-realization. He was completely aloof from the bodily conception; therefore he immediately took this position and convinced the King that whatever contradictory things the King had said about his body did not actually apply to him as a spirit soul.

TEXT 10

स्थौल्यं कार्श्यं व्याधय आधयश्च
क्षुत्तृड् भयं कलिरिच्छा जरा च ।
निद्रा रतिर्मन्युरहंमदः शुचो
देहेन जातस्य हि मे न सन्ति ॥१०॥

sthaulyaṁ kārśyaṁ vyādhaya ādhayaś ca
kṣut tṛḍ bhayaṁ kalir icchā jarā ca
nidrā ratir manyur ahaṁ madaḥ śuco
dehena jātasya hi me na santi

sthaulyam—being very stout and strong; *kārśyam*—being skinny and weak; *vyādhayaḥ*—the pains of the body, such as disease; *ādhayaḥ*—the pains of the mind; *ca*—and; *kṣut tṛṭ bhayam*—hunger, thirst and fear; *kaliḥ*—quarrels between two persons; *icchā*—desires; *jarā*—old age; *ca*—and; *nidrā*—sleep; *ratiḥ*—attachment for sense gratification; *manyuḥ*—anger; *aham*—false identification (in the bodily concept of life); *madaḥ*—illusion; *śucaḥ*—lamentation; *dehena*—with this body; *jātasya*—of one who has taken birth; *hi*—certainly; *me*—of me; *na*—not; *santi*—exist.

TRANSLATION

Fatness, thinness, bodily and mental distress, thirst, hunger, fear, disagreement, desires for material happiness, old age, sleep, attachment for material possessions, anger, lamentation, illusion and identification of the body with the self are all transformations of the material covering of the spirit soul. A person absorbed in the material bodily conception is affected by these things, but I am free from all bodily conceptions. Consequently I am neither fat nor skinny nor anything else you have mentioned.

PURPORT

Śrīla Narottama dāsa Ṭhākura has sung: *deha-smṛti nāhi yāra, saṁsāra-bandhana kāhāṅ tāra.* One who is spiritually advanced has no connection with the body or with the bodily actions and reactions. When one comes to understand that he is not the body and therefore is neither fat nor skinny, one attains the topmost form of spiritual realization. When one is not spiritually realized, the bodily conception entangles one in the material world. At the present moment all human society is laboring under the bodily conception; therefore in the *śāstras* people in this age are referred to as *dvipada-paśu,* two-legged animals. No one can be happy in a civilization conducted by such animals. Our Kṛṣṇa consciousness movement is trying to raise fallen human society to the status of spiritual understanding. It is not possible for everyone to become immediately self-realized like Jaḍa Bharata. However, as stated in *Śrīmad-Bhāgavatam* (1.2.18): *naṣṭa-prāyeṣv abhadreṣu nityaṁ bhāgavata-sevayā.* By spreading the *Bhāgavata* principles, we can raise human society to the platform of perfection. When one is not affected by the bodily conceptions, one can advance to the Lord's devotional service.

naṣṭa-prāyeṣv abhadreṣu
nityaṁ bhāgavata-sevayā
bhagavaty uttamaśloke
bhaktir bhavati naiṣṭikī

The more we advance our freedom from the bodily conception, the more we are fixed in devotional service, and the more we are happy and peaceful. In this regard, Śrīla Madhvācārya says that those who are too materially affected continue the bodily conception. Such persons are concerned with different bodily symptoms, whereas one freed from bodily conceptions lives without the body even in the material condition.

TEXT 11

जीवन्मृतत्वं नियमेन राजन्
आद्यन्तवद्यद्विकृतस्य दृष्टम् ।
स्वस्वाम्यभावो ध्रुव ईड्य यत्र
तर्ह्युच्यतेऽसौ विधिकृत्ययोगः ॥११॥

jīvan-mṛtatvaṁ niyamena rājan
ādyantavad yad vikṛtasya dṛṣṭam
sva-svāmya-bhāvo dhruva īḍya yatra
tarhy ucyate 'sau vidhikṛtya-yogaḥ

jīvat-mṛtatvam—the quality of being dead while living; *niyamena*—by the laws of nature; *rājan*—O King; *ādi-anta-vat*—everything material has a beginning and an end; *yat*—because; *vikṛtasya*—of things that are transformed, such as the body; *dṛṣṭam*—is seen; *sva-svāmya-bhāvaḥ*—the condition of servanthood and mastership; *dhruvaḥ*—unchangeable; *īḍya*—O you who are worshiped; *yatra*—wherein; *tarhi*—then; *ucyate*—it is said; *asau*—that; *vidhi-kṛtya-yogaḥ*—fitness of order and duty.

TRANSLATION

My dear King, you have unnecessarily accused me of being dead though alive. In this regard, I can only say that this is the case everywhere because everything material has its beginning and end. As far as your thinking that you are the king and master and are thus trying to order me, this is also incorrect because these positions are temporary. Today you are a king and I am your servant, but tomorrow the position may be changed, and you may be my servant and I your master. These are temporary circumstances created by providence.

PURPORT

The bodily conception is the basic principle of suffering in material existence. In Kali-yuga especially, people are so uneducated that they cannot even understand that the body is changing at every moment and that the ultimate change is called death. In this life one may be a king, and in the next life one may be a dog, according to *karma.* The spirit soul is in a deep slumber caused by the force of material nature. He is put in one type of condition and again changed into another type. Without self-realization and knowledge, conditional life continues, and one falsely claims himself a king, a servant, a cat or a dog. These are simply different transformations brought about by the supreme arrangement. One should not be misled by such temporary bodily conceptions. Actually no one is master within the material world, for everyone is under the control of material nature, which is under the control of the Supreme Personality of Godhead. Therefore the Supreme Personality of Godhead, Kṛṣṇa, is the ultimate master. As explained in *Caitanya-caritāmṛta, ekale īśvara kṛṣṇa, āra saba bhṛtya:* the only master is Kṛṣṇa, and everyone else is His servant. Forgetfulness of our relationship with the Supreme Lord brings about our suffering in the material world.

TEXT 12

विशेषबुद्धेर्विवरं मनाक् च
पश्याम यन्न व्यवहारतोऽन्यत् ।
क ईश्वरस्तत्र किमीशितव्यं
तथापि राजन् करवाम किं ते ॥१२॥

viśeṣa-buddher vivaraṁ manāk ca
paśyāma yan na vyavahārato 'nyat
ka īśvaras tatra kim īśitavyaṁ
tathāpi rājan karavāma kiṁ te

viśeṣa-buddheḥ—of the conception of the distinction between master and servant; *vivaram*—the scope; *manāk*—a little; *ca*—also; *paśyāmaḥ*—I see; *yat*—which; *na*—not; *vyavahārataḥ*—than the temporary usage or convention; *anyat*—other; *kaḥ*—who; *īśvaraḥ*—the master; *tatra*—in this; *kim*—who; *īśitavyam*—is to be controlled; *tathāpi*—nevertheless; *rājan*—O King (if you still think that you are master and I am servant); *karavāma*—I may do; *kim*—what; *te*—for you.

TRANSLATION

My dear King, if you still think that you are the King and that I am your servant, you should order me, and I should follow your order. I can then say that this differentiation is temporary, and it expands only from usage or convention. I do not see any other cause. In that case, who is the master, and who is the servant? Everyone is being forced by the laws of material nature; therefore no one is master, and no one is servant. Nonetheless, if you think that you are the master and that I am the servant, I shall accept this. Please order me. What can I do for you?

PURPORT

It is said in *Śrīmad-Bhāgavatam, ahaṁ mameti:* One thinks, "I am this body, and in this bodily relationship he is my master, he is my servant, she is my wife, and he is my son." All these conceptions are temporary due to the inevitable change of body and the arrangement of material nature. We are gathered together like straws floating in the waves of an ocean, straws that are inevitably separated by the laws of the waves. In this material world, everyone is floating on the waves of the ocean of nescience. As described by Bhaktivinoda Ṭhākura:

(miche) māyāra vaśe, yāccha bhese',
khāccha hābuḍubu, bhāi
(jīva) kṛṣṇa-dāsa, e viśvāsa,
karle ta' āra duḥkha nāi

Śrīla Bhaktivinoda Ṭhākura states that all men and women are floating like straws on the waves of material nature. If they come to the understanding that they are the eternal servants of Kṛṣṇa, they will put an end to this floating condition. As stated in *Bhagavad-gītā* (3.37): *kāma eṣa krodha eṣa rajoguṇa-samudbhavaḥ.* Due to the mode of passion, we desire many things, and according to our desire or anxiety and according to the order of the Supreme Lord, material nature gives us a certain type of body. For some time we play as master or servant, as actors play on the stage under someone else's direction. While we are in the human form, we should put an end to this nonsensical stage performance. We should come to our original constitutional position, known as Kṛṣṇa consciousness. At the present moment, the real master is material nature. *Daivī hy eṣā guṇamayī mama māyā duratyayā* (Bg. 7.14). Under the spell of material nature, we are becoming servants and masters, but if we agree to be controlled by the Supreme Personality of Godhead and His eternal servants, this temporary condition ceases to exist.

TEXT 13

उन्मत्तमत्तजडवत्स्वसंस्थां
गतस्य मे वीर चिकित्सितेन ।
अर्थः कियान् भवता शिक्षितेन
स्तब्धप्रमत्तस्य च पिष्टपेषः ॥१३॥

unmatta-matta-jaḍavat sva-saṁsthāṁ
gatasya me vīra cikitsitena
arthaḥ kiyān bhavatā śikṣitena
stabdha-pramattasya ca piṣṭapeṣaḥ

unmatta—madness; *matta*—a drunkard; *jaḍa-vat*—like a dunce; *sva-saṁsthām*—situation in my original constitutional position; *gatasya*—of one who has obtained; *me*—of me; *vīra*—O King; *cikitsitena*—by your chastisement; *arthaḥ*—the meaning or purpose; *kiyān*—what; *bhavatā*—by you; *śikṣitena*—by being instructed; *stabdha*—dull; *pramattasya*—of a crazy man; *ca*—also; *piṣṭa-peṣaḥ*—like grinding flour.

TRANSLATION

My dear King, you have said, "You rascal, you dull, crazy fellow! I am going to chastise you, and then you will come to your senses." In this regard, let me say that although I live like a dull, deaf and dumb man, I am actually a self-realized person. What will you gain by punishing me? If your calculation is true and I am a madman,

then your punishment will be like beating a dead horse. There will be no effect. When a madman is punished, he is not cured of his madness.

PURPORT

Everyone in this material world is working like a madman under certain impressions falsely acquired in the material condition. For example, a thief who knows that stealing is not good and who knows that it is followed with punishment by a king or by God, who has seen that thieves are arrested and punished by the police, nonetheless steals again and again. He is obsessed with the idea that by stealing he will be happy. This is a sign of madness. Despite repeated punishment, the thief cannot give up his stealing habit; therefore the punishment is useless.

TEXT 14

श्रीशुक उवाच

एतावदनुवादपरिभाषया प्रत्युदीर्य मुनिवर उपशमशील उपरतानात्म्य-
निमित्त उपभोगेन कर्मारब्धं व्यपनयन् राजयानमपि तथोवाह ॥१४॥

śrī-śuka uvāca
etāvad anuvāda-paribhāṣayā pratyudīrya muni-vara upaśama-śīla uparatānātmya-nimitta upabhogena karmārabdhaṁ vyapanayan rāja-yānam api tathovāha.

śrī-śukaḥ uvāca—Śukadeva Gosvāmī continued to speak; *etāvat*—so much; *anuvāda-paribhāṣayā*—by explanatory repetition of words spoken previously by the King; *pratyudīrya*—giving replies one after another; *muni-varaḥ*—great sage Jaḍa Bharata; *upaśama-śīlaḥ*—who was calm and peaceful in character; *uparata*—ceased; *anātmya*—things not related to the soul; *nimittaḥ*—whose cause (ignorance) for identification with things not related to the soul; *upabhogena*—by accepting the consequences of his *karma; karma-ārabdham*—the resultant action now attained; *vyapanayan*—finishing; *rāja-yānam*—the palanquin of the King; *api*—again; *tathā*—as before; *uvāha*—continued to carry.

TRANSLATION

Śukadeva Gosvāmī said: O Mahārāja Parīkṣit, when King Rahūgaṇa chastised the exalted devotee Jaḍa Bharata with harsh words, that peaceful, saintly person tolerated it all and replied properly. Nescience is due to the bodily conception, and Jaḍa Bharata was not affected by this false conception. Out of his natural humility, he never considered himself a great devotee, and he agreed to suffer the results of his past karma. Like an ordinary man, he thought that by carrying the palanquin, he was destroying the reactions of his past misdeeds. Thinking in this way, he began to carry the palanquin as before.

PURPORT

An exalted devotee of the Lord never thinks that he is a *paramahaṁsa* or a liberated person. He always remains a humble servant of the Lord. In all reverse conditions, he agrees to suffer the results of his past life. He never accuses the Lord of putting him into a distressed condition. These are the signs of an exalted devotee. *Tat te 'nukampāṁ susamīkṣyamāṇaḥ.* When suffering reversed conditions, the devotee always considers that the reverse conditions are the Lord's concessions. He is never angry with his master; he is always satisfied with the position his master offers. In any case, he continues performing his duty in devotional service. Such a person is guaranteed promotion back home, back to Godhead. As stated in *Śrīmad-Bhāgavatam* (10.14.8):

tat te 'nukampāṁ susamīkṣamāṇo
bhuñjāna evātma-kṛtaṁ vipākam
hṛd-vāg-vapurbhir vidadhan namas te
jīveta yo mukti-pade sa dāya-bhāk

"My dear Lord, one who constantly waits for Your causeless mercy to be bestowed upon him and who goes on suffering the reactions of his past misdeeds, offering You respectful obeisances from the core of his heart, is surely eligible for liberation, for it has become his rightful claim."

TEXT 15

**स चापि पाण्डवेय सिन्धुसौवीरपतिस्तत्त्वजिज्ञासायां सम्यक्श्रद्धयाधिकृताधिकार-
स्तद्धृदयग्रन्थिमोचनं द्विजवच आश्रुत्य बहुयोगग्रन्थसम्मतं त्वरयावरुह्य
शिरसा पादमूलमुपसृतः क्षमापयन् विगतनृपदेवस्मय उवाच ॥ १५ ॥**

*sa cāpi pāṇḍaveya sindhu-sauvīra-patis tattva-jijñāsāyāṁ samyak-
śraddhayādhikṛtādhikāras tad dhṛdaya-granthi-mocanaṁ dvija-vaca
āśrutya bahu-yoga-grantha-sammataṁ tvarayāvaruhya śirasā pāda-
mūlam upasṛtaḥ kṣamāpayan vigata-nṛpa-deva-smaya uvāca.*

saḥ—he (Mahārāja Rahūgaṇa); *ca*—also; *api*—indeed; *pāṇḍaveya*—O best of the Pāṇḍu dynasty (Mahārāja Parīkṣit); *sindhu-sauvīra-patiḥ*—the King of the states known as Sindhu and Sauvīra; *tattva-jijñāsāyām*—in the matter of inquiring about the Absolute Truth; *samyak-śraddhayā*—by faith consisting of complete control of the senses and the mind; *adhikṛta-adhikāraḥ*—who attained the proper qualification; *tat*—that; *hṛdaya-granthi*—the knot of false conceptions within the heart; *mocanam*—which eradicates; *dvija-vacaḥ*—the words of the *brāhmaṇa* (Jaḍa Bharata); *āśrutya*—hearing; *bahu-yoga-grantha-sammatam*—approved by all yogic processes and their scriptures; *tvarayā*—very hastily; *avaruhya*—getting down (from the palanquin); *śirasā*—by his head; *pāda-mūlam*—at the lotus feet; *upasṛtaḥ*—falling down flat to offer obeisances; *kṣamāpayan*—obtaining pardon for his offense; *vigata-nṛpa-deva-smayaḥ*—giving up the false pride of being the King and therefore being worshipable; *uvāca*—said.

TRANSLATION

Śukadeva Gosvāmī continued: O best of the Pāṇḍu dynasty [Mahārāja Parīkṣit], the King of the Sindhu and Sauvīra states [Mahārāja Rahūgaṇa] had great faith in discussions of the Absolute Truth. Being thus qualified, he heard from Jaḍa Bharata that philosophical presentation which is approved by all scriptures on the mystic yoga process and which slackens the knot in the heart. His material conception of himself as a king was thus destroyed. He immediately descended from his palanquin and fell flat on the

ground with his head at the lotus feet of Jaḍa Bharata in such a way that he might be excused for his insulting words against the great brāhmaṇa. He then prayed as follows.

PURPORT

In *Bhagavad-gītā* (4.2) Lord Kṛṣṇa says:

evaṁ paramparā-prāptam
imaṁ rājarṣayo viduḥ
sa kāleneha mahatā
yogo naṣṭaḥ parantapa

"This supreme science was thus received through the chain of disciplic succession, and the saintly kings understood it in that way. But in course of time the succession was broken, and therefore the science as it is appears to be lost."

Through the disciplic succession the royal order was on the same platform as great saintly persons (*rāja-ṛṣis*). Formerly they could understand the philosophy of life and knew how to train the citizens to come to the same standard. In other words, they knew how to deliver the citizens from the entanglement of birth and death. When Mahārāja Daśaratha ruled Ayodhyā, the great sage Viśvāmitra once came to him to take away Lord Rāmacandra and Lakṣmaṇa to the forest to kill a demon. When the saintly person Viśvāmitra came to the court of Mahārāja Daśaratha, the King, in order to receive the saintly person, asked him, *aihiṣṭaṁ yat tat punar-janma-jayāya.* He asked the sage whether everything was going on well in his endeavor to conquer the repetition of birth and death. The whole process of Vedic civilization is based on this point. We must know how to conquer the repetition of birth and death. Mahārāja Rahūgaṇa also knew the purpose of life; therefore when Jaḍa Bharata put the philosophy of life before him, he immediately appreciated it. This is the foundation of Vedic society. Learned scholars, *brāhmaṇas,* saintly persons and sages who were fully aware of the Vedic purpose advised the royal order how to benefit the general masses, and by their cooperation, the general masses were benefited. Therefore everything was successful. Mahārāja Rahūgaṇa attained this perfection of understanding the value of human life; therefore he regretted his insulting words to Jaḍa Bharata, and he immediately descended from his palanquin and fell down at the lotus feet of Jaḍa Bharata in order to be excused and to hear from him further about the values of life known as *brahma-jijñāsā* (inquiry into the Absolute Truth). At the present moment, high government officials are ignorant of the values of life, and when saintly persons endeavor to broadcast the Vedic knowledge, the so-called executives do not offer their respectful obeisances but try to obstruct the spiritual propaganda. Thus one can say that the former kingly government was like heaven and that the present government is like hell.

TEXT 16

कस्त्वं निगूढश्चरसि द्विजानां
बिभर्षि सूत्रं कतमोऽवधूतः ।
कस्यासि कुत्रत्य इहापि कस्मात्
क्षेमाय नश्चेदसि नोत शुक्लः ॥१६॥

kas tvaṁ nigūḍhaś carasi dvijānāṁ
bibharṣi sūtraṁ katamo 'vadhūtaḥ
kasyāsi kutratya ihāpi kasmāt
kṣemāya naś ced asi nota śuklaḥ

kaḥ tvam—who are you; *nigūḍhaḥ*—very much covered; *carasi*—you move within this world; *dvijānām*—among the *brāhmaṇas* or saintly persons; *bibharṣi*—you also wear; *sūtram*—the sacred thread belonging to the first-class *brāhmaṇas; katamaḥ*—which; *avadhūtaḥ*—highly elevated person; *kasya asi*—whose are you (whose disciple or son are you); *kutratyaḥ*—from where; *iha api*—here in this place; *kasmāt*—for what purpose; *kṣemāya*—for the benefit; *naḥ*—of us; *cet*—if; *asi*—you are; *na uta*—or not; *śuklaḥ*—the personality of the pure mode of goodness (Kapiladeva).

TRANSLATION

King Rahūgaṇa said: O brāhmaṇa, you appear to be moving in this world very much covered and unknown to others. Who are

you? Are you a learned brāhmaṇa and saintly person? I see that you are wearing a sacred thread. Are you one of those exalted, liberated saints such as Dattātreya and other highly advanced, learned scholars? May I ask whose disciple you are? Where do you live? Why have you come to this place? Is your mission in coming here to do good for us? Please let me know who you are.

PURPORT

Mahārāja Rahūgaṇa was very anxious to receive further enlightenment in Vedic knowledge because he could understand that Jaḍa Bharata belonged to a *brāhmaṇa* family either by disciplic succession or by birth in a *brāhmaṇa* dynasty. As stated in the *Vedas: tad vijñānārthaṁ sa gurum evābhigacchet.* Rahūgaṇa was accepting Jaḍa Bharata as a *guru,* but a *guru* must prove his position not only by wearing a sacred thread but by advancing knowledge in spiritual life. It is also significant that Rahūgaṇa asked Jaḍa Bharata which family he belonged to. There are two types of families—one according to dynasty and the other according to disciplic succession. In either way, one can be enlightened. The word *śuklaḥ* refers to a person in the mode of goodness. If one wants to receive spiritual knowledge, he must approach a bona fide *brāhmaṇa-guru,* either in the disciplic succession or in a family of learned *brāhmaṇas.*

TEXT 17

नाहं विशङ्के सुरराजवज्रा-
न त्र्यक्षशूलान्न यमस्य दण्डात् ।
नाग्न्यर्कसोमानिलवित्तपास्त्रा-
च्छङ्के भृशं ब्रह्मकुलावमानात् ॥१७॥

nāhaṁ viśaṅke sura-rāja-vajrān
na tryakṣa-śūlān na yamasya daṇḍāt
nāgny-arka-somānila-vittapāstrāc
chaṅke bhṛśaṁ brahma-kulāvamānāt

na—not; *aham*—I; *viśaṅke*—am afraid; *sura-rāja-vajrāt*—from the thunderbolt of the King of heaven, Indra; *na*—nor; *tryakṣa-śūlāt*—

from the piercing trident of Lord Śiva; *na*—nor; *yamasya*—of the superintendent of death, Yamarāja; *daṇḍāt*—from the punishment; *na*—nor; *agni*—of fire; *arka*—of the scorching heat of the sun; *soma*—of the moon; *anila*—of the wind; *vitta-pa*—of the owner of riches, Kuvera, the treasurer of the heavenly planets; *astrāt*—from the weapons; *śaṅke*—I am afraid; *bhṛśam*—very much; *brahma-kula*—the group of the *brāhmaṇas; avamānāt*—from offending.

TRANSLATION

My dear sir, I am not at all afraid of the thunderbolt of King Indra, nor am I afraid of the serpentine, piercing trident of Lord Śiva. I do not care about the punishment of Yamarāja, the superintendent of death, nor am I afraid of fire, scorching sun, moon, wind, nor the weapons of Kuvera. Yet I am afraid of offending a brāhmaṇa. I am very much afraid of this.

PURPORT

When Śrī Caitanya Mahāprabhu was instructing Rūpa Gosvāmī at the Daśāśvamedha-ghāṭa in Prayāga, He pointed out very clearly the seriousness of offending a Vaiṣṇava. He compared the *vaiṣṇava-aparādha* to *hātī mātā*, a mad elephant. When a mad elephant enters a garden, it spoils all the fruits and flowers. Similarly, if one offends a Vaiṣṇava, he spoils all his spiritual assets. Offending a *brāhmaṇa* is very dangerous, and this was known to Mahārāja Rahūgaṇa. He therefore frankly admitted his fault. There are many dangerous things—thunderbolts, fire, Yamarāja's punishment, the punishment of Lord Śiva's trident, and so forth—but none is considered as serious as offending a *brāhmaṇa* like Jaḍa Bharata. Therefore Mahārāja Rahūgaṇa immediately descended from his palanquin and fell flat before the lotus feet of the *brāhmaṇa* Jaḍa Bharata just to be excused.

TEXT 18

तद्‍ ब्रूह्यसङ्गो जडवन्निगूढ-
विज्ञानवीर्यो विचरस्यपारः ।

वचांसि योगग्रथितानि साधो
न नः क्षमन्ते मनसापि भेत्तुम् ॥१८॥

tad brūhy asaṅgo jaḍavan nigūḍha-
vijñāna-vīryo vicarasy apāraḥ
vacāṁsi yoga-grathitāni sādho
na naḥ kṣamante manasāpi bhettum

tat—therefore; *brūhi*—please speak; *asaṅgaḥ*—who have no association with the material world; *jaḍa-vat*—appearing like a deaf and dumb man; *nigūḍha*—completely hidden; *vijñāna-vīryaḥ*—who have full knowledge of the spiritual science and are thus very powerful; *vicarasi*—you are moving; *apāraḥ*—who possess unlimited spiritual glories; *vacāṁsi*—the words uttered by you; *yoga-grathitāni*—bearing the complete meaning of mystic *yoga; sādho*—O great, saintly person; *na*—not; *naḥ*—of us; *kṣamante*—are able; *manasā api*—even by the mind; *bhettum*—to understand by analytical study.

TRANSLATION

My dear sir, it appears that the influence of your great spiritual knowledge is hidden. Factually you are bereft of all material association and fully absorbed in the thought of the Supreme. Consequently you are unlimitedly advanced in spiritual knowledge. Please tell me why you are wandering around like a dullard. O great, saintly person, you have spoken words approved by the yogic process, but it is not possible for us to understand what you have said. Therefore kindly explain it.

PURPORT

Saintly people like Jaḍa Bharata do not speak ordinary words. Whatever they say is approved by great *yogīs* and those advanced in spiritual life. That is the difference between ordinary people and saintly people. The listener must also be advanced to understand the words of such exalted, spiritually advanced people as Jaḍa Bharata. *Bhagavad-gītā* was spoken to Arjuna, not to others. Lord Kṛṣṇa especially selected

Arjuna for instruction in spiritual knowledge because Arjuna happened to be a great devotee and confidential friend. Similarly, great personalities also speak to the advanced, not to *śūdras, vaiśyas,* women or unintelligent men. Sometimes it is very risky to give great philosophical instructions to ordinary people, but Śrī Caitanya Mahāprabhu, for the benefit of the fallen souls of Kali-yuga, has given us a very nice instrument, the chanting of the Hare Kṛṣṇa *mantra.* The general mass of people, although *śūdras* and less, can be purified by chanting this Hare Kṛṣṇa *mantra.* Then they can understand the exalted philosophical statements of *Bhagavad-gītā* and *Śrīmad-Bhāgavatam.* Our Kṛṣṇa consciousness movement has therefore adopted the chanting of the Hare Kṛṣṇa *mahā-mantra* for the general masses. When people gradually become purified, they are instructed in the lessons of *Bhagavad-gītā* and *Śrīmad-Bhāgavatam.* Materialistic people like *strī, śūdra* and *dvija-bandhu* cannot understand words of spiritual advancement, yet one can take to the shelter of a Vaiṣṇava, for he knows the art of enlightening even *śūdras* in the highly elevated subject matter spoken in *Bhagavad-gītā* and *Śrīmad-Bhāgavatam.*

TEXT 19

अहं च योगेश्वरमात्मतत्त्व-
विदां मुनीनां परमं गुरुं वै ।
प्रष्टुं प्रवृत्तः किमिहारणं तत्
साक्षाद्धरिं ज्ञानकलावतीर्णम् ॥१९॥

ahaṁ ca yogeśvaram ātma-tattva-
vidāṁ munīnāṁ paramaṁ guruṁ vai
praṣṭuṁ pravṛttaḥ kim ihāraṇaṁ tat
sākṣād dhariṁ jñāna-kalāvatīrṇam

aham—I; *ca*—and; *yoga-īśvaram*—the master of all mystic power; *ātma-tattva-vidām*—of the learned scholars who are aware of the spiritual science; *munīnām*—of such saintly persons; *paramam*—the best; *gurum*—the preceptor; *vai*—indeed; *praṣṭum*—to inquire; *pravṛttaḥ*—engaged; *kim*—what; *iha*—in this world; *araṇam*—the most secure shelter; *tat*—that which; *sākṣāt harim*—directly the Supreme Personality of Godhead; *jñāna-kalā-avatīrṇam*—who has descended as the incarnation of complete knowledge in His plenary portion known as Kapiladeva.

TRANSLATION

I consider your good self the most exalted master of mystic power. You know the spiritual science perfectly well. You are the most exalted of all learned sages, and you have descended for the benefit of all human society. You have come to give spiritual knowledge, and you are a direct representative of Kapiladeva, the incarnation of God and the plenary portion of knowledge. I am therefore asking you, O spiritual master, what is the most secure shelter in this world?

PURPORT

As Kṛṣṇa confirms in *Bhagavad-gītā:*

yoginām api sarveṣāṁ
mad-gatenāntarātmanā
śraddhāvān bhajate yo māṁ
sa me yuktatamo mataḥ

"Of all *yogīs,* he who abides in Me with great faith, worshiping Me in transcendental loving service, is most intimately united with Me in *yoga* and is the highest of all." (Bg. 6.47)

Jaḍa Bharata was a perfect *yogī.* He was formerly the emperor Bharata Mahārāja, and he was now the most exalted personality among learned sages and the master of all mystic powers. Although Jaḍa Bharata was an ordinary living entity, he had inherited all the knowledge given by the Supreme Personality of Godhead, Kapiladeva. He could therefore be taken directly as the Supreme Personality of Godhead. As confirmed by Śrīla Viśvanātha Cakravartī Ṭhākura in his stanzas to the spiritual master: *sākṣād-dharitvena samasta-śāstraiḥ.* An exalted personality like Jaḍa Bharata is as good as the Supreme Personality of Godhead because he fully represents the Lord by giving knowledge to others. Jaḍa Bharata is herein accepted as the direct representative of the Supreme Personality of Godhead because he was imparting knowledge on behalf of the Supreme Lord. Therefore Mahārāja Rahūgaṇa concluded that it was appropriate to ask him about *ātma-tattva*, the spiritual science. *Tad-vijñānārthaṁ sa gurum evābhigacchet.* This Vedic injunction is also confirmed herein. If anyone is at all interested in knowing the spiritual science (*brahma-jijñāsā*), he must approach a *guru* like Jaḍa Bharata.

TEXT 20

स वै भवाँल्लोकनिरीक्षणार्थ-
मव्यक्तलिङ्गो विचरत्यपिस्वित् ।
योगेश्वराणां गतिमन्धबुद्धिः
कथं विचक्षीत गृहानुबन्धः ॥२०॥

sa vai bhavāl̐ loka-nirīkṣaṇārtham
avyakta-liṅgo vicaraty api svit
yogeśvarāṇāṁ gatim andha-buddhiḥ
kathaṁ vicakṣīta gṛhānubandhaḥ

saḥ—that Supreme Personality of Godhead or His incarnation Kapiladeva; *vai*—indeed; *bhavān*—your good self; *loka-nirīkṣaṇa-artham*—just to study the characteristics of the people of this world; *avyakta-liṅgaḥ*—without manifesting your real identity; *vicarati*—are traveling in this world; *api svit*—whether; *yoga-īśvarāṇām*—of all the advanced *yogīs; gatim*—the characteristics or actual behavior; *andha-buddhiḥ*—who are illusioned and have become blind to spiritual knowledge; *katham*—how; *vicakṣīta*—may know; *gṛha-anubandhaḥ*—I who am bound by attachment to family life, or worldly life.

TRANSLATION

Is it not a fact that your good self is the direct representative of Kapiladeva, the incarnation of the Supreme Personality of Godhead? To examine people and see who is actually a human being and who is not, you have presented yourself to be a deaf and dumb person. Are you not moving this way upon the surface of the

world? I am very attached to family life and worldly activities, and I am blind to spiritual knowledge. Nonetheless, I am now present before you and am seeking enlightenment from you. How can I advance in spiritual life?

PURPORT

Although Mahārāja Rahūgaṇa was playing the part of a king, he had been informed by Jaḍa Bharata that he was not a king nor was Jaḍa Bharata deaf and dumb. Such designations were simply coverings of the spirit soul. Everyone must come to this knowledge. As confirmed in *Bhagavad-gītā* (2.13): *dehino 'smin yathā dehe.* Everyone is encased within the body. Since the body is never identical with the soul, the bodily activities are simply illusory. In the association of such a *sādhu* as Jaḍa Bharata, Mahārāja Rahūgaṇa came to the awareness that his activities as a royal authority were simply illusory phenomena. He therefore agreed to receive knowledge from Jaḍa Bharata, and that was the beginning of his perfection. *Tad-vijñānārthaṁ sa gurum evābhigacchet.* A person like Mahārāja Rahūgaṇa, who was very inquisitive to know the value of life and the spiritual science, must approach a personality like Jaḍa Bharata. *Tasmād guruṁ prapadyeta jijñāsuḥ śreya uttamam* (*Bhāg.* 11.3.21). One must approach a *guru* like Jaḍa Bharata, a representative of the Supreme Personality of Godhead, to inquire about the goal of human life.

TEXT 21

दृष्टः श्रमः कर्मत आत्मनो वै
भर्तुर्गन्तुर्भवतश्चानुमन्ये
यथासतोदानयनाद्यभावात्
समूल इष्टो व्यवहारमार्गः ॥२१॥

dṛṣṭaḥ śramaḥ karmata ātmano vai
bhartur gantur bhavataś cānumanye
yathāsatodānayanādy-abhāvāt
samūla iṣṭo vyavahāra-mārgaḥ

dṛṣṭaḥ—it is experienced by everyone; *śramaḥ*—fatigue; *karmataḥ*—from acting in some way; *ātmanaḥ*—of the soul; *vai*—indeed; *bhartuḥ*—of one who is carrying the palanquin; *gantuḥ*—of one who is moving; *bhavataḥ*—of yourself; *ca*—and; *anumanye*—I guess like that; *yathā*—as much as; *asatā*—with something that is not an actual fact; *uda*—of water; *ānayana-ādi*—of the bringing and other such tasks; *abhāvāt*—from the absence; *sa-mūlaḥ*—based on evidence; *iṣṭaḥ*—respected; *vyavahāra-mārgaḥ*—phenomenon.

TRANSLATION

You have said, "I am not fatigued from labor." Although the soul is different from the body, there is fatigue because of bodily labor, and it appears to be the fatigue of the soul. When you are carrying the palanquin, there is certainly labor for the soul. This is my conjecture. You have also said that the external behavior exhibited between the master and the servant is not factual, but although in the phenomenal world it is not factual, the products of the phenomenal world can actually affect things. That is visible and experienced. As such, even though material activities are impermanent, they cannot be said to be untrue.

PURPORT

This is a discussion on impersonal Māyāvāda philosophy and the practical philosophy of Vaiṣṇavas. The Māyāvāda philosophy explains this phenomenal world to be false, but Vaiṣṇava philosophers do not agree. They know that the phenomenal world is a temporary manifestation, but it is not false. A dream that we see at night is certainly false, but a horrible dream certainly affects the person seeing it. The soul's fatigue is not factual, but as long as one is immersed in the illusory bodily conception, one is affected by such false dreams. When dreaming, it is not possible to avoid the actual facts, and the conditioned soul is forced to suffer due to his dream. A waterpot is made of earth and is temporary. Actually there is no waterpot; there is simply earth. However, as long as the waterpot can contain water, we can use it in that way. It cannot be said to be absolutely false.

TEXT 22

स्थाल्यग्नितापात्पयसोऽभिताप-
स्तत्तापतस्तण्डुलगर्भरन्धिः
देहेन्द्रियास्वाशयसन्निकर्षात्
तत्संसृतिः पुरुषस्यानुरोधात् ॥२२॥

sthāly-agni-tāpāt payaso 'bhitāpas
tat-tāpatas taṇḍula-garbha-randhiḥ
dehendriyāsvāśaya-sannikarṣāt
tat-saṁsṛtiḥ puruṣasyānurodhāt

sthāli—on the cooking pot; *agni-tāpāt*—because of the heat of fire; *payasaḥ*—the milk put into the pot; *abhitāpaḥ*—becomes hot; *tat-tāpataḥ*—because of the milk's becoming hot; *taṇḍula-garbha-randhiḥ*—the center of the rice within the milk becomes cooked; *deha-indriya-asvāśaya*—the bodily senses; *sannikarṣāt*—from having connections with; *tat-saṁsṛtiḥ*—the experience of fatigue and other miseries; *puruṣasya*—of the soul; *anurodhāt*—from compliance due to being grossly attached to the body, senses and mind.

TRANSLATION

King Rahūgaṇa continued: My dear sir, you have said that designations like bodily fatness and thinness are not characteristics of the soul. That is incorrect because designations like pain and pleasure are certainly felt by the soul. You may put a pot of milk and rice within fire, and the milk and rice are automatically heated one after the other. Similarly, due to bodily pains and pleasures, the senses, mind and soul are affected. The soul cannot be completely detached from this conditioning.

PURPORT

This argument put forward by Mahārāja Rahūgaṇa is correct from the practical point of view, but it arises from an attachment to the bodily conception. It can be said that a person sitting in his car is certainly different from his car, but if there is damage to the car, the owner of the car, being overly attached to the car, feels pain. Actually, the damage done to the car has nothing to do with the car's proprietor, but because the proprietor has identified himself with the interest of the car, he feels pleasure and pain connected with it. This conditional state can be avoided if attachment is withdrawn from the car. Then the proprietor would not feel pleasure or pain if the car is damaged or whatever. Similarly, the soul has nothing to do with the body and the senses, but due to ignorance, he identifies himself with the body, and he feels pleasure and pain due to bodily pleasure and pain.

TEXT 23

शास्ताभिगोप्ता नृपतिः प्रजानां
यः किङ्करो वै न पिनष्टि पिष्टम् ।
स्वधर्ममाराधनमच्युतस्य
यदीहमानो विजहात्यघौघम् ॥२३॥

śāstābhigoptā nṛpatiḥ prajānāṁ
yaḥ kiṅkaro vai na pinaṣṭi piṣṭam
sva-dharmam ārādhanam acyutasya
yad īhamāno vijahāty aghaugham

śāstā—the governor; *abhigoptā*—a well-wisher of the citizens as a father is the well-wisher of his children; *nṛ-patiḥ*—the king; *prajānām*—of the citizens; *yaḥ*—one who; *kiṅkaraḥ*—order carrier; *vai*—indeed; *na*—not; *pinaṣṭi piṣṭam*—grinds what is already ground; *sva-dharmam*—one's own occupational duty; *ārādhanam*—worshiping; *acyutasya*—of the Supreme Personality of Godhead; *yat*—which; *īhamānaḥ*—performing; *vijahāti*—they are released from; *agha-ogham*—all kinds of sinful activity and faulty action.

TRANSLATION

My dear sir, you have said that the relationship between the king and the subject or between the master and the servant are not eter-

nal, but although such relationships are temporary, when a person takes the position of a king, his duty is to rule the citizens and punish those who are disobedient to the laws. By punishing them, he teaches the citizens to obey the laws of the state. Again, you have said that punishing a person who is deaf and dumb is like chewing the chewed or grinding the pulp; that is to say, there is no benefit in it. However, if one is engaged in his own occupational duty as ordered by the Supreme Lord, his sinful activities are certainly diminished. Therefore if one is engaged in his occupational duty by force, he benefits because he can vanquish all his sinful activities in that way.

PURPORT

This argument offered by Mahārāja Rahūgaṇa is certainly very effective. In his *Bhakti-rasāmṛta-sindhu* (1.2.4), Śrīla Rūpa Gosvāmī says, *tasmāt kenāpy upāyena manaḥ kṛṣṇe niveśayet:* somehow or other, one should engage in Kṛṣṇa consciousness. Actually every living being is an eternal servant of Kṛṣṇa, but due to forgetfulness, a living entity engages himself as an eternal servant of *māyā.* As long as one is engaged in *māyā's* service, he cannot be happy. Our Kṛṣṇa consciousness movement aims at engaging people in Lord Kṛṣṇa's service. That will help them become freed from all material contamination and sinful activity. This is confirmed in *Bhagavad-gītā* (4.10): *vīta-rāga-bhaya-krodhāḥ.* By becoming detached from material activities, we will be freed from fear and anger. By austerity, one becomes purified and eligible to return home, back to Godhead. The duty of the king is to rule his citizens in such a way that they can become Kṛṣṇa conscious. This would be very beneficial for everyone. Unfortunately the king or president engages people in sense gratification instead of the Lord's service, and such activities are certainly not beneficial for anyone. King Rahūgaṇa tried to engage Jaḍa Bharata in carrying the palanquin, which is a form of sense gratification for the King. However, if one is engaged as a palanquin carrier in the Lord's service, that is certainly beneficial. In this godless civilization, if a president engages people somehow or other in devotional service or the awakening of Kṛṣṇa consciousness, he renders the very best service to the citizens.

TEXT 24

तन्मे भवान्नरदेवाभिमान-
मदेन तुच्छीकृतसत्तमस्य ।
कृषीष्ट मैत्रीदृशमार्तबन्धो
यथा तरे सदवध्यानमंहः ॥२४॥

tan me bhavān nara-devābhimāna-
madena tucchīkṛta-sattamasya
kṛṣīṣṭa maitrī-dṛśam ārta-bandho
yathā tare sad-avadhyānam aṁhaḥ

tat—therefore; *me*—unto me; *bhavān*—your good self; *nara-deva-abhimāna-madena*—by madness due to having the body of a king and thus being proud of it; *tucchīkṛta*—who has insulted; *sat-tamasya*—you who are the best among human beings; *kṛṣīṣṭa*—kindly show; *maitrī-dṛśam*—your causeless mercy upon me like a friend; *ārta-bandho*—O friend of all distressed persons; *yathā*—so; *tare*—I can get relief from; *sat-avadhyānam*—neglecting a great personality like you; *aṁhaḥ*—the sin.

TRANSLATION

Whatever you have spoken appears to me to be contradictory. O best friend of the distressed, I have committed a great offense by insulting you. I was puffed up with false prestige due to possessing the body of a king. For this I have certainly become an offender. Therefore I pray that you kindly glance at me with your causeless mercy. If you do so, I can be relieved from sinful activities brought about by insulting you.

PURPORT

Śrī Caitanya Mahāprabhu has said that by offending a Vaiṣṇava, one finishes all his spiritual activities. Offending a Vaiṣṇava is considered the mad elephant offense. A mad elephant can destroy an entire garden which has been developed with great labor. One may attain the topmost platform of devotional service, but somehow or other if he offends a

Vaiṣṇava, the whole structure collapses. Unconsciously, King Rahūgaṇa offended Jaḍa Bharata, but due to his good sense, he asked to be excused. This is the process by which one can be relieved from a *vaiṣṇava-aparādha*. Kṛṣṇa is always very simple and by nature merciful. When one commits an offense at the feet of a Vaiṣṇava, one must immediately apologize to such a personality so that his spiritual advancement may not be hampered.

TEXT 25

न विक्रिया विश्वसुहृत्सखस्य
साम्येन वीताभिमतेस्तवापि ।
महद्विमानात् स्वकृताद्धि माद‍ृङ्
नङ्‌क्ष्यत्यदूरादपि शूलपाणिः ॥२५॥

na vikriyā viśva-suhṛt-sakhasya
sāmyena vītābhimates tavāpi
mahad-vimānāt sva-kṛtād dhi mādṛṅ
naṅkṣyaty adūrād api śūlapāṇiḥ

na—not; *vikriyā*—material transformation; *viśva-suhṛt*—of the Supreme Personality of Godhead, who is a friend to everyone; *sakhasya*—of you, the friend; *sāmyena*—because of your mental equilibrium; *vīta-abhimateḥ*—who has completely forsaken the bodily concept of life; *tava*—your; *api*—indeed; *mahat-vimānāt*—of insulting a great devotee; *sva-kṛtāt*—from my own activity; *hi*—certainly; *mādṛk*—a person like me; *naṅkṣyati*—will be destroyed; *adūrāt*—very soon; *api*—certainly; *śūla-pāṇiḥ*—even though as powerful as Lord Śiva (Śūlapāṇi).

TRANSLATION

O my dear lord, you are the friend of the Supreme Personality of Godhead, who is the friend of all living entities. You are therefore equal to everyone, and you are free from the bodily conception. Although I have committed an offense by insulting you, I know that there is no loss or gain for you due to my insult. You are

fixed in your determination, but I have committed an offense. Because of this, even though I may be as strong as Lord Śiva, I shall be vanquished without delay due to my offense at the lotus feet of a Vaiṣṇava.

PURPORT

Mahārāja Rahūgaṇa was very intelligent and conscious of the inauspicious effects arising from insulting a Vaiṣṇava. He was therefore very anxious to be excused by Jaḍa Bharata. Following in the footsteps of Mahārāja Rahūgaṇa, everyone should be very cautious not to commit an offense at the lotus feet of a Vaiṣṇava. Śrīla Vṛndāvana dāsa Ṭhākura in the *Caitanya-bhāgavata* (*Madhya* 13) says:

śūlapāṇi-sama yadi bhakta-nindā kare
bhāgavata pramāṇa——tathāpi śīghra mare

hena vaiṣṇavere ninde sarvajña ha-i
se janera adhaḥ-pāta sarva-śāstre ka-i

"Even if one is as strong as Lord Śiva, who carries a trident in his hand, one will nonetheless fall down from his spiritual position if he tries to insult a Vaiṣṇava. That is the verdict of all Vedic scriptures." He also says this in *Caitanya-bhāgavata* (*Madhya* 22).

vaiṣṇavera nindā karibeka yāra gaṇa
tāra rakṣā sāmarthya nāhika kona jana

śūlapāṇi-sama yadi vaiṣṇavere ninde
tathāpiha nāśa yāya——kahe śāstra-vṛnde

ihā nā māniyā ye sujana nindā kare
janme janme se pāpiṣṭha daiva-doṣe mare

"One who blasphemes a Vaiṣṇava cannot be protected by anyone. Even if a person is as strong as Lord Śiva, if he blasphemes a Vaiṣṇava, he is sure to be destroyed. This is the verdict of all *śāstras*. If one does not care for the verdict of the *śāstras* and dares blaspheme a Vaiṣṇava, he suffers life after life because of this."

Thus end the Bhaktivedanta purports of the Fifth Canto, Tenth Chapter, of the Śrīmad-Bhagavatam, *entitled, "The Discussion Between Jaḍa Bharata and Mahārāja Rahūgaṇa."*

CHAPTER ELEVEN

Jaḍa Bharata Instructs King Rahūgaṇa

In this chapter the *brāhmaṇa* Jaḍa Bharata instructs Mahārāja Rahūgaṇa in detail. He tells the King: "You are not very experienced, yet you pose yourself as a learned person because you are very proud of your knowledge. Actually a person who is on the transcendental platform does not care for social behavior that sacrifices spiritual advancement. Social behavior comes within the jurisdiction of *karma-kāṇḍa*, material benefit. No one can spiritually advance by such activities. The conditioned soul is always overpowered by the modes of material nature, and consequently he is simply concerned with material benefits and auspicious and inauspicious material things. In other words, the mind, which is the leader of the senses, is absorbed in material activities life after life. Thus he continuously gets different types of bodies and suffers miserable material conditions. On the basis of mental concoction, social behavior has been formulated. If one's mind is absorbed in these activities, he certainly remains conditioned within the material world. According to different opinions, there are eleven or twelve mental activities, which can be transformed into hundreds and thousands. A person who is not Kṛṣṇa conscious is subjected to all these mental concoctions and is thus governed by the material energy. The living entity who is free from mental concoctions attains the platform of pure spirit soul, devoid of material contamination. There are two types of living entities—*jīvātmā* and *paramātmā*, the individual soul and the Supreme Soul. That Supreme Soul in His ultimate realization is Lord Vāsudeva, Kṛṣṇa. He enters into everyone's heart and controls the living entity in his different activities. He is therefore the supreme shelter of all living entities. One can understand the Supreme Soul and one's position in relationship with Him when one is completely freed from the unwanted association of ordinary men. In this way one can become fit to cross the ocean of nescience. The cause of conditional life is attachment to the external energy. One has to conquer these mental concoctions; unless one does so, he will never be freed from material anxieties. Although mental concoctions have no value, their influence is still very formidable. No one should neglect to control the mind. If one does, the mind becomes so powerful that one immediately forgets his real position. Forgetting that he is an eternal servant of Kṛṣṇa and that service to Kṛṣṇa is his only business, one is doomed by material nature to serve the objects of the senses. One should kill mental concoctions by the sword of service to the Supreme Personality of Godhead and His devotee [*guru-kṛṣṇa-prasāde pāya bhakti-latā-bīja*]."

TEXT 1

ब्राह्मण उवाच
अकोविदः कोविदवादवादान्
वदस्यथो नातिविदां वरिष्ठः ।
न सूरयो हि व्यवहारमेनं
तत्त्वावमर्शेन सहामनन्ति ॥ १ ॥

brāhmaṇa uvāca
akovidaḥ kovida-vāda-vādān
vadasy atho nāti-vidāṁ variṣṭhaḥ
na sūrayo hi vyavahāram enaṁ
tattvāvamarśena sahāmananti

brāhmaṇaḥ uvāca—the *brāhmaṇa* said; *akovidaḥ*—without having experience; *kovida-vāda-vādān*—words used by experienced persons; *vadasi*—you are speaking; *atho*—therefore; *na*—not; *ati-vidām*—of those who are very experienced; *variṣṭhaḥ*—the most important; *na*—not; *sūrayaḥ*—such intelligent persons; *hi*—indeed; *vyavahāram*—mundane and social behavior; *enam*—this; *tattva*—of the truth; *avamarśena*—fine judgment by intelligence; *saha*—with; *āmananti*—discuss.

TRANSLATION

The brāhmaṇa Jaḍa Bharata said: My dear King, although you are not at all experienced, you are trying to speak like a very ex-

perienced man. Consequently you cannot be considered an experienced person. An experienced person does not speak the way you are speaking about the relationship between a master and a servant or about material pains and pleasures. These are simply external activities. Any advanced, experienced man, considering the Absolute Truth, does not talk in this way.

PURPORT

Kṛṣṇa similarly chastised Arjuna. *Aśocyān anvaśocas tvaṁ prajñā-vādāṁś ca bhāṣase:* "While speaking learned words, you are lamenting for what is not worthy of grief." (Bg. 2.11) Similarly, among people in general, 99.9 percent try to talk like experienced advisers, but they are actually devoid of spiritual knowledge and are therefore like inexperienced children speaking nonsensically. Consequently their words cannot be given any importance. One has to learn from Kṛṣṇa or His devotee. If one speaks on the basis of this experience—that is, on the basis of spiritual knowledge—one's words are valuable. At the present moment, the entire world is full of foolish people. *Bhagavad-gītā* describes these people as *mūḍhas.* They are trying to rule human society, but because they are devoid of spiritual knowledge, the entire world is in a chaotic condition. To be released from these miserable conditions, one has to become Kṛṣṇa conscious and take lessons from an exalted personality like Jaḍa Bharata, Lord Kṛṣṇa and Kapiladeva. That is the only way to solve the problems of material life.

TEXT 2

तथैव राजन्नुरुगार्हमेध-
वितानविद्योरुविजृम्भितेषु ।
न वेदवादेषु हि तत्त्ववादः
प्रायेण शुद्धो नु चकास्ति साधुः ॥२॥

tathaiva rājann uru-gārhamedha-
vitāna-vidyoru-vijṛmbhiteṣu
na veda-vādeṣu hi tattva-vādaḥ
prāyeṇa śuddho nu cakāsti sādhuḥ

tathā—therefore; *eva*—indeed; *rājan*—O King; *uru-gārha-medha*—rituals related to material household life; *vitāna-vidyā*—in knowledge that expands; *uru*—very greatly; *vijṛmbhiteṣu*—among those interested; *na*—not; *veda-vādeṣu*—who speak the version of the *Vedas; hi*—indeed; *tattva-vādaḥ*—the spiritual science; *prāyeṇa*—almost always; *śuddhaḥ*—free from all contaminated activities; *nu*—indeed; *cakāsti*—appear; *sādhuḥ*—a person who is advanced in devotional service.

TRANSLATION

My dear King, talks of the relationship between the master and the servant, the king and the subject and so forth are simply talks about material activities. People interested in material activities, which are expounded in the Vedas, are intent on performing material sacrifices and placing faith in their material activities. For such people, spiritual advancement is definitely not manifest.

PURPORT

In this verse, two words are significant—*veda-vāda* and *tattva-vāda.* According to *Bhagavad-gītā,* those who are simply attached to the *Vedas* and who do not understand the purpose of the *Vedas* or the *Vedānta-sūtra* are called *veda-vāda-ratāḥ.*

yām imāṁ puṣpitāṁ vācaṁ
pravadanty avipaścitaḥ
veda-vāda-ratāḥ pārtha
nānyad astīti vādinaḥ

kāmātmānaḥ svarga-parā
janma-karma-phala-pradām
kriyā-viśeṣa-bahulāṁ
bhogaiśvarya-gatiṁ prati

"Men of small knowledge are very much attached to the flowery words of the *Vedas,* which recommend various fruitive activities for elevation to heavenly planets, resultant good birth, power and so forth. Being desirous of sense gratification and opulent life, they say there is nothing more than this." (Bg. 2.42-43)

The *veda-vāda* followers of the *Vedas* are generally inclined to *karma-kāṇḍa*, the performance of sacrifice according to the Vedic injunctions. They are thereby promoted to higher planetary systems. They generally practice the Cāturmāsya system. *Akṣayyaṁ ha vai cāturmāsya-yājinaḥ sukṛtaṁ bhavati:* one who performs the *cāturmāsya-yajña* becomes pious. By becoming pious, one may be promoted to the higher planetary systems (*ūrdhvaṁ gacchanti sattva-sthāḥ*). Some of the followers of the *Vedas* are attached to *karma-kāṇḍa*, the fruitive activities of the *Vedas*, in order to be promoted to a higher standard of life. Others argue that this is not the purpose of the *Vedas*. *Tad yathaiveha karma-jitaḥ lokaḥ kṣīyate evam evam utra puṇya-jitaḥ lokaḥ kṣīyate.* In this world someone may become very highly elevated by taking birth in an aristocratic family, by being well educated, beautiful or very rich. These are the gifts for pious activities enacted in the past life. However, these will be finished when the stock of pious activity is finished. If we become attached to pious activities, we may get these various worldly facilities in the next life and may take birth in the heavenly planets. But all this will eventually be finished. *Kṣīṇe puṇye martya-lokaṁ viśanti* (Bg. 9.21): when the stock of pious activity is finished, one again has to come to this *martya-loka*. According to the Vedic injunctions, the performance of pious activity is not really the objective of the *Vedas*. The objective of the *Vedas* is explained in *Bhagavad-gītā*. *Vedaiś ca sarvair aham eva vedyaḥ:* the objective of the *Vedas* is to understand Kṛṣṇa, the Supreme Personality of Godhead. Those who are *veda-vādīs* are not actually advanced in knowledge, and those who are followers of *jñāna-kāṇḍa* (Brahman understanding) are also not perfect. However, when one comes to the platform of *upāsanā* and accepts the worship of the Supreme Personality of Godhead, he becomes perfect (*ārādhanānāṁ sarveṣāṁ viṣṇor ārādhanaṁ param*). In the *Vedas* the worship of different demigods and the performance of sacrifice are certainly mentioned, but such worship is inferior because the worshipers do not know that the ultimate goal is Viṣṇu (*na te viduḥ svārtha-gatiṁ hi viṣṇum*). When one comes to the platform of *viṣṇor ārādhanam*, or *bhakti-yoga*, one has attained the perfection of life. Otherwise, as indicated in *Bhagavad-gītā*, one is not a *tattva-vādī* but a *veda-vādī*, a blind follower of the Vedic injunctions. A *veda-vādī* cannot be purified from material contamination unless he becomes a *tattva-vādī*, that is, one who knows *tattva*, the Absolute Truth. *Tattva* is also experienced in three features—

brahmeti paramātmeti bhagavān iti śabdyate. Even after coming to the platform of understanding *tattva,* one must worship Bhagavān, Viṣṇu and His expansions, or one is not yet perfect. *Bahūnāṁ janmanām ante jñānavān māṁ prapadyate:* after many births, one who is actually in knowledge surrenders unto Kṛṣṇa. The conclusion is that unintelligent men with a poor fund of knowledge cannot understand Bhagavān, Brahman or Paramātmā, but after studying the *Vedas* and attaining the understanding of the Absolute Truth, the Supreme Personality of Godhead, one is supposed to be on the platform of perfect knowledge.

TEXT 3

न तस्य तत्त्वग्रहणाय साक्षाद्
वरीयसीरपि वाचः समासन् ।
स्वप्ने निरुक्त्या गृहमेधिसौख्यं
न यस्य हेयानुमितं स्वयं स्यात् ॥ ३ ॥

na tasya tattva-grahaṇāya sākṣād
varīyasīr api vācaḥ samāsan
svapne niruktyā gṛhamedhi-saukhyaṁ
na yasya heyānumitaṁ svayaṁ syāt

na—not; *tasya*—of him (a student studying the *Vedas*); *tattva-grahaṇāya*—for accepting the real purpose of Vedic knowledge; *sākṣāt*—directly; *varīyasīḥ*—very exalted; *api*—although; *vācaḥ*—words of the *Vedas; samāsan*—sufficiently became; *svapne*—in a dream; *niruktyā*—by example; *gṛha-medhi-saukhyam*—happiness within this material world; *na*—not; *yasya*—of him who; *heya-anumitam*—concluded to be inferior; *svayam*—automatically; *syāt*—become.

TRANSLATION

A dream becomes automatically known to a person as false and immaterial, and similarly one eventually realizes that material happiness in this life or the next, on this planet or a higher planet, is insignificant. When one realizes this, the Vedas, although an ex-

cellent source, are insufficient to bring about direct knowledge of the truth.

PURPORT

In *Bhagavad-gītā* (2.45), Kṛṣṇa advised Arjuna to become transcendental to the material activities impelled by the three material modes of nature (*traiguṇya-viṣayā vedā nistraiguṇyo bhavārjuna*). The purpose of Vedic study is to transcend the activities of the three modes of material nature. Of course in the material world the mode of goodness is accepted as the best, and one can be promoted to the higher planetary systems by being on the *sattva-guṇa* platform. However, that is not perfection. One must come to the conclusion that even the *sattva-guṇa* platform is also not good. One may dream that he has become a king with a good family, wife and children, but immediately at the end of that dream he comes to the conclusion that it is false. Similarly, all kinds of material happiness are undesirable for a person who wants spiritual salvation. If a person does not come to the conclusion that he has nothing to do with any kind of material happiness, he cannot come to the platform of understanding the Absolute Truth, or *tattva-jñāna. Karmīs, jñānīs* and *yogīs* are after some material elevation. The *karmīs* work hard day and night for some bodily comfort, and the *jñānīs* simply speculate about how to get out of the entanglement of *karma* and merge into the Brahman effulgence. The *yogīs* are very much addicted to the acquisition of material perfection and magical powers. All of them are trying to be materially perfect. but a devotee very easily comes to the platform of *nirguṇa* in devotional service, and consequently for the devotee the results of *karma, jñāna* and *yoga* become very insignificant. Therefore only the devotee is on the platform of *tattva-jñāna,* not the others. Of course the *jñānī's* position is better than that of the *karmī* but that position is also insufficient. The *jñānī* must actually become liberated. and after liberation he may be situated in devotional service (*mad-bhaktiṁ labhate parām*).

TEXT 4

यावन्मनो रजसा पूरुषस्य
सत्त्वेन वा तमसा वानुरुद्धम् ।

चेतोभिराकूतिभिरातनोति
निरङ्कुशं कुशलं चेतरं वा ॥ ४ ॥

yāvan mano rajasā pūruṣasya
sattvena vā tamasā vānuruddham
cetobhir ākūtibhir ātanoti
niraṅkuśaṁ kuśalaṁ cetaraṁ vā

yāvat—as long as; *manaḥ*—the mind; *rajasā*—by the mode of passion; *pūruṣasya*—of the living entity; *sattvena*—by the mode of goodness; *vā*—or; *tamasā*—by the mode of darkness; *vā*—or; *anuruddham*—controlled; *cetobhiḥ*—by the knowledge-acquiring senses; *ākūtibhiḥ*—by the senses of action; *ātanoti*—expands; *niraṅkuśam*—independent like an elephant not controlled by a trident; *kuśalam*—auspiciousness; *ca*—also; *itaram*—other than auspiciousness, sinful activities; *vā*—or.

TRANSLATION

As long as the mind of the living entity is contaminated by the three modes of material nature (goodness, passion and ignorance), his mind is exactly like an independent, uncontrolled elephant. It simply expands its jurisdiction of pious and impious activities by using the senses. The result is that the living entity remains in the material world to enjoy and suffer pleasures and pains due to material activity.

PURPORT

In *Caitanya-caritāmṛta* it is said that material pious and impious activities are both opposed to the principle of devotional service. Devotional service means *mukti*, freedom from material entanglement, but pious and impious activities result in entanglement within this material world. If the mind is captivated by the pious and impious activities mentioned in the *Vedas*, one remains eternally in darkness; one cannot attain the absolute platform. To change the consciousness from ignorance to passion or from passion to goodness does not really solve the problem. As stated in *Bhagavad-gītā* (14.26), *sa guṇān samatītyaitān brahma-*

bhūyāya kalpate. One must come to the transcendental platform; otherwise life's mission is never fulfilled.

TEXT 5

स वासनात्मा विषयोपरक्तो
गुणप्रवाहो विकृतः षोडशात्मा ।
बिभ्रत्पृथङ्नामभि रूपभेद-
मन्तर्बहिष्ट्वं च पुरैस्तनोति ॥ ५ ॥

sa vāsanātmā viṣayoparakto
guṇa-pravāho vikṛtaḥ ṣoḍaśātmā
bibhrat pṛthaṅ-nāmabhi rūpa-bhedam
antar-bahiṣṭvaṁ ca purais tanoti

saḥ—that; *vāsanā*—endowed with many desires; *ātmā*—the mind; *viṣaya-uparaktaḥ*—attached to material happiness, sense gratification; *guṇa-pravāhaḥ*—driven by the force of either *sattva-guṇa, rajo-guṇa* or *tamo-guṇa; vikṛtaḥ*—transformed by lust and so on; *ṣoḍaśa-ātmā*—the chief of the sixteen material elements (the five gross elements, the ten senses and the mind); *bibhrat*—wandering; *pṛthak-nāmabhiḥ*—with separate names; *rūpa-bhedam*—assuming different forms; *antaḥ-bahiṣṭvam*—the quality of being first-class or last-class; *ca*—and; *puraiḥ*—with different bodily forms; *tanoti*—manifests.

TRANSLATION

Because the mind is absorbed in desires for pious and impious activities, it is naturally subjected to the transformations of lust and anger. In this way, it becomes attracted to material sense enjoyment. In other words, the mind is conducted by the modes of goodness, passion and ignorance. There are eleven senses and five material elements, and out of these sixteen items, the mind is the chief. Therefore the mind brings about birth in different types of bodies among demigods, human beings, animals and birds. When the mind is situated in a higher or lower position, it accepts a higher or lower material body.

PURPORT

Transmigration among the 8,400,000 species is due to the mind's being polluted by certain material qualities. Due to the mind, the soul is subjected to pious and impious activities. The continuation of material existence is like the waves of material nature. In this regard, Śrīla Bhaktivinoda Ṭhākura says, *māyāra vaśe yāccha bhese', khāccha hābuḍubu, bhāi:* "My dear brother, the spirit soul is completely under the control of *māyā*, and you are being carried away by its waves." This is also confirmed in *Bhagavad-gītā:*

prakṛteḥ kriyamāṇāni
guṇaiḥ karmāṇi sarvaśaḥ
ahaṅkāra-vimūḍhātmā
kartāham iti manyate

"The bewildered spirit soul, under the influence of the three modes of material nature, thinks himself the doer of activities, which are in actuality carried out by nature." (Bg. 3.27)

Material existence means being fully controlled by material nature. The mind is the center for accepting the dictations of material nature. In this way the living entity is carried away in different types of bodies continuously, millennium after millennium.

kṛṣṇa bhuli' sei jīva anādi-bahirmukha
ataeva māyā tāre deya saṁsāra-duḥkha
(*Caitanya-caritāmṛta, Madhya* 20.117)

Due to the living entity's forgetfulness of Kṛṣṇa, one is bound by the laws of material nature.

TEXT 6

दुःखं सुखं व्यतिरिक्तं च तीव्रं
कालोपपन्नं फलमाव्यनक्ति ।
आलिङ्ग्य मायारचितान्तरात्मा
स्वदेहिनं संसृतिचक्रकूटः ॥ ६ ॥

duḥkhaṁ sukhaṁ vyatiriktaṁ ca tīvraṁ
kālopapannaṁ phalam āvyanakti
āliṅgya māyā-racitāntarātmā
sva-dehinaṁ saṁsṛti-cakra-kūṭaḥ

duḥkham—unhappiness due to impious activities; *sukham*—happiness due to pious activities; *vyatiriktam*—illusion; *ca*—also; *tīvram*—very severe; *kāla-upapannam*—obtained in the course of time; *phalam*—the resultant action; *āvyanakti*—creates; *āliṅgya*—embracing; *māyā-racita*—created by material nature; *antaḥ-ātmā*—the mind; *sva-dehinam*—the living being himself; *saṁsṛti*—of the actions and reactions of material existence; *cakra-kūṭaḥ*—which deceives the living entity into the wheel.

TRANSLATION

The materialistic mind covering the living entity's soul carries it to different species of life. This is called continued material existence. Due to the mind, the living entity suffers or enjoys material distress and happiness. Being thus illusioned, the mind further creates pious and impious activities and their karma, and thus the soul becomes conditioned.

PURPORT

Mental activities under the influence of material nature cause happiness and distress within the material world. Being covered by illusion, the living entity eternally continues conditioned life under different designations. Such living entities are known as *nitya-baddha*, eternally conditioned. On the whole, the mind is the cause of conditioned life; therefore the entire yogic process is meant to control the mind and the senses. If the mind is controlled, the senses are automatically controlled, and therefore the soul is saved from the reactions of pious and impious activity. If the mind is engaged at the lotus feet of Lord Kṛṣṇa (*sa vai manaḥ kṛṣṇa-padāravindayoḥ*), the senses are automatically engaged in the Lord's service. When the mind and senses are engaged in devotional service, the living entity naturally becomes Kṛṣṇa conscious. As soon as one always thinks of Kṛṣṇa, he becomes a perfect *yogī*, as confirmed in *Bhagavad-gītā* (*yoginām api sarveṣāṁ mad-gatenāntarātmanā*). This *antarātmā*, the mind, is conditioned by material nature. As stated here, *māyā-racitāntarātmā sva-dehinaṁ saṁsṛti-cakra-kūṭaḥ:* the mind, being most powerful, covers the living entity and puts him in the waves of material existence.

TEXT 7

तावानयं व्यवहारः सदाविः
क्षेत्रज्ञसाक्ष्यो भवति स्थूलसूक्ष्मः ।
तस्मान्मनो लिङ्गमदो वदन्ति
गुणागुणत्वस्य परावरस्य ॥ ७ ॥

tāvān ayaṁ vyavahāraḥ sadāviḥ
kṣetrajña-sākṣyo bhavati sthūla-sūkṣmaḥ
tasmān mano liṅgam ado vadanti
guṇāguṇatvasya parāvarasya

tāvān—until that time; *ayam*—this; *vyavahāraḥ*—the artificial designations (being fat or skinny, or belonging to the demigods or human beings); *sadā*—always; *āviḥ*—manifesting; *kṣetra-jña*—of the living entity; *sākṣyaḥ*—testimony; *bhavati*—is; *sthūla-sūkṣmaḥ*—fat and skinny; *tasmāt*—therefore; *manaḥ*—the mind; *liṅgam*—the cause; *adaḥ*—this; *vadanti*—they say; *guṇa-aguṇatvasya*—of being absorbed in material qualities or devoid of material qualities; *para-avarasya*—and of lower and higher conditions of life.

TRANSLATION

The mind makes the living entity within this material world wander through different species of life, and thus the living entity experiences mundane affairs in different forms as a human being, demigod, fat person, skinny person and so forth. Learned scholars say that bodily appearance, bondage and liberation are caused by the mind.

PURPORT

Just as the mind is the cause of bondage, it can also be the cause of liberation. The mind is described here as *para-avara. Para* means transcendental, and *avara* means material. When the mind is engaged in the Lord's service (*sa vai manaḥ kṛṣṇa-padāravindayoḥ*), it is called *para*, transcendental. When the mind is engaged in material sense gratification, it is called *avara*, or material. At the present moment, in our conditioned state, our mind is fully absorbed in material sense gratification, but it can be purified and brought to its original Kṛṣṇa consciousness by the process of devotional service. We have often given the example of Ambarīṣa Mahārāja. *Sa vai manaḥ kṛṣṇa-padāravindayor vacāṁsi vaikuṇṭha-guṇānuvarṇane.* The mind must be controlled in Kṛṣṇa consciousness. The tongue can be utilized to spread the message of Kṛṣṇa and glorify the Lord or take *prasāda*, the remnants of food offered to Kṛṣṇa. *Sevonmukhe hi jihvādau:* when one utilizes the tongue in the service of the Lord, the other senses can become purified. As stated in the *Nārada-pañcarātra, sarvopādhi-vinirmuktaṁ tat-paratvena nirmalam:* when the mind and senses are purified, one's total existence is purified, and one's designations are also purified. One no longer considers himself a human being, a demigod, cat, dog, Hindu, Muslim and so forth. When the senses and mind are purified and one is fully engaged in Kṛṣṇa's service, one can be liberated and return home, back to Godhead.

TEXT 8

गुणानुरक्तं व्यसनाय जन्तोः
क्षेमाय नैर्गुण्यमथो मनः स्यात् ।
यथा प्रदीपो घृतवर्तिमश्नन्
शिखाः सधूमा भजति ह्यन्यदा स्वम् ।
पदं तथा गुणकर्मानुबद्धं
वृत्तीर्मनः श्रयतेऽन्यत्र तत्त्वम् ॥ ८ ॥

guṇānuraktaṁ vyasanāya jantoḥ
kṣemāya nairguṇyam atho manaḥ syāt
yathā pradīpo ghṛta-vartim aśnan
śikhāḥ sadhūmā bhajati hy anyadā svam
padaṁ tathā guṇa-karmānubaddhaṁ
vṛttīr manaḥ śrayate 'nyatra tattvam

guṇa-anuraktam—being attached to the material modes of nature; *vyasanāya*—for the conditioning in material existence; *jantoḥ*—of the living entity; *kṣemāya*—for the ultimate welfare; *nairguṇyam*—being unaffected by the material modes of nature; *atho*—thus; *manaḥ*—the mind; *syāt*—becomes; *yathā*—as much as; *pradīpaḥ*—a lamp; *ghṛta-vartim*—a wick within clarified butter; *aśnan*—burning; *śikhāḥ*—the flame; *sādhūmāḥ*—with smoke; *bhajati*—enjoys; *hi*—certainly; *anyadā*—otherwise; *svam*—its own original; *padam*—position; *tathā*—so; *guṇa-karma-anubaddham*—bound by the modes of nature and the reactions of material activities; *vṛttīḥ*—various engagements; *manaḥ*—the mind; *śrayate*—takes shelter of; *anyatra*—otherwise; *tattvam*—its original condition.

TRANSLATION

When the living entity's mind becomes absorbed in the sense gratification of the material world, it brings about his conditioned life and suffering within the material situation. However, when the mind becomes unattached to material enjoyment, it becomes the cause of liberation. When the flame in a lamp burns the wick improperly, the lamp is blackened, but when the lamp is filled with ghee and is burning properly, there is bright illumination. Similarly, when the mind is absorbed in material sense gratification, it causes suffering, and when detached from material sense gratification, it brings about the original brightness of Kṛṣṇa consciousness.

PURPORT

It is therefore concluded that the mind is the cause of material existence and liberation also. Everyone is suffering in this material world because of the mind; it is therefore proper to train the mind or to cleanse the mind from material attachment and engage it fully in the Lord's service. This is called spiritual engagement. As confirmed in *Bhagavad-gītā:*

māṁ ca yo 'vyabhicāreṇa
bhakti-yogena sevate
sa guṇān samatītyaitān
brahma-bhūyāya kalpate

"One who engages in full devotional service, who does not fall down in any circumstance, at once transcends the modes of material nature and thus comes to the level of Brahman." (Bg. 14.26)

We should engage the mind fully in Kṛṣṇa conscious activities. Then it will be the cause of our liberation, for our returning home, back to Godhead. However, if we keep the mind engaged in material activities for sense gratification, it will cause continuous bondage and will make us remain in this material world in different bodies, suffering the consequences of our different actions.

TEXT 9

एकादशासन्मनसो हि वृत्तय
आकूतयः पञ्च धियोऽभिमानः ।
मात्राणि कर्माणि पुरं च तासां
वदन्ति हैकादश वीर भूमीः ॥ ९ ॥

ekādaśāsan manaso hi vṛttaya
ākūtayaḥ pañca dhiyo 'bhimānaḥ
mātrāṇi karmāṇi puraṁ ca tāsāṁ
vadanti haikādaśa vīra bhūmīḥ

ekādaśa—eleven; *āsan*—there are; *manasaḥ*—of the mind; *hi*—certainly; *vṛttayaḥ*—activities; *ākūtayaḥ*—senses of action; *pañca*—five; *dhiyaḥ*—senses for gathering knowledge; *abhimānaḥ*—the false ego; *mātrāṇi*—different sense objects; *karmāṇi*—different material activities; *puram ca*—and the body, society, nation, family or place of nativity; *tāsām*—of those functions; *vadanti*—they say; *ha*—oh; *ekādaśa*—eleven; *vīra*—O hero; *bhūmīḥ*—fields of activity.

TRANSLATION

There are five working senses and five knowledge-acquiring senses. There is also the false ego. In this way, there are eleven items for the mind's functions. O hero, the objects of the senses [such as sound and touch], the organic activities [such as

evacuation] and the different types of bodies, society, friendship and personality are considered by learned scholars the fields of activity for the functions of the mind.

PURPORT

The mind is the controller of the five knowledge-acquiring senses and the five working senses. Each sense has its particular field of activity. In all cases, the mind is the controller or owner. By the false ego one thinks oneself the body and thinks in terms of "my body, my house, my family, my society, my nation" and so on. These false identifications are due to the expansions of the false ego. Thus one thinks that he is this or that. Thus the living entity becomes entangled in material existence.

TEXT 10

गन्धाकृतिस्पर्शरसश्रवांसि
विसर्गरत्यर्त्यभिजल्पशिल्पाः ।
एकादशं स्वीकरणं ममेति
शय्यामहं द्वादशमेक आहुः ॥१०॥

gandhākṛti-sparśa-rasa-śravāṁsi
visarga-raty-arty-abhijalpa-śilpāḥ
ekādaśaṁ svīkaraṇaṁ mameti
śayyām ahaṁ dvādaśam eka āhuḥ

gandha—smell; *ākṛti*—form; *sparśa*—touch; *rasa*—taste; *śravāṁsi*—and sound; *visarga*—evacuating; *rati*—sexual intercourse; *arti*—movement; *abhijalpa*—speaking; *śilpāḥ*—grasping or releasing; *ekādaśam*—eleventh; *svīkaraṇam*—accepting as; *mama*—mine; *iti*—thus; *śayyām*—this body; *aham*—I; *dvādaśam*—twelfth; *eke*—some; *āhuḥ*—have said.

TRANSLATION

Sound, touch, form, taste and smell are the objects of the five knowledge-acquiring senses. Speech, touch, movement, evacuation and sexual intercourse are the objects of the working senses.

Besides this, there is another conception by which one thinks, "This is my body, this is my society, this is my family, this is my nation," and so forth. This eleventh function, that of the mind, is called the false ego. According to some philosophers, this is the twelfth function, and its field of activity is the body.

PURPORT

There are different objects for the eleven items. Through the nose we can smell, by the eyes we can see, by the ears we can hear, and in this way we gather knowledge. Similarly, there are the *karmendriyas*, the working senses—the hands, legs, genitals, rectum, mouth and so forth. When the false ego expands, it makes one think, "This is my body, family, society, country," etc.

TEXT 11

द्रव्यस्वभावाशयकर्मकालै-
रेकादशामी मनसो विकाराः ।
सहस्रशः शतशः कोटिशश्च
क्षेत्रज्ञतो न मिथो न स्वतः स्युः ॥११॥

dravya-svabhāvāśaya-karma-kālair
ekādaśāmī manaso vikārāḥ
sahasraśaḥ śataśaḥ koṭiśaś ca
kṣetrajñato na mitho na svataḥ syuḥ

dravya—by physical objects; *sva-bhāva*—by nature as the cause of development; *āśaya*—by culture; *karma*—by predestined resultant actions; *kālaiḥ*—by time; *ekādaśa*—eleven; *amī*—all these; *manasaḥ*—of the mind; *vikārāḥ*—transformations; *sahasraśaḥ*—in thousands; *śataśaḥ*—in hundreds; *koṭiśaḥ ca*—and in millions; *kṣetra-jñataḥ*—from the original Supreme Personality of Godhead; *na*—not; *mithaḥ*—one another; *na*—nor; *svataḥ*—from themselves; *syuḥ*—are.

TRANSLATION

The physical elements, nature, the original cause, culture, destiny and the time element are all material causes. Agitated by

these material causes, the eleven functions transform into hundreds of functions and then into thousands and then into millions. But all these transformations do not take place automatically by mutual combination. Rather, they are under the direction of the Supreme Personality of Godhead.

PURPORT

One should not think that all the interactions of the physical elements, gross and subtle, that cause the transformation of mind and consciousness are working independently. They are under the direction of the Supreme Personality of Godhead. In *Bhagavad-gītā* (15.15), Kṛṣṇa says that the Lord is situated in everyone's heart (*sarvasya cāhaṁ hṛdi sanniviṣṭo mattaḥ smṛtir jñānam apohanaṁ ca*). As mentioned herein, Supersoul (*kṣetrajña*) is directing everything. The living entity is also *kṣetrajña*, but the supreme *kṣetrajña* is the Supreme Personality of Godhead. He is the witness and order giver. Under His direction, everything takes place. The different inclinations of the living entity are created by his own nature or his expectations, and he is trained by the Supreme Personality of Godhead through the agency of material nature. The body, nature and the physical elements are under the direction of the Supreme Personality of Godhead. They do not function automatically. Nature is neither independent nor automatic. As confirmed in *Bhagavad-gītā*, the Supreme Personality of Godhead is behind nature.

mayādhyakṣeṇa prakṛtiḥ
sūyate sa-carācaram
hetunānena kaunteya
jagad viparivartate

"This material nature is working under My direction, O son of Kuntī, and it is producing all moving and unmoving beings. By its rule this manifestation is created and annihilated again and again." (Bg. 9.10)

TEXT 12

क्षेत्रज्ञ एता मनसो विभूती-
जीवस्य मायारचितस्य नित्याः ।

आविर्हिताः क्वापि तिरोहिताश्च
शुद्धो विचष्टे ह्यविशुद्धकर्तुः ॥१२॥

kṣetrajña etā manaso vibhūtīr
jīvasya māyā-racitasya nityāḥ
āvirhitāḥ kvāpi tirohitāś ca
śuddho vicaṣṭe hy aviśuddha-kartuḥ

kṣetra-jñaḥ—the individual soul; *etāḥ*—all these; *manasaḥ*—of the mind; *vibhūtīḥ*—different activities; *jīvasya*—of the living entity; *māyā-racitasya*—created by the external, material energy; *nityāḥ*—from time immemorial; *āvirhitāḥ*—sometimes manifested; *kvāpi*—somewhere; *tirohitāḥ ca*—and not manifested; *śuddhaḥ*—purified; *vicaṣṭe*—sees this; *hi*—certainly; *aviśuddha*—unpurified; *kartuḥ*—of the doer.

TRANSLATION

The individual soul bereft of Kṛṣṇa consciousness has many ideas and activities created in the mind by the external energy. They have been existing from time immemorial. Sometimes they are manifest in the wakening state and in the dream state, but during deep sleep [unconsciousness] or trance, they disappear. A person who is liberated in this life [jīvan-mukta] can see all these things vividly.

PURPORT

As stated in *Bhagavad-gītā* (13.3), *kṣetrajñaṁ cāpi māṁ viddhi sarva-kṣetreṣu bhārata.* There are two kinds of *kṣetrajña,* or living beings. One is the individual living being, and the other is the supreme living being. The ordinary living being knows about his body to some extent, but the Supreme, Paramātmā, knows the condition of all bodies. The individual living being is localized, and the Supreme, Paramātmā, is all-pervading. In this *śloka* the word *kṣetrajña* refers to an ordinary living being, not the supreme living being. This ordinary living being is of two kinds—*nitya-baddha* or *nitya-mukta.* One is eternally conditioned and the other eternally liberated. The eternally liberated living beings are in the Vaikuṇṭha *jagat*, the spiritual world, and they never fall into the material world. Those in the material world are conditioned souls, *nitya-baddha.* The *nitya-baddhas* can become liberated by controlling the mind because the cause of conditioned life is the mind. When the mind is trained and the soul is not under the mind's control, the soul can be liberated even in this material world. When it is liberated, one is called *jīvan-mukta.* A *jīvan-mukta* knows how he has become conditioned; therefore he tries to purify himself and return home, back to Godhead. The eternally conditioned soul is eternally conditioned because he is controlled by the mind. The conditioned state and liberated state are compared to the sleeping, unconscious state and the awakened state. Those who are sleeping and unconscious are eternally conditioned, but those who are awake understand that they are eternally part and parcel of the Supreme Personality of Godhead, Kṛṣṇa. Therefore even in this material world, they engage in Kṛṣṇa's service. As confirmed by Śrīla Rūpa Gosvāmī: *īhā yasya harer dāsye.* If one takes to Kṛṣṇa's service, he is liberated, even though he appears to be a conditioned soul within the material world. *Jīvan-muktaḥ sa ucyate.* In any condition, one is to be considered liberated if his only business is to serve Kṛṣṇa.

TEXTS 13-14

क्षेत्रज्ञ आत्मा पुरुषः पुराणः
साक्षात्स्वयंज्योतिरजः परेशः ।
नारायणो भगवान् वासुदेवः
स्वमाययाऽऽत्मन्यवधीयमानः ॥१३॥
यथानिलः स्थावरजङ्गमाना-
मात्मस्वरूपेण निविष्ट ईशेत् ।
एवं परो भगवान् वासुदेवः
क्षेत्रज्ञ आत्मेदमनुप्रविष्टः ॥१४॥

kṣetrajña ātmā puruṣaḥ purāṇaḥ
sākṣāt svayaṁ jyotir ajaḥ pareśaḥ
nārāyaṇo bhagavān vāsudevaḥ
sva-māyayātmany avadhīyamānaḥ

yathānilaḥ sthāvara-jaṅgamānām
ātma-svarūpeṇa niviṣṭa īśet
evaṁ paro bhagavān vāsudevaḥ
kṣetrajña ātmedam anupraviṣṭaḥ

kṣetra-jñaḥ—the Supreme Personality of Godhead*; *ātmā*—all-pervading, present everywhere; *puruṣaḥ*—the unrestricted controller, who has unlimited power; *purāṇaḥ*—the original; *sākṣāt*—perceivable by hearing from the authorities and by direct perception; *svayam*—personal; *jyotiḥ*—manifesting His bodily rays (the Brahman effulgence); *ajaḥ*—never born; *pareśaḥ*—the Supreme Personality of Godhead; *nārāyaṇaḥ*—the resting place of all living entities; *bhagavān*—the Personality of Godhead with six full opulences; *vāsudevaḥ*—the shelter of everything, manifested and nonmanifest; *sva-māyayā*—by His own potency; *ātmani*—in His own self, or in the ordinary living entities; *avadhīyamānaḥ*—existing as the controller; *yathā*—as much as; *anilaḥ*—the air; *sthāvara*—of nonmoving living entities; *janīgamānām*—and of the moving living entities; *ātma-svarūpeṇa*—by His expansion as the Supersoul; *niviṣṭaḥ*—entered; *īśet*—controls; *evam*—thus; *paraḥ*—transcendental; *bhagavān*—the Supreme Personality of Godhead; *vāsudevaḥ*—the shelter of everything; *kṣetra-jñaḥ*—known as *kṣetrajña; ātmā*—the vital force; *idam*—this material world; *anupraviṣṭaḥ*—entered within.

TRANSLATION

There are two kinds of kṣetrajña—the living entity, as explained above, and the Supreme Personality of Godhead, who is explained as follows. He is the all-pervading cause of creation. He is full in Himself and is not dependent on others. He is perceived by hearing and direct perception. He is self-effulgent and does not experience birth, death, old age or disease. He is the controller of all the demigods, beginning with Lord Brahmā. He is called Nārāyaṇa, and He is the shelter of living entities after the annihilation of this material world. He is full of all opulences, and He is the resting

---

*In text 12 the word *kṣetrajña* described the living being, but in this verse the word *kṣetrajña* indicates the Supreme Person.

place of everything material. He is therefore known as Vāsudeva, the Supreme Personality of Godhead. By His own potency, He is present within the hearts of all living entities, just as the air or vital force is within the bodies of all beings, moving and nonmoving. In this way He controls the body. In His partial feature, the Supreme Personality of Godhead enters all bodies and controls them.

PURPORT

This is confirmed in *Bhagavad-gītā* (15.15). *Sarvasya cāhaṁ hṛdi sanniviṣṭo mattaḥ smṛtir jñānam apohanaṁ ca.* Every living being is controlled by the supreme living being, Paramātmā, who resides within everyone's heart. He is the *puruṣa*, the *puruṣa-avatāra*, who creates this material world. The first *puruṣa-avatāra* is Mahā-Viṣṇu, and that Mahā-Viṣṇu is the plenary portion of the plenary portion of the Supreme Personality of Godhead, Kṛṣṇa. Kṛṣṇa's first expansion is Baladeva, and His next expansions are Vāsudeva, Saṅkarṣaṇa, Aniruddha and Pradyumna. Vāsudeva is the original cause of the *brahmajyoti*, and the *brahmajyoti* is the expansion of the rays of the body of Vāsudeva.

yasya prabhā prabhavato jagad-aṇḍa-koṭi-
koṭiṣv aśeṣa-vasudhādi-vibhūti-bhinnam
tad brahma niṣkalam anantam aśeṣa-bhūtaṁ
govindam ādi-puruṣaṁ tam ahaṁ bhajāmi

"I worship Govinda, the primeval Lord, who is endowed with great power. The glowing effulgence of His transcendental form is the impersonal Brahman, which is absolute, complete and unlimited and which displays the varieties of countless planets, with their different opulences, in millions and millions of universes." (*Brahma-saṁhitā* 5.40) The Supreme Personality of Godhead is thus described in *Bhagavad-gītā:*

mayā tatam idaṁ sarvaṁ
jagad avyakta-mūrtinā
mat-sthāni sarva-bhūtāni
na cāhaṁ teṣv avasthitaḥ

"By Me, in My unmanifested form, this entire universe is pervaded. All beings are in Me, but I am not in them." (Bg. 9.4)

This is the position of the plenary expansions of Kṛṣṇa as the all-pervading Vāsudeva, Saṅkarṣaṇa, Pradyumna and Aniruddha.

TEXT 15

न यावदेतां तनुभृन्नरेन्द्र
विधूय मायां वयुनोदयेन ।
विमुक्तसङ्गो जितषट्सपत्नो
वेदात्मतत्त्वं भ्रमतीह तावत् ॥१५॥

na yāvad etāṁ tanu-bhṛn narendra
vidhūya māyāṁ vayunodayena
vimukta-saṅgo jita-ṣaṭ-sapatno
vedātma-tattvaṁ bhramatīha tāvat

na—not; *yāvat*—as long as; *etām*—this; *tanu-bhṛt*—one who has accepted a material body; *narendra*—O King; *vidhūya māyām*—washing away the infection accumulated because of contamination by the material world; *vayunā udayena*—by awakening of transcendental knowledge due to good association and study of the Vedic literatures; *vimukta-saṅgaḥ*—free from all material association; *jita-ṣaṭ-sapatnaḥ*—conquering the six enemies (the five knowledge-acquiring senses and the mind); *veda*—knows; *ātma-tattvam*—spiritual truth; *bhramati*—he wanders; *iha*—in this material world; *tāvat*—until that time.

TRANSLATION

My dear King Rahūgaṇa, as long as the conditioned soul accepts the material body and is not freed from the contamination of material enjoyment, and as long as he does not conquer his six enemies and come to the platform of self-realization by awakening his spiritual knowledge, he has to wander among different places and different species of life in this material world.

PURPORT

When one's mind is absorbed in the material conception, he thinks that he belongs to a particular nation, family, country or creed. These are all called *upādhis,* designations, and one has to become freed from them (*sarvopādhi-vinirmuktam*). As long as one is not freed, he has to continue conditioned life in material existence. The human form of life is meant for cleansing away these misconceptions. If this is not done, one has to repeat the cycle of birth and death and thus suffer all material conditions.

TEXT 16

न यावदेतन्मन आत्मलिङ्गं
संसारतापावपनं जनस्य ।
यच्छोकमोहामयरागलोभ-
वैरानुबन्धं ममतां विधत्ते ॥१६॥

na yāvad etan mana ātma-liṅgaṁ
saṁsāra-tāpāvapanaṁ janasya
yac choka-mohāmaya-rāga-lobha-
vairānubandhaṁ mamatāṁ vidhatte

na—not; *yāvat*—as long as; *etat*—this; *manaḥ*—mind; *ātma-liṅgam*—existing as the false designation of the soul; *saṁsāra-tāpa*—of the miseries of this material world; *āvapanam*—the growing ground; *janasya*—of the living being; *yat*—which; *śoka*—of lamentation; *moha*—of illusion; *āmaya*—of disease; *rāga*—of attachment; *lobha*—of greed; *vaira*—of enmity; *anubandham*—the consequence; *mamatām*—the sense of ownership; *vidhatte*—gives.

TRANSLATION

The soul's designation, the mind, is the cause of all tribulations in the material world. As long as this fact is unknown to the conditioned living entity, he has to accept the miserable condition of the material body and wander within this universe in different positions. Because the mind is affected by disease, lamentation, illu-

sion, attachment, greed and enmity, it creates bondage and a false sense of intimacy within this material world.

PURPORT

The mind is the cause of both material bondage and liberation. The impure mind thinks, "I am this body." The pure mind knows that he is not the material body; therefore the mind is considered to be the root of all material designations. Until the living entity is aloof from the association and contaminations of this material world, the mind will be absorbed in such material things as birth, death, disease, illusion, attachment, greed and enmity. In this way the living entity is conditioned, and he suffers material miseries.

TEXT 17

भ्रातृव्यमेनं तदद‍्भ्रवीर्य-
मुपेक्षयाध्येधितमप्रमत्तः ।
गुरोर्हरेश्चरणोपासनास्त्रो
जहि व्यलीकं स्वयमात्ममोषम् ॥१७॥

bhrātṛvyam enaṁ tad adabhra-vīryam
upekṣayādhyedhitam apramattaḥ
guror hareś caraṇopāsanāstro
jahi vyalīkaṁ svayam ātma-moṣam

bhrātṛvyam—the formidable enemy; *enam*—this mind; *tat*—that; *adabhra-vīryam*—very, very powerful; *upekṣayā*—by neglecting; *adhyedhitam*—unnecessarily increased in power; *apramattaḥ*—one who is without illusion; *guroḥ*—of the spiritual master; *hareḥ*—of the Supreme Personality of Godhead; *caraṇa*—of the lotus feet; *upāsanā-astraḥ*—applying the weapon of worshiping; *jahi*—conquer; *vyalīkam*—false; *svayam*—personally; *ātma-moṣam*—which covers the constitutional position of the living entity.

TRANSLATION

This uncontrolled mind is the greatest enemy of the living entity. If one neglects it or gives it a chance, it will grow more and

more powerful and will become victorious. Although it is not factual, it is very strong. It covers the constitutional position of the soul. O King, please try to conquer this mind by the weapon of service to the lotus feet of the spiritual master and of the Supreme Personality of Godhead. Do this with great care.

PURPORT

There is one easy weapon with which the mind can be conquered—neglect. The mind is always telling us to do this or that; therefore we should be very expert in disobeying the mind's orders. Gradually the mind should be trained to obey the orders of the soul. It is not that one should obey the orders of the mind. Śrīla Bhaktisiddhānta Sarasvatī Ṭhākura used to say that to control the mind one should beat it with shoes many times just after awakening and again before going to sleep. In this way one can control the mind. This is the instruction of all the *śāstras.* If one does not do so, one is doomed to follow the dictations of the mind. Another bona fide process is to abide strictly by the orders of the spiritual master and engage in the Lord's service. Then the mind will be automatically controlled. Śrī Caitanya Mahāprabhu has instructed Śrīla Rūpa Gosvāmī:

brahmāṇḍa bhramite kona bhāgyavān jīva
guru-kṛṣṇa-prasāde pāya bhakti-latā-bīja

When one receives the seed of devotional service by the mercy of the *guru* and Kṛṣṇa, the Supreme Personality of Godhead, one's real life begins. If one abides by the orders of the spiritual master, by the grace of Kṛṣṇa he is freed from service to the mind.

Thus end the Bhaktivedanta purports of the Fifth Canto, Eleventh Chapter of the Śrīmad-Bhāgavatam, *entitled "Jaḍa Bharata Instructs King Rahūgaṇa."*

CHAPTER TWELVE

Conversation Between Mahārāja Rahūgaṇa and Jaḍa Bharata

Because Mahārāja Rahūgaṇa was still doubtful about his enlightenment, he asked the *brāhmaṇa* Jaḍa Bharata to repeat his instructions and clarify ideas he could not understand. In this chapter, Mahārāja Rahūgaṇa offers his respectful obeisances to Jaḍa Bharata, who was concealing his real position. The King could understand by his speech how exalted and advanced he was in spiritual knowledge. He very much regretted his offense against him. Mahārāja Rahūgaṇa was bitten by the serpent of ignorance, but was cured by the nectarean words of Jaḍa Bharata. Later, because he was doubtful about the subjects discussed, he made further inquiries, one question after another. First he wanted to be released from the offense he had committed at the lotus feet of Jaḍa Bharata.

Mahārāja Rahūgaṇa was somewhat unhappy at not being able to grasp Jaḍa Bharata's instructions, which were full of meaning that could not be understood by a materialistic person. Therefore Jaḍa Bharata repeated his instructions more clearly. He said that on the surface of the globe all living entities, moving and unmoving, were but transformations of the earth in different ways. The King was very proud of his king's body, but that body was simply another transformation of the earth. Out of his false prestige, the King was misbehaving toward the palanquin carrier, as a master toward a servant, and he was actually very unkind to other living entities. Consequently King Rahūgaṇa was unfit to give protection to the citizens, and because he was ignorant, he was unfit to be counted among advanced philosophers. Everything in the material world is but a transformation of the earth, although things have different names according to their transformations. Actually the varieties are one and the same, and ultimately all these varieties are vanquished into atoms. Nothing is permanent in this material world. The variety of things and their distinctions are simply mental concoctions. The Absolute Truth is beyond illusion and is manifest in three features—impersonal Brahman, localized Paramātmā and the Supreme Personality of Godhead. Ultimate realization of the Absolute Truth is the Supreme Personality of Godhead, called Vāsudeva by His devotees. Unless one is blessed with the dust from the feet of a pure devotee on his head, one cannot possibly become a devotee of the Supreme Personality of Godhead.

Jaḍa Bharata also told about his own previous birth and informed the King that by the grace of the Lord he still remembered all the incidents of his past life. Due to the activities of his past life, Jaḍa Bharata was being very cautious and was therefore assuming the characteristics of a deaf and dumb man to avoid mingling with the material world. Association with the material modes of nature is very powerful. The bad association of materialistic men can be avoided only in the association of devotees. In the association of devotees, one is given an opportunity to render devotional service in nine different ways—*śravaṇaṁ kīrtanaṁ viṣṇoḥ smaraṇaṁ pāda-sevanam arcanaṁ vandanaṁ dāsyaṁ sakhyam ātma-nivedanam.* In this way, in the association of devotees, one can pass over material association, cross over the ocean of nescience and return home, back to Godhead.

TEXT 1

रहूगण उवाच
नमो नमः कारणविग्रहाय
स्वरूपतुच्छीकृतविग्रहाय ।
नमोऽवधूत द्विजबन्धुलिङ्ग-
निगूढनित्यानुभवाय तुभ्यम् ॥ १ ॥

rahūgaṇa uvāca
namo namaḥ kāraṇa-vigrahāya
svarūpa-tucchīkṛta-vigrahāya
namo 'vadhūta dvija-bandhu-liṅga-
nigūḍha-nityānubhavāya tubhyam

rahūgaṇaḥ uvāca—King Rahūgaṇa said; *namaḥ*—my respectful obeisances; *namaḥ*—obeisances; *kāraṇa-vigrahāya*—to one whose body emanates from the Supreme Person, the cause of all causes; *svarūpa-*

tucchīkṛta-vigrahāya—who has completely removed all the contradictions of the scriptures by manifesting his true self; *namaḥ*—respectful obeisances; *avadhūta*—O master of all mystic power; *dvija-bandhu-liṅga*—by the characteristics of a person born in a *brāhmaṇa* family but not executing the duties of a *brāhmaṇa; nigūḍha*—covered; *nitya-anubhavāya*—to him whose eternal self-realization; *tubhyam*—to you.

TRANSLATION

King Rahūgaṇa said: O most exalted personality, you are not different from the Supreme Personality of Godhead. By the influence of your true self, all kinds of contradiction in the śāstras have been removed. In the dress of a friend of a brāhmaṇa, you are hiding your transcendental blissful position. I offer my respectful obeisances unto you.

PURPORT

From the *Brahma-saṁhitā* we understand the Supreme Personality of Godhead is the cause of all causes (*sarva-kāraṇa-kāraṇam*). Ṛṣabhadeva was the direct incarnation of the Supreme Personality of Godhead, the cause of all causes. His son, Bharata Mahārāja, who was now acting as the *brāhmaṇa* Jaḍa Bharata, had received his body from the cause of all causes. Therefore he is addressed as *kāraṇa-vigrahāya.*

TEXT 2

ज्वरामयार्तस्य यथागदं सत्
निदाघदग्धस्य यथा हिमाम्भः ।
कुदेहमानाहिविदष्टदृष्टेः
ब्रह्मन् वचस्तेऽमृतमौषधं मे ॥ २ ॥

jvarāmayārtasya yathāgadaṁ sat
nidāgha-dagdhasya yathā himāmbhaḥ
kudeha-mānāhi-vidaṣṭa-dṛṣṭeḥ
brahman vacas te 'mṛtam auṣadhaṁ me

jvara—of a fever; *āmaya*—by the disease; *ārtasya*—of a distressed person; *yathā*—just as; *agadam*—the medicine; *sat*—right; *nidāgha-*

dagdhasya—of one scorched by the heat of the sun; *yathā*—just as; *hima-ambhaḥ*—very cold water; *ku-deha*—in this body made of matter and full of dirty things such as stool and urine; *māna*—of pride; *ahi*—by the serpent; *vidaṣṭa*—bitten; *dṛṣṭeḥ*—of one whose vision; *brahman*—O best of the *brāhmaṇas; vacaḥ*—words; *te*—your; *amṛtam*—nectar; *auṣadham*—medicine; *me*—for me.

TRANSLATION

O best of the brāhmaṇas, my body is filled with dirty things, and my vision has been bitten by the serpent of pride. Due to my material conceptions, I am diseased. Your nectarean instructions are the proper medicine for one suffering from such a fever, and they are cooling waters for one scorched by the heat.

PURPORT

The conditioned soul has a body full of dirty things—bones, blood, urine, stool and so forth. Nonetheless, the most intelligent men in this material world think they are these combinations of blood, bone, urine and stool. If this is so, why can't other intelligent men be made with these ingredients, which are so readily available? The entire world is going on under the bodily conception and creating a hellish condition unfit for any gentleman's living. The instructions given to King Rahūgaṇa by Jaḍa Bharata are very valuable. They are like the medicine that can save one from a snakebite. The Vedic instructions are like nectar and cool water for one suffering from scorching heat.

TEXT 3

तस्माद्भवन्तं मम संशयार्थं
प्रक्ष्यामि पश्चादधुना सुबोधम् ।
अध्यात्मयोगग्रथितं तवोक्त-
माख्याहि कौतूहलचेतसो मे ॥ ३ ॥

tasmād bhavantaṁ mama saṁśayārthaṁ
prakṣyāmi paścād adhunā subodham

adhyātma-yoga-grathitaṁ tavoktam
ākhyāhi kautūhala-cetaso me

tasmāt—therefore; *bhavantam*—to you; *mama*—of me; *saṁśaya-artham*—the subject matter that is not clear to me; *prakṣyāmi*—I shall submit; *paścāt*—afterwards; *adhunā*—now; *su-bodham*—so that it can be clearly understood; *adhyātma-yoga*—of mystic instruction for self-realization; *grathitam*—as composed; *tava*—your; *uktam*—speech; *ākhyāhi*—please explain again; *kautūhala-cetasaḥ*—whose mind is very inquisitive to understand the mystery of such statements; *me*—to me.

TRANSLATION

Whatever doubts I have about a particular subject matter I shall ask you about later. For the time being, these mysterious yoga instructions you have given me for self-realization appear very difficult to understand. Please repeat them in a simple way so that I can understand them. My mind is very inquisitive, and I want to understand this clearly.

PURPORT

The Vedic literature instructs: *tasmād guruṁ prapadyeta jijñāsuḥ śreya uttamam.* An intelligent man must be very inquisitive to know the transcendental science deeply. Therefore one must approach a *guru,* a spiritual master. Although Jaḍa Bharata explained everything to Mahārāja Rahūgaṇa, it appears that his intelligence was not perfect enough to understand clearly. He therefore requested a further explanation. As stated in *Bhagavad-gītā* (4.34): *tad viddhi praṇipātena paripraśnena sevayā.* The student must approach a spiritual master and surrender unto him fully (*praṇipātena*). He must also question him in order to understand his instructions (*paripraśnena*). One should not only surrender to the spiritual master but also render loving service unto him (*sevayā*) so that the spiritual master will be pleased with the student and explain the transcendental subject matter more clearly. A challenging spirit before the spiritual master should be avoided if one is at all interested in learning the Vedic instructions in depth.

TEXT 4

यदाह योगेश्वर दृश्यमानं
क्रियाफलं सद्व्यवहारमूलम् ।
न ह्यञ्जसा तत्त्वविमर्शनाय
भवानमुष्मिन् भ्रमते मनो मे ॥ ४ ॥

yad āha yogeśvara dṛśyamānaṁ
kriyā-phalaṁ sad-vyavahāra-mūlam
na hy añjasā tattva-vimarśanāya
bhavān amuṣmin bhramate mano me

yat—that which; *āha*—have said; *yoga-īśvara*—O master of mystic power; *dṛśyamānam*—being clearly seen; *kriyā-phalam*—the results of moving the body here and there, such as feeling fatigue; *sat*—existing; *vyavahāra-mūlam*—whose basis is etiquette alone; *na*—not; *hi*—certainly; *añjasā*—on the whole, or in fact; *tattva-vimarśanāya*—for understanding the truth by consultation; *bhavān*—your good self; *amuṣmin*—in that explanation; *bhramate*—is bewildered; *manaḥ*—mind; *me*—my.

TRANSLATION

O master of yogic power, you said that fatigue resulting from moving the body here and there is appreciated by direct perception, but actually there is no fatigue. It simply exists as a matter of formality. By such inquiries and answers, no one can come to the conclusion of the Absolute Truth. Because of your presentation of this statement, my mind is a little disturbed.

PURPORT

Formal inquiries and answers about the bodily conception do not constitute knowledge of the Absolute Truth. Knowledge of the Absolute Truth is quite different from the formal understanding of bodily pains and pleasures. In *Bhagavad-gītā* Lord Kṛṣṇa informs Arjuna that the pains and pleasures experienced in relation to the body are temporary; they come and go. One should not be disturbed by them but should tolerate them and continue with spiritual realization.

TEXTS 5-6

ब्राह्मण उवाच
अयं जनो नाम चलन् पृथिव्यां
यः पार्थिवः पार्थिव कस्य हेतोः ।
तस्यापि चाङ्घ्र्योरधि गुल्फजङ्घा-
जानूरुमध्योरशिरोधरांसाः ॥ ५ ॥
अंसेऽधि दार्वी शिबिका च यस्यां
सौवीरराजेत्यपदेश आस्ते ।
यस्मिन् भवान् रूढनिजाभिमानो
राजास्मि सिन्धुष्विति दुर्मदान्धः ॥ ६ ॥

brāhmaṇa uvāca
ayaṁ jano nāma calan pṛthivyāṁ
yaḥ pārthivaḥ pārthiva kasya hetoḥ
tasyāpi cāṅghryor adhi gulpha-jaṅghā-
jānūru-madhyora-śirodharāṁsāḥ

aṁse 'dhi dārvī śibikā ca yasyāṁ
sauvīra-rājety apadeśa āste
yasmin bhavān rūḍha-nijābhimāno
rājāsmi sindhuṣv iti durmadāndhaḥ

brāhmaṇaḥ uvāca—the *brāhmaṇa* said; *ayam*—this; *janaḥ*—person; *nāma*—celebrated as such; *calan*—moving; *pṛthivyām*—on the earth; *yaḥ*—who; *pārthivaḥ*—a transformation of the earth; *pārthiva*—O King, who possesses a similar earthly body; *kasya*—for what; *hetoḥ*—reason; *tasya api*—of him also; *ca*—and; *aṅghryoḥ*—feet; *adhi*—above; *gulpha*—ankles; *jaṅghā*—calves; *jānu*—knees; *uru*—thighs; *madhyora*—waist; *śiraḥ-dhara*—neck; *aṁsāḥ*—shoulders; *aṁse*—shoulder; *adhi*—upon; *dārvī*—made of wood; *śibikā*—palanquin; *ca*—and; *yasyām*—on which; *sauvīra-rājā*—the King of Sauvīra; *iti*—thus; *apadeśaḥ*—known as; *āste*—there is; *yasmin*—in which; *bhavān*—Your Lordship; *rūḍha*—imposed upon; *nija-abhimānaḥ*—having a conception of false prestige; *rājā asmi*—I am the King; *sindhuṣu*—in the state of Sindhu; *iti*—thus; *durmada-andhaḥ*—captivated by false prestige.

TRANSLATION

The self-realized brāhmaṇa Jaḍa Bharata said: Among the various material combinations and permutations, there are various forms and earthly transformations. For some reason, these move on the surface of the earth and are called palanquin carriers. Those material transformations which do not move are gross material objects like stones. In any case, the material body is made of earth and stone in the form of feet, ankles, calves, knees, thighs, torso, throat and head. Upon the shoulders is the wooden palanquin, and within the palanquin is the so-called King of Sauvīra. The body of the King is simply another transformation of earth, but within that body Your Lordship is situated and falsely thinking that you are the King of the state of Sauvīra.

PURPORT

After analyzing the material bodies of the palanquin carrier and the palanquin passenger, Jaḍa Bharata concludes that the real living force is the living entity. The living entity is the offshoot or offspring of Lord Viṣṇu; therefore within this material world, among moving and non-moving things, the real principle is Lord Viṣṇu. Due to His presence, everything is working, and there are actions and reactions. One who understands Lord Viṣṇu as the original cause of everything is to be understood to be perfectly situated in knowledge. Although he was falsely proud of being a king, King Rahūgaṇa was not really situated in knowledge. Therefore he was rebuking the palanquin carriers, including the self-realized *brāhmaṇa*, Jaḍa Bharata. This is the first accusation Jaḍa Bharata made against the King, who was daring to talk to a learned *brāhmaṇa* from the flimsy ground of ignorance, identifying everything with matter. King Rahūgaṇa argued that the living entity is within the body and that when the body is fatigued the living entity within must therefore be suffering. It is clearly explained in the following verses that the living entity does not suffer due to the body's fatigue. Śrīla Viśvanātha Cakravartī gives an example of a child heavily decorated with ornaments; although the child's body is very delicate, he does not feel fatigue, nor do the parents think that his ornaments should be taken away. The living entity has nothing to do with bodily pains and pleasures. These are simply mental concoctions. An intelligent man will find the original cause of everything. Material combinations and permutations may be a matter of fact in worldly dealings, but actually the living force, the soul, has nothing to do with them. Those who are materially upset take care of the body and manufacture *daridra-nārāyaṇa* (poor Nārāyaṇa). However, it is not a fact that the soul or Supersoul becomes poor simply because the body is poor. These are the statements of ignorant people. The soul and Supersoul are always apart from bodily pleasure and pain.

TEXT 7

शोच्यानिमांस्त्वमधिकष्टदीनान्
विष्टया निगृह्णन्निरनुग्रहोऽसि ।
जनस्य गोप्तास्मि विकत्थमानो
न शोभसे वृद्धसभासु धृष्टः ॥ ७ ॥

śocyān imāṁs tvam adhikaṣṭa-dīnān
viṣṭyā nigṛhṇan niranugraho 'si
janasya goptāsmi vikatthamāno
na śobhase vṛddha-sabhāsu dhṛṣṭaḥ

śocyān—lamentable; *imān*—all these; *tvam*—you; *adhi-kaṣṭa-dīnān*—poor persons suffering more pains because of their poverty-stricken position; *viṣṭyā*—by force; *nigṛhṇan*—seizing; *niranugrahaḥ asi*—you have no mercy in your heart; *janasya*—of the people in general; *goptā asmi*—I am the protector (king); *vikatthamānaḥ*—bragging; *na śobhase*—you do not look very good; *vṛddha-sabhāsu*—in the society of learned persons; *dhṛṣṭaḥ*—simply impudent.

TRANSLATION

It is a fact, however, that these innocent people carrying your palanquin without payment are certainly suffering due to this

injustice. Their condition is very lamentable because you have forcibly engaged them in carrying your palanquin. This proves that you are cruel and unkind, yet due to false prestige you were thinking that you were protecting the citizens. This is ludicrous. You were such a fool that you could not have been adored as a great man in an assembly of persons advanced in knowledge.

PURPORT

King Rahūgaṇa was proud of being king, and he felt he had the right to control the citizens as he liked, but actually he was engaging men in carrying his palanquin without payment, and therefore he was causing them trouble without reason. Nonetheless, the King was thinking that he was the protector of the citizens. Actually the king should be the representative of the Supreme Personality of Godhead. For this reason he is called *nara-devatā,* the Lord among human beings. However, when a king thinks that because he is the head of the state, he can utilize the citizens for his sense gratification, he is in error. Such an attitude is not appreciated by learned scholars. According to the Vedic principles, the king should be advised by learned sages, *brāhmaṇas* and scholars, who advise him according to the injunctions given in the *dharma-śāstra.* The duty of the king is to follow these instructions. Learned circles do not appreciate the king's utilizing public endeavor for his own benefit. His duty is to give protection to the citizens instead. The king should not become such a rogue that he exploits the citizens for his own benefit.

It is stated in *Śrīmad-Bhāgavatam* that in Kali-yuga the heads of government will be plunderers and thieves. These thieves and plunderers take the money and property of the public by force or connivance. Therefore it is said in *Śrīmad-Bhāgavatam, rājanyair nirghṛṇair dasyu-dharmabhiḥ.* As Kali-yuga advances, we can see that these characteristics are already visible. We can certainly imagine how deteriorated human civilization will be by the end of Kali-yuga. Indeed, there will no longer be a sane man capable of understanding God and our relationship with Him. In other words, human beings will be just like animals. At that time, in order to reform human society, Lord Kṛṣṇa will come in the form of the Kalki *avatāra.* His business will be to kill all the atheists because ultimately the real protector is Viṣṇu, or Kṛṣṇa.

The Lord incarnates and sets things in order when things are mismanaged by so-called kings and heads of government. As Kṛṣṇa says in *Bhagavad-gītā, yadā yadā hi dharmasya glānir bhavati bhārata.* Of course this takes many years, but the principle is there. When the king or governmental head does not follow the proper principles, nature deals out the punishments in the forms of war, famine and so forth. Therefore if the governmental head is not aware of life's goal, he should not take charge of ruling the people. Actually the supreme proprietor of everything is Lord Viṣṇu. He is the maintainer of everyone. The king, the father, and the guardian are simply representatives of Lord Viṣṇu, empowered by Him to look after the management and maintain things. It is therefore the duty of the head of the state to maintain the general populace in such a way that people will ultimately know the goal of life. *Na te viduḥ svārtha-gatiṁ hi viṣṇum.* Unfortunately the foolish governmental head and the general populace do not know that the ultimate goal of life is to understand and approach Lord Viṣṇu. Without this knowledge, everyone is in ignorance, and all society is crowded with cheaters and cheated.

TEXT 8

यदा क्षिताचेव चराचरस्य
विदाम निष्ठां प्रभवं च नित्यम् ।
तन्नामतोऽन्यद् व्यवहारमूलं
निरूप्यतां सत्क्रिययानुमेयम् ॥ ८ ॥

yadā kṣitāv eva carācarasya
vidāma niṣṭhāṁ prabhavaṁ ca nityam
tan nāmato 'nyad vyavahāra-mūlaṁ
nirūpyatāṁ sat-kriyayānumeyam

yadā—therefore; *kṣitau*—in the earth; *eva*—certainly; *cara-acarasya*—of different bodies, some moving and some not moving; *vidāma*—we know; *niṣṭhām*—annihilation; *prabhavam*—appearance; *ca*—and; *nityam*—regularly by the principles of nature; *tat*—that; *nāmataḥ*—than simply by name; *anyat*—other; *vyavahāra-mūlam*—cause of material activities; *nirūpyatām*—let it be ascertained; *sat-kriyayā*—by actual employment; *anumeyam*—to be inferred.

TRANSLATION

All of us on the surface of the globe are living entities in different forms. Some of us are moving and some not moving. All of us come into existence, remain for some time and are annihilated when the body is again mingled with the earth. We are all simply different transformations of the earth. Different bodies and capacities are simply transformations of the earth that exist in name only, for everything grows out of the earth and when everything is annihilated it again mingles with the earth. In other words, we are but dust, and we shall but be dust. Everyone can consider this point.

PURPORT

In the *Brahma-sūtra* it is said: *tad-ananyatvam ārabhambhaṇa-śabdādibhyaḥ* (2.1.14). This cosmic manifestation is a mixture of matter and spirit, but the cause is the Supreme Brahman, the Supreme Personality of Godhead. Therefore in *Śrīmad-Bhāgavatam* (1.5.20) it is said: *idaṁ hi viśvaṁ bhagavān ivetaraḥ.* The entire cosmic manifestation is but a transformation of the energy of the Supreme Personality of Godhead, but because of illusion, no one can appreciate that God is nondifferent from the material world. Actually He is not different, but this material world is simply a transformation of His different energies: *parāsya śaktir vividhaiva śrūyate.* There are also other versions of this in the *Vedas: sarvaṁ khalv idaṁ brahma.* Matter and spirit are all nondifferent from the Supreme Brahman, Bhagavān. Lord Śrī Kṛṣṇa confirms this statement in the *Bhagavad-gītā* (7.4): *me bhinnā prakṛtir aṣṭadhā.* The material energy is Kṛṣṇa's energy, but it is separated from Him. The spiritual energy is also His energy, but it is not separated from Him. When the material energy is engaged in the service of the Supreme Spirit, so-called material energy is also transformed into spiritual energy, just as an iron rod becomes fire when placed in contact with fire. When we can understand by an analytical study that the Supreme Personality of Godhead is the cause of all causes, our knowledge is perfect. Simply understanding the transformations of different energies is partial knowledge. We must come to the ultimate cause. *Na te viduḥ svārtha gatiṁ hi viṣṇum.* The knowledge of those who are not interested in knowing the original cause of all emanations is never perfect knowledge.

There is nothing in the phenomenal world that is not produced by the supreme energy of the Supreme Personality of Godhead. Aromas from the earth are different scents manufactured and used for different purposes, but the original cause is the earth, nothing else. A waterpot made of earth can be used to carry water for some time, but ultimately the pot is nothing but earth. Therefore there is no difference between the pot and its original ingredient, earth. It is simply a different transformation of the energy. Originally the cause or primary ingredient is the Supreme Personality of Godhead, and the varieties are only by-products. In the *Chāndogya Upaniṣad* it is stated: *yathā saumy ekena mṛt-piṇḍena sarvaṁ mṛnmayaṁ vijñātaṁ syād vācārambhaṇaṁ vikāro nāmadheyaṁ mṛttikety eva satyam.* If one studies the earth, he naturally understands the by-products of the earth. The *Vedas* therefore enjoin, *yasmin vijñāte sarvam evaṁ vijñātaṁ bhavati:* if one simply understands the original cause, Kṛṣṇa, the cause of all causes, then naturally everything else is understood, although it may be presented in different varieties. By understanding the original cause of different varieties, one can understand everything. If we understand Kṛṣṇa, the original cause of everything, we do not need to separately study the subsidiary varieties. Therefore from the very beginning it is said: *satyaṁ paraṁ dhīmahi.* One has to concentrate one's understanding on the Supreme Truth, Kṛṣṇa or Vāsudeva. The word Vāsudeva indicates the Supreme Personality of Godhead, who is the cause of all causes. *Mat-sthāni sarva-bhūtāni na cāhaṁ teṣv avasthitaḥ.* This is a summary of phenomenal and noumenal philosophy. The phenomenal world depends on the noumenal existence; similarly, everything exists by virtue of the potency of the Supreme Lord, although due to our ignorance the Supreme Lord is not perceived in everything.

TEXT 9

एवं निरुक्तं क्षितिशब्दवृत्त-
मसन्निधानात्परमाणवो ये ।
अविद्यया मनसा कल्पितास्ते
येषां समूहेन कृतो विशेषः ॥ ९ ॥

evaṁ niruktaṁ kṣiti-śabda-vṛttam
asan nidhānāt paramāṇavo ye

avidyayā manasā kalpitās te
yeṣāṁ samūhena kṛto viśeṣaḥ

evam—thus; *niruktam*—falsely described; *kṣiti-śabda*—of the word "earth"; *vṛttam*—the existence; *asat*—not real; *nidhānāt*—from the dissolution; *parama-aṇavaḥ*—atomic particles; *ye*—all of which; *avidyayā*—because of less intelligence; *manasā*—in the mind; *kalpitāḥ*—imagined; *te*—they; *yeṣām*—of which; *samūhena*—by the aggregate; *kṛtaḥ*—made; *viśeṣaḥ*—the particulars.

TRANSLATION

One may say that varieties arise from the planet earth itself. However, although the universe may temporarily appear to be the truth, it ultimately has no real existence. The earth was originally created by a combination of atomic particles, but these particles are impermanent. Actually the atom is not the cause of the universe, although some philosophers think so. It is not a fact that the varieties found in this material world simply result from atomic juxtaposition or combination.

PURPORT

Those who follow the atomic theory think that the protons and electrons of atoms combine in such a way as to bring all material existence into being. However, the scientists fail to discover the cause of atomic existence itself. Under these circumstances, we cannot accept that the atom is the cause of the universe. Such theories are advanced by unintelligent people. According to real intelligence, the real cause of the cosmic manifestation is the Supreme Lord. *Janmādy asya yataḥ:* He is the original cause of all creation. As stated in *Bhagavad-gītā* (10.8): *ahaṁ sarvasya prabhavo mattaḥ sarvaṁ pravartate.* Kṛṣṇa is the original cause. *Sarva-kāraṇa-kāraṇam:* He is the cause of all causes. Kṛṣṇa is the cause of atoms, the material energy.

bhūmir āpo 'nalo vāyuḥ
khaṁ mano buddhir eva ca
ahaṅkāra itīyam me
bhinnā prakṛtir aṣṭadhā (Bg. 7.4)

The ultimate cause is the Supreme Personality of Godhead, and only those in ignorance try to find out other causes by posing different theories.

TEXT 10

एवं कृशं स्थूलमणुर्बृहद्यद्
असच्च सज्जीवमजीवमन्यत् ।
द्रव्यस्वभावाशयकालकर्म-
नाम्नाजयावेहि कृतं द्वितीयम् ॥१०॥

evaṁ kṛśaṁ sthūlam aṇur bṛhad yad
asac ca saj jīvam ajīvam anyat
dravya-svabhāvāśaya-kāla-karma-
nāmnājayāvehi kṛtaṁ dvitīyam

evam—thus; *kṛśam*—skinny or short; *sthūlam*—fat; *aṇuḥ*—tiny; *bṛhat*—big; *yat*—which; *asat*—impermanent; *ca*—and; *sat*—existing; *jīvam*—the living entities; *ajīvam*—inanimate, lifeless matter; *anyat*—other causes; *dravya*—phenomena; *sva-bhāva*—nature; *āśaya*—disposition; *kāla*—time; *karma*—activities; *nāmnā*—only by such names; *ajayā*—by material nature; *avehi*—you should understand; *kṛtam*—done; *dvitīyam*—duality.

TRANSLATION

Since this universe has no real ultimate existence, the things within it—shortness, differences, grossness, skinniness, smallness, bigness, result, cause, living symptoms, and materials—are all imagined. They are all pots made of the same substance, earth, but they are named differently. The differences are characterized by the substance, nature, predisposition, time and activity. You should know that all these are simply mechanical manifestations created by material nature.

PURPORT

The temporary manifestations and varieties within this material world are simply creations of material nature under various circumstances:

prakṛteḥ kriyamāṇāni guṇaiḥ karmāṇi sarvaśaḥ. The actions and reactions carried out by the material nature are sometimes accepted as our scientific inventions; therefore we want to take credit for them and defy the existence of God. This is described in *Bhagavad-gītā* (3.27), *ahaṅkāra-vimūḍhātmā kartāham iti manyate:* due to being covered by the illusory external energy, the living entity tries to take credit for the differentiated creations within the material world. Actually all these are being created automatically by the material force set in motion by the energy of the Supreme Personality of Godhead. Therefore the ultimate cause is the Supreme Person. As stated in *Brahma-saṁhitā:*

īśvaraḥ paramaḥ kṛṣṇaḥ
sac-cid-ānanda-vigrahaḥ
anādir ādir govindaḥ
sarva-kāraṇa-kāraṇam

He is the cause of all causes, the ultimate cause. In this regard Śrīla Madhvācārya says: *evaṁ sarvaṁ tathā prakṛtvayai kalpitaṁ viṣṇor anyat. evaṁ prakṛtyādhāraḥ svayam ananyādhāro viṣṇur eva. ataḥ sarva-śabdāś ca tasminn eva.* Actually the original cause is Lord Viṣṇu, but out of ignorance people think that matter is the cause of everything.

rājā goptāśrayo bhūmiḥ
śaraṇaṁ ceti laukikaḥ
vyavahāro na tat satyaṁ
tayor brahmāśrayo vibhuḥ

Things are contemplated on the ephemeral or external platform, but actually this is not the truth. The actual protector and shelter of everyone is Brahman, the Supreme, not the king.

goptrī ca tasya prakṛtis
tasyā viṣṇuḥ svayaṁ prabhuḥ
tava goptrī tu pṛthivī
na tvaṁ goptā kṣiteḥ smṛtaḥ

ataḥ sarvāśrayaiś caiva
goptā ca harir īśvaraḥ

sarva-śabdābhidheyaś ca
śabda-vṛtter hi kāraṇam
sarvāntaraḥ sarva-bahir
eka eva janārdanaḥ

The actual protectress is the material nature, but Viṣṇu is her Lord. He is the Lord of everything. Lord Janārdana is the director both externally and internally. He is the cause of the function of words and what is expressed in all sound.

śirasodhāratā yadvad
grīvāyās tadvad eva tu
āśrayatvaṁ ca goptṛtvam
anyeṣām upacārataḥ

Lord Viṣṇu is the resting place of the entire creation: *brahmaṇo hi pratiṣṭhāham* (Bg. 14.27). On Brahman, everything is resting. All the universes are resting on the *brahmajyoti*, and all the planets are resting on the universal atmosphere. In each and every planet there are oceans, hills, states and kingdoms, and each planet is giving shelter to so many living entities. They are all standing on the earth of feet and legs, torso and shoulders, but actually everything is resting ultimately on the potencies of the Supreme Personality of Godhead. Therefore He is known ultimately as *sarva-kāraṇa-kāraṇam*, the cause of all causes.

TEXT 11

ज्ञानं विशुद्धं परमार्थमेक-
मनन्तरं त्वबहिर्ब्रह्म सत्यम् ।
प्रत्यक् प्रशान्तं भगवच्छब्दसंज्ञं
यद्वासुदेवं कवयो वदन्ति ॥११॥

jñānaṁ viśuddhaṁ paramārtham ekam
anantaraṁ tv abahir brahma satyam
pratyak praśāntaṁ bhagavac-chabda-saṁjñaṁ
yad vāsudevaṁ kavayo vadanti

jñānam—the supreme knowledge; *viśuddham*—without contamination; *parama-artham*—giving the ultimate goal of life; *ekam*—unified; *anantaram*—without interior, unbroken; *tu*—also; *abahiḥ*—without exterior; *brahma*—the Supreme; *satyam*—Absolute Truth; *pratyak*—inner; *praśāntam*—the calm and peaceful Supreme Lord, worshiped by the *yogīs; bhagavat-śabda-saṁjñam*—known in the higher sense as Bhagavān, or full of all opulences; *yat*—that; *vāsudevam*—Lord Kṛṣṇa, the son of Vasudeva; *kavayaḥ*—the learned scholars; *vadanti*—say.

TRANSLATION

What, then, is the ultimate truth? The answer is that nondual knowledge is the ultimate truth. It is devoid of the contamination of material qualities. It gives us liberation. It is the one without a second, all-pervading and beyond imagination. The first realization of that knowledge is Brahman. Then Paramātmā, the Supersoul, is realized by the yogīs who try to see Him without grievance. This is the second stage of realization. Finally, full realization of the same supreme knowledge is realized in the Supreme Person. All learned scholars describe the Supreme Person as Vāsudeva, the cause of Brahman, Paramātmā and others.

PURPORT

In *Caitanya-caritāmṛta* it is said: *yad advaitaṁ brahmopaniṣadi tad apy asya tanu-bhā.* The impersonal Brahman effulgence of the Absolute Truth consists of the bodily rays of the Supreme Personality of Godhead. *Ya ātmāntaryāmī puruṣa iti so 'syāṁśa-vibhavaḥ.* What is known as *ātmā* and *antaryāmī,* the Supersoul, is but an expansion of the Supreme Personality of Godhead. *Ṣaḍ-aiśvaryaiḥ pūrṇo ya iha bhagavān sa svayam ayam.* What is described as the Supreme Personality of Godhead, complete with all six opulences, is Vāsudeva, and Śrī Caitanya Mahāprabhu is nondifferent from Him. Great learned scholars and philosophers accept this after many, many births. *Vāsudevaḥ sarvam iti sa mahātmā sudurlabhaḥ* (Bg. 7.19). The wise man can understand that ultimately Vāsudeva, Kṛṣṇa, is the cause of Brahman, and Paramātmā, the Supersoul. Thus Vāsudeva is *sarva-kāraṇa-kāraṇam,* the cause of all causes. This is confirmed in *Śrīmad-Bhāgavatam.* The real *tattva,* Absolute Truth, is Bhagavān, but due to incomplete realization of the Absolute Truth, people sometimes describe the same Viṣṇu as impersonal Brahman or localized Paramātmā.

vadanti tat tattva-vidas
tattvaṁ yaj jñānam advayam
brahmeti paramātmeti
bhagavān iti śabdyate
(*Bhāg.* 1.2.11)

From the very beginning, *Śrīmad-Bhāgavatam* says, *satyaṁ paraṁ dhīmahi:* we meditate on the supreme truth. The supreme truth is explained here as *jñānaṁ viśuddhaṁ satyam.* The Absolute Truth is devoid of material contamination and is transcendental to the material qualities. It gives all spiritual success and liberation from this material world. That Supreme Absolute Truth is Kṛṣṇa, Vāsudeva. There is no difference between Kṛṣṇa's inner self and outward body. Kṛṣṇa is *pūrṇa,* the complete whole. There is no distinction between His body and soul as there is between ours. Sometimes so-called scholars, not knowing the constitutional position of Kṛṣṇa, mislead people by saying that the Kṛṣṇa within is different from the Kṛṣṇa without. When Kṛṣṇa says, *man-manā bhava mad-bhakto mad-yājī māṁ namaskuru,* so-called scholars advise the reader that it is not the person Kṛṣṇa to whom we must surrender but the Kṛṣṇa within. So-called scholars, Māyāvādīs, cannot understand Kṛṣṇa with their poor fund of knowledge. One should therefore approach an authorized person to understand Kṛṣṇa. The spiritual master has actually seen Kṛṣṇa; therefore he can explain Him properly.

tad viddhi praṇipātena
paripraśnena sevayā
upadekṣyanti te jñānaṁ
jñāninas tattva-darśinaḥ
(Bg. 4.34)

Without approaching an authorized person, one cannot understand Kṛṣṇa.

TEXT 12

रहूगणैतत्तपसा न याति
न चेज्यया निर्वपणाद् गृहाद्वा ।
नच्छन्दसा नैव जलाग्निसूर्यै-
र्विना महत्पादरजोऽभिषेकम् ॥१२॥

rahūgaṇaitat tapasā na yāti
na cejyayā nirvapaṇād gṛhād vā
na cchandasā naiva jalāgni-sūryair
vinā mahat-pāda-rajo-'bhiṣekam

rahūgaṇa—O King Rahūgaṇa; *etat*—this knowledge; *tapasā*—by severe austerities and penances; *na yāti*—does not become revealed; *na*—not; *ca*—also; *ijyayā*—by a great arrangement for worshiping the Deity; *nirvapaṇāt*—or from finishing all material duties and accepting *sannyāsa; gṛhāt*—from ideal householder life; *vā*—or; *na*—nor; *chandasā*—by observing celibacy or studying Vedic literature; *na eva*—nor; *jala-agni-sūryaiḥ*—by severe austerities such as keeping oneself in water, in a burning fire or in the scorching sun; *vinā*—without; *mahat*—of the great devotees; *pāda-rajaḥ*—the dust of the lotus feet; *abhiṣekam*—smearing all over the body.

TRANSLATION

My dear King Rahūgaṇa, unless one has the opportunity to smear his entire body with the dust of the lotus feet of great devotees, one cannot realize the Absolute Truth. One cannot realize the Absolute Truth simply by observing celibacy [brahmacarya], strictly following the rules and regulations of householder life, leaving home as a vānaprastha, accepting sannyāsa, or undergoing severe penances in winter by keeping oneself submerged in water or surrounding oneself in summer by fire and the scorching heat of the sun. There are many other processes to understand the Absolute Truth, but the Absolute Truth is only revealed to one who has attained the mercy of a great devotee.

PURPORT

Actual knowledge of transcendental bliss can be bestowed upon anyone by a pure devotee. *Vedeṣu durlabham adurlabham ātma-bhaktau.* One cannot attain the perfection of spiritual life simply by following the directions of the *Vedas.* One has to approach a pure devotee: *anyābhilāśitā-śūnyaṁ jñāna-karmādy-anāvṛtam.* By the grace of such a devotee, one can understand the Absolute Truth, Kṛṣṇa, and one's relationship with Him. A materialistic person sometimes thinks that simply by executing pious activities and remaining at home one can understand the Absolute Truth. That is denied in this verse. Nor can one understand the Absolute Truth simply by observing the rules and regulations of *brahmacarya* (celibacy). One only has to serve the pure devotee. That will help one understand the Absolute Truth without fail.

TEXT 13

यत्रोत्तमश्लोकगुणानुवादः
प्रस्तूयते ग्राम्यकथाविघातः ।
निषेव्यमाणोऽनुदिनं मुमुक्षो-
र्मतिं सतीं यच्छति वासुदेवे ॥ १३॥

yatrottamaśloka-guṇānuvādaḥ
prastūyate grāmya-kathā-vighātaḥ
niṣevyamāṇo 'nudinaṁ mumukṣor
matiṁ satīṁ yacchati vāsudeve

yatra—in which place (in the presence of exalted devotees); *uttama-śloka-guṇa-anuvādaḥ*—discussion of the pastimes and glories of the Supreme Personality of Godhead; *prastūyate*—is presented; *grāmya-kathā-vighātaḥ*—due to which there is no chance of talking of worldly matters; *niṣevyamāṇaḥ*—being heard very seriously; *anudinam*—day after day; *mumukṣoḥ*—of persons who are very serious about getting out of material entanglement; *matim*—meditation; *satīm*—pure and simple; *yacchati*—is turned; *vāsudeve*—unto the lotus feet of Lord Vāsudeva.

TRANSLATION

Who are the pure devotees mentioned here? In an assembly of pure devotees, there is no question of discussing material subjects like politics and sociology. In an assembly of pure devotees, there is discussion only of the qualities, forms and pastimes of the Supreme Personality of Godhead. He is praised and worshiped with full attention. In the association of pure devotees, by constantly hearing such topics respectfully, even a person who wants to merge into the existence of the Absolute Truth abandons this idea and gradually becomes attached to the service of Vāsudeva.

PURPORT

The symptoms of pure devotees are described in this verse. The pure devotee is never interested in material topics. Śrī Caitanya Mahāprabhu has strictly prohibited His devotees to talk about worldly matters. *Grāmya-vārtā nā kahibe:* one should not indulge in talking unnecessarily about news of the material world. One should not waste time in this way. This is a very important feature in the life of a devotee. A devotee has no other ambition than to serve Kṛṣṇa, the Supreme Personality of Godhead. This Kṛṣṇa consciousness movement was started to engage people twenty-four hours daily in the service of the Lord and in His glorification. The students in this institution engage in the cultivation of Kṛṣṇa consciousness from five in the morning to ten at night. They actually have no opportunity to waste their time unnecessarily by discussing politics, sociology and current events. These will go their own way. A devotee is concerned only with serving Kṛṣṇa positively and seriously.

TEXT 14

अहं पुरा भरतो नाम राजा
विमुक्तदृष्टश्रुतसङ्गबन्धः ।
आराधनं भगवत ईहमानो
मृगोऽभवं मृगसङ्गाद्धतार्थः ॥१४॥

ahaṁ purā bharato nāma rājā
vimukta-dṛṣṭa-śruta-saṅga-bandhaḥ

ārādhanaṁ bhagavata īhamāno
mṛgo 'bhavaṁ mṛga-saṅgād dhatārthaḥ

aham—I; *purā*—formerly (in my previous birth); *bharataḥ nāma rājā*—a King named Mahārāja Bharata; *vimukta*—liberated from; *dṛṣṭa-śruta*—by experiencing personally through direct association, or by getting knowledge from the *Vedas; saṅga-bandhaḥ*—bondage by association; *ārādhanam*—the worship; *bhagavataḥ*—of the Supreme Personality of Godhead, Vāsudeva; *īhamānaḥ*—always performing; *mṛgaḥ abhavam*—I became a deer; *mṛga-saṅgāt*—because of my intimate association with a deer; *hata-arthaḥ*—having neglected the regulative principles in the discharge of devotional service.

TRANSLATION

In a previous birth I was known as Mahārāja Bharata. I attained perfection by becoming completely detached from material activities through direct experience, and through indirect experience I received understanding from the Vedas. I was fully engaged in the service of the Lord, but due to my misfortune, I became very affectionate to a small deer, so much so that I neglected my spiritual duties. Due to my deep affection for the deer, in my next life I had to accept the body of a deer.

PURPORT

The incident herein described is very significant. In a previous verse it is stated, *vinā mahat-pāda-rajo-'bhiṣekam:* one cannot attain perfection without smearing the dust from the lotus feet of an exalted devotee on his head. If one always follows the orders of the spiritual master, there is no question of falling down. As soon as a foolish disciple tries to overtake his spiritual master and becomes ambitious to occupy his post, he immediately falls down. *Yasya prasādād bhagavat-prasādo yasyāprasādān na gatiḥ kuto 'pi.* If the spiritual master is considered an ordinary man, the disciple surely loses his chance to advance further. Despite a very rigid life in devotional service, Bharata Mahārāja did not consult a spiritual master when he became overly attached to a deer. Consequently he became strongly attached to the deer, and, forgetting his spiritual routine, he fell down.

TEXT 15

सा मां स्मृतिर्मृगदेहेऽपि वीर
कृष्णार्चनप्रभवा नो जहाति ।
अथो अहं जनसङ्गादसङ्गो
विशङ्कमानोऽविवृतश्चरामि ॥१५॥

sā māṁ smṛtir mṛga-dehe 'pi vīra
kṛṣṇārcana-prabhavā no jahāti
atho ahaṁ jana-saṅgād asaṅgo
viśaṅkamāno 'vivṛtaś carāmi

sā—that; *mām*—me; *smṛtiḥ*—remembrance of the activities of my previous life; *mṛga-dehe*—in the body of a deer; *api*—although; *vīra*—O great hero; *kṛṣṇa-arcana-prabhavā*—which appeared because of the influence of sincere service to Kṛṣṇa; *no jahāti*—did not leave; *atho*—therefore; *aham*—I; *jana-saṅgāt*—from the association of ordinary men; *asaṅgaḥ*—completely detached; *viśaṅkamānaḥ*—being afraid; *avivṛtaḥ*—unobserved by others; *carāmi*—I go here and there.

TRANSLATION

My dear heroic King, due to my past sincere service to the Lord, I could remember everything of my past life even while in the body of a deer. Because I am aware of the falldown in my past life, I always keep myself separate from the association of ordinary men. Being afraid of their bad, materialistic association, I wander alone unnoticed by others.

PURPORT

In *Bhagavad-gītā* it is said: *svalpam apy asya dharmasya* (Bg. 2.40). It is certainly a great fall to go from human life to animal life, but in the case of Bharata Mahārāja or any devotee, devotional service to the Lord never goes in vain. As stated in *Bhagavad-gītā* (8.6): *yaṁ yaṁ vāpi smaran bhāvaṁ tyajaty ante kalevaram.* At the time of death, by nature's law the mind is absorbed in a certain type of thinking. This may lead one to animal life, yet for a devotee there is no loss. Even though

Bharata Mahārāja received the body of a deer, he didn't forget his position. Consequently, in the body of a deer he was very careful to remember the cause of his downfall. As a result, he was given a chance to be born in a family of very pure *brāhmaṇas.* Thus his service to the Lord never went in vain.

TEXT 16

तस्मान्नरोऽसङ्गसुसङ्गजात-
ज्ञानासिनेहैव विवृक्णमोहः ।
हरिं तदीहाकथनश्रुताभ्यां
लब्धस्मृतिर्यात्यतिपारमध्वनः ॥१६॥

tasmān naro 'saṅga-susaṅga-jāta-
jñānāsinehaiva vivṛkṇa-mohaḥ
hariṁ tad-īhā-kathana-śrutābhyāṁ
labdha-smṛtir yāty atipāram adhvanaḥ

tasmāt—for this reason; *naraḥ*—every person; *asaṅga*—by detachment from the association of worldly people; *su-saṅga*—by the association of devotees; *jāta*—produced; *jñāna-asinā*—by the sword of knowledge; *iha*—in this material world; *eva*—even; *vivṛkṇa-mohaḥ*—whose illusion is completely cut to pieces; *harim*—the Supreme Personality of Godhead; *tad-īhā*—of His activities; *kathana-śrutābhyām*—by the two processes of hearing and chanting; *labdha-smṛtiḥ*—the lost consciousness is regained; *yāti*—achieves; *atipāram*—the ultimate end; *adhvanaḥ*—of the path back home, back to Godhead.

TRANSLATION

Simply by associating with exalted devotees, anyone can attain perfection of knowledge and with the sword of knowledge can cut to pieces the illusory associations within this material world. Through the association of devotees, one can engage in the service of the Lord by hearing and chanting [śravaṇaṁ kīrtanam]. Thus one can revive his dormant Kṛṣṇa consciousness and, sticking to the cultivation of Kṛṣṇa consciousness, return home, back to Godhead, even in this life.

PURPORT

To become liberated from material bondage, one must give up the association of worldly people and accept the association of devotees. Positive and negative processes are mentioned in this regard. Through the association of devotees, one develops Kṛṣṇa consciousness, which is dormant within. This Kṛṣṇa consciousness movement is giving this chance to everyone. We are giving shelter to everyone who is serious about progressing in Kṛṣṇa consciousness. We arrange for their lodging and board so that they can peacefully cultivate Kṛṣṇa consciousness and return home, back to Godhead, even in this life.

Thus end the Bhaktivedanta purports of the Fifth Canto, Twelfth Chapter of the Śrīmad-Bhāgavatam, *entitled, "The Conversation Between Mahārāja Rahūgaṇa and Jaḍa Bharata."*

CHAPTER THIRTEEN

Further Talks Between King Rahūgaṇa and Jaḍa Bharata

The *brāhmaṇa* Jaḍa Bharata became very kind to King Rahūgaṇa, and to disassociate him from the material world, he spoke figuratively of the forest of the material world. He explained that this material world is like a great forest in which one becomes entangled due to association with material life. In this forest there are plunderers (the six senses) as well as carnivorous animals like jackals, wolves and lions (wife, children and other relatives) who are always anxious to suck the blood from the head of the family. The forest plunderers and the carnivorous blood-sucking animals combine to exploit the energy of a man within this material world. In this forest there is also a black hole, covered by grass, into which one may fall. Coming into the forest and being captivated by so many material attractions, one identifies himself with this material world, society, friendship, love and family. Having lost the path and not knowing where to go, being harassed by animals and birds, one is also victimized by many desires. Thus one works very hard within the forest and wanders here and there. He becomes captivated by temporary happiness and becomes aggrieved by so-called distress. Actually one simply suffers in the forest from so-called happiness and distress. Sometimes he is attacked by a snake (deep sleep), and due to the snakebite he loses consciousness and becomes puzzled and bewildered about discharging his duties. Sometimes he is attracted by women other than his wife, and thus he thinks he enjoys extramarital love with another woman. He is attacked by various diseases, by lamentation and by summer and winter. Thus one within the forest of the material world suffers the pains of material existence. Expecting to become happy, the living entity changes his position from one place to another, but actually a materialistic person within the material world is never happy. Being constantly engaged in materialistic activities, he is always disturbed. He forgets that one day he has to die. Although he suffers severely, being illusioned by the material energy, he still hankers after material happiness. In this way he completely forgets his relationship with the Supreme Personality of Godhead.

By hearing this from Jaḍa Bharata, Mahārāja Rahūgaṇa revived his Kṛṣṇa consciousness and thus benefited from Jaḍa Bharata's association. He could understand that his illusion was over, and he begged pardon from Jaḍa Bharata for his misbehavior. All this was told to Mahārāja Parīkṣit by Śukadeva Gosvāmī.

TEXT 1

ब्राह्मण उवाच
दुरत्ययेऽध्वन्यजया निवेशितो
रजस्तमःसत्त्वविभक्तकर्मदृक् ।
स एष सार्थोऽर्थपरः परिभ्रमन्
भवाटवीं याति न शर्म विन्दति ॥ १ ॥

brāhmaṇa uvāca
duratyaye 'dhvany ajayā niveśito
rajas-tamaḥ-sattva-vibhakta-karmadṛk
sa eṣa sārtho 'rtha-paraḥ paribhraman
bhavāṭavīṁ yāti na śarma vindati

brāhmaṇaḥ uvāca—the *brāhmaṇa* Jaḍa Bharata continued to speak; *duratyaye*—which is very difficult to traverse; *adhvani*—on the path of fruitive activities (performing actions in this life, creating a body in the next life by those actions, and in this way continuously accepting birth and death); *ajayā*—by *māyā*, the external energy of the Supreme Personality of Godhead; *niveśitaḥ*—caused to enter; *rajaḥ-tamaḥ-sattva-vibhakta-karma-dṛk*—a conditioned soul who sees only immediately beneficial fruitive activities and their results, which are divided into three groups by the modes of goodness, passion and ignorance; *saḥ*—he; *eṣaḥ*—this; *sa-arthaḥ*—the living entity falsely seeking sense gratification; *artha-paraḥ*—intent upon gaining wealth; *paribhraman*—wandering all over; *bhava-aṭavīm*—the forest known as *bhava*, which means the repetition of birth and death; *yāti*—enters; *na*—not; *śarma*—happiness; *vindati*—obtains.

TRANSLATION

Jaḍa Bharata, who had fully realized Brahman, continued: My dear King Rahūgaṇa, the living entity wanders on the path of the material world, which is very difficult for him to traverse, and he accepts repeated birth and death. Being captivated by the material world under the influence of the three modes of material nature (sattva-guṇa, rajo-guṇa and tamo-guṇa), the living entity can see only the three fruits of activities under the spell of material nature. These fruits are auspicious, inauspicious and mixed. He thus becomes attached to religion, economic development, sense gratification and the monistic theory of liberation (merging with the Supreme). He works very hard day and night exactly like a merchant who enters a forest to acquire some articles to sell later for profit. However, he cannot really achieve happiness within this material world.

PURPORT

One can very easily understand how difficult and insurmountable the path of sense gratification is. Not knowing what the path of sense gratification is, one becomes implicated in the repetition of birth and accepts different types of bodies again and again. Thus one suffers in material existence. In this life one may think that he is very happy being an American, Indian, Englishman or German, but in the next life one has to accept another body among 8,400,000 species. The next body has to be immediately accepted according to *karma.* One will be forced to accept a certain type of body, and protesting will not help. That is the stringent law of nature. Due to the living entity's ignorance of his eternal blissful life, he becomes attracted to material activities under the spell of *māyā.* In this world, he can never experience happiness, yet he works very hard to do so. This is called *māyā.*

TEXT 2

यस्यामिमे षण्नरदेव दस्यवः
सार्थं विलुम्पन्ति कुनायकं बलात् ।
गोमायवो यत्र हरन्ति सार्थिकं
प्रमत्तमाविश्य यथोरणं वृकाः ॥ २ ॥

yasyām ime ṣaṇ nara-deva dasyavaḥ
sārthaṁ vilumpanti kunāyakaṁ balāt
gomāyavo yatra haranti sārthikaṁ
pramattam āviśya yathoraṇaṁ vṛkāḥ

yasyām—in which (in the forest of material existence); *ime*—these; *ṣaṭ*—six; *nara-deva*—O King; *dasyavaḥ*—the plunderers; *sa-artham*—the conditioned souls, who are interested in false ideas; *vilumpanti*—plunder, regularly taking away all the possessions; *ku-nāyakam*—who are always misguided by so-called *gurus,* or spiritual masters; *balāt*—by force; *gomāyavaḥ*—exactly like foxes; *yatra*—in which forest; *haranti*—they take away; *sa-arthikam*—the conditioned soul who is seeking material profits to maintain the body and soul; *pramattam*—who is a crazy man not knowing his self-interest; *āviśya*—entering the heart; *yathā*—just as; *uraṇam*—nicely protected lambs; *vṛkāḥ*—the tigers.

TRANSLATION

O King Rahūgaṇa, in this forest of material existence there are six very powerful plunderers. When the conditioned soul enters the forest to acquire some material gain, the six plunderers misguide him. Thus the conditioned merchant does not know how to spend his money, and it is taken away by these plunderers. Like tigers, jackals and other ferocious animals in a forest that are ready to take away a lamb from the custody of its protector, the wife and children enter the heart of the merchant and plunder him in so many ways.

PURPORT

In the forest there are many plunderers, dacoits, jackals and tigers. The jackals are compared to one's wife and children. In the dead of night, jackals cry very loudly, and similarly one's wife and children in this material world also cry like jackals. The children say, "Father, this is wanted; give me this. I am your dear son." Or the wife says, "I am your dear wife. Please give me this. This is now needed." In this way one is plundered by the thieves in the forest. Not knowing the aim of human life, one is constantly being misguided. The aim of life is Viṣṇu (*na te viduḥ svārtha-gatiṁ hi viṣṇum)*. Everyone works very hard to earn money, but no one knows that his real self-interest is in serving the Supreme Personality of Godhead. Instead of spending money for advancing the Kṛṣṇa consciousness movement, one spends his hard-earned money on clubs, brothels, liquor, slaughterhouses and so forth. Due to sinful activities, one becomes implicated in the process of transmigration and thus has to accept one body after another. Being thus absorbed in a distressed condition, one never attains happiness.

TEXT 3

प्रभूतवीरुत्तृणगुल्मगह्वरे
कठोरदंशैर्मशकैरुपद्रुतः ।
क्वचित्तु गन्धर्वपुरं प्रपश्यति
क्वचित्क्वचिच्चाशुरयोल्मुकग्रहम् ॥ ३ ॥

prabhūta-vīrut-tṛṇa-gulma-gahvare
kaṭhora-daṁśair maśakair upadrutaḥ
kvacit tu gandharva-puraṁ prapaśyati
kvacit kvacic cāśu-rayolmuka-graham

prabhūta—a very large number; *vīrut*—of creepers; *tṛṇa*—of varieties of grass; *gulma*—of thickets; *gahvare*—in bowers; *kaṭhora*—cruel; *daṁśaiḥ*—by bites; *maśakaiḥ*—by mosquitoes; *upadrutaḥ*—disturbed; *kvacit*—sometimes; *tu*—but; *gandharva-puram*—a false palace created by the Gandharvas; *prapaśyati*—he sees; *kvacit*—and sometimes; *kvacit*—sometimes; *ca*—and; *āśu-raya*—very quickly; *ulmuka*—like a meteor; *graham*—a fiend.

TRANSLATION

In this forest there are dense bowers composed of thickets of bushes, grass and creepers. In these bowers the conditioned soul is always disturbed by cruelly biting mosquitoes [envious people]. Sometimes he sees an imaginary palace in the forest, and sometimes he is bewildered by seeing a fleeting fiend or ghost, which appears like a meteor in the sky.

PURPORT

The material household is actually a hole of fruitive activity. To earn a livelihood, one engages in different industries and trades, and sometimes one performs great sacrifices to go to higher planetary systems. Apart from this, at least everyone is engaged in earning a livelihood in some profession or occupation. In these dealings, one has to meet many undesirable people, and their behavior is compared to the biting of mosquitoes. This creates very undesirable conditions. Even in the midst of these disturbances, one imagines that he is going to construct a grand house and live there permanently, although he knows that he cannot. Gold is compared to a quickly fleeting fiend, which appears like a meteor in the sky. It displays itself for a moment and is then gone. Generally *karmīs* are attracted to gold or money, but these are compared herein to ghosts and witches.

TEXT 4

निवासतोयद्रविणात्मबुद्धि-
स्ततस्ततो धावति भो अटव्याम् ।
क्वचिच्च वात्योत्थितपांसुधूम्रा
दिशो न जानाति रजस्वलाक्षः ॥ ४ ॥

nivāsa-toya-draviṇātma-buddhis
tatas tato dhāvati bho aṭavyām
kvacic ca vātyotthita-pāṁsu-dhūmrā
diśo na jānāti rajas-valākṣaḥ

nivāsa—residential place; *toya*—water; *draviṇa*—wealth; *ātma-buddhiḥ*—who considers these material things the *ātma*, or self; *tataḥ tataḥ*—here and there; *dhāvati*—he runs; *bhoḥ*—O King; *aṭavyām*—on that forest path of material existence; *kvacit ca*—and sometimes; *vātyā*—by the whirlwind; *utthita*—raised; *pāṁsu*—by dust; *dhūmrāḥ*—appear smoke-colored; *diśaḥ*—the directions; *na*—not; *jānāti*—knows; *rajaḥ-vala-akṣaḥ*—whose eyes are covered by the dust of the wind or who is captivated by his wife during her menstrual period.

TRANSLATION

My dear King, the merchant on the forest path of the material world, his intelligence victimized by home, wealth, relatives and so forth, runs from one place to another in search of success. Sometimes his eyes are covered by the dust of a whirlwind—that is to say, in his lust he is captivated by the beauty of his wife, especially during her menstrual period. Thus his eyes are blinded, and he cannot see where to go or what he is doing.

PURPORT

It is said that household attraction resides in the wife because sex is the center of household life: *yan maithunādi-gṛhamedhi-sukhaṁ hi tuccham.* A materialistic person, making his wife the center of attraction, works very hard day and night. His only enjoyment in material life is sexual intercourse. Therefore *karmīs* are attracted to women as friends or wives. Indeed, they cannot work without sex. Under the circumstances the wife is compared to a whirlwind, especially during her menstrual period. Those who strictly follow the rules and regulations of householder life engage in sex only once a month, at the end of the menstrual period. As one looks forward to this opportunity, his eyes are overwhelmed by the beauty of his wife. Thus it is said that the whirlwind covers the eyes with dust. Such a lusty person does not know that all his material activities are being observed by different demigods, especially the sun-god, and are being recorded for the *karma* of one's next body. Astrological calculations are called *jyoti-śāstra.* Because the *jyoti,* or effulgence, in the material world comes from the different stars and planets, the science is called *jyoti-śāstra,* the science of the luminaries. By the calculations of *jyoti,* our future is indicated. In other words, all the luminaries—the stars, sun and moon—witness the activities of the conditioned soul. Thus he is awarded a particular type of body. A lusty person whose eyes are covered by the dust of the whirlwind of material existence does not at all consider that his activities are being observed by different stars and planets and are being recorded. Not knowing this, the conditioned soul commits all kinds of sinful activities for the satisfaction of his lusty desires.

TEXT 5

अदृश्यझिल्लीस्वनकर्णशूल
उलूकवाग्भिर्व्यथितान्तरात्मा
अपुण्यवृक्षान् श्रयते क्षुधार्दितो
मरीचितोयान्यभिधावति क्वचित् ॥ ५ ॥

adṛśya-jhillī-svana-karṇa-śūla
ulūka-vāgbhir vyathitāntarātmā
apuṇya-vṛkṣān śrayate kṣudhārdito
marīci-toyāny abhidhāvati kvacit

adṛśya—invisible; *jhillī*—of crickets or a kind of bee; *svana*—by the sounds; *karṇa-śūla*—whose ears are disturbed; *ulūka*—of the owls; *vāgbhiḥ*—by sound vibrations; *vyathita*—very disturbed; *antaḥ-ātmā*—whose mind and heart; *apuṇya-vṛkṣān*—impious trees that have no fruits or flowers; *śrayate*—he takes shelter of; *kṣudha*—from hunger; *arditaḥ*—suffering; *marīci-toyāni*—the waters of a mirage in the desert; *abhidhāvati*—he runs after; *kvacit*—sometimes.

TRANSLATION

Wandering in the forest of the material world, the conditioned soul sometimes hears an invisible cricket making harsh sounds, and his ears become very much aggrieved. Sometimes his heart is pained by the sounds of owls, which are just like the harsh words of his enemies. Sometimes he takes shelter of a tree that has no fruits or flowers. He approaches such a tree due to his strong appetite, and thus he suffers. He would like to acquire water, but he is simply illusioned by a mirage, and he runs after it.

PURPORT

In *Śrīmad-Bhāgavatam* it is said that the *Bhāgavata* philosophy is meant for people who are completely free from envy (*paramo nirmat-sarāṇām*). The material world is full of envious people. Even within one's inner circle there is much backbiting, and this is compared to the sound vibration of a cricket in the forest. One cannot see the cricket, but one hears its sounds and thus becomes aggrieved. When one takes to Kṛṣṇa consciousness, one always hears unpalatable words from relatives. This is the nature of the world; one cannot avoid mental distress due to the backbiting of envious people. Being very much aggrieved, sometimes one goes to a sinful person for help, but he has no means to help because he has no intelligence. Thus the living entity is disappointed. This is like running after a mirage in the desert in an effort to find water. Such activities do not produce any tangible results. Due to being directed by the illusory energy, a conditioned soul suffers in so many ways.

TEXT 6

क्वचिद्वितोयाः सरितोऽभियाति
परस्परं चालषते निरन्धः ।
आसाद्य दावं क्वचिदग्नितप्तो
निर्विद्यते क्व च यक्षैर्हृतासुः ॥ ६ ॥

kvacid vitoyāḥ sarito 'bhiyāti
parasparaṁ cālaṣate nirandhaḥ
āsādya dāvaṁ kvacid agni-tapto
nirvidyate kva ca yakṣair hṛtāsuḥ

kvacit—sometimes; *vitoyāḥ*—without depth to the water; *saritaḥ*—rivers; *abhiyāti*—he goes to bathe or jumps into; *parasparam*—one another; *ca*—and; *ālaṣate*—desires; *nirandhaḥ*—being with no stock of food; *āsādya*—experiencing; *dāvam*—a forest fire in family life; *kvacit*—sometimes; *agni-taptaḥ*—burned by fire; *nirvidyate*—is despondent; *kva*—somewhere; *ca*—and; *yakṣaiḥ*—by kings resembling rogues and thieves; *hṛta*—taken away; *asuḥ*—wealth, which is as dear as one's life.

TRANSLATION

Sometimes the conditioned soul jumps into a shallow river, or being short of food grains, he goes to beg food from people who are not at all charitable. Sometimes he suffers from the burning

heat of household life, which is like a forest fire, and sometimes he becomes sad to have his wealth, which is as dear as life, plundered by kings in the name of heavy income taxes.

PURPORT

When one is hot due to the scorching sun, one sometimes jumps into a river to gain relief. However, if the river is almost dried up and the water is too shallow, one may break his bones by jumping in. The conditioned soul is always experiencing miserable conditions. Sometimes his efforts to get help from friends are exactly like jumping into a dry river. By such actions, he does not derive any benefit. He only breaks his bones. Sometimes, suffering from a shortage of food, one may go to a person who is neither able to give charity nor willing to do so. Sometimes one is stationed in household life, which is compared to a forest fire (*saṁsāra-dāvānala-līḍha-loka*). When a man is heavily taxed by the government, he becomes very sad. Heavy taxation obliges one to hide his income, but despite this endeavor the government agents are often so vigilant and strong that they take all the money anyway, and the conditioned soul becomes very aggrieved.

Thus people are trying to become happy within the material world, but this is like trying to be happy in a forest fire. No one need go to a forest to set it ablaze; fire takes place automatically. Similarly, no one wants to be unhappy in family life or worldly life, but by the laws of nature unhappiness and distress are forced upon everyone. To become dependent on another's maintenance is very degrading; therefore, according to the Vedic system, everyone should live independently. Only the *śūdras* are unable to live independently. They are obliged to serve someone for maintenance. It is said in the *śāstras: kalau śūdra-sambhavāḥ.* In this age of Kali, everyone is dependent on another's mercy for the maintenance of the body; therefore everyone is classified as a *śūdra.* In the Twelfth Canto of *Śrīmad-Bhāgavatam* it is said that in Kali-yuga the government will levy taxes without reciprocally benefiting the citizens. *Anāvṛṣṭyā vinaṅkṣyanti durbhikṣa-kara-pīḍitāḥ.* In this age there will also be a shortage of rain; therefore a scarcity of food will arise, and the citizens will be very much harassed by government taxation. In this way the citizens will abandon their attempts to lead a peaceful life and will leave their homes and hearths and go to the forest in sheer disappointment.

TEXT 7

शूरैर्हृतस्वः क्व च निर्विण्णचेताः
 शोचन् विमुह्यन्नुपयाति कश्मलम् ।
क्वचिच्च गन्धर्वपुरं प्रविष्टः
 प्रमोदते निर्वृतवन्मुहूर्तम् ॥ ७ ॥

śūrair hṛta-svaḥ kva ca nirviṇṇa-cetāḥ
śocan vimuhyann upayāti kaśmalam
kvacic ca gandharva-puraṁ praviṣṭaḥ
pramodate nirvṛtavan muhūrtam

śūraiḥ—by very powerful enemies; *hṛta-svaḥ*—all of whose possessions have been stolen; *kva ca*—sometimes; *nirviṇṇa-cetāḥ*—very morose and aggrieved at heart; *śocan*—deeply lamenting; *vimuhyan*—becoming bewildered; *upayāti*—achieves; *kaśmalam*—unconsciousness; *kvacit*—sometimes; *ca*—also; *gandharva-puram*—an imaginary city in the forest; *praviṣṭaḥ*—having entered; *pramodate*—he enjoys; *nirvṛta-vat*—exactly like a person who has achieved success; *muhūrtam*—for a moment only.

TRANSLATION

Sometimes, being defeated or plundered by a superior, powerful agent, a living entity loses all his possessions. He then becomes very morose, and lamenting their loss, he sometimes becomes unconscious. Sometimes he imagines a great palatial city in which he desires to live happily with his family members and riches. He thinks himself fully satisfied if this is possible, but such so-called happiness continues only for a moment.

PURPORT

The word *gandharva-puram* is very significant in this verse. Sometimes in the forest a very big castle appears, and this is called a castle in the air. Actually this castle does not exist anywhere but in one's imagination. This is called *gandharva-pura.* In the material forest, the conditioned soul sometimes contemplates great castles and skyscrapers, and he wastes his energy for such things, hoping to live in them very peacefully with his family forever. However, the laws of nature do not allow this. When he enters such castles, he temporarily thinks that he is very happy, even though his happiness is impermanent. His happiness may last for a few years, but because the owner of the castle has to leave the castle at the time of death, everything is eventually lost. This is the way of worldly transactions. Such happiness is described by Vidyāpati as the happiness one derives upon seeing a drop of water in the desert. The desert is heated by scorching sunshine, and if we want to reduce the desert temperature, we need huge amounts of water—millions and millions of gallons. What effect will one drop have? Water certainly has value, but one drop of water cannot reduce the heat of the desert. In this material world everyone is ambitious, but the heat is very scorching. What will an imaginary castle in the air do to help? Śrīla Vidyāpati has therefore sung: *tāṭala saikate, vāri-bindu-sama, suta-mita-ramaṇi-samāje.* The happiness of family life, friends and society is compared to a drop of water in the scorching desert. The entire material world is busy trying to attain happiness because happiness is the prerogative of the living being. Unfortunately, due to falling in contact with the material world, the living entity simply struggles for existence. Even if one becomes happy for a while, a very powerful enemy may plunder everything. There are many instances in which big businessmen suddenly become paupers in the street. Yet the nature of material existence is such that foolish people are attracted to these transactions and they forget the real business of self-realization.

TEXT 8

चलन् क्वचित्कण्टकशर्कराङ्घ्रि-
नगारुरुक्षुर्विमना इवास्ते ।
पदे पदेऽभ्यन्तरवह्निनार्दितः
कौटुम्बिकः क्रुध्यति वै जनाय ॥ ८ ॥

calan kvacit kaṇṭaka-śarkarāṅghrir
nagāruruksur vimanā ivāste
pade pade 'bhyantara-vahninārditaḥ
kauṭumbikaḥ krudhyati vai janāya

calan—wandering; *kvacit*—sometimes; *kaṇṭaka-śarkara*—pierced by thorns and small stones; *aṅghriḥ*—whose feet; *naga*—the hills; *āruruk-ṣuḥ*—one desiring to climb; *vimanāḥ*—disappointed; *iva*—like; *āste*—becomes; *pade pade*—step by step; *abhyantara*—within the abdomen; *vahninā*—by the strong fire of appetite; *arditaḥ*—being fatigued and aggrieved; *kauṭumbikaḥ*—a person living with his family members; *krudhyati*—becomes angry; *vai*—certainly; *janāya*—at the family members.

TRANSLATION

Sometimes the merchant in the forest wants to climb the hills and mountains, but due to insufficient footwear, his feet are pricked by small stone fragments and by thorns on the mountain. Being pricked by them, he becomes very aggrieved. Sometimes a person who is very attached to his family becomes overwhelmed with hunger, and due to his miserable condition he becomes furious with his family members.

PURPORT

The ambitious conditioned soul wants to be very happy in this material world with his family, but he is compared to a traveler in the forest who desires to climb a hill full of thorns and small stones. As stated in the previous verse, the happiness derived from society, friendship and love is like a drop of water in the scorching heat of the desert. One may want to become very great and powerful in society, but this is like attempting to climb a hill full of thorns. Śrīla Viśvanātha Cakravartī Ṭhākura compares one's family to high mountains. Becoming happy in their association is like a hungry man's endeavoring to climb a mountain full of thorns. Almost 99.9 percent of the population is unhappy in family life, despite all the attempts being made to satisfy the family members. In the Western countries, due to the dissatisfaction of the family members, there is actually no family life. There are many cases of divorce, and out of dissatisfaction, the children leave the protection of their parents. Especially in this age of Kali, family life is being reduced. Everyone is becoming self-centered because that is the law of nature. Even if one has sufficient money to maintain a family, the situation is such that no one is happy in family life. Consequently according to the *varṇāśrama* institution, one has to retire from family life in middle age: *pañcāśordhvaṁ vanaṁ vrajet.* One should voluntarily retire from family life at the age of fifty and go to Vṛndāvana or a forest. This is recommended by Śrīla Prahlāda Mahārāja (*Bhāg.* 7.5.5):

tat sādhu manye 'sura-varya dehināṁ
sadā samudvigna-dhiyām asad-grahāt
hitvātma-pātaṁ gṛham andha-kūpaṁ
vanaṁ gato yad dharim āśrayeta

There is no benefit in transferring from one forest to another. One must go to the Vṛndāvana forest and take shelter of Govinda. That will make one happy. The International Society for Krishna Consciousness is therefore constructing a Kṛṣṇa-Balarāma temple to invite its members as well as outsiders to come and live peacefully in a spiritual atmosphere. That will help one become elevated to the transcendental world and return home, back to Godhead. Another sentence in this verse is very significant: *kauṭumbikaḥ krudhyati vai janāya.* When one's mind is disturbed in so many ways, he satisfies himself by becoming angry with his poor wife and children. The wife and children are naturally dependent on the father, but the father, being unable to maintain the family properly, becomes mentally distressed and therefore chastises the family members unnecessarily. As stated in *Śrīmad-Bhāgavatam* (12.2.9): *ācchinna-dāra-draviṇā yāsyanti giri-kānanam.* Being disgusted with family life, one separates from the family by divorce or some other means. If one has to separate, why not separate willingly? Systematic separation is better than forced separation. Forced separation cannot make anyone happy, but by mutual consent or by the Vedic arrangement one must separate from his family affairs at a certain age and fully depend on Kṛṣṇa. This makes one's life successful.

TEXT 9

क्वचिन्निगीर्णोऽजगराहिना जनो
नावैति किञ्चिद्विपिनेऽपविद्धः ।
दष्टः स्म शेते क्व च दन्दशूकै-
रन्धोऽन्धकूपे पतितस्तमिस्रे ॥ ९ ॥

kvacin nigīrṇo 'jagarāhinā jano
nāvaiti kiñcid vipine 'paviddhaḥ
daṣṭaḥ sma śete kva ca danda-śūkair
andho 'ndha-kūpe patitas tamisre

kvacit—sometimes; *nigīrṇaḥ*—being swallowed; *ajagara-ahinā*—by the great snake known as the python; *janaḥ*—the conditioned soul; *na*—not; *avaiti*—understands; *kiñcit*—anything; *vipine*—in the forest; *apaviddhaḥ*—pierced by arrows of suffering; *daṣṭaḥ*—being bitten; *sma*—indeed; *śete*—lies down; *kva ca*—sometimes; *danda-śūkaiḥ*—by other kinds of snakes; *andhaḥ*—blind; *andha-kūpe*—in a blind well; *patitaḥ*—fallen; *tamisre*—in a hellish condition of life.

TRANSLATION

The conditioned soul in the material forest is sometimes swallowed by a python or crushed. At such a time he is left lying in the forest like a dead person, devoid of consciousness and knowledge. Sometimes other poisonous snakes bite him. Being blind to his consciousness, he falls down into a dark well of hellish life with no hope of being rescued.

PURPORT

When one becomes unconscious due to being bitten by a snake, one cannot understand what is taking place outside the body. This unconscious condition is the condition of deep sleep. Similarly, the conditioned soul is actually sleeping on the lap of the illusory energy. Bhaktivinoda Ṭhākura has sung, *kata nidrā yāo māyā-piśācīra kole:* "O living entity, how long will you sleep in this condition on the lap of the illusory energy?" People do not understand that they are actually sleeping in this material world, being devoid of knowledge of spiritual life. Caitanya Mahāprabhu therefore says:

enechi auṣadhi māyā nāśibāra lāgi'
hari-nāma-mahā-mantra lao tumi māgi'

"I have brought medicine to awaken every living being from perpetual sleep. Please receive the holy name of the Lord, the Hare Kṛṣṇa *mahā-mantra*, and awaken." The *Kaṭha Upaniṣad* (1.3.14) also says, *uttiṣṭha jāgrata prāpya varān nibodhata:* "O living entity, you are sleeping in this material world. Please get up and take advantage of your human form of life." The sleeping condition means loss of all knowledge. In *Bhagavad-gītā* (2.69) it is also said, *yā niśā sarva-bhūtānāṁ tasyāṁ jāgarti saṁyamī:* "What is night for all beings is the time of awakening for the self-controlled." Even in the higher planets, everyone is under the spell of the illusory energy. No one is really interested in the real values of life. The sleeping condition, called *kāla-sarpa* (the time factor), keeps the conditioned soul in a state of ignorance, and therefore pure consciousness is lost. In the forest there are many blind wells, and if one falls down in one there is no chance of being rescued. In a state of sleep, one remains perpetually bitten by some animals, especially snakes.

TEXT 10

कर्हि स्म चित्क्षुद्ररसान् विचिन्वं-
स्तन्मक्षिकाभिर्व्यथितो विमानः ।
तत्रातिकृच्छ्रात्प्रतिलब्धमानो
बलाद्विलुम्पन्त्यथ तं ततोऽन्ये ॥१०॥

karhi sma cit kṣudra-rasān vicinvaṁs
tan-makṣikābhir vyathito vimānaḥ
tatrāti-kṛcchrāt pratilabdhamāno
balād vilumpanty atha taṁ tato 'nye

karhi sma cit—sometimes; *kṣudra*—very insignificant; *rasān*—sexual enjoyment; *vicinvan*—searching for; *tat*—of those women; *makṣikābhiḥ*—by honeybees, or the husbands or family members; *vyathitaḥ*—very much aggrieved; *vimānaḥ*—insulted; *tatra*—in that; *ati*—very much; *kṛcchrāt*—with difficulty because of spending money; *pratilabdhamānaḥ*—obtaining sexual enjoyment; *balāt*—by force; *vilumpanti*—kidnapped; *atha*—thereafter; *tam*—the object of sense enjoyment (the woman); *tataḥ*—from him; *anye*—another debauchee.

TRANSLATION

Sometimes, in order to have a little insignificant sex enjoyment, one searches after debauched women. In this attempt, one is insulted and chastised by the women's kinsmen. This is like going to take honey from a beehive and being attacked by the bees. Sometimes, after spending lots of money, one may acquire another woman for some extra sense enjoyment. Unfortunately, the object of sense enjoyment, the woman, is taken away or kidnapped by another debauchee.

PURPORT

In a great forest, honeycombs are very important. People often go there to collect honey from the combs, and sometimes the bees attack and punish them. In human society, those who are not Kṛṣṇa conscious remain in the forest of material life simply for the honey of sex life. Such debauchees are not at all satisfied with one wife. They want many women. Day after day, with great difficulty, they try to secure such women, and sometimes, while trying to taste this kind of honey, one is attacked by a woman's kinsmen and chastised very heavily. By bribing others, one may secure another woman for enjoyment, yet another debauchee may kidnap her or offer her something better. This woman hunting is going on in the forest of the material world, sometimes legally and sometimes illegally. Consequently in this Kṛṣṇa consciousness movement the devotees are forbidden to have illicit sex. Thus they avoid so many difficulties. One should remain satisfied with one woman, being duly married. One can satisfy one's lusty desires with his wife without creating disturbances in society and being punished for doing so.

TEXT 11

क्वचिच्च शीतातपवातवर्ष-
प्रतिक्रियां कर्तुमनीश आस्ते ।
क्वचिन्मिथो विपणन् यच्च किञ्चिद्
विद्वेषमृच्छत्युत वित्तशाठ्यात् ॥११॥

kvacic ca śītātapa-vāta-varṣa-
pratikriyāṁ kartum anīśa āste
kvacin mitho vipaṇan yac ca kiñcid
vidveṣam ṛcchaty uta vitta-śāṭhyāt

kvacit—sometimes; *ca*—also; *śīta-ātapa-vāta-varṣa*—of freezing cold, scorching heat, strong wind and excessive rainfall; *pratikriyām*—counteraction; *kartum*—to do; *anīśaḥ*—being unable; *āste*—remains in misery; *kvacit*—sometimes; *mithaḥ*—one another; *vipaṇan*—selling; *yat ca*—whatever; *kiñcit*—a little bit; *vidveṣam*—mutual enmity; *ṛcchati*—obtain; *uta*—it is so said; *vitta-śāṭhyāt*—because of cheating one another merely for money.

TRANSLATION

Sometimes the living entity is busy counteracting the natural disturbances of freezing cold, scorching heat, strong wind, excessive rainfall and so forth. When he is unable to do so, he becomes very unhappy. Sometimes he is cheated in business transactions one after another. In this way, by cheating, living entities create enmity among themselves.

PURPORT

This is an example of the struggle for existence, the attempt to counteract the onslaught of material nature. This creates enmity in society, and consequently society is filled with envious people. One person is envious of another, and this is the way of the material world. The Kṛṣṇa consciousness movement aims at creating an atmosphere of non-envy. Of course it is not possible for everyone to become Kṛṣṇa conscious, but the

Kṛṣṇa consciousness movement can create an exemplary society wherein there is no envy.

TEXT 12

क्वचित्क्वचित्क्षीणधनस्तु तस्मिन्
शय्यासनस्थानविहारहीनः ।
याचन् परादप्रतिलब्धकामः
पारक्यदृष्टिर्लभतेऽवमानम् ॥१२॥

kvacit kvacit kṣīṇa-dhanas tu tasmin
śayyāsana-sthāna-vihāra-hīnaḥ
yācan parād apratilabdha-kāmaḥ
pārakya-dṛṣṭir labhate 'vamānam

kvacit kvacit—sometimes; *kṣīṇa-dhanaḥ*—becoming bereft of all riches; *tu*—but; *tasmin*—in that forest; *śayyā*—of bedding for lying down; *āsana*—of a sitting place; *sthāna*—of a residential house; *vihāra*—of enjoyment with a family; *hīnaḥ*—being bereft; *yācan*—begging; *parāt*—from others (friends and relatives); *apratilabdha-kāmaḥ*—not getting his desires fulfilled; *pārakya-dṛṣṭiḥ*—becomes greedy for the wealth of others; *labhate*—he obtains; *avamānam*—dishonor.

TRANSLATION

On the forest path of material existence, sometimes a person is without wealth and due to this does not have a proper home, bed or sitting place, nor proper family enjoyment. He therefore goes to beg money from others, but when his desires are not fulfilled by begging, he wants to borrow or steal the property of others. Thus he is insulted in society.

PURPORT

The principles of beg, borrow or steal are very appropriate in this material world. When one is in want, he begs, borrows or steals. If begging is unsuccessful, he borrows. If he cannot pay, he steals, and when he is caught, he is insulted. This is the law of material existence. No one can live here very honestly; therefore by trickery, cheating, begging, borrowing or stealing, one tries to satisfy his senses. Thus no one in this material world is living peacefully.

TEXT 13

अन्योन्यवित्तव्यतिषङ्गवृद्ध-
वैरानुबन्धो विवहन्मिथश्च ।
अध्वन्यमुष्मिन्नुरुकृच्छ्रवित्त-
बाधोपसर्गैर्विहरन् विपन्नः ॥१३॥

anyonya-vitta-vyatiṣaṅga-vṛddha-
vairānubandho vivahan mithaś ca
adhvany amuṣminn uru-kṛcchra-vitta-
bādhopasargair viharan vipannaḥ

anyonya—with one another; *vitta-vyatiṣaṅga*—by monetary transactions; *vṛddha*—increased; *vaira-anubandhaḥ*—one is encumbered by enmity; *vivahan*—sometimes marrying; *mithaḥ*—one another; *ca*—and; *adhvani*—on the path of material existence; *amuṣmin*—that; *uru-kṛcchra*—by great difficulties; *vitta-bādha*—by scarcity of money; *upasargaiḥ*—by diseases; *viharan*—wandering; *vipannaḥ*—one becomes fully embarrassed.

TRANSLATION

Due to monetary transactions, relationships become very strained and end in enmity. Sometimes the husband and wife walk on the path of material progress, and to maintain their relationship they work very hard. Sometimes due to scarcity of money or due to diseased conditions, they are embarrassed and almost die.

PURPORT

In this material world, there are many transactions between peoples and societies as well as between nations, but gradually these end in enmity between the two parties. Similarly, in the marriage relationship, monetary transactions are sometimes overpowered by the dangerous conditions of material life. One then becomes diseased or monetarily embarrassed. In the modern age most countries have developed economically, but due to business exchanges, relationships seem to be strained. Finally wars are declared between nations, and as a result of these upheavals there is destruction all over the world, and people suffer heavily.

TEXT 14

तांस्तान् विपन्नान् स हि तत्र तत्र
विहाय जातं परिगृह्य सार्थः ।
आवर्ततेऽद्यापि न कश्चिदत्र
वीराध्वनः पारमुपैति योगम् ॥१४॥

tāṁs tān vipannān sa hi tatra tatra
vihāya jātaṁ parigṛhya sārthaḥ
āvartate 'dyāpi na kaścid atra
vīrādhvanaḥ pāram upaiti yogam

tān tān—all of them; *vipannān*—embarrassed in various ways; *saḥ*—the living being; *hi*—certainly; *tatra tatra*—here and there; *vihāya*—giving up; *jātam*—those who are newly born; *parigṛhya*—taking; *sa-arthaḥ*—the living being searching for his own interest; *āvartate*—wanders in this forest; *adya api*—even until now; *na*—not; *kaścit*—any of them; *atra*—here in this forest; *vīra*—O hero; *adhvanaḥ*—of the path of material life; *pāram*—the ultimate end; *upaiti*—gets; *yogam*—the process of devotional service to the Supreme Personality of Godhead.

TRANSLATION

My dear King, on the forest path of material life, first a person is bereft of his father and mother, and after their death he becomes attached to his newly born children. In this way he wanders on the path of material progress and is eventually embarrassed. Nonetheless, no one knows how to get out of this, even up to the moment of death.

PURPORT

In this material world, family life is an institution of sex. *Yan maithunādi-gṛhamedhi-sukham* (*Bhāg.* 7.9.45). Through sex, the father and mother beget children, and the children get married and go down the same path of sexual life. After the death of the father and mother, the children get married and beget their own children. Thus generation after generation these things go on in the same way without anyone's attaining liberation from the embarrassment of material life. No one accepts the spiritual processes of knowledge and renunciation, which end in *bhakti-yoga.* Actually human life is meant for *jñāna* and *vairāgya,* knowledge and renunciation. Through these one can attain the platform of devotional service. Unfortunately people in this age avoid the association of liberated people (*sādhu-saṅga*) and continue in their stereotyped way of family life. Thus they are embarrassed by the exchange of money and sex.

TEXT 15

मनस्विनो निर्जितदिग्गजेन्द्रा
ममेति सर्वे भुवि बद्धवैराः ।
मृधे शयीरन्न तु तद्व्रजन्ति
यन्न्यस्तदण्डो गतवैरोऽभियाति ॥१५॥

manasvino nirjita-dig-gajendrā
mameti sarve bhuvi baddha-vairāḥ
mṛdhe śayīran na tu tad vrajanti
yan nyasta-daṇḍo gata-vairo 'bhiyāti

manasvinaḥ—very great heroes (mental speculators); *nirjita-dik-gajendrāḥ*—who have conquered many other heroes as powerful as elephants; *mama*—my (my land, my country, my family, my community, my religion); *iti*—thus; *sarve*—all (great political, social and religious leaders); *bhuvi*—in this world; *baddha-vairāḥ*—who have created enmity among themselves; *mṛdhe*—in battle; *śayīran*—fall dead on the ground; *na*—not; *tu*—but; *tat*—the abode of the Supreme Personality of Godhead; *vrajanti*—approach; *yat*—which; *nyasta-daṇ-*

ḍaḥ—a *sannyāsī; gata-vairaḥ*—who has no enmity throughout the whole world; *abhiyāti*—attains that perfection.

TRANSLATION

There were and are many political and social heroes who have conquered enemies of equal power, yet due to their ignorance in believing that the land is theirs, they fight one another and lay down their lives in battle. They are not able to take up the spiritual path accepted by those in the renounced order. Although they are big heroes and political leaders, they cannot take to the path of spiritual realization.

PURPORT

Big political leaders might be able to conquer equally powerful political enemies, but unfortunately they cannot subdue their strong senses, the enemies that always accompany them. Not being able to conquer these nearby enemies, they simply try to conquer other enemies, and ultimately they die in the struggle for existence. They do not take to the path of spiritual realization or become *sannyāsīs.* Sometimes these big leaders take up the guise of a *sannyāsī* and call themselves *mahātmās,* but their only business is conquering their political enemies. Because they spoil their lives with the illusion of "this is my land and my family," they cannot progress spiritually and attain liberation from the clutches of *māyā.*

TEXT 16

प्रसज्जति क्वापि लताभुजाश्रय-
स्तदाश्रयाव्यक्तपदद्विजस्पृहः ।
क्वचित्कदाचिद्धरिचक्रतस्त्रसन्
सख्यं विधत्ते बककङ्कगृध्रैः ॥१६॥

prasajjati kvāpi latā-bhujāśrayas
tad-āśrayāvyakta-pada-dvija-spṛhaḥ
kvacit kadācid dhari-cakratas trasan
sakhyaṁ vidhatte baka-kaṅka-gṛdhraiḥ

prasajjati—becomes more and more attached; *kvāpi*—sometimes; *latā-bhuja-āśrayaḥ*—who takes shelter of the soft arms of his beautiful wife which are like creepers; *tat-āśraya*—who are sheltered by such creepers; *avyakta-pada*—who sing unclear songs; *dvija-spṛhaḥ*—desiring to hear birds; *kvacit*—sometimes; *kadācit*—somewhere; *hari-cakrataḥ trasan*—being afraid of the roaring sound of a lion; *sakhyam*—friendship; *vidhatte*—makes; *baka-kaṅka-gṛdhraiḥ*—with cranes, herons and vultures.

TRANSLATION

Sometimes the living entity in the forest of material existence takes shelter of creepers and desires to hear the chirping of the birds in those creepers. Being afraid of roaring lions in the forest, he makes friends with cranes, herons and vultures.

PURPORT

In the forest of the material world there are many animals and birds, trees and creepers. Sometimes the living entity wants to take shelter of the creepers; in other words, he wants to be happy by being embraced by the creeperlike arms of his wife. Within the creepers there are many chirping birds; this indicates that he wants to satisfy himself by hearing the sweet voice of his wife. In old age, however, he sometimes becomes afraid of imminent death, which is compared to a roaring lion. To save himself from the lion's attack, he takes shelter of some bogus *svāmīs*, *yogīs*, incarnations, pretenders and cheaters. Being misled by the illusory energy in this way, he spoils his life. It is said, *hariṁ vinā mṛtiṁ na taranti:* no one can be saved from the imminent danger of death without taking shelter of the Supreme Personality of Godhead. The word *hari* indicates the lion as well as the Supreme Lord. To be saved from the hands of Hari, the lion of death, one must take shelter of the supreme Hari, the Supreme Personality of Godhead. People with a poor fund of knowledge take shelter of nondevotee cheaters and pretenders in order to be saved from the clutches of death. In the forest of the material world, the living entity first of all wants to be very happy by taking shelter of the creeperlike arms of his wife and hearing her sweet voice. Later, he sometimes takes shelter of so-called *gurus* and *sādhus* who are like cranes, herons and vultures. Thus he is cheated both ways by not taking shelter of the Supreme Lord.

TEXT 17

तैर्वञ्चितो हंसकुलं समाविश-
न्नरोचयन् शीलमुपैति वानरान् ।
तज्जातिरासेन सुनिर्वृतेन्द्रियः
परस्परोद्वीक्षणविस्मृतावधिः ॥१७॥

tair vañcito haṁsa-kulaṁ samāviśann
arocayan śīlam upaiti vānarān
taj-jāti-rāsena sunirvṛtendriyaḥ
parasparodvīkṣaṇa-vismṛtāvadhiḥ

taiḥ—by them (the cheaters and pretenders, the so-called *yogīs*, *svāmīs*, incarnations and *gurus*); *vañcitaḥ*—being cheated; *haṁsa-kulam*—the association of great *paramahaṁsas*, or devotees; *samāviśan*—contacting; *arocayan*—not being satisfied with; *śīlam*—their behavior; *upaiti*—approaches; *vānarān*—the monkeys, which are all debauchees with no good character; *tat-jāti-rāsena*—by sense gratification in the association of such debauchees; *sunirvṛta-indriyaḥ*—being very satisfied with getting the opportunity of sense gratification; *paraspara*—of one another; *udvīkṣaṇa*—by seeing the faces; *vismṛta*—who has forgotten; *avadhiḥ*—the end of life.

TRANSLATION

Being cheated by them, the living entity in the forest of the material world tries to give up the association of these so-called yogīs, svāmīs and incarnations and come to the association of real devotees, but due to misfortune he cannot follow the instructions of the spiritual master or advanced devotees; therefore he gives up their company and again returns to the association of monkeys who are simply interested in sense gratification and women. He derives satisfaction by associating with sense gratifiers and

enjoying sex and intoxication. In this way he spoils his life simply by indulging in sex and intoxication. Looking into the faces of other sense gratifiers, he becomes forgetful and thus approaches death.

PURPORT

Sometimes a foolish person becomes disgusted with bad association and comes to the association of devotees and *brāhmaṇas* and takes initiation from a spiritual master. As advised by the spiritual master, he tries to follow the regulative principles, but due to misfortune he cannot follow the instructions of the spiritual master. He therefore gives up the company of devotees and goes to associate with simian people who are simply interested in sex and intoxication. Those who are so-called spiritualists are compared to monkeys. Outwardly, monkeys sometimes resemble *sādhus* because they live naked in the forest and pick fruits, but their only desire is to keep many female monkeys and enjoy sex life. Sometimes so-called spiritualists seeking a spiritual life come to associate with Kṛṣṇa conscious devotees, but they cannot execute the regulative principles or follow the path of spiritual life. Consequently they leave the association of devotees and go to associate with sense gratifiers, who are compared to monkeys. Again they revive their sex and intoxication, and looking at one another's faces, they are thus satisfied. In this way they pass their lives up to the point of death.

TEXT 18

द्रुमेषु रंस्यन् सुतदारवत्सलो
व्यवायदीनो विवशः स्वबन्धने ।
क्वचित्प्रमादाद्गिरिकन्दरे पतन्
वल्लीं गृहीत्वा गजभीत आस्थितः ॥१८॥

drumeṣu raṁsyan suta-dāra-vatsalo
vyavāya-dīno vivaśaḥ sva-bandhane
kvacit pramādād giri-kandare patan
vallīṁ gṛhītvā gaja-bhīta āsthitaḥ

drumeṣu—in the trees (or in houses standing like trees in which monkeys jump from one branch to another); *raṁsyan*—enjoying; *suta-*

dāra-vatsalaḥ—being attached to the children and wife; *vyavāya-dīnaḥ*—who is poorhearted because of acting on the platform of sex desire; *vivaśaḥ*—unable to give up; *sva-bandhane*—in bondage to the reactions of one's own activities; *kvacit*—sometimes; *pramādāt*—from fear of imminent death; *giri-kandare*—in a cave in a mountain; *patan*—falling down; *vallīm*—the branches of a creeper; *gṛhītvā*—capturing; *gaja-bhītaḥ*—being afraid of the elephant of death; *āsthitaḥ*—remains in that position.

TRANSLATION

When the living entity becomes exactly like a monkey jumping from one branch to another, he remains in the tree of household life without any profit but sex. Thus he is kicked by his wife just like the he-ass. Unable to gain release, he remains helplessly in that position. Sometimes he falls victim to an incurable disease, which is like falling into a mountain cave. He becomes afraid of death, which is like the elephant in the back of that cave, and he remains stranded, grasping at the twigs and branches of a creeper.

PURPORT

The precarious condition of a householder's life is described herein. A householder's life is full of misery, and the only attraction is sex with the wife who kicks him during sexual intercourse, just as the she-ass does her mate. Due to continuous sex life, he falls victim to many incurable diseases. At that time, being afraid of death, which is like an elephant, he remains hanging from the twigs and branches of the tree, just like a monkey.

TEXT 19

अतः कथञ्चित्स विमुक्त आपदः
पुनश्च सार्थं प्रविशत्यरिन्दम ।
अध्वन्यमुष्मिन्नजया निवेशितो
भ्रमञ्जनोऽद्यापि न वेद कश्चन ॥१९॥

ataḥ kathañcit sa vimukta āpadaḥ
punaś ca sārthaṁ praviśaty arindama

adhvany amuṣminn ajayā niveśito
bhramañ jano 'dyāpi na veda kaścana

ataḥ—from this; *kathañcit*—somehow; *saḥ*—he; *vimuktaḥ*—liberated; *āpadaḥ*—from the danger; *punaḥ ca*—again; *sa-artham*—taking interest in that life; *praviśati*—begins; *arim-dama*—O King, killer of the enemies; *adhvani*—on the path of enjoyment; *amuṣmin*—that; *ajayā*—by the influence of the illusory energy; *niveśitaḥ*—being absorbed; *bhraman*—traveling; *janaḥ*—the conditioned soul; *adya api*—even up to death; *na veda*—does not understand; *kaścana*—anything.

TRANSLATION

O killer of enemies, Mahārāja Rahūgaṇa, if the conditioned soul somehow or other gets out of his dangerous position, he again returns to his home to enjoy sex life, for that is the way of attachment. Thus, under the spell of the Lord's material energy, he continues to loiter in the forest of material existence. He does not discover his real interest even at the point of death.

PURPORT

This is the way of material life. When one is captured by sexual attraction, he becomes implicated in so many ways and cannot understand the real aim of life. Therefore *Śrīmad-Bhāgavatam* (7.5.31) says, *na te viduḥ svārtha-gatiṁ hi viṣṇum:* generally people do not understand the ultimate goal of life. As stated in the *Vedas, oṁ tad viṣṇoḥ paramaṁ padaṁ sadā paśyanti sūrayaḥ:* those who are spiritually advanced simply look to the lotus feet of Viṣṇu. The conditioned soul, however, not being interested in reviving his relationship with Viṣṇu, becomes captivated by material activities and remains in everlasting bondage, being misled by so-called leaders.

TEXT 20

रहूगण त्वमपि ह्यध्वनोऽस्य
संन्यस्तदण्डः कृतभूतमैत्रः ।
असज्जितात्मा हरिसेवया शितं
ज्ञानासिमादाय तरातिपारम् ॥२०॥

rahūgaṇa tvam api hy adhvano 'sya
sannyasta-daṇḍaḥ kṛta-bhūta-maitraḥ
asaj-jitātmā hari-sevayā śitaṁ
jñānāsim ādāya tarāti-pāram

rahūgaṇa—O King Rahūgaṇa; *tvam*—you; *api*—also; *hi*—certainly; *adhvanaḥ*—of the path of material existence; *asya*—this; *sannyasta-daṇḍaḥ*—having given up the king's rod for punishing criminals; *kṛta-bhūta-maitraḥ*—having become friendly to everyone; *asat-jita-ātmā*—whose mind is not attracted to the material pleasure of life; *hari-sevayā*—by the means of loving service to the Supreme Lord; *śitam*—sharpened; *jñāna-asim*—the sword of knowledge; *ādāya*—taking in hand; *tara*—cross over; *ati-pāram*—to the ultimate end of spiritual existence.

TRANSLATION

My dear King Rahūgaṇa, you are also a victim of the external energy, being situated on the path of attraction to material pleasure. So that you may become an equal friend to all living entities, I now advise you to give up your kingly position and the rod by which you punish criminals. Give up attraction to the sense objects and take up the sword of knowledge sharpened by devotional service. Then you will be able to cut the hard knot of illusory energy and cross to the other side of the ocean of nescience.

PURPORT

In *Bhagavad-gītā* Lord Kṛṣṇa compares the material world to a tree of illusion from which one must cut oneself free:

na rūpam asyeha tathopalabhyate
nānto na cādir na ca sampratiṣṭhā
aśvattham enaṁ suvirūḍha-mūlam
asaṅga-śastreṇa dṛḍhena chittvā

tataḥ padaṁ tat parimārgitavyaṁ
yasmin gatā na nivartanti bhūyaḥ
tam eva cādyaṁ puruṣaṁ prapadye
yataḥ pravṛttiḥ prasṛtā purāṇī

"The real form of this tree cannot be perceived in this world. No one can understand where it ends, where it begins, or where its foundation is. But with determination, one must cut down this tree with the weapon of detachment. So doing, one must seek that place from which, having once gone, one never returns, and there surrender to that Supreme Personality of Godhead from whom everything has begun and in whom everything is abiding since time immemorial." (Bg. 15.3-4)

TEXT 21

राजोवाच
अहो नृजन्माखिलजन्मशोभनं
किं जन्मभिस्त्वपरैरप्यमुष्मिन् ।
न यद्धृषीकेशयशःकृतात्मनां
महात्मनां वः प्रचुरः समागमः ॥२१॥

rājovāca
aho nṛ-janmākhila-janma-śobhanaṁ
kiṁ janmabhis tv aparair apy amuṣmin
na yad dhṛṣīkeśa-yaśaḥ-kṛtātmanāṁ
mahātmanāṁ vaḥ pracuraḥ samāgamaḥ

rājā uvāca—King Rahūgaṇa said; *aho*—alas; *nṛ-janma*—you who have taken birth as a human being; *akhila-janma-śobhanam*—the best of all species of life; *kim*—what need; *janmabhiḥ*—with births in a higher species like the demigods in the heavenly planets; *tu*—but; *aparaiḥ*—not superior; *api*—indeed; *amuṣmin*—in the next birth; *na*—not; *yat*—which; *hṛṣīkeśa-yaśaḥ*—by the glories of the Supreme Personality of Godhead, Hṛṣīkeśa, the master of all senses; *kṛta-ātmanām*—of those whose hearts are purified; *mahā-ātmanām*—who are actually great souls; *vaḥ*—of us; *pracuraḥ*—abundant; *samāgamaḥ*—the association.

TRANSLATION

King Rahūgaṇa said: This birth as a human being is the best of all. Even birth among the demigods in the heavenly planets is not

as glorious as birth as a human being on this earth. What is the use of the exalted position of a demigod? In the heavenly planets, due to profuse material comforts, there is no possibility of associating with devotees.

PURPORT

Human birth is a great opportunity for self-realization. One may take birth in a high planetary system among the demigods, but due to the profusion of material comforts, one cannot gain release from material bondage. Even on this earth those who are very opulent do not generally care to take to Kṛṣṇa consciousness. An intelligent person actually interested in getting freed from the material clutches must associate with pure devotees. By such association, one can gradually become detached from the material attraction of money and women. Money and women are the basic principles of material attachment. Śrī Caitanya Mahāprabhu therefore advised those who are actually serious about returning back to Godhead to give up money and women in order to be fit to enter the kingdom of God. Money and women can be fully utilized in the service of the Lord, and one who can utilize them in this way can become freed from material bondage. *Satāṁ prasaṅgān mama vīrya-saṁvido bhavanti hṛt-karṇa-rasāyanāḥ kathāḥ* (*Bhāg.* 3.25.25). Only in the association of devotees can one relish the glorification of the Supreme Personality of Godhead. Just through a little association with a pure devotee, one can become successful in his journey back to Godhead.

TEXT 22

न ह्यद्भुतं त्वच्चरणाब्जरेणुभि-
र्हतांहसो भक्तिरधोक्षजेऽमला ।
मौहूर्तिकाद्यस्य समागमाच्च मे
दुस्तर्कमूलोऽपहतोऽविवेकः ॥२२॥

na hy adbhutaṁ tvac-caraṇābja-reṇubhir
hatāṁhaso bhaktir adhokṣaje 'malā
mauhūrtikād yasya samāgamāc ca me
dustarka-mūlo 'pahato 'vivekaḥ

na—not; *hi*—certainly; *adbhutam*—wonderful; *tvat-caraṇa-abja-reṇubhiḥ*—by the dust of your lotus feet; *hata-aṁhasaḥ*—who am completely freed from the reactions of sinful life; *bhaktiḥ*—love and devotion; *adhokṣaje*—unto the Supreme Personality of Godhead, who is beyond the capture of experimental knowledge; *amalā*—completely freed from all material contamination; *mauhūrtikāt*—momentary; *yasya*—of whom; *samāgamāt*—by the visit and association; *ca*—also; *me*—my; *dustarka*—of false arguments; *mūlaḥ*—the root; *apahataḥ*—completely vanquished; *avivekaḥ*—not discriminating.

TRANSLATION

It is not at all wonderful that simply by being covered by the dust of your lotus feet, one immediately attains the platform of pure devotional service to Adhokṣaja, which is not available even to great demigods like Brahmā. By associating with you just for a moment, I am now freed from all argument, false prestige and lack of discrimination, which are the roots of entanglement in the material world. Now I am free from all these problems.

PURPORT

Association with pure devotees certainly frees one from the material clutches. This is certainly true of King Rahūgaṇa's association with Jaḍa Bharata. King Rahūgaṇa was immediately freed from the misgivings of material association. The arguments offered by pure devotees to their disciples are so convincing that even a dull-headed disciple is immediately enlightened with spiritual knowledge.

TEXT 23

नमो महद्भ्योऽस्तु नमः शिशुभ्यो
नमो युवभ्यो नम आवटुभ्यः ।
ये ब्राह्मणा गामवधूतलिङ्गा-
श्चरन्ति तेभ्यः शिवमस्तु राज्ञाम् ॥२३॥

namo mahadbhyo 'stu namaḥ śiśubhyo
namo yuvabhyo nama āvaṭubhyaḥ

ye brāhmaṇā gām avadhūta-liṅgāś
caranti tebhyaḥ śivam astu rājñām

namaḥ—all obeisances; *mahadbhyaḥ*—unto the great personalities; *astu*—let there be; *namaḥ*—my obeisances; *śiśubhyaḥ*—unto those great personalities who appear as boys; *namaḥ*—respectful obeisances; *yuvabhyaḥ*—unto those who appear as young men; *namaḥ*—respectful obeisances; *ā-vaṭubhyaḥ*—unto those who appear as children; *ye*—all those who; *brāhmaṇāḥ*—self-realized in transcendental knowledge; *gām*—the earth; *avadhūta-liṅgāḥ*—who remain hidden under different bodily guises; *caranti*—they traverse; *tebhyaḥ*—from them; *śivam astu*—let there be all good fortune; *rājñām*—unto the royal dynasties or kings (who are always very puffed up).

TRANSLATION

I offer my respectful obeisances unto the great personalities, whether they walk on the earth's surface as children, young boys, avadhūtas or great brāhmaṇas. Even if they are hidden under different guises, I offer my respects to all of them. By their mercy, may there be good fortune in the royal dynasties that are always offending them.

PURPORT

King Rahūgaṇa was very repentant because he had forced Jaḍa Bharata to carry his palanquin. He therefore began offering prayers to all kinds of *brāhmaṇas* and self-realized persons, even though they might be playing like children or hiding in some guises. The four Kumāras walked everywhere in the guise of five-year-old boys, and similarly there are many *brāhmaṇas*, knowers of Brahman, who traverse the globe either as young men, children or *avadhūtas*. Being puffed up due to their position, the royal dynasties generally offend these great personalities. Therefore King Rahūgaṇa began to offer his respectful obeisances unto them so that the offensive royal dynasties might not glide down into a hellish condition. If one offends a great personality, the Supreme Personality of Godhead does not excuse one, although the great personalities themselves might not take offense. Mahārāja Ambarīṣa was offended by Durvāsā, who even approached Lord Viṣṇu for pardon. Lord Viṣṇu would not grant him pardon; therefore he had to fall down at the lotus feet of Mahārāja Ambarīṣa, even though Mahārāja Ambarīṣa was a *kṣatriya-gṛhastha.* One should be very careful not to offend the lotus feet of Vaiṣṇavas and *brāhmaṇas.*

TEXT 24

श्रीशुक उवाच

इत्येवमुत्तरामातः स वै ब्रह्मर्षिसुतः सिन्धुपतय आत्मसतत्त्वं विगणयतः परानुभावः परमकारुणिकतयोपदिश्य रहूगणेन सकरुणमभिवन्दित चरण आपूर्णार्णव इव निभृतकरणोर्म्याशयो धरणिमिमां विचचार ॥२४॥

śrī-śuka uvāca
ity evam uttarā-mātaḥ sa vai brahmarṣi-sutaḥ sindhu-pataya ātma-satattvaṁ vigaṇayataḥ parānubhāvaḥ parama-kāruṇikatayopadiśya rahūgaṇena sakaruṇam abhivandita-caraṇa āpūrṇārṇava iva nibhṛta-karaṇormy-āśayo dharaṇim imāṁ vicacāra.

śrī-śukaḥ uvāca—Śrī Śukadeva Gosvāmī said; *iti evam*—in this way; *uttarā-mātaḥ*—O Mahārāja Parīkṣit, son of mother Uttarā; *saḥ*—that *brāhmaṇa; vai*—indeed; *brahma-ṛṣi-sutaḥ*—Jaḍa Bharata, the son of a highly educated *brāhmaṇa; sindhu-pataye*—unto the king of the province of Sindhu; *ātma-sa-tattvam*—the actual constitutional position of the soul; *vigaṇayataḥ*—although insulting Jaḍa Bharata; *para-anubhāvaḥ*—who was very exalted in spiritual realization; *parama-kāruṇikatayā*—by his quality of being very kind to the fallen souls; *upadiśya*—instructing; *rahūgaṇena*—by King Rahūgaṇa; *sa-karuṇam*—piteously; *abhivandita-caraṇaḥ*—whose lotus feet were worshiped; *āpūrṇa-arṇavaḥ iva*—like the full ocean; *nibhṛta*—completely silenced; *karaṇa*—of the senses; *ūrmi*—the waves; *āśayaḥ*—possessing a heart in which; *dharaṇim*—the earth; *imām*—this; *vicacāra*—continued to roam.

TRANSLATION

Śrīla Śukadeva Gosvāmī continued: My dear King, O son of mother Uttarā, there were some waves of dissatisfaction in the

mind of Jaḍa Bharata due to his being insulted by King Rahūgaṇa, who made him carry his palanquin, but Jaḍa Bharata neglected this, and his heart again became calm and quiet like an ocean. Although King Rahūgaṇa had insulted him, he was a great paramahaṁsa. Being a Vaiṣṇava, he was naturally very kindhearted, and he therefore told the King about the constitutional position of the soul. He then forgot the insult because King Rahūgaṇa pitifully begged pardon at his lotus feet. After this, he began to wander all over the earth, just as before.

PURPORT

In *Śrīmad-Bhāgavatam* (3.25.21), Kapiladeva describes the symptoms of great personalities: *titikṣavaḥ kāruṇikāḥ suhṛdaḥ sarva-dehinām.* A saintly devotee is certainly very tolerant. He is the friend of all living entities, and he does not create enemies within the world. A pure devotee has all the qualities of a *sādhu.* Jaḍa Bharata is an example of this. Due to the material body, his senses were certainly agitated when he was insulted by King Rahūgaṇa, but later, due to the King's humble submission, Jaḍa Bharata excused him. It is the duty of everyone desiring to return to Godhead to become submissive like King Rahūgaṇa and beg pardon of Vaiṣṇavas one may have offended. Vaiṣṇavas are generally very kindhearted; therefore if one immediately submits himself at the lotus feet of a Vaiṣṇava, one is immediately cleared of offensive reactions. If one does not do so, the reactions will remain, and the results will not be very palatable.

TEXT 25

सौवीरपतिरपि सुजनसमवगतपरमात्मसतत्त्व आत्मन्यविद्याध्यारोपितां च देहात्ममतिं विससर्ज । एवं हि नृप भगवदाश्रिताश्रितानुभावः ॥२५॥

sauvīra-patir api sujana-samavagata-paramātma-satattva ātmany avidyādhyāropitāṁ ca dehātma-matiṁ visasarja. evaṁ hi nṛpa bhagavad-āśritāśritānubhāvaḥ.

sauvīra-patiḥ—the King of the state of Sauvīra; *api*—certainly; *sujana*—from an elevated person; *samavagata*—having completely understood; *paramātma-sa-tattvaḥ*—the truth of the constitutional position of the spirit soul and the Supersoul; *ātmani*—in himself; *avidyā*—by nescience; *adhyāropitām*—erroneously attributed; *ca*—and; *deha*—in the body; *ātma-matim*—the concept of the self; *visasarja*—completely gave up; *evam*—thus; *hi*—certainly; *nṛpa*—O King; *bhagavat-āśrita-āśrita-anubhāvaḥ*—the consequence of taking shelter of a devotee who has similarly taken shelter of a spiritual master in the *paramparā* system (one is sure to get out of the great nescience of the bodily concept of life).

TRANSLATION

After receiving lessons from the great devotee Jaḍa Bharata, King Rahūgaṇa of the state of Sauvīra became completely aware of the constitutional position of the soul. He thus gave up the bodily conception completely. My dear King, whoever takes shelter of the servant of the servant of the Lord is certainly glorified because he can without difficulty give up the bodily conception.

PURPORT

As stated in *Caitanya-caritāmṛta* (*Madhya* 22.54):

"sādhu-saṅga", "sādhu-saṅga"——sarva-śāstre kaya
lava-mātra sādhu-saṅge sarva-siddhi haya

It is a fact that if one takes shelter of a pure devotee, one attains all perfection, even if the association is a short one. A *sādhu* is a pure devotee of the Lord. It has been our practical experience that the first instruction of our spiritual master infused us with Kṛṣṇa consciousness so that now we are at least on the path of Kṛṣṇa consciousness and can understand the philosophy. As a result, there are many devotees engaged in this Kṛṣṇa consciousness movement. The whole world is revolving under the bodily conception; therefore there must be devotees all over the world to deliver people from the false bodily conception and fully engage them in Kṛṣṇa consciousness.

TEXT 26

राजोवाच

यो ह वा इह बहुविदा महाभागवत त्वयाभिहितः परोक्षेण वचसा जीवलोकभवाध्वा स ह्यार्यमनीषया कल्पितविषयो नाञ्जसाव्युत्पन्नलोकसमधिगमः । अथ तदेवैतद्दुरवगमं समवेतानुकल्पेन निर्दिश्यतामिति ॥२६॥

rājovāca
ya ha vā iha bahu-vidā mahā-bhāgavata tvayābhihitaḥ parokṣeṇa vacasā jīva-loka-bhavādhvā sa hy ārya-manīṣayā kalpita-viṣayo nāñjasāvyutpanna-loka-samadhigamaḥ. atha tad evaitad duravagamaṁ samavetānukalpena nirdiśyatām iti.

rājā uvāca—King Parīkṣit said; *yaḥ*—which; *ha*—certainly; *vā*—or; *iha*—in this narration; *bahu-vidā*—who are aware of many incidents of transcendental knowledge; *mahā-bhāgavata*—O great devotee sage; *tvayā*—by you; *abhihitaḥ*—described; *parokṣeṇa*—figuratively; *vacasā*—by words; *jīva-loka-bhava-adhvā*—the path of material existence of the conditioned soul; *saḥ*—that; *hi*—indeed; *ārya-manīṣayā*—by the intelligence of advanced devotees; *kalpita-viṣayaḥ*—the subject matter is imagined; *na*—not; *añjasā*—directly; *avyutpanna-loka*—of persons who are not very experienced or intelligent; *samadhigamaḥ*—the complete understanding; *atha*—therefore; *tat eva*—because of that; *etat*—this matter; *duravagamam*—which is difficult to understand; *samaveta-anukalpena*—by substituting the direct meaning of such incidents; *nirdiśyatām*—let it be described; *iti*—thus.

TRANSLATION

King Parīkṣit then told Śukadeva Gosvāmī: My dear lord, O great devotee sage, you are omniscient. You have very nicely described the position of the conditioned soul, who is compared to a merchant in the forest. From these instructions intelligent men can understand that the senses of a person in the bodily conception are like rogues and thieves in that forest, and one's wife and children are like jackals and other ferocious animals. However, it

is not very easy for the unintelligent to understand the purport of this story because it is difficult to extricate the exact meaning from the allegory. I therefore request Your Holiness to give the direct meaning.

PURPORT

There are many stories and incidents in *Śrīmad-Bhāgavatam* that are described figuratively. Such allegorical descriptions may not be understood by unintelligent men; therefore it is the duty of the student to approach a bona fide spiritual master for the direct explanation.

Thus end the Bhaktivedanta purports of the Fifth Canto, Thirteenth Chapter, of the Śrīmad-Bhāgavatam, *entitled, "Further Talks Between King Rahūgaṇa and Jaḍa Bharata."*

The Author

His Divine Grace A. C. Bhaktivedanta Swami Prabhupāda appeared in this world in 1896 in Calcutta, India. He first met his spiritual master, Śrīla Bhaktisiddhānta Sarasvatī Gosvāmī, in Calcutta in 1922. Bhaktisiddhānta Sarasvatī, a prominent devotional scholar and the founder of sixty-four Gauḍīya Maṭhas (Vedic Institutes), liked this educated young man and convinced him to dedicate his life to teaching Vedic knowledge. Śrīla Prabhupāda became his student, and eleven years later (1933) at Allahabad he became his formally initiated disciple.

At their first meeting, in 1922, Śrīla Bhaktisiddhānta Sarasvatī Ṭhākura requested Śrīla Prabhupāda to broadcast Vedic knowledge through the English language. In the years that followed, Śrīla Prabhupāda wrote a commentary on the *Bhagavad-gītā,* assisted the Gauḍīya Maṭha in its work and, in 1944, without assistance, started an English fortnightly magazine, edited it, typed the manuscripts and checked the galley proofs. He even distributed the individual copies freely and struggled to maintain the publication. Once begun, the magazine never stopped; it is now being continued by his disciples in the West.

Recognizing Śrīla Prabhupāda's philosophical learning and devotion, the Gauḍīya Vaiṣṇava Society honored him in 1947 with the title "Bhaktivedanta." In 1950, at the age of fifty-four, Śrīla Prabhupāda retired from married life, and four years later he adopted the *vānaprastha* (retired) order to devote more time to his studies and writing. Śrīla Prabhupāda traveled to the holy city of Vṛndāvana, where he lived in very humble circumstances in the historic medieval temple of Rādhā-Dāmodara. There he engaged for several years in deep study and writing. He accepted the renounced order of life (*sannyāsa*) in 1959. At Rādhā-Dāmodara, Śrīla Prabhupāda began work on his life's masterpiece: a multivolume translation and commentary on the eighteen thousand verse *Śrīmad-Bhāgavatam* (*Bhāgavata Purāṇa*). He also wrote *Easy Journey to Other Planets.*

After publishing three volumes of *Bhāgavatam,* Śrīla Prabhupāda came to the United States, in 1965, to fulfill the mission of his spiritual master. Since that time, His Divine Grace has written over forty volumes of authoritative translations, commentaries and summary studies of the philosophical and religious classics of India.

In 1965, when he first arrived by freighter in New York City, Śrīla Prabhupāda was practically penniless. It was after almost a year of great difficulty that he established the International Society for Krishna Consciousness in July of 1966. Under his careful guidance, the Society has grown within a decade to a worldwide confederation of almost one hundred *āśramas*, schools, temples, institutes and farm communities.

In 1968, Śrīla Prabhupāda created New Vṛndāvana, an experimental Vedic community in the hills of West Virginia. Inspired by the success of New Vṛndāvana, now a thriving farm community of more than one thousand acres, his students have since founded several similar communities in the United States and abroad.

In 1972, His Divine Grace introduced the Vedic system of primary and secondary education in the West by founding the *Gurukula* school in Dallas, Texas. The school began with 3 children in 1972, and by the beginning of 1975 the enrollment had grown to 150.

Śrīla Prabhupāda has also inspired the construction of a large international center at Śrīdhāma Māyāpur in West Bengal, India, which is also the site for a planned Institute of Vedic Studies. A similar project is the magnificent Kṛṣṇa-Balarāma Temple and International Guest House in Vṛndāvana, India. These are centers where Westerners can live to gain firsthand experience of Vedic culture.

Śrīla Prabhupāda's most significant contribution, however, is his books. Highly respected by the academic community for their authoritativeness, depth and clarity, they are used as standard textbooks in numerous college courses. His writings have been translated into eleven languages. The Bhaktivedanta Book Trust, established in 1972 exclusively to publish the works of His Divine Grace, has thus become the world's largest publisher of books in the field of Indian religion and philosophy. Its latest project is the publishing of Śrīla Prabhupāda's most recent work: a seventeen-volume translation and commentary—completed by Śrīla Prabhupāda in only eighteen months—on the Bengali religious classic *Śrī Caitanya-caritāmṛta.*

In the past ten years, in spite of his advanced age, Śrīla Prabhupāda has circled the globe twelve times on lecture tours that have taken him to six continents. In spite of such a vigorous schedule, Śrīla Prabhupāda continues to write prolifically. His writings constitute a veritable library of Vedic philosophy, religion, literature and culture.

References

The statements of *Śrīmad-Bhāgavatam* are all confirmed by standard Vedic authorities. The following authentic scriptures are quoted in this book on the pages listed.

Bhagavad-gītā, 10, 21, 23, 28, 41, 45, 69, 80 81, 90, 113, 114, 117, 122, 129, 135, 150, 172, 173, 181, 183, 187, 189, 192, 197, 199, 201, 211, 222, 223, 229, 239-240, 244, 245, 255, 274, 276, 278, 279, 309-310, 314-315, 319, 341, 350, 351, 361, 377, 379, 383, 386, 390, 408-409, 410, 412, 422, 453

Bhakti-rasāmṛta-sindhu (Rūpa Gosvāmī), 5, 19, 150, 181, 367

Brahma-saṁhitā, 17, 52, 57, 112, 116, 159, 191, 204, 254, 260, 267, 287, 295, 394, 401, 414

Bṛhan-nāradīya Purāṇa, 31

Caitanya-bhāgavata (Vṛndāvana dāsa Ṭhākura), 370

Caitanya-candrāmṛta (Prabodhānanda Sarasvatī), 85

Caitanya-caritāmṛta (Kṛṣṇadāsa Kavirāja), 89, 127-128, 168, 174, 217, 320

Chāndogya Upaniṣad, 145-146, 411

Garga Upaniṣad, 23

Gautamīya-tantra, 117

Hari-bhakti-vilāsa (Sanātana Gosvāmī), 117

Īśopaniṣad, 20-21

Jyotir Veda, 59-60

Glossary

A

Ācārya—a spiritual master who teaches by his own example.
Adhokṣaja—the Supreme Lord, who cannot be seen with material eyes.
Ahaṁ brahmāsmi—the realization that "I am spirit soul."
Ahaṁ mameti—the false conception of "I" and "mine."
Akāma—freedom from material desire.
Ānanda—spiritual bliss.
Apavarga—liberation from *pavarga*, the miseries of material existence.
Apipātā—desiring only to perform devotional service to Kṛṣṇa.
Aprākṛta—transcendental to material nature.
Aprameya—immeasurable.
Apsarās—the society girls of the heavenly planets.
Arcā-vigraha—the Deity form of the Lord.
Artha—economic development.
Asat—temporary.
Āśrama—one of the four orders of spiritual life.
Ātmā—the self.
Ātma-tattva—spiritual science.
Avadhūta—a great saintly person who has surpassed the need for regulative principles.
Avara—material.
Avatāra—an incarnation of the Lord who descends from the spiritual sky.

B

Bhagavad-bhakti—See: Bhakti-yoga.
Bhagavān—Kṛṣṇa, who is full in six opulences.
Bhakta—a devotee.
Bhakti-yoga—devotional service to Kṛṣṇa.
Brahma-bandhu—a fallen member of a *brāhmaṇa* family.
Brahma-bhūta—the joyful state of being free from material contamination.
Brahmacarya—the vow of strict abstinence from sex indulgence.

Brahma-jijñāsā—inquiry into the Absolute Truth.
Brahmajyoti—the effulgence emanating from the body of the Lord.
Brahma-satra—meditating on the Supreme Lord always.
Brahmacārī—a celibate student under the care of a bona fide spiritual master.
Brāhmaṇa—the intelligent class of men.

C

Caṇḍāla—an outcaste or untouchable; a dog-eater.

D

Daiva-varṇāśrama—the transcendental system of four social orders and four spiritual orders.
Dama—sense control; a quality of *brāhmaṇas.*
Daṇḍavat—offering respect to a superior by falling flat like a stick.
Dasyu-dharma—the occupational duty of rogues and thieves.
Devas—demigods.
Dharā-maṇḍala—a planet.
Dharma—the capacity to render service, which is the essential quality of a living being.
Dharmānvekṣamāṇaḥ—strictly according to religious principles.
Dhīra—a sober person who has controlled senses.
Dvija—a *brāhmaṇa.*
Dvija-bandhu—See: Brahma-bandhu.

G

Garbhādhāna-saṁskāra—Vedic ceremony of purification performed by the parents before conceiving a child.
Govinda—a name of Kṛṣṇa meaning He who gives pleasure to the cows and the senses.
Gṛhastha—one who lives in God conscious married life.
Gṛhavrata—one who has taken a vow to execute family duties.

Guṇas—the modes of nature.

Guru—a bona fide spiritual master.

Guru-dakṣiṇā—a gift given to one's spiritual master.

Gurukula—the place of the spiritual master, where his disciples come to study and perform devotional service.

H

Hari—a name of Kṛṣṇa meaning He who removes all inauspicious things from the heart.

Hari-nāma-saṅkīrtana—See: Saṅkīrtana.

Hṛdaya-granthi—the hard knot of family attachment in the heart.

I

Īśitva—in mystic *yoga*, the perfection of control over others.

J

Jīvan-mukta—a person who is already liberated even while living in this body.

Jitendriya—one who has conquered the senses.

Jñāna-kāṇḍa—the division of the *Vedas* dealing with empirical speculation in pursuit of the truth.

Jñānī—one who is engaged in the cultivation of knowledge.

Jyoti-śāstra—the Vedic science of astronomy.

K

Kaitava-dharma—cheating religion.

Kāla-sarpa—the snakelike time factor.

Kāma—lust.

Karma—fruitive activities and their subsequent reactions.

Karma-bandha—the bondage of fruitive activities.

Karma-kāṇḍa—the performance of fruitive sacrifices according to Vedic injunctions.

Karmātmaka—one whose mind is colored with fruitive activity.
Karmendriyas—the working senses.
Karmīs—fruitive workers.
Kīrtana—the devotional process of chanting.
Kṛpā-siddhi—perfection attained simply by the blessings of a superior person.
Kṣatriya—the administrative class of men.
Kuṅkuma—a red cosmetic powder.

L

Laghimā—in mystic *yoga,* the perfection of becoming the heaviest.

M

Mahā-bhāgavata—a great devotee.
Mahā-mantra—the great chanting for deliverance: Hare Kṛṣṇa, Hare Kṛṣṇa, Kṛṣṇa Kṛṣṇa, Hare Hare/ Hare Rāma, Hare Rāma, Rāma Rāma, Hare Hare.
Mahātmā—a great soul.
Manīṣayā—by intelligence.
Mantra—a transcendental sound heard and chanted to purify one's consciousness and raise it to the spiritual platform.
Martya-loka—the earth planet, where death is very prominent.
Māyā—the energy of the Lord which deludes the living entities who desire to forget Him.
Mlecchas—those who cannot follow Vedic regulative principles; meat-eaters.
Moha—illusion.
Mokṣa—liberation.
Mūḍhas—fools and rascals.
Mukti—liberation from material bondage.
Muni—a sage or self-realized soul.
Muni-putra—the son of a saintly person.

N

Naiṣṭhika-brahmacārī—one who has been celibate since birth.
Nirguṇa—without material qualities.

Niṣkiñcana—having no desire for material comfort.
Nistraiguṇya—the transcendental position above the three modes of nature.
Nitya-baddha—an eternally conditioned soul.
Nitya-mukta—an eternally liberated soul.
Nivṛtti-mārga—the path of renouncing sense enjoyment.

O

Oṁkāra—the primal sound chanted in Vedic hymns which represents Kṛṣṇa.

P

Pāñcarātrika-vidhi—the devotional process of Deity worship.
Para—transcendental.
Parā bhakti—transcendental devotional service of the Supreme Lord.
Paramahaṁsa—a *sannyāsī* or devotee on the highest spiritual platform.
Paramātmā—the Supersoul, the localized aspect of the Supreme Lord.
Piṇḍa—*prasāda* from Lord Viṣṇu offered to the forefathers.
Pitās—forefathers.
Pitṛloka—the planet where the forefathers live in great delight as long as they are remembered by their descendants.
Prakāmya—in mystic *yoga*, the perfection of automatically realizing any desire.
Pramatta—one who is crazy because he cannot control his senses.
Prajāpatis—the progenitors of mankind.
Prāpti—in mystic *yoga*, the perfection of obtaining anything simply by reaching out.
Prasāda—the remnants of food offered to Kṛṣṇa.
Pravṛtti-mārga—the path by which the living entities are given a chance to enjoy and at the same time are regulated so that they can eventually come to spiritual life.
Puṁścalī—a woman who is easily carried away by men, not to be trusted.
Pūrṇa—the complete whole, Kṛṣṇa.
Puruṣa-avatāras—the primary Viṣṇu expansions of Kṛṣṇa who are involved in the creation of the universe.
Puruṣottama—the greatest living personality, Kṛṣṇa.

R

Rājarṣis—great saintly kings.
Rajo-guṇa—the material mode of passion.

S

Śabda-brahma—transcendental sound vibration.
Sac-cid-ānanda-vigraha—the eternal form of the Lord which is full of bliss and knowledge.
Sādhu—a great saintly person.
Sādhu-saṅga—the association of liberated persons.
Śālagrāma-śilā—a Deity incarnation of Nārāyaṇa in the form of a stone.
Śama—fixed in mind control; a quality of *brāhmaṇas.*
Sama-darśinaḥ—seeing with equal vision.
Samādhi—trance, absorption in God consciousness.
Samprekṣya nāsikāgram—keeping eyes half-open in practice of *yoga.*
Saṁsāra—the cycle of birth and death in the material world.
Saṅkīrtana—congregational chanting of the holy name of the Lord.
Sannyāsī—one in the renounced order of life.
Śānta—peaceful.
Sārva-kāraṇa-kāraṇam—the cause of all causes, Kṛṣṇa.
Śāstras—revealed scriptures.
Sattva-guṇa—the material mode of goodness.
Satya—truthfulness; a quality of *brāhmaṇas.*
Satya-kāma—all of one's desires being directed to the Supreme Truth.
Sevā—devotional service.
Sevaka—a servant.
Sevya—one who is served.
Siddhis—mystic powers or perfections.
Śivatama—the most auspicious.
Smṛti—scriptures compiled by living entities under transcendental direction.
Śrāddha ceremony—the offering of *viṣṇu-prasāda* to one's forefathers.
Śravaṇa—the devotional process of hearing.
Śrīvatsa—the sign of the goddess of fortune on the chest of Viṣṇu.

Śruti—scriptures received directly from God.
Strī—woman.
Śūdra—the laborer class of men.
Śukla—a person in the mode of goodness; also a name of Viṣṇu.
Sukṛtinaḥ—pious persons.
Svāṁśa—nondifferent plenary expansions of the Lord.
Svarūpa-vismṛti—forgetting one's real constitutional position.

T

Tamo-guṇa—the material mode of ignorance.
Tapasya—voluntary acceptance of some material trouble for progress in spiritual life.
Tilaka—sacred clay used to mark twelve temples of Viṣṇu on the body of a devotee.
Titikṣā—tolerance; a quality of *brāhmaṇas.*
Tulasī—Kṛṣṇa's favorite plant.

U

Ugra-karma—horrible activities which are the basis of a demoniac civilization.
Upāsanā-kāṇḍa—worship of demigods, ultimately of Viṣṇu, as prescribed in the *Vedas.*
Upādhis—material designations.
Urukrama—Kṛṣṇa, who performs wonderful feats.

V

Vaikuṇṭha—the spiritual sky, where there is no anxiety.
Vairāgya—the spirit of renunciation.
Vaiṣṇava—a devotee of Lord Viṣṇu.
Vaiṣṇava-aparādha—an offense at the lotus feet of a Vaiṣṇava.
Vaiśya—the class of men involved in business and farming.
Vānaprastha—retired life in which one travels to holy places in preparation for the renounced order of life.

Varṇa—the four divisions of society according to quality of work and situation in the modes of nature.
Varṇa-saṅkara—unwanted children produced from illicit sex.
Varṇāśrama-dharma—See Daiva-varṇāśrama.
Vibhinnāṁśa—separated expansions of the Lord, the minute living entities.
Vidagdha—one who is expert in the art of flattering women.
Vidūra-vigata—See: Caṇḍāla.
Vijara—not subjected to the miseries of old age.
Vijighatsa—free from desire for material enjoyment.
Vijñāna—practical knowledge.
Vimṛtyu—not subjected to death and rebirth.
Vimūḍha—See: Pramatta.
Viṣaya—material affairs of sense gratification.
Viṣaya-taraṅga—the waves of material existence.
Viśoka—callous to material distress and happiness.
Viṣṇu-tattvas—the innumerable plenary expansions of Kṛṣṇa, each of whom is also God.

Y

Yajña—Vedic sacrifice.
Yajña-puruṣa—the enjoyer of all Vedic sacrifices, Viṣṇu.
Yogamāyā—the internal potency of the Lord.
Yogeśvara—Kṛṣṇa, who is the master of all mystic powers.
Yojana—eight miles.
Yuga—the four ages of the universe.

Sanskrit Pronunciation Guide

Vowels

अ a आ ā इ i ई ī उ u ऊ ū ऋ ṛ ॠ ṝ
ऌ ḷ ए e ऐ ai ओ o औ au

ं ṁ *(anusvāra)* ः ḥ *(visarga)*

Consonants

Gutturals:	क ka	ख kha	ग ga	घ gha	ङ ṅa
Palatals:	च ca	छ cha	ज ja	झ jha	ञ ña
Cerebrals:	ट ṭa	ठ ṭha	ड ḍa	ढ ḍha	ण ṇa
Dentals:	त ta	थ tha	द da	ध dha	न na
Labials:	प pa	फ pha	ब ba	भ bha	म ma
Semivowels:	य ya	र ra	ल la	व va	
Sibilants:	श śa	ष ṣa	स sa		
Aspirate:	ह ha	ऽ = ' *(avagraha)* - the apostrophe			

The vowels above should be pronounced as follows:

a – like the *a* in org*a*n or the *u* in b*u*t.
ā – like the *ā* in f*a*r but held twice as long as *a*.
i – like the *i* in p*i*n.
ī – like the *ī* in p*i*que but held twice as long as *i*.
u – like the *u* in p*u*sh.
ū – like the *ū* in r*u*le but held twice as long as *u*.

ṛ – like the *ri* in *Ri*ta (but more like French *ru*).
ṝ – same as *ṛi* but held twice as long.
ḷ – like *lree (lruu).*
e – like the *e* in they.
ai – like the *ai* in *ai*sle.
o – like the *o* in g*o*.
au – like the *ow* in h*ow*.
ṁ *(anusvāra)* – a resonant nasal like the *n* in the French word *bon.*
ḥ *(visarga)* – a final *h*-sound: *aḥ* is pronounced like *aha; iḥ* like *ihi.*

The consonants are pronounced as follows:

k – as in *k*ite
g – as in *g*ive
ṅ – as in si*ng*
ch – as in staun*ch-h*eart
jh – as in he*dgeh*og
ṭ – as in *t*ub
ṇ – as *rn*a (prepare to say the *r* and say *na*).
kh – as in Ec*kh*art
gh – as in di*g-h*ard
c – as in *ch*air
j – as in *j*oy
ñ – as in ca*ny*on
ṭh – as in ligh*t-h*eart
ḍha- as in re*d-h*ot
ḍ – as in *d*ove

Cerebrals are pronounced with tongue to roof of mouth, but the following dentals are pronounced with tongue against teeth:

t – as in *t*ub but with tongue against teeth.
th – as in ligh*t-h*eart but tongue against teeth.
d – as in *d*ove but tongue against teeth.
dh – as in re*d-h*ot but with tongue against teeth.
n – as in *n*ut but with tongue in between teeth.
p – as in *p*ine
b – as in *b*ird
m – as in *m*other
r – as in *r*un
v – as in *v*ine.
ph – as in u*p-h*ill (not *f*)
bh – as in ru*b-h*ard
y – as in *y*es
l – as in *l*ight
s – as in *s*un
ś (palatal) – as in the *s* in the German word *sprechen*
ṣ (cerebral) – as the *sh* in *sh*ine
h – as in *h*ome

There is no strong accentuation of syllables in Sanskrit, only a flowing of short and long (twice as long as the short) syllables.

Index of Sanskrit Verses

This index constitutes a complete listing of the first and third lines of each of the Sanskrit poetry verses and the first line of each Sanskrit prose verse of this volume of *Śrīmad-Bhāgavatam*, arranged in English alphabetical order. In the first column the Sanskrit transliteration is given, and in the second and third columns respectively the chapter-verse references and page number for each verse are to be found.

A

U

V

Y

General Index

Numerals in boldface type indicate references to translations of the verses of *Śrīmad-Bhāgavatam.*

A

Absolute Truth
brahma-jijñāsā as search for, 183
descriptions in Vedic literature give one conception of, 116
is Bhagavān, 416-417
only revealed to one who has mercy of great devotee, 418
three features of, 377-378
Ācāryas
cited on mother's breast milk, 106
give instruction on offering obeisances, **115**
Ācchinna-dāra-draviṇā
quoted, 438
Activities
bewildered people rotting in material, 91
knowledge destroys reactions to material, 172
living entities bound by due to modes of nature, 309
performed in this life enjoyed or suffered in next, 187
performed to satisfy *yajña-puruṣa,* 33
Ṛṣabhadeva performed wonderful, **217**
should be performed for benefit of soul, 182
society divided according to people's, 78
Adāhyo' yam
quoted, 229
Adānta-gobhir viśatāṁ tamisram
quoted, 7
Adhokṣaja
as name of Kṛṣṇa, **456**
Adhyātma
quoted on becoming desireless, 181
Affection
for devotees as cause of Supreme Lord's appearance, **111**
Aggressor
can be killed according to *Vedas,* 327
Agni
one should offer respects to, 255
ten names of, **48**
Āgnīdhra Mahārāja
appreciated beauty of Pūrvacitti, 100
as example of fallen *yogī,* 86
as father of Nābhi, **110, 133**
as King of Jambūdvīpa, **103**
as son of Priyavrata, **48, 78,** 81
began appreciating Pūrvacitti's glance, **92**
begot nine sons, **104**
Brahmā understood desire of, **82**-83
compared Pūrvacitti's eyebrows to stringless bows, **89**-90
gave protection to inhabitants of Jambūdvīpa, **78**
hears tinkling of Pūrvacitti's bangles, **84**-86
kingdoms in Jambūdvīpa received by sons of, **106**
knew art of flattering women, **102**
praises Pūrvacitti's breasts, **95**-96
promoted to Pitṛloka, **107**
questioned Pūrvacitti about workings of *māyā,* 91
worshiped Brahmā, **80**
Ahaṁ sarvasya prabhavo mattaḥ
quoted, 197, 412
Ahaṅkāra-vimuḍhātmā kartāham
quoted, 414
Aihiṣṭaṁ yat tat punar-janma
quoted, 355

Beauty
as one of six opulences of God, 139
as result of austerities and penances, **100**
displayed on Viṣṇu's chest, **113**
of Apsarā's movements, **87**
of Pūrvacitti's face, **98**
Pūrvacitti attracted by Āgnīdhra's, **103**
Bhadrā
as daughter of Meru, **108**
Bhadra Kālī
emerged from diety to protect Jaḍa Bharata, 327
śūdra leader of dacoits wanted to worship, **320**
Bhadrasena
as son of Ṛṣabhadeva, **152**
Bhadrāśva
as son of Pūrvacitti and Āgnīdhra, **104**
Bhagavad-gītā
Arjuna addresses Kṛṣṇa as *puruṣam ādyam* in, 82
characteristic *dharma* explained in, 194
cited on good rebirth of a devotee, 307
cited on practicing *yoga* with half-open eyes, 85
cited on temporary pains and pleasures, 404
quoted on acting for satisfaction of the Lord, 33
quoted on activities performed for satisfaction of Kṛṣṇa, 147
quoted on association with material nature, 309
quoted on attaining certain bodies after death, 107
quoted on attainment of Kṛṣṇa's abode, 227
quoted on bewilderment of soul, 382
quoted on bodily encagement, 363
quoted on coming to transcendental platform, 33, 380-381
quoted on constant hearing and chanting, 300
quoted on control of Lord over living entities, 394
Bhagavad-gītā
quoted on creations of modes of nature, 67
quoted on demigod worship, 15
quoted on detachment from material activities, 367
quoted on devotees as never lost, 9, 10
quoted on devotees' indifference to material opulences, 75
quoted on devotees' not falling down, 37-38
quoted on devotional service as greatest gain, 241
quoted on devotional service as never in vain, 422
quoted on difficulty of overcoming divine energy, 127
quoted on disciplic succession, 40, 355
quoted on encouraging ignorant to work in spirit of devotion, 186
quoted on experiencing higher taste, 6
quoted on faithless rituals, 255
quoted on falldown of devotee, 66
quoted on flowery words of *Vedas*, 376
quoted on full surrender to Kṛṣṇa, 30
quoted on full surrender to spiritual master, 403
quoted on giving up all varieties of religion, 136
quoted on goal of living entities, 244
quoted on happiness and distress, 274
quoted on highest *yogī*, 45, 361
quoted on immortality of soul, 341
quoted on incarnation to rectify mismanagement, 408-409
quoted on inexpensive worship of the Lord, 262
quoted on knowing that Kṛṣṇa is everything, 172
quoted on knowledge destroying reactions to material activities, 172
quoted on Kṛṣṇa as friend to devotee, 122
quoted on Kṛṣṇa as original cause, 412
quoted on Kṛṣṇa as source of spiritual and material worlds, 197

C

E

F

Fruitive activities
color mind of person engaged in *karma*, **171**
encouraged by *Ṛg*, *Sāma* and *Yajur Vedas*, **316**
inhabitants of Pitṛloka in category of, 80
Jaḍa Bharata knew results of, 311
mind of ignorant living entity subjugated to, **173**
performed for self-interest, 119
priests considered themselves under influence of, 130
should be avoided by ignorant people, **185**
Śukrācārya inclined to, 189
unalloyed devotee untouched by, 175

G

Gaṇḍakī River
Bharata Mahārāja collected water of, **262**
Bharata sat by to chant, **270**
śālagrāma-śilās found in, **261**
Gandhamādana Hill
as place of Priyavrata's meditation, 15, **16,** 19
Gandharvaloka
residents of expert in musical science, 17
Gandharvas
as superior to ghosts, **196**
Ganges
origin of, 63
Garbhādhāna-saṁskāra
performance of, 81
Garbhodakaśāyī Viṣṇu
merges in body of Mahā-Viṣṇu, 52
Garga Upaniṣad
quoted on control of Lord over everything, 23
Gata-saṅgasya muktasya
verses quoted, 256
Gautamīya-tantra
quoted on devotees' offerings to Kṛṣṇa, 117
Gāyatrī *mantra*
Hiraṇmaya worshiped by, 265-266
Jaḍa Bharata did not learn, **313**
quoted on planetary systems, 59
Ghost
as superior to human being, **196**
Ṛṣabhadeva appeared as if haunted by, **213**
Ṛṣabhadeva passed through human society like a, **208**
Ghṛtapṛṣṭha
as son of Priyavrata, **48**
Giridhara Gosvāmī
cited on Āgnīdhra as product of lusty conception, 81
Goddess of fortune
Govinda served by, 116
Goloka Vṛndāvana
mahā-mantra imported from, 44
promotion to, **107**
Golokera prema-dhana, hari-nāma
verse quoted, 43
Goodness, mode of
accepted as best in material world, 379
Goptrī ca tasya prakṛtis
verses quoted, 414
Gosvāmīs
gave up exalted positions to become mendicants, 49
Govinda
as name of Kṛṣṇa, 159
as primeval Lord, 116
Govindam ādi-puruṣaṁ tam
quoted, 82, 159
Gṛhastha
as division of society, 78
can conquer lusty desires of youth, 36
observes religious principles, **135**
needs encouragement of his wife, 55
should have enough money to maintain body and soul together, 169
Gṛhe vā vanete thāke, 'hā gaurāṅga
quoted, 34
Guru
must prove his position, 357
necessity of approaching, 362

Guru
to become attached to devotional service on must contact, 173
one must approach a, 403
See also: Spiritual master

H

Happiness
devotees not entangled by material, 82
enjoyed according to destiny, 214
eternal, blissful life as transcendental to material, **165**
Lord as bestower of all heavenly, **202**
material as insignificant, **378-379**
material comes without effort, 279
material compared to drop of water in desert, 436
none in material world, **427**
nonpermanent appearance and disappearance of, 211
one is fit for eternal life if he is callous to, 319-320
Pūrvacitti and Āgnīdhra enjoyed heavenly, **103**
saṅkīrtana-yajña must be performed in order to get material, 141-142
sought by living entity life after life, 166
two types of *mahātmās* want eternal, 168
Harer nāma harer nāma harer namaiva
verse quoted, 31
Hari
becomes visible to His devotee, **260**
can save one from death, 448
See also: Kṛṣṇa
Hari-bhakti-vilāsa
quoted on devotees' offerings to Kṛṣṇa, 117
Haridāsa Ṭhākura
Caitanya accepted as *nāmācārya*, 311
grace of saves on from allurement of women, 224
Harivarṣa
as son of Āgnīdhra and Pūrvacitti, **104**
Havi
as son of Ṛṣabhadeva, **153**
Hearing
householder should have full opportunity for, 169
Heart
a *yogī* always thinks of Supreme Lord within his, 85
becomes peaceful from eating grains, 199
cleansed by constant chanting, 123
everyone's desires fulfilled by Lord in, 122
of Bharata like a lake of ecstatic love, 264
of Ṛṣabhadeva composed of *dharma*, 192
son born from father's, **193-194**
Viṣṇu informs Brahmā from within, 83
of male and female tied together in material existence, **176**
of Ṛṣabhadeva as spiritual, **191**
purified by penance and austerity, **165**
slackening of knot in, **177**
Heaven
See: Heavenly planets
Heavenly planets
Āgnīdhra prepared to go to, 102
developing interest in promotion to, 173
Indra as King of, **202**
Lord can offer elevation to, **125**
return of Menakā to, 105
Hell
Āgnīdhra prepared to go to, 102
associates of people fond of women and sex are on path to, **167**
Hippies
originated from King Arhat, 232
Hiraṇmaya
as Lord Nārāyaṇa within the sun, 265
as son of Pūrvacitti and Āgnīdhra, **104**
Hiraṇyagarbhaḥ samavartatāgre
prayer quoted, 19
Hiraṇyakaśipu and Hiraṇyākṣa
were formerly Jaya and Vijaya, 9
Hiraṇyaretā
as son of Priyavrata, **48**

N

O

Q

R

Religion
devoted to worship of demigods, 181
God doesn't belong to particular, 132
Kṛṣṇa advents Himself to re-establish principles of, 122
Ṛṣabhadeva appeared to preach principles of, 136
Renunciation
as one of six opulences of God, 139
attachments in stage of, 176
of sacrifice, charity and penance not recommended, 222
Priyavrata speaks in spirit of, **65-69**
Ṛg Veda
encourages fruitive activity, **316**
hymns to Nārāyaṇa given in, **265**
Ṛṣabhadeva
appeared in dynasty of Priyavrata, **237**
appeared to preach principles of religion, 136
as incarnation of the Supreme Lord, 141, 401
as master of all mystic power, **141**
as plenary expansion of Vāsudeva, **227**
as Supersoul, 229
as well-wisher of everyone, **207**
auspicious narration of pastimes of, **239**
Bharata as firstborn son of, 307
considered His body material, **228**
description of bodily features of, **212-213**
enthroned as emperor of the world, **144**
incarnated to deliver people from *māyā*, **234**
instructs sons on engaging in penance and austerity, **164-165**
instructs sons on giving up false ego, **180**-182
poured water on Ajanābha by His own prowess, **141**
qualities of, **139**-140
refused to manifest mystic yogic perfections, 221
satisfied Viṣṇu in every respect, **158-159**
strictly followed principles of *varṇāśrama-dharma*, **155-156**
Ṛṣabhadeva
transcendental signs on feet of, 139
Rūpa Gosvāmī
cited on offering food, 118
quoted on approaching spiritual master, 181
quoted on devotee as liberated, 392
quoted on liberated person, 34-35
quoted on real intelligence, 23
quoted on understanding Kṛṣṇa with material senses, 116

S

Sac-cid-ānanda-vigraha
can't be seen by us, 121
looks like human form, **191**
Sacrifice
kinds of performed by Bharata Mahārāja, **251**
Lord pleased by sages at, **135**
method of offering part of *brahmacarya* rules, **314**
not being performed at present, 199
of a man not mentioned in any *śāstras*, 324
of man-animal to Bhadra Kālī, 321-322
of man or animal before deity forbidden, 329
performed by Nābhi, 112
performed to acquire son, **129**
seven means to obtain Lord's mercy in performance of, **111**
Viṣṇu as master and enjoyer of all, **110**
Ṣaḍ-aiśvaryaiḥ pūrṇo ya iha
quoted, 416
Sādhu
freedom from material conception by association with, 177
necessity of association with, 128
"Sādhu-saṅga", "sādhu-saṅga"-sarva-śāstre
verse quoted, 128, 460
Sādhyaloka
residents of are all great saints, 17

T

U

V

Y